Dictionary of Italian Literature

DICTIONARY OF ITALIAN LITERATURE

Peter Bondanella
Julia Conaway Bondanella
co-editors

GREENWOOD PRESS WESTPORT, CONNECTICUT

Library of Congress Cataloging in Publication Data

Main entry under title:

Dictionary of Italian literature.

   Bibliography: p.
   Includes index.
   1. Italian literature—Dictionaries.
I. Bondanella, Peter E., 1943–   II. Bondanella,
Julia Conaway.
PQ4006.D45   850'.3   78-4022
ISBN 0-313-20421-7

Library of Congress Catalog Card Number: 78-4022
ISBN: 0-313-20421-7

First published in 1979

Greenwood Press, Inc.
51 Riverside Avenue, Westport, Connecticut 06880

Printed in the United States of America

10 9 8 7 6 5 4 3 2 1

CONTENTS

Contents

xi

THE EDITORS

PETER BONDANELLA is Director of the Center for Italian Studies at Indiana University, where he teaches Renaissance literature, comparative literature, and Italian cinema. A Younger Humanist Fellow of the National Endowment for the Humanities, he is the author, editor, or translator of *Machiavelli and the Art of Renaissance History* (1974), *Francesco Guicciardini* (1976), *The Decameron: A Norton Critical Edition* (1977), *Federico Fellini: Essays in Criticism* (1978), and *The Portable Machiavelli* (1979). He is presently completing a study of Italian neorealism and a translation of Boccaccio's *Decameron* with a commentary.

JULIA CONAWAY BONDANELLA is Assistant Professor in the Honors Division and Coordinator of the Freshman Honors Seminars at Indiana University. By training a comparatist with interests in medieval and Renaissance literature and the history of ideas, she is the author of *Petrarch's Visions and Their Renaissance Analogues* (1978) and a number of articles on Petrarch, Ronsard, and Spenser. At present she is completing a translation and critical edition of Rousseau's works.

THE CONTRIBUTORS

CHANDLER B. BEALL is Professor Emeritus of Romance Languages at the University of Oregon, where he founded both the Program in Comparative Literature and the journal *Comparative Literature,* of which he was editor from 1947 until 1972. A recipient of fellowships from the Fulbright Commission and the American Council of Learned Societies, he has served as President of the American Comparative Literature Association and Vice-President of the International Comparative Literature Association. He is the author of *Chateaubriand et le Tasse* (1934), *La Fortune du Tasse en France* (1942), and numerous articles on Petrarchism, Tasso, Dante, Montale, and topics in comparative literature.

THOMAS GODDARD BERGIN is Sterling Professor Emeritus of Romance Languages at Yale University. An authority on Old Provençal, Medieval, and contemporary Italian literature, he is the author, translator, or editor of a number of books, including *Giovanni Verga* (1931, rpt. 1969), *Anthology of the Provençal Troubadours* (1941, rpt. 1973), *The New Science of Giambattista Vico* (1941), *Petrarch* (1970), *Petrarch's Bucolicum Carmen* (1974), and *Petrarch's Africa* (1977). He has received a number of fellowships and special awards, including a Fulbright Fellowship and the Dante Medal from the Dante Society of America, and is past President of the American Association of Teachers of Italian.

ALDO S. BERNARDO is Professor of Romance Languages at the State University of New York at Binghamton, where he teaches Dante, Petrarch, and medieval literature. He has been awarded fellowships from the American Council of Learned Societies, the John Simon Guggenheim Foundation, and the Fulbright Commission and served as the Co-Director of the World Petrarch Congress at the Folger Library in 1974. He is the author of a number of scholarly studies, including *Petrarch, Scipio and "Africa"* (1962), *Petrarch, Laura, and the "Triumphs"* (1974), and *Petrarch's "Rerum Familiarium" Libri I-VIII* (1975)

GIAN-PAOLO BIASIN is Professor of Italian and Comparative Literature at the University of Texas in Austin. A specialist in literature of the nineteenth and twentieth centuries as well as contemporary criticism, he is a member of the editorial or advisory boards of several scholarly journals and is the author of various books and articles, including *The Smile of the Gods: A Thematic Study of Cesare Pavese's Works* (1968) and *Literary Diseases: Theme and Metaphor in the Italian Novel* (1975).

GLAUCO CAMBON is Professor of Romance Languages and Comparative Literature at the University of Connecticut. He is the editor of *Eugenio Montale: Selected Poems* (1965) and *Pirandello: A Collection of Critical Essays* (1967) and the author of a great many studies, including *Tematica e sviluppo della poesia americana* (1956), *La lotta con Proteo* (1963), *Giuseppe Ungaretti* (1967), and *Eugenio Montale* (1973).

ERNESTO G. CASERTA is Assistant Professor of Romance Languages at Duke University, where he teaches nineteenth- and twentieth-century Italian literature, aesthetics, and criticism. The recipient of an American Philosophical Society Fellowship, Professor Caserta has published *Croce critico letterario* (1972), *Manzoni's Christian Realism* (1977), and a translation of Leopardi's *War of the Mice and the Crabs* (1976), as well as numerous articles on Croce, Leopardi, and Silone.

S. BERNARD CHANDLER is Professor and Chairman of the Department of Italian Studies at the University of Toronto. He is the author or editor of a number of scholarly studies, including *The World of Dante: Six Studies in Language and Thought* (1966), *Alessandro Manzoni* (1974), and *Italians in the Modern World* (1978). Since 1973, he has been one of the International Vice-Presidents of the Associazione Internazionale per gli Studi di Lingua e Letteratura Italiana.

PAOLO CHERCHI is Professor of Romance Languages at the University of Chicago, where he teaches medieval Italian and Provençal literature as well as eighteenth-century Spanish literature. He is the editor of an edition of the works of Tommaso Garzoni (1972) and the author of *Capitoli di critica cervantina* [*1605–1784*] (1977) and *Ricerche e interpretazioni romanze* (1978).

FREDI CHIAPPELLI is Professor of Italian and Director of the Center for Medieval and Renaissance Studies at the University of California at Los Angeles. A specialist in Italian Renaissance literature, stylistics, and linguistics, he has received fellowships from the National Endowment for the

Humanities, the John Simon Guggenheim Foundation, and the Italian government; in addition, he is a fellow of such European academies as the Crusca (Italy), Vaucluse (France), Ciencias (Portugal), and Buenas Letras (Spain). Professor Chiappelli is the author or editor of numerous publications, including the first volumes of a major edition of Machiavelli's diplomatic writings (1971, 1973), *Studi sul linguaggio del Machiavelli* (1952), *Nuovi studi sul linguaggio del Machiavelli* (1969), *Studi sul linguaggio del Petrarca* (1971), *Machiavelli e la lingua fiorentina* (1974), and a forthcoming study of Torquato Tasso.

GUSTAVO COSTA is Professor of Italian literature at the University of California at Berkeley and a specialist in Vico, intellectual history, and the history of criticism. He has received fellowships from the Istituto Italiano per gli Studi Storici and the John Simon Guggenheim Foundation and is the author of *La leggenda dei secoli d'oro nella letteratura italiana* (1972), *Le antichità germaniche nella cultura italiana da Machiavelli a Vico* (1977), and numerous articles and monographs dedicated mainly to the authors and problems of eighteenth-century culture and literature.

TERESA de LAURETIS is Associate Director of the Center for Twentieth-Century Studies and Professor of Italian at the University of Wisconsin-Milwaukee. A specialist in contemporary literature, criticism, and film, she has written numerous articles on these subjects and a semiotic study of Italo Svevo entitled *La sintassi del desiderio: struttura e forme del romanzo sveviano* (1976).

ANDREA di TOMMASO is Associate Professor of Romance and Germanic Languages at Wayne State University, where he teaches Renaissance literature and Italian cinema. A recipient of a fellowship from the Fulbright Commission, he is the author of *Structure and Ideology in Boiardo's Orlando Innamorato* (1972) and articles on Renaissance literature. At present, he is Managing Editor of *Italian Culture*.

ROBERT S. DOMBROSKI is Associate Professor of Italian at the University of Connecticut. He is the author of *Introduzione allo studio di Carlo Emilio Gadda* (1974) and *Ideologia e forma nel romanzo di Pirandello* (1978), and is the editor of *Critical Perspectives on the Decameron* (1976). He has published a number of major essays on modern and contemporary Italian literature and literary sociology.

DENNIS J. DUTSCHKE is Assistant Professor of French and Italian at the University of California at Davis. He is the author of *Francesco Petrarca:*

Canzone XXIII from First to Final Version (1977) and a number of articles on Boccaccio and Petrarch. At present he is completing a study of Matteo Bandello.

SILVANO GAROFALO is Associate Professor of French and Italian at the University of Wisconsin-Madison, where he specializes in Italian literature since the eighteenth century. He is the author of *Conversiamo un po'* (1969), several studies of Leopardi, Unamuno, and Manzoni, and a forthcoming book entitled *The Dictionaries of Gianfrancesco Pivati*.

GUIDO GUARINO is Professor of Italian and Chairman of the Department of Italian at Rutgers University. He is the author of a number of articles on the Italian Renaissance and several major translations: Giovanni Boccaccio's *Concerning Famous Women* (1963) and *The Albertis of Florence: Leon Battista Alberti's Della famiglia* (1971).

EMMANUEL S. HATZANTONIS is Professor of Italian at the University of Oregon. A specialist in Italian Renaissance literature and the literary relations between classical Greece and modern European nations, he is the author of scholarly studies on the Circe myth in world literature, Verga, Dante, and Hellenic literature.

ANTONIO ILLIANO is Associate Professor of Romance Languages at the University of North Carolina at Chapel Hill, where he teaches modern Italian and comparative literature. He is the author of a number of works in this area, including a translation of Pirandello's *On Humor* (1974), *Introduzione alla critica pirandelliana* (1976), and essays on the Italian absurd, Calvino, Pirandello, and Alfieri.

LOUIS KIBLER is Associate Professor of Romance and Germanic Languages at Wayne State University, where he teaches modern Italian literature. He is a coauthor of *Giorno per giorno* (1971) and has published a number of studies devoted to Pavese and Moravia.

CHRISTOPHER KLEINHENZ is Associate Professor of French and Italian and Chairman of the Medieval Studies Program at the University of Wisconsin-Madison. A recipient of a Fellowship from the Institute for Research in the Humanities, he is the author of a number of books and articles on medieval literature, including *Medieval Manuscripts and Textual Criticism* (1976) and *Boccacciana: Bibliografia delle edizioni e degli scritti critici [1939–1974]* (1976).

ANNA M. LAWTON is Assistant Professor of Foreign Languages and Literatures at Purdue University. A specialist in contemporary Russian literature and cinema as well as the literary relations between Italy and Russia, she is the author of a number of articles on European futurism and film.

BEN LAWTON is Assistant Professor of Foreign Languages and Literatures at Purdue University, where he teaches Italian literature and film. He is the editor of *Film Studies Annual* and the author of a number of articles on Italian literature and cinema. At present he is completing a study of Italian neorealism.

GIANCARLO MAIORINO is Associate Professor of French and Italian and Comparative Literature at Indiana University, where he teaches Italian literature, literature and the other arts, and the history of ideas. He is the author of a number of articles on Alberti, Da Vinci, Bruno, and Montaigne and is at present completing a study of Renaissance and modern aesthetics.

ALBERT N. MANCINI is Professor of Romance Languages at Ohio State University, where he teaches Italian Renaissance and Baroque literature and serves as Coordinator of the Italian program. An associate editor of *Forum Italicum* and a member of the Delegate Assembly of the Modern Language Association of America, he is the author of several major studies on Italian Seicento literature.

MARK MUSA is Professor of Italian at Indiana University, where he teaches medieval literature. A recipient of fellowships from the Fulbright Commission and the John Simon Guggenheim Foundation, he is the author, editor, or translator of *Essays on Dante* (1964), *The Poetry of Panuccio Del Bagno* (1965), *Dante's Inferno* (1971), *Dante's Vita Nuova: A Translation and an Essay* (1973), *Advent at the Gates: Dante's Comedy* (1974), *The Decameron: A Norton Critical Edition* (1977), and *The Portable Machiavelli* (1979). He is presently completing a translation of Dante's *Purgatory* and a translation of Boccaccio's *Decameron* with a commentary.

RALPH NASH is a Professor of English and former Chairman of the Department of English at Wayne State University. An authority on Renaissance literature, including Neo-Latin and Anglo-Italian literary relationships, he is the author of a number of scholarly articles in this field and is the translator of Sannazaro's *Arcadia*.

NICOLAS J. PERELLA is Professor of Italian at the University of California at Berkeley where he teaches Italian and Comparative Literature as well as the history of ideas. A fellow of the John Simon Guggenheim Foundation, he is the author of numerous articles and books, including *The Kiss Sacred and Profane* (1969), *Night and the Sublime in Giacomo Leopardi* (1970), *The Critical Fortune of Battista Guarini's Pastor Fido* (1973), and *Midday in Italian Literature* (1978).

JOY HAMBUECHEN POTTER is Associate Professor of Italian at the University of Texas in Austin, where she teaches medieval literature and the modern novel. A recipient of a National Endowment Fellowship for Independent Study and Research, she is the author of articles on Vittorini and Boccaccio as well as a forthcoming book on Vittorini. She is currently completing a study of Boccaccio.

DOUGLAS RADCLIFF-UMSTEAD is Professor of Romance Languages and Chairman of that department at Kent State University. A specialist in Italian Renaissance drama, Romanticism, and Pirandello, he has received awards from the Fulbright Commission, the National Endowment for the Humanities, and the John Simon Guggenheim Foundation; for six years he was the Director of the Center for Medieval and Renaissance Studies at the University of Pittsburgh. He is the author of *The Birth of Modern Comedy in Renaissance Italy* (1969), *Ugo Foscolo* (1970), *The Mirror of Our Anguish, A Study of Pirandello's Narrative Works* (1978), and various critical essays.

OLGA RAGUSA is Professor of Italian and Chairman of the Italian Department at Columbia University, editor of *Italica,* and a former member of the Executive Council of the Modern Language Association of America. A recipient of awards from the American Council of Learned Societies and the Fulbright Commission, she is the author of many books and articles, including *Mallarmé in Italy* (1957), *Verga's Milanese Tales* (1964), *Luigi Pirandello* (1968), and *Narrative and Drama: Essays in Modern Italian Literature from Verga to Pasolini* (1975).

WAYNE A. REBHORN is Associate Professor of English at the University of Texas in Austin, where he teaches Renaissance literature. He has received a fellowship from the American Council of Learned Societies and is the author of articles on Erasmus, Milton, and More and *Courtly Performances: Masking and Festivity in Baldassare Castiglione's Book of the Courtier* (1978).

ALDO D. SCAGLIONE is W. R. Kenan Professor of Romance Languages and Comparative Literature at the University of North Carolina at Chapel Hill. He has received major fellowships and research grants from the Fulbright Commission, the John Simon Guggenheim Foundation, the

Newberry Library, the Southeastern Institute for Medieval and Renaissance Studies, and the Deutscher Akademischer Austauschdienst. Professor Scaglione is the author or editor of many scholarly works, including Boiardo's *Orlando Innamorato* (1951; rpt. 1963,1966,1973); *Nature and Love in the Late Middle Ages: An Essay on the Cultural Context of the Decameron* (1963; rpt. 1966); *Ars grammatica* (1970); *The Classical Theory of Composition from Its Origins to the Present* (1972); *Francis Petrarch, Six Centuries Later* (1975); and *Ariosto 1974 in America* (1976).

SARA STURM-MADDOX is Professor of French and Italian at the University of Massachusetts in Amherst, where she teaches medieval French literature as well as medieval and Renaissance Italian literature. She is the author of *The Lay of Guingamor: A Study* (1969), *Lorenzo de' Medici* (1975), and numerous articles on Dante, Petrarch, and Old French. At present she is completing a monographic study of Petrarch's lyrics.

JOSEPH TUSIANI is Professor of Romance Languages at Herbert H. Lehman College of the City University of New York. He is the author, editor, or translator of *Lust and Liberty: The Poems of Machiavelli* (1963), *The Complete Poems of Michelangelo* (1969), *Jerusalem Delivered* (1970), Boccaccio's *Nymphs of Fiesole* (1971), and three anthologies spanning from the inception of Italian poetry to the Futurist Manifesto of 1909—*The Age of Dante, Italian Poets of the Renaissance,* and *From Marino to Marinetti* (1971, 1974). A poet in his own right, he has recorded selections of his verse for the Library of Congress.

TIBOR WLASSICS is Professor of Italian at the University of Pittsburgh, where he teaches Dante as well as early Baroque and twentieth-century Italian literature. He has published in many European and American periodicals and is the author of several books, including *Da Verga a Sanguineti* (1973), *Galilei critico letterario* (1974), and *Dante narratore: Studi sullo stile della Commedia* (1975).

EDITORS' PREFACE

The first short reference guide to Italian literature in the English language, the *Dictionary of Italian Literature* provides within a single volume an introduction to major and minor Italian writers from the twelfth century to the present, to Italian metrics and poetic forms or genres, and to literary or critical schools, periods, problems, and movements. The three hundred and sixty-two entries, arranged alphabetically and cross-referenced for the reader's convenience, cover a wide range of subjects divided into the eight categories listed in Appendix B: two groups of entries on subjects which cross chronological boundaries (genres, periods, movements, and the like); and six groups on the writers from the basic chronological periods. Inevitably, some areas receive less attention than others. For example, although no individual entries are devoted to literary reviews or academies, these subjects are treated, whenever appropriate, within entries on the writers, movements, or periods to which they are directly related.

Two criteria determined the selection of subjects: their intrinsic importance to the history of Italian literature or culture; and their relevance to other national literatures, cultures, or art forms. It was our aim to present Italian literature from a comparative perspective and to go beyond Italian literary tastes or received critical opinion. Merely to have transposed an Italian reference dictionary into English would not have fully served English-speaking readers. Thus, while the relative space assigned to various writers, periods, or movements may reflect the most recent critical views in Italian scholarship, the editors and the other contributors have not hesitated to question or to modify standard interpretations, either explicitly in the text or implicitly by the relative space devoted to a particular item.

Although this dictionary is not designed solely for those who know little or no Italian, it is most probable that a majority of its users will fall into this category. In addition, many readers coming from fields outside Italian literature or literature in general will require information on the relationships of Italian literature to nonliterary disciplines such as the fine arts, music (especially opera), social thought, and history. Although most Italian reference guides naturally concentrate upon the Italian context of an individual author, period, or movement, we have felt it necessary, whenever possible and limitations of space permitting, to refer not only to the Italian literary context but also to the international context, to a writer's links to music, art, the cinema, or other literatures, and to his or her translations from other authors. English translations of Italian literary works are noted in the bibliographies accompanying each entry to enable those who have studied little or no Italian to enjoy this wealth of good reading.

Finally, the present work does not pretend to be comprehensive; it aims, rather, to be the most useful initial reference tool for the general public and the specialist. Furthermore, this dictionary is a reference work and not a literary history of Italy. We have included entries on poetic genres that are easily defined in a brief space and are most typical of specific chronological periods, but no broad and comprehensive treatments of literary modes such as the novel, the drama, or the lyric are presented. It will be possible to trace the evolution of such topics by following individual entries through the appropriate periods, but no attempt has been made to produce a book which would replace comprehensive critical works. The dictionary format has its advantages, however, since separate entries provide the reader with more succinct and authoritative factual information and interpretative material and more detailed bibliographies than could a literary history in a narrative format. In addition, the dictionary supplies a selective list of general guides for the study of Italian literature and culture, all of which contain references to extensive bibliographies; standard works on Italian metrics and versification; authoritative literary histories of Italy; encyclopedias and dictionaries of value for the study of Italian literature; and scholarly periodicals which publish regular bibliographical supplements on research in the field.

Finally, to set the entries within the proper historical perspective, a timeline from the twelfth century to the present has been included (Appendix A), so that the reader can compare at a glance developments in Italian literature and culture with those in Western literature, political thought, history, religion, philosophy, science, and the arts. This chronological chart notes general trends and crucial events in Western thought, but it does not provide a complete account of developments in any particular field of study. For the reader's convenience, all entries are indexed at the end of the work and are arranged according to subject matter or chronological period in Appendix B. It is our hope that the user of this work will find it readable, reliable, self-contained, and, above all, a useful guide to the wealth of information available on Italy's brilliant literary heritage.

The thirty-five contributors to this dictionary represent a distinguished cross-section of North American Italianists and comparatists; they include most of the established critics in the field as well as some promising younger members of the profession. These contributors are the authors of the signed articles, usually those on major writers, periods, or movements. The co-editors have shared the responsibility of writing the remaining unsigned articles, of choosing the entries to be included or excluded, of distributing the various entries among the contributors, and of editing the complete work. The spirit of cooperation and professionalism among the contributors to this dictionary speaks well for the future of Italian studies on this continent, and the editors are most grateful for their scholarly support.

Peter Bondanella

Julia Conaway Bondanella

February 1978

HOW TO USE THIS DICTIONARY

I. Style of Entries

1. Books and articles are given first in their original Italian form following Italian rules of capitalization. Books are set in italics, poems within quotation marks.
2. Following the Italian titles of books or poems, the reader will find within parentheses, first, the date of composition and or publication of that work (if known or applicable); and second, an English translation of the title. If an English translation of a book has been published, the title of this publication is set in italics; if a poem has been published in English, its specific title or first line is set within quotation marks. It should be noted that published titles may not correspond literally to the Italian original.
3. If no published English version of a book or poem exists, a literal English translation is provided for the reader's convenience. To indicate that these titles have not been published, book titles are left in Roman type and the titles or first lines of poems appear without quotation marks.
4. In addition to the index by subject and period at the end of the dictionary, entries are cross-referenced within the body of the text. Whenever an asterisk (*) appears, this indicates that an entry on this topic is to be found elsewhere in the dictionary. If information in other entries is pertinent to a particular topic, the reader's attention is drawn to these entries by a reference at the end of the article.

II. Bibliographical Style

1. All bibliographical entries are complete, including the full titles, the complete data of publication, and the names of editors or translators, if available, to simplify locating these works, especially if the reader must rely heavily upon interlibrary loans.

2. In general, the bibliography for each entry is arranged alphabetically in the following order: (a) Italian editions of primary texts, if any, listed first by title and then, whenever necessary, by editor; (b) English translations of primary texts listed first by title and then, whenever necessary, by editor or translator; (c) critical studies, books and articles, in a variety of languages, ordered by author or, whenever necessary, by title.

3. In some cases where no single Italian critical edition of an author's works exists, there may be few or no Italian texts cited while English translations may be rather numerous. In such instances, the critical works listed give detailed accounts of the standard Italian texts.

4. The bibliographies also refer whenever possible to currently available reprints of scholarly works or English translations, the original edition of which may be out of print. In these instances, only the original publication date will be listed, followed by "rpt." and the complete bibliographical information on the publisher of the reprint to facilitate the purchase of such works by readers or librarians.

Dictionary of
Italian
Literature

A

ALAMANNI, LUIGI (1495–1556), Florentine poet and statesman. Alamanni was a frequent visitor to the Orti Oricellari, the circle of young republican intellectuals which included Cosimo Rucellai (1495–1519) and Niccolò Machiavelli.* Alamanni was deeply involved in the unsuccessful conspiracy of 1522 against Giulio de' Medici, the future Pope Clement VII. Fleeing to Venice and then to France when Giulio became pope, Alamanni returned to Florence after the brief interval of republican freedom to serve in the city's government from 1527 to 1530, when he was once again forced to go into exile in France where he enjoyed the patronage of Francis I, Henry II, and Catherine de' Medici. His presence at the French court was partially responsible for the Italianate cultural influence, so important during the mid-sixteenth century. His ties to the French monarchy enabled him to return to Italy on numerous occasions and to establish contacts with Bembo,* Varchi,* Speroni,* and others who were to be central figures in the history of Franco-Italian intellectual and literary relationships during the Renaissance.*

Machiavelli valued Alamanni's friendship enough to make him one of the speakers in his *Arte della guerra (The Art of War)*, and he also dedicated his *Vita di Castruccio Castracani (The Life of Castruccio Castracani)* to him. Alamanni himself produced several influential, if minor, literary works. Besides a number of eclogues, Petrarchan lyrics, and satires, his best compositions are *Antigone* (1556, Antigone), a tragedy after Sophocles; *Flora* (1549, Flora), a comedy in the Roman style; and *Avarchide* (1570, The Avarchide), a minor epic* poem in imitation of the *Iliad* which deals with the siege of Bourges by King Arthur. His most famous work, one which retained a certain popularity long after his death, was *La coltivazione* (1546, Cultivation), a didactic poem in blank verse in imitation of Virgil's *Georgics*. Here, amidst many erudite references to the classics, several passages of genuine poetry stand out—Alamanni's praise of the country life, his description of the Golden Age as contrasted to the corrupt present, and his nostalgia for an Italy freed from foreign domination.

See also MACHIAVELLI, Niccolò.

Bibliography: Versi e prose di Luigi Alamanni, ed. Pietro Raffaelli (Florence: Le Monnier, 1859); Henri Hauvette, *Un exilé florentin à la cour de France au XVIe siècle, Luigi Alamanni (1495–1556); sa vie et son oeuvre* (Paris: Hachette, 1903).

ALBERTI, LEON BATTISTA (1404–1472), Florentine humanist, architect, art theorist, poet, painter, and mathematician. Alberti was born in Genoa and was the second natural son of the exiled Florentine, Lorenzo Alberti, and the Bolognese widow, Bianca di Carlo Fieschi. Battista Alberti, who later added Leo or Leon to his name, belonged to one of the most prominent and prosperous merchant and banking families of the bourgeois aristocracy of Florence. That family, however, like others which had aligned themselves with the "popular" political factions, had been banished from Florence in 1387 for opposing the ruling faction headed by the oligarchical Albizzi family. In 1406, at the time of the plague which took their mother's life, Lorenzo removed his sons, Battista and Carlo, first to Venice and then to Padua, where the young Alberti, like other prominent educators and humanists of his generation, received the finest available classical literary education. In 1421, at the age of seventeen, Leon Battista went to Bologna to study canon law. In the same year, both his father and his paternal uncle died. His relatives soon appropriated the inheritance left to him and his brother, and refused to support him. Whether they did so from malice or because Alberti refused to assume a role in the family business is not clear. The following years were difficult ones in which Leon Battista was dogged by poverty and illness. Nonetheless, he persevered in his studies and continued also to read the Greek and Latin classics so dear to him. It was perhaps this personal experience of hardship which confirmed in him the belief, echoed in his later writings, that one is the product of one's own will and effort, and that fortune, fickle and hostile, only defeats those who let themselves be defeated. His views on the difficulties faced by the intellectual in society are first expressed in the early work *De commodis et incommodis literarum* (1430, The Pains and Pleasures of a Man of Letters). Earlier, in the period 1424–26, Alberti had authored a Latin comedy, *Philodoxeos* (Philodoxus), which he passed off successfully as the work of a classical Roman poet named Lepidus.

In 1432, Alberti was in Rome, where he had been granted the first benefice of his ecclesiastical career—an appointment as apostolic abbreviator, or secretary, in the papal chancery at the court of Pope Eugenius IV. He was to hold that position until 1464. Enchanted by Rome, Alberti spent the following two years studying its ancient monuments, from which he was to derive some, perhaps too many, of his own architectural principles. In 1435, the sentence of banishment having been lifted, Alberti went to Florence with the pope. There, as he tells us in the dedicatory letter to Filippo Brunelleschi which precedes his treatise *De pictura* (1436, *On Painting*), he was greatly impressed with the genius of that city's artists, including Donatello, Masaccio, Ghiberti, Luca della Robbia, and Brunelleschi himself. From then on he would spend most of his time in Florence or in Rome. In 1447, he became architectural advisor to the new pope, Nicholas V, whom Alberti knew from their student years together in Bologna. Throughout his life he dedicated himself to exploring numerous fields of knowledge, and as a result of his contributions to the arts, to the sciences, and to letters, he has been acclaimed as the embodiment of the Renaissance* ideal of the "universal man."

If there is one notion which provides a unifying element in Alberti's thought, it is the belief that nature is a rationally ordered system which can serve as a heuristic model for man in his attempt to put order into human existence. According to Alberti, it is the imitation of nature which allows man to discover and to employ his own rationality, which in turn is the source of that inner strength, or *virtù,* which will enable him to become the master of his own destiny. When Alberti, in his treatise *On Painting,* advises the painter to imitate nature, it is the *process* of nature that he means for him to imitate. While the painter should not simply copy what he sees, neither should he give form to what cannot be seen in nature. To the painter and sculptor alike, Alberti recommends the use of live models, in order to avoid growing used to one's own errors. By conquering space and time, painting will give to the painter a divine perspective, and ultimately, he says, the painter will be praised as though he were a god. Significantly, Alberti's treatise on painting was a departure from the recipe books of the past and was instrumental in changing the status of the painter from that of craftsman to that of the inspired creative artist.

While painting is important for Alberti, insofar as it idealizes that which it shows and teaches both the viewer and the painter, perhaps architecture is the most important of the arts in his intensely practical vision of life. Architecture, born both of necessity and of a natural instinct to build, serves as a unifying force which regulates and harmonizes the activity of the city. In his *De iciarchia* (circa 1470, On Governing a Household), Alberti draws an analogy between the family, the republic, and the human body. Likewise, in *De re aedificatoria* (begun in 1449 but not printed until 1485, *Ten Books of Architecture*), he compares the human body to a building. There is in Alberti's thought a psychophysical parallelism which suggests that the state of mind is reflected in the condition of the physical being. This applies not only to the individual but to the family and to society as a whole as well. Physical education, family management, and urban planning are thus linked in an aesthetic vision of a world which, like a work of art, is governed by human reason. Understandably, in his work *Della famiglia* (1433–39, *The Family in Renaissance Florence*), Alberti reverses his earlier view on the acquisition of wealth and implies that poverty is a kind of disfigurement which is to be avoided. The individual, whose principal aim is to be a good citizen, is not only expected to make the most of himself, but also, as Alberti often repeats, to be useful to others.

In addition to his influential treatises on art and on the family, Alberti wrote several vernacular dialogues including *Theogenius* (circa 1440, Theogenius) and *Profugiorum ab aerumna* (1441–42, Flight from Hardship), which deal with the conflict between *virtù* and fortune and reaffirm the importance of reason as a guide and source of comfort in adversity. He also composed *Intercenales* (circa 1441, *Convivial Dialogues*), a grammar of the Tuscan language, and several amorous writings in prose and verse which reflect his personal experience in love and his misogyny. His many interests were joined by his belief that literature, art, and science can serve the useful civic function of improving the quality of human life.

See also HUMANISM.

Bibliography: Opere volgari, ed. Cecil Grayson, 3 vols. (Bari: Laterza, 1960, 1966, 1973); *The Albertis of Florence: Leon Battista Alberti's Della Famiglia,* trans. Guido Guarino (Lewisburg, Pa.: Bucknell University Press, 1971); *The Family in Renaissance Florence,* trans. Renée Watkins (Columbia, S.C.: University of South Carolina Press, 1969); *On Painting and on Sculpture,* trans. Cecil Grayson (London: Phaidon, 1972); Joan Gadol, *Leon Battista Alberti: Universal Man of the Renaissance* (Chicago: University of Chicago Press, 1969).

Andrea di Tommaso

ALCIATI, ANDREA (1492–1550), legal scholar and writer of emblems. Alciati was born near Milan. A precocious student of classical languages, he received a doctorate in law in 1514 and practiced in Milan until he was called to Avignon as a professor. Having returned to Milan for a number of years, he was again summoned to assume a position in the French university in Bourges, this time by King Francis I himself. A friend of Erasmus, Alciati was a stalwart defender of the revival of classical learning, which was the core of the humanist philosophy. Partially as a result of his interest in the classics, he wrote his most influential work, the *Emblematum liber* (1531, Emblem Book), the first of several editions to appear in his lifetime. Alciati's original conception of an emblem was poetic and referred only to a special kind of epigram; indeed, one-fifth of the two hundred and twenty emblems in the first edition were translations or imitations of the *Greek Anthology*. The highly pictorial epigrams led the printer to add visual illustrations of the ideas expressed in the epigrams to the 1531 edition. Although Alciati seems to have had little regard for this part of his writing, the vogue of emblem books in sixteenth- and seventeenth-century Europe was phenomenal. Despite his original intention, the genre came to have a tripartite structure: caption, illustration, and epigram. Important poets were directly or indirectly influenced by the genre, and some modern scholars have tried to link Baroque* or metaphysical imagery to that of the widely popular emblems.

Bibliography: Robert J. Clements, *Picta Poesis: Literary and Humanistic Theory in Renaissance Emblem Books* (Rome: Edizioni di storia e letteratura, 1960); Henry Green, *Andrea Alciati and His Books of Emblems* (London: Trubner, 1872); Elizabeth K. Hill, "What Is an Emblem?," *Journal of Aesthetics and Art Criticism* 29 (1971), 261–65; Hessel Miedema, "The Term *Emblema* in Alciati," *Journal of the Warburg and Courtauld Institutes* 31 (1968), 234–50; Giuliano Pellegrini, "Introduzione alla letteratura degli emblemi," *Rivista di letterature moderne e comparate* 29 (1976), 5–26, 85–98; Mario Praz, *Studies in Seventeenth-Century Imagery* (Rome: Edizioni di storia e letteratura, 1964)—includes illustrations and an extensive bibliography of emblem books.

ALEARDI, ALEARDO (1812–1878), poet and patriot. Born in Verona, Aleardi studied law at the University of Padua but soon turned to a literary career, even changing his original name Gaetano to Aleardo because of its musical effect. He collaborated with Giovanni Prati* on a Paduan periodical, *Il Caffè Pedrocchi,* which the Austrians suppressed in 1847 for its liberal leanings. Aleardi took an active part in the uprisings of 1848–49 and was sent by the Venetian Republic to request assistance against the Austrians. Arrested in 1852 and again in 1859, he was released after the Treaty of Villafranca. After Italian unification, he became a member of Italy's Parliament, a senator, and eventually professor of aesthetics at the University of Florence (1864–74).

Aleardi's first major work was an historical poem, "Arnalda di Roca" (1844, Arnalda di Roca), the story of a girl from a noble family who is captured by the Turks after the fall of Cyprus (1570), and who saves herself from a life in a harem by setting fire to the powder magazine of the ship which is transporting her to captivity. Another poem, "Le città italiane marinare e commercianti" (1856, Italian Maritime and Commercial Cities), evokes the image of free city-states in the Middle Ages, while "Il Monte Circello" (1852, Mount Circello) celebrates the draining of the Pontine Marshes that was one result of Italian reunification. Much of Aleardi's poetry was written in a patriotic vein and was influenced by Lord Byron as well as French and German writers. His work is a typical expression of Risorgimento sentiment and the love of country which does not always yield great poetic results. His major poems were collected and published together in 1864 under the title *Canti* (Songs).

Bibliography: Canti scelti, ed. Luigi Grilli (Turin: UTET, 1944); *From Marino to Marinetti,* trans. Joseph Tusiani (New York: Baroque Press, 1974).

ALERAMO, SIBILLA, pen-name of Rina Faccio (1876–1960), novelist and poet. Aleramo, born in Alessandria, was never formally educated and lived through an unfortunate youth: her mother went insane, her father deserted the family, and she was seduced as an adolescent and constrained to marry a man she did not love. She had a number of love affairs, including relationships with Dino Campana* and Vincenzo Cardarelli.* These experiences have figured in her fiction, much of which is written from a feminist perspective. One of the signers of Croce's* antifascist manifesto in 1925, Aleramo joined the Communist party after the fall of fascism and became one of its most militant supporters until her death.

Her first novel, *Una donna* (1906, *A Woman at Bay*), is an obviously autobiographical account of a world in which women are exploited by men and treated as objects. Its protagonist lives through many of the events experienced by the author and evolves from a meek, naive girl into a woman with a profession and mission in life, achieved only at the expense of abandoning her husband and son. None of Aleramo's other fictional works matches *Una donna*. Two later works—*Il frustino* (1932, The Whip), and *Amo, dunque sono* (1927, I Love, Therefore I Am)—reflect the influence of Ibsen and D'Annunzio.* During her career, Aleramo translated the love letters of George Sand and Alfred de Musset, as well as Madame de Lafayette's *The Princess of Clèves*. Some of the most revealing material about her life is contained in her personal diary, *Dal mio diario* (1945, From My Diary), and in a collection of letters she exchanged with her lover Dino Campana.

Bibliography: Dal mio diario (1940-45) (Rome: Tumminelli, 1945); *Una donna* (Milan: Mondadori, 1944); *A Woman at Bay,* trans. Maria Lansdale (New York: Putnam's, 1908); Sergio Pacifici, *The Italian Novel from Capuana to Tozzi* (Carbondale, Ill.: Southern Illinois University Press, 1973).

ALFIERI, VITTORIO (1749–1803), dramatist and poet. Born to an aristocratic family in Asti on 16 January 1749, Alfieri was raised in a cultural environment affected by French language and traditions. In a proto-romantic spirit, as Benedetto Croce* has defined it, Alfieri spent the rest of his life searching for his Italian roots and a libertarian consciousness.

From his early years at the military academy in Turin (1759–66), Alfieri rebelled against a pedantic and antiquated system of education. His military career was short-lived; having been granted permission by the king in 1766 to travel in Italy and abroad, Alfieri undertook a series of journeys throughout the peninsula and then to France, England, Germany, Russia, Spain, and Portugal (1767–72). In an age of travel and cosmopolitanism, few men of letters could match Alfieri's peregrinations. Always intolerant of authoritarianism and militarism, Alfieri labeled Frederick II of Prussia the head of a military camp. Before Beethoven, Alfieri indignantly commented on Metastasio's* servile genuflection in the presence of Maria Theresa.

Alfieri returned to Turin in 1772, and spent the next three years alternating love affairs, theatres, and literary circles. In 1795, he presented his first tragedy, *Cleopatra (Cleopatra),* at the Carignano Theatre; its public success was minimized by the author himself. Yet, it was at that time that Alfieri began to dedicate all his energies to the study of Italian literature and language. His initial readings of Ariosto* and Metastasio were followed by those of Rousseau, Voltaire, Montaigne, and Plutarch. The study of Petrarch,* Tasso,* and Dante* marked further steps in his attempts to *spiemontizzarsi,* or to drop Piedmontese habits. In search of an Italian tragic style, Alfieri moved to Florence, where he met Francesco Gori Gandellini, who encouraged him to read Machiavelli* and to write a tragedy on the subject of the Pazzi revolt. The result, however, was a political treatise, *Della tirannide* (1789, *On Tyranny*), in which Alfieri presented the very core of his literary inspiration: hatred of tyranny and an inexhaustible thirst for freedom.

The most productive and happy years of Alfieri's life began in 1777, when his lifelong relationship with Luisa Stolberg D'Albany flourished. By 1780, his tragedies also enjoyed public acclaim. Alfieri traveled again to England (1783–84) and France (1787–92), where he worked on a new edition of his nineteen tragedies, which followed the unsatisfactory and incomplete Siena edition of 1783 that included only ten plays. In Paris, Alfieri witnessed the early developments of the French Revolution. His love of freedom had already produced five *Odi* to America (1781–83, *America the Free: Five Odes*), which were then followed by his *Parigi sbastigliata* (1789, Paris without the Bastille). Yet, the violent and bloody events of those years shattered his ideal and abstract notion of liberty to the point that, after visits to England and Holland, Alfieri returned to Florence in 1792. The entrance of the French into that Italian city in 1798 reinforced his anti-Gallic attitude. During the last years of his life, Alfieri finished the *Vita (Memoirs)* and appointed himself knight of the self-created order of Homer. He died on 8 August 1803 and was buried in Santa Croce in Florence, as a lasting example to the new Italian spirit that was to inspire Foscolo* and the Risorgimento.

Aside from his theatrical works, Alfieri's production includes poetry, satires, treatises, and a prototype of the romantic autobiography, the *Vita.* The first part of the *Vita* was completed in 1799, and the second in Florence by 1803. A document of the times in the tradition of Cellini's* *Vita,* Alfieri's *Vita* aims at unearthing the organic growth of artistic consciousness. At the time of Schiller and Goethe, Alfieri set out to portray the growth of the artistic mind—the *pianta uomo*—as an organic alternative to the mechanistic views of the eighteenth century. To this extent, the poet represents the final product of a genetic evolution that includes psychological memories from his adolescence, which already suggest the sensibility and relentlessness of his character. The *Vita* is divided into four epochs. The first presents nine years of "vegetation." The second narrates his life at the Academy, his first love, and his trips to Milan, Florence, Rome, and Genoa, where he was impressed by the tumultuous immensity of the sea. The third epoch deals with his journeys throughout Europe. (Remarkable are his descriptions of the wind, indicative of a response to the ineffable that was to be popularized in England through a number of poems on breezes and western winds.) The fourth epoch analyzes the literary activities of the writer. In terms of the portrait of the artist, the *Vita* presents interesting parallels with basic attitudes of the *Sturm und Drang*.

Alfieri's pursuit of political freedom was institutionalized in his political treatises. The two books of *Della tirannide* were written in 1777, and then published in 1789. Inspired by Machiavelli, they celebrate the concept of liberty above all forms of government. At the very outset, Alfieri differentiates between the tyrant and the king: the tyrant has an unlimited power to do evil, whereas the king is an objective executor of the laws. Feeding on religion and the aristocracy, modern tyrants last longer than their ancient predecessors because it is difficult to find a new Brutus. Alfieri therefore seems to favor an ideal form of republic, although he regretfully realized that people were not yet ready for democracy, as the events of the French Revolution had shown. The three books of *Del principe e delle lettere* (1785–86, *The Prince and Letters*) deal with the mission of literature with regard to society and politics. In the first book, the traditional antinomy prince-poet is resolved in cooperation between the two, since the poet can bring glory and fame to tyranny. In the second book, Alfieri confronts the writer's duty to perform in public office with freedom of judgment. From a literary standpoint, tyranny can only promote imitative poetry, and the true poet must fight the tyrant.

Even Alfieri's comedies treat political subjects. Written between 1800 and 1803, *L'uno (The One)* presents the dangers of tyranny, *I pochi (The Few)*, those of oligarchy, and *I troppi (The Too Many)*, those of democracy. As an alternative, Alfieri proposes in *L'Antidoto (The Antidote)* a form of constitutional monarchy patterned after the English model. Two other comedies, *La finestrina* (circa 1800, *The Little Window*) and *Il divorzio* (circa 1800, *The Divorce*), are more moralistic and satirical; the first exposes human vices, and the second attacks contemporary customs like *cicisbeismo* (the largely Venetian custom of allowing a young gallant, a "cavalier servente," to escort a married woman in society). This satirical vein reappears in the nineteen satires (1786–93), in which Alfieri attacks all social classes and institutions. Their harsh and epigrammatic style also characterizes *Il misogallo* (1793–99, The Gaul-Hater), which expresses— and even exaggerates—his anti-French feelings. Alfieri's more lyrical poetry reflects his superior individualism in the forms of the Petrarchan tradition, which he injects with a characteristic virility and abruptness.

Alfieri's nineteen tragedies were written from 1775 to 1786. The definitive and complete edition of them was printed in Paris between 1787 and 1789. All have been translated by Lloyd and Bowring. They deal with the ancient world (*Saul, Saul; Mirra, Myrrha; Ottavia, Octavia*), medieval and Renaissance* times (*Don Garzia, Don Garzia; Congiura de' Pazzi, The Pazzi Conspiracy; Rosmunda, Rosmunda*), and the modern age (*Maria Stuarda, Mary Stuart; Filippo, Philip II*). All of these tragedies follow the classical organization of French tragedy, although the Alfierian theatre is characterized by a more rapid development and a minimal number of protagonists. Usually, the first and last acts are very short, and the dramatic action is largely resolved in the dialogues and frequent monologues that economize on the French use of informers and secondary figures. Alfieri explains that he wrote in three stages: first, he put down subject matter and division into acts; then he wrote the dialogues in prose; and finally he wrote in verse. The most homogeneous group of tragedies is that based on the theme of political freedom: *Virginia (Virginia), Ottavia, Bruto primo (The First Brutus), Bruto secondo (The Second Brutus), Timoleone (Timoleon), Filippo, Congiura de' Pazzi.* Although Alfieri's masterpieces, *Mirra* and *Saul,* deal with ancient themes, they reflect projections of the artist's fundamental struggle between tyranny and freedom. This tension is ready to explode at the beginning of each work, which does not really present any character development. After Alfieri delineates a heroic humanity removed from common people, he develops the conflict between freedom and tyranny within the only superhuman and complex protagonist of Alfierian tragedy: the tyrant himself. Saul becomes the object of the greatest love and hatred, the only character capable of expressing the superhuman passions of Alfieri himself. His tragic doom exemplifies the writer's unresolved conflict between a superior individualism and his passionate, yet abstract, love for a theoretical notion of freedom.

Bibliography: Opere di Vittorio Alfieri da Asti, ed. Luigi Fassò et al., 26 vols. to date (Asti: Casa d'Alfieri, 1951–75); *America the Free: Five Odes,* trans. Joseph Tusiani (New York: Italian-American Center for Urban Affairs, 1975); *Memoirs,* trans. anonymous, ed. E. R. Vincent (Oxford: Oxford University Press, 1961); *The Prince and Letters,* trans. Beatrice Corrigan and Julius Molinaro (Toronto: University of Toronto Press, 1972); *The Tragedies of Vittorio Alfieri,* trans. Charles Lloyd and Edgar A. Bowring, 2 vols. (1876; rpt. Westport, Conn.: Greenwood Press, 1970); *Of Tyranny,* trans. Julius Molinaro and Beatrice Corrigan (Toronto: University of Toronto Press, 1961); Walter Binni, *Saggi alfieriani* (Florence: La Nuova Italia, 1969); Benedetto Croce, *Poesia e non poesia* (Bari: Laterza, 1923); Mario Fubini, *Ritratto dell'Alfieri* (Florence: La Nuova Italia, 1967).

Giancarlo Maiorino

ALVARO, CORRADO (1895–1956), novelist and journalist. After an education in Naples and Rome, Alvaro served in World War I as an infantryman and was seriously wounded. After graduating with a degree in literature and philosophy from the University of Milan (1920), he worked on the *Corriere della sera* and *Il Mondo* (1922–26). As foreign correspondent for *La Stampa*, he traveled to Germany, Turkey, Greece, France, and the Soviet Union, and during the fascist period he published several travel books which attempted to explain foreign countries usually obscured by fascist propaganda. After the war, Alvaro continued his journalistic career and contributed regularly to *Il Mondo* and other periodicals.

Alvaro's chief novel is *Gente in Aspromonte* (1930, *Revolt in Aspromonte*), a short narrative depicting the tribulations of a Calabrian driven to banditry by a cruel landlord, which decries rural injustice at a time when taking such a position was often dangerous. It was Alvaro's intent to arouse the conscience of right-thinking people against social injustices in his native Calabria, as would Carlo Levi* in *Cristo si è fermato a Eboli (Christ Stopped at Eboli)* after the fall of fascism. Some critics saw in this tale of rural primitivism and power a veiled, allegorical reference to Italy under Mussolini. A novel produced some years later, *L'uomo è forte* (1938, *Man Is Strong*), seems to have been inspired by Alvaro's journey to the Soviet Union; it pictures life in a Kafkaesque dictatorship and is a covert indictment of fascism. In addition to these two major works, Alvaro wrote many other novels, several plays—including a contemporary interpretation of an ancient Greek myth, *La lunga notte di Medea* (1949, *The Long Night of Medea*)—and a personal journal, *Quasi una vita* (1950, Almost a Life), which was awarded the Strega Prize for Literature in 1952.

Bibliography: Man Is Strong, trans. Frances Frenaye (New York: Knopf, 1948); *Plays for a New Theatre: Playbook 2* (New York: New Directions, 1966)—includes *The Long Night of Medea; Revolt in Aspromonte,* trans. Frances Frenaye (New York: New Directions, 1962); Domenico Cara, *Corrado Alvaro* (Florence: La Nuova Italia, 1968).

AMMIRATO, SCIPIONE (1531–1601), political writer, historian, and poet. Ammirato was born in Lecce and studied law in Naples, Rome, and Padua before becoming secretary to Alessandro Contarini, a Venetian patrician. In Venice, his literary interests developed after he became acquainted with Pietro Aretino,* Sperone Speroni,* and Vittoria Colonna.* Forced to abandon Contarini's service because of a scandal, he returned to Lecce long enough to found the Accademia dei Trasformati. Earlier, he had aspired to the post of official historian for the city of Naples, but since this post was not offered him, he came to Florence in 1569, where Grand Duke Cosimo I proposed the task of writing a history of Florence, which he agreed to undertake. One of the guiding forces behind the Florentine Accademia degli Alterati, Ammirato became a powerful figure in the culture of Florence at that time.

Ammirato's literary production was vast. Besides many rather mediocre poems, several *novelle,** dialogues, *canzoni,** and a comedy, Ammirato wrote a series of orations addressed to King Philip II of Spain and Pope Clement VIII—the *Filippiche* and the *Clementine* (1640, The Philippines, The Clementines), in which he urged the two men to organize a crusade against the Turks. Of most significance were the *Istorie fiorentine* (1600–41, The History of Florence) and his masterpiece, the *Discorsi sopra Cornelio Tacito* (1594, Discourses on Cornelius Tacitus). The *Istorie* covered the city's history until 1574 but was a poor successor to the greater efforts of Machiavelli* or Guicciardini.* The *Discorsi,* an influential commentary composed of one hundred and forty-three discourses, shifted from Machiavelli's earlier republican bias in his *Discorsi* on Livy towards a more fashionable reliance upon Tacitus, the historian of the Roman Empire and a thinker better attuned to the political climate of the Florentine Duchy in particular and to the period of the Counter-Reformation in general. Neither the commentary nor the history contained the sophisticated argumentation or brilliant analysis that had characterized earlier political thought or historiography in Florence, but Ammirato's commentary remained rather well known abroad as long as the vogue of political theory inspired by Tacitus endured.

See also MACHIAVELLI, Niccolò.

Bibliography: Discorsi di Scipione Ammirato sopra Cornelio Tacito and *Istoria fiorentine,* ed. Luciano Scarabelli (Turin: Pomba, 1853); Eric Cochrane, *Florence in the Forgotten Centuries: 1527–1800* (Chicago: University of Chicago Press, 1973); Rofoldo De Mattei, *Il pensiero politico di Scipione Ammirato con discorsi inediti* (Milan: Giuffrè, 1963); Giuseppe Toffanin, *Machiavelli e il "Tacitismo"* (1921; rpt. Naples: Guida, 1972).

ANDREINI, GIOVAN BATTISTA (1576–1654), actor and dramatist. Born in Florence, Andreini was the son of a famous theatrical couple. In 1594, he began an early career on the stage with his father's company, the Gelosi, usually playing the role of the young man in love. In 1600, he formed his own theatrical company, the Fedeli, and served the Gonzaga family of Mantua for more than thirty years until approximately 1640. He and his company made numerous tours within Italy and abroad, most often to the court of France where Andreini was popular with Louis XIII. His long career coincided with the triumph of the Italian *commedia dell'arte** throughout Europe.

Andreini authored numerous plays, including *Florinda* (1606, Florinda), a tragedy in the Senecan style set in Scotland; *La Maddalena* (1610, Mary

Magdalen), a play reflecting the Baroque* fascination with this New Testament character; and *La Maddalena lasciva e penitente* (1617, Mary Magdalen, Wanton and Penitent), another drama on the same theme, notable for its music which was composed by Monteverdi and others. His fame rests primarily upon his drama *L'Adamo* (1613, Adam), a religious play which treats the creation story, the expulsion from the Garden of Eden, Satan's Infernal Council, and many other scenes, all of which are vaguely similar to passages in Milton's *Paradise Lost* (1667). In his essay on epic* poetry, Voltaire first suggested Andreini as one of Milton's sources. Paolo Rolli,* who translated Milton into Italian in 1729, believed that Milton had seen the play performed during his Italian visit of 1638–39. This idea was popularized by William Hayley's *Life of Milton* (1796), which contained the first English translations of the crucial scenes from the Italian play. Although Cambridge University's Trinity College possesses a manuscript in which Milton outlines a projected tragedy on Adam and Eve during the years 1641 and 1642, possibly reflecting Andreini's direct influence, the relationship between Milton's epic poem and Andreini's religious drama is, nonetheless, quite uncertain; Milton could have found some of the material attributed to Andreini in the epic poetry of Tasso.*

See also COMMEDIA DELL'ARTE.

Bibliography: L'Adamo, ed. Ettore Allodoli (Lanciano: Carabba, 1913); William Hayley, *The Life of Milton* (1796; rpt. New York: Garland, 1971).

ANGIOLIERI, CECCO (circa 1260–1313), poet. Little is known of this lyric poet who belonged to a wealthy Guelph family in Siena. He took part in several campaigns with Sienese troops, notably at the battle of Campaldino, and, during this time, apparently became acquainted with Dante Alighieri.* Several documents testify that he was absolved of a lawsuit for criminal assault in 1291 and that his five sons renounced their inheritance upon his death to avoid his heavy debts. It is also supposed that he left Siena and spent some time in Rome at the court of Cardinal Riccardo Petroni. Evidently, his life was marked by wild escapades and brushes with the law; his bad reputation was sufficiently widespread to cause Boccaccio* to recount one of his misadventures in *The Decameron* (IX,4). Scholars generally attribute one hundred and twenty-eight sonnets* to Cecco, some of which are still disputed. We have no reliable information on the dates of their composition. Although many critics have spoken of a *Canzoniere,* or songbook, by Cecco as if he had produced a coherent body of poetry analogous to that of Petrarch,* the only formal organization of the poems has been imposed by modern editors. Because he was long considered a kind of Italian François Villon, Cecco's poems were often read as autobiographical documents rather than as poems produced by a sophis-

ticated and imaginative artist working out of the literary traditions of Latin
Goliardic poetry and the love poetry which originated in Provence and
spread to Sicily and Tuscany.

Cecco's poetry is often identified with the realistic verse of the Italian
tradition known as *poesia giocosa* (jocose poetry), but it is now clear that
the best of these poems are heavily indebted to the medieval Latin
Goliardic poets for many of their themes and techniques. Other sonnets—
notably "I' ho sì gran paura di fallare" ("I have so great a fear of being
amiss"), "Sonetto, da poi ch'i' non trovo messo" ("Sonnet, since I cannot
find messenger"), and "Qualunque ben si fa, naturalmente" ("Whatever
virtue in this world there is")—demonstrate his mastery of the technical
vocabulary, imagery, and themes of the Sicilians and of the Tuscan *dolce
stil nuovo** and his positive acceptance of their conventions. Since we do
not know whether Cecco progressed from this love poetry within the
courtly tradition to his realistic and comic works, or whether he simply
wrote different kinds of poems at the same time, studies which assume
either possibility are purely speculative.

Although Cecco appreciated this courtly tradition and addressed three
sonnets to his friend Dante, the realistic sonnets, in which he parodies the
themes, vocabulary, and situations common to Tuscan love lyrics of the
period, are the real expression of his genius. Dante's Beatrice, an instrument for that poet's salvation, is reduced to Cecco's Becchina, the
daughter of a cobbler who seems to have been sent to punish rather than to
bless him. Instead of keeping the respectful distance between lover and
lady found in Dante's *Vita nuova,* Cecco quarrels with his lady in poems
commonly written in the form of a *contrasto,* or argument, such as "Bec-
chin' amore, i' ti solev'odiare" ("Becchina love, one time I did hate you").
Whereas Dante and his followers had stressed the extraordinary effects of
the lady upon the lover, Cecco frequently abandons the measured vocabulary of his Tuscan contemporaries, juxtaposing the courtly and more
vulgar or commonplace terms, concepts, and images. The most famous of
his sonnets are anthology pieces such as "S'i' fosse fuoco, arderei 'l
mondo" ("If I were fire, I would burn up the world"), "Tre cose so-
lamente mi sò in grado" ("Three things, and three alone do I desire"), and
"I' ho un padre si complessionato" ("I have a sire, and of such kidney
he"). These sonnets create the *persona* of a poet who is poverty-stricken
because of his stingy parents and who is primarily engaged in drinking,
brawling in taverns, and pursuing charming women. So convincing was this
literary creation that generations of critics accepted it as authentic without
perceiving its connection to literary tradition.

Bibliography: Poeti giocosi del tempo di Dante, ed. Mario Marti (Milan: Rizzoli,
1956); *The Sonnets of a Handsome and Well-Mannered Rogue,* trans. Thomas C.

Chubb (New York: Archon, 1970); Peter E. Bondanella, "Cecco Angiolieri and the Vocabulary of Courtly Love," *Studies in Philology* 69 (1972), 55–71; Mario Marti, *Cultura e stile nei poeti giocosi del tempo di Dante* (Pisa: Nistri-Lischi, 1953).

ANTONELLI, LUIGI (1882–1942), playwright and journalist. Born at Castilenti, Antonelli founded a periodical in the Abruzzi before traveling to Argentina in 1912 as a journalist. Throughout his literary career, he combined writing with editorial work and journalism and composed some thirty plays during his lifetime. His early works went almost unnoticed until the appearance of his single masterpiece, *L'uomo che incontrò se stesso* (1918, The Man Who Met Himself), which critics have placed within the tradition of *teatro grottesco.* * Several lesser known plays in the same vein are *La fiaba dei tre magi* (1919, The Fable of the Three Magicians), *L'isola delle scimmie* (1922, Monkey Island), and *La rosa dei venti* (1928, The Compass Rose). Like Pirandello* and other *grotteschi,* Antonelli rejected the subject matter and form of the typical bourgeois drawing-room comedy and proposed, instead, more cerebral plays with human characters who often represent or embody philosophical abstractions and ideas.

L'uomo che incontrò se stesso is not only an early Italian example of absurdist literature but also reflects some knowledge of psychoanalysis. Antonelli defines the work as a tragedy of a man who tries to reshape his past (this is also the theme of his play *La rosa dei venti*). The plot involves a bifurcated protagonist—one character a man of middle age, another representing the same man in his youth—who has been betrayed by his wife and who fails to avoid the repetition of this betrayal when the ruler of a mysterious island, Dr. Climt (perhaps the typical German psychoanalyst), offers him an opportunity to relive the incident. *La fiaba dei tre magi* is a contemporary version of the "ship of fools" theme, where Justice, Truth, and Poetry descend upon an ocean liner to investigate a murder on board; only Poetry succeeds in alleviating the tragedy. *L'isola delle scimmie* is a fanciful description of the disruptive effects of humanity upon a utopian colony of monkeys. Although Antonelli's best work was written in the pre-absurdist tradition of the *teatro grottesco,* he also wrote many more traditional bourgeois plays based upon the amorous triangle of husband, wife, and lover. One later work, *Il Maestro* (1933, The Master), is worthy of note for its rejection of the elements of illusion and fantasy which are central to his best works.

See also TEATRO GROTTESCO.

Bibliography: Teatro grottesco del Novecento: antologia, ed. Gigi Livio (Milan: Mursia, 1965); Silvio D'Amico, *Storia del teatro drammatico* (Milan: Garzanti, 1953); Lander MacClintock, *The Age of Pirandello* (Bloomington, Ind.: Indiana University Press, 1954).

ARCADIA, a still extant literary society founded in Rome in 1690 by fourteen men of letters who had gathered around Christina of Sweden (died 1689). The Accademia dell'Arcadia was supposed to continue the anti-baroque trend initiated by the former queen's Royal Academy (created in 1674). Among the most prominent founders were Giambattista Felice Zappi (1667–1719), Giovan Mario Crescimbeni (1663–1728), and Gian Vincenzo Gravina.* Gravina styled in Latin the society's by-laws and included such relevant ideas as the return to nature, which influenced the thought of Jean-Jacques Rousseau. Indeed, on one hand, the Arcadia is the last manifestation of a pastoral* tradition, connected with the idea of the Golden Age, which goes back to the Renaissance* and was codified by Sannazaro.* On the other hand, it signals the beginning of a new era, characterized by empirical and rationalistic thought, and from this point of view, it can be considered the first phase of the Enlightenment* in Italy.

One of the most striking aspects of this society was its rapid expansion and its rigorously centralized organization. Rome was the seat of its president or *Custode Generale* (general keeper) and of its central branch or *Serbatoio* (reservoir). Chapters were soon created all over Italy under the ambitious title "Arcadic Colonies." In this way, the Arcadia became a literary phenomenon of considerable magnitude which exerted a deep influence on Italian culture during the first half of the eighteenth century. Its immediate purpose was the elimination of the so-called bad taste of the Baroque,* and from this point of view it is considered the first reaction to the Marinism (*see* MARINO, GIAMBATTISTA) which prevailed in seventeenth-century Italian literature. But the role of the Arcadia transcends the boundaries of literature and can be fully understood only from an interdisciplinary viewpoint, taking into account the history of philosophy as well as the history of science. The achievements of Arcadia in the field of literature mainly concern poetry and criticism, including the rise of literary historiography. The most important writer in the first field was Pietro Metastasio,* a pupil of Gravina, who, until the last decade of the eighteenth century, retained his international reputation as a sublime poet, fostered by admirers such as Voltaire and Rousseau. Other notable representatives of Arcadian poetry were Paolo Rolli* and Carlo Innocenzo Frugoni (1692–1768), not to mention a host of minor versifiers who share with their greater fellow members the credit for having firmly established a poetic language and technique whose influence can be traced not only in Parini* but also in Carducci.* As to the academy's contribution in the field of criticism, there is no doubt that Gravina, Muratori,* Pietro Calepio (1693–1762), and Antonio Conti (1677–1749) played an important role in the rise of new approaches to literary works, founded on a more or less original assessment of the power of imagination and of primitive poetry. Last but not least, Arcadia originated the history of Italian literature, as exemplified by Crescimbeni's *Istoria della volgar poesia* (1698; 2nd ed.,

1714, History of Italian Poetry), which paved the way to Girolamo Tiraboschi's* *Storia della letteratura italiana* (History of Italian Literature), a classic work in its genre (1772–82; 2nd ed., 1787–94).

The society, created in the midst of the Counter-Reformation, became an essential part of the Catholic establishment and enjoyed the protection of the popes. The strictly orthodox façade, however, covered an intense intellectual activity that did not fit into the traditional values. It has been noted that some prominent scientists belonging to the school of Galileo,* the great victim of the Roman Inquisition, were members of the Arcadia (e.g., Francesco Redi,* Marcello Malpighi, 1628–94; Lorenzo Bellini, 1643–1704; and Vincenzo Viviani, 1622–1703). It should be added that the most significant representatives of the intellectual revival of the South, studied by Nicola Badaloni (1923–   ) in an important work (*Introduzione a G. B. Vico* [Milan: Feltrinelli, 1961]), were active members of Arcadia: from Francesco D'Andrea (1625–98) to Gravina and Giuseppe Valletta (1636–1714), not to mention Vico* himself. The Arcadian world is a labyrinth of crosscurrents and intellectual exchanges, encompassing not only the Italian territory but also the most vital intellectual centers of Europe, such as Paris, London, and Zurich. Prudence dictated by the heavy regime of the Counter-Reformation did not prevent the assimilation of scientific and philosophic ideas which eroded the foundation of traditional Christianity. Descartes, Gassendi, Boyle, Newton, Locke, Leibniz, and Spinoza were studied and discussed in a new clime of free research, which marked the beginning of the Italian Enlightenment. It has been said that the philosophy prevailing in Arcadia was Cartesian rationalism. This is only a half-truth, since the empirical component of modern thought also had many followers among the Arcadians and was frequently combined with rationalism in a syncretistic approach.

The denigrators of Arcadia have criticized its outward appearance without taking into account its inner complexities. In 1757, Saverio Bettinelli (1718–1808) chastised the proliferation of mediocre versifiers under the Arcadian aegis, when he wrote in his *Lettere virgiliane* (Virgilian Letters) that the society should be closed for a period of fifty years and should not create other chapters or send diplomas for a period of one hundred years. In 1763, Giuseppe Baretti* violently attacked Arcadia in *La frustra letteraria* (Literary Whip), setting a pattern for the adverse criticism that prevailed until World War II and prevented a genuine historical appreciation of the role played by the society in the history of Italian literature and culture. This trend was challenged by Benedetto Croce* in an address delivered in 1945, which broke new ground in the field of early eighteenth-century studies. In recent years, Croce's interpretation has been further developed by Mario Fubini (1900–1977) who established a continuum between the first and second halves of the eighteenth century, i.e., between

Arcadia and the Enlightenment, and by Walter Binni (1913–) who has pointed out the importance of the origins to be found in Tuscan and northern literary milieux. This point of view has been opposed by Giuseppe Petronio (1909–) and by other critics whose writings have stirred a still undecided dispute, showing in various cases a strange ignorance of the Anglo-American theories of pastoral* poetry and of its relevance in Western culture.

See also BAROQUE; ENLIGHTENMENT; NEOCLASSICISM; PASTORAL.

Bibliography: Benedetto Croce, *La letteratura italiana del Settecento* (Bari: Laterza, 1949); Mario Fubini, *Dal Muratori al Baretti,* 2nd ed. (Bari: Laterza, 1954); Violet Paget (pseud. Vernon Lee), *Studies of the Eighteenth Century in Italy,* 2nd ed. (London: Unwin, 1907); Antonio Pironalli, *L'Arcadia* (Palermo: Palumbo, 1963).

Gustavo Costa

ARETINO, PIETRO (1492–1556), poet and prose writer, journalist, and self-professed "flagello divino" ("divine scourge") of princes. Although Aretino (his name assumed from his native Arezzo) came from a rather modest family background (his father was a cobbler), as a youth he was able to receive schooling in poetry and painting in Perugia. In 1517, he made his way to Rome where he secured the protection of the Chigi banking family and a position of favor within the papal court of Leo X and Cardinal Giulio de' Medici. Upon the death of Leo X (1521) and during the subsequent election of his successor, Hadrian VI, Aretino began to acquire a certain notoriety with his publicly voiced opposition to Hadrian and his supporters; at the foot of the statue of Pasquino, Aretino attached his *Pasquinate* (lampoons) which became popular reading throughout the city of Rome. Aretino quickly became *persona non grata,* especially with the papal court, and he prudently left Rome to seek his fortune in various northern Italian cities. Availing himself of his contacts with the Medici family, Aretino was introduced to the Gonzaga family of Mantua by Giulio de' Medici. Also at this time, Aretino met and became friends with the Medici *condottiere* Giovanni delle Bande Nere. With the election of Pope Clement VII, a Medici, Aretino was able to return to Rome; however, he was unable to keep away from the public arena, and he quickly rekindled old hatreds. The breaking point came when Aretino wrote sonnets* to accompany a series of erotic designs which a friend, Marcantonio Raimondi, had made. The papal datary Giovanni Matteo Giberti, an enemy of former times, learned of the sonnets and threatened to harm Aretino either politically or physically. Again Aretino left Rome to avoid the confrontation. His absence was brief, however, and upon his return to Rome, he was greeted with an armed attack by men Giberti hired. Seriously wounded, Aretino fought back with his most effective weapon, the pen, attacking Giberti and even the papacy. Following this episode, Aretino retreated to the protection of Giovanni delle Bande Nere. The date was 1525 and, except for a brief excursion late in life (Aretino traveled to Rome in 1553 in hopes of being elected cardinal), he never again returned to Rome. Shortly after the death of Giovanni delle Bande Nere in 1526, Aretino established what was to become his permanent residence in the city of Venice. He was then thirty-five years old, on the threshold of an active, often tumultuous life as a writer, bon vivant, and friend or foe to popes, princes, and artists.

Venice proved to be the ideal city for Aretino. His popularity was widespread, he was protected by the Doge Andrea Gritti, and he lived in a handsome house ("Casa Aretina") next to the Rialto Bridge. He enjoyed a wide variety of social contacts as well as romances with both men and women. Relatively free to spend his time and utilize his talents, Aretino amassed a sizable fortune with his hired pen by either praising possible benefactors or blackmailing enemies. He became privy to important information about key figures which he wove into his *giudizi* ("judgments"), *pronostici* ("prognostications"), and letters. Aretino won the favor, if not the friendship, of such noted men as Francis I, Clement VII, Charles V, Cosimo de' Medici, Titian, and Sansovino. A visit to Aretino's house became mandatory for any dignitary passing through Venice, and, as he himself boasted, he became "Secretary of the World." An outward display of Aretino's notoriety is the gold chain which Francis I bequeathed to Aretino in 1533, a somewhat dubious distinction given the motto engraved on the chain: "Lingua eius loquetur mendacium" ("His tongue speaks a lie"). Aretino, who had entreated Francis to send him the promised chain, retorted in his characteristically witty fashion, stating that if the motto were true, then he must be lying whenever he praised Francis. Titian and Sansovino appear to have been more generously motivated when the former painted Aretino's portrait in 1545 and the latter sculpted a bust of him. Life in Venice was not without its difficulties: Aretino's prognostications and lampoons caused him the loss of friendships such as that with the powerful Gonzaga family, led to a second attempt on his life, turned his former secretary Nicolò Franco into an enemy, and brought on the slanderous accusations of Antonio Francesco Doni* in his *Terremoto* (1556, Earthquake). Aretino never lost his zest for life, however, and he continued to write and seek the company of others. Having outlived many of his former benefactors and friends, Aretino died of apoplexy in 1556. His epitaph reads: "Here lies the Tuscan poet Aretino./ He slandered all but God, Whom he left out/ because, he pleaded, Well, I never knew him."

Aretino was first drawn to poetry, especially to antiliterary and anti-Petrarchan poetry. His favorite meter was the sonnet* with prolonged *coda,* and the subject matter was occasional and often lascivious. In 1529, he attempted a more ambitious poem, the *Marfisa* (name of the heroine), which he had envisioned as an extension of Ludovico Ariosto's* *Orlando furioso (The Frenzy of Orlando).* He copyrighted and published the work even though it was never completed. Aretino soon turned to prose, especially the theatre. He wrote his first comedy *La Cortigiana (The Courtezan)* in 1525 (published in 1534). It remains one of his most popular comedies, depicting with vivid realism a Sienese visitor in Rome who endeavors to become a cardinal and is taught the rather seamy side of court life. In this work, Aretino's polemical stance and his penchant for comic satire provide a scathing portrait of sixteenth-century Roman life. Five other plays followed: *Marescalco* (The Stablemaster), written in 1527, published in 1533: *Ipocrito* (1542, The Hypocrite); *Talanta* (1542, Talanta); *Filosofo* (1546, The Philosopher); and a tragedy written in hendecasyllables, *Orazia* (1546, The Horatii). Paradoxically, during this same period of time, Aretino wrote a series of religious prose works, treating the lives of Jesus, the Virgin Mary, St. Catherine of Siena, and St. Thomas Aquinas.

A literary form which proved most congenial to Aretino's personality was the dialogue. The *Ragionamenti (Dialogues),* written in 1534 (first part) and 1536 (second part), are a notoriously realistic and ribald parody of the Platonic dialogue. Blending elements of comedy and the *novella,** Aretino portrays an old prostitute, Nanna, as she instructs her daughter Pippa on the lives of nuns, wives, and whores, encouraging her to adopt the last-named profession. Aretino wrote other dialogues, one of which, *Le carte parlanti* (1543, The Speaking Cards), is based on the ingenious pretext of a discussion between ordinary playing cards and Tarot cards which explain their symbolic meaning and reveal the fates of their players, including Charles V.

Much of what Aretino wrote, especially the numerous lampoons and eulogies, is no longer extant. However, if one is to consider his letters, a sizable amount of representative material has survived. There are six volumes of Aretino's personal letters, numbering approximately three thousand. Published over a twenty-year period (1537–57), they touch on all walks of life, especially Renaissance* Venice, art (over six hundred letters), good food, wine, and company; many are adulatory petitions for money, others are elaborate letters of gratitude for gifts received.

In his writings, as in his multifaceted and colorful life, Aretino did not present a unified front. He not only treated a wide range of topics, but also adopted numerous and varied styles of writing. He was attracted to both poetry and prose, to sacred as well as to profane subjects. Although his works often show a rather superficial inspiration, they always demonstrate Aretino's unique quality for judging human nature and events, a polemical intent, an antiliterary stance, a journalistic approach, and an effort to entertain.

Bibliography: Aretino's Dialogues, trans. Raymond Rosenthal (New York: Stein & Day, 1971); *Aretino: Selected Letters,* trans. George Bull (Harmondsworth: Penguin, 1976); Thomas Caldecot Chubb, ed., *The Letters of Pietro Aretino* (New York: Archon, 1967); Samuel Putnam, ed., *The Works of Aretino,* 2 vols. (Chicago: Pascal Covici, 1926); Thomas Caldecot Chubb, *Aretino, Scourge of Princes* (New York: Reynal & Hitchcock, 1940); James Cleugh, *The Divine Aretino* (New York: Stein & Day, 1966); Edward Hutton, *Pietro Aretino, The Scourge of Princes* (London: Constable, 1922).

Dennis Dutschke

ARIOSTO, LUDOVICO (1474–1533), poet and playwright. While the records indicate that his mother, Daria Malaguzzi Valeri, was of noble extraction and that his father, Count Nicolò Ariosto, could trace his distinguished family back at least to twelfth-century Bologna, Ludovico did not grow up to think of himself as a nobleman. Unlike his literary predecessor in the Este court of Ferrara, Matteo Maria Boiardo,* count of Scandiano, he had no use for titles (as when signing his correspondence) and found his career as a gentleman servant of the court to be both burdensome and an impediment to his literary vocation. Born in his mother's home town of Reggio, where his father was captain of the citadel and which he would later remember as a joyful place, Ludovico began at an early age to show an inclination to poetry and drama. When, sometime in 1484 or 1485, Nicolò moved his family to Ferrara, where he was to become head of the municipal administration, the cultural benefits of that splendid Renaissance* city were soon made available to his children. It was on 25 January 1486 that Ludovico and his brother Gabriele were taken by their father to the opening performance of Plautus's *Menaechmi.* The experience apparently proved to be so delightful that it inspired Ludovico to write parts, which he then directed his brothers and sisters to recite in a "little theatre" in their home. But Nicolò had other plans for his oldest son and in 1489, at his father's insistence, Ludovico entered the University of Ferrara as a student of the law, a subject for which he had little appreciation. Five years later, he was able to convince his father to allow him to abandon his legal studies in order that he might devote himself to the study of the classical Latin authors. This he undertook to do under the tutelage of the Augustinian friar, Gregorio da Spoleto, who served as tutor to the young princes of the Este household and, later, to Francesco Sforza in Milan. Gregorio's departure from Ferrara deprived Ariosto of the opportunity to learn Greek, and the death of his father in 1500 obliged him to abandon his literary pursuits and the pleasant life of an aspiring poet and lover of Latin, in order to take over the management of family affairs and to provide for the welfare of his nine brothers and sisters. After a period of public employment as the captain of the citadel in Canossa, in October 1503 Ariosto entered the service of Cardinal Ippolito d'Este (son of Duke Ercole and brother of Alfonso, who was to become duke of Este in 1505), as a courtier and servant whose duties would range from important diplomatic missions to Pope Julius II to the most humble domestic services. The cardinal retained the poet in his service until 1517 and assumed the expenses of publishing the 1516 edition of the *Orlando furioso* (1516, 1521, 1532, *The Frenzy of Orlando*). It may be somewhat misleading, however, to think of him as Ariosto's patron, since he apparently had and showed little appreciation for his poetry, did not pay him to be a poet, and paid him with no conscientious regularity for the services which were exacted from him.

In 1518, Ariosto refused to accompany Ippolito on a journey to Hungary and was dismissed. In April of that year, he passed into the service of the cardinal's brother, Duke Alfonso, and while his fortunes improved momentarily, he continued to find court service distasteful. In 1522, financial exigency forced Ariosto to accept the post of commissary of the remote and hostile Garfagnana district, where he remained until July 1525, far from Ferrara and from Alessandra Benucci, a Florentine resident of Ferrara to whom he had been devoted at least since the death of her husband, Tito Strozzi, in 1515. Alessandra and Ludovico were secretly married sometime between 1526 and 1530. His last years were relatively tranquil ones during which he retreated into independent retirement in a modest house in via Mirasole in Ferrara. He died there, apparently with his wife and his illegitimate son, Virginio, at his side, on or about the sixth of July in his fifty-ninth year. He is entombed at the Biblioteca Comunale Ariostea, housed in the Palazzo Paradiso in Ferrara.

As a writer, Ariosto is best remembered as the author of the *Orlando furioso,* a poetic masterpiece which stands unchallenged as the highest literary achievement of an age which was more successfully given to visual expression. But even as a verbal creation, Ariosto's romantic epic* succeeded in giving, at least to some sixteenth-century readers, the feeling that to read the *Furioso* was to see the events as though they were occurring before one's very eyes. Such was the impression of the critic Lodovico Dolce (1508–68). Ariosto thus proved to be an excellent example of the kind of writer who satisfied the Renaissance intellectual's need to associate the skills of a poet of vivid descriptive ability with those of the painter, not unlike Homer, whom Petrarch* called the "best of painters." In a sense, this impression has been reconfirmed by recent readings, which disclose that some of the most essential elements of the poem (such as Orlando's madness) are presented in iconic and figurative terms (Orlando's nudity as a sign of madness, for example) rather than through verbal enunciations. Madmen, it would appear, did not gain a literary voice, however rudimentary, until the age of Elizabeth in England and that of Cervantes in Spain.

Having started out, ostensibly, like others, to continue and bring to a conclusion the unfinished *Orlando innamorato* (1483, Orlando in Love, Books I and II; 1495, complete edition) of Matteo Maria Boiardo, Ariosto in fact succeeds in creating a vividly real microcosm of which he is the omnipotent master, "the Providence of the little world of the poem," as he has been called. That world is one which combines classical elements derived from Virgil, Ovid, Catullus, Horace, Statius, and others with material taken from Carolingian epics and legends and from the Celtic tales of the Arthurian cycle. It is the world of paladins and knights affected by love and magic. In addition, it bears the influence of Dante,* Petrarch,* Boccaccio,* Leon Battista Alberti,* and, of course, Boiardo, as well as others. It can be and has been said that very little of the material of the poem was invented by Ariosto himself. Even in his own century, which could still distinguish between poetic invention and disposition, Ariosto was accused of being a robber of tales. Nonetheless, he remains the master of that world, a kind of demiurge who is able to control and dominate the activities of its inhabitants, shifting from scene to scene at will, abandoning his creatures, and returning to them according to his own whim as if to suggest that the cosmic instability, which is reflected in Orlando's erotomania, is itself a reflection of the supreme artificer's own instability. It is the poet himself, in fact, who confesses to his audience that love threatens at every moment to destroy his creative powers. As he works to refine his verse, his beloved continues to file away at his wits, so that he too, like Orlando, may become a frenzied lover, caught up in a dance of folly which is the human condition itself.

Still, behind the veil of madness and mutability, of inconstancy and infidelity, Ariosto seems to suggest that reason and stability are as much the real focus of his poem as frenzy and folly. Reminiscent of Seneca's *Hercules furens* (The Frenzy of Hercules), the title of Ariosto's poem metaphorically links Hercules to Orlando and Ruggiero in their roles as heroes at the crossroads in search of the path of human virtue. If the heroes are temporarily led astray, there is an underlying belief that reason, despite its limitations, will allow them to regain their senses, as in fact happens to both. And Ariosto's portrait of Bradamante, sister of Rinaldo, future wife of Ruggiero (converted to Christianity), and illustrious ancestor of the Este family, is even more encouraging. She is a model of constancy, loyalty, magnanimity, and compassion. So cleverly has Ariosto constructed the world of Orlando and Angelica, of Ruggiero and Bradamante, that even today critics only hesitatingly assert that there is not some hidden allegory lying dormant in it, waiting to be uncovered.

Ariosto's other works include the fragmentary *Cinque canti* (1545, Five Cantos), which the author may have intended to incorporate into the *Furioso* but which are far different in tone; a collection of Latin and Italian lyrics; *Le Satire* (1534, *The Satires*); and four comedies—*La Cassaria (The Coffer)*, first performed in 1508 for Cardinal Ippolito, *I Suppositi (The Pretenders)*, performed in Ferrara in 1509 and in Rome for Pope Leo X in 1519, *Il Negromante (The Necromancer)*, produced for the first time at the carnival of 1529 in Ferrara (although conceived in 1509) and *La Lena (Lena)*, presented at the carnival of 1528 in Ferrara. There is also an unfinished play, *I Studenti (The Students)*, for which his son Virginio and his brother Gabriele each wrote separate conclusions. As an innovative playwright, Ariosto is recognized as a master whose comedies were surpassed in his day only by the single example of Machiavelli's* *La Mandragola (The Mandrake Root)*. In addition, Ariosto wrote numerous letters.

Most interesting for the glimpse they give us of the private world of the author are *Le Satire*, which recall specific incidents and situations out of Ariosto's past. They are written in tercets, and the poet uses them as occasions to remember first his break with Ippolito in 1517, and then, in the second satire, a trip to Rome in the same year to defend a benefice sought by another who knew he had forgotten to pay his registration taxes. The third recalls his entry in 1518 into the service of Alfonso, and the fourth how, like a bird who changes cages and for several days cannot sing, he left Ferrara in 1522 to assume his duties in the Garfagnana. The fifth satire is addressed to his cousin who is about to take a wife, while the sixth is to Pietro Bembo,* asking him to help with his son Virginio's education. The last, written in his forty-ninth year, concerns his refusal of an offer to be made ambassador to Pope Clement VII.

See also BOIARDO, Matteo Maria; TASSO, Torquato.

Bibliography: The Comedies of Ariosto, trans. Edmond M. Beame and Leonard G. Sbrocchi (Chicago: University of Chicago Press, 1975); *Orlando Furioso*, trans. Guido Waldman (London: Oxford University Press, 1974); *Orlando Furioso (The Frenzy of Orlando)*, 2 vols., trans. Barbara Reynolds (Baltimore: Penguin, 1975–77); *The Satires of Ariosto: A Renaissance Autobiography*, trans. Peter DeSa Wiggins (Athens, Ohio: Ohio University Press, 1976); C. P. Brand, *Ludovico Ariosto: A Preface to the 'Orlando Furioso'* (Edinburgh: University of Edinburgh Press, 1974); Robert Durling, *The Figure of the Poet in Renaissance Epic* (Cambridge, Mass.: Harvard University Press, 1965); Edmund G. Gardner, *The King of Court Poets: A Study of the Work, Life, and Times of Ludovico Ariosto* (1906; rpt. Westport, Conn.: Greenwood Press, 1969); Robert Griffin, *Ludovico Ariosto* (New York: Twayne, 1974); Graham Hough, *A Preface to 'The Faerie Queene'* (New York: Norton, 1963); Aldo Scaglione, ed., *Ariosto 1974 in America* (Ravenna: Longo, 1977).

Andrea di Tommaso

B

BACCHELLI, RICCARDO (1891–), poet, novelist, journalist, dramatist, critic, and editor. Bacchelli was born in Bologna. Leaving the local university in 1912 without obtaining a degree, Bacchelli contributed a number of articles to *La Voce,* was one of the founders of *La Ronda,* and eventually became drama critic for *La Fiera letteraria* and a member of several of Italy's most prestigious academies. His first poetry, *Poemi lirici* (1914, Lyric Poems), reflects his ties to the poets associated with *La Voce* in Florence. An early play, *Amleto* (1919, Hamlet), which was published by *La Ronda,* modifies the Shakespearean character, presenting him as a modern antihero, a figure akin to Borgese's* Rubè. One of his best works is the satirical novel entitled *Lo sa il tonno* (1923, The Tuna Knows), a philosophical or moral tale related by a tuna encountered at a fish market; this novel owes an obvious debt to the animal fables of Leopardi* (the model for prose style in the circle of writers associated with *La Ronda*). Besides contributing substantive critical essays to *La Ronda* and a number of other literary reviews on a wide variety of writers (Leopardi, Shakespeare, Goldoni,* Ibsen, and Verga*), Bacchelli began his highly successful experiments with the genre of the historical novel in *Il diavolo al Pontelungo* (1927, *The Devil at the Long Bridge*). Set around Locarno and Bologna between 1873 and 1876, the work recounts the events leading up to the unsuccessful uprising in Bologna of 1874. Its major protagonists are historical figures, the Russian anarchist Bakunin, his follower Carlo Cafiero, and the leaders of the uprising, Andrea Costa and Abdon Negri. An account of a peasant legend concerning a visit of the devil to the same region one hundred years before the time of the story introduces the tale and inspires its title.

After a number of critical essays, lyrics, and novels, between 1938 and 1940 Bacchelli published his greatest work, a historical novel in three parts under the general title of *Il mulino del Po (The Mill on the Po): Dio ti salvi (God Save You), La miseria viene in barca (Trouble Travels by Water),* and *Mondo vecchio sempre nuovo (Nothing New Under the Sun).* The novel's scope is extremely ambitious. After Napoleon's retreat from Moscow in 1812, a young man named Lazzaro Scacerni returns to Italy with enough money from his army pay to purchase a mill on the Po River. The reader follows the saga of the Scacerni family from the Napoleonic period through the Risorgimento until the last Lazzaro Scacerni's death at the front near the Piave in 1918 closes the trilogy. While owing an obvious debt to Manzoni's* historical novel (another favorite model for the *La Ronda* group), Bacchelli's work avoids servile imitation and brings an entire century to life with the epic sweep of its prose. The success of the novel established Bacchelli's fame and earned him a place in the Accademia d'Italia (1940).

Shortly thereafter, Bacchelli published *Rossini* (1941, Rossini), a biography of the composer worthy of comparison to the well-known volume by Stendhal. An earlier historical work, *La congiura di Don Giulio d'Este* (1931, The Conspiracy of Don Giulio d'Este), is an admirable reconstruction of the atmosphere in Ferrara at the time of Ariosto.* Combining his love for history with his sense of literary style, Bacchelli successfully returned to the genre of the historical novel with *I tre schiavi di Giulio Cesare* (1947, The Three Slaves of Julius Caesar), a tale indebted to Suetonius which traces the lives of three of Caesar's slaves who bring his dead body home to his wife; and *Non ti chiamerò più padre* (1959, No Longer Shall I Call You Father), the fictional reconstruction of the life and times of Pietro Bernardone, the father of St. Francis of Assisi,* which shows the saint in a rather untraditional light, devoid of his humility.

Age has not slowed Bacchelli's prodigious productivity. His latest works include *Rapporto segreto* (1967, Secret Report), a satirical novel about space flight in an unnamed country (obviously the United States) and several volumes of his memoirs.

Bibliography: Tutte le opere di Riccardo Bacchelli, 29 vols.—a few as yet unpublished (Milan: Mondadori, 1958–); *The Devil at the Long Bridge,* trans. Orlo Williams (New York: Longmans, 1929); *The Mill on the Po,* trans. Frances Frenaye (1950; rpt. Westport, Conn.: Greenwood Press, 1975)—contains the first two parts of the trilogy; *Nothing New Under the Sun,* trans. Stuart Hood (New York: Pantheon, 1955); Mario Saccenti, *Riccardo Bacchelli* (Milan: Mursia, 1973).

BALLATA or CANZONE A BALLO ("dance song"), an ancient lyric genre originally intended to be set to music for dancing. Appearing first in Florence and Bologna in the thirteenth century, the form was perfected by the poets of the *dolce stil nuovo,** Dante,* and Petrarch,* and was to be employed by poets in all periods, including Poliziano,* Lorenzo de' Medici,* Pascoli,* Carducci,* and D'Annunzio.* Its metrical and stanzaic structure is rather intricate. The ballata consists of a refrain (*ripresa* or *ritornello*), usually of one to five lines, repeated at the end of each stanza, and an indeterminant number of stanzas. When set to music, the chorus usually sings the refrains while a soloist renders the stanzas. The stanzas may be divided into what are termed *mutazioni* ("variations") or *piedi* ("feet") and a *volta* ("turn"); the *mutazioni* have the same meter and number of lines, while the *volta* repeats the number of lines and the rhyme of the refrain. The last line of the refrain and the last line of the *volta* rhyme, as do the last line of the *mutazioni* and the first line of the *volta*. A typical arrangement of a *ballata* might be: *xy yx / ab ab bc cx xy yx / de de effx xy yx/* etc. Typical of this lyric are lines with eleven, seven, eight, or a mixture of eleven and seven syllables. There are a number of variant forms, which differ according to the number of lines in the refrain: the *ballata grande* (four lines); the *ballata mezzana* (three lines); the *ballata minore* (two lines); the *ballata piccola* (a single line of eleven syllables); the *ballata minima* (a single line of less than eleven syllables); and the *ballata stravagante* (more than four lines). This form should not be confused with the *ballata romantica* or "romantic ballad" composed by such poets as Berchet,* Carrer,* and Prati* in imitation of German or English models of the nineteenth century.

Bibliography: Sir Maurice Bowra, "Songs of Dance and Carnival," in *Italian Renaissance Studies,* ed. E. F. Jacob (London: Faber & Faber, 1960); Lydia Meierhans, *Die Ballata* (Bern: Francke Verlag, 1956); Raffaele Spongano, *Nozioni ed esempi di metrica italiana* (Bologna: Pàtron, 1966).

BANDELLO, MATTEO (1485–1561), churchman and writer of *novelle.** Bandello was born at Castelnuovo Scrivia and received a religious education in the Milanese monastery of Santa Maria delle Grazie where his uncle was prior and where, as a child, he apparently observed Da Vinci* painting *The Last Supper.* Subsequently, he attended the University of Pavia. During the opening years of the sixteenth century, Bandello followed his uncle, who was then the general of the Dominican order, all over Italy and France, acquiring a vast knowledge of the many important cities in Italy and being exposed to a great number of narrative traditions both erudite and popular in character. When his uncle died in 1506, Bandello returned to Milan and began his literary career. He served a great number of patrons in his lifetime: Alessandro Bentivoglio, Massimiliano Sforza, Isabella d'Este, Francesco Gonzaga, Giovanni delle Bande Nere (in whose camp he apparently met Machiavelli*), Cesare Fregoso (and later his widow Costanza Rangone), and finally Henry II of France, who made him bishop of Agen (1550), a post he held until his death.

Among Bandello's minor works are *Le tre Parche* (1531, The Three Fates), a poem in *terza rima** in honor of the first son of Fregoso and his wife Costanza; the *Canti XI* (1536–38, Eleven Cantos), a poem in *ottava rima** which praised Lucrezia Gonzaga, true love, and modesty; a collection of Petrarchan verse entitled *Alcuni fragmenti de le rime* (1544, Some Fragments of the Rhymes), which was dedicated to Marguerite de Navarre, sister of King Francis I of France and the author of the *Heptameron,* a collection of tales inspired by Boccaccio;* a Latin version of one of Boccaccio's *novelle* (X,8); a series of letters; and a version in the vernacular of Euripides's *Hecuba*. His reputation, however, rests upon his *Novelle (The Novels)*, three parts of which appeared in 1554, with the final section (some thirty *novelle*) appearing after his death in 1573. The stories number two hundred and fourteen in all, and unlike many of the other collections from Boccaccio's to Bandello's day, there is no frame-story within which the *novelle* are told. Instead, each one was supposedly told in Bandello's company, and he later committed them to paper from memory. Every tale is prefaced by a dedicatory letter to a person of importance—a group of people which comprises a cross-section of the important courtiers, noblemen, and churchmen of his day. The variety of the collection is astounding; it includes historical, romantic, tragic, or anecdotal tales. Unlike Boccaccio, who carefully groups his stories by day and topic, Bandello covers various topics at random—love, jests, justice, descriptions of clergymen, and many other themes. He is primarily concerned with love and death, which are often described in the most minute detail with a sensuality that is lacking in Boccaccio and a tone that often borders upon that of the *fabliaux* tradition.

The most striking characteristic of this collection is its contemporary quality. Although the stories range in setting from antiquity to the Renaissance,* the most interesting *novelle* and their dedications usually give the reader a vivid impression of current events and contemporary historical protagonists—Pope Leo X, Machiavelli,* Da Vinci,* Castiglione,* Martin Luther, Lorenzo de' Medici,* Henry VIII, the Sack of Rome, the siege of Vienna, and the Protestant Reformation. For Bandello, storytelling is at its best when it underlines unusual occurrences in everyday life which produce a sense of the marvelous. With his intention to amuse by the presentation of his chronicle of Renaissance society and his avoidance of pedantic literary language, Bandello achieves a narrative style in the *novella* form which, if less aesthetically pleasing than that of his predecessor Boccaccio, is, nevertheless, also more accessible to the reader of both his time and our own day. His *novelle* were not without their influence upon European literature. In France, Pierre Boaistuau published loose translations of six of his stories in 1559, François Belleforest published translations of some seventy others by 1570, and part four of the *Novelle* appeared in an anonymous translation in 1573. Writers in Elizabethan England were thus able to read Bandello both in the original Italian and in French translations. William Painter's *Palace of Pleasure* (1566–67) presented twenty-five of his stories; Geffraie Fenton's *Tragicall Discourses* (1567) are derived from him indirectly through the Belleforest version. Most importantly, Elizabethan dramatists used the stories as direct or indirect sources to produce some of the greatest plays of the period, including Shakespeare in *Much Ado About Nothing* (1598), *Twelfth Night*

(1600), and *Romeo and Juliet* (1596) (Bandello's version was itself based upon Da Porto's* original) and Webster in the *Duchess of Malfi* (produced 1616?, printed 1623).

See also DA PORTO, Luigi; NOVELLA.

Bibliography: Tutte le opere di Matteo Bandello, ed. Francesco Flora, 2 vols. (Milan: Mondadori, 1972); *Certain Tragicall Discourses of Bandello,* trans. Geffraie Fenton, 2 vols. (London: Nutt, 1889); *The Novels of Matteo Bandello,* trans. John Payne, 6 vols. (London: Villon Society, 1890); Letterio di Francia, *Novellistica,* 2 vols. (Milan: Vallardi, 1924–25); T. Gwynfor Griffith, *Bandello's Fiction: An Examination of the Novelle* (Oxford: Blackwell, 1955); Yvonne Rodax, *The Real and the Ideal in the Novella of Italy, France, and England* (Chapel Hill, N.C.: University of North Carolina Studies in Comparative Literature, No. 44, 1968); René Sturel, *Bandello en France au XVIe siècle* (1918; rpt. Geneva: Slatkine, 1970).

BANTI, ANNA, pseudonym of Lucia Longhi Lopresti (1895–   ), novelist, critic, and biographer. Born in Florence and educated primarily in art history, Banti married Robert Longhi, the distinguished art historian, and became the literary editor of *Paragone,* an important journal devoted to both art and literature. Her first works were collections of short stories—*Itinerario di Paolina* (1937, Guide to Paolina), *Il coraggio delle donne* (1940, The Courage of Women), and *Le monache cantano* (1942, The Nuns Sing)—and a novel, *Sette lune* (1941, Seven Moons). The status of women in Italy evolved as one of her main themes. After the war, partly inspired by her husband's interest in Caravaggio, Banti published her best known novel, *Artemisia* (1947, Artemisia), a fictional recreation of the life of Artemisia Gentileschi, a sixteenth-century painter and a follower of Caravaggio, who was one of the first women in the arts to proclaim the equality of the sexes. This work was followed by a collection of stories, *Le donne muoiono* (1951, The Women Die) which won the Viareggio Prize the next year.

Besides biographies of Fra Angelico, Lorenzo Lotto, Velásquez, and Monet, as well as a major study of Matilde Serao,* between 1953 and 1965, Banti continued to publish important fiction, including *Il bastardo* (1953, The Bastard), *Allarme sul lago* (1954, Alarm on the Lake), *La monaca di Sciangai* (1957, The Nun of Shanghai, which was awarded the Veillon Prize), *Le mosche d'oro* (1962, The Golden Flies), *Je vous écris d'un pays lointain* (1971, I Write You from a Far-Off Land), and *La camicia bruciata* (1973, The Burned Shirt). With her preoccupation with the place of the modern Italian woman in a changing society and her intelligent, masterful narrative style, Anna Banti has established herself as one of the most perceptive contemporary voices for the feminine point of view in Italian literature. In addition to her own literary or scholarly works, she has translated Thackeray's *Vanity Fair* and Virginia Woolf's *Jacob's Room.*

Bibliography: Artemisia (Milan: Mondadori, 1953); *La camicia bruciata* (Milan: Mondadori, 1973); *Matilde Serao* (Turin: UTET, 1965); *La Fiera letteraria* 3 (1957), special issue on Anna Banti.

BARETTI, GIUSEPPE (1719–1789), scholar, linguist, poet, translator, and journalist. Born in Turin, the first of four brothers, Baretti inherited an ecclesiastical benefice and began his education with the Jesuits. An avid traveler even in his youth, he lived in Milan, Venice, and Turin until his trip to England in 1751. In each of these Italian cities, he met and became a friend of the major literary figures of his day. His own literary works began with translations of Ovid and the tragedies of Pierre Corneille (1747–48), and a volume of poetry entitled *Le piacevoli poesie di Giuseppe Baretti torinese* (1750, The Pleasing Poetry of Giuseppe Baretti of Turin).

After his arrival in London, Baretti first supported himself with a position at the Italian Opera and then by giving private lessons in Italian. He soon mastered the English language so thoroughly that he began to publish scholarly works on Italian poetry, language, and grammar, some of which became quite influential. His Italian-English, English-Italian dictionary in two volumes with a dedication to Samuel Johnson, which appeared in 1760, remained the standard reference work on these two languages until the beginning of the twentieth century. Besides these many publications written in English during the period 1753–60, Baretti translated Johnson's *Rasselas* Into French (but left it unpublished) and became the friend of such notables as Johnson, Henry Fielding, and William Pitt. Although Baretti was never the intellectual equal of many of his friends or even his opponents, he did not hesitate to react against what he considered to be unreasonable attacks upon Italian literature and the decadent state of Italian culture in Voltaire's *Essay on Epic Poetry* (1727). Thus, in *A Dissertation upon the Italian Poetry* (1753), Baretti attacked the celebrated French writer for his "impertinence" and for uttering "contemptuous reflections" in a language (English) that he had dishonored by his false and prejudicial opinions. Baretti also accused him of not even knowing the Italian language. This brief and polemical essay is still interesting for its spirited defense of Dante's* poetry and for Baretti's interesting suggestion that John Milton might well have been inspired by Dante's epic* before he composed his own Christian epic, *Paradise Lost* (1667).

Baretti returned to Italy in 1760 through Portugal, Spain, and France, a journey which was to be described in a diary entitled *A Journey from London to Genoa* (1770). Establishing himself in Venice, he initiated the publication of the famous periodical *La frustra letteraria* (The Literary Whip) under the pseudonym of Aristarco Scannabue, or "Aristarchus the Ox-Slayer," by the end of 1763. The journal was published each fortnight for approximately a year, resulting in twenty-five separate issues and bitter polemics before he abandoned Venice and his violent critics. Baretti then moved near Ancona, where eight additional issues were printed. Although *La frustra's* limitations become obvious when compared to such publications as *The Spectator* in England, the journal provided Baretti with a forum for his passionate literary debates, his attacks upon the French influence in Italian culture, his praise of the dramatic works of Carlo Gozzi,* and his always provocative literary judgments. Returning to London in 1766, Baretti rejoined Johnson's circle and became the friend of Oliver Goldsmith, Edmund Burke, James Boswell, and Joshua Reynolds. After the publication of Samuel Sharp's *Letters from Italy* (1766), a work he viewed as an attack upon Italy and her culture, Baretti counted with *An Account of the Manners and Customs of Italy* (1768). He was shortly thereafter named secretary for foreign correspondence of the Royal Academy of Painting, Sculpture, and Architecture, headed at the time by Sir Joshua Reynolds.

Soon after being appointed to this important position, Baretti was accosted by a prostitute in Haymarket; his abrupt manner caused her procurers to attack him, one of whom Baretti managed to kill with a fruit knife. Charged by the authorities with homicide, Baretti directed his own defense in Old Bailey, and with such character witnesses as Goldsmith, Johnson, and Reynolds—the cream of London's intellectual community—he was easily acquitted. Much of the rest of his life was spent among these English friends and in writing and publishing various literary and scholarly works, including a noteworthy three-volume edition of the Italian works of Machiavelli* (1772), a Spanish-English dictionary, a translation into Italian of Reynolds's essays on art, and other minor works. During this latter phase of his career, he was also offered a university position in Dublin, which he refused, and in 1782 he was granted a royal pension. A quarrel over losses in chess caused a break with his friend Samuel Johnson; Johnson's death in 1784 prohibited any reconciliation.

Besides his many linguistic publications and his private lessons, which enabled many of the English intelligentsia of the epoch to read and speak Italian, Baretti's most memorable achievement was a French essay entitled *Discours sur Shakespeare et sur Monsieur de Voltaire* (1777, Discourse on Shakespeare and Mr. Voltaire). In this work, Baretti expressed a pre-romantic predilection for the very unclassical qualities in Shakespeare's style which neoclassical critics had censured. Moreover, Baretti rejected the idea that a universal standard of taste existed, a concept crucial to any neoclassical poetics. Instead, he argued that literary standards were relative and reflected national backgrounds and traditions. For Baretti, the goal of the theatre was to please, not to follow abstract rules of dramatic construction set down by Aristotle or his French and Italian commentators; he believed that Shakespeare managed to please his audience by employing a natural language and by ignoring the rules.

Baretti died in London in 1789 and was buried there. Although not a great writer or a highly original thinker himself, his importance as a bridge between Italian and English culture cannot be underestimated. His presence in Enlightenment* England was at least partially responsible for the increasing interest in Italian culture and literature which characterizes the pre-romantic and romantic periods in England.

See also ENLIGHTENMENT.

Bibliography: Opere, ed. Franco Fido (Milan: Rizzoli, 1967); *Opere scelte di Giuseppe Baretti,* ed. Bruno Maier, 2 vols. (Turin: UTET, 1972); *Epistolario,* ed. Luigi Piccioni, 2 vols. (Bari: Laterza, 1932), *La frustra letteraria,* 2 vols. (Bari: Laterza, 1932), and *Prefazioni e polemiche* (Bari: Laterza, 1933)—all of which contain Italian, French, and English works; *An Account of the Manners and Customs of Italy,* 2 vols. (London: Davies, 1768); *A Dictionary of English and Italian Languages,* 2 vols. (London: Hitch & Hawes, 1760); *A Journey from London to Genoa* (London: Davies, 1770); Lacy Collison-Morley, *Giuseppe Baretti and His Friends* (London: John Murray, 1909); Norbert Jonard, *Giuseppe Baretti (1719–1789): l'homme et l'oeuvre* (Clermont-Ferrand: De Bussac, 1963).

BAROQUE. In Italy, the Baroque Age flourished from 1545, the year the Council of Trent convened, until 1690, the year the Arcadian Academy* was founded. Out of the Council of Trent, which was called into session between 1545 and 1563, came a rigorous program for the Catholic Reformation to renew religious fervor, correct clerical abuses, institute a redefinition and affirmation of principles of faith, and combat the menace of Protestantism. The missionary zeal of the Catholic Revival to reawaken faith in the purified church was reflected in the work of the Society of Jesus to promote education as a means of spiritual enlightenment. Every facet of culture in Catholic countries was expected to express the enthusiasm for reform and renewal: literature, theatre, architecture, sculpture, painting, and music. Traditional artistic forms gave way to new styles, genres, and media which represented the aspiration toward a grandiose assertion of religious doctrine and spiritual dedication. Churches with undulating façades and interiors with a dramatic interplay of darkness and brilliant illumination were to impress the faithful with the Passion of Christ, emphasizing the physical reality of the suffering which made possible salvation for all believers. The sculptor and architect Gian Lorenzo Bernini (1598–1680) sought to fashion a painterly form of sculpture, as in his *Ecstasy of St. Teresa,* which would portray the intense rapture of mystical experience. In the design of the plaza of St. Peter's, he attempted with the great colonnade to show how the true church embraced worshippers. In painting, the desire for dramatic contrast resulted in *chiaroscuro* canvases which highlighted moments of deep emotion against a dark background where the shadows themselves reinforced the scene's theatricality. Opera, the art form which unites music, drama, poetry, and dance (*see* MELODRAMA), was perhaps the most typical expression of Baroque spirit, as in the works of Claudio Monteverdi (1547–1643), especially the *Orfeo* (Orpheus) of 1607 which represented an effort to revive Greek tragedy. Baroque art in all its manifestations was profoundly sensual, attempting to arouse powerful feelings of religious ardor and exaltation.

Frequently, the art forms of the second half of the sixteenth century and of the entire seventeenth century were so extravagant that they received the derisive label "Baroque." This term may derive from the Portuguese and Spanish *barrueco* to designate a pearl so oddly shaped that it would appear about to burst apart. In that sense, the "Baroque" would indicate something exaggerated, bizarre, distorted, floridly decadent, irregular, bewildering, monstrous, or grotesque. In Italy, long before the introduction of the Portuguese-Spanish term, there existed the word *baroco* as the name for an extremely strained mode of syllogism. The twisted logic of the Italian term extended to an *argomento in baroco* (a rather forced demonstration) and then to *discorsi barocchi* (subtle discussions), so that in literature the "Baroque" implies a frenetic search for ever new subtleties of expression at the risk of distorting language in its syntax and imagery. The Baroque depends on a confused harmony achieved through an aesthetic balance that rests upon a structural tension which forever threatens to explode. Although the term has been used by historians and critics to describe the artistic aspirations of Europe and Latin America toward a dazzling style in literature, music, architecture, and the graphic arts during the period running from the early years of the Catholic Reformation to the start of the eighteenth century, it may also apply to the art forms of other eras such as that of Hellenistic Greece or Imperial Rome at the time of Caracalla. One may speak also of a "baroque mind" or "baroque soul" existing at any time or in any country, always in quest of creating wondrous works of art.

In Italian literature of the late sixteenth century and the first quarter of the seventeenth century, the writer who best expressed the Baroque desire to transform poetry into a medium to fashion the marvelous was Giambattista Marino.* The term *marinismo* came to mean a highly musical and extremely sensual form of poetry whose end was to arouse wonder through extravagant metaphors, strained conceits, hyperbole, startling word plays, and totally original myths. The novel Marinist language was intended to surprise the poetic audience with unexpected melodies, boldly colorful images, and enchanting descriptions of voluptuous experiences. This quest for a stupefying poetic style betrayed a need on the part of Marino and his imitators to surpass poets of earlier periods like Petrarch.* As the Marinist manner came to dominate the literary forms of the seventeenth century, it is often called *secentismo* to describe the major style of the 1600s. The fact that there were movements parallel to Marinism outside of Italy, such as *gongorismo* in Spain, *préciosité* in France, and euphuism in England (although differing from each other in certain emphases and verbal articulation), attested to a need to recreate an unstable reality through language with astounding metaphors and subtle conceits. In hundreds of sonnets,* madrigals,* and long narrative poems, the Marinists orchestrated a new poetic music that expressed an awareness of the world and life as existing in crisis; Baroque poetry sought to reestablish lost sensuous contacts with elemental life. The search for the marvelous compels readers or listeners to reexamine reality and to try to forge concrete links with a universe in continual flux.

Marino and his contemporaries all participated in the *querelle des anciens et des modernes*—the battle of the books between admirers of the writers of antiquity and the proponents of the superiority of modern writers. Even authors who openly acknowledged their debt to classical antiquity still believed that they could equal the greatness of Greek and Roman writers and introduce new themes characteristic of their own times. The poet Gabriello Chiabrera,* while attempting to fuse the solidity of the Horatian ode with the grace of Ronsard's noble odes, saw himself as a Columbus in verse discovering the "new worlds of poetry" by celebrating Christian naval victories over Turkish fleets, singing the praises of Italian prelates and rulers, and producing gallant *canzonette* in honor of a beautiful woman's smile or fleeting loveliness. Throughout this period, there was an overriding conviction that writers must invent new linguistic means for their creative capacities, whether or not they might ever attain the heights of the ancients or the classical figures of Italian literature like Petrarch or Tasso.* A literature built on the subtlety of complex conceits would offer a way to freedom from the constricting modes of the past.

Writers during Italy's Baroque Age recognized that they had a public role to fulfill. They put themselves at the service of the court, the church, or some patrician family. This public art was manifested in the importance of opera, courtly spectacles, and Jesuit dramas. Poets affirmed the heroic virtues of rulers who invited them to their courts and honored them with titles and administrative positions. The centers of cultural life in Italy during the Baroque Age were Milan under a Spanish viceroy, Turin under the gradually ascendant House of Savoy, Venice moving into economic decline but still offering refuge to exiles from the Inquisition, and the newly purified Rome of the Catholic Reformation with its clerics zealously combatting dissent. While the mercantile values of the middle class which had dominated northern and central Italian life in the Middle Ages and Renaissance* vanished in the midst of economic and commercial disintegration, neofeudalism emerged as families of wealth and social influence attempted to enhance their power with noble titles. For this neofeudal public, writers were expected to provide delight or to exalt the glory of a noble heritage.

Literary critics also affirmed the importance of poetry in responding to the new public taste for the marvelous and the heroic. In attacking the Petrarchistic tradition, the critic Alessandro Tassoni* established in his *Considerazioni sopra le Rime del Petrarca* (1602, Considerations on Petrarch's Poetry) the relationship between self-creation and artistic creation. In this relationship, a poet must express the needs of his own times and his immediate public rather than modeling himself on the style of a writer who had achieved success several centuries before by proclaiming a theory of love and human relationships which no longer corresponded to social conditions in seventeenth-century Italy. Baroque critics had before them the ideal of an Aristotelian humanism, reaffirmed at the Council of Trent, that called writers to the moral responsibility of fashioning works inspired by a sense of majesty, passion, virtue, and glory. The serious social awareness of the role played by literature provided the background for the fierce polemic over Marino's lengthy narrative poem *Adone* (1623, *Adonis*), which the critic Tommaso Stigliani (1573–1651) denounced as a lascivious display of technical virtuosity. Marino's linguistic genius found its most complete critical vindication in the writings of Emanuele Tesauro,* who in his *Il Cannocchiale Aristotelico* (1654, The Aristotelian Telescope) defended the invention of conceits which would offer a newly magnified visual power to lovers of poetry. Refined conceits with the scintillating subtleties would make possible escape from the limitations of everyday existence. The reading public would find delight in the refreshing ornamentation of the new literature.

By the final decade of the seventeenth century, literary taste had moved away from the passionate excesses of Marinism. In 1690, a group of poets, among them the jurist Gian Vincenzo Gravina,* gathered in Rome to found the Arcadian Academy with the intention of rescuing poetry from Marino's sensualism, while preserving the love of musicality which enlivened the best verse of that age. By that moment, literature was passing from the grandiosity of the Baroque to the dream of an idyllic pastoral harmony.

See also ARCADIA; CHIABRERA, Gabriello; MARINO, Giambattista; MELODRAMA; TASSONI, Alessandro.

Bibliography: Benedetto Croce, *Storia dell'età barocca in Italia* (Bari: Laterza, 1929); Franco Croce, "Critica e trattatistica del barocco," *Storia della Letteratura Italiana: Il Seicento,* eds. Emilio Cecchi and Natalino Sapegno (Milan: Garzanti, 1967); Eugenio Donato, "Tesauro's Poetics: Through the Looking Glass," *Mod-*

ern Language Notes 78 (1963), 15–30; Giovanni Getto, "La Polemica sul Barocco," *Letteratura Italiana: Le Correnti* (Milan: Marzorati, 1956); Helmut Hatzfeld, "A Clarification of the Baroque Problem in the Romance Literatures," *Comparative Literature* 1 (1949), 113–39; *Trattatisti e Narratori del Seicento,* ed. Ezio Raimondi (Milan: Ricciardi, 1960); Frank J. Warnke, *Versions of Baroque: European Literature in the Seventeenth Century* (New Haven, Conn.: Yale University Press, 1972); René Wellek, "The Concept of Baroque in Literary Scholarship," *Journal of Aesthetics and Art Criticism* 5 (1946), 77–109.

Douglas Radcliff-Umstead

BASILE, GIAMBATTISTA (circa 1575–1632), soldier, courtier, and poet. Born in Naples, Basile left the city for a number of years and earned his living as a soldier, first in the Venetian Republic (1604–07) and then in Naples and Calabria (1608–12). Finally, with the assistance of his sister Adriana, who had become a singer of some renown, he secured a position in the Gonzaga court in Mantua, as well as a title, and he remained there briefly until 1613. The rest of his life was spent fulfilling the duties of several minor governmental posts and writing.

In 1613, Basile collected many of his works, previously published separately between 1608 and 1612, in a volume entitled *Opere* (Works). This edition included a series of encomiastic madrigals* and odes; various eclogues; a musical drama in five acts entitled *La Venere addolorata* (Sorrowful Venus); and *Il pianto della Vergine* (The Lament of the Virgin), an imitation of the fashionable lacrimonious poetry of Luigi Tansillo,* *Le lacrime di San Pietro* (1585, The Tears of St. Peter). In 1616, he published an edition of Pietro Bembo's* poetry which included a commentary; this was followed in 1617 by an edition of Giovanni della Casa's* lyrics and by the first edition of the poetry of Galeazzo di Tarsia (1520–53). In spite of this erudite interest in the fashionable courtly lyric of Italy's literary class, Basile's true literary talents would be expressed in dialect, an impulse which was apparently awakened in him by the example of his friend, Giulio Cesare Cortese (1575–circa 1627).

The first result of Basile's interest in literature written in dialect was *Le muse napolitane* (1635, Neapolitan Muses), which appeared under the name Gian Alessio Abbattutis and was popular enough to be printed in six other editions during the seventeenth century alone. The work consists of nine eclogues containing two or three characters, each dedicated to one of the poetic Muses. The intent of the collection is both moralistic and scholarly. It is still interesting for its vivid portrayals of popular scenes from contemporary life and for its preservation of the beauties of ancient Neapolitan dialects.

Basile's masterpiece in dialect, published only after his death, is *Lo cunto de li cunti overo lo trattenemiento de li peccerille* (1634–36, The

Story of Stories, or the Entertainment of the Little Ones). This work is best known to popular tradition and literary history alike as the *Pentamerone (The Pentameron),* a title employed in an important early edition (1674) and later in the influential Italian translation done by Benedetto Croce* (1925). The Greek title, like that of Boccaccio's* *Decameron,* refers to the five days of storytelling in the narration. Like Boccaccio's model, Basile's collection of tales is set within a frame, and the occasion for the storytelling reflects a new interest in magic and popular folklore as well as an increased Oriental influence: a Moorish slave girl gains, by deceit, the rightful place of a princess and marries her prince; after the marriage, the couple is entertained by ten women who tell one story on each day for a total of fifty; on the last day, however, the tenth story is narrated by the princess who, as a result, is restored to her rightful position while the imposter is punished. The gracious storytellers of Boccaccio's *novelle* * are replaced by women whose class origins and names—limping Zeza, crocked Cecca, long-nosed Tolla, hunchbacked Popa, hairless Ciommetella, and so on—set the tone and language of Basile's *fiabe* (fables) apart from the more genteel Tuscan tradition. Each day is introduced by a banquet; after the first day of stories is completed, music, games, and dancing precede the banquet on the other four days.

Basile's *Pentamerone* reached a European audience because of the romantic interest in folklore and dialect. The predominantly popular plots of his fables, many of which possess Oriental antecedents or parallels, became extremely popular among children, and their importance was confirmed by the praise of the brothers Grimm in their famous collection of children's stories in 1822. Basile's versions of such classics as Cinderella, Puss-in-Boots, Beauty and the Beast, and The Three Oranges would later inspire Perrault, Tieck, and Carlo Gozzi* among others. The reputation of the collection was enhanced by the popular translations into German by Felix Liebrecht (1846) and into English by Sir Richard Burton, the well-known translator of *The Arabian Nights* (1893). Far from being a mere collection of fairy tales for children, however, Basile's work was considered by no less a critic than Benedetto Croce as the central literary contribution of the Italian Seicento. Other critics of the *Pentamerone* have pointed out the Oriental elements, the interest in magic, the concern for the representation of everyday reality without Boccaccio's elevated tone, the use of dialect, the taste for parody as well as paradoxical metaphor and simile, the concern for justice, and the tales with happy endings as typical of the Baroque* period style.

See also NOVELLA; STRAPAROLA, Gian Francesco.

Bibliography: Il Pentamerone ossia La fiaba delle fiabe, ed. Benedetto Croce, 3 vols. (Bari: Laterza, 1974); *The Pentamerone of Giambattista Basile,* trans. N. M.

Penzer, 2 vols. (1932; rpt. Westport, Conn.: Greenwood Press, 1975); Benedetto Croce, *Saggi sulla letteratura italiana del Seicento* (Bari: Laterza, 1962); Giovanni Getto, *Barocco in prosa e in poesia* (Milan: Rizzoli, 1969).

BASSANI, GIORGIO (1916–   ), novelist, poet, essayist, critic, and editor. Bassani spent most of his childhood in Ferrara. His Jewish heritage and the portrayal of the Jewish community there figure prominently in his works, for he is one of the few Italian Jewish writers to make this fact of birth a central theme. After studying literature at the University of Bologna, Bassani started writing verse under a pseudonym (Giacomo Marchi) to avoid difficulties with the fascist racial laws.

Bassani began to acquire a reputation as a critic in 1948 when he became the editor of the international literary journal *Botteghe oscure*. In this post, he helped to publish some of the best avant-garde literature by contemporary European writers. Later, in 1960, he joined the editorial staff of *Paragone*. As a journalist, he has been associated with many major Italian periodicals, including *La Fiera letteraria, Il Mondo, Nuovi argomenti,* and the *Corriere della sera.* Perhaps his most outstanding achievement in his capacity as editorial consultant for the Feltrinelli publishing house was the "discovery" of Giuseppe Tomasi di Lampedusa.* After Lampedusa's novel *Il gattopardo* (1958, *The Leopard*) had been rejected by other publishers, Bassani's recommendation made possible its tremendous popular and critical success.

Bassani's first major work was *Cinque storie ferraresi* (1956, *Five Stories of Ferrara*), for which he received the prestigious Strega Prize in 1956. Each story focuses upon the Ferrara of the past, and each analyzes a single character. Through this portrait of Ferrara, a whole series of critical historical issues—fascism, anti-Semitism, the Resistance—is reduced to its human proportions. Only one of the five stories is told in the first person; the others are related from the viewpoint of a more objective, omniscient narrator, reflecting the fact that historical representation tends to motivate this early work.

Bassani received widespread recognition and the Viareggio Prize in 1962 for his masterful novel *Il giardino dei Finzi-Contini* (1962, *The Garden of the Finzi-Continis*); Vittorio De Sica's film (1970) further increased the book's fame. The work continues the Ferraran setting of Bassani's stories, but the style embodies a completely subjective narrative voice skillfully employed to capture the nostalgia both Bassani and his characters feel for their past. Rather than employing a strictly chronological structure, the memory of the unnamed narrator orders the events of the novel and gives them meaning. The novel analyzes the cloistered life of an aristocratic Jewish family which is contrasted to the more modern and progressive Jewish family of the narrator. After a gradual decline during the early years of fascist restrictions upon Jews, the Finzi-Continis finally disappear in German concentration camps in 1943. Micòl, the beautiful daughter of this family with whom the narrator falls in love, is one of the most appealing female figures in recent literature.

Although most of Bassani's works deal with Ferrara and its Jewish community, one of the best of his recent novels is *L'Airone* (1968, *The Heron*), a portrait of a lonely man's encounter with anguish and solitude. Here Bassani departs from the urban atmosphere of his studies of the ghetto in prewar Ferrara and employs an essentially philosophical or existential rather than an elegiac tone.

Much of Bassani's critical work has been collected in one volume, *Le parole preparate* (1966, The Prepared Words). Dedicated to Benedetto Croce,* the essays range over a wide variety of topics, from a scholarly treatment of the image of Venice in world literature to perspicacious reviews of contemporary novels. Of some interest are Bassani's statements on the relationship of literature and the cinema, since Bassani has collaborated with several Italian directors in their productions as scriptwriter or dubbing editor.

Bassani received the Nelly Sachs International Prize in 1969 for his collected works and is universally recognized as one of contemporary Italy's best writers of prose fiction. Most of his major works have been published in a one-volume edition entitled *Il romanzo di Ferrara* (1974, The Novel of Ferrara). His literary portrait of Ferrara transcends narrow religious or political issues and represents an elegiac portrait of a mythical city and community whose literary function as a symbol for man's loneliness and suffering overshadows any hint of parochial regionalism or local color.

Bibliography: Il romanzo di Ferrara (Milan: Mondadori, 1974); *Five Stories of Ferrara,* trans. William Weaver (New York: Harcourt, 1971); *The Garden of the Finzi-Continis,* trans. William Weaver (New York: Harcourt, 1977); *The Heron,* trans. William Weaver (New York: Harcourt, 1970); Marianne Shapiro, "The *Storie ferraresi* of Giorgio Bassani," *Italica* 49 (1972), 30–48, and Marilyn Schneider, "Mythical Dimensions of Micòl Finzi-Contini," *Italica* 51 (1974), 43–67.

BECCARIA, CESARE (1738–1794), political writer and penal reformer. Beccaria, the son of an aristocratic Milanese family, was educated at a Jesuit college in Parma and graduated from the University of Padua in 1758. Moving to Milan, he joined a fashionable literary academy, the Accademia dei Trasformati, where he met Giuseppe Parini* and Pietro Verri;* when Verri established the rival Accademia dei Pugni, Beccaria accompanied him. Verri's influence upon Beccaria was decisive. At his suggestion, Beccaria composed and published his first work, *Del disordine e de' rimedii delle monete nello stato di Milano nell'anno 1762* (1762, On

Remedies for the Monetary Disorders of Milan in the Year 1762), a study of the economic problems caused by the free circulation of many different coins which encouraged speculation and fluctuations of exchange rates. Again at Verri's suggestion, Beccaria began a second work, a study of criminal justice. Alessandro Verri,* Pietro's brother, helped him gain permission to visit the prisons of the city. *Dei delitti e delle pene (On Crimes and Punishments)* appeared anonymously in 1764 and was an instant sensation all over Europe. As the author of this work, Beccaria was invited to Paris in 1766 and was warmly welcomed by the most prominent figures in the intellectual community. In 1768, he was named to the chair of public economy and commerce at the Palatine School in Milan and held the post until 1770. The remainder of his life was spent in various government posts. He also composed several minor treatises, including *Ricerche intorno alla natura dello stile* (1770, Research on the Nature of Style) and *Elementi di economia pubblica* (1804, Elements of Public Economy), the posthumously published lecture notes from his course on economics.

Beccaria's *Dei delitti e delle pene* was sufficient to establish his reputation as one of the foremost thinkers of the European Enlightenment* and as the best known Italian reformer of his day. Crucial to his analyses were the fundamental principles that law should be the result of a free agreement made by men in a state of equality and that the concept of utility should govern human affairs. As he put it, men should examine their actions rationally from a single viewpoint: "la massima felicità divisa nel maggior numero" ("the greatest happiness shared by the greatest number"). He speaks of a "geometric precision" which must be applied to social problems, and he argues for a thorough, logical study of the question of criminal punishments. At the same time, his calm argumentation gives way to the impassioned indignation he felt over the abuses he describes.

After discussing the origin of society in a social contract, Beccaria asserts that an unjust punishment is one in which the punishment fails either to prevent new crimes by the same criminal or to deter other crimes by other criminals; punishments must create the greatest possible impression on the mind but must not do any more damage to the body than is necessary. In keeping with his geometric analogy, Beccaria claims that a hedonistic calculus may be established to determine the proper punishment; the pain the punishment inflicts must only just barely exceed the advantage derived from the crime, and the punishment must be prompt and certain. Furthermore, he demands that punishments be appropriate to the crime, providing a classic attack on the death penalty and suggesting that long prison terms are more effective deterrents, since they instill more prolonged terror than brief executions. The logic of his argument has not been fundamentally altered by the many contemporary arguments against capital punishment based upon sociological or statistical studies. Beccaria also rejects the usefulness of oaths, believing self-interest to govern most legal testimony, and he replaces sin with utility as the sole criterion for determining the nature of a crime.

Beccaria's views on man's equality before the law and his hedonistic basis for penal justice struck a responsive chord. Although the tract was placed on the Index in 1766, his ideas were discussed and sometimes even accepted by the philosophers and crowned heads of Europe, including Catherine the Great, Frederick the Great, Maria Theresa of Austria, and the grand duke of Tuscany. Many, however, were unwilling to go so far as to abolish the death penalty. Voltaire wrote a commentary on the work which was often reprinted with the original, especially in England and America. Thomas Jefferson copied entire sections of the original Italian text in his notebooks, and John Adams cited Beccaria in his defense of the British soldiers involved in the Boston Massacre. Perhaps Beccaria's most lasting influence, outside the realm of practical penal reform all over Europe, was upon Jeremy Bentham's philosophy of utilitarianism. In his *Introduction to the Principles of Morals and Legislation* (1789), Bentham not only repeats the concept of the greatest happiness for the greatest number, but he further develops the notion of a hedonistic calculus. Beccaria's influence can also be traced in the American Constitution and in the Declaration of the Rights of Man.

See also ENLIGHTENMENT; VERRI, Pietro.

Bibliography: On Crime and Punishments, trans. Henry Paolucci (Indianapolis, Ind.: Bobbs-Merrill, 1963); Marcello Maestro, *Cesare Beccaria and the Origins of Penal Reform* (Philadelphia: Temple University Press, 1973), and *Voltaire and Beccaria as Reformers of Criminal Law* (New York: Columbia University Press, 1942); Franco Venturi, *Italy and the Enlightenment* (New York: New York University Press, 1972).

BELLI, GIUSEPPE GIOACCHINO (1791–1863), poet. As a young boy, Belli was forced to flee his native Rome with his mother, when in 1799 French troops occupied the city, and to live in Naples in poverty for some years. During that time, his father died of cholera, and after 1801 he lived with his mother in Rome. Relatively little is known of his education, but after his mother's death in 1807, he supported himself with a series of minor clerical positions. By 1807, he had already begun writing uninspired poetry in Italian; eventually, he joined Arcadia,* and he was later among the founders of the Accademia Tiberina. His early works included several plays, a poem in *terzine* in imitation of both Dante* and Monti,* entitled *La pestilenza stata in Firenze l'anno di nostra salute 1348* (1816, The Plague in Florence in the Year of Our Lord 1348), and a number of still less important writings.

A fortunate marriage in 1816 to Maria Conti, the rich widow of a wealthy nobleman, granted Belli a measure of security and the time to travel and write. After several visits to Milan, Belli came under the influence of Carlo Porta,* and Porta's works in dialect furnished the model for his Roman sonnets.* His first poem in Roman dialect was composed in 1816, and after 1828 he devoted most of his energy to the composition of over two thousand such poems. With the death of his wife in 1837, Belli was forced to go to work to care for his son Ciro, and he found employment within the papal bureaucracy. During the revolutionary upheavals in Rome in 1848–49, he personally witnessed attacks upon church property. Although his poetry often supplied ample justification for these attacks, Belli was terrified by this violent popular outburst, and he experienced a spiritual crisis. Renouncing his sonnets in dialect and burning many of them, he even became a censor of theatrical works after the revolutionary movements were suppressed and the control of the church was restored. Only with the posthumous publication of his uncensored Roman sonnets in 1886–89 did the literary public become fully aware of the breadth and scope of his talent.

Belli's fame rests squarely upon his sonnets in Roman dialect. While his poetry in Italian reflects a conventional, even reactionary attitude, his dialect poetry presents an entirely different vision of the world. Post-Napoleonic and pre-Risorgimento Rome was one of the most corrupt and poorly administered areas of Italy, the perfect target for any reformer or anticlerical liberal. Belli's early readings of the French *philosophes* and their Italian counterparts encouraged his anticlerical stance in the poems, a position he rejected in his later, more conservative years. His introduction to the collection reflects the romantic elements in his poetics—his desire to leave behind him a "monument" to the Roman plebeians and his philological interest in their particular linguistic forms.

In the hundreds of sonnets Belli wrote, there is a remarkable vitality and zest for linguistic expression. Every facet of Roman life is depicted. The portrait of this priest-ridden and morally bankrupt society is always interesting, if never pretty. His topics include such unlikely subjects as a slightly off-color version of the creation story, "La creazzione der monno" (The Creation of the World); a comparison of God on Judgment Day to a mother hen scattering her chicks between the roof and the cellar in "Er giorno der giudizzio" ("Judgment Day"); a series of outrageous portraits of various popes; an endless stream of brief comments upon every possible dogma, sacrament, institution, and personality connected with the church; and an infinite variety of personality types, including prostitutes, cardinals, nuns, beggars, police informers, witches, and servants. Belli's humor is undeniable: in "S.P.Q.R.," he explains that this ancient republican symbol actually signifies "soli preti qui rreggneno" (here, only priests rule); in

"Er bordello scuperto" ("The Whorehouse Raid"), he provides a comic picture of a shameless cardinal caught up in a police raid on a brothel.

Perhaps his greatest single poem, if only one can be chosen from the many hundreds Belli composed, is "Er caffettiere filosofo" ("The Coffee-House Philosopher"). Although written in dialect and concerned with a seemingly frivolous comparison between the human condition and beans in a coffee-grinder, the sonnet is the product of a keen and learned mind, and it owes something to a variety of literary sources, including a Baroque* sonnet by Ciro di Pers (1599–1663) and a striking image from one of Erasmus's Latin works. Its conclusion—that all mankind is destined to a common fate in death just as the coffee beans, no matter how large or small, all end their existence as a finely ground powder—is a typical Bellian combination of popular language, graphic and compelling comparisons, and a pessimistic tone. The portrait of Rome under Gregory XVI and Pius X calls up the grotesque scenes from Dante's* *Inferno,* the expressionistic imagery of Federico Fellini's Roman tableaux, and the linguistic experimentation of a Rabelais or a Joyce. Joyce was only one of many great writers who have admired Belli's Roman sonnets; others include Stendhal, Gogol, St. Beuve, Pier Paolo Pasolini,* Carlo Emilio Gadda,* and Alberto Moravia.*

See also PORTA, Carlo.

Bibliography: I sonetti di Giuseppe Gioacchino Belli, ed. Giorgio Vigolo, 3 vols. (Milan: Mondadori, 1952); *From Marino to Marinetti,* trans. Joseph Tusiani (New York: Baroque Press, 1974); *The Roman Sonnets of G. G. Belli,* trans. Harold Norse (London: Perivale Press, 1974); Federico A. Leoni, *Concordanze belliane,* 2 vols. (Göteborg: Romantica Gothoburgensia, 1970); Carlo Muscetta, *Cultura e poesia di G. G. Belli* (Milan: Feltrinelli, 1961); *Studi belliani nel centenario di Giuseppe Gioacchino Belli* (Rome: Editore Carlo Colombo, 1965).

BEMBO, PIETRO (1470–1547), poet, courtier, and humanist. Bembo was born in Venice on 20 May 1470 to a patrician family. He was soon initiated into humanistic studies, mostly by his teacher Giovanni Aurelio Augurello (1440–1524), a well-known humanist, but also by the stimulating presence in his home of some distinguished men of letters like Ermolao Barbaro (1453–94) and Girolamo Donato. In 1487, Bembo followed his father to Rome where he stayed for one year, having the opportunity to admire the classical, Christian, and humanistic features of the Eternal City. Back in Venice in 1490, Bembo was officially initiated into the city's political life with disastrous failures. In 1491, a meeting with Poliziano* was probably decisive in his definitive orientation towards humanistic studies, and the same year, he left for Messina to study Greek under the famous Grecian Constantine Lascaris. During the trip, Bembo met Pontano* in Naples, who dedicated the last book of his *De rebus coelestibus* (On Heavenly

Bodies) to him. After two years of fruitful meditation and studies in Messina, Bembo returned to Venice where he collaborated with the great publisher Aldo Manuzio* (Aldus Manutius) and became the editor of Lascaris's Greek grammar. At this press, Bembo published his first work, *De Aetna* (1496, On Aetna), a dialogue with his father on an ascent of Mount Aetna. In 1497, he followed his father to Ferrara where he studied philosophy under Niccolò Leoniceno (1428–1524) whose lessons he had already followed at Padua. Bembo lived for two years in Ferrara and there conceived and began to write *Gli Asolani (Gli Asolani)*. Back in Venice in 1499, he presented his candidacy for several political offices, but he was repeatedly defeated. In 1501, Manuzio published his editions of Petrarch's* lyrics and Dante's* *Divine Comedy,* or, as Bembo called it, *Terze Rime* (1502, Terze Rime); these editions are extremely important because they indicate a new awareness of vernacular poetry. In 1505, Bembo published his first major work, *Gli Asolani,* dedicated to Lucrezia Borgia who reciprocated his love. The following year, he accepted the hospitality of the duchess of Urbino, and for six years resided at that court, where he conceived and almost completed his *Prose della volgar lingua* (Writings in the Vernacular Language). In 1512, Bembo moved to Rome, and there published the *De imitatione* (1513, On Imitation) which became the manifesto for Ciceronian humanism. The fame of this work prompted Pope Leo X to put him in charge of writing the *Brevi* (briefs) for the Roman Curia. In 1521, Bembo left Rome since, after the death of his close friend Cardinal Bibbiena* and the ascent of a new pope, the Roman atmosphere was no longer congenial. Bembo retired to Padua. In 1525, his book *Prose della volgar lingua* appeared in Venice, and in 1530, the *Rime* (Rhymes). The same year he was nominated historian and librarian of the Republic of Venice. In 1539, he was made cardinal and moved to Rome where he died on 18 January 1547.

Bembo's most important works are *Gli Asolani,* the *Prose,* and the *Rime.* The first, probably composed between 1497 and 1502, and revised in 1503 and 1504, consists of three dialogues held among three noblemen and three noble ladies who meet in the villa of Caterina Cornaro at Asolo. The first gentleman maintains that love is the source of all evil; the second sees in love the origin of all joys; and the third asserts that love is the source of all goodness when it is turned to God who shines in earthly beauty. The third dialogue contains the main thesis of the book: an exaltation of Platonic love along the lines indicated by Ficino* and present, in one way or another, in the whole of humanistic thought. Bembo's systematization, however, was extremely influential upon writers such as Ariosto,* Castiglione,* and Tasso.*

The *Prose della volgar lingua* is also a dialogue divided into three books and set in Venice from the tenth to the twelfth of December. The first book examines the origins of Italian language and literature seen mostly in their relationship to the language and literature of Provence. Here Bembo also defines the language of the courts with their eclectic nature and gives a profile of what a literary language should be. The second book analyzes, with a finesse unknown to the humanistic tradition (which was concerned mostly with the content of a literary work), problems of style, metrics, and diction, drawing examples from Petrarch's *Canzoniere (Lyric Poems)* and Boccaccio's* works. The third book presents many observations on grammatical problems, relying again on the major *Trecento* models. At the same time, the work is the first history of Italian literature, after Dante's *De vulgari eloquentia,* and a manifesto which promotes the usage of an "ideal language" as opposed to the languages used in the courts (which had produced the Petrarchism* of the Quattrocento) and to the anarchistic tendencies of the popular poetry of that time (Burchiello,* Pulci,* and the like). This "ideal language" is basically the Tuscan as it had been used by Petrarch and Boccaccio, a language purified of all barbarism and dialectalism, a language that fulfills all the requirements of control, decorum, and liveliness without a trace of vulgarity—a language, in essence, which represents the Renaissance* ideal of equilibrium and classical beauty. Such a language could be a national language and could realize the aspirations of a vernacular humanism. The impact of this work on the writers of the Renaissance was immense, and it gave life to endless controversies which lasted until the nineteenth century.

The publication of the *Rime* in 1530 (a second enlarged edition was published in 1535 and a third in 1548) marks the birth of fashionable Petrarchism. The imitation of Petrarch—according to the theories exposed in the *Prose*—is transparent in the style, the lexicon, and the themes. Yet, it is also obvious that Bembo differs from his model. Petrarch's existential quest and his tormented living between two loves have no authentic echo in Bembo who reveals, instead, some hedonistic features and a markedly naturalistic and secular morality. In his search for equilibrium, Bembo reduces his model to a moderate containment, pleased only with his imitation, which is the true aspiration of this poetry.

Bibliography: Opere, ed. A. F. Seghezzi, 4 vols. (Venice: Hertzhauser, 1729); *Prose e rime,* ed. Carlo Dionisotti (Turin: UTET, 1966); *Pietro Bembo's Gli Asolani,* trans. Rudolf Gottfried (1953; rpt. Freeport: Books for Libraries Press, 1971); Vittorio Cian, *Un decennio della vita di M. Pietro Bembo (1521–1531)* (Turin: Loescher, 1885); Dante Della Terza, *"Imitatio:* Theory and Practice—The Example of Bembo the Poet," *Yearbook of Italian Studies 1* (1971), 119–41; Giorgio Santangelo, *Il petrarchismo del Bembo e di altri poeti del '500* (Rome: IECF, 1967); Mario Santoro, *Pietro Bembo* (Naples: Morano, 1937); Bernard Weinberg, *A History of Literary Criticism in the Italian Renaissance,* 2 vols. (Chicago: University of Chicago Press, 1960).

Paolo Cherchi

BENELLI, SEM (1877–1949), poet and playwright. Benelli was born near Prato and was primarily self-taught. He became a journalist and first appeared in print with a poem published in 1905. After that time, he devoted most of his writing to the theatre. An interventionist, Benelli was wounded twice in the Great War, decorated, and a participant in the seizure of Fiume after hostilities had ceased. Initially favorable to fascism and elected to Parliament on the fascist ticket, Benelli rejected the party after the Matteotti assassination, although he did fight in the Ethiopian War as a volunteer. Afterwards, he left Italy for Switzerland and returned only after Mussolini's fall.

Critics usually divide Benelli's many plays into three groups: verse dramas on historical topics; fantasies with philosophical themes; and prose plays on contemporary topics with a moral purpose. Benelli's greatest triumphs came with works in the first category, and he earned an international reputation with *La cena delle beffe* (1909, *The Jest*), a play based upon one of Grazzini's* *Novelle* set in Renaissance* Florence. Dealing with the horrible revenge of Gianetto on two brothers, *La cena* attracted the talents of such great actors as John Barrymore and Sarah Bernhardt (who played the male role of Gianetto). Other noteworthy plays in this same vein include *La maschera di Bruto* (1908, The Mask of Brutus), in which Lorenzaccio, the murderer of Duke Alessandro de' Medici, is compared to the classical tyrannicide Brutus; and *L'amore dei tre re* (1910, *The Love of the Three Kings*), a lyrical drama with music by Italo Montemezzi. Some of Benelli's plays in the other two and less successful categories include the fantasies *Orfeo e Proserpina* (1928, Orpheus and Proserpina), *Adamo e Eva* (1932, Adam and Eve), and *L'elefante* (1937, The Elephant). *L'elefante* is a timeless work about a boy with a talent for music who is forced to become a scientist by his father. Although many critics reject Benelli's rhetorical costume dramas as examples of the worst kind of fustian, Benelli—like D'Annunzio,* his more famous master— composed plays which expressed the Italians' need to examine their historical past and to discover new pride in their native traditions.

Bibliography: The Jest, trans. Marjorie Bowen (London: Odhams, 1922); *The Love of the Three Kings*, trans. Howard M. Jones, in T. H. Dickinson, ed., *Chief Contemporary Dramatists* (Boston: Houghton-Mifflin, 1930); Lander McClintock, *The Age of Pirandello* (Bloomington, Ind.: Indiana University Press, 1951).

BENIVIENI, GIROLAMO (1453–1542), poet. This Florentine poet, a close friend of Lorenzo de' Medici,* Marsilio Ficino,* Poliziano,* and Giovanni Pico della Mirandola,* was part of the Platonic Academy of Florence. As a result, he participated in the philosophical and literary discussions of that group. Ficino's influential commentary in Latin on Plato's *Symposium* was completed in 1469, and by 1474 he had completed an Italian translation of this seminal work on Neo-Platonism, calling it *Il libro dello amore* (The Book of Love). In 1486, Benivieni began to condense the vast corpus of Ficino's remarks into a poem which appeared around 1487 as "Canzone d'amore composta per Hieronymo Beniviena Cittadino Fiorentino, secondo la mente et oppinione de' Platonici" ("Ode of Love Composed by Jerome Beniviena, Florentine Citizen, according to the Mind and Opinion of Platonists"). In its philosophical tone, the work recalls Cavalcanti's* "Donna mi prega" ("Because a lady asks me") and other works of Dante* and the *stilnovisti*. None of Benivieni's various other lyrics and eclogues equals its importance.

Benivieni's fame was assured when Pico included a commentary on this work in the third book of a more general treatment of Neo-Platonic philosophy (1522, *A Platonick Discourse Upon Love*). Printed together with the discourse in numerous editions all over Europe, Benivieni's poem had an enormous impact upon writers and poets who were influenced by Neo-Platonism. Edmund Spenser's *Fowre Hymnes* (1596), in particular, reflect the direct influence of both Benivieni's *canzone** and Pico's commentary. In 1651, Thomas Stanley published a translation of Pico's commentary and the poem (mistakenly called a sonnet* rather than a *canzone* or ode). Its appearance gained a wide audience for Benivieni's masterpiece in Renaissance* England.

See also FICINO, Marsilio; DELLA MIRANDOLA, Giovanni Pico.

Bibliography: Giovanni Pico della Mirandola, *A Platonick Discourse Upon Love,* trans. Thomas Stanley (Boston: Merrymount, 1914); Jefferson Butler Fletcher, *The Religion of Beauty in Woman* (New York: Millian, 1911)—contains a translation of the ode; John Charles Nelson, *Renaissance Theory of Love* (New York: Columbia University Press, 1958).

BEOLCO, ANGELO: *See* RUZZANTE.

BERCHET, GIOVANNI (1783–1851), poet, translator, and literary critic. Berchet was born in Milan, the first of eight brothers. An early classical education was, on his father's advice, supplemented by the serious study of modern foreign languages which provided him with immediate access to the essential critical and literary documents of the romantic movement in English, German, and French. Some of his earliest literary works were Italian translations from the works of Thomas Gray (1807), Schiller (1810), and Goldsmith (1810). Berchet became one of the most vigorous voices for change, in response to Madame de Staël's call in 1816 for Italian writers to translate Shakespeare and recent German or English poetry rather than to remain preoccupied with the classical tradition and its mythology.

While still employed as a German translator by the Austrian authorities in Milan, Berchet published one of the fundamental manifestoes of the Italian romantic movement, *Sul "Cacciatore feroce" e sulla "Eleonora" di Goffredo Augusto Bürger: Lettera semiseria di Grisostomo al suo figliuolo* (1816, On the "Fierce Hunter" and "Leonora" of G. A. Bürger: The Semiserious Letter from Chrysostom to His Son). Intended as an introduction to prose translations of two ballads by Bürger, Berchet's treatise presented the German poems as exemplary specimens of romantic literature based upon popular tradition rather than upon classical models. His basic position, one already expounded by various literary critics beyond the Alps, including Herder and Schlegel, is that poetry should be universal, popular, modern, and useful. Classical works are identified with the "poetry of the dead," while the kind of verse represented by Bürger's ballads is linked to the "poetry of the living." Berchet urges Italian poets to reject classical motifs and the neoclassical rules for poetic composition, including the dramatic unities. As a result of his beliefs, Berchet became closely associated with Ludovico di Breme,* Silvio Pellico,* Ermes Visconti (1784–1841), and other Italian intellectuals gathered around the focal point of Milanese romanticism,* the periodical *Il Conciliatore* (1818–19).

Berchet and many other Italian romantics felt that a literary revival in Italy presupposed a political upheaval and national independence. Thus, he quite naturally became involved with the forces working against the Austrians for Italian freedom. Between 1819 and 1820, he composed a patriotic poem entitled "I profughi di Parga" (1823, The Refugees of Parga), later published in Paris. In this poem, an exile recounts to an Englishman the story of how a small section of Epirus, once owned by Venice, was ceded to Turkey by the English, forcing many of its inhabitants to go into exile rather than to live under Turkish oppression. Implicated in anti-Austrian activities in 1821, Berchet was forced to flee the country. He passed through Switzerland and Paris before settling in London in 1822, where he remained for seven years working as a translator in an Italian bank.

In London, Berchet composed his most distinguished poetry, including six *romanze* or romantic ballads on various historical subjects. These include "Clarina" ("Clarina"), a tale set against the background of the Piedmontese revolt in 1821; "Il romito di Cenisio ("The Hermit of Mount Cenis"), a lament for the imprisoned poet, Silvio Pellico; and "Il trovatore" ("The Troubadour"), a romantic view of an ill-fated medieval singer and his courtly lady. Another work in the same vein is *Le fantasie* (1829, The Visions), a description of an Italian exile's dreams which evokes ancient Lombard glory and contrasts that happy state to modern Italian decadence. Berchet left England in 1829 to travel across Europe. While in Belgium, he wrote one of the most popular Italian patriotic odes,

"All'armi! All'armi!" ("To arms, to arms") in reaction to uprisings in various Italian cities. Of greater literary import was a collection of translations entitled *Vecchie romanze spagnuole* (1835, Old Spanish Ballads) and an unfinished Italian version of the German *Niebelungenlied*. His interest in medieval poetic forms thus remained constant throughout his entire career, and he was ever marked by his early encounter with the German folklorists and romantic critics.

When Milan was liberated briefly in 1848, Berchet returned there, but was again forced into exile once Austrian rule was restored. He was elected a deputy to the Sub-Alpine Parliament, but his increasingly conservative opinions isolated him from many of his former admirers. After passing his last days in Pisa, Florence, Vichy, and Nice, he died in Turin. Berchet's talents as an original poet never matched those of his more illustrious counterparts in the romantic movement. However, he provided a crucial link between the Italian romantics and their compatriots beyond the Alps, and his own poetry helped to popularize in Italy the ballad form with its historical, medieval, or patriotic themes.

See also PELLICO, Silvio; ROMANTICISM.

Bibliography: Opere, ed. Marcello Turchi (Naples: F. Rossi, 1972); *From Marino to Marinetti,* trans. Joseph Tusiani (New York: Baroque Press, 1974); Vittore Branca and T. Kardos, *Il romanticismo* (Budapest: Akademiai Kiado, 1968); Mario Fubini, *Romanticismo italiano* (Bari: Laterza, 1953).

BERNARI, CARLO (1909–   ), largely self-taught Neapolitan novelist. Bernari's early political and literary ideas were indebted to the antifascist views of Benedetto Croce.* After a brief visit to Paris (1930–31) where he met André Breton and other surrealist writers, he returned to Italy and began his influential novel entitled *Tre operai* (1934, Three Workers). It first appeared in a series edited for Rizzoli by Cesare Zavattini (1902–   ), who soon became a major influence upon the neorealist cinema of the postwar period. In a preface to the definitive edition of 1965, Bernari explains the circumstances surrounding the composition of the book. It was begun in a first draft as *Tempo passato* (Past Time), its protagonist was originally a petit bourgeois, and its narrative style was objective and naturalistic. This initial draft was changed, the characters were drawn from the lower working class, and the style combined direct and indirect discourse, literary language, and dialect, in a narrative in the present tense designed to give a sense of immediacy to his condemnation of the prefascist society in Italy. In eighteen brief chapters, Bernari sets forth the unhappy experiences of three southern workers, Teodoro Barrin, Marco De Martino, and Anna Giordano, and traces their tragic fates through a series of personal failures. The book was received by fascist critics and censors with some displeasure, since it failed to conform to the regime's ideal of a contented working class happily supporting the fascist economic system. Later, certain postwar critics proclaimed it one of the first significant neorealist narratives and compared its subject matter and style to the crucial novels and films of that decade.

Since the appearance of *Tre operai*, Bernari has written a number of novels, including *Quasi un secolo* (1940, Almost a Century), a vast panorama of three generations of Neapolitan life, from the fall of the Bourbons to the beginning of the twentieth century; and *Speranzella* (1949, Speranzella Street), a tale of postwar Naples, awarded the Viareggio Prize in 1950 and considered his finest work by most critics. During most of his life, Bernari has served as a journalist for various periodicals and has collaborated on a number of films. In 1955, he completed a voyage to China for *L'Europeo* which he described in a successful travel book entitled *Il gigante Cina* (1957, China the Giant).

See also NEOREALISM.

Bibliography: Speranzella (Milan: Mondadori, 1949); *Tre operai* (Milan: Mondadori, 1965); Emilio Pesce, *Bernari* (Florence: La Nuova Italia, 1970); *La Fiera letteraria* (2 February 1958)—Bernari issue.

BERNI, FRANCESCO (1497 or 1498–1535), humorous poet and courtier. Born in Lamporecchio of a noble Florentine family, Berni completed his studies in Florence where he wrote his first literary work, *La Caterina* (1516?, Catherine), a rustic drama in *ottava rima.* * In 1517, he went to the Rome of Pope Leo X (one of the Medici) and entered the service of Cardinal Bernardo Dovizi da Bibbiena,* a distant relative and the author of *La Calandria* (1521, *The Follies of Calandro*). Berni passed into the service of Bibbiena's nephew Angelo Dovizi when Bibbiena died in 1520. The brief pontificate of the Dutch pope, Hadrian VI, provoked one of his most famous satires, but with the ascent of another Medici (Clement VII) to the throne of St. Peter, Berni returned to favor at the papal court and entered the service of the bishop of Verona, Giovan Matteo Giberti. After suffering through the Sack of Rome (1527) and traveling all over Italy in Giberti's service, Berni found a patron in Cardinal Ippolito de' Medici. After the death of Clement VII, Berni apparently became caught in the middle of the struggle between Ippolito and his cousin Alessandro for control of Florence, and his life was ended by poisoning in the palace of Cardinal Cybo.

Besides very minor poetry in Latin, Berni wrote but one long poem, a Tuscan version of Boiardo's* *Orlando innamorato* (Orlando in Love) written to remove the Ferrarese flavor of the original and to make it acceptable to Italian readers. Boiardo was known through this version until the nineteenth century, when scholars and readers returned to the original. Berni's most characteristic lyric poetry was written in two particular forms, the *capitolo** in *terza rima** and the *sonetto caudato,* or "tailed" sonnet,* which he frequently extended far beyond the fourteen-line norm. His poetry follows and expands the tradition of Domenico di Giovanni,* Luigi Pulci,* and such medieval predecessors as Rustico di Filippo* or Cecco Angiolieri,* a tradition of humorous vernacular poetry which may employ biting satire. No subject was too frivolous, no person too exalted for his poetic barbs. Some well-known poems attack Hadrian VI, the blind followers of Aristotle, the greed and gluttony of the priests at the papal court, the lack of decisiveness on the part of Clement VII, and the pomposity of typical courtiers. The poetry often borders on the obscene or the off-color, and the subjects treated may vary from a *capitolo* on a urinal to others dealing with eels, jelly, the plague, married life, and a multitude of humorous topics.

As a poet with close ties to the popular vernacular tradition, Berni attacked the conventions of the dominant poetic mode, the Petrarchan lyric; he is one of the great anti-Petrarchan poets in Italy. Like Du Bellay and Shakespeare, who wrote verse which has often mistakenly been interpreted as a total rejection of their master Petrarch,* Berni was too able a poet to blame all the faults and superficialities of the lyric tradition upon its founder. Most famous of these poems is a parody of Pietro Bembo's* classic Petrarchan lyric "Crin d'oro crespo e d'ambra tersa e pura" ("A Curly Hair of Gold"), which Berni rendered ridiculous in a brilliant parody entitled "Chiome d'argento fine, irte ed attorte" ("The Beauty of His Lady"), by confusing the attributes enumerated in typical Petrarchan descriptions of the lady. Thus, the woman in Berni's description possesses ebony teeth, snowy eyebrows, and eyes of pearls. Berni's works were first edited by Anton Francesco Grazzini* in 1548, a Florentine poet who was one of Berni's great successors in humorous Italian verse.

See also BEMBO, Pietro; BOIARDO, Matteo Maria; PETRAR-CHISM.

Bibliography: Rime, ed. Giorgio Bàrberi Squarotti (Turin: Einaudi, 1969); *Italian Poets of the Renaissance,* trans. Joseph Tusiani (Long Island City, N.Y.: Baroque Press, 1971); Andrea Sorrentino, *Francesco Berni: poeta della scapigliatura del Rinascimento* (Florence: Sansoni, 1933).

BERTO, GIUSEPPE (1914–   ), novelist and playwright. Berto was born in Mogliana Veneto and educated in literature at the University of Padua. He served in both the Abyssinian War and the North African campaign of 1941–43 before he was captured in Tunisia and imprisoned for thirty months at a prisoner-of-war camp in Hereford, Texas. There, Berto turned to writing and completed twelve short stories and two novels, *Le opere di Dio* (1948, *The Works of God*) and *Il cielo è rosso* (1947, *The Sky is Red*).

The latter novel achieved great critical and commercial success both in Italy and abroad and earned him the Premio Letterario Firenze in 1948. Both novels are normally placed within the neorealist tradition, because of their apparent debt to American writers and their extensive treatment of World War II. After a less successful novel, *Il brigante* (1951, *The Brigand*), Berto published a penetrating account of his experiences in the African campaign, *Guerra in camicia nera* (1955, War in a Black Shirt). In this work, Berto readily admits his own complicity in the fascist experiment, picturing himself (like many others of his generation) as a young man who put himself at its service, although he was in many ways dissatisfied with fascist ideology.

Berto's early neorealism has been abandoned in his latest and most impressive works. The author's own personal emotional crisis coincided with the writing and publication of his best novel, *Il male oscuro* (1964, *Incubus*), a psychological study influenced both by Freud and Joyce's stream-of-consciousness narrative style. It has been widely acclaimed as a masterpiece and was awarded two major literary prizes in 1964, the Viareggio and the Campiello. Another less distinguished novel appeared in 1966, although begun in 1958— *La cosa buffa (Antonio in Love)*. Here, Berto explores the implications of Conrad's statement that "life is a funny thing" ("è una cosa buffa"). Besides these narratives, Berto has written several plays, among them *Anonimo veneziano* (1971, *Anonymous Venetian*) and *La passione secondo noi stessi* (1972, The Passion According to Ourselves), a children's novel, and numerous film scripts.

See also NEOREALISM.

Bibliography: Antonio in Love, trans. William Weaver (London: Hodder & Stoughton, 1968); *Incubus,* trans. William Weaver (New York: Knopf, 1966); *The Sky Is Red,* trans. Angus Davidson (New York: New Directions, 1948); *The Works of God and Other Stories,* trans. Angus Davidson (Norfolk, Conn.: New Directions, 1950); Donald Heiney, *America in Modern Italian Literature* (New Brunswick, N.J.: Rutgers University Press, 1964); Corrado Piancastelli, *Berto* (Florence: La Nuova Italia, 1970).

BETOCCHI, CARLO (1899–   ), poet and editor. Born in Turin and trained as a surveyor and engineer before finally turning to a permanent journalistic and literary career, Betocchi served at the Austrian front and in Libya during World War I. Although much of his life has been spent as a worker in heavy construction, Betocchi is one of the most well-read Italian poets. His favorite foreign poets are Rimbaud, Shelley, Keats, Eliot, Hopkins, and Dickinson, although he is most indebted to Dante,* Ungaretti,* Montale,* Luzi,* and Sereni* in Italian literature. As a result of his wide reading and keen sensibilities, Betocchi managed to master his craft without the benefit of advanced formal education.

Betocchi's first poetry was collected in a book entitled *Realtà vince il sogno* (1932, Reality Conquers the Dream) and was published in connection with *Il Frontispizio,* a journal established by Piero Bargellini (1897–   ) as an organ for Catholic artists. Betocchi's metaphysical and philosophical themes imbued with a genuine Christian faith suggest to some critics an indebtedness to Clemente Rèbora* and the *crepuscolari,* or "twilight" poets. Three other volumes appeared between 1933 and 1954. When all his poems were published in a collection called *Poesie* (1955, Poetry), they were awarded the prestigious Viareggio Prize. This honor was a belated recognition of Betocchi's talents which were, in large measure, expressed outside any particular literary school or fashionable stylistic movement. His next major collection, *L'estate di San Martino* (1961, Indian Summer), met with critical acclaim, and the poet's entire opus was awarded the Montefeltro and Dante Alighieri prizes in that year. Some of his individual poems—"Un dolce pomeriggio d'inverno" ("A Gentle Afternoon in Winter"), "Alla sorella" ("To Sister"), "Il cacciatore d'allodole" ("Hunter of Skylarks"), "Dell'ombra" ("Shade and Shadow"), "Rovine" ("Ruins"), and "Vetri" ("Windows")—are numbered among the masterpieces of twentieth-century Italian poetry. At present, Betocchi works on several important literary journals in Italy.

See also RÈBORA, Clemente.

Bibliography: Carlo Betocchi: Poems, trans. I. L. Solomon (New York: Clarke, 1964): Gianni Pozzi, *La poesia italiana del Novecento* (Turin: Einaudi, 1955); Valerio Volpini, *Betocchi* (Florence: La Nuova Italia, 1971); *La Fiera letteraria* (1968)—special issue on Betocchi.

BETTI, UGO (1892–1953), dramatist, poet, jurist, and journalist. Born in Camerino in the Marches, Betti moved with his family in 1901 to Parma where he was educated for the law. He volunteered for the army soon after taking his degree in 1914, and he served with distinction as an artillery officer until his capture by the Austrians during the retreat from Caporetto in 1917. He was interned for the remainder of the war in a prison camp, where two of his fellow prisoners were Carlo Emilio Gadda* and Bonaventura Tecchi.* Upon his repatriation, Betti continued his legal studies, specializing in railroad law. During the 1920s, he secured an appointment as a magistrate, first in the province of Parma and then in the city of Parma itself. He married in 1930 and was transferred to Rome as a judge in the Appellate Court, a post he held until 1943. In the postwar era, Betti's former position as an official of the fascist judicial system, together with his public statements in favor of Mussolini's regime, drew much criticism. His adherence to fascism, however, appears to have been perfunctory; certainly, the absence of propagandistic elements in his plays is notable.

Although Betti was employed as a legal archivist and advisor during the last decade of his life, most of his energies were directed toward his work as a dramatist and a journalist.

Betti's career as a creative writer began in 1922, when he published a volume of wartime poems, *Il re pensieroso* (The Pensive King). Two other works of poetry appeared during his lifetime, but his most respected collection is the *Ultime liriche* (Last Poems), which were written between 1937 and 1953 and published posthumously in 1957. Although the public and critical reception of Betti's poetry has in general been lukewarm, a few critics, notably Eurialo De Michelis (1904–   ) and Attilio Momigliano (1883–1952), have held it in high esteem, Betti also published three volumes of undistinguished short stories and one novel. His place in literature rests principally on his dramatic works. If one excludes the revolutionary creations of Pirandello,* Betti's twenty-five plays constitute the most significant Italian contribution to the theatre of this century.

For his first play, *La padrona* (1926, The Mistress), Betti was awarded a prize offered by a Roman periodical. Its success, however, was mixed: most Romans liked it, but the Milanese did not. In form, *La padrona* is a rather conventional naturalist play in which passions and sensuality within a family lead to suffering. Yet, some of the work's qualities and themes announce the more mature Betti: the atmosphere of cruelty and violence, the probing of marital relations, and, above all, the intense egoism of the characters, an egoism so profound that it seems a curse of Satan. Typical, too, is Betti's language which, even in this early work, is remarkable for its dramatic concision relieved by moments of lyricism. The plays which immediately followed *La padrona* are of interest primarily as examples of the theatrical experiments Betti conducted at the outset of his career: symbolic dramas, a farce, and a ballet-drama. During the 1930s, he also wrote a trilogy of comedies, two of which deserve mention: *I nostri sogni* (1936, Our Dreams) and *Il paese delle vacanze* (1937, *Summertime*).

Some have regarded *Frana allo scalo nord* (1932, *Landslide*) as Betti's masterpiece; it is certainly his first important work. The scene is an inquiry into the causes of a landslide which has killed some railway workers. The duty of Parsc, the examining magistrate, is to fix responsibility and an appropriate sentence. Betti's legal background might lead one to expect a traditional courtroom drama. The facts of the case, however, are scarcely mentioned, and by setting the play in an unidentified foreign city, Betti transcends legal questions. The courtroom, then, becomes the scene of an inquiry into the nature and needs of human beings. As in *La padrona*, egoism is revealed as the root of evil, a kind of original sin inherent in all and concretized on the stage by the Bettian symbol of the blotch *(macchia)*. But with *Frana* a new element appears: man's egoism is tempered by his equally strong need for justice, justice not at a social or legal level but on a spiritual plane. Consonant with his spiritual concern is the conclusion of the judge, who rules that responsibility cannot be attributed to one person or group, for all are guilty, all have been caught up in the "mesh of gears" *(ingranaggio)*, which in Betti's world represents the complex machinery of evil. The play offers no simple solution to the problems of evil and suffering; they can only be alleviated and perhaps made bearable by pity for one's fellow human beings.

Although Betti maintained (and many of his critics have agreed) that his plays were written to prove the existence of God, the Christian message is not usually apparent. Church doctrine is absent, God is seldom mentioned, and no Divine Grace descends to illumine souls or to relieve the anguish of men. On the contrary, Betti's characters confront moral and spiritual dilemmas with only those resources available to all: their conscience and their compassion. The results are frequently unconventional, sometimes illegal, and certainly un-Christian. Yet, however strange they may appear, Betti's solutions to human anguish are, within the limits of the play, satisfying and even inevitable. Thus, in what is his best-known work, *Corruzione al Palazzo di Giustizia* (1944, *Corruption in the Palace of Justice*), the suicide of the innocent Elena is necessary not only to rid the Palace of Justice of its corruption but also to relieve the suffering of the guilty. In *Delitto all' isola delle capre* (1946, *Goat Island*), love transcends the murder of a man by his beloved, and Elsa in *Lotta fino all' alba* (1945, *Struggle Till Dawn*) mercifully poisons her husband in order to still his moral torment. A poor prostitute in *La regina e gli insorti* (1949, *The Queen and the Rebels*) affirms human dignity with her self-willed death, while political martyrdom is sanctified in *L'aiuola bruciata* (1951–52, *The Burnt Flowerbed*). *L'aiuola bruciata, Acque turbate* (1951, *Troubled Waters*), and *La fuggitiva* (1952–53, *The Fugitive*) constitute Betti's spiritual testament, his belief in the necessity of faith in God.

Despite Betti's success in getting most of his plays produced, he enjoyed little critical and even less popular acclaim in Italy during his life. His dark dramas lacking in realism conceded nothing to popular taste, and his contempt for the Italian literary milieu alienated many influential critics. Like Pirandello,* he attracted international attention and rose in the esteem of his countrymen only when his works were performed and acclaimed in Paris in the early 1950s.

Bibliography: Teatro completo (Bologna: Cappelli, 1971); *The New Theatre of Europe,* ed. Robert W. Corrigan (New York: Delta, 1962); *Three Plays by Ugo Betti: The Queen and the Rebels, The Burnt Flowerbed, Summertime,* trans. Henry Reed (New York: Grove, 1956); *Three Plays on Justice: Landslide, Struggle Till Dawn, The Fugitive,* trans. G. H. McWilliam (San Francisco: Chandler, 1964); *Ugo Betti: Three Plays,* trans. Gino Rizzo, et al. (New York: Hill & Wang, 1966); Antonio di Pietro, *L'opera di Ugo Betti,* 2 vols. (Bari: Centro Librario, 1966–68);

G. H. McWilliam, "Introduction" to *Ugo Betti: Two Plays* (Manchester: University of Manchester Press, 1965); J. A. Scott, "The Message of Ugo Betti," *Italica* 37 (1960), 44–57.

Louis Kibler

BIBBIENA: *See* DOVIZI, BERNARDO.

BILENCHI, ROMANO (1909–), journalist and novelist. Bilenchi was born in Colle Val d'Elsa. As a young journalist, he worked on various periodicals, including *Selvaggio* (a journal reflecting the radical tendencies of early Italian fascism, which criticized the regime's conformism after coming to power); *L'Universale* (which Bilenchi directed for a time); *Campo di Marte* (an essentially antifascist forum, which brought Bilenchi into contact with its editors Alfonso Gatto* and Vasco Pratolini*); *Letteratura;* and *Solaria.* In the 1930s, Bilenchi wrote several short stories as well as his first novel, *Conservatorio di Santa Teresa* (1940, The Conservatory of Santa Theresa), republished in 1973. An earlier collection of eight short stories, *Il capofabbrica* (1935, The Foreman), aroused the censors for its subversive tone and appeared only after changes were made. He reissued the collection with his original text in *Racconti* (1958, Short Stories). Bilenchi's fictional portrayal of a society devoid of authentic human relationships begins to merge into his personal life with two long tales written in 1941, *La siccità* (Drought) and *La miseria* (Misery).

Besides enlisting in the Italian Communist party in 1939, Bilenchi took part in antifascist partisan uprisings in Florence (1943–44). After the war, he continued a fruitful journalistic career, founding and directing *Il Nuovo corriere* (1948–56). The Hungarian Revolt of 1957 caused him to withdraw from the Communist party and active political life, although he prepared new editions of earlier works and became director of the *terza pagina* (literary page) for the Florentine newspaper *La Nazione.* Returning to narrative fiction after a number of years, Bilenchi wrote his best work, *Il bottone di Stalingrado* (1972, The Stalingrad Button), which was awarded the Viareggio Prize in that year. The novel's title refers to a button taken by an Austrian soldier (whose father was killed by the fascists) from the body of a Russian soldier killed at the battle of Stalingrad. The button, given to Marco, the book's protagonist, becomes a symbol for his political awakening. Marco's life is traced from his fascist schooldays through the war, the resistance, and the early years of the postwar economic crisis. The evolution of his political ideals seems to reflect the changes in Bilenchi's own thinking. During that same year, he rejoined the Communist party with an open letter to *Unità,* affirming that he saw the organization as the only hope for progressive political change in Italy.

Bibliography: Il bottone di Stalingrado (Florence: Vallecchi, 1972); *Racconti* (Florence: Vallecchi, 1958); Paolo Petroni, *Romano Bilenchi* (Florence: La Nuova Italia, 1972).

BIONDO, FLAVIO (1392–1463), humanist, historian, and antiquarian. Born at Forlì of a well-known but poor family, Biondo followed his father into public service after acquiring a humanistic education in Cremona. By 1422, he was Forlì's ambassador to Milan, but when he took part in an unsuccessful uprising against the Ordelaffi, the ruling family of that city, he was forced into exile and lived in Imola, Ferrara, Venice, and other Italian cities until he came to Rome as a notary to the Curia at the beginning of the pontificate of Eugenius IV in 1433. He later fell into disfavor under Pope Nicholas V but returned to court under Pope Pius II* in 1458. He died in Rome while completing a massive study of Roman history.

Biondo's first critical effort precipitated a polemic with Leonardo Bruni.* In *De verbis romanae locutionis* (1435, On the Words of Roman Speech), he argued that the Italian vernacular had branched off from Latin during the period when Roman Italy was being changed by Germanic invasions. Therefore, Biondo reasoned, the vernacular was a bastard language created by the contamination of the purer Latin tongue, which he regarded as the only language suitable to cultivated men. Bruni had proposed, on the other hand, that the vernacular was itself a product of classical antiquity and had always existed as a popular form of speaking, even in the days of Cicero.

More essential to the development of humanistic thought about the past were Biondo's two antiquarian works—*Roma instaurata* (1444–46, Rome Restored) and *Roma triumphans* (1453–59, Rome Triumphant). The first work analyzes the topography of ancient Rome and occasionally refers to its institutions, while the second inspects the public and private life of the ancient city and provides precise archaeological descriptions of palaces and buildings. Following Poggio Bracciolini's* *De varietate fortunae* (The Inconstancy of Fortune), Biondo employs philological and archaeological sources in a strict and scholarly manner unequaled before him. He was well aware of the chronological gap separating the classical and medieval civilizations. His sensitivity to this historical discontinuity led him, like many other humanists, to advocate the imitation of the classical past. This new understanding of the ruins of Rome and their proper reconstruction helped to transform the sense of history not only in works of scholarship and social thought but also in the arts, particularly in the work of Andrea Mantegna (1431–1506). It also led to the development of what Renaissance* thinkers termed "chorography," that is, the study of geohistory or local history emphasizing the physical remains surviving from past ages. This historical discipline was applied to the entire Italian peninsula when Biondo used the methods of *Roma instaurata* in *L'Italia illustrata* (1453, Italy Illustrated) to study the fourteen ancient regions of the country. Biondo's important history, *Historarum ab inclinatione romani imperii decades* (1452-53, The Decades), which comprised thirty-two books and narrated the history of Italy from the invasion of the Goths and the destruction of Rome (A.D. 410) to his own times, was left incomplete at his death. Biondo follows typical humanist historiographical methods, imitating the classical model of Livy. Apparently, the work was intended to rival Bruni's *De bello italico adversus Gothos* (1470, *The historie, concerning the warres betwene the Imperialles and the Gothes*).

See also BRACCIOLINI, Poggio; BRUNI, Leonardo; HUMANISM.

Bibliography: Bartolomeo Nogara, ed., *Scritti inediti e rari di Flavio Biondo* (Rome: Tipografia poliglotta Vaticana, 1927); Peter Burke, *The Renaissance Sense of the Past* (New York: St. Martin's, 1969); Roberto Weiss, *The Renaissance Discovery of Classical Antiquity* (Oxford: Blackwell, 1969).

BOCCACCIO, GIOVANNI (1313–1375), narrator, poet, and humanist. The greatest Italian storyteller, possibly the greatest of all time, was born in Florence, or perhaps the nearby village of Certaldo. He was the illegitimate son of an unknown mother, probably of humble origin, and of Boccaccio di Chellino, a successful merchant associated with the Bardi Company of Florence, the largest bank of the period. Having legally adopted him, his father probably took him along when in 1327 he moved to Naples, a region greatly influenced by Florentine businessmen, to represent the Bardi interests there as councilor and chamberlain to Naples' King Robert of Anjou. Trained as an apprentice and, later, a junior member of his father's firm, Boccaccio learned accounting, exchange, and general business administration. However, his heart was not in business, and as he repeatedly asserted throughout his life, from his earliest years he had a constant and ineradicable passion for poetry and gave all his spare time to the gathering, copying, and studying of ancient and medieval books, both in Latin and in the vernaculars of Italy and France. Unable to dissuade him from his literary pursuits by steering him into canon law, which he studied between the ages of eighteen and twenty-three, his father had to leave Boccaccio on his own when business interests caused him to leave Naples for Paris in 1332.

Boccaccio continued his happy years of independence in Naples until 1340. He divided his free time between the bustling city and the splendid countryside with its seaside villas and gardens, in the company of associates, friends, and customers or acquaintances even from the royal court. He soon started writing and produced various works destined to open up new vistas for Italian and European literature. The *Caccia di Diana* (1334?, Diana's Hunt) adopts Dante's* *terzina,* while the *Filocolo* (1336?, Love's Labor), in prose, is the first artistic Italian novel. Through a mass of

adventurous, chivalrous tales fraught with learned literary and biographical allusions, the *Filocolo* narrates the French story of Florio and Bi-
ancofiore's long frustrated and finally happy love. The *Filostrato*
(1335–36?, *Filostrato*, or "Prostrated by Love"), composed in the octave
derived from the popular romances, introduces on the literary scene a
fragment of the post-Homeric Trojan cycles, dealing with Criseida's passionate love for Troiolo and her later betrayal of him, a subject exploited by
Chaucer and Shakespeare. From these early works on, Boccaccio's vernacular fiction constantly revolves around the motif of love, with its illusions and delusions of faithfulness and treachery, happiness and tragedy.
Even to the point of contravening the specific conventions of the individual
genres, this theme is central to all his works, whether they take the form of
romance, comedy, epic,* allegorical vision, or short story.

The economic crisis of the 1340s and the first difficulties of the Bardi
Company forced Boccaccio's return to Florence at the end of 1340. There
he completed the *Teseida* (1340–41, *The Book of Theseus*), the first Italian
epic in octaves, dealing with the love of Arcita and Palemone for Emilia,
another story reelaborated by Chaucer. He again turned to emulating
Dante in the *Commedia delle ninfe* (1341–42, The Comedy of the Nymphs
of Florence), written in prose mixed with verse, and in the *Amorosa visione*
(1342–43, Amorous Vision), written in *terzine,* where through Tuscan
allegory he presents love as an ennobling, religious force. The *Visione*
inspired Petrarch's* *Trionfi (Triumphs).* The *Elegia di Madonna Fiammetta* (1343–44, *Amorous Fiammetta*) is the first modern novel in
epistolary form which concentrates upon the inner events of the character's psyche. In this stylistic tour de force, the role of Fiammetta, who in
Boccaccio's literary career corresponds, *mutatis mutandis,* to Dante's
Beatrice and Petrarch's Laura, and who appears constantly in Boccaccio's
fiction except in the *Caccia,* the *Filostrato,* and the *Corbaccio,* is curiously
but most effectively reversed: she, rather than the man (who is sometimes
understood as Boccaccio himself), is the jilted one. The *Ninfale fiesolano*
(1344–46?, *The Nymph of Fiesole*) is a charming poem in octaves combining etiological fable, pastoral* idyll, and a rather rare motif in literature—
paternal and maternal love. Boccaccio's masterpiece, *The Decameron*
(1349–50), begins with the celebrated description of the Black Death, the
disastrous plague witnessed by the author in Florence which affected that
city in even more tragic proportions than the rest of Europe.

A decisive turning point in Boccaccio's life came during those years of
plague when he met Petrarch (1350). Without giving up his interest in the
vernacular, after that date and under the clear influence of Petrarch,
Boccaccio devoted himself to his Latin humanistic scholarship. Until the
end of his life, he almost continuously worked on the vast and influential
encyclopedia of ancient mythology, the *Genealogia deorum gentilium*

(1350–75, *The Genealogies of the Gentile Gods*); the *De casibus virorum illustrium* (1355–74?, *The Fates of Illustrious Men*); the *De mulieribus claris* (1361–75?, *Concerning Famous Women*); and an inventory of ancient and contemporary topography, the *De montibus silvis, fontibus, lacubus etc.* (1355–74?, Concerning Mountains, Forests, Springs, Lakes, etc.). The *Bucolicum carmen* (1351–66?, Pastoral Songs), like the bucolic eclogues of Dante and Petrarch, inspired the long Renaissance* tradition of that classical genre which had disappeared during the Middle Ages. Besides an important correspondence and scattered *Rime* or lyrical poems in Italian, he produced a strange misogynous work, the *Corbaccio* (1356?, 1366? *The Corbaccio,* or "The Bad Raven"), a sort of tense exercise in the genres of satire and invective, and, finally, the last acts in his lifelong devotion to Dante, namely, the *Trattatello in laude di Dante* (three versions of 1351, 1360, and 1373, *In Praise of Dante*), as well as the *Esposizioni* or commentary on the first seventeen cantos of the *Divina Commedia* (1374), the result of his appointment as public lecturer on Dante in the church of Santo Stefano di Badia (1373–74).

During the latter part of his life, Boccaccio, who since the late 1350s had held minor orders of the clergy, was afflicted by a painful, prolonged illness which combined a form of dropsy with scabies. Nonetheless, between 1340 and 1371 he engaged in numerous travels and an active public life. Appointed to several important diplomatic missions by the Florentine government, he met with heads of state and high church officials. In 1351, he was sent to offer Petrarch full restoration of his confiscated patrimony if he should take up residence in Florence. Although the independent Prince of Humanists refused, Boccaccio visited Petrarch several more times in Padua, Milan, and Venice. His friendship with Petrarch ended only with the death of his friend and master, a loss which saddened the last year of his life.

The Decameron, Boccaccio's most famous work, is a collection of one hundred short stories or *novelle** told by a company of seven young ladies and three young men, ten each day, during a retreat to the hills of Fiesole above Florence in order to escape from the plague-ridden city in 1348. The general introduction describing the plague and the meeting of the young people as well as the introductions and epilogues to the several days constitute the frame. Its function goes well beyond that of a frame-story as found in other collections such as the *Arabian Nights.* It creates a climate of honest escape and healthy withdrawal that places the storytelling and the daily activities of the youngsters on a special plane, within an almost surrealistic setting against which the exemplary yet realistic stories are made to stand out. In this one respect, it is curiously analogous to the pilgrimage of the *Divina Commedia.*

Although the popular reader has traditionally concentrated on the sensual and jestful aspects of the collection as a hymn to the joy of living, the critical reader makes no such distortion. The book is richly articulated along some basic motifs whose clear pattern of distribution is an essential part of its overall structure. Thus, after a first day of satirical glimpses at the vices of men, especially of the higher classes, the external forces of destiny, namely fortune or *caso,* are brought into play, first as they triumph over the men and women that have become their playthings (second day) and then as they are overcome by human will and industry (third day). Next, the internal forces of instinct (typically, love) and talent (*ingegno,* intellect, wit) are given the field. The fourth and fifth days show the workings of love, first unhappy, then happy, while on the sixth day *ingegno* triumphs in the form of witty sayings or of jests performed either as ends in themselves or as a means of overcoming a difficult situation or, more specifically, to give way to a passion by removing a social obstacle through a clever trick. Jests are played by women on their husbands (seventh day) or "by a woman on a man, a man on a woman, or a man on another" (eighth day). Although the ninth day, like the first day, is ostensibly without a set theme, it in fact recapitulates by offering once again the sequence of the three basic motifs. The tragic and heroic themes of the last day offer a counterpoint to the comedy of the first by presenting exemplary cases of lofty human virtues: magnanimity, liberality, endurance.

This grandiose, unprecedentedly varied "human comedy," therefore, acts on the reader through a subtle and effective contrapuntal play of opposite possibilities. Life is pictured as a dialectical whole of ups and downs, victories and defeats, joys and sorrows which can be understood and accepted once we see its wholeness through the harmonious interplay of its apparently contradictory symmetries. While earlier criticism dwelled on the work's ribald and sensual farces, much of recent criticism has in contrast focused on the richness and versatility of Boccaccio's realism, the fullness of his human comedy. The flexibility of the content is perfectly matched by that of the stylistic and linguistic forms, as Petrarch was the first to note. The secret of the book's unsurpassed readability, as well as its success as a canonical reference text—the ideal linguistic model of Italian prose writing from Bembo's* time to the early eighteenth century—depends to a large extent on its unprecedented mixture of styles. The language always bends to fit the subject, unafraid of the most drastic adjustments that may be called for. Thus, Boccaccio could provide a valid and enduring lesson of highly literate writing, indeed, even academic to the point of being long regarded as Ciceronian, and at the same time create some of the most popular scenes and characters of all literature.

Bibliography: Amorous Fiammetta, trans. Bartholomew Young (1926; rpt. Westport, Conn.: Greenwood Press, 1970); *Boccaccio on Poetry,* trans. Charles Osgood (Indianapolis, Ind.: Bobbs-Merrill, 1956); *The Book of Theseus,* trans. Bernadette McCoy (New York: Medieval Text Association, 1974); *Concerning Famous Women,* trans. Guido Guarino (New Brunswick, N.J.: Rutgers University Press, 1963); *The Corbaccio,* trans. Anthony Cassell (Urbana, Ill.: Illinois University Press, 1975); *The Decameron,* trans. G. A. McWilliam (Baltimore: Penguin, 1972); *The Decameron: A Norton Critical Edition,* eds. and trans. Mark Musa and Peter E. Bondanella (New York: Norton, 1977); *The Fates of Illustrious Men,* trans. Louis Hall (New York: Ungar, 1965); *The Filostrato of Giovanni Boccaccio,* trans. N. E. Griffin and A. B. Myrick (New York: Biblo & Tannen, 1967); *Giovanni Boccaccio's Thirteen Questions of Love,* ed. Harry Carter (New York: Potter, 1974)—excerpts from the *Filocolo; The Nymph of Fiesole,* trans. Daniel Donno (1960; rpt. Westport, Conn.: Greenwood Press, 1974); Vittore Branca, *Boccaccio medievale* (Florence: Sansoni, 1958); Giovanni Getto, *Vita di forme e forme di vita nel Decameron* (Turin: Petrini, 1958); A. C. Lee, *The Decameron: Its Sources and Analogues* (1909; rpt. New York: Haskell, 1972); Aldo D. Scaglione, *Nature and Love in the Late Middle Ages: An Essay on the Cultural Context of The Decameron* (1963; rpt. Westport, Conn.: Greenwood Press, 1976); *Studi sul Boccaccio* (Florence, 1963–); E. F. Tuttle and Marga Cottino-Jones, eds., *Boccaccio: Secoli di vita* (Ravenna: Longo, 1977); Herbert G. Wright, *Boccaccio in England from Chaucer to Tennyson* (London: Athlone, 1957).

Aldo D. Scaglione

BOCCALINI, TRAIANO (1556–1613), political thinker and essayist. Born in Loreto, Boccalini spent the early part of his life studying law and letters at Perugia and Padua. In 1584, he moved to Rome, where he spent much of the rest of his life. There, he enjoyed the patronage of Cardinals Scipione Borghese and Bonifazio Caetani, and Pope Gregory XIV named him governor of Benevento, a post he filled for a brief period. Returning to Rome, he fell out of favor at court, perhaps because of his friendship with Paolo Sarpi.* In 1612, he went to Venice, where the suddenness of his death the following year seemed to confirm the rumor spread by his children that the Spanish had killed him because of his strong opposition to their Italian policies.

Boccalini's political ideas reflect the debate of the time over the doctrine of *ragion di stato* and the implications of Machiavelli's* republican theories for a world increasingly composed of absolutist, nonrepublican nation states. He opposed the justification of evil deeds in the name of "reason of state" and most frequently criticized the Spanish for the corruption and political strife in Italy during the Counter-Reformation. Like the works of Ammirato* and Botero,* Boccalini's *Commentari sopra Cornelio Tacito* (1677, Commentary on Cornelius Tacitus) evinces the predilection of his contemporaries for the historian of the Roman Empire, in contrast to the humanist writings of the Quattrocento and Cinquecento and especially to those of Machiavelli, which are more concerned with the works of Livy, the historian of the Roman Republic. For Boccalini, the ideal state was that of republican Venice. His attacks upon tyrannical governments in this commentary did not overlook Machiavelli's views on government in *The Prince*. Boccalini construed this work not as a handbook for the absolute ruler but rather as a warning to the people about the true nature of princely absolutism. This view of Machiavelli was later revived by Foscolo* and the romantics.

In 1605, Boccalini began his most popular work, the *Ragguagli di Parnaso (Advertisements from Parnassus),* portions of which he gave Cardinal Borghese and the king of France two years later. Two hundred of these "dispatches" had been published by the year of his death, and thirty-one appeared posthumously under the title *Pietra del paragone politico* (1615, *Politick Touchstone*). This last group was by far the most contentious and the most violently anti-Spanish. In these reports, Boccalini envisions himself the observer of events taking place in the imaginary realm of Parnassus, a kingdom governed by Apollo and populated by poets, politicians, great men, personified states and human qualities. Boccalini's dispatches cover all conceivable topics—literary questions such as the import of Aristotle's *Poetics,* neoclassicism,* the relative merits of brevity or prolixity in writing, philosophical or political problems, and general topics of interest, such as academicians, pedants, and life in society. The breadth of the subject matter and Boccalini's sometimes playful, sometimes biting satire guaranteed their success within Italy. Abroad, they received numerous translations in the major European languages (including one in English as early as 1622) and influenced, among others, Cervantes, Swift, and Addison.

See also AMMIRATO, Scipione; BOTERO, Giovanni; MACHIA-VELLI, Niccolò.

Bibliography: Ragguagli di Parnaso e Pietra del Paragone, ed. Giuseppe Rua, 2 vols. (Bari: Laterza, 1910–12); *Ragguagli di Parnaso e scritti minori,* ed. Luigi Firpo, 3 vols. (Bari: Laterza, 1948); *Advertisements from Parnassus . . . Together with the author's Politick touchstone; his Secretaria di Apollo* (London: R. Smith, 1704); William H. Irving, "Boccalini and Swift," *Eighteenth-Century Studies* 7 (1973–74), 143–60; Friedrich Meinecke, *Machiavellism: The Doctrine of Raison d'État and Its Place in Modern History,* trans. D. Scott (London: Routledge & Kegan Paul, 1957); Giuseppe Toffanin, *Machiavelli e il "Tacitismo"* (1921; rpt. Naples: Guida, 1972).

BOIARDO, MATTEO MARIA (1441–1494), count of Scandiano, poet, and courtier. Often spoken of as an ancient and noble family, the Boiardi were prominent in the society surrounding the Este court of Ferrara in the fifteenth century. Niccolò II d'Este had made Selvatico and Feltrino

Boiardi the feudal lords of Rubiera in 1362. The Boiardi held that position until 1423, at which time Feltrino the younger (grandfather of Matteo Maria) ceded Rubiera to Niccolò III in exchange for the lordship of Arceto, Scandiano, Gesso, and Torricella. In the same year, by declaration of the duke of Milan, those estates were severed from the territories of Reggio, and Feltrino was proclaimed the first count of Scandiano as well as lord of the other towns. Feltrino's oldest son, Giovanni, married Lucia Strozzi, of Florentine descent and sister of the distinguished poet-humanist Tito Vespasiano Strozzi (1442–1505). Their first son, Matteo Maria, probably born at Scandiano in the spring of 1441, was to become the finest lyric poet of his day, and a man known for his gentility and compassion.

Matteo Boiardo spent most of his early childhood in Ferrara. He acquired a good classical education, learned Greek and Latin, and studied philosophy and law at the University of Ferrara. He served the Este family as a poet, courtier, and administrator. His earliest works include Virgilian eclogues, the *Carmina de Laudibus Estensium* (1463–64, Songs in Praise of Ercole d'Este), and other verse, as well as translations and adaptations of works by classical Greek and Latin authors. As a courtier he enjoyed the benefits of the courts of the Dukes Borso, Ercole, and Sigismondo in Ferrara, Modena, and Reggio. In Ferrara, he undoubtedly had access to the Estense Library and its rich collections of romances, while it was in Sigismondo's court in Reggio that, in 1469, Boiardo met and fell in love with Antonia Caprara, to whom he was to dedicate his *Amorum libri* (1499, Three Books of Love Songs), a memorable collection of one hundred and eighty Petrarchan lyrics. His service as a gentleman of the court placed him at Borso's reception of Emperor Frederick III at Ferrara in 1469; in Rome with Borso in 1471; and in Naples in 1473 as part of a cortège of five hundred sent to escort Eleanor of Aragon, the fiancée of Ercole, back to Ferrara. It was Ercole, then duke of Ferrara, who, in 1480, appointed Boiardo governor of Modena and, in 1487, governor of Reggio. He held the former office until 1483 and the latter until his death.

While Boiardo was fond of the Este family and served them loyally, he was equally fond of Scandiano, his birthplace, where he enjoyed the natural beauty and simple country diversions. It was also a peaceful place which he found more suitable for writing poetry. It was in Scandiano that Boiardo could be found in 1479, now married to Taddea Gonzaga of Novellara, working on his masterful romance epic,* the *Orlando innamorato* (Books I and II, 1483; complete edition, 1495, Orlando in Love).

As a lyric poet, Boiardo is surpassed by none of his contemporaries. His *Amorum libri* are the best and most important examples of fifteenth-century love poetry written in the Petrarchan manner. They are an intimate portrait of intense personal sentiments, full of originality and vitality. It is the *Orlando innamorato*, however, which reveals Boiardo's poetic powers of invention in their full richness. Begun around 1472 and interrupted early in the third book by the author's death, the *Innamorato* is a romantic epic, or chivalric romance, which revived a faltering literary tradition and served as a source and constant point of reference for Ariosto's* *Orlando furioso* (*The Frenzy of Orlando*). The poem is a rich amalgam of Arthurian romance, Carolingian epic, and popular inspiration. It has been said, for example, that some of the Saracen warriors were named after peasants in the author's service. The nationalistic and religious fervor of the militant medieval epic gives way, in the *Innamorato,* to the Ovidian belief that love conquers all, in spite of the fact that the poet spends much of his time describing armed conflicts. The power of love turns the mood of the poem from that of a predominantly male-centered medieval epic world to that of a chivalric microcosm in which courtly love, complemented by humanistic learning, begins to contribute to the formation of the Renaissance* ideal of the perfect courtier, later to be described in Castiglione's* *Book of the Courtier.*

Boiardo's narrative skill and inventiveness enabled him to weave a tapestry of tales which, in its intricate variety, reveals the author's aristocratic temperament, his feeling for nature, and his attachment to his characters, who, as they move about in an enchanted and enchanting world, entice the spellbound listener/reader into a labyrinth of adventure and diversion. Nevertheless, the *Innamorato,* which, to be sure, has some serious stylistic shortcomings, fell victim to Tuscan cultural hegemony and was rejected because of its local flavor (a result of its linguistic regionalism) and its lack of conceptual unity. It was thereafter ignored or subjected to revision and rewriting. Not until the rediscovery of Boiardo's original by Antonio Panizzi (1797–1879) in the nineteenth century did the *Orlando innamorato,* until then known primarily through Francesco Berni's* and Ludovico Domenichi's (1515–64) Tuscanized versions, begin to regain some of the reputation it had enjoyed with its original audience at the Este court in fifteenth-century Ferrara.

See also ARIOSTO, Ludovico.

Bibliography: Tutte le opere di Matteo Maria Boiardo, ed. Angelandrea Zottoli, 2 vols. (Milan: Mondadori, 1936–37); *Orlando Innamorato: Translated into Prose from the Italian of Francesco Berni . . . by William Stewart Rose* (Edinburgh: W. Blackwood and London: T. Cadell, 1823); Andrea di Tommaso, *Structure and Ideology in Boiardo's Orlando Innamorato* (Chapel Hill, N.C.: University of North Carolina Press, 1972); Robert Durling, *The Figure of the Poet in Renaissance Epic* (Cambridge, Mass.: Harvard University Press, 1965); E. W. Edwards, *The Orlando Furioso and Its Predecessor* (Cambridge: Cambridge University Press, 1924); Giovanni Ponte, *La personalità e l'opera del Boiardo* (Genoa: Tilgher, 1972).

Andrea di Tommaso

BOITO, ARRIGO (1842–1918), composer, librettist, and poet. Born in Padua, Boito attended the Conservatory of Music in Milan, where he met Emilio Praga.* A scholarship enabled him to study in Paris, where he met Baudelaire, Rossini, Berlioz, and Verdi. Upon his return to Milan, he became a leading figure in the *scapigliatura*,* a bohemian gathering of artists and intellectuals in the city. He also saw military service against the Austrians in the northern campaigns of 1866. His first opera, *Mefistofele* (1868, *Mephistopheles*), was greeted with jeers and whistles at La Scala because of its supposedly Wagnerian qualities. However, seven years later it triumphed in Bologna. Another opera, *Nerone* (Nero), planned as early as 1861, was performed at La Scala in 1924 only after the composer's death.

When Boito met the famous actress Eleonora Duse in 1884, she became his mistress for a time. Duse was instrumental in showing the young man the importance of Shakespeare's theatre; two of Boito's most important *libretti* for Giuseppe Verdi—*Othello* and *Falstaff*—were both derived from Shakespearean sources. Besides these two well-known operas, Boito wrote the *libretti* of a number of minor operas for other Italian composers. Although he always considered his poetry less important than his music, Boito's two collections of poetry—*Re Orso* (1865, King Bear) and *Il libro dei versi e Re Orso* (1877, The Book of Verses and King Bear)—are outstanding examples of the kind of lyric poetry produced by members of the *scapigliatura*. While other poets of the movement experimented with the effects of painting, Boito attempted to incorporate musical qualities into his poetry.

See also SCAPIGLIATURA.

Bibliography: Tutti gli scritti, ed. Piero Nardi (Milan: Mondadori, 1942); *Mefistofele,* English and Italian version (New York: Fred Rullman, 1920); Giuseppe Verdi, *Seven Verdi Librettos,* trans. William Weaver (New York: Norton, 1973)—includes English and Italian *libretti* for *Othello* and *Falstaff.*

BOITO, CAMILLO (1836–1914), architect, art historian, and writer. A native of Rome and the older brother of Arrigo,* the poet, Boito studied architecture in Venice at the Accademia di Belle Arti but fled to Tuscany in 1856 when his political beliefs aroused the ire of the Austrian authorities. He moved to Milan in 1859 and occupied the chair of architecture at the Accademia di Brera from 1860 until 1908. As a critic and art historian, Boito's renown came from his scholarly works on the architecture of medieval Italy (1880) and on Milan's duomo (1889). His popular *novelle,** stories which sometimes reflect the thematic concerns of the *scapigliatura** movement usually connected with his more famous brother, are basically studies in ambience or atmosphere concentrating upon feminine characters of great beauty and passion. "Un corpo" (1870, A Corpse) exemplifies Boito's art. It describes a beautiful woman named Carlotta who is loved by both a painter and a student of anatomy; the student comes upon her in a morgue, and the traumatic event is described in masterful fashion by Boito. His most famous tale, "Senso" (1882, "A Thing Apart"), tells of a Venetian noblewoman and her Austrian lover. Although Lieutenant Remigio Ruz is as handsome as Adonis, he is a coward who uses jewels and money obtained from his mistress to bribe army doctors into granting him a certificate of illness. Once the countess discovers he has been unfaithful, she denounces his cowardice to his commanding officer, who is forced to have him executed as a deserter; the countess witnesses his death by invitation. The story's fame was redoubled by Luchino Visconti's beautiful but controversial film of the same title in 1954. The tone of the original story and its decadent atmosphere perfectly complemented Visconti's pessimistic interpretation of the Risorgimento in both *Senso* and his even more famous filmic version of Lampedusa's* *Il gattopardo* (1963).

Bibliography: "Senso" e altre storielle vane, ed. Piero Nardi (Florence: Le Monnier, 1961); *Italian Regional Tales of the Nineteenth Century,* eds. Archibald Colquhoun, et al. (London: Oxford University Press, 1961); *Senso di Luchino Visconti,* ed. G. B. Cavallaro (Bologna: Cappelli, 1955); Geoffrey Nowell-Smith, *Luchino Visconti* (New York: Viking, 1973).

BONAGIUNTA ORBICCIANA DA LUCCA (thirteenth century), poet. Because several other Luccans bore the same name, some confusion has arisen over the poet's identity. Probably a notary whose official documents were written between 1242 and 1257, he may have lived into the last quarter of the century, since he reproaches Guinizzelli* in a poem which was very likely written in the early 1270s. Largely ignored until the nineteenth century, Bonagiunta went through a phase of Sicilian imitation which led another poet, possibly Chiaro Davanzati,* to accuse him of plagiarizing Giacomo da Lentino.* Bonagiunta's poetry shows the influence of both Guittone* and the *stilnovisti,* but he probably was not a follower of either.

Although he was competent technically, Bonagiunta's poetry is largely derivative. He played but a minor role in the development of the Italian lyric, for he put forth no new themes and made no real stylistic innovations. Ironically, Dante* in *Purgatory* XXIV has Bonagiunta speak the words which signal the end of the Sicilian-Provençal tradition and the rise of a new and significant poetic style, the so-called *dolce stil nuovo*. Whether or not Dante wished so to classify the group of poets of which he was a member, the encounter of the pilgrim and Bonagiunta is an important event in Italian literary history and one which called attention to Bonagiunta's own work.

See also DOLCE STIL NUOVO.

Bibliography: Poeti del Duecento, ed. Gianfranco Contini, 2 vols. (Milan: Ricciardi, 1960); Frederick Goldin, *German and Italian Lyrics of the Middle Ages*

(Garden City, N.Y.: Doubleday, 1973); Kenneth W. Miller, "A Critical Edition of the Poetry of Bonagiunta da Lucca," Ph.D. Dissertation, Indiana University, 1973.

BONTEMPELLI, MASSIMO (1878-1960), novelist, playwright, and journalist. Bontempelli was a native of Como and attended the University of Turin, fought as an artillery officer in World War I, and collaborated on a number of Florentine publications *(Il Marzocco, La Nazione)* and *La Nuova antologia* in Rome. In 1922, he published *La scacchiera davanti allo specchio* (The Chess-Board in Front of the Mirror), a fantasy obviously indebted to *Alice in Wonderland*, telling of a young child who enters a miraculous mirror and lives through an extraordinary adventure. Between 1926 and 1929, Bontempelli directed (for a time with Curzio Malaparte*) the journal *900*, a review designed to move Italian culture beyond its stuffy provincialism. He then completed the novels *Il figlio di due madri* (1929, The Son of Two Mothers), a tale of a reincarnation, and *Vita e morte di Adria e dei suoi figli* (1930, The Life and Death of Adria and Her Sons), a strange tale of a woman whose desire is to fix her perfect beauty in time. Made a member of the Accademia d'Italia in 1930, Bontempelli spent the next decade in various cities, both Italian and foreign, and continued to work as a journalist and writer. Although he usually supported the fascist regime during the early part of his career, he was suspended for a year from his journalistic profession for participating in the commemoration of D'Annunzio's* death in 1938. He passed the war years in Venice and was afterwards elected senator on the Popular Front ticket, only to see the election invalidated as a result of what was considered his fascist background.

In addition to his poetry and several excellent biographical studies of Scarlatti, Verdi, Verga,* Leopardi,* and Pirandello,* certain of Bontempelli's dramatic works merit reading. The best plays recall the fabulous atmosphere of the grotesque theatre.* Perhaps most worthy of note is *Nostra Dea* (1925, Our Dea), a philosophical parody of the view that human beings are the products of their environment. In the comedy, Dea's personality changes with her changes in clothes (she is domineering in riding gear, religious in priestly garb, a nonentity in underwear). Although usually recognized for what he wrote during the fascist period, Bontempelli was awarded the Strega Prize for Literature in 1953 for *L'amante fedele* (1953, The Faithful Lover), a later collection of short stories in a surrealist vein.

Bibliography: L'Avventura novecentista (Florence: Vallecchi, 1974); *Racconti e romanzi*, ed. Paola Masino, 2 vols. (Milan: Mondadori, 1961); Luigi Baldacci, *Massimo Bontempelli* (Turin: Borla, 1967); Fernando Tempesti, *Massimo Bon-*

tempelli (Florence: La Nuova Italia, 1974); Domenico Vittorini, *The Modern Italian Novel* (1930; rpt. New York: Russell & Russell, 1967).

BORGESE, GIUSEPPE ANTONIO (1881–1952), essayist, literary critic, poet, novelist, teacher, and political activist. Borgese was born near Palermo in Sicily and completed his university training in Florence. His thesis, highly praised by Benedetto Croce,* was published by *La critica* as *Storia della critica romantica in Italia* (1905, History of Romantic Criticism in Italy). In Florence, Borgese collaborated on a number of literary reviews, including *Leonardo* and *Il Regno,* and he founded another, *Hermes,* which appeared between 1904 and 1906. His early nationalist and imperialist views had changed to some extent by 1909, for during that year he published a study of D'Annunzio* which was critical of his patriotic ideology. Borgese was unusually attuned to writers whose merits were overlooked by other critics. Some of his essays, many originally published in Milan's *Corriere della sera,* were collected in three volumes entitled *La vita e il libro* (1910–13, Life and Books), in *Studi di letterature moderne* (1920, Studies of Modern Literatures) and in *Tempo di edificare* (1924, Time to Build). Besides coining the critical term *crepuscolari* ("twilight poets"), now commonly employed in all discussions of the works of such poets as Guido Gozzano* and Sergio Corazzini,* Borgese practically discovered Federigo Tozzi* and encouraged such promising authors as Moravia,* Soldati,* and Piovene.*

Although he also published poetry, other minor novels, plays, and several translations, Borgese's chief literary creation is the novel *Rubè* (1921, *Rubè*). The protagonist, a decadent European youth whose excessive tendencies to self-analysis have rendered him unfit for living, is related to the many inept antiheroes in the fiction of the next generation. Rubè dies during a political demonstration in Bologna, clutching the black and red flags of the Fascist and Communist parties, a victim of two political ideologies he can neither understand nor accept.

Borgese began his teaching career in Turin and Milan, holding a chair of German literature and then of aesthetics. An antifascist of the liberal persuasion, he refused to sign the required oath of allegiance to the Fascist party and left Italy to go into self-imposed exile in the United States where he taught Italian and literature at Smith College and the Universities of California and Chicago. He married Elizabeth Mann, the daughter of the novelist, and became an eloquent antifascist spokesman; his *Goliath, The March of Fascism* (1937) was a forceful plea for the recognition that fascism posed a threat to liberal democracy. In his last years, Borgese worked for a committee formed to establish a world constitution. He returned to Italy in 1947, but his university position was never restored to him.

Bibliography: Foundations of the World Republic (Chicago: University of Chicago Press, 1953); *Goliath, The March of Fascism* (New York: Viking, 1937); *Rubè,* trans. Isaac Goldberg (New York: Harcourt, 1923); Sarah D'Alberti, *Giuseppe Antonio Borgese* (Palermo: Flaccovio Editore, 1971); Sergio Pacifici, *The Modern Italian Novel from Capuana to Tozzi* (Carbondale, Ill.: Southern Illinois University Press, 1973).

BORSIERI, PIETRO (1786–1852), poet and patriot. Born in Milan, Borsieri studied law in Pavia and worked in the Ministry of Justice. Following the publication in 1816 of Madame de Staël's provocative article, "On the Method and Value of Translations," in which she urged Italian writers to rid themselves of the pedantry and outmoded conventions of their national literature by translating the great writers from abroad, Borsieri reacted positively to this advice and eventually composed the influential *Avventure letterarie di un giorno* (1816, Literary Adventures of a Day), which became one of the key manifestoes of the Italian romantic movement. In this work, Borsieri defended Madame de Staël, attacked her Italian critics, and recommended that Italian writers open their minds to the contemplation of forms of poetic beauty known only in foreign literatures.

Borsieri was also a major contributor to the Milanese journal, *Il Conciliatore* (1818–19). This periodical published the essays of Silvio Pellico,* Giovanni Berchet,* and many others, and was regarded as an organ for social, political, or literary reform and for the new romantic movement. Borsieri not only wrote the journal's opening statement but also contributed many articles in literary criticism, ranging from discussions of works by Sheridan, Baretti,* Hume, and Sismondi (1773–1842) to those of Firenzuola.*

Arrested in 1822, Borsieri was sentenced to prison for twenty years for his political beliefs, but the Austrian authorities commuted the sentence to deportation in 1836, and Borsieri spent two years in America supporting himself miserably as a teacher of Italian before returning to Europe in 1838. He was unable to pick up his once promising literary career when he returned after his many years of prison and exile. He died in Belgirate, a poor and deserted man, a victim of the political changes which swept over Italy in the nineteenth century.

See also ROMANTICISM.

Bibliography: Avventure letterarie di un giorno, ed. Giorgio Alessandrini (Rome: Ateneo, 1967).

BOTERO, GIOVANNI (1544–1617), political writer. Born in the Piedmont region, Botero received a Jesuit education and became a teacher of rhetoric and philosophy in both Italy and France. Recalled from Paris in 1569 for his anti-Spanish sentiment, he once again caused difficulties for himself with church officials by preaching a sermon against the papacy's temporal power in the presence of the archbishop of Milan, the future Saint Charles Borromeo, nephew of Pope Pius IV. However, Borromeo hired Botero as his personal secretary (1582), and in 1586 he became an assistant to Borromeo's nephew Federico, eventually moving to Rome with Federico when he became a cardinal. After 1599, Botero became the tutor of the three oldest sons of the duke of Savoy, in whose service he remained until 1610.

Botero's years in the papal city stimulated his literary activity. One of his earliest works, *Delle cause della grandezza e magnificenza delle città* (1588, *The Greatness of Cities*) appeared there, as did *Della ragion di stato* (1588, *Reason of State*) and some portions of *Relazioni universali* (1591–96, *An Historicall Description of the most famous Kingdomes and Common-weales in the Worlde*). The first of these provides various geographical descriptions in a treatment of the most suitable sites for founding cities, remarks concerning the role of economics in determining a city's greatness, and comments upon many other matters pertaining to urban life. It was translated into English by Robert Peterson in 1606. *Della ragion di stato,* a work in ten books which popularized the expression "reason of state," is a typical Counter-Reformation tract which stresses the value of religious uniformity and warns of the menace of the Turks to Christianity, a religion Botero viewed as the one most likely to guarantee the obedience of a prince's subjects. Although Botero claimed to refute Machiavelli's* theories, he was influenced not only by the Florentine secretary but also by Bodin, Livy, and Tacitus. In line with the tendency of his day toward absolutism, Botero cited Tacitus, the historian of the Roman Empire, almost twice as frequently as Livy, the historian of the Roman Republic. Whereas Machiavelli's *Discorsi* emphasized the foundation of a republican form of government, Botero's "reason of state" assumed the existence of state and ruler and studied the means for their preservation or extension. This treatise became extremely popular. During the author's lifetime, it appeared in over twenty editions in Italian, Spanish, French, and Latin. Finally, the *Relazioni,* written in five parts, attempts to provide a geographical, political, and economic picture of the various countries in the world based upon many of the assumptions contained in his earlier works.

See also MACHIAVELLI, Niccolò.

Bibliography: Scrittori politici del '500 e del '600, ed. Bruno Widmar (Milan: Rizzoli, 1964); *An Historicall Description of the most famous Kingdomes and Common-Weales in the Worlde,* trans. Robert Johnson (London: Haviland, 1630); *The Reason of State & The Greatness of Cities,* trans. P. J. and D. P. Waley and Robert Peterson (New Haven, Conn.: Yale University Press, 1956); Friedrich Meinecke, *Machiavellism: The Doctrine of Raison D'État and Its Place in Modern*

History (London: Routledge & Kegan Paul, 1957); Giuseppe Toffanin, *Machiavelli e il "Tacitismo"* (1921; rpt. Naples: Guida, 1972).

BRACCIOLINI, POGGIO (1380–1459), humanist, statesman, and historian. Born at Terranuova in Tuscany, Bracciolini came to Florence to complete his studies as a notary and attracted the attention and protection of Coluccio Salutati,* a noted humanist and Florentine chancellor, as well as the friendship of Niccolò Niccoli (circa 1365–1437), one of the Renaissance's* most assiduous seekers of rare manuscripts and the man who built up the famous library of Cosimo de' Medici. With Salutati's backing, he secured a post in Rome, becoming secretary to Pope Boniface IX. He continued his work under the antipope John XXIII, whom he accompanied to the Council of Constance in 1414, where his patron was deposed. Bracciolini was associated with the Roman Curia until 1453, except for a five-year period spent in England (1418–23). In 1453, he moved from the papal service to succeed Carlo Marsuppini as chancellor of the Florentine Republic, finally retiring from an active life one year before his death.

Bracciolini's contributions to Italian humanism* loom large. Perhaps most importantly for posterity, Bracciolini, under the influence of his friend Niccoli, whose enthusiasm for rare manuscripts was contagious, spent a great deal of time searching through various French, Swiss, German, Italian, and Burgundian monasteries. The results of his labors were staggering. To his efforts, we owe Lucretius's *De rerum natura,* a complete Quintilian, many orations of Cicero, the *Silvae* of Statius, several comedies by Plautus, and other less essential works. Bracciolini's many letters, addressed to the most prominent historical and literary figures of his day and often describing in great detail key historical events such as the burning of Jerome of Prague or the personalities of important churchmen, bankers, and statesmen, have proved invaluable to contemporary historians in their efforts to reconstruct life in Bracciolini's time.

Like most humanists of his day, Bracciolini rejected the vernacular and always used Latin as his literary medium. Most of his works appeared in an edition published in Basel in 1538. His dialogue, *De varietate fortunae* (1431–48, The Inconstancy of Fortune), reflects the many hours he spent in Rome contemplating the ancient ruins. Not only is it one of the first discerning studies of these ancient edifices, but it also reflects a Stoic attitude toward parrying the blows of fortune, a philosophical topic of much interest to humanists. The fourth part of the dialogue contains an account of the merchant Niccolò de' Conti's twenty-five year voyage to India and Java. Other works include *De avaritia* (1428–29, On Avarice), a dialogue devoted to the advantages and drawbacks of this Christian vice; and *Contra ypocritas* (1448, Against Hypocrisy), a dialogue between Poggio, Marsuppini, and a humanist Benedictine abbot set in Marsuppini's library which attacks the hypocrisy of the Roman churchmen. No less anticlerical in tone is Bracciolini's dialogue *De infelicitate principum* (1440, On the Unhappy Lot of a Ruler), a discussion between Cosimo de' Medici, Marsuppini, and Niccoli in which the pope's indifference to Bracciolini's crucial discoveries of lost manuscripts in Germany suggests the futility of believing that true nobility arises from personal merit rather than birth. *Liber facetiarum* (1438–52, *The Facetiae*), a collection of jests and anecdotes often obscene or anticlerical in tone, was one of Bracciolini's most popular works. In addition to these original compositions, he translated Xenophon's *Cyropaedia*.

The work which still attracts scholarly attention is his *Historia fiorentina* (1476, History of Florence), a history of the city between 1350 and 1455 which continued the long-standing tradition of historiography among the humanists within the Florentine Chancellery and was eventually to influence the even more luminous works in the vernacular by Machiavelli* and Guicciardini.* While Bracciolini seems to continue the history of Florence which Leonardo Bruni* had produced earlier, he actually narrows the scope of his own undertaking to consider a series of wars waged with the Visconti of Milan and makes a radical departure from Bruni's model Livy, preferring Sallust's *Bellum Jugurthinum* (Jugurthine War) as a guide to the form of his own narrative. Bracciolini emphasizes foreign affairs, for which Machiavelli criticized him in justifying the composition of his new history of Florence. Bracciolini's analysis of the motivations of historical protagonists reveals a serious interest in psychological explanations. For him, desire and anger as well as the hope for revenge constitute man's most compelling motives for action, and in larger terms, he pictures human history as a product of human self-interest. This is particularly true in his pro-Florentine critique of the foreign policy of the city's enemies, which he declares is motivated by greed as opposed to Florentine policies whose end is simply the defense of liberty. At its best, Bracciolini's Latin prose was admired by his contemporaries as well as by writers for several centuries to come who chose to express their thoughts in that universal language of the Renaissance. His history of Florence is one of the monuments to the rhetorical prose tradition of the Florentine Chancellery.

See also BRUNI, Leonardo; HUMANISM.

Bibliography: Opera omnia, ed. Riccardo Fubini (Turin: Bottega d'Erasma, 1964); *The Facetiae,* trans. B. J. Hurwood (New York: Award, 1968); *Travelers in Disguise: Narratives of Eastern Travel by Poggio Bracciolini and Ludovico de Varthema,* trans. J. W. Jones (Cambridge, Mass.: Harvard University Press, 1963); *Two Renaissance Book Hunters: The Letters of Poggius Bracciolini to Nicolaus di Niccolis,* trans. Phyllis Gordon (New York: Columbia University Press, 1974); Nancy S. Struever, *The Language of History in the Renaissance* (Princeton, N.J.: Princeton University Press, 1970); E. Walser, *Poggius Flor-*

entinus: Leben und Werke (Berlin: Teubner, 1914); Donald J. Wilcox, *The Development of Florentine Humanist Historiography in the Fifteenth Century* (Cambridge, Mass.: Harvard University Press, 1969).

BRACCO, ROBERTO (1862–1943), dramatist. Bracco was born in Naples. Deeply indebted to the drama of Ibsen, Bracco attempted to bring to the Italian theatre a deeper awareness of the crisis in European culture, which he felt was ignored by the popular drawing-room comedies of the period. His first one-act plays appeared in 1887. Particularly timely were those plays which analyzed the dilemma of women in modern society who are trapped within a social system insensitive to their aspirations or talents: *Tragedie dell'anima* (1899, Tragedies of the Soul); *Sperduti nel buio* (1901, Lost in the Darkness); *La piccola fonte* (1905, *The Hidden Spring*); and *I fantasmi* (1906, *Phantasms*). His most famous work, *Il piccolo santo* (1910, The Little Saint), anticipates the direction of much modern drama. As the first Italian play to examine the unconscious, it owes much to Freudian ideas. The play concerns a village priest named Don Fiorenzo and his ambivalent affection for a young girl named Annita (originally the daughter of a woman the priest loved in his youth, but now his ward who is engaged to his brother, Giulio). The mentally deficient Barbarello somehow intuits Don Fiorenzo's suppressed love for Annita and in his devotion to the priest murders Giulio. In the end, Don Fiorenzo dies from grief and guilt.

Bracco's career in the theatre was cut short by the advent of fascism. His vigorous opposition to their cause led the fascists to persecute him and to boycott his works. Bracco was an extremely popular dramatist with a worldwide reputation at the outbreak of World War I, but his critical reputation has never regained the ground it lost after he withdrew from writing for the theatre in 1922.

Bibliography: Teatro, 10 vols. (Milan: Remo Sandron, 1922); *The Hidden Spring,* trans. Dirce St. Cyr, in *Poet Lore* 18 (1907), 143–86, and *Phantasms,* trans. Dirce St. Cyr, in *Poet Lore* 19 (1908), 241–92; Silvio D'Amico, *Il teatro italiano del Novecento* (Milan: Treves, 1939); Maddalena Kuitunen, "Ibsen and the Theatre of Roberto Bracco," pp. 187–202, in *Petrarch to Pirandello: Studies in Italian Literature in Honor of Beatrice Corrigan,* ed. Julius A. Molinaro (Toronto: University of Toronto Press, 1973); Pasquale Parisi, *Roberto Bracco, la sua vita, la sua arte, i suoi critici* (Milan: Remo Sandron, 1923).

BRANCATI, VITALIANO (1907–1954), critic, playwright, and novelist. A native of Sicily, Brancati obtained a university degree in literature and joined the Fascist party in 1922, attracted to the movement by its apparent vitality and revolutionary character. Two early plays—*Feodor* (1928, Feodor) and *Piave* (1932, Piave)—as well as an early novel—*L'amico del* *vincitore* (1932, The Friend of the Winner)—reflect this affinity for fascism. *Piave* actually includes Mussolini as one of a group of soldiers whose bravery at the battle of Piave is its subject, and for this drama Brancati was awarded a literary prize reserved for writers favorable to the regime. However, at this time, Brancati, coming under the more liberal influence of Giuseppe Borgese,* began gradually to reject fascism and its literary myths.

Gli anni perduti (1935, Lost Years) marks Brancati's turning away from D'Annunzio* and fascism towards a satirical narrative style employing specifically Sicilian themes. In this novel, the representation of southern decadence, sensuality, *gallismo* (excessive preoccupation with sex, boasting of sexual prowess), and immobility attains philosophical proportions and indirectly provides a critique of the fascist regime and its mentality. His major novels in this vein—*Don Giovanni in Sicilia* (1941, Don Juan in Sicily), *Il bell'Antonio* (1949, *Antonio, The Great Lover*), and *Paolo il caldo* (1955, Paolo the Hot)—all explore these themes in a tragicomic tone. Usually considered his masterpiece, *Il bell'Antonio* describes a handsome man whose reputation as a womanizer conceals his impotence, the discovery of which embarrasses his family, his town, and even the Fascist party. One of his antifascist stories, *Il vecchio con gli stivali* (1945, The Old Man with the Boots), was filmed as *Anni difficili* (1948, Difficult Years) by Luigi Zampa.

Bibliography: Opere, ed. Angelo Guglielmi (Milan: Bompiani, 1974); *Il borghese e l'immensità: scritti 1930–1954*, eds. Sandro De Feo and G. A. Cibotto (Milan: Bompiani, 1973); *Antonio, The Great Lover*, trans. Vladimir Kean (London: Dobson, 1952); Robert Dombroski, "Brancati and Fascism: A Profile," *Italian Quarterly* 13 (1969), 41–63; Claire L. Huffman, "Vitaliano Brancati: A Reassessment," *Forum Italicum* 6 (1972), 356–77.

BRUNETTO LATINI (circa 1220–circa 1295), poet, scholar, and diplomat. Brunetto, the son of Bonaccorso Latini, was probably born in Florence. Official documents attest to his endeavors both professionally as a notary and politically as a Guelph partisan who served his city well. An envoy to the court of Alfonso X of Castille, he sought aid against Manfred and the Ghibellines. However, after the rout of Montaperti (1260), he was forced to seek refuge in France where he remained for seven years, living among Florentine merchants and financiers. When a victory at Benevento in 1266 returned power to the Guelphs, Brunetto returned to Florence, serving his city by assuming important diplomatic and administrative duties until his death.

As an early Italian man of letters and an elder statesman, he was esteemed by his countrymen. Villani* describes him as a great philosopher and a master of rhetoric who believed with Cicero and Aristotle that the use of reason and the art of speaking well were fundamental to human society. It was he who taught the Florentines how best to govern themselves in the republican manner. Although condemned for the sin of sodomy in Dante's* *Inferno* (XV), Brunetto is portrayed in high fashion. Dante the Pilgrim addresses the man whose works profoundly influenced him with reverence and gratitude and recalls him as the fatherly tutor who had shown him "how man makes himself eternal."

During his years in France, Brunetto learned the language and literature of Occitania, and translated and composed works in Latin, French, and Italian. His role in the revival of interest in classical learning stems first from his *Rhetoric,* a translation with commentary of the first seventeen chapters of Cicero's *De inventione* (On Invention) done during his first year in exile. In his attempt to discuss the various divisions of human knowledge, he brings together many sources. In his translations of some of Cicero's orations, he was able to reproduce the style of the original in the vernacular, and thus he contributed to the development of Italian prose. His first important work, written in southern French prose, entitled *Li Tresors* (circa 1260, The Treasure), is an encyclopedia of human knowledge accumulated to that time. The first book consists of a history of the world, a theological summary, and detailed information from the fields of astronomy, geography, and natural history; the second, of a partial translation and commentary upon the *Nichomachean Ethics* which becomes a treatise on virtue and vice; and the third of a rhetoric and politics which depicts communal Italian democracy as the most perfect form of government by contrasting it with the French monarchy. The work was quickly translated into Italian and had a wide reception throughout Europe. His second major work, the *Tesoretto* (after 1282, Little Treasure), is an unfinished allegorical poem in Italian modeled after the *Roman de la Rose;* it contains biographical material reflecting the traumatic experience of living in exile. It is historically important because it is the first Italian poem showing the influence of the French *Roman,* and it also influenced Dante. Brunetto also wrote the *Favolello* (after 1282, Little Poem), letters in verse to Rustico di Filippo* on the theme of friendship.

Bibliography: Li Livres dou Tresor, ed. Frances J. Carmody (Berkeley, Calif.: University of California Press, 1948); Bianca Ceva, *Brunetto Latini: l'uomo e l'opera* (Milan: Ricciardi, 1965); Charles T. Davis, "Brunetto Latini and Dante," *Studi Medievali* 8 (1967), 421–50.

BRUNI, LEONARDO (1370 or 1373–1444), humanist, historian, and statesman. Born in Arezzo (and thus often known as Leonardo Aretino Bruni), Bruni moved to Florence as a young man and studied under Coluccio Salutati,* Giovanni Malpaghini (1346–1417), and Manuel Chrysoloras (circa 1350–1415), noted humanists and classical scholars. This training gave Bruni access to the works of both Plato and Aristotle, and was to influence his own political and historical works in Latin. In 1405, Bruni left Florence to serve as apostolic secretary to Pope Innocent VII. He remained in Rome for the next ten years, except for a brief interval (1410–11) as head of the Florentine Chancellery. He accompanied the antipope John XXIII to the Council of Constance but was forced to flee when the council turned against his patron. Returning to Florence, he served the city in many ways, most notably as chancellor of the Republic from 1427 until his death.

Bruni was one of the most learned men of his times, the typical representative of what modern scholarship has come to term "civic humanism." His writings encompass several disciplines, to all of which he made significant and lasting contributions. Besides his indispensable Latin translations of Aristotle's *Ethics* (1417) and *Economics* (1420–21), he also translated works by Demosthenes, Aeschylus, and Plutarch, and provided Latin paraphrases of some of the writings of Polybius and Xenophon. He also composed influential brief biographies of both Dante* and Petrarch,* and produced a Latin version of one of Boccaccio's* *novelle** (IV,1) which, like the more famous Latin version of the Griselda story by Petrarch (X, 10), enjoyed a wide audience. His *De bello italico adversus Gothos* (1470, *The historie, concerning the warres betwene the Imperialles and the Gothes*) represents a rather free interpretation of an earlier classical history by Procopius. An important Latin comedy based upon classical models, *Poliscena* (1478, Poliscena), a story of the seduction of a young girl by the same name, has sometimes (but probably erroneously) been attributed to him. The *De militia* (1421, On Knighthood) examines the allegedly classical origins of this medieval institution and is a forerunner of Machiavelli's* attempts to combine citizenship with active military service. His *De studiis et litteris* (1423–26, *Concerning the Study of Literature*), is one of the first treatises on education addressed to a woman (Baptista di Montefeltro) and shows a clear concern for classical study among the intelligent women of the early Quattrocento.

Bruni's most important works are inspired by his love for his adopted city and his position as an official representative of the Florentine Republic. The longest of them is the *Historiae Florentini populi* (History of the Florentine People), begun as early as 1415; by 1429, the first six books had been published, and in 1439, the first nine books were formally presented to the city government. Three other books were finished before Bruni died, but the work was never completed. Its subject matter is the history of Florence. After a brief consideration of the period from its Roman origins to its emergence as a free Commune in the thirteenth century, the rest of the work concentrates upon the period from 1250 to the death of

Gian Galeazzo Visconti of Milan (1402). The history is based upon both Latin models and the medieval chronicle of Giovanni Villani,* but its political intent and its superiority to preceding Italian histories are evident in Bruni's transformation of the medieval chronicle into a compelling account of the struggle between a free city (Florence) and a tyranny (Milan), which cannot help but remind the reader of that other memorable struggle of Sparta and Athens. Florence's ability to resist the superior forces of her enemies is explained by her civic virtue and her republican form of government. Because the city of Florence was interested in the widest possible dissemination of the ideas embodied in Bruni's history, it commissioned Donato Acciaiuoli (1429–78) to make an Italian translation of the work which, by 1473, was completed. It was bound together with an Italian translation of Bracciolini's* history of the city, and in the vernacular form, the two works attracted a wide public long before printed versions of the original Latin manuscripts were available.

Bruni's view of Florence as a bastion of civic freedom is echoed in a funeral oration delivered in 1427, the *Oratio Funebris* (Funeral Oration) for Nanni degli Strozzi, a general who had served Florence in her alliance against the Visconti of Milan. Like the famous oration by Pericles in Thucydides which inspired it, Bruni's speech praised Florence for her role as the teacher of freedom to all the world and for the institutions which allowed every citizen free access to public offices and honors. Both this oration and his monumental humanist history of the city owe much of their ideology and outlook to one of his early works, the *Laudatio Florentinae Urbis* (In Praise of the City of Florence). This key work written between 1403 and 1404 provides the first literary portrait of Florence's political institutions and geographical location. It first expressed Bruni's ideas on "civic humanism" in the claim that Florence had saved Italian liberty and was heir both to the republican tradition of the Romans and to the humanistic tradition of classical Athens. In this regard, two Latin dialogues—*Dialogi ad Petrum Paulum Histrum* (1401 and 1405, Dialogues Dedicated to Pier Paolo Vergerio)—suggest the real merits of modern writers, such as the "three crowns of Florence" (Dante, Petrarch, and Boccaccio*), and modify both Dante's glorification of Caesar and his view of Caesar's republican assassins in *The Divine Comedy*. When Bruni died, the city revived the custom of granting the classical symbol of esteem, the laurel leaf, to honor him. Giannozzo Manetti* gave the funeral oration in the church of Santa Croce, and Bruni's grave was marked with an important sculpture by Bernardo Rossellino.

See also BRACCIOLINI, Poggio; HUMANISM; SALUTATI, Coluccio.

Bibliography: Istoria fiorentina, eds. G. Mancini, et al., 3 vols. (Florence: Le

Monnier, 1855–60); *Prosatori latini del Quattrocento,* ed. Eugenio Garin (Milan: Ricciardi, 1952); Giovanni Boccaccio and Leonardo Bruni, *The Earliest Lives of Dante* (New York: Ungar, 1963); *Vittorino da Feltre and Other Humanist Educators,* ed. W. H. Woodward (New York: Teachers College, Columbia University, 1963); C. C. Bayley, *War and Society in Florence: The "De Militia" of Leonardo Bruni* (Toronto: University of Toronto Press, 1961); Hans Baron, *The Crisis of the Early Italian Renaissance: Civic Humanism and Republican Liberty in an Age of Classicism and Tyranny* (Princeton, N.J.: Princeton University Press, 1966); Donald J. Wilcox, *The Development of Florentine Humanist Historiography in the Fifteenth Century* (Cambridge, Mass.: Harvard University Press, 1969).

BRUNO, GIORDANO (1548–1600), theologian-philosopher and prose writer. Bruno was born in Nola near Naples, at the beginning of 1548, and baptized as Filippo. In 1565, he entered the Dominican order in the Convent of S. Domenico Maggiore in Naples, where he changed his first name to Giordano, perhaps in honor of one of his teachers. He was ordained in 1571. Because of his clandestine readings of prohibited works (among them, Erasmus's commentary on St. Jerome), the Dominican order brought charges against him in 1575, but at the beginning of the following year, just when the trial was to begin, Bruno escaped to Rome where he was again indicted by the order. Bruno then left the priesthood, moved to Genoa, Turin, Venice, Padua, Milan, and to Geneva (1578) where he accepted Calvinism, but was then abruptly excommunicated. He next moved to Lyons and Toulouse where he taught philosophy, and finally to Paris (1581) where he came into close contact with the court of Henry III. In Paris in 1582, Bruno published the first of his works that still survive: *De umbris idearum* (Shadows of Ideas); *Ars memoriae* (Art of Memory); *Cantus Circaeus* (The Incantation of Circe); and *De compendiosa architectura et complemento artis Lullii* (On the Complete Architecture with an Addition of Lull's Art). All of them deal with the problems of mnemonic technique, along the lines of Ramon Lull (1235–1316) but with strong Platonic influences. Protected by the king, Bruno taught philosophy at the Sorbonne, taking the side of a group of teachers opposed to Aristotelianism. In 1582, he published his only comedy, *Il Candelaio (The Candle Bearer),* a bitter satire against pedantry and homosexuality.

In 1583, Bruno went to London under the protection of the French ambassador. There he got in touch with the Oxford group and was allowed to teach a course. But after three lessons the course was suspended because Bruno professed the Copernican theories. Returning to London, he continued his anti-Aristotelian campaign and produced what are known as "Italian dialogues": *La Cena delle ceneri* (1584, *The Ash Wednesday Supper*), a cosmological work in which Bruno accepts Copernicus's heliocentrism but also surpasses it by hypothesizing a plurality of worlds; *De la causa, principio et uno* (1584, *Cause, Principle, and Unity*); and *De l'infinito universo et mondi* (1584, *On the Infinite Universe and Worlds*), in which the relationships between philosophy and religion are explained and in which he insists upon the previous ideas of the plurality of the worlds and the immanence of the Divinity. In *Lo spaccio della bestia trionfante* (1584, *The Expulsion of the Triumphant Beast*), *Cabala del cavallo pegaseo con l'aggiunta dell'Asino cillenico* (1584, The Intrigue of the Winged Horse), and *Degli eroici furori* (1585, *The Heroic Frenzies*), Bruno strives for human activism rather than for a contemplative passivity; analyzes the relationship between the soul and the infinite One; and pronounces some very important principles of poetics: "poetry is not born out of souls, but souls derive from poetry . . . there can be as many types of poets as there can be ways of feeling and kinds of human inventiveness" *(Degli eroici furori).*

These works provoked a scandal, and Bruno had to go back to France (1585). But the new political atmosphere, as well as some heated diatribes that Bruno directed against the followers of Aristotle, obliged him to leave Paris. For two years (1586–88) he resided in Wittenberg, where he taught philosophy and wrote many works on different subjects (physics, magic, rhetoric). After a brief stay in Prague (1588), Bruno moved to Helmsted (1589–90) and Frankfurt (1590) where he published the *De triplici minimo et mensura* (On the Three-fold Minimum and Measure), *De monade, numero et figura* (On the Monad, Number, and Figure), and *De immenso, innumerabilibus et infigurabilibus* (On the Immeasurable and the Innumerable), three poems in which Bruno develops his ideas about matter, the nature of the atom, and the monad.

When the Senate of Frankfurt denied Bruno residence in that city, he moved to Zurich, and from there, solicited by the patrician Giovanni Mocenigo, he went to Venice (1591). Betrayed by his patron, he was arrested on 23 May 1592. The trial lasted for nine months, and Bruno seemed to admit to some of the accusations of heresy. Extradited to Rome, he underwent a second trial that lasted for seven years (1593–1600), but he did not admit any guilt. He was condemned as a heretic to be burned alive. The sentence was carried out on 17 February 1600 in Campo dei Fiori.

Bruno's interests were far-flung, ranging from art of memory, physics, poetics, creative writing to ethics. The complexity of his thought derives from the fact that he was seldom a systematic thinker; from the occasional nature of his writings; and from the fact that the lines of several philosophical systems—the Neo-Platonism* of Cusano, the naturalism of Telesio, Pythagorean atomism, Copernican heliocentrism, and even Thomism—are present in his works. However, a consistent theme in Bruno's writings is a firm opposition to Aristotelianism and a desire for knowledge which can be achieved only through human means.

From Neo-Platonism, Bruno derives his idea of the infinity of Divinity, but this Divinity is present in the world as an internal *artifex* and not as a transcendental entity. Hence, he formulated his theory of the infinity of the worlds, all of them living in one as their divine principle. This theory—which is very close to the modern conception of the universe—transcends both Neo-Platonism and the Copernician theory because of its principle of the immanence of Divinity and because of the plurality of worlds. This immanence explains Bruno's interest in magic and his aversion to Aristotelianism with its division between form and matter, which, according to Bruno, cannot be separated. This immanence also explains the nature of Bruno's investigation: for him, the philosopher is kindled by admiration and ardor both for the living natural unity and for the progressive revelation of the infinity of the mind's power. Bruno constantly exalts human freedom, which becomes possible only through speculation. Be it of a mathematical or magical nature, this speculation is nothing but *eroico furore,* that is, obedience to a vitalistic *élan* towards the Beautiful and the True. In this process, man realizes himself in a final affirmation of his belonging to nature and of his participation in the essence of Divinity.

This celebration of man and nature is the surest Renaissance* mark on Bruno's thought. Yet, it was bound to influence deeply philosophy from Descartes, Galileo,* Spinoza, Leibniz up to the modern understanding of the nature of the universe. Moreover, his work had a strong influence (which has not yet been fully studied) on the libertine thought of the seventeenth and eighteenth centuries.

As a writer, Bruno stands far from the Renaissance rules of decorum, and he is considered a Baroque* figure. Yet, his imaginative and dense style, full of plebeian expressions, does not belong to any school. If anything, it is another revolt against the tyranny of models and against authority. In his writings, reason and fantasy, images and logical argumentations, rare Latinisms and vernacular words of low style mingle together in a fascinating prose with a delirious discourse which expresses at the same time the aggressive anxiety of the searcher for Beauty and Truth, and the rational instruments with which he pursues them.

Bibliography: Dialoghi italiani, ed. Giovanni Aquilecchia (Florence: Sansoni, 1972); *Opere latine conscripta,* ed. Felice Tocco, et al., 3 vols. (1879–91; rpt. Stuttgart: Holzboog, 1962); *The Ash Wednesday Supper,* trans. Stanley Jaki (The Hague: Mouton, 1975); *Cause, Principle, and Unity,* trans. Jack Lindsay (1962; rpt. Westport, Conn.: Greenwood Press, 1976); *The Expulsion of the Triumphant Beast,* trans. Arthur Imerti (New Brunswick, N.J.: Rutgers University Press, 1964); *The Genius of the Italian Theater,* ed. Eric Bentley (New York: Mentor, 1964); *The Heroic Frenzies,* trans. Paul Memmo (Chapel Hill, N.C.: University of North Carolina Press, 1964); Giancarlo Maiorino, "The Breaking of the Circle: Giordano Bruno and the Poetics of Immeasurable Abundance," *Journal of the*

History of Ideas 38 (1977), 317–27; Daniel Massa, "Giordano Bruno's Ideas in Seventeenth-Century England," *Journal of the History of Ideas* 38 (1977), 227–42; Dorothea Singer, *Giordano Bruno: His Life and Thought* (1950; rpt. Westport, Conn.: Greenwood Press, 1977—contains a translation of *On the Infinite Universe and Worlds*); Vincenzo Spampanato, *Vita di Giordano Bruno,* 2 vols. (Messina: Principato, 1921); Frances A. Yates, *Giordano Bruno and the Hermetic Tradition* (Chicago: University of Chicago Press, 1964).

Paolo Cherchi

BUONARROTI, MICHELANGELO (1475–1564), Renaissance* sculptor, painter, architect, and poet. Apprenticed as a youth to Bertoldo and Ghirlandaio, Michelangelo early enjoyed the patronage of Lorenzo de' Medici* in Florence, where he met many of the most famous humanists and writers of his day, among them Marsilio Ficino,* Angelo Poliziano,* and Giovanni Pico della Mirandola.* During periods of residence alternating chiefly between Rome and Florence, he completed works commissioned by both secular and ecclesiastical patrons, including the famed statue of David, the frescoes of the Sistine Chapel, the cupola of St. Peter's Cathedral in Rome, and the Medici funeral chapel in Florence. He lived in Rome from 1534 until his death, a period which coincides with that of his poetic maturity.

Michelangelo repeatedly deprecated his poetic production, maintaining that he was merely an amateur poet. Nonetheless, his poetic composition spans most of his life and includes more than three hundred extant poems as well as numerous fragments. His *canzoniere* or collection of *rime* was assembled and ordered by later editors, not by the poet himself; many poems were composed with apparent haste on the backs of letters or on artistic or architectural sketches, while others were laboriously revised. The acclaim of his contemporaries, their record of the pleasure he derived from composing verses, and the poems themselves attest to his devotion to poetic activity. While they represent an avocation in relation to his prodigious achievement in other areas, they merit serious attention. A few of his compositions rank among the finest of his day.

Michelangelo's early poems, of which many remained incomplete, appear to be generally derivative and conventional. Traces of his wide reading in earlier poetry, both Italian and Latin, are to be found throughout his works. As in his sculpture, however, he readily assimilated these early influences in the creation of a personal idiom. The style of his mature poetry, while it still owes much to Dante* and more to Petrarch,* frequently appears notably original in the context of the imitative verse of most of his Italian contemporaries. This poetry is characterized by complex *concetti* (conceits) as well as by complicated and frequently difficult syntactical patterns. Critics have associated a number of its characteristics with those of the European Baroque* movement. Michelangelo cast his poems almost exclusively in the form of sonnets* and madrigals.* The madrigals, marked by metric innovations or irregularities, were frequently the vehicle for his wit and for a display of inventiveness in the use of conventional images and themes. The collection also yields a number of poems which develop patterns of recurring images, such as those of light, fire, and stone. An effective and important group of poems on Night reflects the theme of the sculpture in the Medici Chapel in Florence and suggests the relation between his literary and artistic conceptions.

Michelangelo's late love for the poetess Vittoria Colonna* and his equally intense love and admiration for the young Roman nobleman Tommaso Cavalieri inspired a large number of poems on beauty, love, passion, and their ultimate implications for the human soul. The tension between the attraction of beauty as a work of God and, therefore, as a human manifestation of the Divine, and the apprehension that the love and desire inspired by human beauty might instead lead away from God, clearly recall the inner tension of Petrarch's* *Canzoniere (Lyric Poems)* inspired by the obsessive image of Laura. Michelangelo was more than sixty years old when he began to write poems and letters to Vittoria, and he generally casts her in the role of intermediary in his striving toward the Christian ideal of love.

The poems on human beauty give expression to perhaps the most original and characteristic of Michelangelo's themes, that of the creation of beauty in a work of art. The dialectic of the love experience is compared to that of creation and destruction for both lover and beloved. Often celebrated as postulations of his theory and philosophy of art, Michelangelo's poems about the artist's struggle reveal his preoccupation with the nature and modes of aesthetic creativity, and in them the Renaissance Platonism of the content is particularly pronounced. The artist who conceives an image and strives to realize it in his sculpture or painting participates, however partially, in the work of nature and works as God's intermediary. It is often observed that Michelangelo's poetry reflects little appreciation for the natural world and little concern for the larger political questions of his day; his focus rather is on the individual human subject, frequently perceived in relation to the Creator. In the timelessness of his own creation, the artist on occasion opposes his monument to the inevitable ravages of time. In a famed sonnet to Vittoria, the poet declares that in contrast to human mortality the created image endures; "thus Nature is vanquished by art." This process, however, is often incomplete, as the artist's medium resists the thrust of the ideal which he attempts to impose upon it.

After the death of Vittoria in 1547, Michelangelo's poems not only lament her loss but also reflect an increasing preoccupation with redemption, in confessional or penitential invocations to Christ for aid in over-coming the contradictions inherent in human passions. Deeply impressed during his youth in Florence by the preaching of Savonarola,* Michelangelo was continually preoccupied with the expression of his religious ideal. Like his artistic works, his poetry reflects the attempt of the Neo-Platonic writers to effect a reconciliation and synthesis of classical culture and the Christian faith.

See also BAROQUE; COLONNA, Vittoria; FICINO, Marsilio; MEDICI, Lorenzo de'.

Bibliography: Rime, ed. Enzo Girardi (Bari: Laterza, 1960); *The Complete Poems,* trans. Joseph Tusiani (New York: Noonday Press, 1960); *Complete Poems and Selected Letters of Michelangelo,* trans. Creighton Gilbert (New York: Modern Library, 1965); Alma Altizer, *Self and Symbolism in the Poetry of Michelangelo, John Donne, and Agrippa d'Aubigné* (The Hague: Nijhoff, 1973); *Michelangelo: A Self-Portrait,* ed. R. J. Clements (Englewood Cliffs, N.J.: Prentice-Hall, 1963); R. J. Clements, *The Poetry of Michelangelo* (New York: New York University Press, 1965); E. N. Girardi, *Studi sulle Rime di Michelangelo* (Milan: L'Eroica, 1964).

Sara Sturm-Maddox

BUONARROTI, MICHELANGELO IL GIOVANE (**"The Younger"**) (1568–1646), academician, poet, dramatist, and grandnephew of the famous artist and sculptor. Educated at the Medici court in Florence, Buonarroti became a member of the influential Accademia della Crusca, participating in the formulation of the first and second editions of its famous *Vocabulario* (1612, 1623, Dictionary). He was a typical court poet of the period, often composing occasional lyrics and allegorical works for the entertainment of the royalty and dignitaries who visited his Medici patrons. Devoted to his ancestor's memory, he helped to found the Galleria Buonarroti and edited the first printed edition of Michelangelo's* lyric poetry in 1623, bringing together manuscripts preserved in the family archives and those stored in the Vatican. Unfortunately, his scholarly methods were affected by his fear of scandal and the influence of his rather conservative milieu. He tampered with the texts in his possession and even altered those in the Vatican, often suppressing and revising those poems which Michelangelo had originally addressed to men. A more accurate edition became available only in 1863.

In spite of his scholarly shortcomings, Buonarroti composed nine excellent satires in the Horatian style and is still remembered for two comedies—*La Tancia* (1612, Tancia) and *La fiera* (1619, The Fair). The first, a five-act play written in *ottava rima,** treats the love of a city dweller for a peasant girl named Tancia and successfully presents the contrasting forms of language spoken by the different characters. Some critics contend that this linguistic experimentation, inspired by his work on the Crusca dictionary, was his sole purpose in composing the play. The second comedy, employing alternating lines of eleven- and seven-syllable verse, describes the happenings at a fair in the imaginary city of Pandora and is divided into five days, each of which contains five acts. Again, Buonarroti's contribution to the art of comedy in this play is his clever use of language in creating the flavor of the dialects which might have been spoken at such a fair in Florence by various social groups.

Bibliography: Teatro del Seicento, ed. Luigi Fassò (Milan: Ricciardi, 1956); U. Limentani, *La satira nel Seicento* (Milan: Ricciardi, 1961); M. G. Masera, *Michelangelo Buonarroti il Giovane* (Turin: Rosenberg & Sellier, 1941).

BURCHIELLO: *See* DOMENICO DI GIOVANNI.

BUZZATI, DINO (1906–1972), journalist, playwright, and novelist. Buzzati came from Belluno in the Dolomite Alps, the setting which has lent an air of mystery to many of his narrative works. After earning a law degree from the University of Milan in 1928, Buzzati became a journalist with the *Corriere della sera,* a career he never entirely abandoned even after he achieved fame as a writer. His first two novels, *Bàrnabo delle montagne* (1933, Bàrnabo of the Mountains) and *Il segreto del Bosco Vecchio* (1935, The Secret of the Old Wood), present fables or Nordic myths set among the forbidding forests and imposing mountain ranges that were to characterize much of his best work, including his masterpiece, *Il deserto dei Tartari* (1940, *The Tartar Steppe*). Three collections of short stories followed the publication of this important novel—*I sette messaggeri* (1943, The Seven Messengers); *Paura alla Scala* (1949, The Scala Scare); and *Il crollo della Baliverna* (1957, The Collapse of the Baliverna). The stories from these three collections were reprinted in 1958 in a book entitled *Sessanta racconti* (Sixty Stories) and awarded the Strega Prize for Literature in 1958. It contains some of Buzzati's greatest short stories, such as "Sette piani" ("Seven Floors")—revised to form the play *Un caso clinico* (A Clinical Case) in 1953; "Il cane che ha visto Dio" (The Dog That Saw God); "Appuntamento con Einstein" (Appointment with Einstein); and "Il mantello" (The Cloak). Buzzati also wrote and illustrated a successful children's book entitled *La famosa invasione degli orsi in Sicilia* (1945, The Famous Invasion of the Bears in Sicily).

    Il deserto dei Tartari is one of the most original twentieth-century Italian novels. It treats the life of Giovanni Drogo, a lieutenant who is stationed at a bleak border fort to await the attack of the Tartars from the north. This obscure enemy is never seen and, indeed, never attacks during Drogo's entire lifetime. Buzzati accentuates the mystery inherent in everyday reality and articulates man's obsession with guilt and death in a Kafkaesque manner reminiscent of *The Trial* and *The Castle*. The work has an allegorical character, and Drogo's fruitless wait represents human existence without purpose or transcendental meaning. Buzzati's evocation of the uncanny, the fantastic, and the marvelous is likewise intrinsic to his best short stories.

With his critical reputation secure, Buzzati began to write in a number of different styles and genres. *Il grande ritratto* (1960, *Larger Than Life*) is a science fiction novel about the construction of a huge electronic brain which assumes a human personality. *Un amore* (1963, *A Love Affair*) is a novel written in a more conventional style which describes a love affair between an architect named Antonio Dorigo and a ballerina named Laide, a girl less than half his age. Returning to a more experimental narrative style with *Poema a fumetti* (1969, Comic Strip Poem), Buzzati presents a pop version of the ancient legend of Orpheus and Eurydice through the contemporary medium of the comic strip. He transforms the classical singer into Orfi, a rock-and-roll artist, and gives a new twist to the ancient myth. *Miracoli di Val Morel* (1971, The Miracles of the Val Morel Mortuary), one of the last works published before his death, is a collection of sketches concerning thirty-nine imaginary votive offerings placed in a mortuary. Since 1972, two important posthumous works have appeared—*Cronache terrestri* (1972, Earthly Chronicles), a collection of previously unpublished stories and essays; and *Dino Buzzati: un autoritratto* (1973, Dino Buzzati: A Self-Portrait), an autobiography transcribed from taped conversations.

Buzzati's early reputation as the "Italian Kafka" (a comparison which Buzzati did not appreciate and which, in many respects, was an insufficient assessment of his own originality) has been corrected by recent critics, who have tried to assess Buzzati's original contributions to narrative techniques and themes. Buzzati's fascination with philosophical fables and metaphysical allegories provides an interesting contrast to the more poetic and fanciful treatment of the marvelous in the works of Italo Calvino.*

Bibliography: Il deserto dei Tartari (Milan: Mondadori, 1970); *Sessanta racconti* (Milan: Mondadori, 1958); *Catastrophe: The Strange Stories of Dino Buzzati,* trans. Judith Landry and Cynthia Jolly (London: Calder & Boyars, 1966); *Larger Than Life,* trans. Henry Reed (London: Secker & Warburg, 1962); *A Love Affair,* trans. Joseph Green (New York: Farrar, Straus, 1964); *The Tartar Steppe,* trans. Stuart C. Hood (New York: Noonday, 1965); Elain D. Cancalon, "Spatial Structures in the Narrative of Dino Buzzati," *Forum Italicum* 11 (1977), 36–46; Antonia Veronese Arslan, *Invito alla lettura di Dino Buzzati* (Milan: Mursia, 1974).

C

CACCIA (the word means ''hunt''), a poetic form of popular origin which may employ any meter without a fixed rhyme scheme. The form is defined primarily by its content, which usually concerns a hunt or some outside activity, enlivened by a goodly number of shouts and cries. First appearing in thirteenth-century France, the genre flourished in the following century in Italy and survived until the sixteenth century. Of the few *caccie* which have come down to us, Franco Sacchetti's* ''Passando con pensier per un boschetto'' (''Through the Woods One Day'') is considered the best.

Bibliography: Raffaele Spongano, *Nozioni ed esempi di metrica italiana* (Bologna: Pàtron, 1966).

CALVINO, ITALO (1923–   ), novelist, essayist, critic, editor, and translator. Born in Santiago de Las Vegas, Cuba, of Italian parents, both scientists, Calvino spent his childhood and youth in San Remo, which he understandably claims as his ''truer'' birthplace. During World War II, Calvino joined the resistance movement and fought as a *partigiano*—a vital experience from which he drew inspiration for his first stories. In the fall of 1945, Calvino moved to Turin, where he attended the university, became militantly involved in left-wing politics, and began working for Einaudi, his future publisher. In 1947, he graduated from the University of Turin with a dissertation on Joseph Conrad's work.

Pavese* and Vittorini* were the first to recognize Calvino's literary talent. Pavese recommended one of Calvino's first stories to *Aretusa*, while Vittorini published another of his stories in *Il Politecnico* as early as December 1945. Shortly after the publication of Calvino's first novel, *Il sentiero dei nidi di ragno* (1947, *The Path to the Nest of Spiders*), which portrays some aspects of the resistance as seen through the eyes of a small boy, it was again Pavese who provided the first valuable, and still valid, insights into Calvino's ''astuteness'' in relieving the realistic portrayal with fable-like twists in a manner typical of and innate to his narrative vocation. Pavese also noted the ''Ariostoesque flavor'' of the story. The commitment to neorealism also alternates with fantasy in his short stories, collected in *Ultimo viene il corvo* (1949, *Adam, One Afternoon, and Other Stories*) and in the comprehensive edition of *I racconti* (1958, *Short Stories*). In his major novels, the ''fable'' generally gains the upper hand and becomes an integral component of the complex structure of such un-expected creations as *Il visconte dimezzato* (1952, *The Cloven Viscount*), *Il barone rampante* (1957, *The Baron in the Trees*), and *Il cavaliere in-esistente* (1959, *The Non-Existent Knight*), three novels reissued in 1960 as a trilogy with the title *I nostri antenati* (Our Forefathers).

These creations are no extravagant frolics but rather are signs of the constant tension between man's conscience and the disfiguring power of a reality which defies his understanding. The ideological nature of Calvino's concerns becomes polemically active in his creative process, a complex *modus creandi* which blends the fabulous, the surrealistic, and the absurd with an authentic vocation for wit and satire in the best European tradition from Ariosto* to G. B. Shaw.

One of Calvino's original contributions to modern fiction is to be found in his unorthodox method of attributing a real consistence to the un-predictable creations of his poetic fantasy. That is, he starts with a wild invention, treats it as if it were quite real, and eventually draws it to its "logical" conclusion. This drastic and narrowly idealistic process is often effective because it conveys, and is inherently justified by, a basic alle-gorical intention whose function and motivations are overtly defined by the writer himself in his preface to *I nostri antenati*. Hence, the unlikely predicament of the viscount, cloven in two vertical sections one good one bad, is basically an ironic figuration of modern man in his ludicrous state of alienated mutilation, while the baron who lives in trees is a man who seeks his Tarzan-like exile not out of a need for mere rebellion or misanthropic isolation but because he wants to dramatize, through his actual escape into nature, the kind of critical detachment that is necessary to attain a measure of true communication. As for the knight who exists only as pure will inside a geometric armor, it may be said that he represents the nothingness of contemporary man who, deprived of all power to relate to the world, has reached a stage of nonexistence because he identifies with material prod-ucts and is reduced either to a mere function or to a sort of existential fiction. The allegorical intention also suggests a possible guideline for the ultimate recovery of completeness and harmony through a rational understanding of freedom. Thus, (1) the hope for completeness beyond the mutilations imposed by society may reawaken (2) the need for self-determination and eventually lead to (3) a new and truer sense of being. The philosophical intention, however, is cleverly attuned to a complex narrative mechanism which elicits a plurality of meanings. The treatment of the good-evil theme, for instance, while suggesting a parody of the Christian parable, may also call for·an interpretation of the good-evil polarity in terms of involvement and ignorance. This contextual openness is sustained and enhanced by Calvino's dazzling style—a special manner of writing characterized by a smoothly winding syntax, articulate yet smugly sensitive to all rhythms of speech—and by a constant sense of irony which mirrors its own self-consciousness in a mood of literate detachment and playful complacency.

The ideological commitment also characterizes *La giornata di uno scrutatore* (1963, *The Watcher*) and the stories of *Marcovaldo ovvero le stagioni in città* (1963, Marcovaldo, or the Seasons in the City) with their satiric indictment of urban alienation. However, it is in *Le cosmicomiche* (1965, *Cosmicomics*)—a type of stream-of-consciousness narrative of the creation and evolution of the universe through the eyes of a man-formula called Qfwfq who acts as a kind of cosmic conscience—that Calvino has reached the highest degree of demythization of the anthropocentric syndrome with which mankind is accustomed to look at reality and knowledge. In spite of recurring influences from varied sources (Borges, de Saussure, Carroll, Barthes, the cartoon strip, semiotics,* structuralism,* Propp, Lévi-Strauss, Robbe-Grillet, algebra, formal logic, astronomy), the narrative of the *Cosmicomiche* (or *comicosmiche* with convertible terms and parodic play of words) is the expression of a new kind of cosmogonic humor which is unlike anything ever written before. The connecting link and unifying element is the filtered voice-personality of Qfwfq, the epistemic cell that lived and lives in the first protozoan and in all later stages and forms of evolution (from mollusk to dinosaur to moon farmer, etc.), the graph of all that man has been and will be, the embryo of life, the primeval oneness, the atavistic gene in its archetypal form and perceptive everpresence.

From this brilliant premise, which can be construed as a subtly humorous but unusually effective attempt to recapture the dawn of life in the seething interplay of all its ancestral elements (biological, logical, and psychological), Calvino's perception evolves towards more complex and increasingly more abstract and theoretical forms of pluralism and relativism. In the four episodes of *Ti con zero* (1967, *t zero*), the clever interlocking of time, space, and motion is at the core of a constantly changing frame of reference in which diverse or opposite concepts and values (unity and multiplicity, past and present, chaos and order, probability and certainty, play and serious argumentation) are made to coexist and often to coincide. This trend leads, on one hand, to *Il castello dei destini incrociati* (1969, *The Castle of Crossed Destinies*), which originated as a narrative *tour de force* for the richly illustrated *I tarocchi* (1969, The Tarot Cards) of Franco M. Ricci and gradually turns into a spectacular game with the Tarot cards used as both tools and emblems for a sort of structuralistic game on human destiny; and, on the other, to *Le città invisibili* (1972, *Invisible Cities*), a masterpiece of unprecedented rigor and symmetry that challenges all rhetorical conventions of, and preconceived notions about, the craft of fiction. This time the reader is faced with an imaginary Marco Polo who describes to an imaginary Kublai Khan the "invisible" cities of his vast empire in nine chapters. Each of the chapters contains a number of short narratives symmetrically distributed (ten in the first and last chapters, five in the intervening ones), each preceded and followed by brief commentaries based on imaginary dialogues and discussions between the great traveler and the great listener. Within the framework of each chapter, the descriptions of the cities are distributed according to headings or categories which recur throughout the book and whose context is deliberately designed to allow for a maximal freedom in the method of approaching and reading the texts. The task and opportunity of providing meaning(s) for the stories (cities) is given, through the listening and arguing function of the great Khan, to the reader himself, who is brought into the narrative process as an active contributor. In fact, each and every reader is free to do as he or she pleases: as a traveler, he can stay, move about, get lost, leave, or whatever; as a reader-writer, he can change, alter, rearrange, replace, exchange. He can even rewrite the narratives or extend them beyond the limits of suggestive figurations and into the alluringly generous white space that surrounds them. Creativity may be the ultimate response to alienation.

Bibliography: The Baron in the Trees, trans. Archibald Colquhoun (New York: Harcourt, 1977); *The Castle of Crossed Destinies,* trans. William Weaver (New York: Harcourt, 1977); *Cosmicomics,* trans. William Weaver (New York: Collier, 1970); *Invisible Cities,* trans. William Weaver (New York: Harcourt, 1974); *The Nonexistent Knight and the Cloven Viscount,* trans. Archibald Colquhoun (New York: Harcourt, 1977); *The Path to the Nest of Spiders,* trans. Archibald Colquhoun (New York: Ecco Press, 1976); *The Watcher and Other Stories,* trans. William Weaver and Archibald Colquhoun (New York: Harcourt, 1971); Giuseppe Bonura, *Invito alla lettura di Calvino* (Milan: Mursia, 1972); Contardo Calligaris, *Italo Calvino* (Milan: Mursia, 1973); Italo Calvino, "Notes Towards a Definition of the Narrative Form as a Combinative Process," *20th Century Studies* 1 (1970), 93–101; Gore Vidal, "Fabulous Calvino," *New York Review of Books,* 30 May 1974, pp. 13–21.

Antonio Illiano

CAMPANA, DINO (1885–1932), poet. Born in Marradi near Florence, Campana left his university studies in chemistry (1903–06) and wandered all over Europe and South America (1908), spending time in prisons (1903) and mental institutions (1906, 1909). He returned to Italy in time to be rejected for military service in World War I.

Campana first presented his *Canti orfici* (1914, *Orphic Songs*) to Papini* and Soffici,* then co-directors of the avant-garde periodical *Lacerba.* The original manuscript was lost by Soffici, however, and Campana was forced to rewrite from memory the collection that later won him a critical reputation as one of the foremost innovators in contemporary Italian verse. The original manuscript was rediscovered in 1971. The first edition was actually hawked around Florentine cafes by its author, whose rather disreputable appearance and eccentric habits reminded many of Walt Whitman, whose *Songs of Myself* he always carried about with him. In 1918, Campana entered a mental hospital and remained there until his death, writing no further poetry.

Canti orfici is a singular work in Italian literature, a collection of lyrics that are often fragmentary, nihilistic, and intensely personal. At their best they achieve a lucidity of imagery and color and an emotional power unsurpassed among his contemporaries or the poets who contributed to the Florentine journal *La Voce* (Rèbora,* Jahier,* and Sbarbaro*), with whom Campana is often associated. Several of the lyrics from his collection—in particular "La chimera" ("The Chimera"), "Giardino autunnale" ("Autumnal Garden"), "L'invetriata" ("The Glass Window"), and "Viaggio a Montevideo" ("Journey to Montevideo")—number among the most beautiful and influential lyrics of the early twentieth century.

Although largely ignored by academic scholars until after his death, Campana owes his recent popularity among the critics to their acceptance of hermeticism* in lyric poetry and to their search for the precursors of this movement. Campana, however, is greatly indebted to the more conventional lyrics of Carducci* as well as to the philosophical influence of Nietzsche; *Canti orfici* was actually dedicated to Kaiser Wilhelm of Germany. His strange and tragic life, a reflection of his art, has often been compared to those of Rimbaud and Georg Trakl.

See also HERMETICISM.

Bibliography: Opere e contributi, ed. Enrico Falqui, 2 vols. (Florence: Vallecchi, 1973); *Dino Campana: Orphic Songs,* trans. I. L. Salomon (New York: October House, 1968); Neuro Bonifazi, *Dino Campana* (Rome: Ateneo, 1964); Cesare Galimberti, *Dino Campana* (Milan: Mursia, 1967); Maura Del Serra, *L'immagine aperta: poetica e stilistica dei "Canti orfici"* (Florence: La Nuova Italia, 1973).

CAMPANELLA, TOMMASO (1568–1639), poet and philosopher. Campanella was the son of an illiterate shoemaker of Stilo (Calabria). His exceptional talents, prodigious memory, and thirst for knowledge had destined him to the only intellectual pursuit open to a man of his social position: Campanella became a Dominican monk. He studied Aristotle's logic and physics in various Calabrese monasteries, but he soon adopted the sensist *De rerum natura* (1565, *On the Nature of Things*) of his countryman Bernardo Telesio (1509–88) as his bible. Praised by the English philosopher Francis Bacon (1561–1626) as "the first of the moderns," Telesio stressed the importance of sense perception in epistemology, rejected a slavish dependence upon Aristotle, and attempted to discover novel theories of natural philosophy. Campanella's first major work, the

Philosophia sensibus demonstrata (1589, Experimental Philosophy), an apology for Telesio's doctrine, ran into ecclesiastical censure. Campanella fled to Naples, printed his work, and was promptly arrested on charges of entertaining a "familiar demon," supposedly concealed in the nail of his little finger. Disobeying the sentence which banished him to Calabria, he traveled to Rome, Florence, and Bologna, studying, seeking protection, and composing treatises. In 1594, he was arrested by the Holy Inquisition in Padua and was charged with heresy, tortured, and transferred to the prisons of the Holy See in Rome, where Giordano Bruno* was awaiting execution. Here he managed to compose the now lost first versions of his later works on physics, physiology, and prosody. He was tortured again and sentenced to a public recantation of his heresy and an indefinite term in his order's custody. Freed, rearrested, and prosecuted again for heresy in 1598, Campanella was definitively ordered back to Calabria.

By now, the utopian ideal of a universal Christian monarchy, which was to dominate Campanella's political thinking to the end of his life, had, in his mind, taken on a communistic tint, resembling that of the theocratic republic described in his later dialogue, *La Città del sole* (1602, *City of the Sun*). The acute social unrest in Calabria, an area oppressed by Spanish rule and ecclesiastical abuse, had catalyzed this idea into a project of popular uprising, and Campanella became the spiritual leader of an ingenuous conspiracy (1599), the stargazing prophet of impending doom. Betrayed by his fellows, the rebellious friar was captured by the Spanish forces, transferred to Naples, and tortured on the rack (1600). After a full confession which assured him the gallows, his total faith in his own messianic mission compelled the persecuted monk to save his life at any cost. Since the insane could not be executed, Campanella set fire to his cell and feigned madness. Put to the test during thirty-six hours of the hardest torture known to his ingenious age, he resisted (1601). Although he was crippled and ill and imprisoned for life, Campanella at once set to work. He completed his *Monarchia di Spagna (A Discourse Touching the Spanish Monarchy)* and *La Città del sole;* he composed his *Metaphysics* and his Telesian treatise *Del senso delle cose e della magia (On the Sense and Feeling in All Things and on Magic);* and he wrote his greatest lyrics.

By the connivance of the Spanish authorities and the Holy See, Campanella was forgotten in his dungeon and left four years in the underground cells of St. Elmo Prison, hands and feet in chains. Viceroys came and went; pontiffs were elected and buried. His hopes renewed at each change, Campanella addressed hundreds of supplications to popes, emperors, kings, cardinals, bishops, friends, and enemies, requesting freedom, transfer to Rome, money for food, the right to say Mass, the *imprimatur* for his works, and promising great revelations, miracles, and sure methods of converting the Jews, the Turks, and the Protestants. Often, the result of these entreaties was a search of his cell, the seizure of his means to write, and the destruction of his manuscripts. In 1613, an admirer, Tobia Adami, managed to smuggle out a number of his works and set to publish them abroad, and Campanella was transferred for another stretch in the hole at St. Elmo. When Galileo* was besieged by the Inquisition, Campanella hastened to his aid with an eloquent *Apologia pro Galileo* (1616, *The Defense of Galileo*). One month after his own liberation in 1626, he was rearrested by that sacred body and transferred in chains to Rome for another three years of captivity and prosecution for heresy. Campanella was freed at last by the vain and superstitious Urban VIII, whose favors Campanella courted with favorable horoscopes and a fawning commentary upon the pontiff's verses. He knew a short period of glory in the papal court, during which he published his *Atheismus triumphatus* (Atheism Conquered) and *Quod reminiscentur* (On Converting the Heathen). Once again, however, the intrigues of his enemies forced him to flee (1634), and he lived out his last five years in Paris. Preceded there by his fame, he was welcomed by Louis XIII and Richelieu, and received with honors at the Sorbonne. He died a good Christian in the monastery of his order in Paris.

In thirty years of captivity, Campanella composed an incredible amount of work, which, in effect, aimed at a total overhaul of human knowledge. Among his writings were an enormous *Theology* in thirty volumes, seven books on various points of religious doctrine, and long treatises on metaphysics, logic, mathematics, economy, medicine, rhetoric, historiography, astronomy, astrology, and so on. *La Città del sole,* still interesting as a curious and contradictory document of the human intellect's never-ceasing effort to devise plans of ideal societies, has a place, somewhere between Plato and Zamyatin, in the history of utopian thought. His *Del senso delle cose* is noteworthy for its lyrical flights of fancy depicting the "secret life" of the inanimate universe. His exceptional and monstrous destiny as a man on this earth will always startle and force the readers of his correspondence to pause.

Still, Campanella's literary fame today rests chiefly on his poems. Judged by preceding generations of critics as almost devoid of interest, a rough stammering, as it were, oppressed by rational excess, his *canzoni** and sonnets,* and especially his beautiful "Hymn to the Sun" (composed in the depths of St. Elmo), strike us today as the "missing link" in Italian poetry: the nearest parallel, in Italian, to the creations of the English Metaphysical poets. Their "antiliterary" quality is deceptive. Campanella's attacks on Baroque* poetry should not mislead us because his utilitarian view of art cannot destroy what is lyrical, irrational, and magical in his inspiration. In some translucent verses, he attains the effect for which Marino* always strove but rarely with success. Campanella's diction reminds us of John Donne: his best poems are passionate but, as it were, subdued "conversations" with an interlocutor who must be gently compelled to consider, come to terms, *accept;* a skeptical interlocutor, who seems to be, and who in fact is, the chained dweller of St. Elmo.

Bibliography: Tutte le opere, ed. Luigi Firpo (Milan: Mondadori, 1954)—of which only the first volume has so far appeared; *Opere di Giordano Bruno e Tommaso Campanella,* ed. Romano Amerio (Milan: Ricciardi, 1956); *The Defense of Galileo,* trans. Grant McColley, *Smith College Studies in History* 22 (1937), 1–93; *A Discourse Touching the Spanish Monarchy,* trans. Edmund Chilmead (London: Stephens, 1654); *Famous Utopias,* ed. Charles Andrews (New York: Tudor, 1937) —contains *The City of the Sun; Renaissance Philosophers: The Italian Philosophers,* eds. Arturo B. Fallico and Herman Shapiro (New York: Random House, 1967); Luigi Amabile, *Fra Tommaso Campanella, la sua congiura, i suoi processi e la sua pazzia,* 3 vols. (Naples: Morano, 1882), and *Tommaso Campanella nei castelli di Napoli, in Roma e in Parigi* (Naples: Morano, 1895); Léon Blanchet, *Campanella* (Paris: Alcan, 1920); Nicola Badaloni, *Tommaso Campanella* (Milan: Feltrinelli, 1965); Edmund Gardner, *Thomas Campanella and His Poetry* (Oxford: Oxford University Press, 1923); Francesco Grillo, *Tommaso Campanella in America: A Critical Bibliography and a Profile* (New York: Vanni, 1954); Attilio Momigliano, "La lirica di Campanella," in *Cinque saggi* (Florence: Sansoni, 1945).

Tibor Wlassics

CANTO CARNASCIALESCO ("Carnival Song"), a festive poetic form characteristic of Tuscan carnival celebrations, usually meant to be sung by celebrants riding the decorated carnival carts in pre-Lenten processions. In most cases, the singers also wore special costumes and masks and participated in *trionfi* (triumphs), special processions devoted to popular fables or classical myths almost always involving the theme of love. The popularity of this poetic genre may have stimulated the growth of the Italian musical theatre. A number of musicians were associated with the carnival songs of the Medici era, including Antonio Squarcialupi and two Dutch musicians, Heinrich Isaak (called Arrigo Tedesco by the Florentines) and Alexander Agricola. Structurally, carnival songs resemble the *ballata** and generally include a central theme, which is modified or elaborated by the singers, as well as the obligatory refrain repeated after every stanza. Edited by Anton Francesco Grazzini,* the first authoritative printed collection of these works appeared in 1559. The songs by Lorenzo de' Medici,* "Il Magnifico," are perhaps the best known. However, a list of the authors of these lively works reveals that the most distinguished Florentine citizens contributed to the development of the genre and includes, besides a number of anonymous composers, such names as Bernardo Rucellai (1448–1514), Biagio Buonaccorsi (1472–1526), Lorenzo di Filippo Strozzi (1483–1541), Jacopo Nardi,* Benedetto Varchi,* and Giovan Battista Gelli.*

See also BALLATA; MEDICI, Lorenzo de'.

Bibliography: Canti carnascialeschi del Rinascimento, ed. C. S. Singleton (Bari: Laterza, 1936); Jean-Pierre Barricelli, "Revisiting the Canti Carnascialeschi," *Italian Quarterly* 11 (1967), 43–61; Sir Maurice Bowra, "Songs of Dance and Carnival," in *Italian Renaissance Studies,* ed. E. F. Jacob (London: Faber, 1967).

CANZONE, a term reflecting that link between poetry and music common to a group of vernacular lyric poems such as the Provençal *canso,* the German *minnesong,* and the Italian *canzone.* It defines a number of verse forms with varying metrical patterns, the *canzone a ballo* or *ballata,** the *frottola, barzelletta,* the *canto carnascialesco,** and the *lauda sacra.* In its most refined form, it came to be known as the *canzone petrarchesca,* after its creator. In his *De vulgari eloquentia* (II), Dante* describes the form and metrics of the *canzone,* drawing no distinction between the practice of the poets of Provence and those of the Italian peninsula. Before the time of the Sicilian School, the courtly lyrics had become well established by the poets in Provence, northern France, and Germany, who continued to write throughout the Frederician period. It is generally recognized that the Italian *canzone,* in its Frederician form, was patterned upon the Provençal *canso;* it is also likely that the German *minnesong* had a secondary metrical influence upon its technique. Giraut de Borneil is credited with having developed the pattern which first became popular in Italy. Having begun among the poets of the Sicilian School, it was used by Guittone d'Arezzo* and his followers in Tuscany, by the poets of the *dolce stil nuovo,** and by Petrarch,* Tasso,* Leopardi,* Chiabrera,* and a host of others.

The *canzoni* of different poets display wide variations in structure. It is a short form consisting of equal stanzas and a shorter envoy. Each stanza has a tripartite structure and is divided into two equal parts, or *piedi,* and one unequal part, called the *sirima* or *cauda.* The envoy at the close of the poem bids farewell to the work. The number of lines to the stanza varies from seven to twenty, and in the envoy from three to ten. The lines are ordinarily hendecasyllabic mixed with heptameters and (less frequently) pentameters. Petrarch's *canzoni* have a more or less fixed form and normally consist of five or six stanzas with an envoy.

Dante calls the *canzone* the noblest form of poetry, and its frequent subjects are nature or the more complex human sentiments. Its greatest vogue was during the period of Petrarch's influence, lasting until Tasso's death. After Tasso, under the influence of the French Pléiade, the Pindaric and Anacreontic ode began to modify the form and content of the traditional *canzone.* Chiabrera played a central role in the diffusion of the *canzone,* and he revived the *canzonetta,* originally employed by the Frederician poets, which became favored by Metastasio* and the poets of Arcadia.* Toward the close of the seventeenth century, Alessandro Guidi

(1650–1712) developed the *canzone libera* (free-form canzone), which was perfected in the poetry of Leopardi and displayed a less rigid metrical form than was acceptable in the traditional Petrarchan form. In Great Britain, the Petrarchan *canzone* was employed by William Drummond of Hawthornden, and in Germany by A. W. von Schlegel and other Romantics. It was used to a greater extent only by the poets of Spain and Portugual.

See also CHIABRERA, Gabriello; DA LENTINO, Giacomo; DANTE ALIGHIERI; DOLCE STIL NUOVO; GUITTONE D'AREZZO; LEOPARDI, Giacomo; METASTASIO, Pietro; PETRARCA, Francesco.

Bibliography: Raffaele Spongano, *Nozioni ed esempi di metrica italiana* (Bologna: Pàtron, 1966); Ernest H. Wilkins, "The Canzone and the Minnesong," pp. 41–50, in *The Invention of the Sonnet and Other Studies in Italian Literature* (Rome: Edizioni di storia e letteratura, 1959).

CAPITOLO, a verse form the name of which is derived from the term used by Petrarch* to describe the six parts or "chapters" of his *Trionfi (Triumphs).* The form originated in imitation of Dante's* *terza rima.* There is no essential metrical difference between *terza rima* and the verse of a *capitolo,* although some scholars prefer to discriminate between the *capitolo* and *terza rima,* considering the themes employed in many *capitoli* a corruption of Dante's original and loftier purpose. Indeed, the *capitolo* was originally used for allegorical or moral poetry, but during the Renaissance,* it rapidly developed into the classical verse form for satirical poetry and was successfully adapted by Ariosto,* Berni,* and Lorenzo de' Medici,* among others. Modern poets, including Alfieri,* Leopardi,* and Carducci* have composed *capitoli.* Although satire is their predominant theme, this verse is by no means limited to any particular theme or level of style.

See also TERZA RIMA.

Bibliography: Raffaele Spongano, *Nozioni ed esempi di metrica italiana* (Bologna: Patròn, 1966).

CAPUANA, LUIGI (1839–1915), journalist, critic, and novelist. Born in Mineo in the Sicilian province of Catania, the first of seven sons, Capuana received his early education from members of his family and at a school in Bronte. By the time he enrolled in the faculty of law in Catania in 1857, his interest in Sicilian folklore was already serious and was encouraged by his friendship with Lionardo Vigo (1799–1879). Besides collecting folk ballads from his native region, Capuana was not above playing a practical joke on his scholarly friends by inventing some works of his own. One of his fake Sicilian versions of Dante's* "Donne ch'avete intelletto d'amore"

("Ladies who have intelligence of love") deceived one of Italy's foremost philologists and was included in an anthology of Sicilian verse. After abandoning his studies in 1860, he published his first important work, a patriotic poem entitled *Garibaldi* (1861, Garibaldi).

In 1864, Capuana moved to Florence and took an active part in the intellectual life of the city, becoming the drama critic for *La Nazione*, encountering the works of the French realists for the first time, and meeting prominent critics and writers. Returning to Mineo in 1868, Capuana became involved in local affairs and was, at one time, the mayor of the city. Although he wrote relatively little at this time, Capuana was profoundly influenced by Hegel and De Sanctis* and dabbled in photography, ceramics, drawing, and editing dialect poetry; he also projected the composition of a number of critical essays, *novelle,* * and novels. In 1875, he began a long affair with an illiterate Sicilian domestic (Giuseppina Sansone) which lasted until 1892 and produced several illegitimate children. Some critics have seen in this strange union between entirely different personalities the genesis of his greatest novel, *Il marchese di Roccaverdina* (1901, The Marquis of Roccaverdina).

Returning north in 1875, Capuana became an active contributor to Milan's *Corriere della sera.* A close friend of Giovanni Verga,* Capuana defended Verga's *I Malavoglia* when it was published as the greatest Italian novel since Manzoni.* His own first collection of short stories, which appeared in 1877, *Profili di donne* (Profiles of Women), was followed by his first novel, *Giacinta* (1879, Giacinta), a collection of fables entitled *C'era una volta* (1882, Once Upon a Time), and a collection of cogent essays on Zola, Goncourt, Balzac, and Verga, *Studi sulla letteratura contemporanea* (1880, 1882, Studies on Contemporary Literature). Capuana then moved to Rome, where he met D'Annunzio,* edited a literary magazine, and published more critical essays before returning to Sicily because of his health. Back in Rome in 1888, where he remained for thirteen years, he met Pirandello* and Zola, was appointed to a position in a teacher's college for women in 1890, and published, among other things, six collections of *novelle,* three novels—*Profumo* (1890, Perfume), *La sfinge* (1897, The Sphinx), and his masterpiece, *Il marchese di Roccaverdina*—and three collections of essays, including the important *Gli 'ismi' contemporanei* (1898, Contemporary 'Isms'). Appointed professor of lexicography and stylistics at the University of Catania in 1902, Capuana carried on his prolific literary production with thirteen additional volumes of *novelle,* critical essays, dramatic works in dialect, and a number of fables and stories for children.

Capuana's significance as a critic is directly linked to his views on Italian *verismo.* * Although he dedicated *Giacinta* to Zola, wrote essays on French realism and naturalism, and defended Verga's *verismo,* Capuana was always careful to avoid being identified as too strict an adherent to the French brand of naturalism. He always accepted the emphasis De Sanctis placed upon the concrete nature of art and rejected many of the contemporary literary movements in France as uselessly abstract in their criticism of anything in art which could be called a type and which lacked roots in a specified reality. However, he consistently applauded the general tenets of naturalism—the rejection of symbolism, impersonality of narration, objectivity, and the author's thorough knowledge of his subject matter.

Although his many collections of short stories and fables contain masterful examples of these narrative forms, Capuana's fame today rests mainly upon his criticism and two of his novels—*Giacinta* and *Il marchese di Roccaverdina*. The first work is similar to many naturalist case studies in human heredity and environment. A young girl named Giacinta is raped at the age of fourteen. Years later, when a fortunate inheritance seems to promise her happiness, the traumatic events of her unhappy childhood and family life return to destroy her prospects and her relationship with her lover, Andrea Gerace. Giacinta finally ends her life by taking poison. The novel's original narrative style rejects a strict chronological order and uses flashbacks extensively. The plot of *Il marchese di Roccaverdina* recalls that of *Crime and Punishment* and centers around the problem of human guilt and individual responsibility. It is less concerned with issues of heredity and environment than *Giacinta*. The novel begins with the murder of Rocco Criscione. The two main suspects are his wife, Agrippina Solmo, and Neli Casaccio, who has threatened the victim. Neli is sent to prison for fifteen years for the crime, but the reader soon discovers that the real culprit is the marquis and that his motive is jealousy, for Agrippina has been his mistress for the past ten years. The novel traces the progressive destruction of the marquis by his guilty conscience and provides a convincing indictment of a social order based upon injustice. It is one of the masterpieces of Italy's naturalist tradition, although its probing analysis of the guilty protagonist may be seen as a step toward the psychological novel of the next generation.

See also VERGA, Giovanni; VERISMO.

Bibliography: Capuana: Antologia dagli scritti critici, ed. Walter Mauro (Bologna: Calderini, 1971); *Giacinta ed altri racconti,* ed. Geno Pampaloni (Novara: Vallecchi, 1972); *Il Marchese di Roccaverdina* (Milan: Garzanti, 1969); *Racconti,* ed. Enrico Ghidetti, 3 vols. (Rome: Salerno, 1973–74); Carlo Madrignani, *Capuana e il naturalismo* (Bari: Laterza, 1970); Sergio Pacifici, *The Modern Italian Novel from Capuana to Tozzi* (Carbondale, Ill.: Southern Illinois University Press, 1973); Gino Raya, *Bibliografia di Luigi Capuana (1839–1969)* (Rome: Ciranna, 1969); Vincenzo Traversa, *Luigi Capuana, Critic and Novelist* (The Hague: Mouton, 1968).

CARDARELLI, VINCENZO (1887–1959), lyric poet and editor. Cardarelli was born Nazzareno Caldarelli in Corneto Tarquinia. Essentially self-taught, Cardarelli moved to Rome at the age of nineteen, eventually changed his name, and became a journalist. In 1911, he moved to Florence, where he contributed valuable essays on Ibsen and Péguy to *La Voce* and *Marzocco,* two major literary reviews. The outbreak of the war in 1914 prevented him from pursuing his studies with a fellowship in Germany, and his attempt to volunteer for the army was unsuccessful. In 1919, along with Riccardo Bacchelli,* Emilio Cecchi,* and a number of other young intellectuals, he founded the literary review *La Ronda* in Rome and eventually became its primary spokesman until it ceased publication in 1923. In 1949, Cardarelli became editor of the important literary weekly *La Fiera letteraria* and actively pursued the belles-lettres until his death.

   La Ronda was founded in opposition to the avant-garde movements—futurism* and hermetic poetry in particular. The review opposed modernistic theorists and proposed the restoration of a more traditional standard for poetry and prose and a taste for clarity, simplicity, rational syntax, and eloquence. Leopardi's* prose and verse were usually cited as the example to imitate. In Cardarelli, *La Ronda*'s ideals found their most skillful practitioner. Primarily written in his youth, the best of his lyrics, collected together as *Poesie* (Poems) in 1949, reflect a thematic concern with the seasons and the moods evoked by landscapes at various times of day. Among the best of these poems are "Estiva" ("Summertime"), "Adolescente" ("Adolescent"), "Alba" ("Dawn"), and "Autunno" ("Autumn"), all of which embody the classical simplicity and sensibility of *La Ronda*'s program but which are also the expression of authentic poetic inspiration. Several of Cardarelli's narrative works contain some of the finest examples of twentieth-century prose and have received literary awards. They include *Il sole a picco* (1929, The Sun Overhead), *Cielo sulle città* (1938, The Sky Over the Cities), *Villa Tarantola* (1948, Villa Tarantola), and *Viaggio di un poeta in Russia* (1954, Voyage of a Poet in Russia).

See also FUTURISM; HERMETICISM.

Bibliography: Opere complete, ed. Giuseppe Raimondi (Milan: Mondadori, 1962); *Contemporary Italian Poetry,* ed. Carlo L. Golino (Berkeley, Calif.: University of California Press, 1962); *Twentieth-Century Italian Poetry,* ed. L. R. Lind (Indianapolis, Ind.: Bobbs-Merrill, 1974); Bruno Romani, *Vincenzo Cardarelli* (Florence: La Nuova Italia, 1972); *"La Ronda" 1919–1923,* ed. Giuseppe Cassieri (Turin: ERI, 1969).

CARDUCCI, GIOSUÈ (1835–1907), poet, critic, and scholar. Son of a doctor and the oldest of three children, Carducci spent most of his childhood in Bolgheri, south of Livorno, the setting of two of his finer poems,

"Davanti San Guido" ("Before San Guido") and "Idillio Maremmano" ("The Idyll of Maremma"). His republican political views gave way to acceptance of the monarchy with the annexation of Rome to the Italian kingdom. In 1860, he was appointed professor of Italian literature at the University of Bologna and held this position until 1904, when he retired because of failing health. His accomplishments as a leading poet of the new Italy were recognized by the government, which made him senator for life in 1890. In 1906, he was awarded the Nobel Prize and thus received international recognition.

For nearly forty years, Carducci dominated the Italian literary scene with collections of poems, critical studies, and polemical essays on literary and political subjects. His writings are collected in fifty-two volumes in the Edizione Nazionale. Although his reputation has waned considerably upon the national and international scene, he remains the most important Italian poet of the second half of the nineteenth century. His perceptive scholarship constitutes a significant advance in the field of criticism. The studies on Cino da Pistoia,* Dante,* Petrarch,* Lorenzo il Magnifico,* Poliziano,* Ariosto,* Tasso,* Parini,* and the erotic poets of the eighteenth century retain their value for the contemporary student of Italian literature. Carducci is part of that group of critics who, along with Alessandro D'Ancona (1835–1914), Adolfo Bartoli (1833–1894), and Domenico Comparetti (1835–1927), adhered to the historical approach to a text.

His youthful polemic against the late romantics and romanticism* in general stemmed from his distaste for what he considered alien to the Italian tradition and a distraction from the study of classical writers. To be sure, he did not remain immune to romantic precepts. That he was affected by them is evident in his concept of poetry as a representation of life and its values, his belief in historic progress, and his awareness of the contrast between reality and ideals. Over the years, his views on modern foreign writers were modified, and he came to appreciate them. Carducci, who came to be known as the civic and moral poet of the new Italy, valued literature on strictly utilitarian grounds, i.e., as a means of education and inspiration to noble deeds. His "Inno a Satana" (1863, "Hymn to Satan"), of pantheistic inspiration, is a hymn to the active life, to the exaltation of rationalism over Christian theology, and to the affirmation of the individual as a free agent over his destiny.

Carducci sought to develop a consciousness in the citizens of the newly formed kingdom of Italy which would make them keenly aware of their cultural past. For him this past had its roots in the remote pagan world of Roman antiquity. This link with the past was reinforced by a language and style which refuted the simple and spoken forms advocated by Manzoni* in favor of a native literary flavor. In *Odi barbare* (1877–89, *The Barbarian Odes*), he attempted to recapture the spirit of antiquity by reproducing the rhythmic structure of Greek and Latin verses through concentration on accents rather than syllabic length; hence the title "barbarian." These poems, which are for the most part historical, along with *Rime nuove* (1861–87, *The New Lyrics*) which are of a personal nature, represent his finest poetry. Here his poetic voice achieved its own authentic form. In these two books, the poet has completely freed himself from the classical models, which in varying degrees can be noted in his first three collections: *Juvenilia* (1850–60, Youthful Writings), *Levia gravia* (1861–71, Light and Serious Poems), and *Giambi ed epodi* (1867–79, Iambics and Epodes). A decline in quality characterizes his last collection *Rime e ritmi* (1898, *The Lyrics and Rhythms*), because of a certain mannerism which permeates many of the poems.

Carducci's concept of life is reminiscent of Foscolo's* in the sense that he too sought to overcome the frailty of the human individual through the evocation of exemplary episodes of the past. In a world where the purpose of creation seems to be that of destruction, there is a need for ideals which would assert life over death. Carducci, however, did not go back to the Greeks, but to the Romans and to episodes from medieval and contemporary history. The ancient world takes concrete shape and acquires meaning for the modern reader with "Alle fonti del Clitumno" ("By the Sources of the Clitumnus"), "Dinanzi alle Terme di Caracalla" ("Before the Baths of Caracalla"), and "Nell'annuale della fondazione di Roma" ("On the Anniversary of the Founding of Rome"). Here the ancients' concept of nature is fused with the immediacy of contemporary painting. In vivid colors, he presents the virile magnanimity of the Roman spirit as opposed to the weak, stagnant life of the new Italians. The obvious didactic lesson is the emulation of the ancient Romans. Carducci, who saw a direct link between the Roman spirit, on the one hand, and the Italian Communes and the Renaissance* on the other, believed that this bond should extend to the new Italy. An austere morality and an intrepid love for freedom guides the lives of the people of the Communes in poems such as "Su i campi di Marengo" ("On the Fields of Marengo"), "Comune rustico" ("The Rustic Commune"), and "Faida di comune" ("A Communal Feud").

On the personal level, Carducci revealed the depth of his humanity with "Funere mersit acerbo" ("Plunged in Bitter Death") and "Pianto antico" ("Ancient Lament"), where the desolation of the poet over the sudden death of his three-year-old son reaches moving pathos. The grief which is so intimate and personal becomes universal, as the poet recognizes death as a constant threat against life. As the title of one of the poems indicates, it is an "ancient lament," a grief that has been part of the life process since the beginnings of the human race. Death always destroys regardless of human sentiments.

Nature is a fundamental theme in Carducci's poetry. The emotions which spur the poet at a particular moment of his poetic creation are fused with the natural scene. In "Before San Guido," nature assumes a soothing quality as it reminds the poet of his carefree childhood in the midst of a bucolic countryside. In "Traversando la Maremma Toscana" ("Crossing the Tuscan Maremma"), the tortuous lines of the landscape seem to reflect the tormented soul of the poet. Now that his youthful dreams have failed miserably, the memory of the natural scene where he had spent his childhood inspires peace and tranquility. The autumnal panorama of "San Martino" so vividly captures the scene following grape-gathering that one can nearly smell the fermentation of the wine and feel the chill of that foggy, misty November weather so typical of central and northern Italy. The poems in which the landscape plays a dominant role, regardless of the themes treated within, represent some of Carducci's most beautiful and enduring work.

Bibliography: Edizione nazionale delle opere di Giosuè Carducci (Bologna: Zanichelli, 1935–40); *A Selection of His Poems,* trans. G. L. Bickersteth (London: Longmans, Green, 1913); *From the Poems of Giosuè Carducci,* trans. Romilda Rendel (London: Kegan Paul, Trench, Trubner, 1929); *Poems of Giosuè Carducci,* trans. Frank Sewall (New York: Dodd Mead, 1892); *A Selection from the Poems,* trans. Emily A. Tribe (London: Longmans, 1921); Anne Paolucci, "Moments of the Creative Process in the Literary Criticism of Giosuè Carducci," *Italica* 33 (1956), 110–20; S. E. Scalia, *Carducci: His Critics and Translators in England and America 1881–1932* (New York: Vanni, 1937); Orlo Williams, *Giosuè Carducci* (London: Houghton, 1914).

Silvano Garofalo

CARITEO, BENEDETTO (1450–1514), Catalan poet and courtier. Born Benedetto Gareth in Barcelona, Cariteo (also known as Chariteo) came to the Aragonese court of Naples in 1467–68 where he was warmly received by the humanist Neapolitan Academy. He acquired his new surname in the Academy because his Catalan surname suggested the name "Cariteo" (chosen of the Graces). In the Academy, Cariteo formed close intellectual and personal ties with such eminent figures as Jacopo Sannazaro* and Giovanni Pontano.* He remained a faithful servant of the House of Aragon even after King Ferdinand II was forced into exile by the French invasions and the occupation of Naples by King Louis XII in 1501. He regained his position in Naples after the eventual eclipse of French power in southern Italy and remained there until his death.

Although Cariteo composed some minor poetry in *terza rima,** his most celebrated work is the collection *Endimione* (1506, Endymion), which consists of sonnets* in praise of a woman named Luna as well as numerous sonnets and *canzoni** of an historical and political nature celebrating the House of Aragon or delineating various court personalities. It was his love poetry, however, that made him famous and established him, along with

Tebaldeo* and Serafino Aquilano,* as a model during the sixteenth century for Petrarchan verse. Reaching the heights of popularity during the Renaissance* because of the brilliance of its extravagant poetic conceits, Cariteo's poetry was the kind of Petrarchan verse which prompted Pietro Bembo's* more severely defined Petrarchan classicism. Modern critics have sometimes denigrated his poetry for its emphasis upon the conceit and for its supposed lack of originality, a fate shared by many of the lesser Petrarchan poets of his day; but his merits as a poet were considerable, and he was partly responsible for the vogue of the Petrarchan lyric throughout Europe. He was also one of the first Petrarchans of his time to integrate classical forms and techniques into the evolving tradition of the Renaissance love lyric.

See also PETRARCHISM; SERAFINO AQUILANO, TEBALDEO, Antonio.

Bibliography: Le Rime di Benedetto Gareth, ed. Erasmo Percopo, 2 vols. (Naples: Biblioteca napoletana di storia e letteratura, 1892); Giovanni Getto, "Sulla poesia del Cariteo," *Giornale storico della letteratura italiana* 123 (1946), 53–68; Ernest H. Wilkins, "A General Survey of Renaissance Petrarchism," *Comparative Literature* 2 (1950), 327–42.

CARO, ANNIBALE (1507–1566), poet, translator, and scholar. After studying in Florence, where he befriended Benedetto Varchi,* and living in Naples where he met many of the foremost literary figures of that court, Caro entered the service of Cardinal Pier Luigi Farnese and, after his murder, that of Cardinal Alessandro Farnese. These posts enabled him to obtain benefices and an income sufficient to assure him the tranquility necessary for his literary pursuits.

Caro's numerous letters are an excellent historical source. He also composed a collection of Petrarchan verse (1557), a number of satirical sonnets,* and a prose comedy, *Gli straccioni* (1554, The Ragged Ones), produced by combining two actual figures from the Rome of his day with elements from *The Loves of Leucippe and Clitophon* by Achilles Tatius. Caro's most lasting influence was as a translator. In addition to a version of Longus's *Daphnis and Chloe* (1784) in blank verse, he produced a translation of the *Aeneid* (1581), likewise in blank verse, which became a Renaissance* classic and influenced other Italian epic* poets in their choice of meter. Caro also became embroiled in a heated dispute with Ludovico Castelvetro* over a poem written in 1553 in praise of the royal house of France. Castelvetro attacked the work for its failure to attain an adequately Petrarchan style; Caro and his defenders countered the argument; and the quarrel resulted in the murder of one of Caro's supporters, Alberigo Longo (d. 1555). Accused of this crime as well as that of heresy,

Castelvetro was forced to leave Rome. Having left the service of the Farnese family in 1563, Caro spent the last few years of his life revising his letters and his lyric poems and bringing his version of the *Aeneid* to completion.

See also CASTELVETRO, Ludovico.

Bibliography: Opere, 8 vols. (Milan: Classici italiani, 1807–12); Aulo Greco, *Annibal Caro, cultura e poesia* (Rome: Edizioni di storia e letteratura, 1950); Francesco Sarri, *Annibal Caro: saggio critico* (Milan: L'Università del Sacro Cuore, 1933).

CARRER, LUIGI (1801–1850), poet, translator, and scholar. Born of a humble Venetian family, Carrer studied law but soon turned to literary pursuits after his success in the Venetian salons and the praise of Lord Byron persuaded him to write. Without independent means, Carrer was always forced to work; he was a proofreader, an editor, the secretary to the Istituto Veneto, and finally the director of the Museo Correr, a post he held until his death.

Carrer translated Lucretius and published illuminating biographies of Carlo Goldoni* (1824) and Ugo Foscolo* (1842). His *Ballate* (1834, Ballads) was favorably received by critics and readers, and his use of this form to write poetry with historical or legendary themes was typical of one type of romantic verse. Most representative of these poems are "La vendetta" ("The Revenge"), an enigmatic poem about an ancient love affair shrouded in mystery, and "La sposa dell'Adriatico" (The Bride of the Adriatic), a ballad which explains the symbolic marriage of the Venetian doge to the sea through the fanciful account of an early doge whose mistress was drowned in the ocean. Carrer also composed a Byronic poem entitled *Clotaldo* (1826, Clotaldus) and wrote critical prefaces to the many volumes of Italian classics which he edited.

Bibliography: Poesia dell'Ottocento, eds. Carlo Muscetta and Elsa Sormani, 2 vols. (Turin: Einaudi, 1968); *From Marino to Marinetti,* trans. Joseph Tusiani (New York: Baroque Press, 1974).

CASANOVA, GIACOMO GIROLAMO (1725–1798), adventurer and autobiographer. Born in Venice of a theatrical family, Casanova received the protection and patronage of the owners of the Grimani Theatre upon the death of his father. Sent to Padua for his education by the Grimanis, Casanova became a good student at the university (1738–41), graduated, and received minor orders in preparation for a career in the church. His first love affair was apparently with the sister of his professor Antonio Gozzi, and from that time on, he appeared to have discovered his true calling in life. Returning to Venice, he acquired a new patron, a Venetian senator of standing, and began to find acceptance in polite society. After a series of journeys to various Italian cities and after acquiring a number of aristocratic patrons, he was, at the age of twenty-four, almost adopted by a Venetian patrician, when he was investigated by the Inquisition and forced to flee from Venice in 1749.

The pattern of Casanova's life had, by now, become fixed: a constant parade of travels, mistresses, patrons, and scandals. In the course of his life, he met most of the crowned heads of Europe, gambled away fortunes, dabbled in poetry and drama, directed a lottery, and created for himself a European reputation as a rake, an adventurer, and a worthy successor to Don Juan. Around 1755, he gave himself a title (Chevalier de Seingalt) in order to further his progress in polite society. The most famous escapade of his life was his escape from the dreaded state prison in Venice in 1756. Allowed to return to Venice in 1774, he became a spy for the Inquisition until he was once again banished from Venice in 1782. At that time, he moved to Austria to become the librarian of a nobleman from Bohemia; he remained in Austria until his death.

Casanova's greatest literary work is his autobiography, with its creation of a living myth, its easy hedonism, and its portrayal of eighteenth-century society. Although he apparently collaborated with Lorenzo da Ponte* on the libretto for Mozart's *Don Giovanni* (1787) and attempted a long, philosophical romance, his *Memoires* (1821, *History of My Life*) is one of the best and most massive autobiographies of the century. It became an international best seller when it appeared in the early nineteenth century, despite inadequate translations and partial editions. Although he considered Italian a more beautiful language, Casanova wrote in French to ensure a wider audience. It had reached only the year 1774 when he died and left over four thousand manuscript pages incomplete. Not until 1960 was the original manuscript published in its entirety, having narrowly escaped destruction by Allied bombings in Leipzig during World War II. In a recent film entitled *Casanova* (1976), Federico Fellini gives a novel and controversial interpretation of the character of this legendary eighteenth-century adventurer.

Bibliography: History of My Life, trans. Willard R. Trask, 12 vols. (New York: Harcourt, 1966); Maurice Andrieux,·*Daily Life in Venice in the Time of Casanova* (New York: Praeger, 1972); Peter Bondanella, ed., *Federico Fellini: Essays in Criticism* (New York: Oxford University Press, 1978); John Masters, *Casanova* (New York: Bernard Geis, 1969).

CASSOLA, CARLO (1917–), novelist and journalist. Attracted to literature at an early age, Cassola became part of a literary movement organized at Rome's Liceo Tasso called *novismo*. The members of this group opposed the excesses of futurism* and reflected a mildly antifascist attitude.

During his years as a student before entering the University of Rome, Cassola was associated with an interesting assortment of intellectuals, including Vittorio Mussolini, the dictator's son whose editorship of the film journal *Cinema* from 1938 to 1943 gave dissident elements within fascist culture a focal point for their opposition, and Manlio Cancogni (1916–   ), a now noted journalist and novelist. In the 1930's, Cassola was quite attracted to the works of Proust and Joyce. He enrolled in the School of Law at the University of Rome in 1935, and when he graduated and began to teach, he was gradually drawn to literature. At that time, he began writing short stories which were not published until the war had ended. After the fall of fascism, Cassola participated in the resistance and joined the *Partito d'Azione,* a coalition of antifascist and noncommunist forces. As his reputation as a writer grew, Cassola finally abandoned teaching for permanent work in journalism and writing.

Cassola is one of the most popular and prolific contemporary novelists. In his various works, several distinct stages are discernible. Beginning with his early short stories in 1937 to the time of the novel *Il taglio del bosco* (1954, Timber Cutting), Cassola's works expressed an elegiac tone and a highly pessimistic view of the human condition. In this novel, Cassola portrays a lonely woodsman who, like Cassola, had recently lost his wife. Because of the autobiographical inspiration, Cassola feels much affection for this early work, in spite of the fact that his other novels have generated more critical commentary. Cassola avoids sentimentality in the plot by choosing a working-class protagonist devoid of Cassola's own middle-class values and psychology, who, nevertheless, shares his problems. This novel is said to reflect an existentialist tendency in the literature of the period.

A second and more crucial phase of Cassola's works coincides with the impact of neorealism* in film and literature and deals with political issues and the author's experiences in the resistance. Two of Cassola's best books belong to this period. In *Fausto e Anna* (1952, *Fausto and Anna*), Cassola draws the compelling portrait of an intellectual much like himself who is torn between his desire to participate in the resistance and his antipathy for the communists who control so many of the antifascist forces. Much of the book's appeal lies in his description of partisan life, and its publication gave expression to a widespread sentiment in Italy that the moral and political goals of the resistance had not been fully achieved. *La ragazza di Bube* (1960, *Bebo's Girl*) continued this pessimistic appraisal of the resistance and received the prestigious Strega Prize in 1960 as well as widespread popular acclaim. This novel sets forth a case history of how the resistance twisted the personality of a basically good young man. Bube, a hero of the antifascist struggle, is led to commit a murder partially justified by the rancors of the past conflict. The crime separates him from his fiancée

Mara, who is forced to wait for him for fourteen years before they can be married.

After 1960, Cassola's novels return to the earlier elegiac tone and existential content. Typical of this period is *Un cuore arido* (1961, *An Arid Heart*), a minute analysis of the daily life of one woman, Anna Cavorzio, concentrating upon the gradual but inevitable desiccation of her feelings. *Monte Mario* (1973, *Portrait of Helena*), one of Cassola's most successful recent works, moves away from the Tuscan Maremma region or from the period of the resistance to probe a contemporary relationship. The work unfolds in the urban atmosphere of Rome and describes the unrequited love of Mario Varallo, a captain of the *carabinieri*, for Elena Raicevic, whose style of life reflects the relaxed values of the present but who, nevertheless, remains a virgin until the age of twenty-six.

To date, Cassola's style has evolved through several phases. His ability to participate in and to act as a barometer for various literary trends, while always maintaining his artistic integrity and independence, marks him as one of contemporary Italy's major novelists.

Bibliography: An Arid Heart, trans. William Weaver (New York: Pantheon, 1964); *Bebo's Girl*, trans. Marguerite Waldman (New York: Pantheon, 1962); *Fausto and Anna*, trans. Isabel Quigly (1960; rpt. Westport, Conn.: Greenwood Press, 1975); *Portrait of Helena*, trans. Sebastian Roberts (London: Chatto & Windus, 1975); Gian Carlo Ferretti, *Letteratura e ideologia: Bassani, Cassola, Pasolini* (Rome: Editori Riuniti, 1964); Sergio Pacifici, ed., *From Verismo to Experimentalism: Essays on the Modern Italian Novel* (Bloomington, Ind.: Indiana University Press, 1969).

CASTELVETRO, LUDOVICO (1505–1571), scholar and critic. Born in Modena, Castelvetro studied law and literature at several universities before receiving his degree from the University of Siena and returning to Modena in 1529. Although Castelvetro was one of the most learned men of his time, he also had a difficult personality and often angered fellow scholars. In 1553, his tactless criticism of Annibale Caro's* poem in praise of France ("Venite all'ombra de' gran gigli d'oro," Come to the shade of the great golden lilies), aroused the opposition which eventually developed into an accusation of heresy, precipitating his flight from Modena in 1557. Ultimately excommunicated, he was forced to roam throughout Italy and Europe for the rest of his life.

Most of Castelvetro's works are critical or theoretical, but one of the most influential learned comedies of the Italian Renaissance,* *Gl'ingannati* (1550, *The Deceived*), is often attributed either to him or to Alessandro Piccolomini (1508–78), a Sienese humanist friend. It is one of many comedies which owes its plot to Plautus's *Menaechmi* and has often been discussed as a possible source for Shakespeare's *Twelfth Night*. In the field of literary criticism, Castelvetro produced two important commentaries, one on Petrarch's* lyric poetry (1582) and another on Dante's* *Inferno,* which remained unknown and unpublished until the nineteenth century. One of the best practical critics of the period, he based his observations on careful readings of the texts themselves without totally abandoning the older allegorical methods of textual analysis which he had learned from Cristoforo Landino* and earlier Latin humanists. Castelvetro, however, applied these methods both to modern classics written in the vernacular and to Latin works.

Castelvetro's masterpiece was his lengthy commentary on Aristotle's *Poetics* (1570, 1576) which included the Greek text and an Italian translation. This work continued the tradition begun by Robortello's* first commentary of 1548, incorporated the critical discussion which followed Robortello's work, and produced an original and often controversial interpretation of this central text in Renaissance criticism. While Robortello accepted the Aristotle text as a masterpiece, Castelvetro more often than not used it to build his own theories, and he departs, sometimes drastically, from the intention of the original. First, Castelvetro emphasizes the rhetorical aspects of Aristotle's theory—the relationship of the poem to its audience—and diminishes his attention to formalistic aspects of a literary text. Rejecting any didactic purpose in literature, he states that its sole end is to delight and to give pleasure to its audience. The Aristotelian concept of purgation or catharsis is, for him, simply another means of satisfying this criterion. Furthermore, he believes that literature should appeal to a broad audience, not simply to an elite collection of learned men.

According to Castelvetro, poetry is closest to history, for history presents events in prose which actually happened, while poetry describes events in verse which might have occurred. Poetry is, therefore, in one sense an imitation of history and not an imitation of reality itself. Although he emphasizes this element of verisimilitude in poetry, Castelvetro nevertheless raises the question of the marvelous in poetry, one of the major issues in the poetics of the late Renaissance and Baroque* period. The marvelous in poetry, an element which creates delight and thus satisfies the goal of poetry, is the element which sets poetry apart from history. For him, the good act leading to evil best gives rise to a sense of the marvelous in literature. He devotes a good deal of attention to how this is achieved in *Oedipus the King* as well as in various modern works. This attention to modern literature is one of the features making Castelvetro's criticism unique. By advocating the combination of verisimilitude and the marvelous in poetry, he anticipates the theories of Torquato Tasso,* who, in his own epic* poem, tried to combine the Aristotelian principle of *mimesis* (imitation) with the Christian element of the marvelous. Finally, Castelvetro defines the poet himself not as a divinely inspired writer but, instead, as a careful and precise artisan who writes to delight and, ultimately, to achieve personal glory. Castelvetro actually spends little time in this voluminous commentary dealing with Aristotle's central problem of *mimesis,* but one of his own formulas—the maxim that a tragic work must, of necessity, be limited to a single day's time and to a single place—became accepted practice in most neoclassical works in Italy, France, and England until the eighteenth century. This formula is often erroneously attributed to Aristotle, who actually only stressed the unity of poetic action and never suggested the so-called three unities as a fixed dramatic rule.

Bibliography: Opere varie critiche di Lodovico Castelvetro (Milan: Foppens, 1727) —contains Muratori's biography; *La Poetica d'Aristotile, volgarizzata da Lodovico Castelvetro,* ed. Pietro Metastasio (Milan: Silvestri, 1831); *Le rime del Petrarca brevemente esposte per Lodovico Castelvetro* (Venice: Zatta, 1756); *Sposizione di Lodovico Castelvetro a XXIX canti dell'Inferno,* ed. Giovanni Franciosi (Modena: Società tipografica, 1886); Allan H. Gilbert, ed., *Literary Criticism: Plato to Dryden* (Detroit, Mich.: Wayne State University Press, 1962); R. S. Crane, ed., *Critics and Criticism, Ancient and Modern* (Chicago: University of Chicago Press, 1952); Robert C. Melzi, *Castelvetro's Annotations to the Inferno* (The Hague: Mouton, 1966); Bernard Weinberg, *A History of Literary Criticism in the Italian Renaissance,* 2 vols. (Chicago: University of Chicago Press, 1961).

CASTIGLIONE, BALDESAR (1478–1529), Mantuan courtier, diplomat, writer on courtesy and manners, and occasional poet. Born near Mantua, Castiglione spent his early years in the court there before being sent to the court of Ludovico il Moro at Milan in 1492 in order to finish his education as a courtier. Sojourning in the most brilliant Italian court of the epoch which had attracted humanists and artists like Bramante and Leonardo,* Castiglione threw himself into the study of classical and Italian literature, developed a connoisseur's knowledge of art, and learned the courtier's art of serving a brilliant, though difficult, master. When Milan fell to the French in 1499, Castiglione briefly returned to Mantua. After failing to win the favor of Duke Francesco Gonzaga, he finally obtained permission in 1504 to enter the service of Guidobaldo di Montefeltro, duke of Urbino, on whom he had called several years before. Castiglione considered the period from 1504 to 1513 spent in the service of Guidobaldo and his successor Francesco Maria della Rovere the flower of his life. Guidobaldo was an ideal humanist prince, a soldier, statesman, scholar, and patron of the arts who had assembled a fine library and art collection and whose court attracted the leading luminaries of the day: writers like Pietro Bembo* and Bernardo Bibbiena,* artists like Bramante and Raphael, and important political figures from Florence, Genoa, and Rome. After Francesco Maria became duke in 1508, the court lost some of its luster, but because the duke was the nephew of Pope Julius II, Castiglione found himself repeatedly in Rome on diplomatic missions. There he associated with the humanists at the papal court and developed a close friendship with Raphael. When Leo X became pope in 1513, Castiglione remained in Rome as ambassador, but in 1515, when Urbino was taken from Francesco Maria by papal forces for the pope's nephew, Castiglione returned to Mantua and the service of the duke to whom he had been reconciled. In 1516, he married Ippolita Torelli and returned to Rome as Duke Francesco Gonzaga's ambassador. Four years later, he experienced the double loss of his wife and his friend Raphael. He continued his diplomatic career in Rome, however, and in 1524, he was made papal nunzio to the Spanish court of Charles V. His last years were not especially happy ones. Separated from his loved ones and friends in Italy, saddened by news of the Sack of Rome by troops of Charles V on 6 May 1527, and forced to defend himself from attacks that he had failed to alert the pope to Charles's intentions, Castiglione felt himself in what he called a solitude filled with cares. He was made bishop of Avila in 1528 and died in Spain the following year.

Castiglione was by vocation a courtier and diplomat and only by avocation a writer. He composed verse in Latin and Italian, including several elegies considered among the best neo-Latin poems of the century. He left a large number of letters important for the diplomatic and social history of a period in which he played so central a role. And with his cousin Cesare Gonzaga he wrote an interesting dramatic eclogue *Tirsi* (1506, Tirsi) celebrating the duchess of Urbino and her court; it was first performed during carnival, 1506.

Castiglione's reputation as a writer of world stature rests on a single work, *Il libro del Cortegiano* (1528, *The Book of the Courtier*), which he began writing as early as 1508, finished in a three-book version in 1515, and reworked into its final form between 1521 and 1524, adding the dedicatory letter to Don Michel de Silva, a Portuguese bishop he knew in Rome, probably in 1527. *The Courtier* is largely concerned with defining the qualities of an ideal courtier, with but one of its four books devoted to his female counterpart. Presenting the courtier as a humanist and a knight, Castiglione takes inspiration from the Roman and Ciceronian ideal of the orator—the widely educated, cultured individual whose primary activities were political, legal, and diplomatic. Castiglione's main interest in his book is to define the modes of behavior of his ideal figure, whom he sees as a consummate actor able to manipulate his appearances to suit every situation and person he encounters. In every case, the courtier is expected to manifest a certain grace and dignified gravity, qualities he achieves through self-knowledge and control, perfect mastery of social forms, and what Castiglione dubs *sprezzatura,* roughly translated as "nonchalance." Presenting his ideal figure as an actor, Castiglione argues at the same time that his ideal actions will be informed by moral principles, but on more than one occasion in his book he brings up the issue of morality without definitively resolving it.

Castiglione casts his work in the form of a dialogue. Although strongly influenced by Cicero's *De Oratore (On the Orator),* passages of which are often closely imitated, *The Courtier* is closer in form to the symposium and specifically to Plato's *Symposium* which is recalled in Book IV. The ideal courtier is thus presented through the supposedly real speeches and conversations and debates of the courtiers and ladies who resided at the court of Urbino in March 1507. Their mode of talk is serious but festive, dignified yet informal, just as it is in most symposia. The self-reflexive nature of their subject matter, their sitting around in a circle, their formal sequence of speakers, and the intoxication of their last evening of discussion are also typical of that genre.

By presenting his doctrines in dialogue form, Castiglione not only made his work more literary and readable, thus insuring the tremendous popularity it would enjoy in Europe over the next three centuries, but also enabled him to do considerably more than write a treatise on courtiership. He is able to have his characters engage in lively debates on a host of important issues, from the question of a literary language for Italy through the nature and place of woman in society to the character of the ideal state. By manipulating his dialogue form, he can have his characters challenge accepted truths without committing himself to any particular position, both because such neutrality was politically safer in Renaissance* Italy and because he correctly perceived something of the true complexity of many fundamental issues. Finally, by putting his doctrines in the mouths of the men and women of Urbino whom he so cherished, Castiglione is able to create a moving memorial to that court and a nostalgic tribute to the ideal Renaissance civilization so effectively depicted in his book.

Bibliography: Il libro del cortegiano con una scelta delle opere minori, ed. Bruno Maier (Turin: UTET, 1964); *La seconda redazione del Cortegiano di Baldassarre Castiglione,* ed. Ghino Ghinassi (Florence: Sansoni, 1968); *The Book of the Courtier,* trans. Sir Thomas Hoby (1561; rpt. New York: Dutton, 1974); *The Book of the Courtier,* trans. Charles Singleton (Garden City, N.Y.: Doubleday, 1959); Lawrence Lipking, "The Dialectic of *Il Cortegiano," Publications of the Modern Language Association* 81 (1966), 355–62; Wayne A. Rebhorn, *Courtly Performances: Masking and Festivity in Castiglione's Book of the Courtier* (Detroit, Mich.: Wayne State University Press, 1978), and "Ottaviano's Interruption: Book IV and the Problem of Unity in *Il Libro del Cortegiano," Modern Language Notes* 87 (1972), 37–59; Lawrence V. Ryan, "Book IV of Castiglione's *Courtier:* Climax or Afterthought?" *Studies in the Renaissance* 19 (1972), 156–79.

Wayne A. Rebhorn

CATHERINE OF SIENA (1347–1380), mystic, saint, and writer of letters and religious treatises. Catherine was born the last of twenty-five children as Caterina Benincasa, and first took religious vows in 1362. Her piety soon drew about her a circle of followers who prayed and read Scripture with her while they ministered to the sick and the needy. In 1370, she began to attract the attention of the church hierarchy by urging Christian princes to set aside their temporal differences in a common alliance against the unbelievers who held the Holy Land. Put to an examination by the Dominicans in 1374, she emerged with the complete backing of the order. Moreover, she began to take an active part in the political life of the times and went to Avignon to persuade Gregory XI to return the Holy See to Rome. After his death, Catherine supported the efforts of Pope Urban VII to reunite the feuding branches of the church.

Catherine's writings include almost four hundred letters and a treatise, *Dialogo della divina provvidenza* (1377–78, *A Treatise of Divine Providence*). Central to her religious message is the definition of God's essence as love: through a process of self-analysis and mystic meditation, the human being can come not only to understand the Divine nature but also to love his fellow men. Besides her edifying example and the purity of her call for religious revival in the church, Catherine's private letters reveal a powerful personality, equally at home with the spiritual and temporal rulers of the world or the most humble folk. Typical of her unaffected but authoritative tone is a letter addressed to Giovanni Acuto (Sir John Hawkwood), the English soldier of fortune: "I marvel much that you, having, as I heard, promised to be willing to go to die for Christ in this holy crusade, are wanting to make war in these parts. This is not that holy disposition which God demands from you if you are to go to so holy and venerable a place. It seems to me that you ought now, at this present time, to dispose yourself to virtue . . . and thus you shall show that you are a manly and true knight." Her letters provide the contemporary reader with an intimate view of the spiritual and political life of the late fourteenth century. Immediately after her death, the steps for her canonization were undertaken, an act which finally became official in 1461 under the pontificate of Pius II.*

Bibliography: Le lettere di santa Caterina da Siena, ed. Piero Misciattelli, 6 vols. (Florence: Marzocco, 1940–52); *Libro della divina dottrina, volgarmente detto Dialogo della divina provvidenza,* ed. Matilde Fiorilli (Bari: Laterza, 1928); *The Dialogue of the Seraphic Virgin Catherine of Siena,* trans. Algar Thorold (London: Kegan Paul, 1907); *Saint Catherine of Siena As Seen in Her Letters,* trans. Vida Scudder (New York: Dutton, 1906); Edmund G. Gardner, *Saint Catherine of Siena* (New York: Dutton, 1907).

CAVALCANTI, GUIDO (circa 1240–1300), poet. Born before 1259 to Cavalcante de' Cavalcanti, descendant of a Guelph family of merchants, Cavalcanti was engaged to Bice, daughter of the Ghibelline Farinata degli Uberti, in 1267. It was one of the many engagements celebrated that year in order to bring peace among these political factions in Florence. In 1280,

Cavalcanti was a Guelph guarantor for the peace arranged by Cardinal Latini. In 1284 and 1290, he was a member of the General Council of the Commune. On 24 June 1300, the priors of the Commune banished Cavalcanti as a leader of the White faction, and he was confined to Sarzana. The exile was revoked a month later, but Guido died in Sarzana on 29 August of the same year.

A legend soon flourished around Cavalcanti's personality. Dino Compagni* (*Cronica* I, 20), Giovanni Villani* (*Cronica* VIII), Boccaccio* (*Decameron* VI, 9), and Franco Sacchetti* (*Trecentonovelle* LXVIII), all of them depending, perhaps, on the famous "disdain" that Dante* attributes to Cavalcanti (*Inferno* X, 63), portray the poet as a gentle, cultivated, solitary, choleric, and disdainful man. Yet, the reading of some of his tender ballads (the one on the "foresette," for instance) could noticeably soften this portrait of an artistocratic, disdainful man. It is also true, however, that such a legend could have some basis in certain themes in his lyrics, particularly those in "Donna me prega" ("Because a lady asks me").

Undoubtedly the best Italian poet before Dante, Cavalcanti is the true father of the school of the *dolce stil nuovo.** A total of fifty-two poems have been transmitted to us (sonnets,* ballads, songs, and one *mottetto*). Two more ballads, in collaboration with his brother Jacopo, are doubtfully attributed to him.

One of the most interesting episodes of the Italian literature of the Duecento is his relationship with Dante. They exchanged several sonnets, including Cavalcanti's "I' vengo 'l giorno a te 'nfinite volte" ("I daily come to thee uncounting times"), whose purpose has never been easily identified. Dante dedicated his *Vita nuova* to Cavalcanti, calling him "the first of my friends," but does not mention him in the *De vulgari eloquentia,* or in *The Divine Comedy,* except for the enigmatic episode in the *Inferno.* It is possible, then, to assume that their relationship turned cool, perhaps because Dante oriented himself toward an ethical and civic understanding of literature, whereas Cavalcanti conceived it always as a refined, aristocratic, and self-justifying means of expression. Or, perhaps, a different conception of love and of its function in a spiritual itinerary might have contributed to the cooling of their friendship.

Cavalcanti's ideas about the nature of love and its effects are mostly consigned to the song "Donna me prega," which has been the subject of endless interpretations beginning with the commentary of the fourteenth-century physician Dino del Garbo. Even today the interpretations are controversial. In one instance, the song is interpreted along the lines of Arabic Neo-Platonism, and in others, in terms of the philosophy of Albertus Magnus or that of Aristotelian-Scholasticism, or, what seems more probable, that of Averroism. In this poem, Cavalcanti maintains that love is an accident, not an essence, and dwells in the sensitive soul. It is, therefore, incapable of pure knowledge which can be achieved only by the "possible intellect." Love, depending on a sensitive faculty, judges in an erroneous way, and the substitution of love for reason is often the cause of death (to be understood in a metaphorical way).

From this naturalistic conception of love comes the theme of death that is so intertwined in Cavalcanti's poetry with the theme of love as an exalting joy. Thus, the dominant elements of his poetry are those of crying, puzzlement, and fear. Cavalcanti personified his feelings and viewed their contrasting forces almost as if he were an hallucinating spectator. But this hallucinated observation is often accompanied by a sense of self-pity, extenuation, and melancholy which is reflected in the style and in the rhythm of his poems. Cavalcanti's keen sensitivity to the emotions, particularly that of love, has been discussed by Ezra Pound who characterized Cavalcanti as a great psychologist of the emotions, both sharp in his understanding and precise in his descriptions of emotional states. Pound's affection for his predecessor led him to translate his sonnets, songs, and ballads.

See also DOLCE STIL NUOVO.

Bibliography: Guido Cavalcanti: Rime, ed. Guido Favati (Milan: Ricciardi, 1957); Ezra Pound, *Translations* (New York: New Directions, 1963); Peter Dronke, *Medieval Latin and the Rise of the European Love Lyric,* 2 vols. (Oxford: Clarendon Press, 1968); J. E. Shaw, *Guido Cavalcanti's Theory of Love: The "Canzone d'Amore" and Other Related Problems* (Toronto: University of Toronto Press, 1949).

Paolo Cherchi

CECCHI, EMILIO (1884–1966), Florentine journalist and critic. Cecchi was educated at the University of Florence and collaborated on such literary journals as *La Voce* and *Leonardo* before moving to Rome where he became the critic for *La Tribuna* after 1910. Having served in World War I, Cecchi went to London as a correspondent and met such famous writers as Max Beerbohm, G. K. Chesterton, and Lytton Strachey. Back in Italy in 1919, he was among the founders of *La Ronda,* and, in 1927, he began to write for the prestigious *Corriere della sera* of Milan, a task he carried on until his death. In 1930–31, Cecchi taught Italian culture at the University of California at Berkeley, came back to Italy (where he worked in the cinema), and returned to America in 1937–38. In 1940, he was made a member of the Accademia d'Italia, and, in 1947, of the Accademia dei Lincei. With Benedetto Croce's* support, he received an award from the Lincei in 1952 for his essays.

A number of Cecchi's best essays are in the collections entitled *Pesci rossi* (1920, Goldfish) and *Corse al trotto* (1936, Trotting Races). Besides cultivating the art of the essay, Cecchi was an important critic whose knowledge of the English language made him one of the key interpreters of Anglo-American culture in Italy. His works in this area include an essay on Kipling (1911); *Storia della letteratura inglese nel secolo XIX* (1915, History of Nineteenth-Century English Literature); and, most importantly, *America amara* (1939, Bitter America). Besides translating writers such as Shakespeare, Chesterton, Shelley, and Leibniz, Cecchi was also a distinguished art critic.

Bibliography: America amara (Florence: Sansoni, 1940); *Corse al trotto vecchie e nuove* (Florence: Sansoni, 1941); *Pesci rossi,* 5th ed. (Florence: Vallecchi, 1940); Donald Heiney, *America in Italian Literature* (New Brunswick, N.J.: Rutgers University Press, 1964); Giorgio Luzi, "Cecchi critico," in *Letteratura italiana: i critici* (Milan: Marzorati, 1969), III, 2363–95; Giuliana Scudder, ed., *Bibliografia degli scritti di Emilio Cecchi* (Rome: Edizioni di storia e letteratura, 1970).

CELLINI, BENVENUTO (1500–1571), sculptor, goldsmith, and autobiographer. Cellini is remembered as much for the history of his life as for his artistic works because of its dramatic force and its panoramic account of the manners and morals of rulers and their subjects in the turbulent sixteenth century. Cellini the writer captures the essence of his characters with the bold strokes of his pen, but it is his personality alone that we see in all its dimensions. Much, but certainly not the most memorable, material found in these pages is corroborated in contemporary accounts. The first nineteen and the last twenty-six years of Cellini's life were spent largely in his native Florence. In 1519, he went to Rome, where he served Popes Clement VII and Paul III from 1523 until 1540 (except for visits to Florence and elsewhere, and a disappointing trip to France). Paul III imprisoned Cellini for a time, providing Cellini with an unforgettable episode for his narrative. During the years 1540–45, he remained in France to work for King Francis. Despite his wide travels in search of patronage, and his continued conflicts with the leaders of Florence, his allegiance to his native city never waned. He died there in 1571 and was buried with honors in the church of the Annunziata.

At the age of fifty-eight, Cellini decided to compose his *Vita (Autobiography).* The genesis of this remarkable work was not mere egotism; rather, it sprang from a long and venerable literary tradition, which portrayed the lives of great men in fiction as well as in biography and autobiography. Cellini draws on models as diverse as Plutarch's *Lives,* St. Augustine's *Confessions,* the lives of the saints, pilgrimage stories, and journey-narratives such as Homer's *Odyssey* and Dante's* *Divine Comedy.* Moreover, his *Vita* reflects the impact of the *novella** tradition inaugurated by Boccaccio's* *Decameron* and has a picaresque structure. Cellini adds another dimension to the traditional literary hero, transforming him into an artist of whom Cellini is the preeminent example. The events of his birth foreshadow his special qualities and abilities. With a lineage going back to the foundation of Florence by the Romans, Cellini is named Benvenuto (the "welcome" one) because of his parents' joy at his birth. This auspicious birth, marked by the appearances of the magic scorpion and salamander, opens his tale, the salient feature of which is his intertwining of the rather humble details of everyday life with the climactic turns of events which pit Cellini, the man of *virtù,* against malignant *fortuna.* The conflict of special excellence and fortune, so crucial in the writings of Alberti,* Castiglione,* Guicciardini,* or Machiavelli,* is reconciled in a most original manner by Cellini, who claims that his faith in God provides him the freedom of will necessary to face *fortuna* without being completely determined by her fickle force.

Cellini's autobiography is divided into two parts, recalling Augustine's *Confessions* and the biographies and saints' lives from which Cellini freely borrows. The first part tells of his life prior to his imprisonment by Pope Paul III—his early education and the siege of the Castel Sant'Angelo by Protestant troops during which Cellini displays his heroic prowess—and finally of the trials of that imprisonment, his attempted escape, and religious conversion. The second portion leads Cellini from his conversion through his greatest artistic triumphs, the casting of the *Perseus* in particular, and shows forth the fulfillment of his artistic vocation. The autobiography ends abruptly in 1562, although Cellini continued to live and work for some years afterwards. The manuscript, which was not published until 1728, is written both in Cellini's own hand and in that of a scribe. Had Cellini continued his story past 1562, he would have been forced to discuss a number of misfortunes, such as illness and financial difficulties, which befell him in his old age. Perhaps Cellini permits the narrative to trail off because its central purpose was to thank God and to display his inordinate excellence as a man and an artist.

Cellini's autobiography depicts a genius in conflict with envious rivals, ignorant patrons, and interfering contemporaries. He never found a patron who completely satisfied him, including Pope Clement VII, Pope Paul III, Cosimo I, the grand duke of Tuscany, and King Francis I of France. However, Cellini obviously agreed with one pontiff's remark that men of his talents were above the law and with Francis's judgment that his works surpassed even those of the ancients. Thus, Cellini's autobiography also becomes a narrative describing the triumph of art over life. Its most dramatic moment is that recounting the casting of the *Perseus* in 1557, which now stands in the Loggia dei Lanzi in the Piazza della Signoria of Florence. Besides this most famous bronze, Cellini produced a restoration of an ancient Ganymede; busts of Cosimo I and Bindo Altoviti; the Nymph of Fontainebleau; and a white marble Christ on a black crucifix. In addition, he created manifold medals, vases, dies for mints, candlesticks, and ornaments and jewelry of great beauty, most of which is now lost, with the exception of the spectacular saltcellar he made for Francis now in the Kunsthistorisches Museum of Vienna. His work was characterized by its intricate ornamentation, originality, and its movement and skill; much of its execution is traced in the autobiography.

The *Vita* circulated in manuscript before its publication in 1728, but its literary impact can be traced only from the eighteenth century. Quickly becoming one of the most widely read Italian narratives, it was translated by Goethe (1796) and John Addington Symonds (1888) and made into an opera by Berlioz (1838). Its appearance coincided with a revival of interest in the Italian Renaissance* in Europe. Historians such as Jacob Burckhardt were to see in Cellini's egocentrism and genius both the secret of the greatness and the seeds of the destruction of that brilliant civilization in which Cellini seemed so much at ease. Unlike the modern artist, who is so often alienated from his society and even his public, Cellini emerges from his narrative as the master of any situation. His consummate skill as a storyteller, who moves with ease from the comic to the tragic and displays an ingenious sense of plot and character, language, and suspense, is without parallel in all of sixteenth-century Italian Renaissance fiction. Of less importance to the course of Italian literature, but still of value to art historians, are his treatises on the arts of sculpture and goldsmithing.

Bibliography: Autobiography, trans. George Bull (Baltimore: Penguin, 1956); *The Treatises of Benvenuto Cellini on Goldsmithing and Sculpture,* trans. C. R. Ashbee (New York: Dover, 1967); Jonathan Goldberg, "Cellini's *Vita* and the Conventions of Early Autobiography," *Modern Languages Notes* 89 (1974), 71–83; T. C. Price Zimmermann, "Confession and Autobiography in the Early Renaissance," pp. 121–40, in *Renaissance Studies in Honor of Hans Baron,* eds. Anthony Molho and John A. Tedeschi (Florence: Sansoni, 1971).

CESAROTTI, MELCHIORRE (1730–1808), poet, translator, and scholar. Born in Padua, where he completed his schooling in a seminary and became a teacher of rhetoric, Cesarotti obtained a post in 1768 at the University of Padua teaching Greek and Hebrew. In 1779, he became the secretary to the Venetian Academy of Science, Letters, and Arts, after having joined the Accademia dell'Arcadia* two years earlier with the academic name of Meronte Larisseo.

Cesarotti became the most influential translator of his day. Besides the *Prometheus* by Aeschylus, the poetry of Juvenal, the speeches of Demosthenes, and a partial version of Homer's *Iliad* (1795), Cesarotti translated some works of Voltaire and two immensely influential English poems which affected the course of Italian pre-romantic and romantic verse—

Thomas Gray's "Elegy" (which would also influence Foscolo's* *Dei sepolcri, On Sepulchres*) and James Macpherson's *Ossian*. Extremely popular throughout Italy and Europe, this last work (the translation of which Cesarotti completed by 1772) revived interest in the poetry of nature and in a romanticized view of Europe's medieval past. In 1797, Napoleon granted Cesarotti a pension for his translation of the poems of Ossian, the emperor's favorite poet. In all of Cesarotti's translations, his aim was never simply to render the older text, but, rather, to make it come alive under the impact of a modern sensibility. This involved, his critics felt, a willingness to take too many liberties with his originals.

Cesarotti's major prose work is his *Saggio sulla filosofia delle lingue* (1785, Essay on the Philosophy of Languages) in which he argued that the Italian language was formed by the gradual corruption of classical Latin under the influence of barbarian tongues rather than by a growth from a spoken, idiomatic Latin. He rejected any concept of linguistic purism such as that advocated by the Accademia della Crusca. Cesarotti saw no possibility of maintaining a static, changeless language, because language was the interpreter of thought and could not obey academic rules. He believed that a new word or a foreign word had the right to exist in Italian when it responded to a new reality. Thus, in both his translations and his theoretical treatise on language, Cesarotti worked to break away from the constraints of classicism and to enable Italian poetry and language to embrace new romantic concepts of language and literary style.

See also QUESTIONE DELLA LINGUA; ROMANTICISM.

Bibliography: Opere scelte di Melchiorre Cesarotti, ed. Giuseppe Ortolani, 2 vols. (Florence: Le Monnier, 1945–46); Giulio Marzot, *Il gran Cesarotti* (Florence: La Nuova Italia, 1949); Paul Van Tieghem, *Ossian et l'ossianisme dans la littérature européene au XVIIIᵉ siècle* (Groningen: Wolter, 1920).

CHIABRERA, GABRIELLO (1552–1638), lyric poet. Chiabrera was born in Savona and educated at a Jesuit college after his father's death. He entered the service of Cardinal Cornaro in 1572 and lived in Rome until 1581, when he was forced to flee the city after killing a man in a duel. After that time, he spent most of his life in his native Savona, although he enjoyed the patronage and friendship of many Italian rulers, including three grand dukes of Tuscany, the prince of Savoy, Vincenzo Gonzaga, and Pope Urban VIII. He was considered one of Italy's greatest poets during the Baroque* period, surpassed in fame only by Giambattista Marino,* but as critical fashion shifted and the period style fell into disrepute, his reputation, too, waned.

Chiabrera composed a host of lyric poems, sonnets,* odes, satires, and other literary works, including a brief autobiography. Beginning his literary career as a young man when Torquato Tasso* was Italy's most important poèt, Chiabrera wrote several epic* poems, dedicated to various heads of state. His drama *Il rapimento di Cefalo* (1600, The Abduction of Cephalus) was performed in Florence at the marriage of Maria de' Medici and Henri IV, king of France, accompanied by the music of Giulio Caccini. Chiabrera's best poems include thirty Horatian satires, the *Sermoni* (Sermons), published in a complete edition only in 1718. His lyric poetry appeared in numerous collections that enjoyed many editions and was most original when it reflected the vogue of Anacreontic verse for which Chiabrera found models both in earlier Italian poets and in the French Pléiade (particularly the works of Ronsard and Belleau). Another lyric form he employed with great success was the Pindaric ode, with which he sang the praises of most of the notable figures of his day, embellishing their lives or deeds with mythological imagery and themes. He popularized the *canzonetta* form, a poem often set to music and written in several brief stanzas with short lines (often four to nine syllables instead of the more conventional combination of seven and eleven syllables). Perhaps the best known of these poems are "La violetta/ Che in su l' erbetta" ("The violet/ which opens at/ dawn on the tender grass") and "Belle rose porporine" ("Purple roses, not on bitter/ thorns you glitter"). Besides experimenting with various lyric genres of classical derivation, Chiabrera also wrote verse which shifted the traditional stress upon the next-to-last syllable in the line to other positions, foreshadowing the metric experiments of Carducci* in the nineteenth century. Although Italian critics often contrasted Chiabrera with Marino, both their works reflect the general Baroque period style but retain their own individual flavor.

See also BAROQUE; MARINO, Giambattista.

Bibliogràphy: Opere, ed. Marcello Turchi (Turin: UTET, 1973); *From Marino to Marinetti,* trans. Joseph Tusiani (New York: Baroque Press, 1974); Giovanni Getto, *Barocco in prosa e in poesia* (Milan: Rizzoli, 1969); Francesco L. Mannucci, *La lirica di Gabriello Chiabrera: storia e caratteri* (Naples: Perrella, 1925); Ferdinando Neri, *Il Chiabrera e la Pléiade francese* (Turin: Bocca, 1920).

CHIARELLI, LUIGI (1880–1947), playwright. Born in Trani, Chiarelli was unable to study at a university because of his father's early death. However, he frequented literary circles while beginning a career in journalism. His connections to the theatrical world bore fruit when his first important play, *La maschera e il volto (The Mask and the Face),* was first performed in 1916. The work was an immediate success, not only in Italy but all over the world, and it inaugurated the rise of the *teatro grottesco** in Italy, a movement identified with the works of Chiarelli, Antonelli,* Rosso di San Secondo,* and the early Pirandello.* Chiarelli then entered into several cooperative ventures with the actor Virgilio Talli, founding a theatrical company called Ars Italica (1918) under Talli's direction. After putting together a second company in 1921 and becoming president of the Italian playwrights' union, Chiarelli continued to write a great number of plays and short stories, film reviews for a Roman daily, and various translations from several languages until his death.

La maschera e il volto, Chiarelli's masterpiece, deals with the discrepancy between the attitudes imposed upon man by society and his true feelings. It has come out in several English translations, including one by W. Somerset Maugham. Luigi Pirandello later exploited more successfully and more profoundly this philosophical and psychological dichotomy symbolized by the metaphor of mask and face. Like Pirandello, Chiarelli is most concerned with the absurd, grotesque dilemmas which arise from the conflict of mask and face. His best work probes the tragicomic consequences of Count Paolo Grazia's public declaration that he would kill his wife Savina if she ever betrayed him and his refusal to do so when he discovers that she has been unfaithful. The clash between his private emotions (the "face") and his public pose (the "mask") results in many grotesque situations. Savina is forced to attend her own funeral, and Paolo is threatened with prison for not really murdering his wife, although he had been freed earlier for pretending to have done so. The ultimate solution in the play is pessimistic: both Savina and Paolo flee society to attain authentic personal freedom.

Many of Chiarelli's plays can be classified as belonging to this grotesque tradition: *La scala di seta* (1917, The Silken Stairs); *Chimere* (1919, Chimeras); *Fuochi d'artificio* (1922, Fireworks); and *Jolly* (1928, Joker). Most of his later work did not, however, attain the popular or critical acclaim that greeted his masterpiece. Chiarelli's work represents a crucial development beyond the more traditional themes of nineteenth-century Italian theatre towards the more philosophical theatre of Pirandello and augurs the technical and scenographic innovations that occurred when contemporary theatre rejected the canons of realism.

See also TEATRO GROTTESCO.

Bibliography: Anthony Dent, ed., *International Modern Plays* (New York: Dutton, 1951)—contains *The Mask and the Face;* Lander MacClintock, *The Age of Pirandello* (Bloomington, Ind.: Indiana University Press, 1951); Michael Vena, "Luigi Chiarelli (1880–1947): Profile of a Playwright," *Connecticut Review* 7 (1974), 59–63.

CIELO D'ALCAMO (thirteenth century), poet. Nothing is known of this poet, famous for his *contrasto* "Rosa fresca aulentissima" ("Most fragrant rose of summer"). He was most probably a minstrel of moderate culture, familiar with the courtly conventions, although he was more closely allied to the popular poetic traditions. Written between 1231 and 1250, his *contrasto* is notable as an example of popular poetry. Its language may have a Sicilian base, a dialect spoken around Messina. Composed of one hundred and sixty lines in stanzas of five lines, it includes three alexandrines with identical rhymes and two hendecasyllabic lines with *rime baciate (aa bb)*. In this dialogue between an overconfident man, perhaps the minstrel, and a sprightly young woman of humbler origins, the author employs the conventions of the traditional *débat* and *pastorella* in a modified and more vigorous manner. It is possible that this was a musical mime meant to be acted out by a pair of minstrels. The would-be lover, self-assured, gallant, impudent, now the knight of the *pastorella,* now that of the love song, displays his virtuosity in the art of love. Pleading with her, he hyperbolizes her beauty, proclaims how much he would endure for her, and describes how he fell in love with her at first sight, in tones ranging from gallant to impudent.

The *villana* or country girl has a witty repartee to his every proclamation: she would shave off her hair before loving him; she is a woman of such worth he could not possibly afford her; she warns him by the conventional threat of her relatives; and finally, she tells him he must ask her parents' permission. When she has him where she wants him, she admits to loving him, and when she demands that he swear on the Bible never to fail her, the poem departs from convention and the knight gives in. Once he has properly pledged his fidelity and she has achieved her goal, she too gives in and suggests that they go upstairs, ending the poem with a wish for good fortune. The whole construction of the scene reveals the poet's skill in characterization, dialogue, and creating suspense; it also shows his sensitivity to human psychology, as he brings the scene to a natural conclusion. In *De vulgari eloquentia* (I, xii, 6), Dante* cites the third line of this poem as an example of "mediocre" style, which today remains a valid judgment of the stylistic level of the work.

Bibliography: Poeti del Duecento, ed. Gianfranco Contini, 2 vols. (Milan: Ricciardi, 1960); *The Age of Dante: An Anthology of Early Italian Poetry,* trans. Joseph Tusiani (New York: Baroque Press, 1974).

CIMINELLI, SERAFINO DE': *See* SERAFINO AQUILANO.

CINO DA PISTOIA (circa 1270–circa 1336), lyric poet and lawyer. Cino was born into a rich Pistoian family of the Black faction as Guittoncino di Francesco dei Sigibuldi. After studying law at the University of Bologna, Cino taught in various Italian cities (Siena, Naples, and Perugia). Taking an active role in the politics of the period, he was forced into exile from Pistoia for three years between 1303 and 1306. Like Dante* an ardent supporter of Henry VII and the imperial cause, Cino established himself as a legal scholar with his *Lectura in codicem* (1314, Readings in the Codex), a commentary of fundamental importance upon the first nine books of the *Codex* of Justinian. In 1324, he was granted honorary citizenship by the city of Florence. He died in Pistoia and was buried in a magnificent and still visible tomb in the city cathedral.

Cino's reputation today rests not upon his legal scholarship but upon his poetry. His role as an intermediary between Dante and the *stilnovisti,* on the one hand, and Petrarch,* on the other, has always been emphasized by his critics. A personal friend of both Dante and Petrarch, Cino was praised by Dante in several places in the *De vulgari eloquentia* (I, x, 4; I, xiii, 3; I, xvii, 3; II, v, 4; II, vi, 6) for the musicality of his verse, produced by his frequent use of enjambement, and for his rhetorical skill in a number of poetic forms, the *canzone** in particular. Moreover, Cino and Dante exchanged several sonnets* on various topics, and Cino wrote a song to Dante to console him for the death of Beatrice—"Avvenga ch'io non aggia più per tempo" ("Even if I had not until this day"). Perhaps most famous are the poems which treat the death of his own lady, Selvaggia, such as "Io fui 'n su l'alto e 'n sul beato monte" ("I was on the high and blessed mountain"), or "La dolce vista e 'l bel guardo soave" ("The soothing sight and the most lovely gleam"). The last poem is recalled by Petrarch who pays tribute to his literary predecessors in a famous *canzone* (LXX), four stanzas of which contain concluding lines from his favorite poets (Arnaut Daniel, Dante, Cavalcanti,* and Cino). Beyond the similarities of style and theme, further evidence of Petrarch's esteem for Cino's verse is found in another sonnet (XCII), which Petrarch composed at the time of Cino's death.

See also DOLCE STIL NUOVO.

Bibliography: Poeti del dolce stil nuovo, ed. Mario Marti (Florence: Le Monnier, 1969); *The Age of Dante: An Anthology of Early Italian Poetry,* trans. Joseph Tusiani (New York: Baroque Press, 1974); *German and Italian Lyrics of the Middle Ages,* trans. Frederick Goldin (New York: Doubleday, 1973); Maria Corti, "Il linguaggio poetico di Cino da Pistoia," *Cultura Neolatina* 12 (1952), 185–223; Domenico De Robertis, "Cino e le 'imitazioni' dalle rime di Dante," *Studi danteschi* 29 (1950), 103–77.

CINZIO: *See* GIRALDI, GIAMBATTISTA.

COLLODI, CARLO: *See* LORENZINI, CARLO.

COLONNA, FRANCESCO (1433–1527), prose writer. Colonna was a Dominican monk from the region of Venice, and is traditionally considered the author of the *Hypnerotomachia Poliphili* (1499, *The Strife of Love in a Dreame*). This extraordinary romance whose first edition was brought out by the Aldine Press contains approximately two hundred woodcuts and is one of the most magnificently illustrated books of the Renaissance* as well as one of the first to display hieroglyphics. The work is divided into two books, the first of which relates a dream-journey of Poliphilus. Included in its often obscure and sometimes confusing narrative are many detailed descriptions of imaginary structures, buildings, and statues from classical antiquity. This interest in architecture demonstrates the author's knowledge of Vitruvius and, perhaps, the works of Leon Battista Alberti.* It also parallels that awakening of interest in the ruins of classical antiquity which characterizes Italian humanism.* A further reflection of this humanist revival lies in the work's elaborate triumphs, a poetic theme popularized by *The Triumphs* of Petrarch.* The book had considerable impact upon European culture, influencing Dürer, Rabelais, and numerous poets of Elizabethan England, where it was partially translated in 1592.

Bibliography: Hypnerotomachia: The Strife of Love in a Dreame (1592), trans. Sir Robert Dallington, ed. Lucy Gent (Delmar, N.Y.: Scholars' Facsimiles, 1973); Linda Fierz-David, *The Dream of Poliphilo,* foreword by C. G. Jung (New York: Pantheon, 1950); M. T. Casella and G. Pozzi, *Francesco Colonna: biografia e opere,* 2 vols. (Padua: Editrice Antenore, 1959).

COLONNA, VITTORIA (1492–1547), poet and noblewoman. The daughter of Fabrizio Colonna and Agnese di Montefeltro of Urbino, Vittoria was the product of the union of two of Italy's most illustrious families. For political reasons, she was betrothed at the age of four to Fernando Francesco d'Avalos, the marquis of Pescara, and married him on the island of Ischia at the age of nineteen. This marriage of convenience developed into a marriage of love. When her husband died in 1525, Colonna devoted the rest of her life to works of charity and literary pursuits, spending most of her time in various convents before returning to live in Rome where she died.

Colonna was disturbed by corruption in the church and was acquainted with reformers like Cardinal Pole and Jacopo Sadoleto. Her friendships and correspondents included Pietro Aretino,* Pietro Bembo,* Jacopo Sannazaro,* Bernardo Tasso,* Baldesar Castiglione,* and, most importantly, Michelangelo.* Her relationship with Michelangelo inspired some of that artist's finest poetry. Her major literary work is her *Canzoniere* (1544, Songbook), a collection of lyric poems (mostly sonnets* but also including *canzoni** and *capitoli** in *terza rima**). The first section of the collection was devoted to the memory of her husband, and the second to religious and moral themes. Colonna followed the precepts of Pietro Bembo in her adherence to a classical Petrarchan style.

See also BEMBO, Pietro; BUONARROTI, Michelangelo; PETRARCHISM.

Bibliography: Italian Poets of the Renaissance, trans. Joseph Tusiani (Long Island City, N.Y.: Baroque Press, 1971); Maud F. Jerrold, *Vittoria Colonna* (Freeport: Books for Libraries Reprint, 1969)—contains many translations; Giorgio Sant-angelo, *Il petrarchismo del Bembo e di altri poeti del '500* (Rome: IECE, 1967)—contains Italian selections; Suzanne Therault, *Un Cénacle humaniste de la Renaissance autour de Vittoria Colonna châtelaine d'Ischia* (Paris: Didier, 1968).

COMMEDIA DELL'ARTE. For over two and a half centuries, the influence of Italian theatrical traditions extended across Europe, from London to St. Petersburg, through the efforts of the professional acting companies that from the middle of the sixteenth century to the close of the eighteenth century performed improvised plays in the style which came to be known as the *commedia dell'arte.* The exact origin of this professional tradition, played by *artisti* who created their own drama on the stage according to a skeletal scenario (the *canovaccio* or *soggetto*), will long remain a cause for scholarly debate. One theory traces the *commedia dell'arte* back to Italy's ancient Atellan farce with its grotesque masked characters like Maccus and Buccus, but there is no evidence for a continuous tradition to Renaissance* times. During the Middle Ages in Italy, performances of sacred dramas featured mimes, jugglers, and tumblers, especially in the role of devils, whose spontaneous buffoonery clearly seems to have anticipated the capers of Harlequins and "Zanni" clowns in the *commedia dell'arte.* Throughout the medieval and Renaissance periods, carnival festivities always included acrobatic dancing and slapstick acting by merrily costumed clowns who wore masks. By the early years of the sixteenth century, professional buffoons were appearing not only in public squares but also at the banquets of the nobility and bourgeoisie. The most famous clown of that era, the Venetian Zuan Polo, used to lead public processions, improvise his own comedies, and dazzle his audiences with witty remarks. These buffoons finally came to take part in the spectacular intermezzos during amateur performances of learned comedies (the *commedia erudita*) before the members of literary academies or noble families that were celebrating a wedding or a birthday. This encounter between cultured amateurs and professional entertainers led to a refinement in the tastes and acting style of the improvisational performers. Having won for themselves both academic recognition and noble patronage, the actors soon felt ready to return to the general public. The guilds evolved into wandering companies like the Gelosi, Desiosi, Confidenti, Uniti, Accesi, and Fedeli, all of whom flourished during the second half of the sixteenth century.

To a great extent, the *commedia dell'arte* resulted from an artistic compromise between a popular desire for spontaneity and an academic demand for classical culture. With their reliance on vivid comic action, visual effects, acrobatics, and often vulgar humor, the improvisational actors achieved success before a varied audience. Through its quest for variation and innovation along with fixed masks and pantomime, this professional theatre could appeal to every class. Although abandoning the artistic straitjacket of performance from a complete text, the actors admitted classical material into the dialogue. For the new class of actors who became prominent during the second half of the sixteenth century as well as throughout the following century no longer consisted primarily of mountebanks, but included cultured members of the nobility like Flaminio Scala (dates uncertain), the troupe director who eventually published a collection of fifty scenarios in 1611. With his knowledge of classical characterization, this actor-director transformed the antics of Zanni clowns into the astute stratagems of the servant figures who appear in learned comedies and are modeled on the wily slaves in the comedies of Plautus and Terence. Comic formulas and character-types that had been tried in the learned plays of writers like Machiavelli* and Ariosto* were repeated again and again by the improvisational actors. Pedantic doctors of law, lovers speaking in Petrarchan language, and strutting but cowardly Spanish captains continued to make up the cast of characters. The employment of different dialects on stage remained a standard device to arouse laughter. Many of the scenarios used by the actors of the *commedia dell'arte* were adapted from learned comedies. In addition to deriving plots from the erudite comedies, the professionals acquired a highly developed sense of dramatic construction. In his desire to set high standards, Scala adhered to the three classical unities of time, place, and action. Academic titles and honors attest to the esteem which Scala and other actors such as the versatile Francesco Andreini (1548–1624) and his wife, the poetess Isabella Andreini (1562–1604), enjoyed among the literati. The actors of the *commedia dell'arte* adapted the material of the learned comedy, enriched it with a new tradition of jests (the *lazzi*), and carried Italy's theatrical art to an international audience.

Perhaps the major aesthetic process at work in creating and continuing the *commedia dell'arte* was one of crystallization. The comic materials of the past—from ancient Roman plays and the medieval and Renaissance *novella** as perfected by Boccaccio—became fixed elements in the new theatrical style which relied on the mask and the marionette. The outer form, the stereotype such as the cuckold or the vain attorney, remained the mask to which the talented actor could impart life by employing his vast knowledge of appropriate dialogue and gesture. Although the *commedia dell'arte* represented a theatre of gesture rather than of written word, linguistic virtuosity (lost to the twentieth-century reader of a scenario) was necessary to awaken and to sustain audience interest. The masks reflected the Baroque* longing to hold a distortion mirror before society, so that audiences of the various regions of Italy could see their own foibles in comic exaggeration—for example, the greedy Venetian merchant Pantalone, the Bergamask Zanni clowns, the Bolognese attorney Dr. Graziano, and the delightfully resourceful Harlequin (Arlecchino) that Lombardy and France have both claimed as their original mask. Also, the masks of the *commedia dell'arte* and the Italian puppet theatre developed on parallel lines, and Burattino (the marionette figure) soon came to have the full company of all the stock characters like Pasquariello, the Neapolitan Scaramuccia, and Pulcinella. Out of the crystallized material of the *canovaccio,* the mask and the marionette, the professional artists fashioned a theatre of wit, comic surprise, and facile humor.

It was to an urban culture that the *commedia dell'arte* appealed. Even when religious prelates condemned the theatre as morally licentious and corrupting, the acting troupes found protectors in civil authorities. By the middle of the eighteenth century, the urban audiences became receptive to a more sophisticated drama than that of the improvisational theatre. The Venetian playwright Carlo Goldoni* worked to reform the theatre by eliminating masks, fully writing out the comedies, and avoiding obscenity. Although Goldoni's rival Carlo Gozzi* attempted to revive the decaying spirit of *commedia dell'arte* in plays like *Il Re Cervo (The King Turned Stag),* the golden age of improvisational masked theatre had passed. Today the *commedia dell'arte* continues to live in the Harlequins and Columbines of carnival masks and children's puppet shows.

See also ARIOSTO, Ludovico; GOLDONI, Carlo; GOZZI, Carlo; MACHIAVELLI, Niccolò.

Bibliography: Adolfo Bartoli, *Scenari inediti della Commedia dell'Arte* (Florence: Sansoni, 1880); *The Classic Theatre,* Vol. I, ed. Eric Bentley (Garden City, N.Y.: Doubleday, 1958); Pierre Louis Duchartre, *The Italian Comedy,* trans. R. T. Weaver (1929; rpt. New York: Dover Books, 1966); Joseph S. Kennard, *Masks and Marionettes* (1935; rpt. Port Washington, N.Y.: Kennikat Press, 1967); Kathleen M. Lea, *Italian Popular Comedy* (1934; rpt. New York: Russell & Russell, 1962); Ferdinando Neri, *Scenari delle Maschere in Arcadia* (1913; rpt. Turin: Erasmo, 1961); Allardyce Nicoll, *The World of Harlequin, A Critical Study of the Commedia dell'Arte* (Cambridge: Cambridge University Press, 1963); Giacomo Oreglia, *The Commedia dell'Arte,* trans. Lovett F. Edwards (New York: Hill & Wang, 1968); Vito Pandolfi, *La Commedia dell'Arte: storia e testo,* 3 vols. (Florence: Sansoni, 1957–61); Pamela Robertson, *The Commedia dell'Arte* (Natal: University Press, 1960); Winifred Smith, *The Commedia dell'Arte* (1912; rpt. New York: Blom, 1964); Ferdinando Taviani, *La Commedia dell'Arte e la Società Barocca,* Vol. I, *La Fascinazione del Teatro* (Bulzoni; Rome, 1969).

Douglas Radcliff-Umstead

COMPAGNI, DINO (circa 1255–1324), Florentine historian and poet. Compagni came from a noble and powerful Guelph family and was a key member of the silk guild. In his time, Compagni was considered a good poet, and his contemporaries occasionally compared his lyrics to those of Guinizzelli,* Guittone,* and Cavalcanti.* The anonymous didactic poem *Intelligenza* (Lady Intelligence) is sometimes attributed to him.

Compagni held a number of important civic positions, including that of *gonfaloniere* (standardbearer) of justice and prior. With the defeat in 1301 of the White faction to which he and Dante Alighieri* belonged, Compagni was forced to abandon his governmental post. Although he was permitted to remain in Florence, he was excluded from further participation in public affairs. With the entrance of Emperor Henry VII into Italy (1310–12), the fortunes of Compagni's faction seemed to be on the rise again, and it was at this time that he composed his major historical work, the *Cronica delle cose occorrenti ne' tempi suoi (Chronicle of Events Occurring in His Times)*. Unlike some medieval narratives which began with the biblical origins of humanity, Compagni's work employed a narrower scope, one closer to that of a modern monograph, and focused upon the civil discord in Florence from the time of the formation of the Guelph and Ghibelline factions. Part one deals with the arrival of Charles of Valois in Florence, sent by Pope Boniface VIII to make peace; part two describes the victory of the Black faction over the Whites; and the final section treats Henry VII's descent into Italy. Thus, the first part tells of Florentine affairs at a time when the author was directly involved in them, while the concluding pages, characterized by a clearly partisan spirit, reflect the period of his exile from politics. Memorable passages of the history include character sketches of Pope Boniface and of Corso Donati who was a key figure in the internecine conflicts analyzed in the book. After circulating for many years in manuscript, the work was lost; rediscovered by Muratori,* it was published in 1726 in *Rerum italicarum scriptores* (Historians of Italy). Along with the chronicles of Giovanni and Matteo Villani* and other minor historians, Compagni's history testifies to the growing interest in understanding the historical processes at work in Florence at the beginning of the Trecento, which gave rise to a number of historical masterpieces in both Latin and the vernacular over the next two and one half centuries.

See also MURATORI, Ludovico Antonio; VILLANI, Giovanni; VILLANI, Matteo.

Bibliography: Cronica, ed. Gino Luzzatto (Turin: Einaudi, 1968); *Dino Compagni e la sua Cronica,* ed. Isodoro Del Lungo, 3 vols. (Florence: Le Monnier, 1879–87) —includes Compagni's poetry; *The Chronicle,* trans. Else Benecke and A. G. Ferrers Howell (London: Dent, 1906); Giovanni Pirodda, "Per una lettura della Cronica di Dino Compagni," *Filologia e letteratura* 13 (1967), 337–93.

COMPIUTA DONZELLA, LA (early thirteenth-century), Florentine poetess. Nothing is known of the life of this poetess. Although her actual existence was long doubted, it does not seem reasonable to distrust the manuscript in which the compositions have been preserved. Two sonnets* of Maestro Torrigiano of Florence ("Esser donzella di trovare dotta," or To be a lady skilled in poetry, and "S'una donzella di trovar s'ingegna," or If a lady tries to rhyme) seem to be addressed to her, as was possibly a passage in a letter of Guittone.* It is not known if Compiuta is her real name or a *senhal* (pen name) to indicate her accomplishments and her perfection.

Only three sonnets remain of the work of the first woman known to have written poetry in Italian. Her poems exhibit certain motifs and stylistic devices common to Provençal poetry. However, her womanly concerns lend freshness to the old motifs. She expresses a desire to avoid the world and all its disillusionments in order better to serve God ("Lasciar voria lo mondo e Dio servire," "I wish to leave the world and serve but God"). In "A la stagion che il mondo foglia e fiora" ("The season when the world is leaves and flowers"), the image of a joyous spring is contrasted with the sadness of a young woman who is being forced into a marriage against her wishes.

Bibliography: Gianfranco Contini, ed., *Poeti del Duecento,* 2 vols. (Milan: Ricciardi, 1960); *The Age of Dante: An Anthology of Early Italian Poetry,* trans. Joseph Tusiani (New York: Baroque Press, 1974).

CORAZZINI, SERGIO (1886–1907), Roman lyric poet. Forced to abandon his studies after his family suffered economic setbacks, Corazzini worked for an insurance company in Rome and passed his evenings in the literary cafes of the city. Born into a family haunted by the fear of tuberculosis, Corazzini was destined to die prematurely from this illness and thus had good reason to express the melancholy and morbid sentiments that the critic Giuseppe Antonio Borgese* associated with him and his fellow *crepuscolari* or "twilight poets" in 1910. The tone of his first collection of verse, which appeared in 1904, was bitter and somber, and its major theme, sorrow and death. In the following year, Corazzini met Govoni* and Palazzeschi* and published two new collections, *L'amaro calice* (The Bitter Cup) and *Le aureole* (The Halos), characterized by an even darker mood, which was possibly a reflection of the progression of his illness. Typical is "Sonetto" ("Sonnet"), a poem in which the poet declares: "I should like to die of melancholy." Leaving Rome in 1906 for Nocera and a sanitarium, Corazzini still managed to publish *Piccolo libro inutile* (1906, Useless Little Book), which contains his best known works, including "Desolazione del povero poeta sentimentale" ("Desolation of the Poor Sentimental Poet"). Showing the obvious debt to Pascoli's* poetics typical of much *crepuscolari* verse, this famous lyric is obsessed with the idea of death as the poet's final destiny: "I want to die, simply because I am tired"; "All I know, dear God, is how to die." Corazzini passed away the following year; his last and one of his most beautiful poems, "La morte di Tantalo" (The Death of Tantalus), appeared posthumously. His demise came as a shock to his circle of friends, several of whom—including Fausto Maria Martini (1886–1931) and Alberto Tarchiani (1885–1964), later ambassador to the United States—abandoned Italy afterwards to seek solace in foreign adventure. Corazzini's circle is portrayed in Martini's novel *Si sbarca a New York* (1930, New York Landing).

See also GOZZANO, Guido; PASCOLI, Giovanni.

Bibliography: Poesie edite e inedite, ed. Stefano Jacomuzzi (Turin: Einaudi, 1968); *Contemporary Italian Poetry,* ed. Carlo L. Golino (Berkeley, Calif.: University of California Press, 1962); Luciano Anceschi, *Le poetiche del Novecento in Italia* (Turin: Paravia, 1973); Stefano Jacomuzzi, *Sergio Corazzini* (Milan: Mursia, 1963); Edoardo Sanguineti, *Tra Liberty e crepuscolarismo* (Milan: Mursia, 1970); Aldo Vallone, *I crepuscolari* (Palermo: Palumbo, 1970).

COSSA, PIETRO (1830–1881), playwright. Cossa was born in Rome and was raised by an uncle. His anticlerical and liberal views precipitated his arrest by the papal police, and he was forced to emigrate to South America. There he lived as a singer before returning to Italy, where he supported himself by teaching and eventually by his successful dramatic works.

Cossa represents a moment of transition from Italian romanticism* to *verismo** or naturalism on the stage. Although most of his plays are in verse, the majority of them deal with themes from classical or Italian history, with the lives of romantic writers, or with authors esteemed by the romantic movement. Cossa's plays combine what is very often a neo-classical subject matter with an adherence to the canons of naturalism as applied to drama. In the prologue to his most important play *Nerone* (1872, Nero), Cossa states that he accepts the "laws" of *verismo* and that he has banished from the stage any verse which contains only sound and no ideas; truth alone is beautiful in dramatic art. Other works include *Messalina* (1877, Messalina), *Cleopatra* (1876, Cleopatra), *Cola di Rienzo* (1879, Cola di Rienzo), *Sordello* (1872, Sordello), *Beethoven* (1872, Beethoven), and *I Borgia* (1881, The Borgias). More often than not, Cossa's realism degenerates into a mere transformation of traditional tragic characters into bourgeois figures. Nonetheless, all of his plays reflect his attempt to combine historical topics with realistic dialogue and the generic elements of both comedy and tragedy to produce a new kind of naturalistic theatre.

Bibliography: Eligio Possenti, ed., *Teatro italiano,* Vol. 4 (Milan: Nuova Accademia, 1962).

CREPUSCOLARI POETS ("Twilight poets"): *See* BORGESE, Giuseppe Antonio; CORAZZINI, Sergio; GOZZANO, Guido; MORETTI, Marino; PALAZZESCHI, Aldo.

CROCE, BENEDETTO (1866–1952), philosopher, historian, literary critic, editor, and statesman. Croce was born in Pescasseroli (L'Aquila) into a well-to-do family of landowners and he spent almost his entire life in Naples, where he died. He lost his parents and sister in the earthquake of Casamicciola (1883) and from that experience bore lasting physical and emotional scars. By nature an autodidact, Croce often found his teachers in past generations and among his contemporaries, including Carducci* and De Sanctis,* Vico* and Hegel, Labriola and Gentile.* With these men he established a critical dialogue in the best tradition of European humanism. Better than any other twentieth-century European scholar, Croce himself came to fulfill a similar role for successive generations.

Croce spent two years in Rome (1884–85) as the guest of his uncle, Silvio Spaventa. (For Croce's own description of this early period, see *Contributo alla critica di me stesso, An Autobiography,* 1915). There he met Antonio Labriola (1843–1904), who introduced him to Herbart's philosophy, to problems of morality and art, and in 1895 to Marxism. Back in Naples (1886), Croce plunged into the erudite research of regional history. He visited several European countries and built up a rich library. By 1892, having come to feel suffocated under the weight of erudition, Croce was seeking a new direction to his spiritual quest. Two essays, *La storia ridotta sotto il concetto dell'arte* (1893, *History Brought Under the General Concept of Art)* and *La critica letteraria* (1894, *Literary Criticism),* mark his first decisive steps away from the then dominant positivistic school. Croce's polemics would never cease, not even with the demise of positivism, which reappeared under new names. From 1895 to 1900, Croce conducted a systematic critique of Marxism and concluded by restricting its value to that of a historiographic canon (1900, *Materialismo storico ed economica marxistica, Historical Marxism and the Economics of Karl Marx).* His position towards Marxist doctrine became increasingly negative. Over and over he denounced the propagandistic methods and the systematic falsifications of truth by its leaders (1966, *Essays on Marx and Russia).* From his study of Marx, Croce derived the category of the "useful" and the incentive to study Hegel and Vico, as a result of which he was able to tackle more strictly philosophical problems.

In 1900, Croce published a first sketch of his aesthetic theory, elaborated into *Estetica come scienza dell'espressione e linguistica generale* (1902, *Aesthetic as Science of Expression and General Linguistic),* one of the most important books on art published in this century. He had met Gentile (1895), with whom he had a close intellectual relationship until 1925. They collaborated on the review *La critica* (published 1903–44 without interruption, and succeeded by the *Quaderni della critica,* 1945–51) and on numerous other cultural projects.

In 1904, Croce began his editorial association with G. Laterza of Bari, editing, besides his own works, a series of publications which was to play a decisive role in the formation of contemporary Italian culture: "Scrittori d' Italia" (Writers of Italy), "I classici della filosofia" (The Classics of Philosophy), and "Biblioteca di cultura moderna" (The Library of Modern Culture). In 1905, he published the first sketch of *Logica come scienza del concetto puro (Logic as Science of the Pure Concept),* and in 1907, a section of *Filosofia della practica, economia ed etica (Philosophy of the Practical),* both published in their final form in 1909. The role of intellectual leader which Croce assumed demanded not only a total moral commitment but also continuous revisions and the updating of his own thought, as well as the systematic critique of the philosophy of his idealist teachers: Hegel's idealism (1907, *Ciò che è vivo e ciò che è morto nella filosofia di Hegel, What Is Living and What Is Dead in the Philosophy of Hegel*) and Vico's historicism (1911, *La filosofia di Giambattista Vico, The Philosophy of Giambattista Vico*). From then on, Croce's publications multiplied very rapidly.

Appointed senator for life in 1910, he participated intensely in the political life of his country and served as minister of education in 1920–21. During the Fascist regime, he became the living symbol in Italy of intellectual honesty and moral integrity, the stoic defender of truth and liberty. His courageous denunciation of the fascist dictatorship had a profound effect on many young intellectuals. He spoke against racism, academic formalism, historiography devoid of moral or political commitment, sterile criticism, and decadent literature. With the end of fascism, Croce assumed an active political role. He was a member of the first democratic government in 1944, deputy to the Constituent Assembly (1946), and president of the Liberal party until 1947. In that year, at the age of eighty, he opened in his home a postgraduate school of historical studies, the "Istituto italiano di studi storici," which is still very much alive today.

Croce's "Philosophy of the Spirit" is both antimetaphysical and antimaterialistic. For him reality is Spirit, history in its becoming. The activity of the Spirit takes four distinct forms, two theoretical and two practical: intuition, or knowledge of the particular (art); logic, or knowledge of the universal; the economic (vitality), or the volition of the particular; and ethics, or the volition of the universal. Correcting and integrating Hegel's idealism (for the dialect of opposites, he substituted the dialectic of distinct ethics) and Vico's historicism, Croce arrived at the dynamic identity of history and philosophy and formulated a logic of the concrete universal in contrast to the formalistic logic of the abstract, distinguishing the pure concepts from the pseudoconcepts (scientific, empirical knowledge). Philosophy by its very nature is not eternal, he stated, but nondefinitive, always open to new problems. In *Storia come pensiero e come azione* (1938, *History as the Story of Liberty*), he suggested a revision of the tetradic conception of the Spirit through a redefinition of the form of vitality as a category *sui generis,* an absolute principle present in every form.

According to Croce, aesthetic activity is distinct, yet not separate from the other forms of the Spirit, on account of its unity and circularity. At the auroral level of the cognitive sphere, art is not a logical, moral, or utilitarian act, nor is it a physical fact. It is pure image, intuition-expression, self-sufficient and autonomous; it does not progress, it cannot be translated, compared, classified, or grouped according to extrinsic criteria into schools of historical movements. There can be no history of poetry, only of literature, because no relationship of cause and effect (sources and influences) exists among works of art. He sees the theory of literary genres as well as the subdivision of the arts as empirical classifications with no philosophical basis, because all forms of art have the same source and are differentiated only by the means with which they are materialized. In his 1908 Heidelberg lecture, Croce enucleated the lyrical nature of artistic expression and redefined art as a priori synthesis of image and feeling, of form and content (1913, *Breviario di estetica, The Essence of Aesthetic*). In later studies, he theorized the cosmic nature of lyrical intuition and its character of totality and eternity (1920, *Nuovi saggi di estetica,* New Essays on Aesthetics); art as creation and doing, and the necessity of a moral personality at its foundation (*Aesthetica in nuce,* "Aesthetics," in *Encyclopaedia Britannica,* 14th ed., 1929); and the pseudo-antithesis between classical and romantic art, folk poetry and poets' poetry, the difference between poetry and literature (1936, *La poesia,* Poetry).

For Croce, literary criticism meant to distinguish the pure artistic creation from the spurious nonaesthetic products, and to characterize and judge it. He viewed the critic not as an *artifex additus artefici,* but as a *philosophus additus artefici.* As a literary critic, Croce, better than any other European scholar of his time, attained a vastness of scope and universality of interest, examining literature from the ancient Greek to the contemporary (1941, *Poesia antica e moderna,* Poetry Ancient and Modern), from the great poets of European literature (Dante,* Ariosto,* Shakespeare, Corneille, Goethe) to representatives of specific historical periods (1923, *Poesia e non poesia, European Literature in the Nineteenth Century*), or conducting studies in depth of entire literary epochs: *Poeti e scrittori del pieno e del tardo Rinascimento* (1945–52, Poets and Writers of the High and Late Renaissance, 3 vols.), *La letteratura della nuova Italia,* 6 vols. (1914–40, Literature of Modern Italy). Crocean criticism, though not always acceptable today, always broke new ground, suscitated lively polemics, and rectified erroneous preconcepts, giving new impetus and new direction to the solution of literary problems.

In the field of historiography (1917, *Teoria e storia della storiografia, History: Its Theory and Practice*), Croce's contribution has been no less significant. His concepts of the contemporaneity of history and its essentially ethicopolitical nature, and his distinction between history and chronicle, are positive theoretical conquests. Like literary criticism, historiography demands the total commitment of the historian in whose works philosophy and history are united. From a precise historical perspective, Croce wrote *Storia d'Italia dal 1871 al 1915* (1928, *A History of Italy, 1871–1915*) and *Storia d'Europa nel secolo decimonono* (1932, *History of Europe in the Nineteenth Century*), a passionate evocation of a great era of European and Italian liberalism, in contrast with the fascist dictatorship that followed. Examining other periods, in *Storia del regno di Napoli* (1925, *History of the Kingdom of Naples*), *Storia dell'età barocca in Italia* (1929, History of the Baroque Age in Italy), or in various biographical studies, Croce brought to life the ethicopolitical drama of the past in its present relevancy: history, rather than the execution of the past, is its justification. Croce's Absolute Historicism is one of the most comprehensive syntheses in modern thought, and his answers to problems of art, criticism, and history remain substantially valid today.

Bibliography: Aesthetic as Science of Expression and General Linguistic, trans. Douglas Ainslie (rev. ed. 1922; rpt. New York: Noonday, 1965); "Aesthetics," *Encyclopaedia Britannica*, 14th ed., 1929; *History of Europe in the Nineteenth Century* (New York: Harcourt, 1933); *Philosophy-Poetry-History: An Anthology of Essays*, trans. Cecil Sprigge (London: Oxford University Press, 1965); Silvano Borsari, *L'opera di Benedetto Croce* (Naples: Nella Sede dell'Istituto, 1964); Aloysius R. Caponigri, *History and Liberty: The Historical Writings of B. Croce* (London: Routledge & Kegan Paul, 1955); Gian N. G. Orsini, *Benedetto Croce: Philosopher of Art and Literary Critic* (Carbondale, Ill.: Southern Illinois University Press, 1961); Raffaello Piccoli, *Benedetto Croce* (London: Jonathan Cape, 1922); William K. Wimsatt, Jr. and Cleanth Brooks, *Literary Criticism: A Short History* (New York: Knopf, 1957).

Ernesto G. Caserta

CROCE, GIULIO CESARE (1550–1609), Bolognese poet and *cantastorie* (professional storyteller). The son of a blacksmith, Croce was destined by his father for higher education. After his father's premature death in 1557, he was raised by a paternal uncle but seemed to fare poorly in school. Around 1563, his foster family moved to Medicina where Croce remained until 1568, practicing the art of poet and *cantastorie* among the noble families of Bologna who lived there during the summers. In 1568, he moved to Bologna and supported himself as a blacksmith while he composed dialect verse. By 1575, Croce had married. Shortly thereafter, he abandoned his trade to devote all of his time to poetry, a decision which resulted in great economic deprivation. His poverty was increased by the fact that during the course of his life, he had fourteen children by two wives. Upon his death, Croce left over three hundred works of various lengths, many of which remain unedited in the archives of the University of Bologna.

Croce's literary works belong to the Bolognese branch of Italy's popular literature, better known outside of the country through such writers as the Florentine poets Berni* or Pulci,* the Roman dialect poet Belli,* and the Sienese writer Cecco Angiolieri.* Croce is best remembered for a comic work entitled *Bertoldo e Bertoldino* (1608, Bertoldo and Bertoldino), the tale of a crafty peasant named Bertoldo whose arguments, often set in dialogue form, refute the views of his king and whose conversations are liberally sprinkled with popular proverbs and the folk wisdom of the period. His son Bertoldino, however, is his opposite and a simpleton. Fortunately, his wife Marcolfa resembles her husband and manages to save her son from many of the problems which his lack of intelligence creates. The work became so popular that an abbot from Bologna, Adriano Banchieri (1567–1634), was prompted to continue this same series of adventures by creating a son for Bertoldino named Cacasenno.

Bertoldo, the first part of the book, was inspired by an anonymous medieval Latin work, *Dialogus Salomonis et Marcolphi* (Dialogue Between Solomon and Marcolphus), which treated the proverbial wisdom of King Solomon. It appeared in the late fourteenth century and was translated into Italian (1502) as well as into English, German, and French. The second part, *Bertoldino,* departs from this source and contains an increased number of dialogues based upon popular aphorisms, as well as a number of tales with a moral purpose. Part of its appeal to a popular audience lies in its elevation of the sagacity of the humble, exploited classes above that of their arrogant masters. In fact, Bertoldo dies at court because its way of life and cuisine is antithetical to peasant ways. The work's message seems to be that all social classes have a certain worth and dignity and that the poor are not to be rejected solely because of their economic status. Croce's most typical literary device is that of amplification, one common among poets whose art has a popular, oral basis.

Still another work by Croce has attracted critical attention, one of his several plays in dialect, *La Farinella* (1609, Farinella). This comedy in five acts treats Lelio's love for Ardelia, which is opposed by his father, Messer Zenobio, because of her lack of wealth. Lelio disguises himself as a woman, calls himself Farinella, and joins Ardelia's service, telling her that Lelio has drowned in order to test her love for him. Once he witnesses her sincere sorrow, he reveals his secret. The plot is complicated by Zenobio's infatuation with Farinella, who is actually his son in disguise. The play ends happily, as both the popular tradition of the *commedia dell'arte** and the more erudite tradition of Cinquecento comedy demanded. Both of these different literary traditions form the background to Croce's play, but the author treats his comic language and milieu with a freshness and a vivacity which are often lacking in many of the imitations of classical comedies composed during the Renaissance.

Bibliography: Bertoldo e Bertoldino, ed. Luigi Emery (Florence: Le Monnier, 1951); *Affanni e canzoni del padre di Bertoldo,* ed. Massimo Dursi (Bologna: Alfa, 1966); *La Farinella,* ed. Pietro Cazzani (Turin: Einaudi, 1965); Olindo Guerrini, *La vita e le opere di Guilio Cesare Croce* (Bologna: Forni Editore, 1879); Marcel Tetel, "Giulio Cesare Croce, Cantastorie or Literary Artist?" *Forum Italicum* 4 (1970), 32–38.

D

DA LENTINO, GIACOMO (thirteenth century), notary and lyric poet at the court of Frederick II.* Giacomo was born at Lentino (today Lentini), north of Syracuse in Sicily. The little that is known of his life comes from a few legal documents dating from 1233 and 1240 bearing his signature, and from several references to himself, his birthplace, and contemporary events in his poems. A sonnet* of Bonagiunta,* probably written between 1250 and 1270, mentions his death. That Giacomo was a prominent poet is demonstrated by his substantial body of verse and the testimony of other poets, including Dante,* who singles him out as the foremost Sicilian poet in the *Purgatorio* (XXIV, 55–60) and *De vulgari eloquentia* (I, 12); Petrarch,* who mentions him favorably in the *Trionfo d'amore (Triumph of Love);* and Lorenzo de' Medici,* who set the precedent for collections of Italian poetry by including him in his *canzoniere.* Apparently, Giacomo was also the most prolific poet of the Sicilian School. Of the fifteen *canzoni,* * twenty-two sonnets, two *tenzoni* (poetic debates), and the single *discordo* (poetic disagreement) attributed to him, none survives in the original Sicilian because successive scribes modified the language to conform to their Tuscan standard.

There was no sustained tradition of court poetry in the Italian vernacular before Giacomo's time, but the still flourishing poetry of Provence served in its stead for the poets of the Sicilian School, whose style defined the course of Italian love poetry as it spread northward. In adapting the Provençal style to Italian, Giacomo freely borrows poetic forms, themes, linguistic structures, and the terminology of *fin'amor.* However, his contributions, a new concept of love and a new poetic form, are noteworthy both historically and poetically. Reflective of his independent spirit, the sonnets written in *tenzone* with the abbot of Tivoli and such *canzoni* as "Amor non vole" (Love does not permit me to implore) express his dissatisfaction with imitations of troubadour fashions uninspired by a personal poetic vision. In the *tenzone,* the abbot predictably complains of unrequited love and pledges his fidelity to the god of love in the hope that the lady, like himself, will be stricken by love's arrow. Giacomo replies that the abbot should give up writing such poetry to avoid both artistic and mortal sins. In "Amor non vole," Giacomo criticizes poets who lack personal inspiration and depend solely upon the superficial aspects of courtly verse; courtly love takes a new turn when the lover refuses to beg for pity and mercy, terms which have become essentially void of meaning through overuse. He proposes to develop a new kind of poetry which displays a logical relationship between structure and concept.

Giacomo's conscious efforts to develop such poetry are apparent even in his *canzoni,* the form most closely bound to the Provençal tradition. On the whole, the subject matter of his *canzoni* appears unsurprising: the indecisive and troubled lover adores the lovely but haughty lady, begs for compassion and mercy, praises her beauty, experiences joy when she is near, and suffers when she is far away. Nonetheless, his innovations, both stylistic and conceptual, stand out, as for example in "Maravigliosamente/ un amor me distringe" ("Wonderfully/ a love holds me bound"), a *canzone* in which the poet compares the painter whose painting is only an imperfect copy of an idea to the poet, whose ideal image of his lady perfectly expresses his love only as long as it remains in his heart. Once expressed, its perfection is lost, and he can only approach his beloved by painting her in his imagination. His poetic praises of his beloved become signs *(signa)* of the love for her which he cannot express in her presence. Hence, the poem itself is a representation of the love he holds within his heart, albeit an imperfect one. Likewise, in "Dolce cominciamento" ("A sweet beginning"), the lady's image is so vividly evoked by his memory that it comes to life in the poet's imagination.

Giacomo's most significant achievement was, of course, his development of the sonnet, a form perfectly designed for poetry in which the form is logically related to content. No earlier sonnets have ever been found, and it is customary to regard him as the inventor. Giacomo's sonnets deal mainly with love, although two have a particularly moral end, that of elaborating the themes of friendship and suffering. All the sonnets have fourteen hendecasyllabic lines with two quatrains rhymed *abababab* and sestets in which he uses three rhyme schemes: *cdecde,* in most cases, as well as *cdcdcd* and *ccdccd.* Ordinarily, the sestet and octave are logically divided, and in the early manuscripts the sestets are divided into the two tercets. Giacomo exploits the sonnet's possibilities and gives new life to troubadour commonplaces. Some of the sonnets are didactic and argumentative; the best are lyrical and inspired. The brevity of the sonnet form enables the poet to unify his thought more efficiently than in the longer *canzone.* Giacomo's sonnets display two basic kinds of logical organization. The first is marked by the use of parataxis, and his images and comparisons are loosely enumerated but logically related. The second is characterized by a hypotactic structure in which each part is logically subordinated to a central concept. An example of the first type is "Lo basilico" ("The basilisk"), in which the loose structure reflects a loose comparison between the poet-lover and four unusual creatures from medieval bestiaries with surprising habits, all corresponding to the unusual activities of the lover. The series of four comparisons in the octave is reiterated in the first four lines of the sestet. "Io m'aggio posto in core a Dio servire" ("I have set my heart to serving God") is of the second type, with a complex periodic structure which deals with the problem of the lover's religious devotion to an angelic lady. Throughout, sacred and profane love are juxtaposed by means of a vocabulary combining religious and courtly terminology. A tension arises from the confusion between the real and the poetic heavens, as the poet refuses to go to Paradise without his lady, whose conventional beauty makes him mistake her for an angel. The tense equilibrium is reestablished in the final lines which portray the lady as both an angel and an object of physical desire. The claim that heavenly and romantic or courtly love is not inherently incompatible represents a new theme and provided the basis and inspiration for the intellectualization of love among the poets of the *dolce stil nuovo** in northern Italy.

Generally, Giacomo's poetic efforts reflect his considerable talents. Although he is transposing troubadour terminology into Italian, he is not an inept experimenter. He frequently succeeds in both sonnets and *canzoni* to join stylistic virtuosity and conceptual development intimately together, and he breathes new life into the poetry of love. Style is subordinated to logic and virtuosity becomes meaningful. Not only can he manage the complexities of troubadour verse, but he also demonstrates an independent spirit in his conception of love and poetry.

See also CANZONE; DOLCE STIL NUOVO; FREDERICK II; SONNET.

Bibliography: The Poetry of Giacomo Da Lentino, ed. Ernest Langley (Cambridge, Mass., Harvard University Press, 1915); *German and Italian Lyrics of the Middle Ages,* trans. Frederick Goldin (Garden City, N.Y.: Doubleday, 1973); Christopher Kleinhenz, "Giacomo da Lentino and the Advent of the Sonnet: Divergent Patterns in Early Italian Poetry," *Forum Italicum* 10 (1976), 218–32.

DANIELLO, BERNARDINO (circa 1500–1565), translator, poet, and critic. Daniello was born in Lucca and was a student of the Venetian scholar Trifon Gabriele (circa 1470–1549). Daniello's significant contributions came from his work as a critic and translator, although he wrote some lyric verse in the Petrarchan vein which was printed in several sixteenth-century anthologies. His major treatise *La poetica* (1536, Poetics) is based primarily upon Horace, although the presence of Aristotle is already evident. He repeats Horace's definition of poetry's dual goal of instruction and delight, and he is the first modern writer to mention the concept of verisimilitude. The work is a dialogue in two books, the first of which goes beyond the definition of poetry to discuss two of the three necessary procedures in poetry—invention or the selection of a theme and disposition, or the ordering of the poetic material. The second book explores stylistics and elocution with numerous examples taken from Italian poets, especially Dante,* Petrarch,* and Boccaccio.* Besides this treatise, Daniello published an extremely influential commentary (1541) on Petrarch's *Canzoniere (Lyric Poems)*, which is indispensable to any study of sixteenth-century views of this model poet. He is also the author of a less important commentary on Dante's *Commedia* (1568) and a popular translation of Virgil's *Georgics* into Italian blank verse (1549), which is accompanied by a commentary defending the value of translating the classics into the vernaculars. His use of blank verse in a translation of the second book of Virgil's *Aeneid* (1545) is its first use in Italian epic* poetry, predating Trissino's* *La Italia liberata dai Goti* (1547, Italy Liberated from the Goths), Alamanni's* *Avarchide* (1570, The Avarchide), and Annibale Caro's* famous translation of the *Aeneid* (1581).

See also CARO, Annibale.

Bibliography: La poetica (Munich: Wilhelm Fink, 1968); Ezio Raimondi, "Bernardino Daniello e le varianti petrarchesche," *Studi petrarcheschi* 5 (1952), 95–130; Bernard Weinberg, *A History of Literary Criticism in the Italian Renaissance,* 2 vols. (Chicago: University of Chicago Press, 1961).

D'ANNUNZIO, GABRIELE (1863–1938), poet, novelist, dramatist, and military hero. Born into a well-to-do family in Pescara, D'Annunzio at the age of eleven was sent to secondary school in Prato, where he was a rebellious but brilliant student. He received his diploma in 1881 and then went to Rome. Although he enrolled at the university, he soon abandoned it in order to write for various journals and to begin the series of love affairs which were to characterize his life. Two years after his arrival in the capital, he married the Duchess Maria Hardouin di Gallese, who bore him three children. Marriage did not curb his philandering, and in 1894, he met the actress Eleonora Duse, with whom a year later he began one of the most celebrated romances of *fin de siècle* Europe. Turning briefly to politics, D'Annunzio was elected for one term to the Chamber of Deputies (1897–1900). He aligned himself first with the extreme right and then capriciously moved to the left during the socialist attacks on Pelloux's government. His political career was undistinguished, and ended when he was defeated in the elections of 1900.

Even as a schoolboy, D'Annunzio had always cultivated an extravagant lifestyle, one usually beyond his means. When in 1899 he moved to a luxuriously furnished Tuscan villa, La Capponcina, his way of living became even more lavish. He remained there for a decade, until 1910, when overpowering debts forced him to sell not only the villa but many of his personal possessions as well. Inwardly humiliated and still besieged by creditors, he chose voluntary exile in France, staying briefly in Paris and then establishing a residence at Arcachon where he resumed his princely ways. Probably stirred less by patriotic impulses than by the promise of danger, he returned to Italy in the spring of 1915, just before that country's entrance into the war. In addition to making fiery speeches, the fifty-two-year-old D'Annunzio promptly volunteered for frontline duty, serving with distinct heroism first in the infantry, then in the navy, and finally in the air force. Although he was gravely injured and lost his sight in one eye when his airplane crash-landed, he later returned to the front. Among his exploits were a torpedo boat raid on the Austrian fleet at Buccari and a daring flight over Vienna. Enraged when the postwar treaties did not return the port of Fiume (now Rijeka, Yugoslavia) to Italy, D'Annunzio and a ragtag band of volunteers seized the city in September 1919 and held it for over a year. The author's fierce nationalism and his prestige in Italy were exploited by Mussolini, but D'Annunzio himself, despite his high visibility during the fascist years, occupied no important role in Mussolini's government. After a mysterious fall from a window in 1922, he spent the rest of his years in semiretirement at the Vittoriale, a sumptuous villa on Lake Garda.

Like the events of his life, D'Annunzio's works are many and diverse. He wrote in Italian, French, and even Old French; and he exercised his art in all the creative genres, as well as biography, autobiography, and patriotic literature. D'Annunzio was still a schoolboy when he published *Primo vere* (1879, Early Spring), a collection of verses imitative of Carducci's* *Odi barbare (The Barbarian Odes)*. The poems of *Canto novo* (1882, New Song), however, are the first to give evidence of his poetic genius, and they remain among the best written by D'Annunzio during his long career. *Il piacere* (1889, *The Child of Pleasure*) was D'Annunzio's first novel, and to European readers it seemed to express the quintessence of *la belle époque*. The work depicts the rich costumes and chambers of a decadent aristocracy that lives according to the dictates of the Nietzschean "superman," loves with a passion which oscillates between a morbid sensuality and spiritual rapture, and speaks and writes in phrases which have the vacuous grace of *art nouveau* ironwork. *Il piacere* sets the tone and themes for D'Annunzio's novels, among which are *L'innocente* (1891, *The Intruder*) and *Il trionfo della morte* (1894, *The Triumph of Death*).

Eleonora Duse had inspired D'Annunzio to turn his talents toward the theatre, but it was Sarah Bernhardt who appeared in the premiere of the Italian's first full-length play, *La città morta* (1897, *The Dead City*). The success of many of D'Annunzio's dozen theatrical works must be credited to the author's good fortune in having leading actresses star in his works. Only *La figlia di Jorio* (1904, *The Daughter of Jorio*) has shown lasting dramatic qualities. Set in D'Annunzio's native Abruzzi, the tragedy, despite wooden characters, is notable for its high poetry and folkloristic elements.

D'Annunzio gave evidence of a renewed poetic vitality when he published *Maia* (1903), the first book of *Laudi del cielo, del mare, della terra e degli eroi* (Praises of the Sky, the Sea, the Earth, and Heroes). *Elettra* (Electra) and his masterpiece, *Alcyone* (Alcyone), followed in 1904. *Alcyone* contains the best of D'Annunzio, and poems like "La pioggia nel pineto" ("The Rain in the Pine Forest"), "La sera fiesolana" (Fiesolean Evening), and "Meriggio" (Noon) summarize the poet's qualities: the richness of his vocabulary and the profusion of images which create sensuous and dreamlike landscapes evoking the deep harmony of nature. Above all, *Alcyone* emphasizes the pervasive music of D'Annunzio's verse and his technical mastery of Italian prosody, which is surpassed by no other poet of the language.

The publication of *Contemplazione della morte* (1912, Contemplation of Death) initiated a new phase in D'Annunzio's life work. This work and the other autobiographical volumes, *Notturno* (1921, Nocturne) and *Le faville del maglio* (1924–28, The Sparks from the Hammer), contain the thoughts, impressions, and sometimes the ramblings of a man who, having already immortalized the myth of D'Annunzio, must confront the reality that D'Annunzio the man is mortal. In these pages of the author's finest prose, the reader is sometimes privileged to glimpse a D'Annunzio stripped of his ostentatious trappings and his sempiternal posing.

Although Benedetto Croce's* early judgment of D'Annunzio as a "dilettante of sensations" is too severe, much of the author's work does seem flowery and empty. Yet, the music of his language and the evocative qualities of his images have influenced almost every Italian writer of this century. It is difficult to discern a development in D'Annunzio's work. Its unity lies solely in the stamp of its creator's personality—D'Annunzio is always D'Annunzio. He is also his era. The most famous writer in the world in 1900, D'Annunzio embodied in his works, and even more concretely in his life, a whole social class of turn-of-the-century Europe—its decadence, its extravagance, and its frenzied search for ever more exquisite sensations.

Bibliography: Tutte le opere, ed. Egidio Bianchetti, 10 vols. (Milan: Mondadori, 1939–50); *The Child of Pleasure,* trans. Georgina Harding (New York: Richmond, 1898); *The Daughter of Jorio,* trans. Charlotte Porter (1907; rpt. Westport, Conn.: Greenwood Press, 1969); *The Dead City,* trans. G. Mantellini (Chicago: Laird & Lee, 1902); *The Triumph of Death,* trans. Georgina Harding (1896; rpt. New York: Fertig, 1975); Giovanni Gullace, *Gabriele D'Annunzio in France: A Study in Cultural Relations* (Syracuse, N.Y.: Syracuse University Press, 1966); Philippe Jullian, *D'Annunzio* (New York: Viking, 1973); Mario Praz, *The Romantic Agony,* 2nd ed. (New York: Oxford University Press, 1970).

Louis Kibler

DANTE ALIGHIERI (1265–1321), poet. Dante was born in Florence, the son of Alighiero di Bellincione d'Alighiero. Like most of the city's lesser nobility and artisans, Dante's family was Guelph, in opposition to the feudal aristocracy of the Ghibelline party. His mother died when he was young; his father, whom he seems to avoid mentioning as much as possible, remarried and had nine children. As far as one can tell from his writings, Dante's impressions of family life were happy enough. It is fairly certain that he received a careful education, although little of it is known precisely. He possibly frequented the Franciscan lower schools and, later, their schools of philosophy. He studied rhetoric with Brunetto Latini.*

Dante tells us (*Vita nuova* III, 9) that as a young man he taught himself the art of writing verse. Equally important to him at this time was his friendship with Guido Cavalcanti,* his first real poetic influence. During this period, his father died (by 1283), and soon after Dante married a gentlewoman of the Donati family, Gemma di Manetto Donati, the marriage having been arranged by his father. She bore Dante two sons, Pietro and Jacopo, and possibly two daughters. While his marriage and family seem to have had no influence on him as a poet, a noble Florentine woman of outstanding grace and beauty deeply impressed him. She was Bice, the daughter of Folco Portinari and later the wife of Simone dei Bardi. Dante called her Beatrice, the "bringer of Blessings," one who brought bliss to all who looked upon her. He became convinced that she was the guide of his thoughts and emotions "toward that ideal perfection which is the goal of every noble mind"—the praising of one's lady as a picture of virtue and courtesy. Beatrice's father died first, and then she died on 8 June 1290. Dante was overcome with grief but consoled himself by contemplating her in the glory of Heaven.

Meanwhile, Dante's love of study had grown stronger. His vision had been broadened by his reading of Boethius and Cicero. With the diffusion of Aristotle's physical and metaphysical works, there came the need for harmonizing the thoughts of this "teacher of human reason" with the truth of the Faith. Consequently, in his poetry he was interested in glorifying philosophy as the "mistress of his mind" and in treating subjects of moral philosophy—such as nobility and genuine love courtships—in artistically formed *canzoni*.* But despite this, Love remained for him "the source of every noble action and every high purpose."

Along with his spiritual and intellectual life, Dante led an active public life as well. In 1289, he had fought as a mounted soldier at the battle of Campaldino. In the summer of 1300, he was for two months one of the six priors of Florence. During all this time, Dante made no secret of his opposition to the ambitious policy of the papacy. For this reason, it seems that when Dante was sent as one of three delegates from the Commune to the pontiff at the advent of Charles of Valois, or shortly before, Dante was

held after the first talks. During the time of his absence, the revolution of
the Blacks took place in Florence and he was sentenced to exile. It seems
that he first took refuge with the Scala family at Verona. After the death of
his generous patron, Bartolommeo, in 1304, he is believed to have visited
the university at Bologna, where he had been known since 1287. There is
reason to think that he traveled widely in Italy and that he went to Paris
some time between 1307 and 1309. In 1310, Henry VII descended into Italy
to reunite church and state, restore order, and force various cities to
submit. Dante, who attributed the woes of Florence and all of Italy to lack
of imperial guidance, greeted Henry as a savior. With the emperor's
sudden death in Siena in 1313 went Dante's every hope of restoring himself
to an honorable position in his city, and in 1314 he took refuge with Can
Grande della Scala in Verona.

Sometime later, after he was already well known through his lyrics, his
Convivio, Inferno, and *Purgatorio,* Dante was offered asylum at Ravenna
by Francesco da Rimini's nephew, Guido Novella da Polenta. He maintained his friendship with Can Grande della Scala, captain of the
Ghibelline league, on whom he built great hopes. Ravenna was his home
until his death on either 13 or 14 September 1321.

The *Vita nuova (The New Life),* a combination of prose and poetry and
one of the first important examples of Italian literary prose, was composed
between 1292 and 1300, although many of its poems were written earlier. In
the *Vita nuova,* Dante attempts to sift the poetry he had written over the
preceding ten years and to give it order, form, and meaning. His purpose is
to copy from his "book of memory" only those past experiences that
belong to the period beginning his "new life"—a life made by the poet's
first meeting with Beatrice and the Lord of Love, who together with the
poet are the three main characters in the story. The architecture of the
work, then, consists of selected poems arranged in a certain order, with
bridges of prose between them, bridges that serve (with the exception of
the "essays" represented by Chapters XXV and XXXIX) primarily a
narrative function: to describe those events in the life of the protagonist
which supposedly inspired the poems. By offering in this way a narrative
background, the author was able to make their meaning clearer—or, perhaps, to change their original meaning or purpose.

The *Convivio (The Banquet),* written in Italian between 1304 and 1308, is
a feast of fourteen courses, of which the "meat" of each is a *canzone*
concerning love and virtue, and the "bread" the exposition of it. Mere love
poems to the eye, written to a beautiful woman of flesh and blood and
motivated by sensual passion, they are essentially meant for the "mistress
of his mind," philosophy, and are motivated by virtue. The *Convivio* seems
to be a connecting link between the *Vita nuova* and the *Commedia,* since at
first love seems to have earthly associations, but then turns out to have
religious significance. Furthermore, as Dante lauds reason in this work, so

in the *Commedia* reason in the pursuit of knowledge and wisdom becomes man's sole guide on earth, except for the intervention of Divine Grace or assistance. In this work, too, he declares that the vernacular is suitable for ethical subjects as well as amorous ones. Dante completed only four of the projected fourteen chapters of the *Convivio*.

De monarchia (On World-Government), a Latin treatise of disputed date, is an exposition of Dante's political philosophy and a statement of the principles upon which his ideals rested. In the first book, Dante proves that for the welfare of the world, temporal monarchy is necessary. In the second, he says that the Roman people have justly assumed the monarchic office. In the third, he asserts that the authority of the Roman monarch proceeds directly from God, not through any third party.

De vulgari eloquentia (after 1304, *Eloquence in the Vernacular Tongue*), an unfinished Latin treatise, deals with the origin and history of languages. The first book is devoted to a discussion of dialects and the principles of poetic composition in the vulgar tongue and its use by certain poets. It gives the assurance that the Italian language is suited for only the most elevated subjects such as war, love, and virtue and that the form which one must use is the *canzone*.

The *Canzoniere (Lyric Poetry)* contains many of the poems excluded from the *Vita nuova*, but which were inspired nonetheless by Beatrice; those written for other women; and other lyrics composed at different times in his life. In addition, he wrote some fourteen Latin letters; two Latin eclogues; a scientific essay, *Quaestio de aqua et terra* (1320, *Discourse on the Nature of Water and Earth*); a long sonnet* sequence called *Il Fiore* (The Flower), the authenticity of which has been questioned by a number of scholars; many miscellaneous poems, a dozen or so *canzoni*, half as many *ballate*,* two *sestine*,* and some twenty-five or thirty sonnets; and various *Epistles* of a political nature, written in Latin.

Dante's masterpiece is, of course, the *Commedia* (the word "Divina" was added to "Commedia" by posterity), begun about 1306 and composed while in exile. The purpose of the poem, as Dante reveals in his epistle to Can Grande, is "to remove those living in this life from the state of misery and lead them to the state of felicity."

The poem is divided into three major sections: *Inferno* (Hell), *Purgatorio* (Purgatory), and *Paradiso* (Heaven). Each section contains thirty-three cantos with the exception of Hell, which has thirty-four, the opening canto serving as an introduction to the work as a whole. The measure used throughout the poem is *terza rima*.* The drama or main action of the poem centers on one man's journey to God. It tells how God through the agency of Beatrice drew the poet to salvation. The moral that Dante wishes his reader to keep in mind is that what God has done for one man he will do for everyman, if everyman is willing to make this journey.

With the opening line of the poem, Dante begins to construct his allegory of the double journey; that is, his own personal experience in the world beyond, which is open to everyman or the reader in his own journey through this life. The poet, then, finds himself wandering in a dark woods (the worldly life). He tries to escape by climbing a mountain that is lit from behind by the rays of the sun (God). His journey upwards is impeded by the sudden appearance of three beasts: a leopard, a lion, and a she-wolf (the three major divisions of sin, signifying the major divisions of Hell in reverse order—fraud, violence, and concupiscence). The poet is about to be driven back when, just as suddenly as the three beasts appear, Virgil (reason or human understanding) appears. He has been sent by Beatrice (Divine Revelation) to guide Dante on his journey. The only way to escape from the dark woods is to descend into the *Inferno* (man must first descend in humility before he can raise himself to salvation or God)—the way up the mountain, then, is to go down! The purpose of Dante's journey through Hell is to learn all there is to know about sin, as a necessary preparation for the ascent to God. In fact, from the opening canto of the *Inferno* to the closing one of the *Paradiso,* Dante the poet presents his pilgrim as continuously learning, his spiritual development being the main theme of the entire poem; his progress is slow and there are even occasional backslidings. When the pilgrim and his guide have seen all there is to see of sin (canto 34), they find they must exit from Hell by climbing down Lucifer's monstrous, hairy body.

In the first canto of the *Purgatory,* Dante and Virgil are at the foot of a mountain (again), and the reader is naturally reminded of the first canto of the *Inferno:* it is the same mountain, the one they could not then climb because Dante was not spiritually prepared. But now, having investigated all sin and having shaken off pride during his perilous descent into humility, Dante will be able to make his ascent.

Purgatory is a place of repentance, regeneration, and conversion. Although the punishments inflicted on the penitents here are oftentimes more severe than in Hell, the atmosphere is totally different: it is one of sweet encounters, culminating in Dante's reunion with Beatrice in the earthly paradise and Virgil's elegant disappearance. Brotherly love and humility reign here—necessary qualities for a successful journey of man's mind to God. Everyone here is destined to see God eventually. The predominant image is one of homesickness, a yearning to return to man's real home in the heavens. Toward the close of the *Purgatory,* the time comes for Beatrice (Divine Revelation) to take charge of the pilgrim. Human reason (Virgil) can take man only so far; it cannot show him God or explain His many mysteries.

The *Paradise* is an attempt to describe the religious life, one in which man centers his attentions wholly on God, His divine truths, and ultimate happiness. Only in perfect knowledge of the True Good can man have perfect happiness. The dominant image in this realm is light. God is light, and the pilgrim's goal from the very start was to reach the light.

The formal beauty of the *Commedia* should not be dissociated from its spiritual message. The universal appeal of the poem comes precisely from a combination of the two: poetry and philosophy. For Dante, ultimate truth was known. In principle, it was contained in the *Summa* of St. Thomas Aquinas, and the doctrine of the *Divine Comedy* comes largely from the writings of St. Thomas and the other church fathers. Dante, then, with his special kind of allegory tries to imitate God: the symbolic world he creates in his poem is in principle a real mirror of the actual world created by God Himself.

Bibliography: The Divine Comedy, trans. and ed. Charles S. Singleton, 6 vols. (Princeton, N. J.: Princeton University Press, 1970–75); *Dante's Inferno,* trans. Mark Musa (Bloomington, Ind.: Indiana University Press, 1971); *Dante's Lyric Poetry,* eds. and trans. Kenelm Foster and Patrick Boyde (London: Oxford University Press, 1967); *Dante's Vita Nuova: A Translation and an Essay,* trans. Mark Musa (Bloomington, Ind.: Indiana University Press, 1973); *Literary Criticism of Dante Alighieri,* trans. Robert S. Haller (Lincoln, Neb.: University of Nebraska Press, 1973); *On World-Government,* trans. H. W. Schneider (Indianapolis, Ind.: Bobbs-Merrill, 1957); Thomas G. Bergin, *Dante* (1965; rpt. Westport, Conn.: Greenwood Press, 1976); Robert J. Clements, ed., *American Critical Essays on the Divine Comedy* (New York: New York University Press, 1967); Mark Musa, *Advent at the Gates: Dante's Comedy* (Bloomington, Ind.: Indiana University Press, 1974).

Mark Musa

DA PONTE, LORENZO (1749–1838), poet, librettist, teacher, and memorialist. Born in the Jewish ghetto of Ceneda (today, Vittorio Veneto) as Emanuele Conegliano, Da Ponte was baptized in 1763, changed his name, and studied for the priesthood, taking major orders. In his youth, he was somewhat of a libertine, and his escapades resulted first, in expulsion from a seminary position during 1776 and then, during 1779, in banishment from Venetian territory for fifteen years. Forced to move to Austria, he gained the position of "Poet to the Italian Theatre" in 1782 and won the favor of Emperor Joseph II. He became a successful librettist, collaborating with various musicians during the nine years of his stay at court, including Piticchio, Storace, Righini, Salieri, Martin y Soler, and Gazzaniga. However, it was his fortuitous association with Mozart, whom he met in 1783, which guaranteed him a place in musical history.

For Mozart, Da Ponte composed his three most famous *libretti–Le nozze di Figaro* (1786, *The Marriage of Figaro*), *Il dissoluto punito o sia Il Don Giovanni* (1787, *The Punished Libertine or Don Giovanni*), and *Così fan tutte o sia La scuola degli amanti* (1790, *Women Are Like That*). While all three operas are considered masterpieces, it was Da Ponte's version of the Don Juan theme which had the greatest impact upon literature. In his *libretto,* the Baroque* atheist of Tirso de Molina and the courtly figure of Molière are transformed by the Rococo atmosphere, Da Ponte's comic talent, and the genius of Mozart, breathing new life into the theme and inspiring generations of future imitators. According to some accounts of its composition, Da Ponte wrote the libretto in great haste and had the assistance of his good friend Giacomo Casanova* in revising the last sections of the work.

With the death of Emperor Joseph II, Da Ponte's success in Austria came to an abrupt halt. Forced to leave the court because he lacked the favor of the new emperor, Da Ponte traveled to England, where he lived for some years (1792–1805), finding work at the Drury Lane Theatre as a librettist. However, faced with insurmountable financial burdens in England, he sent his family to America and followed them in 1805. Da Ponte landed first in Philadelphia and then went to New York City to rejoin his family and to seek his fortune. After several sad experiences which ended in financial disaster, he chanced to meet Clement Moore in a Broadway bookstore. A trustee of Columbia College (the future author of "The Night Before Christmas"), Moore befriended Da Ponte and gave him access to the best of New York society. These social contacts enabled Da Ponte to establish himself as a private tutor of Italian language and culture. Eventually, he was named professor of Italian at Columbia College, but the post carried no salary and was valuable only insofar as students choosing the optional Italian courses he offered paid him personally for his services. Although Da Ponte was unable to persuade students to take advantage of this unique opportunity, he located some students outside the university community who wanted to study Italian privately. One of the first professors of Italian in America, Da Ponte's tireless efforts on behalf of Italian culture in America deserve recognition. Late in life, his reputation seemed again on the rise, when the first Italian opera company arrived in America in 1825 and performed, among other numbers, his own *Don Giovanni*. Da Ponte tried to organize an Italian opera in New York, but it was forced to close after two years.

In his old age, Da Ponte published his memoirs in four volumes, the *Memorie di Lorenzo da Ponte* (1823–27, *Memoirs of Lorenzo Da Ponte*). Besides its usefulness as a picture of early nineteenth-century American culture viewed from an Italian perspective, the work can still be read with pleasure as the portrait of a fascinating individual. As a representative autobiography of the Italian Enlightenment,* it is of less literary value than the memoirs of Gozzi,* Vico,* or Casanova. Da Ponte was buried in New York, but no trace of his grave remains.

See also CASANOVA, Giacomo; ENLIGHTENMENT.

Bibliography: Memorie e altri scritti, ed. Cesare Pagnini (Milan: Longanesi, 1971); *The Great Operas of Mozart,* trans. W. H. Auden and others (New York: Norton, 1964)—contains original *libretti* and translations; *Memoirs of Lorenzo Da Ponte,* trans. Elisabeth Abbott (New York: Orion, 1959); April Fitzlyon, *The Libertine Librettist* (London: John Calder, 1955); Oscar Mandel, ed., *The Theatre of Don Juan: A Collection of Plays and Views, 1630–1963* (Lincoln, Neb.: University of Nebraska Press, 1963); Joseph L. Russo, *Lorenzo Da Ponte: Poet and Adventurer* (1922; rpt. New York: AMS Press, 1966).

DA PORTO, LUIGI (1485–1529), writer and soldier. Da Porto was from Vicenza. He began writing as a means of passing the time while recuperating from war wounds. His major literary work is the *novella** entitled *Historia novellamente ritrovata di due nobili amanti* (1530, *Romeo and Juliet*). The story appeared in at least two slightly different versions during the decade following his death, and its influence was fairly extensive. Da Porto found his material in the thirty-third *novella* of Masuccio Salernitano's* *Novellino,* but he transferred the story from Siena to Verona, changed the names of the protagonists to Romeo and Giulietta, and, after a reading of Ovid's tale of Pyramus and Thisbe, modified the ending of Masuccio's tale to one closer to that of Shakespeare's later tragedy. The story was repeated in another famous collection of stories, the *Novelle* of Matteo Bandello* (II, 9), and was to be remembered in works by Pierre Boaistuau, Geffraie Fenton, Luigi Groto (1541–85), and Arthur Brooke, as well as its most famous treatment in Shakespeare. Da Porto also wrote a collection of Petrarchan verse which appeared in 1539. His collection of seventy-nine letters was not published until the nineteenth century.

See also MASUCCIO SALERNITANO; NOVELLA.

Bibliography: Romeo and Juliet, ed. and trans. Maurice Jonas (London: Davis & Orioli, 1921)—contains reproductions of the two early Italian versions with translations; Letterio Di Francia, *Novellistica,* 2 vols. (Milan: Vallardi, 1924).

DA TODI, JACOPONE (circa 1236–1306), poet, mystic, and Franciscan. Little is known with certainty about Jacopone, but his life is surrounded by many legends. He was apparently born in Todi of the noble Benedetti family and earned his living as a lawyer. According to tradition, his wife, who with him enjoyed the worldly pleasures, died in the collapse of a building during a dancing celebration around 1268. Jacopone discovered that she had been wearing a hair shirt under her festive clothes, and it was this event which brought about his religious conversion. For ten years, he lived in seclusion as a penitent and eventually joined the Franciscan order, supporting the faction of that religious group which favored strict adherence to the original rule of absolute poverty. Jacopone's cardinal contribution to Italian literature was his collection of sacred and moralistic poetry in the *lauda** form, a poetic structure popularized in thirteenth-century Umbria by confraternities of laymen devoted to public penitence and spiritual singing. A number of these *laude* were written on the corruption of the Franciscan order and the church, detailing their vices of impatience, hypocrisy, and concern for worldly honors. In 1294, with the elevation of a poor hermit named Pier da Morrone to the papacy as Pope Celestine V, the group of ascetics within the Franciscan order to which Jacopone belonged (often called the "Spirituals" to distinguish them from their laxer brothers, the "Conventuals") received some autonomy within the order as the "Poor hermits of Celestine." Jacopone's poetry in praise of poverty may date from this period.

When Pope Boniface VIII succeeded Celestine V in December 1294, this favored treatment was revoked. Jacopone actively opposed Boniface, and with other like-minded priests and Franciscans (especially from the Colonna family), he signed a document at Lunghezza in 1297 declaring Celestine's abdication and Boniface's election invalid. The rebels were subsequently excommunicated, withdrew to Palestrina, and were beseiged by the pope until they were forced to surrender in 1298. Jacopone was imprisoned, an experience which produced a series of poems addressed to Boniface, begging for absolution, dramatizing the sadness of the lamb excluded from the fold, and attacking the pope as the "new Lucifer." It also resulted in one masterpiece on the theme of imprisonment, "Que farai, fra Jacopone" ("And now what, Fra Jacopone?"), in which a varied range of human experience is reflected—the grimmer details of prison life, psychological and mystical introspection, and ascetic self-denial. As the poem develops, the opening note of complaint changes, as Jacopone begins to realize that his torture actually leads him closer to his ascetic ideal. Eventually, he comes to understand that hatred for his captors must be replaced by hatred for his own personal defects. Jacopone was absolved from excommunication and released from prison by Boniface's successor, Benedict XI. He spent his last years in his native Umbria at the Convent of San Lorenzo in Collazzone.

Jacopone wrote nearly one hundred *laude* on a variety of themes, but with an energetic style and a strong sense of the dramatic unmatched by any of his contemporaries. Although his greatest works deal with religious questions, his poetry evinces the influence of troubadour and courtly verse. In one interesting poem entitled "Senno me pare e cortesia empazir per lo bel Messia" ("Sense and nobleness it seems to me, to go mad for the fair Messiah"), the traditional virtues of courtliness, sense, and moderation (so important in the often dangerous encounters between lover and lady in the courtly literature) are set apart from the necessarily immoderate and excessive behavior of the true lover of Christ, and madness in Christ is defined as the only true wisdom. His greatest poem is undoubtedly the dramatic *lauda* entitled "Donna del paradiso" ("Lady of Paradise"), which presents a small sacred drama of the crucifixion with several speakers (Christ, the Virgin, a messenger, and the crowd) and two main events— a lengthy list of tortures inflicted on Christ reported to Mary by the messenger, and an exchange of final words between Christ and Mary. The two central scenes are linked by the lament of the Virgin, a masterful combination of sorrow and ritual, literary tradition and realism. Jacopone is sometimes reputed to be the author of the Latin sequence, "Stabat mater dolorosa" ("The mother stood grieving"), a work of some sixty lines representing the Virgin at the foot of the cross.

See also LAUDA.

Bibliography: Laude, ed. Franco Mancini (Bari: Laterza, 1974); *Laudi, Trattato e Detti,* ed. Franca Ageno (Florence: Le Monnier, 1953); *The Age of Dante,* trans. Joseph Tusiani (New York: Baroque Press, 1974); *The Penguin Book of Italian Verse,* ed. George Kay (Baltimore: Penguin, 1965); Rosanna Bettarini, *Jacopone e il Laudario Urbinate* (Florence: Sansoni, 1969); Alvaro Bizziccari, "L'amore mistico nel canzoniere di Jacopone da Todi," *Italica* 44 (1968), 1–27; Peter Dronke, *The Medieval Lyric* (New York: Harper, 1969); Evelyn Underhill, *Jacopone da Todi, Poet and Mystic* (New York: Dutton, 1919).

DAVANZATI, CHIARO (circa 1235–1280), Florentine poet. Chiaro probably lived in the quarter of Santa Maria sopra Arno, was married, and had five sons. However, there has been some confusion in identifying him with certainty because documents reveal that another man of the same name lived in the quarter of San Frediano and was still living in 1303. Davanzati's writings reveal his political preoccupations and document his participation in the battle of Montaperti in 1260. In a noted poem, he exalts his Florentine homeland and protests the bargain made by the government of Florence, the Signoria, with Charles of Anjou in 1267.

Comprised of about two hundred poems, Chiaro's *canzoniere* reflects his broad interests as well as a cultural milieu constantly in flux. His poems are written on political, moral, didactic, and amorous subjects, and include two cycles of sonnets* inspired by medieval lapidaries and bestiaries as well as others modeled after the genre of the *contrasto* (debate). Critics have discerned three phases in the evolution of Chiaro's poetry. In his youth, the dominant influences were Provençal and Sicilian, particularly with regard to the style of *trobar leu,* or the light style developed by Peire Roger and Bernard de Ventadour, which led to a renewal of interest in the love song. Chiaro's poetry next shows the influence of Guittone d'Arezzo* in its treatment of political and theological themes. In the final phase, his poetic preferences resemble those of poets such as Guinizzelli* and the serious troubadours such as Guilhem de Montanhagol, for he identifies love for the lady with love of God and affirms that only the gentle heart is capable of such love. He portrays the lady as an angelic being with the power to dispose a man to spiritual concerns. Conservative imagery, graceful phrasing, and new themes and sentiments inspired by personal experiences and ardent patriotism seem to point the early Italian lyric in a new direction. Because he avoids wholly conventional treatments of old themes, Davanzati is sometimes viewed as a precursor of the group known as the poets of the *dolce stil nuovo.** Oddly, he seems to have had no real influence on the poets of his day with whom he corresponded, and he was largely ignored by following generations.

See also DOLCE STIL NUOVO.

Bibliography: Chiaro Davanzati, Rime, ed. Aldo Menichetti (Bologna: Commissione per i Testi di Lingua, 1965); Frederick Goldin, *German and Italian Lyrics of the Middle Ages* (Garden City, N.Y.: Doubleday, 1973).

DA VINCI, LEONARDO (1452–1519), artist, scientist, and writer. Leonardo came from Vinci, near Florence and was the illegitimate son of a notary. As a boy Leonardo was placed in the workshop of Andrea Verrocchio, where he obtained a predominantly technical education. The paintings from his early years in Florence include the *Annunciation* and the incomplete *Adoration of the Magi.* In 1482, Leonardo moved to the court of Ludovico Sforza (Il Moro) in Milan, where he hoped to erect a huge equestrian statue of Francesco Sforza and to work as an engineer. He remained in Milan until 1499, painting as well as studying the human body in relentless dissections. He also participated in the life of the court, contriving marvelous machines for courtly entertainment, all the while adding observations, drawings, and questions to the voluminous notebooks which he wrote backwards in order to conceal his thoughts from others. During this period, he completed the *Virgin of the Rocks* and the fresco of the *Last Supper* in the church of Santa Maria delle Grazie. His dream of completing the enormous equestrian statue in bronze was never realized, however, because of Ludovico's urgent need to use his casting metal for making canon to defend the duchy. After Ludovico's fall, Leonardo left Milan and traveled throughout Italy for several years, living in Mantua, Venice, and then Florence. He served Cesare Borgia for a time as a military engineer and then returned to Florence, where he met Machiavelli* and entered into a contest with Michelangelo,* painting an interpretation of the Battle of Anghiari opposite Michelangelo's version in the Palazzo Vecchio. This work was marred by the failure to prepare the fresco properly. In 1506, he returned to Milan at the invitation of Charles d'Amboise, the French king's representative, and remained there until

1513. After a brief sojourn in Rome, Leonardo moved to France in 1517, where Francis I valued his work most highly. He died at one of the royal residences in 1519, attended by his faithful friend Francesco Melzi.

Leonardo's genius was unquestioned even in his own time, but his personality presented an enigma which has puzzled both his contemporaries and the most perspicacious scholars of all ages. A major problem involves the state of Leonardo's writings, for the Vincian manuscripts are so scattered and often so provisional that it is impossible to identify even one authentic chapter, not to mention a separate book on a single subject. Often a drawing accompanying an idea or a remark is of more importance to his argument than his exposition. When Leonardo died, the manuscripts he possessed were inherited and carried to Italy by Francesco Melzi, who put them into order, read them all, and compiled the passages related to painting into a treatise entitled *Trattato della pittura* (1651, Treatise on Painting). Although first published over a century after Leonardo's death, this work was known in manuscript form by his contemporaries and was the only aspect of his voluminous writings which influenced artists or writers of his era. Since almost three-quarters of the material in Melzi's compilation cannot be traced to the Vincian manuscripts extant today, an unknown quantity of priceless writing obviously disappeared after the manuscripts were dispersed following Melzi's death. Some twelve hundred folios were assembled by the sixteenth-century collector Pompeo Leoni to form what is known as the Codex Atlanticus (now in the Ambrosiana Library in Milan). Other important codices include the Codex Trivulzianus at the Trivulziana Library in Milan; a small codex on the flight of birds in Turin; a group of drawings in Venice; a rich collection of drawings in the royal collection at Windsor Castle; and several codices in England. Twelve of the thirteen manuscripts Napoleon removed from the Ambrosiana Library remain in Paris. In 1965, two crucial notebooks (Codex Madrid I and II) were rediscovered in Spain after having been lost for one hundred and thirty-five years. Their reappearance has forced Vincian scholars to revise many of their ideas concerning Leonardo's intellectual development, his originality, and his place in the culture of his times.

Leonardo's contributions to painting and science are far more decisive than his contribution to Italian literature, primarily because the manuscript tradition of his notebooks and manuscripts prevented any true appreciation of his ideas during a period when his major works of art were available for consultation (and imitation) by the major artists of his times. Yet, the enigma of Leonardo which has attracted generations of scholars is perhaps best revealed by the curious notebooks which treat a myriad of topics and put forward an impressive number of heuristic ideas. As Sigmund Freud, one of his most original and controversial interpreters remarked, "he was like a man who awoke too early in the darkness, while the others were still asleep." A single letter he addressed to Ludovico Sforza, detailing his countless talents, is perhaps the best example we have of the self-conscious "universal man," the model of excellence in many complicated sciences and arts which made Leonardo the envy both of his contemporaries and of modern specialists. Although Leonardo necessarily absorbed the lessons of the Florentine Quattrocento concerning the scientific organization of pictorial space and the art of perspective, he never abandoned the direct observation of nature which, according to him, was organized in terms of the language of mathematics. As one recent intellectual historian has perceived, it was Leonardo's achievement to discover that nature speaks to man in detail. In Leonardo the eye of the artist was joined to that of the empirical scientist, and although he discovered no universal laws equivalent to those proposed later by Galileo,* Newton, or Kepler, his empirical observations were centuries ahead of his time in a variety of fields—architecture, mechanics, transportation (the Madrid Codices reveal that he apparently invented the bicycle), anatomy, and so on.

So far as we now know, Leonardo never produced a literary work in a major genre, but his notebooks reveal him to be a masterful prose stylist and a far more learned man than his famous self-description as a "homo sanza lettere" ("man without letters") would suggest. A dominant theme running throughout all his works is his general antipathy to the common humanistic assumption that book learning could explain the secrets of nature. As Leonardo himself aptly expressed it, "he who has access to the fountain does not go to the water-pot." Leonardo turned instead to the book of the world but viewed it in an essentially modern fashion, far removed from his medieval predecessors who may have spoken of the universe as God's book in terms very similar to those Leonardo uses. Numerous interesting but nonscientific subjects are treated in the notebooks: a collection of humorous remarks on the life and habits of animals, in which Leonardo depicts various human characteristics (gratitude, wrath, generosity, and so forth) in terms of traits common to animals; various interesting fables, also predominantly based upon the use of animals in the tradition of Aesop; a number of prophecies; and a collection of humorous tales and jokes ("If Petrarch was so fond of the laurel, it was because it is good in sausage and tuna; I cannot value any of this nonsense.").

With all his genius, Leonardo was a profoundly tragic figure, who never completed a host of important projects and often concealed from the rest of an admiring world the full scope of his originality. Although his few public works aroused the wonder of an age which was impressed only by authentic genius, Leonardo could nevertheless include in one of his last notebooks a note of despair which questioned the value of it all: "Tell me if anything was ever done." Perhaps his own evaluation of his life, which lay hidden in the Codex Madrid I for a number of years, is his best epitaph: "Peruse me, o reader, if you find delight in my work, since this profession very seldom returns to this world, and the perseverance to pursue it and to invent such things anew is found in few people. And come men, to see the wonders which may be discovered in nature by such studies."

See also HUMANISM, RENAISSANCE.

Bibliography: The Madrid Codices, ed. Ladislao Reti, 5 vols. (New York: McGraw-Hill, 1974); *The Notebooks of Leonardo Da Vinci,* ed. Jean Paul Richter, 2 vols. (New York: Dover, 1970)—dual language edition; Jacob Bronowski and Bruce Mazlish, *The Western Intellectual Tradition from Leonardo to Hegel* (New York: Harper, 1975); Kenneth Clark, *Leonardo da Vinci* (Baltimore: Penguin, 1973); Giancarlo Maiorino, "Toward a Definition of Leonardo da Vinci's *Anti-Umanesimo,*" *Canadian Review of Comparative Literature* 3 (1976), 236-52; Carlo Pedretti, *Leonardo: A Study in Chronology and Style* (Berkeley, Calif.: University of California Press, 1973); Ladislao Reti, ed., *The Unknown Leonardo* (New York: McGraw-Hill, 1974).

D'AZEGLIO, MASSIMO TAPPARELLI, MARCHESE (1798–1866), nobleman, painter, statesman, memorialist, and historical novelist. D'Azeglio was born in Turin of a noble and ancient family of French origin. He began his education in Florence after his family was exiled from Piedmont in the wake of the Napoleonic invasions of Italy. He returned to Turin in 1805 after Napoleon obliged the northern aristocracy to swear an oath of allegiance to his government. Although not a gifted student, he enrolled at the University of Turin in 1811, but his university career ended in 1816 when he enlisted in the Civil Guard of the city after Napoleon's downfall. After a brief visit to Rome, where he began to paint, he persuaded his father to allow him to resign his military commission. He returned to Rome in 1820 to pursue an artistic career, with his father's blessing but a rather insubstantial allowance.

In Rome, D'Azeglio set about to study English and even composed an unfinished *novella** in that language. While he learned his new profession, he engaged in a series of passionate love affairs. One of these involved the birth of an illegitimate daughter, Bice, whom he acknowledged. After a number of years spent in painting and courting, he returned to Turin, where he remained until his father's death. He was annoyed by the conservatism of the Piedmontese aristocracy and bored by the lack of cultural attractions in his native city. He managed to win critical acclaim as an artist there with a canvas based upon an incident from the Crusades ("The Death of Montmorency") as well as a book describing the history of a nearby monastery which contained a series of fashionable lithographs.

Of more importance for the future was another painting depicting an episode from the French invasion of Italy in the early sixteenth century, an incident in which thirteen Italian knights were challenged to defend Italian honor and military prowess at Barletta in 1503 by an equal number of French soldiers. With the encouragement of his cousin Cesare Balbo, D'Azeglio transposed this theme from canvas to a historical novel entitled *Ettore Fieramosca o la sfida di Barletta* (1833, *Ettore Fieramosca, or the Challenge of Barletta*). Against the historical background of this famous challenge from which the Italian knights emerged victorious, the author focuses upon the individual life of Ettore Fieramosca, one of the group, and upon his unhappy love affair with Ginevra, the wife of an Italian fighting for the French. Ginevra is eventually ravished by the infamous Cesare Borgia (immortalized by Machiavelli's* *Principe* and the rumors reported in Guicciardini's* *Storia d'Italia*). After her death, Ettore joins her by committing suicide. D'Azeglio had begun the first section of the novel by 1830.

After D'Azeglio moved to Milan, he married Giulietta, the eldest daughter of Alessandro Manzoni,* Italy's most renowned historical novelist and representative of the romantic movement. There he also became acquainted with Tommaso Grossi,* another key figure in the development of Italian romanticism* and the Italian historical novel. After Giulietta's death in 1834, D'Azeglio remarried, but he never abandoned his ties to Manzoni throughout the rest of his life.

D'Azeglio continued to paint and to exhibit his works in Milan until 1843. His most typical subjects continued to be landscapes or themes taken from history or literature (Ariosto,* in particular), many of which have overtly patriotic connotations. A second historical novel, *Niccolò de' Lapi (Palleschi e Piagnoni)* (1841, *Niccolo dei Lapi; or, The Last Days of the Florentine Republic*),added to his widespread popularity as a writer. Similar in theme to Guerrazzi's* *L'Assedio di Firenze,* this work describes the siege of Florence in 1530 and the misfortunes suffered by a former supporter of Savonarola* and his family as a result of their resistance to the Medici invaders. Although D'Azeglio's skill at blending historical themes with the private lives of his fictional characters is admirable, his novels fell far short of the literary achievements of Manzoni or Sir Walter Scott. Nonetheless, their patriotic themes made them quite popular in an age when Italian political independence was a daily preoccupation.

After 1844, D'Azeglio's interests turned away from art or literature towards politics, and he set out to back up his fervent belief in Italian independence with deeds as well as words. He became a key figure in Risorgimento history, fighting bravely in the war of 1848 against the Austrians and receiving wounds in military actions. He preceded Cavour as Piedmontese prime minister and acted as an ambassador for King Victor Emanuel during the next decade. Of most interest to modern readers, however, is his last literary work, the posthumous autobiography entitled *I miei ricordi* (1868, *Things I Remember*) which traces his life until 1845. It is a major source of historical information from the early Risorgimento period, but more importantly, it outlines D'Azeglio's belief in the need for a moral revolution to parallel the political upheavals in the peninsula. For him, the liberation of Italy entailed the creation of a new kind of Italian, an individual with a clear conception of national duty and a strong, lofty character. He saw his country's unregenerate citizens, and not the Austrians, as the chief obstacle to the creation of a free Italy.

See also GUERRAZZI, Francesco Domenico; MANZONI, Alessandro; ROMANTICISM.

Bibliography: *Tutte le opere letterarie,* ed. A. M. Ghisalberti, 2 vols. (Milan: Mursia; 1966);*Ettore Fieramosca, or The Challenge of Barletta,* trans. C. Edwards Lester (New York: Paine & Burgess, 1854); *Niccolò dei Lapi,* trans. H. Hallet (Philadelphia: Lippincott, 1850); *Things I Remember,* trans. E. R. Vincent (Oxford: Oxford University Press, 1966); Ronald Marshall, *Massimo D'Azeglio: An Artist in Politics, 1798–1866* (London: Oxford University Press, 1966).

DE AMICIS, EDMONDO (1846–1908), soldier, novelist, and journalist. After an education in Cueno and Turin, De Amicis was admitted to the military school in Modena and received his commission in the artillery in time to participate in the 1866 campaign against Austria and the conclusion of the wars of independence. When the fighting ended, he moved to Florence to edit an official publication of the Italian Ministry of War. There, he met many of the outstanding literary figures of the day and became interested in Manzoni* and his views on the *questione della lingua.** Drawing upon his own personal experiences, De Amicis published a collection of sketches entitled *La vita militare* (1868, *Military Life in Italy*) which was so successful that it moved him to abandon his military career and to become a professional writer.

De Amicis was highly skillful in assembling various sketches, stories, vignettes, or impressions around a general theme (military life, observations of a foreign country or city, school life). He employed this technique in all his future works. Although many critics consider the schematic structure and its consequent lack of unity to be an obvious defect in his literary works, this style was perfectly adapted to De Amicis's travel memoirs which were extremely popular in the nineteenth century. These include *Spagna* (1873, *Spain and the Spaniards*), *Olanda* (1874, *Holland and Its People*), *Constantinopoli* (1878–79, *Constantinople*), and *Ricordi di Parigi* (1879, *Studies of Paris*). Although sometimes superficial in his observations, De Amicis did not remain unaware of critical social and economic problems. His *Sull'Oceano* (1889, *On the Ocean*) is a sympathetic treatment of Italian emigrants going to America. Eventually, he became a socialist (1891). All his life, De Amicis insisted that an improved educational system in Italy would be the most effective means of changing social conditions in the post-Risorgimento era.

Besides his travel books, memoirs, and literary sketches, De Amicis published a Manzonian treatise on language (1905) and several literary works focusing upon matters of education and the public schools: *Il romanzo d'un maestro* (1890, *The Romance of a Schoolmaster*); *Fra scuola e casa* (1892, Between School and Home); and *La maestrina degli operai* (1895, *Won by a Woman*). Most significant is *Cuore* (1886, *Heart: A School Boy's Journal*), a somewhat sentimental description of the academic life of an Italian boy named Enrico. The novel immediately became the most popular children's book in Italy after Collodi's* *Pinocchio;* it was published in dozens of Italian editions and translated into over twenty-five foreign languages. Present-day readers, however, may view the work's overtly bourgeois ideology and its often philistine sentimentality as an unacceptable picture of public education, but the ideological qualities which make the work objectionable to some today are precisely those which guaranteed its phenomenal success when it first appeared. De Amicis's sincere hope was to stimulate the growth of a strong, healthy Italian nation through improving the quality of moral as well as academic education in the schools. *Cuore* continues to be used in the Italian public schools as a reader for younger students.

Bibliography: De Amicis, ed Antonio Baldini, 2 vols. (Milan: Garzanti, 1948); *Heart: A School Boy's Journal,* trans. Isabel Hapgood (New York: Crowell, 1922); *Military Life in Italy,* trans. W. C. Cady (New York: Putnam's, 1882); Benedetto Croce, *Letteratura della nuova Italia,* Vol. 1 (Bari: Laterza, 1956); Luigi Russo, *I narratori* (Milan: Principato, 1951).

DECADENTISMO, a movement which flourished in Italy during the last decade of the nineteenth century as a reaction to the ideological, social, and moral tenets of positivism. While its origins can be traced to a definite historical period, its chronological extension remains an open question. Science and reason, the forces which were to unveil the mysteries of life and of the universe, had failed to provide adequate answers in the eyes of writers who felt alienated and isolated from institutions dominated by scientists and by government which tended to perpetuate social injustices. The incapacity to relate to human history, nature, and other people heightened the individual's sense of solitude and alienation. Solutions were sought by probing the subconscious in the belief that it represented new dimensions in the human spirit capable of unveiling the mysteries which nature withheld. The role of the poet as society's guiding force was reconfirmed.

It was the subconscious, the irrational, the instincts which provided breakthroughs in knowledge, as opposed to reason. The idea of the dynamic evolution of history as an ever-changing force was rejected in favor of a concept of life whereby sporadic and sudden revelations resulted in a mystic union of the individual with the unknown—outside of time and history. Life and the universe were conceived of as mystery. Thus, it was the exceptional individual endowed with superior prowess and sensitivity who experienced moments of supreme inspiration and made meaningful discoveries. Since the creative process was the result of sudden flashes of insight into the unknown, the traditional forms of prosody underwent significant changes. Symbolic expression of pure rhythm which evoked and suggested indefinite emotions replaced concrete images and sentiments. The fleeting beatings of the subconscious were expressed through analogies. The syntactic link was reduced to a minimum. The word was used in such a way as to fuse together phonic, visual, and auditory values. It was no longer one of the elements in logical discourse, but encompassed in itself ideas and impressions.

The ramifications of *decadentismo* are varied, and major Italian writers associated with this movement have quite different conceptions of life and of the role of literature. Each writer reveals an existential crisis which he seeks to resolve by a subjective interpretation of society and the universe. Antonio Fogazzaro* is perhaps the writer who most acutely experienced the clash between faith and reason. Although he was fundamentally religious, his Catholicism was not based on concrete moral dogma, but rather on personal, ineffable, and mystic religious experiences. In his writings, he sought to establish a delicate balance which could be maintained only through the weakening of rational forces; these ideas caused consternation in the Catholic hierarchy. Another writer associated with the movement, Giovanni Pascoli,* saw all of life as mysterious. He believed that meaningful discoveries could be made by looking at the world through the eyes of a child and that the voice of innocence (a child) was within every adult. By being receptive to this voice, knowledge could be acquired. He modified traditional prosody to comply with a vision where there were glimpses of knowledge that could be recorded in a suggestive language. Another writer, Gabriele D'Annunzio,* sought to unveil the mysteries which engulf the essence of man and the universe through the senses and instincts. According to D'Annunzio, eroticism and sensuality were often means of penetrating and understanding the innermost sentiments of the self. In his writings, these intimate feelings were made to coincide with the ineffable rhythms of nature. A direct fusion of the self with nature was established by bypassing reason and science in favor of one's own impulsive and illogical temperament. Form and content were dictated by the will of an exceptional individual whose ways distinguished him from other men; his refined sensitivity and his physical sophistication and taste set him apart from others. Italo Svevo,* as opposed to the above writers, who in varying degrees mythicized and exalted the self or the human condition, sought demystification, dissolution, and irony in his writings. His tireless and rigorous questioning is reminiscent of the relativism of his contemporary, Luigi Pirandello.* In his efforts to create a literature that would more accurately reflect the human condition, Svevo meticulously probed into the workings of the human psyche. The individual as master of himself and confident of his future is absent from his writings. His research on the human psyche revealed a being frequently in contradiction with itself, wanting to do one thing but ending up doing something else. There seemed to be no direct correlation between one's innermost feelings and his outward behavior.

Benedetto Croce's* vitriolic commentaries on Italian and European *decadentismo* set the tone for the negative criticism which ensued in Italy for nearly fifty years. He labeled these writings false and artificial, and questioned their ability to convey authentic human sentiments. Since many of these writers sought to project the unusual and the refined, Croce felt that creative spontaneity was sacrificed in favor of stylistic, melodic, and contextual considerations which writers had decided to accomplish a priori. Needless to say, this conception of literature was in direct opposition to Croce's aesthetic based on a delicate synthesis of form and content.

A more objective interpretation is provided by Walter Binni (1913–   ) who rejects the negative moral judgment which had been cast on the decadent writers. It is absurd, he argues, to speak of decadence in literature, since each historical moment is unique and should be judged on its own merits without aesthetic prejudices. Through a careful reading of the literature of the period, he concludes that the decadents created a literature which was entirely original for its mysterious and musical qualities.

Carlo Salinari (1919–77) offers a Marxist interpretation of the period. After reaffirming the close correlation between literature and society, he concludes that Pascoli's child, Fogazzaro's saint, D'Annunzio's superman, and Pirandello's alienated man were literary and social figures who reflected the crisis of the bourgeois society. Again the term *decadent* came to have a negative connotation; for Salinari, however, it was not the writer who was in crisis but an entire society.

Bibliography: Walter Binni, *La poetica del decadentismo italiano* (Florence: Sansoni, 1949); Arcangelo Leone de Castris, *Il decadentismo italiano: Svevo, Pirandello, D'Annunzio* (Bari: De Donato, 1974); Mario Praz, *The Romantic Agony*, 2nd ed. (New York: Oxford University Press, 1970); Carlo Salinari, *Miti e coscienza del decadentismo italiano* (Milan: Feltrinelli, 1960).

Silvano Garofalo

DE CÉSPEDES, ALBA (1911–   ), Cuban-born novelist and journalist from a distinguished Cuban family, numbering two presidents of the Cuban republic in its history. Although De Céspedes's three early novels and poetry attracted little attention, *Nessuno torna indietro* (1938, *There's No Turning Back*), a minute examination of eight women, was an international success with twenty-four different translations. It was banned by the fascists in 1940, along with her next novel *Fuga* (1940, Flight), a collection of stories. During the resistance, De Céspedes broadcast for the partisans with the code-name Clorinda. Her experiences during the war inspired *Dalla parte di lei* (1949, *The Best of Husbands*), a probing study of the rights of women within marriage. This work was far ahead of its time in its portrayal of a strong feminine protagonist. The examination of the dilemma of the modern woman and her search for individual self-expression is continued in a number of De Céspedes's works, including *Quaderno proibito* (1952, *The Secret*), *Prima e dopo* (1955, *Between Then and Now*), and *Il rimorso* (1963, *Remorse*). *La bambolona* (1967, *La Bambolona*—the "big doll") marks De Céspedes's shift to a male protagonist and is a comic portrayal of a man whose love for a much younger woman of a lower social class causes his ruin. She has written plays and poems (some in French), and her by-line appears regularly in major Italian periodicals. In spite of her undeniable narrative talents and her perceptive treatment of feminist questions, De Céspedes has not yet received serious consideration from Italian critics and is almost as well known abroad as in Italy. Her works have received a remarkable number of English translations, which is perhaps a testament to the current appeal of her themes.

Bibliography: The Best of Husbands, trans. Frances Frenaye (New York: Macmillan, 1952); *Between Then and Now,* trans. Isabel Quigly (London: Jonathan Cape, 1959); *La Bambolona,* trans. Isabel Quigly (London: Michael Joseph, 1969); *Remorse,* trans. William Weaver (Garden City, N.Y.: Doubleday, 1967); *The Secret,* trans. Isabel Quigly (London: Harvill Press, 1957); *There's No Turning Back,* trans. Jan Nobel (London: Jarrolds, 1941).

DE FILIPPO, EDUARDO (1900–), Neapolitan playwright and the most distinguished member of a family of actors and showpeople. De Filippo's theatrical debut took place in 1906 with a small role in a play by Eduardo Scarpetta (1853–1925), and he continued to perform in a number of companies with his brother Peppino and his sister Titina. After the three formed their own company, first the Teatro Umoristico di Eduardo De Filippo con Titina e Peppino, and then the Teatro Umoristico I De Filippo, their tour of Italy in 1931–32 was so successful that it launched a theatrical venture which lasted for twelve years. At this time, Peppino left the troupe to perform at the Teatro Nuovo in Milan, and De Filippo formed another company, Il Teatro di Eduardo, which made a successful debut with *Napoli milionaria!* (1945, Naples' Millionaires!). De Filippo is generally regarded as this century's best dialect playwright and a dramatic writer exceeded in importance by only Pirandello and Betti in the twentieth century. He has also published a volume of poetry, written several filmscripts, and produced or directed the works of many other dramatists, including those of Betti,* Pirandello,* and Molière.

De Filippo's dramatic output is impressive. The plays usually regarded as his best are *Sik-Sik, l'artefice magico* (1929, *Sik-Sik, The Masterful Magician*); *Questi fantasmi!* (1946, *Oh, These Ghosts!*); *Filumena Marturano* (1946, *Filumena Marturano*), also the basis of Vittorio De Sica's well-known film, *Marriage Italian Style* (1964); *Grande magìa* (1948, *Grand Magic*); *Le voci di dentro* (1948, The Voices from Within); *Sabato, domenica e lunedí* (1959, *Saturday, Sunday, Monday*), a work which received the London drama critics' award in 1973; *Il sindaco del Rione Sanità* (1960, *The Local Authority*); and *L'arte della commedia* (1964, The Art of Comedy). His works are greatly indebted to a number of popular and learned or literary sources, including the *commedia dell'arte;** his own experience in the Neapolitan dialect theatre of Scarpetta, Salvatore Di Giacomo,* and Raffaelo Viviani (1888–1950); the music halls and vaudeville acts popular between the world wars; and the example of Pirandello, whose *Liolà* he produced in 1933 and with whom he collaborated on the writing of a play in dialect just before the Nobel laureate's death.

Because of his deep roots in the dialect theatre of Naples, De Filippo's plays tend to stress vivid characterization over plot; to employ typically Neapolitan locales, characters, and language; and to embody a tragicomic view of the world which owes as much to his birthplace as to Pirandello's *umorismo* ("the sentiment of the contrary"). He tends to build his plots around the dialectic of illusion and reality (typical of his master), and both De Filippo and Pirandello find the greatest source of their dramatic material in the institution of the family. Indeed, the family may constitute the key to De Filippo's dramaturgy and serves as the only firm metaphysical support for his characters. In *Filumena Marturano* and *Il sindaco del Rione Sanità*, De Filippo demonstrates how both a kept woman and a powerful Camorra gangster bow to the compelling authority of the nuclear family and its moral demands upon the individual. In *Questi fantasmi!*, a man named Pasquale pretends to believe his wife's lover to be a ghost in order to avoid the necessity of renouncing her, thereby revealing his kinship to the suffering *raisonneurs* of Pirandello's early works. Moved by compassion for Pasquale's situation, the lover/ghost abandons Maria to her husband, but the threat of another potential "ghost" at the end of the play belies any note of optimism. *Le voci di dentro* dramatizes the bad faith existing within an entire family after it is accused of the murder a man has witnessed them committing in a dream. The family's reactions to this accusation reveal their lack of confidence in each other and their inability to communicate—the crime for which they are ultimately guilty. One of the most imaginative of De Filippo's characters appears in this work—Uncle Nicola, a man who has abandoned normal conversation with his fellows and who expresses himself only with fireworks. Recalling Goldoni's* play of the same title, *L'arte della commedia* may be considered De Filippo's theoretical but comical statement upon the nature of the theatre and upon the Pirandellian theme of illusion and reality he so often employed in his own works.

See also COMMEDIA DELL'ARTE; PIRANDELLO, Luigi.

Bibliography: I capolavori di Eduardo, 2 vols. (Turin: Einaudi, 1973); *Oh, These Ghosts!,* in *Tulane Drama Review* 8 (1964), 118–62; *Saturday, Sunday, Monday,* trans. Keith Waterhouse and Willis Hall (London: Heinemann, 1974); *Sik-Sik, The Masterful Magician,* trans. Robert G. Bender, *Italian Quarterly* 11 (1967), 19–42; *Three Plays,* trans. Carlo Ardito (London: Hamilton, 1976); Robert G. Bender, "A Critical Estimate of Eduardo De Filippo," *Italian Quarterly* 11 (1967), 3–18, and "Pulcinella, Pirandello, and Other Influences on De Filippo's Dramaturgy," *Italian Quarterly* 12 (1968), 39–71; Luciano Codignola, "Reading De Filippo," *Tulane Drama Review* 8 (1964), 108–17; Mario B. Mignone, *Il teatro di Eduardo De Filippo: critica sociale* (Rome: Trevi, 1974).

DEL BAGNO, PANUCCIO, (circa 1215 to 1234–circa 1276), Pisan lyric poet. Twenty-two of Panuccio's lyrics (including sonnets* and *canzoni**) remain in two extant manuscripts which represent the largest collection of lyrics from any Pisan poet of his day. While literary historians often dismiss him as obscure (a reference to his unusual word order) or difficult (his particular language is translated into standard Italian in most editions), recent criticism has discovered in Panuccio's lyrics a number of important and original features: a highly organized *canzoniere* (albeit composed of only a few poems) wherein the individual works reflect stages in the spiritual development treated in the poetry; a concept of the painful nature of the beloved's image based upon its ultimate origin in the poet's imagination (a link to Cavalcanti*); and a view of love as a potential threat to the "true good" of human reason. A number of his Pisan and Pistoian contemporaries, including Geri Giannini (dates uncertain), Galletto Pisano (died circa 1301), and Meo Abbracciavacca (died circa 1313), reflect his influence, although most literary historians have described Panuccio himself as a mere follower of Guittone d'Arezzo.* While he wrote relatively few poems in comparison to his contemporaries in Tuscany or Sicily, his *canzoniere* moves beyond the "vain" love of the courtly and troubadour tradition and points to the much greater and more profound lyrics of both Dante* and Petrarch.*

See also GUITTONE D'AREZZO.

Bibliography: Mark Musa, *The Poetry of Panuccio del Bagno* (Bloomington, Ind.: Indiana University Press, 1965)—contains both texts and a critical study of the poetry.

DELEDDA, GRAZIA (1871–1936), novelist and Nobel laureate. Born in Nuoro (Sardinia) into a middle-class family, Deledda never had a formal university education but was an avid reader of nineteenth-century fiction (especially works by Russian novelists, Balzac, whom she eventually translated, Fogazzaro,* Carducci,* D'Annunzio,* Verga,* and De Amicis*). Set in the Sardinian locale that was to become identified with her greatest writing, her first short stories appeared during 1888–89 in magazines published in Rome and Milan. Deledda's early works attracted the attention of a number of critics, most of whom saw her as a regional writer in the naturalist tradition of Verga and Capuana.* Besides her early *novelle** and novels, she published an article on the folk customs of her native Nuoro in 1883 which contains a reference to Tolstoy, the first indication we have of her interest in the Russian fiction of the period. Her fame was assured by the publication of the novel *Anime oneste* (1885, Honest People), prefaced with an admiring essay by a well-known scholar of the period, and then, by Luigi Capuana's favorable review of *La via del male* (1886, The Path of Evil).

In 1899, Deledda met Palmiro Madesani in Cagliari and married him in the following year; the couple then moved to Rome, where Deledda lived for the rest of her life. In the next decade, she published some of her most important novels, including *Dopo il divorzio* (1902, *After the Divorce*); *Elias Portolu* (1903, Elias Portolu); and *Cenere* (1904, *Ashes*). The first recounts the story of Costantino Ledda, a man condemned to a long prison term for a murder he did not commit. His wife Giovanna finally decides to divorce him and to marry a rich landowner, but a deathbed confession by the actual murderer frees Costantino and presents the couple with a moral dilemma. Deledda's intimate and sympathetic descriptions of Sardinian customs constitute the most interesting element of this novel. With its similar setting and theme, *Elias Portolu* tells of another man unjustly imprisoned who returns home to Sardinia and falls in love with his brother's fiancée. To escape this temptation, he decides to become a priest, but just before his ordination, his brother dies. Yet, he cannot bring himself to follow the tradition of marrying a dead brother's wife to care for his family, and the woman marries another man. Here, as elsewhere in the works treating Sardinia, social customs and traditions seem to conspire against the characters' quest for happiness. Regarded as one of Deledda's masterpieces, *Elias Portolu* exemplifies her interest in a tragic cycle of innocence, sin, suffering, and expiation. *Cenere,* the fame of which was magnified by a film version in 1916 starring Eleonora Duse, perpetuates Deledda's pessimism and her view of life dominated by a sense of guilt and a search for expiation from sin. In this novel, everything about life is shown to have no meaning other than the symbol of death (ashes) in the title.

The period between *Cenere* and 1927, the year Deledda received the Nobel Prize for Literature for 1926, witnessed the publication of many books, including *L'edera* (1906, Ivy); *Colombi e sparvieri* (1912, Doves and Sparrowhawks); *Canne al vento* (1913, Reeds in the Wind); *La madre* (1920, *The Mother*); and *Il segreto dell'uomo solitario* (1921, The Secret of the Solitary Man). Of this group, *La madre* is the most famous and the work most responsible for the award of the Nobel Prize; a preface to the English edition by D. H. Lawrence greatly assisted its reception abroad. Possessing a simplicity of plot and the tone of a classical tragedy, it narrates the story of Paulo, a priest, who falls in love with one of his parishioners, Agnese. His passion is discovered by his mother, who tries to persuade him to abandon this illicit love and to remain faithful to his spiritual vocation. The novel thus combines Deledda's usual focus upon sin and expiation with the conflict between love and duty. Paulo visits Agnese one final time, resists temptation, and returns to his spiritual mission, but Agnese threatens to denounce him on the following day at Mass. The woman is strangely unable to carry out her threat when she approaches the altar during the service, but the possibility has caused his mother so much anguish that she dies during the service while he looks on from the altar.

After 1921, the themes and narrative structures in Deledda's fiction were modified in some respects: the later novels embody a less naturalistic style and give less attention to the description of her familiar Sardinian landscapes. Most critics agree that these later novels are somewhat less successful. Among them are *La fuga in Egitto* (1925, The Flight into Egypt); *Il vecchio e i fanciulli* (1928, The Old Man and the Children); and *Cosima* (1937, Cosima), an autobiographical novel which appeared posthumously.

Deledda's many prose works, a total of some forty volumes of *novelle* and novels, reflect various literary currents. Her interest in violent passion and its tragic effects is romantic, while her sense of fate or destiny and her attention to the customs of her native Sardinia embody the concerns of the Italian *veristi*. Furthermore, many critics link her to *decadentismo* because of her emphasis upon the power of the instincts and irrational forces. She remains the only Italian woman, and one of the few female writers of any nation, to have been awarded the Nobel Prize for Literature.

See also DECADENTISMO; VERISMO.

Bibliography: Romanzi e novelle, ed. Natalino Sapegno (Milan: Mondadori, 1971); *After the Divorce,* trans. Maria Lansdale (New York: Holt, 1905); *Ashes,* trans. Helen Colvill (New York: John Lane, 1908); *The Mother,* trans. Mary Steegman (1923; rpt. Dunwoody, Ga.: Berg, 1974); Carolyn Balducci, *A Self-Made Woman* (Boston: Houghton-Mifflin, 1975); Euralio De Michelis, *Grazia Deledda e il Decadentismo* (Florence: La Nuova Italia, 1938); Sergio Pacifici, *The Modern Italian Novel from Capuana to Tozzi* (Carbondale, Ill.: Southern Illinois University Press, 1973).

DELLA CASA, GIOVANNI (1503–1556), Florentine poet, writer on manners and morals, ecclesiastic, and diplomat. Born most likely at Mugello into a rich Florentine family, Della Casa spent his formative years in Bologna where he studied law and especially literature, becoming part of a literary circle that included Pietro Bembo* and Ludovico Beccadelli (1501–72). He spent 1526 and 1527 with Beccadelli at his family estate in Mugello exclusively reading Cicero and then, in 1528, went with his friend to Padua in order to complete his humanist education by learning Greek. Della Casa settled in Rome after 1532, where, under the protection of the powerful Alessandro Farnese, he began an ecclesiastical and diplomatic career. He became clerk of the Apostolic Chamber in 1538, papal emissary to Florence in 1541, and archbishop of Benevento and papal nunzio to Venice in 1544. When Farnese fell from power at the accession of Julius III to the papacy in 1551, Della Casa retired to Venice and occupied himself with his writing. He was recalled to Rome in 1555 by the new pope, Paul IV, made secretary of state to the Vatican, but failed to obtain a desired cardinalship before his death a year later.

Except for a handful of fairly licentious, comic, youthful poems written at Rome in the 1530s under the inspiration of his friend, the comic poet Francesco Berni,* most of Della Casa's *Rime* (1558, Lyric Poems) were produced during his stay in Venice between 1551 and 1555. Although he closely imitated Petrarch's* style and diction, and followed the literary advice of Bembo, Della Casa gave his lyrics a novelty widely acclaimed in the Renaissance* through his careful manipulation of their style. He dramatized Petrarch's images by placing them in unexpected contexts, rendered them more concrete by extending them literally, and generally made what he imitated thoroughly his own possession. He was most praised, especially by the greatest lyric poet of the century, Torquato Tasso,* for the gravity of his style. He achieved this quality by the introduction of dramatic pauses into the verse, by frequent enjambement of both lines and stanzas, and by mild distortions of normal word order. All of Della Casa's poems express a fundamental anxiety and an inquietude about love or ambition which are often coupled with a longing for release, peace, and even death. The combination of this troubled content and the sublime style made Della Casa's fewer than eighty lyrics among the best of the sixteenth century.

Although he wrote several formal, Ciceronian orations, many letters, and a Latin treatise on the relations between friends of unequal status, Della Casa's enduring prose work is *Il Galateo, ovvero de' Costumi* (1558, *Galateo, of manners and behaviour*), a work whose title is now used to designate any book of etiquette as well as good manners themselves. It was named after Galeazzo (*Lat.* Galatheus) Florimonte, the bishop of Sessa who suggested the project to the author during his Venetian sojourn of 1551–55. In this work, Della Casa generally eschews the Ciceronianism of his earlier orations; his style is informal, spontaneous, and lively, characterized by vigorous colloquial expressions and popular idioms. Although the book shows the influence of Ciceronian and Aristotelian moral philosophy, it is also largely indebted to Boccaccio's* *Decameron* for its familiar style, for specific examples of characters engaged in ideal and un-ideal behavior, and for its use of stories and anecdotes to illustrate moral principles. Presented as the advice of an old, illiterate gentleman to a young student, Della Casa's work concerns itself with a wide range of subjects from table manners and personal appearance to the modes of behavior among people of different social ranks. The *Galateo* is pragmatic and realistic, oriented toward the concrete realities of its own society, and aims to teach the individual how to manipulate his behavior so as to please all those around him. At the same time, it is not a defense of pure opportunism, for it is based on the assumption that the individual's exterior equilibrium and charm will be a reflection of an interior moral harmony. Della Casa assumes the existence of a class-structured society and equates desirable behavior with upper-class norms, condemning the undesirable as common or plebeian and arguing instead for the ancient, aristocratic, and Aristotelian ideals of moderation *(misura)*, tact, and discretion. Like the other great treatise on manners from the Italian Renaissance, Baldesar Castiglione's* *Libro del Cortegiano* (1528, *The Book of the Courtier*), Della Casa's work ultimately suggests, even if it never describes, an ideal, elite society of cultivated courtiers, ladies, and gentlemen. It is informed by the conviction that good manners and civil conversation are essential for human beings if they are to endure the endless troubles and cares of their condition.

See also BEMBO, Pietro; BERNI, Francesco; CASTIGLIONE, Baldesar; PETRARCA, Francesco; PETRARCHISM; TASSO, Torquato.

Bibliography: Galateo ovvero de' costumi, ed. Bruno Maier (Milan: Mursia, 1971); *Galateo, of manners and behaviour*, trans. Robert Peterson (1576), ed. with an introduction by Joel E. Spingarn (Boston: Merrymount, 1914); Ettore Bonora, "Aspetti della prosa del Rinascimento: Il boccaccismo del 'Galateo'," *Giornale storico della letteratura italiana*, 133 (1956), 349–63; W. L. Bullock, "The Lyric Innovations of G. Della Casa," *Publications of the Modern Language Association*, 41 (1926), 82–90; Adriano Seroni, "Sulle *Rime morali* di G. Della Casa," *Paragone*, 226 (1968), 112–23.

Wayne A. Rebhorn

DELLA MIRANDOLA, GIOVANNI PICO (1463–1494), humanist and Neo-Platonist. Pico, the younger son of a wealthy and noble feudal family, was born in Mirandola near Modena in northern Italy and received a humanistic education (including Latin and perhaps Greek) at home. Destined by his mother for the church, he went to Bologna in 1477 to study canon law but left to take up philosophy at the universities in Ferrara and Padua. After 1482, he traveled to Paris and frequently to Florence, and began to learn Hebrew and Arabic. In his early years, Pico wrote poetry and letters in both Latin and Italian, reflecting his humanist upbringing. In 1485, he engaged in a correspondence with Ermolao Barbaro (1453–94) over the merits of humanism* and Scholasticism, in which he defended the worth of Scholasticism against Barbaro's contempt without denying his humanist beliefs. Pico's defense of Scholasticism is but one instance of his syncretism.

After this time, Pico devoted himself to the study of philosophy. Convinced that all philosophers, thinkers, and theologians participated in the one universal truth, he eventually concluded that philosophical knowledge and human reason must be supplemented by religion and revelation which would guide man to God. Although his personal library included works in Italian, Latin, Greek, Hebrew, Arabic, and Aramaic, most of his books were classical and medieval texts in Latin. The Christian Latin tradition was always to provide him with a frame of reference for his writing. In addition, Pico embraced the occult or hermetic tradition of religious truth deriving from Hermes Trismegistus, Orpheus, Pythagoras, and the major Greek philosophers whose secret meanings could be culled from the text by allegorical interpretation. His study of Hebrew brought him into contact with the Cabala, a Jewish tradition of biblical interpretation, which he utilized as another tool in scriptural exegesis. In general, Pico used Greek and Jewish sources of wisdom insofar as they agreed with his own basically Christian principles. This broad historical and philosophical syncretism goes beyond the ecclecticism of Nicholas of Cusa (1401–64) and Ficino* and is, perhaps, Pico's crucial contribution to Renaissance* thought.

Pico's diverse interests led to the writing of nine hundred theses or *Conclusiones,* printed in December 1486 and presented in Rome for public debate among scholars in January 1487. Unfortunately, the debate was never held, for the commission appointed by Pope Innocent VIII to investigate the theses condemned thirteen propositions. Pico subsequently became embroiled in a conflict with church authorities and tried to flee to France, where he was eventually arrested and imprisoned. At the behest of several Italian princes, he was paroled and remained under the protection of Lorenzo de' Medici* until his untimely death in 1494. In 1493, he was finally cleared of all charges by Pope Alexander VI. To introduce this proposed debate, Pico prepared his famous *Oratio* (1486, *Oration*), commonly referred to as the *Oratio de hominis dignitate (Oration on the Dignity of Man);* it was not printed until after his death in an edition of 1495–96 in the care of his nephew. Since this work justifies the study and practice of philosophy as the worthiest human undertaking and proposes the idea of a universal harmony among philosophies, the addition to the title is somewhat misleading. However, the introductory passage to which it refers contains Pico's highly optimistic account of human nature and human potential which makes this his best known work. Although man was defined as a kind of afterthought in creation, because he was made after the other creatures had been placed in the highest, middle, and lowest orders, Pico considered man to be God's finest inspiration. Not only could he admire and comprehend God's handiwork, the universe, but similar to Proteus, he could also fashion himself in whatever form he wished. Through freedom of choice, he could degenerate to the bestial level or ascend to the Divine, and Pico emphasizes human freedom and creativity as a reflection of Divine powers.

Although less famous, other works by Pico are worthy of mention. The *Heptaplus* (1489, *The Sevenfold Narration of the Six Days of Genesis*), dedicated to his patron Lorenzo de' Medici, is a commentary on the first book of the Bible which illustrates his method of interpreting the Scriptures. Pico finds Genesis to be the source of the medieval cosmology which divided the creation into three levels of existence—the intelligences, the heavenly bodies, and the corruptible earthly bodies. Moses, Pico claimed, had anticipated both the findings of Greek natural science and the Platonic view of man as the intermediary between the physical and spiritual worlds, to which he compares the biblical notion that human beings were created in the Divine image. It is Pico's view that the physical order is a reflection of philosophic and religious truth. In this work, the Cabalistic method of interpretation leads him to assign the scriptural texts multiple meanings. The short treatise *De Ente et Uno* (1491, *On Being and the One*), dedicated to the poet Poliziano,* manifests his belief that there was a basic agreement between Plato and Aristotle. Thus, Pico joins a long tradition which held that the two greatest thinkers of classical antiquity actually expressed the same basic ideas. Pico's last book, the *Disputationes adversus astrologiam divinatricem* (Disputations Against Astrology), which death prevented him from revising, deals with yet another topic of interest to Renaissance thinkers. The study summarizes the astrological literature of previous centuries (both favorable and critical) and concludes that the stars act upon earthly things only through light and heat, not through any occult qualities that are mistakenly attributed to them. Pico's chief objection to astrology is religious, not scientific, but even a scientist of the stature of Kepler modified his initial belief in astrology under Pico's influence.

Although Pico died before he had time to complete his ambitious synthesis of Plato and Aristotle, his influence grew among a number of later humanists. Sir Thomas More, who admired Pico's works, wrote an English translation of the biography written by Pico's nephew entitled *The Life of John Picus, Earl of Mirandula*. The *Disputationes* influenced not only

Kepler but also alchemists such as John Dee and Robert Fludd. Thomas Stanley, editor of Aeschylus and mid-seventeenth-century historian and poet, translated Pico's commentary on the *canzone* of Girolamo Benivieni* (1486), which became an important source of Neo-Platonic thought abroad. The metaphysical poet Thomas Traherne and a group of Platonists at Cambridge during this same period were influenced by the *Oratio*.

See also BENIVIENI, Girolamo; FICINO, Marsilio; MEDICI, Lorenzo de'; POLIZIANO, Angelo.

Bibliography: On the Dignity of Man, On Being and the One, Heptaplus, trans. Paul J. W. Miller, et al. (Indianapolis, Ind.: Bobbs-Merrill, 1965); *Renaissance Philosophy: The Italian Philosophers,* eds. Arturo B. Fallico and Herman Shapiro (New York: Random House, 1967)—contains the *Oratio* and the letter to Ermolao Barbaro; *L'opera e il pensiero di Giovanni Pico Della Mirandola nella storia dell'umanesimo* (Florence: Istituto nazionale di studi sul Rinascimento, 1965); Eugenio Garin, *Portraits from the Quattrocento* (New York: Harper, 1972); Sears Jayne, "Ficino and the Platonism of the English Renaissance," *Comparative Literature* 4 (1952), 214–38; Paul Kristeller, *Eight Philosophers of the Italian Renaissance* (Stanford, Calif.: Stanford University Press, 1964); Nesca Robb, *Neoplatonism of the Italian Renaissance* (1935; rpt. New York: Octagon, 1968); Charles Trinkaus, *In Our Image and Likeness: Humanity and Divinity in Italian Renaissance Thought,* 2 vols. (Chicago: University of Chicago Press, 1970).

DELLA PORTA, GIAMBATTISTA (1535–1615), scientist and playwright. Born into a Neapolitan patrician family, Della Porta apparently had the benefit of an extensive private education in the sciences and the humanities. At an early age, he seems to have acquired a taste for magic and the occult as well as for science, and the closely related subjects occupied most of his lifetime. He considered his dramatic works primarily a pastime. Between 1558 and 1578, Della Porta was denounced before the Neapolitan Inquisition for his interest in magic, but his lack of interest in the theological or philosophical implications of science saw him through the experience with no ill effects. In 1558, his *Magiae naturalis (Natural Magick)* appeared, joining his *L'arte del ricordare* (1556, The Art of Memory), and was followed by a treatise on cryptography, *De furtivis literarum* (1563, On Secret Writing). Between 1566 and 1583, he published nothing but conducted numerous scientific experiments and obtained the patronage of Cardinal Luigi d'Este. Although his search for the philosopher's stone was a failure, he produced many learned works: *Pomarium* (1583, The Orchard), a work on fruit-growing; *Olivetum,* (1584, The Olive-Grove), a companion piece on trees; *De humana physiognomonia* (1586, On Human Physiognomy), a treatise devoted to the characterization of personality traits from facial features; *Phytognomonica* (1583, The Physiognomy of Plants); *De refractione* (1593, On Refraction), a treatise on optics which

after 1611 figured in the polemical debate over the invention of the telescope; and other works on hydraulics, the art of prophecy and free will,
chemistry and alchemy, and fortifications. Della Porta was one of the
earliest members of the Accademia de' Lincei, which was to include
Galileo* and most of the other important Italian scientists of the period.
His scientific work, even when bordering on the eccentric, reflected an
emphasis upon observation rather than authority and always aimed at a
practical application of scientific knowledge.

Della Porta's scientific work is now of interest only to specialists in the
history of science, but his plays have retained an importance that their
author would never have imagined possible. His first play appeared in print
in 1589, and by the time of his death, fourteen comedies, along with several
tragedies or tragicomedies, had been published. He left behind a number of
unpublished plays and incomplete works which included the comedies of
Plautus in Italian translation. His *Penelope* (1591, Penelope), a drama
based on the *Odyssey,* has, in keeping with the theories of Giraldi,* a happy
ending and a Counter-Reformation moralistic tone. For a man who had
devoted his life to studying the occult, it is also no surprise that in this play
he attempts to evoke the marvelous, that central concern of Baroque*
literary theory and practice. Besides this tragicomedy, Della Porta wrote a
sacred tragedy about St. George, *Il Giorgio* (1611, St. George), and
L'Ulisse (1614, Ulysses), a tragedy which celebrates neither the Greek
hero's wartime exploits nor his return home, but rather his death at the
hands of his son Telemachus.

Della Porta's comedies are classified by most critics as "serious"
comedy, that is, comedy which employs potentially tragic situations but
which avoids the suffering and death normal to a tragedy by resolving
the conflicts in a happy way. Although learned comedy often takes its
plots and characters from Latin models while serious comedy usually
borrows from *novelle** and romances, this division cannot be sustained
with Della Porta, for he used both Latin models and prose sources. For
Della Porta, comedy involved a search for a novel, marvelous, pleasing,
and well-constructed plot with an emphasis upon peripety in the fourth act,
a view he reiterates in prefaces to *I due fratelli rivali* (1601, The Two Rival
Brothers) and *La carbonaria* (1606, Blackface). He adopts the stock character types found in the *commedia dell'arte,** but he often exaggerates
their traits and places them in plays with coherent structures and polished
language. *La fantasca* (1592, The Maidservant), for example, contains two
excellent versions of the braggart soldier. *La sorella* (1589, The Sister)—
one of his most influential works abroad—employs the clever servant, the
braggart soldier, and the parasite. Based either upon one of Bandello's*
novelle (I, 22) or upon an episode in Ariosto's* *Orlando furioso* (The
Frenzy of Orlando) which finds parallels in Shakespeare's *Much Ado*

About Nothing and Spenser's *Faerie Queene, I due fratelli rivali* displays not only type-characters but also intricate complications and a series of comic reversals. Other comedies of special interest include *L'astrologo* (1606, The Astrologer), *La Cintia* (1601, Cintia), and *La trappolaria* (1596, The Comedy of Trappola).

Della Porta's early translations of Plautus always guided his work, for he was no original genius, but it was precisely this element of classicism in his works that attracted foreign readers. In France, several of his plays were adapted by Jean Routrou. In England, at least five of his works were adapted into either Latin or English. There were versions of *La Cintia, La sorella,* and *La trappolaria* by Walter Hawkesworth, Samuel Brooke, and George Ruggle, respectively. Furthermore, Thomas Tomkis's *Albumazar* (1615) was based upon *L'astrologo,* while Thomas Middleton's *No Wit, No Help Like a Woman's* (1610) was taken from *La sorella.* In addition, his *Magiae naturalis* underwent an anonymous English translation in 1658, while many of his Latin works attracted an even wider audience.

Bibliography: Le commedie, ed. Vincenzo Spampanato, 2 vols. (Bari: Laterza, 1910–11); *Natural Magick,* ed. Derek Price (New York: Basic Books, 1957); Louise George Clubb, *Giambattista Della Porta, Dramatist* (Princeton, N.J.: Princeton University Press, 1965).

DELLA VALLE, FEDERICO (circa 1560–circa 1628), dramatist, poet, and author of orations. Della Valle was born near Asti in the region of Piedmont and became administrator of cavalry in Turin for Duchess Catherine, daughter of King Philip II of Spain and wife of Duke Charles Emmanuel I. Upon the death of his patroness in 1597, Della Valle left the inhospitable atmosphere of the court of the House of Savoy to live in Milan under the protection of Spanish nobles. The experience of working at a court where his talents were never fully appreciated embittered Della Valle, who came to view involvement in political and all worldly affairs as a vain and painful career ending in total disillusionment. As a courtier, he composed an epithalamium for the royal wedding, *intermezzi* for official occasions, and sonnets* and madrigals* in honor of nobles and prelates. In his verse dramas of hendecasyllabic and septenary lines, he showed himself a spokesman for the Catholic Reformation, expressing the anguished conscience of an age of religious dissent, fierce political ambition, and an intense longing for the spiritual peace offered by a pure faith. Reflecting the Baroque* awareness of the world as torn by oppositions, Della Valle upheld an unshakeable confidence in God's goodness while acknowledging and portraying the wretchedness of human existence.

Through Milanese and Turinese editions of 1627 and 1629 as well as from original manuscripts, Della Valle's plays have come to be recognized as major expressions of a tragic comprehension of human destiny. Although all of his plays (at least in their original versions) belong to his Turinese period, only one of them, the tragicomedy *Adelonda di Frigia* (Adelonda of Phrygia), was actually performed during his lifetime. Piedmontese nobles presented the play in 1595 to honor a visit by Archduke Albert Cardinal of Austria on his way home from Spain. Despite its happy outcome, *Adelonda di Frigia* anticipated the content of all Della Valle's dramatic works, with its focus on a heroine resisting adverse circumstances, the capriciousness of fortune, the responsibilities of political power, and the belief in an eternal order of Divine justice. Modeled on Euripides's *Iphigenia in Tauris,* this play contrasts a world of barbaric customs and human sacrifices with an ideal of civilized rightness and true faith as represented by the heroine Adelonda, princess of Phrygia, before her cruel captors, the Amazons. On the way to wed Prince Mirmirano of Pontos, a storm at sea forces Adelonda to land on the Amazon island, where she has had to become priestess in the temple where female warriors sacrifice male victims. At the center of the play is a conflict born of Adelonda's insistence on law as a principle of both human and heavenly justice as opposed to the rule of absolute force by the Amazon Queen Antiope. A tragic crisis occurs when Adelonda has to preside over the execution of her fiancé and his friend Almaro, who arrive on the island to rescue the princess. However, since this play was intended for a festive occasion, its resolution is serene as Adelonda escapes in the company of Mirmirano, Almaro, and her ladies-in-waiting, while the idol worshipped by the Amazons orders the warrior women to change their ways in favor of peace and love. This restoration of a society based on just laws and a religion of charity was not to characterize Della Valle's tragic vision of life, where victory through individual initiative as well as Divine intervention would merely be interpreted as one moment in a life of struggle.

Doubtless, the most important of all Della Valle's plays is *La Reina di Scozia (The Queen of Scotland),* which the author first wrote in 1591, just four years after the execution of Mary Stuart, Queen of Scots. Late in his life, Della Valle prepared a definitive version of the play, in which he toned down his criticism of Queen Elizabeth I of England in order to concentrate on the martyrdom of a monarch unswerving in her Roman Catholic faith. Unlike the later tragedy of moral error by Friedrich von Schiller on the same subject, Della Valle's play presents Mary Stuart as a saint sacrificed by the agents of a heretical religion. This tragedy's structure is a perfect model of classical construction: events take place at the dusk of Mary's last day of life, and the scene is the narrow courtyard of the English castle where the queen and her tiny court are held captive. Although the Catholic ruler and her devoted ladies-in-waiting dream of the lovely fields and rivers of their native Scotland, their fate is either the scaffold or prison.

Spatial constriction also characterizes the play *Ester (Esther),* taken from the Bible. Here the drama occurs in the antechamber of the Persian King Assuero (Ahasuerus) at Susa, where the courtly environment is one of absolute corruption without the redeeming ideal of royal generosity which Mary Stuart represented. The chief agent of the politics of force and oppression, but ironically also its main victim, is the vizier Aman (Haman), whose arrogance nearly brings about the destruction of all the Hebrews in the Persian realm but ultimately results in his own crucifixion. Opposed to the haughty vizier is Mardocheo (Mordecai), Esther's uncle and guardian. Although officially the queen of the Persian nation, Esther recognizes herself to be no more than a slave in her husband's palace, which through Aman's ambitions has become a zone of jealousy and hatred as courtiers conspire to assassinate the monarch. In contrast to Racine's play of the same title, Della Valle's drama illustrates the inconstancy of human behavior. The despotic Assuero commands Aman's execution, elevates Mardocheo to the highest courtly position, and allows the Hebrews to live after Esther has revealed her Jewish origin. Cruelty, capriciousness, and slavery predominate over Divine glory, which awaits the faithful in a realm beyond the miserable confines of a royal court.

Its dramatic portrayal of the triumphant spirit on earth sustained by God makes *Iudit (Judith)* the most militant of Della Valle's dramas in proclaiming the battle against false faith and barbarian ferocity. As master of the forces of savagery, the Assyrian General Oloferne (Holofernes) represents confidence in human ability and destiny without the uplifting support of a just Divinity. As an instrument of God's will, the widow Judith succeeds in seducing and beheading Holofernes in order to lift the siege of the Hebrew town of Bethulia. As go-between for these two heroic figures is the debased courtier Vagao, procurer to the general's pleasures and the personification of the depravity of court life. Unlike Della Valle's other plays where the chorus supports the heroine, here the chorus is composed of poor Assyrian soldiers who appear as victims of the ambition for territorial aggrandizement. This drama of victorious faith, as announced in the prologue by an angel, follows the classical unity of time to move from a night of tense darkness through a day of sensual blandishment to an evening promising voluptuous fulfillment but ending in the annihilation of the enemy of the chosen people. Holofernes's fate illustrates that of all rulers with their courts: humans are the most wretched children of Eve condemned to exile except through the redemption offered by God in Heaven.

See also BAROQUE.

Bibliography: Tutte le Opere di Federico Della Valle, ed. P. Cazzani (Milan: Mondadori, 1955); Pietro Cazzani, "Federico Della Valle," *Enciclopedia dello Spettacolo* 4 (1957), 407–11; Franco Croce, *Federico Della Valle* (Florence: La Nuova Italia, 1965); Giovanni Getto, "Federico Della Valle," in *Letteratura italiana: I Minori* (Milan: Marzorati, 1961); James E. Phillips, *Images of a Queen:*

Mary Stuart in Sixteenth-Century Literature (Berkeley, Calif.: University of California Press, 1964); Claudio Varese, "Federico Della Valle," in *Storia della letteratura italiana: Il Seicento*, eds. Emilio Cecchi and Natalino Sapegno, Vol. V (Milan: Garzanti, 1967).

Douglas Radcliff-Umstead

DE MARCHI, EMILIO (1851–1901), novelist and teacher. A native of Milan, De Marchi completed his education at the Liceo Beccaria and earned a degree in literature from the Accademia Scientifico-Letteraria of Milan in 1874. After graduation, he began a career as a teacher, first in a private college, then in his old *liceo,* and finally at the Accademia, becoming its secretary in 1879. The most formative literary influence upon De Marchi was Alessandro Manzoni,* although he read and was inspired by Scott, Gogol, Balzac, and Tolstoy as well. Among his close friends in Milan could be numbered the foremost writers of the period, including Verga,* Capuana,* Fogazzaro,* Giacosa,* and Paolo Ferrari* (his teacher and the person who encouraged him to write for the theatre). In 1874, De Marchi's first short stories appeared, and two years later, he and two friends founded a literary review, *La Vita Nuova,* which appeared for two years. During the next ten years, De Marchi published several volumes of short fiction, a monograph on literature of the Italian Enlightenment,* a study of Carlo Maria Maggi,* an Italian translation of La Fontaine's fables with illustrations by Gustave Doré, and a number of plays, sketches, and monologues, some of which were written especially for children.

De Marchi owes his reputation to several novels: *Il cappello del prete* (1888, The Priest's Hat); *Demetrio Pianelli* (1890, *Demetrio Pianelli*); and *Arabella* (1893, Arabella). The first two books, which are usually considered his masterpieces, originally appeared in serial form in magazines. *Il cappello del prete* was a commercial success which earned him the esteem of the northern Italian middle class. It recounts the tale of how Carlo Coriolano, baron of Santafusca, murders the priest Don Cirillo for a large sum of money. Although the murderer disposes of the priest's body, the prelate's new hat continually reappears on the scene and eventually drives the baron to confess his crime. The novel's source was an actual event, the murder of a priest by a man who committed suicide in prison upon the eve of his sentence. It was written after a friend challenged De Marchi to demonstrate that a good *romanzo d'appendice* (serial story) could be published in Italy without recourse to French authors.

Demetrio Pianelli reflects its author's personal experience. Like his protagonist, De Marchi spent five long and boring hours each day working in his office, surrounded by the paperwork required in his position at the

Accademia. Like his fictional creation, De Marchi experienced the weariness of office work and described it better and in greater detail than any other Italian writer before Svevo.* Demetrio's half-brother Cesarino commits suicide when it is discovered that he has embezzled a large sum of money from the bank which employs him. Demetrio, a character prone to the self-abnegation admired by De Marchi, decides to support his brother's family and, in the process, falls in love with his sister-in-law Beatrice, an insensitive woman who never appreciates his sacrifices on her behalf. For defending her honor after one of his superiors has made improper advances, Demetrio is punished and is transferred out of town and away from Beatrice and all his friends. Nonetheless, he arranges Beatrice's marriage to his rich cousin Paolino and thereby denies his own feelings for her future well-being.

Demetrio Pianelli was intended to be the first in a cycle which was continued with *Arabella* but thereafter abandoned. *Arabella* follows the life of Cesarino's daughter. Like Demetrio, the protagonist of this work performs an act of renunciation which De Marchi describes in all its tragic implications. In one of his last works, *Giacomo l'idealista* (1897, Giacomo the Idealist), De Marchi creates a protagonist who embodies, rather unsuccessfully, his sentiment of moral idealism.

De Marchi is often identified as a "Manzoniano," but his works lack the sweep or moral certitude of *I promessi sposi*. Still, his best novels dissect the normal lives of characters living in the late nineteenth century, individuals similar in background and attitude to his reading public, rather than the lives of historical figures from a distant past which people the historical novels of Manzoni and many of his followers. De Marchi's style is characterized by a clarity, simplicity, and keenness of observation matched by few other writers of the period. Preoccupied with moral problems, he accepts Manzoni's general view that art should have a moral, didactic purpose, and he successfully infuses the prosaic existence of his characters with a measure of dignity and nobility, presenting them to his audience as models of simple goodness. De Marchi's aspirations to serve his public took concrete shape in a periodical he founded in 1898 called *La buona parola,* which was intended to educate the urban masses to a truer sense of their rights and responsibilities.

Bibliography: Opere complete, ed. Giansiro Ferrata, 4 vols. (Milan: Mondadori, 1959–63); *Demetrio Pianelli,* trans. M. Nowett (1905; rpt. New York: Fertig, 1977); Marcella Cecconi Gorria, *Il primo De Marchi fra storia, cronaca e poesia* (Florence: La Nuova Italia, 1963); Sergio Pacifici, *The Modern Italian Novel from Manzoni to Svevo* (Carbondale, Ill.: Southern Illinois University Press, 1967); Vittorio Spinazzola, *Emilio De Marchi romanziere popolare* (Milan: Comunità, 1971).

DE ROBERTO, FEDERICO (1861–1927), journalist, critic, and novelist. After completing a technical education in Catania, De Roberto cultivated an active interest in literature. Much of his life was spent in Milan, where he met Verga,* Boito,* Rovetta,* and Capuana* and worked for the *Corriere della sera* as a literary critic. His first work, a collection of short stories, *La sorte* (1886, Fate), owed much to the early naturalism of Verga's *novelle.** From this time on, he and his writing were associated with regional novels of Sicily and with the naturalist movement in Italy, *verismo.** He wrote a number of novels between 1889 and 1894—including *Ermanno Raeli* (Ermanno Raeli), *L'illusione* (The Illusion), and *L'impero* (The Empire, published in 1924)—as well as several minor plays and critical essays. His literary fame, however, rests upon a single masterful historical novel, *I viceré* (1894, *The Viceroys*), which has slowly been recognized as one of the finest works in prose produced in Italy during the nineteenth century.

I viceré reflects De Roberto's cosmopolitan culture and his wide readings as the translator of Baudelaire and the author of critical articles on such diverse figures as Tolstoy, Maeterlinck, Nietzsche, and many others. The novel, with its scrupulous observation of details and the psychological introspection of its characters, also shows him as an undogmatic advocate of *verismo*. Rather than accepting the kind of scientific approach to writing suggested by Zola, De Roberto embraced literary realism in order to avoid romantic rhetoric and sentimentalism. Moving away from the simple folk of Verga's fictional universe, De Roberto was also forced to depart from the strict canons of impersonal narration and a literary language shaped by the diction and cadence of local dialects. However, he enlarged his horizons to encompass a whole society and an entire historical period in a single work, completing the study of a world which Verga's projected but unfinished cycle of five novels never managed to reach.

The history of Sicily and that of the Risorgimento, covering the period 1855 to 1882, supplies the structure of *I viceré*. The main characters are the Uzeda family, descendants of the viceroys of Spain, and the story of the family's members is intertwined with the historical development of an entire epoch. The opening section of the novel leads to a description of the fall of the Kingdom of the Two Sicilies and an early election. The second part concludes with the taking of Rome by republican forces and the conversion to liberalism of Don Blasco, a Benedictine monk and former supporter of the Bourbons and the pope, who buys up church lands confiscated by the new state and supports the liberal government in order to guarantee his newfound wealth. The final section of the work describes the first Italian general elections under almost universal suffrage and the victory of the cynical Consalvo, prince of Francalanza, who has decided to support the new political system in order to exploit it.

De Roberto places the entire Risorgimento on trial in this novel. One character expresses this view when he adapts to his own selfish purposes the famous remark of Massimo D'Azeglio* concerning the making of Italian citizens: "Now that Italy is made, we must see about our business affairs." For De Roberto, the Risorgimento (especially in southern Italy) was a "rivoluzione mancata," a revolution that failed. His novel pictures egoism as the single determinant of human affairs in which no social reform is ultimately possible. This pessimistic outlook sets him apart from the French naturalists and is more typical of Italian *verismo*. His single-minded emphasis upon self-interest has caused some critics to accuse him of creating monotonous characters who suffer from the same passions and are moved by the same motives. In *I vicerè* De Roberto manages to combine the form of the historical novel, popularized in Italy by Manzoni* and his followers, with naturalistic themes and narrative techniques. However, rather than writing in a literary Tuscan, as Manzoni did, or in an experimental language reflecting the influence of regional dialects, as Verga chose to do, De Roberto combines many forms of literary language in an essentially antirhetorical prose, perfectly suited to his pessimistic subject matter.

Overshadowed for many years in Italian criticism by his master Verga, De Roberto is today recognized both in Italy and abroad as the author of a masterpiece. His influence can be detected in the prose of many contemporary Sicilian novelists, most particularly in Tomasi di Lampedusa's* *Il gattopardo*. Lampedusa's work accepts De Roberto's view of the Risorgimento and continues his unique combination of the historical reconstruction of the recent past and the psychological investigation of historical characters.

See also TOMASI DI LAMPEDUSA, Giuseppe; VERGA, Giovanni; VERISMO.

Bibliography: The Viceroys, trans. Archibald Colquhoun (New York: Harcourt, 1962); Carlo A. Madrignani, *Illusione e realtà nell'opera di Federico De Roberto* (Bari: De Donato, 1972); Tom O'Neill, "Lampedusa and De Roberto," *Italica* 42 (1970), 170–82; Sergio Pacifici, *The Modern Italian Novel from Manzoni to Svevo* (Carbondale, Ill.: Southern Illinois University Press, 1967); Vittorio Spinazzola, *Federico De Roberto e il verismo* (Milan: Feltrinelli, 1961).

DE SANCTIS, FRANCESCO (1817–1883), critic, essayist, and literary historian. De Sanctis was born in Morra Irpino, the eldest son of a family of small landowners. He was sent to Naples for his schooling (1826–37), where he subsequently attended the school of Basilio Puoti, the then-famous champion of the purists, and began his long and successful teaching career. He taught first in private schools, which then constituted a vital alternative to the public schools controlled by the Bourbons, and later accepted a position at the military college of Nunziatella. Following his active participation in the uprising of 1848, he was arrested and imprisoned for three years (1850–53). Exiled, he lived in Turin (1853–56) and then moved to Zurich, where he taught Italian literature at the federal Poli- technic Institute (1856–60) and met other French, German, and Italian expatriates. In 1860, again following the call of political involvement, he returned to Naples shortly before Garibaldi* liberated the city. Garibaldi named him governor of Avellino. This was the first of a long series of important political and administrative appointments (he served as minister of education in 1861–62, 1878, and 1879–81) which gave him the oppor- tunity of contributing with courage and enlightened dedication to the organization of the newly established Kingdom of Italy.

The intense pace of his political career did not keep De Sanctis from his cherished studies. After revising and collecting his lessons and articles from the Turin-Zurich period in *Saggi critici* (1867, Critical Essays), he published such masterful works as *Saggio critico sul Petrarca* (1869, Critical Essay on Petrarch) and *Storia della letteratura italiana* (1870–71, *History of Italian Literature*). In 1871, he was called to a chair of "compar- ative" literature at the University of Naples, and he dedicated some of the last years of his life to teaching and research. *Nuovi saggi critici* (New Critical Essays) appeared in 1872, while other important writings of that period were published posthumously. Among the latter is the fundamental *Studio su Giacomo Leopardi* (1885, A Study of Giacomo Leopardi).

De Sanctis's thought as a literary critic is essentially characterized by a stage of apprenticeship in the tradition of Vico* and Hegel, and sub- sequently by an original development. Partly by breaking away from that tradition, he established and asserted the basic principles of art as form (e.g., as integral unity of form and content) and of the autonomy of art in relation to morality, science, philosophy, and other disciplines.

De Sanctis did not claim or wish to be a systematic theorist of literature. Nor can he be regarded as a literary historian in the specialized and narrowly professional connotation of the term. Instead, he was a complex and complete figure of teacher, citizen, man of action, and man of letters— a true intellectual of the old democratic school in the romantic and Maz- zinian sense. That is, he was a man whose teachings and writings were the foremost expressions of his moral integrity and civic commitment to the welfare of his country and of society as a whole. Only such a man could conceive and draft a history of Italian literature which is inherently and unequivocally a history of the origin and development of Italian culture and of the conscience of the Italians as a people and a nation. He has produced a coherent and all-encompassing scheme in which the periods of literary "decadence" coincide naturally with moments of moral and political deca- dence and with the widening drift between the idealistic and formalistic tendency of creativity on one hand and the inalienable presence of human, social, and historical realities on the other. From this perspective, inspired by the noble zest of the true educator and humanist, he views the *Divina Commedia* as the masterwork in which the Middle Ages are "realized as art." After Dante* came ages of decline. Petrarch* was a great artist but lacked that "serious and profound faith" that made Dante a poet, while Boccaccio,* shunning the supernatural, created the "earthly" comedy. The first signs of a new science that will eventually lead to moral and political rebirth are in Machiavelli's* work, which counterbalances the formalistic tradition of the Renaissance* by subordinating imagination to the fundamental need of experience and to the observation of reality, and in other thinkers and writers such as Bruno,* Galileo,* Campanella,* Sarpi,* and Vico.* Consequently, the new literature, the literature of the re-awakening, begins with Goldoni's* restoration of the guiding principles of truth and nature, and culminates in Manzoni,* the man who was able to look at humanity from above, with the eye of the next world, and to infuse the ideal into the real. In his twenty chapters on the history of Italian literature, De Sanctis's critical intelligence has provided modern literary historiography with a vast and breathtaking synthesis which, in spite of inevitable gaps and shortcomings, has justly been recognized as one of the best histories of any literature ever written.

The first edition of De Sanctis's works was published by Morano of Naples in 1869–76. Publication continued after his death with *Studio su G. Leopardi, Studi critici* (1886, Critical Studies); *La giovinezza* (1889, Youth), an autobiographical fragment on his youth and intellectual formation; *La letteratura italiana del secolo XIX* (1897, Italian Literature of the Nineteenth Century); *Scritti varii inediti e rari* (1898, Miscellaneous Unedited Works); and *Beatrice* (1914, Beatrice). The bulk of the critic's work has also been collected in subsequent incomplete editions (Naples: Morano, 1930–40; Bari: Laterza, 1949–55; and Turin: Einaudi, 1951–   ).

Bibliography: History of Italian Literature, trans. Joan Redfern, 2 vols. (1931; rpt. New York: Basic Books, 1968); *De Sanctis on Dante,* trans. Joseph Rossi and Alfred Galpin (Madison, Wis.: University of Wisconsin Press, 1957); Elena and Alda Croce, *Francesco De Sanctis* (Turin: UTET, 1964); René Wellek, *A History of Modern Criticism: The Later Nineteenth Century* (New Haven, Conn.: Yale University Press, 1965).

                                                                  Antonio Illiano

DESSÌ, GIUSEPPE (1901–1977), Sardinian novelist. Dessì was born near Cagliari and received a degree from the University of Pisa in 1936 with a thesis on Manzoni.* He left the university in 1936 and earned his living as a teacher and school superintendent.

Dessì's first novel, *San Silvano* (1939, San Silvano), reminds some prominent critics of Joyce and Proust in its treatment of past time. Its setting in the Sardinian countryside was to become a consistent element in Dessì's fiction. A number of Sardinian novels soon followed, including *Michele Boschino* (1942, Michele Boschino); *I passeri* (1955, The Sparrows), a story dealing with the Allied occupation of the island in 1943 which develops the story of Count Massimo Scarbo, who lost a son in the Spanish Civil War and is waiting only for death; and *Il disertore* (1961, *The Deserter*), a novel which takes place after the end of World War I and pictures the life of a poor woman, Maria Angela, whose son has been decorated as a war hero but who is, in reality, only a deserter and a criminal (a truth known only to the mother and to her priest, Pietro Coi).

Dessì's most important work, *Paese d'ombre* (1972, *The Forests of Norbio*) was awarded the Strega Prize in 1972. It is a historical novel set in Sardinia between the end of the Risorgimento and the first part of the twentieth century. Its five sections correspond to various stages in the life of its protagonist, Angelo Uras, a poor boy who eventually inherits some property and becomes the town's mayor. Dessì shows that the region around Norbio, traditionally a source of charcoal for the mainland, has been exploited by the economic policies of the Crispi government. Dessì intended this work to provide the same kind of fictional reconstruction and historical critique of the past which De Roberto* and Tomasi di Lampedusa* so successfully accomplished for the Sicilian experience. The sections of the book treating the central historical and economic problems and their impact upon the book's characters, however, are less successful than those which depict the youth of the protagonist.

Bibliography: The Deserter, trans. Donata Origo (London: Harvill, 1962); *The Forests of Norbio,* trans. Frances Frenaye (New York: Harcourt, 1975); A. De Lorenzo, *Dessì* (Florence: La Nuova Italia, 1971).

DI BREME, LUDOVICO (1781–1820), romantic polemicist and man of letters. Di Breme was born in Turin to a noble family and took religious orders. He held a number of important offices in Milan during the period of Napoleonic rule in Italy, but lost these posts upon the return of the Austrians. Nonetheless, he remained in Milan after the restoration because of the city's cosmopolitan, intellectual climate. In 1815, he met Madame de Staël and A. W. Schlegel and became a close friend of Silvio Pellico,* whose successful tragedy, *Francesca da Rimini*, he edited in 1818. As a result of the literary debate which followed the publication of Madame de Staël's "On the Method and Value of Translations" in the *Biblioteca italiana* in 1816, Di Breme defended the new romantic ideas in his *Discorso intorno all'ingiustizia di alcuni giudizi letterari italiani* (1816, Discourse Concerning the Injustice of Some Italian Literary Judgments). Like similar statements by Pietro Borsieri* and Giovanni Berchet,* this document is a major manifesto of Italian romanticism,* in which Di Breme rejects a preoccupation with the classical Italian poets of the distant past and argues that new times require new themes and poetic forms.

Di Breme also endeavored to bring Italian culture together with that from beyond the Alps. Besides his ties to Madame de Staël and Schlegel, Di Breme introduced Lord Byron to Milanese society. He was acquainted with many of the foreigners traveling through Italy or residing there, including Lady Hamilton, Lord Brougham, and Lady Sidney Morgan, all of whom would play a role in expanding romantic influence in the peninsula.

Besides a large number of letters, many of which are an invaluable source of information concerning the genesis of Italian romanticism, Di Breme published an autobiographical work in French entitled *Grand Commentaire* (1817, Grand Commentary) which discusses the political, religious, and cultural situation in Italy from the time of the Napoleonic Empire to the restoration.

See also ROMANTICISM.

Bibliography: Grand Commentaire, ed. Giovanni Amoretti (Milan: Marzorati, 1970); *Lettere,* ed. Pietro Camporesi (Turin: Einaudi, 1966); *I manifesti romantici,* ed. Carlo Calcaterra (Turin: UTET, 1951); Wolfram Krömer, *Ludovico Di Breme 1780–1820: Der Erste Theoretiker Der Romantik in Italien* (Geneva: Droz, 1961).

DI GIACOMO, SALVATORE (1860–1934), Neapolitan playwright and poet. Passing from medical school to journalism, Di Giacomo served as a librarian for most of his life and began his literary career with the publication of *Sonetti* (1884, Sonnets) in Neapolitan dialect. He continued writing such lyrics until the definitive collection of his poetry appeared in 1926. Among the best known are a group of sonnets,* *'O fùnneco verde* (1886, The Green Alley), the vivid portrait of a Neapolitan slum; a long poem, *'O munasterio* (1887, The Monastery), depicting a jilted sailor who enters a monastery; and *A San Francisco* (1895, In San Francisco Prison), which describes prison life. Besides the poetry which impressed such noted critics as Croce,* Luigi Russo (1892–1961), and Francesco Flora (1891–1962), Di Giacomo wrote some notable dramas, short stories, and studies of Neapolitan culture and history, including an account of prostitution in Naples from the fifteenth through the seventeenth centuries.

Di Giacomo's prose works mark him as a follower of Italian *verismo* * and of Verga* in particular. His *novelle* * and plays written in the local dialect deal with a world of poverty, the Camorra, and typical Neapolitan customs and characters. Di Giacomo described himself as a "sentimental" *verista* or naturalist, and his naturalism is most often tempered by a lyricism unknown to either Capuana* or Verga. Critics consider his best plays to be *'O voto* (1910, The Vow), the story of a dyer who promises the Madonna to marry a prostitute if his health is restored, and *Assunta Spina* (1910, Assunta Spina), a drama of jealousy and murder centering around the female protagonist of the same name.

Di Giacomo was made a member of the Accademia d'Italia in 1929. In addition to his literary works, he made an invaluable contribution to the art of Neapolitan song. Many of his poems in dialect were set to music, and he experimented with a number of poetic forms (including the *canzonetta* of Metastasio*). Only Eduardo De Filippo* rivals Di Giacomo's pre-eminence in Neapolitan literature in this century.

Bibliography: Opere, eds. Francesco Flora and Mario Vinciguerra, 2 vols. (Milan: Mondadori, 1946); *Poesie,* ed. Francesco Flora and Mario Vinciguerra (Milan: Mondadori, 1970); *From Marino to Marinetti,* trans. Joseph Tusiani (New York: Baroque Press, 1974); F. E. Albi, "Neapolitan and Di Giacomo," *Forum Italicum* 8 (1974), 390–400; Salvatore Rossi, *Salvatore Di Giacomo: Storia della critica (1903–1966)* (Catania: Grannotta, 1968); Franco Schlitzer, *Salvatore Di Giacomo: ricerche e note bibliografiche* (Florence: Sansoni, 1966).

DOLCE STIL NUOVO, a term commonly designating a loosely organized group of late thirteenth-century love poets and describing the special character of their lyric production. The existence of such a group has been advanced by modern critics who, lacking support from contemporary historical documents, have based their hypothesis on purely literary evidence (similarities in style, imagery, language, themes, and the like). They have appropriated the phrase *dolce stil nuovo* ("sweet new style") from its place in *Purgatory* XXIV. In that context, Bonagiunta Orbicciani da Lucca* addresses Dante* with the following words:

> "But, tell me, do I not see here before me
> him who brought forth the new poems that begin:
> 'Ladies who have intelligence of Love.' "

to which Dante responds:

> I said to him, "I am a person who,
> when Love breathes into me, takes note and then,
> gives form to what he dictates in my heart."

Bonagiunta then elaborates:

> "My brother, now I see," he said, "the knot
> that held Guittone and the Notary
> and me back from the sweet new style I hear!

> Now, I see very clearly how your wings
>   fly straight behind the one who dictates to you—
>   this, certainly, could not be said of us;
>
> and no one who examines the two styles
>   can clarify the difference more than I have."

(lines 49–62)

This famous, important, and difficult passage has given rise to numerous and varying interpretations. Some critics construe Dante's words as referring to a clearly defined, single-minded group composed of the following poets: Guido Guinizzelli,* Guido Cavalcanti,* Lapo Gianni,* Gianni degli Alfani,* Dino Frescobaldi,* Cino da Pistoia,* and Dante himself. Others prefer to read the passage in *Purgatory* as a restrictive statement of Dante's personal poetics, declaring that, if the school of the *dolce stil nuovo* does exist, then Dante is its sole member.

While the significance and applicability of the episode in *Purgatory* XXIV within both contexts—specific (the *Divine Comedy*) and general (the literature of the Duecento)—are still the subject of much debate, there are at least three historical/critical elements contained therein which allow invaluable insights into the literature of the period: (1) the crucial position of Dante's *canzone* * "Donne ch'avete intelletto d'amore" ("Ladies who have intelligence of Love") in his literary career; (2) the distinct separation of the earlier poetic schools (Sicilian and Guittonian) from later developments in the love lyric, described in artistic terms as the *dolce stil nuovo;* and (3) the new conception of love, the *dittator,* who provides the inspiration for a higher, more refined amorous poetry. Moreover, there is general agreement that in these verses Bonagiunta points toward the wide chasm separating his poetic style *(stil)* (and that of the Notary and Guittone*) from Dante's (and that of other poets?), and defines the latter as audibly and intellectually pleasing *(dolce)* and original *(nuovo)* in concept and manner. Indeed, the indication here of the new poetic style corresponds to the revolution begun by Guido Guinizzelli in Bologna, which, effectively changing the course of poetry in the Duecento, found its complete expression in Dante. To obtain the proper historical perspective, a brief sketch of the Sicilian and Guittonian schools must precede an examination of these points.

The earliest manifestation of an organized and concentrated effort to produce a body of literature in the Italian vernacular (albeit in Sicilian dialect) was at the Imperial court of Frederick II* of Hohenstaufen in Palermo in the years between 1220 and 1250. There, individuals of diverse nationalities, professions, and interests gathered and composed, in their spare time as it were, a large and rich corpus of lyric poetry, the subject of which was, for the most part, love. The so-called Sicilian School relied on the metrical, thematic, and conceptual models provided them by the Provençal troubadours and, to a lesser degree, the northern French *trouvères* and German *minnesinger*. They sang the praises of their beloved, wrote of their constant service and unswerving devotion to these distant and haughty ladies, and lamented the personal anguish caused by unrequited or deceitful love. This is not to say, however, that the Sicilians were unimaginative imitators who repeated *ad nauseam* time-worn cliches and took refuge in artifical conventions and modes, for they did exhibit certain original tendencies, both in formal composition (the invention of the sonnet*) and in thematic conception. All of these elements, then, imitative and innovative, were important in establishing the foundation of the Italian literary tradition.

Toward midcentury a large number of poets (Bonagiunta da Lucca among them) began composing lyrics in central Italy (especially Tuscany) under the tutelage of Guittone d'Arezzo. Generally speaking, they were avid but arid imitators of their Sicilian and Provençal forerunners. Moreover, they were interested above all in obtaining formal elegance and rhetorical and linguistic virtuosity in their poetry. This overriding concern renders much, if not most, of their work inaccessible, unintelligible, or uncongenial (at least to modern readers). Unlike his Sicilian predecessors who generally restricted their poetry to love, Guittone expands his repertory to include amorous, moral, religious, and political subjects, which, while new to Italy, were commonplace in Provence. Resounding with the heavy metrical, verbal, and thematic influence of the troubadours and the Latin rhetorical tradition, Guittone's lyrics also bear the mark of his bourgeois culture and direct experience with life in the Italian Communes. For the audience to whom he directed his lyrics no longer belonged to the aristocracy, the landed nobility, or the imperial court, but rather to the teeming residents of Italy's city-states. Virtually every poet (Dante included) of the second half of the Duecento owed some debt to Guittone, and rightly so, for he demonstrated what form(s) the courtly lyric could assume when there was no longer any court to nurture it. However, some of Guittone's early followers became disenchanted with his rhetorical and linguistic bombast, arduous hermetic stylizations, and cold conventions, and openly moved away from his oppressive, artistically stifling influence.

Dissatisfaction with one literary movement and attitude usually results in the rise of another, which opposes it in some way; thus, through the endless process of reaction → action, the literary tradition continually renews and recreates itself. A case in point is the advent of the *dolce stil nuovo*. Around the third quarter of the century, Guido Guinizzelli, a Ghibelline judge from Bologna, while acknowledging his early intentions to Guittone (cf. the sonnet addressed to him which begins "O caro padre meo," Oh my dear father), began to compose lyrics which varied greatly from those of his predecessors in style, theme, and conception. In a well-known sonnet exchange, Bonagiunta da Lucca addresses the Bolognese poet as the one who had changed the style of pleasing love poetry from what it once was. For his key role in the transformation and renewal of the Italian lyric tradition, Guinizzelli has generally been recognized as the "Father" of the *dolce stil nuovo* (cf. *Vita nuova* XX, and *Purgatory* XXVI, 94–99). In his doctrinal *canzone* "Al cor gentil rempaira sempre amore" ("Love seeks its dwelling always in the gentle heart"), he addresses himself to certain fundamental problems regarding the definition of human nobility, the nature of the beloved lady, and the value of earthly love. The worth of an individual does not depend on wealth, lineage, and other external circumstances, but rather on one's natural disposition; thus, the capacity to love with pure and noble sentiments is reserved for those to whom nature has given the "gentil cuore" (gentle heart). Unlike her passive predecessor in the lyric tradition, Guinizzelli's lady assumes, in the elaborate analogies of the poem, a power and status equal to that of God and is responsible for activating that innate potential to love in her admirer. She becomes a true *donna angelicata,* comparable to the angelic intelligences which move the eternal spheres. Given the philosophical pretensions and the numerous metaphysical parallels and analogies of the *canzone,** Guinizzelli obviously had in mind to ennoble human love by transforming it into a sort of secular *caritas.* However, recognizing the impossibility of his task, he concludes the poem with a tragicomic scene in which the poet is rebuked by God Himself for having dared to use Him as a term of comparison for a vain, earthly love *(vano amor).* Therefore, although unsuccessful in his attempt to reconcile human affection for woman and Divine love for God, Guinizzelli at least indicated the new direction for poets to follow in their amorous poetry. It is to this model that Dante turns in his own poetic experience of the *Vita nuova,* when he decides to write "only those words that praise" his lady (Beatrice) and begins this new stage in his career with the canzone "Donne ch'avete intelletto d'amore," to which Bonagiunta refers in *Purgatory* XXIV. The praise accorded Beatrice in the *Vita nuova* and the *Divine Comedy,* and her role there as Dante's personal bearer of the spiritual salvation *(salute),* fulfill the lofty, but unrealized aspirations of Guinizzelli and represent the supreme achievement of the *dolce stil nuovo.*

The major representative of the Florentine "branch" of this movement is Guido Cavalcanti, whom Dante terms his "first friend" in the *Vita nuova,* and who played an active part in the political events and internecine strife which rent that Tuscan city in the last two decades of the Duecento. With a few notable exceptions, Cavalcanti's poetry does not follow the main characteristics of Guinizzelli's model. Indeed, he is much more concerned with the psychology of love, with the inner struggle of the soul afflicted by contrasting emotions (personified as *spiritelli*, "little spirits"), and with the tragic plight of man, which he captures in moving, hauntingly beautiful verse. Cavalcanti's preoccupation with the mental and physical anguish induced by love permeates his poetry and gives it a morbid and mournful quality which often mirrors the abject state of the lover. Revealing his profound indebtedness to philosophical and scientific treatises in the doctrinal *canzone* "Donna me prega" ("Because a lady asks me"), he presents, as it were, a natural demonstration directed toward elucidating the origin, nature, and effects of love. Although the exact meaning and sources of the *canzone* are still the subject of much debate, certain points emerge clearly: the lover, gazing upon a real woman, formulates within himself his own idea of beauty, and this ideal conception then completely dominates his mind, causing him to strive anxiously and ceaselessly to obtain its earthly manifestation, i.e., a real woman. The anguish and torment of this vain pursuit (vain because the real can never measure up to the ideal) ultimately deprives the lover of reason and causes death. For the most part, the subject of Cavalcanti's poetry is the externalization, with appropriate personifications, of this inner struggle. In the first part of the *Vita nuova,* Dante reveals the influence of the Cavalcantian mode and situation with his attention to the dire and debilitating effects of love on his person and mind.

Another major exponent of the *dolce stil nuovo* is Cino da Pistoia, who was an intimate acquaintance of Dante and an active participant in the political events of his native city. Cino's lyric production is the largest of the *stilnovisti* (Dante included) and reflects virtually all of the major themes, images, and concepts. In addition to harmonizing these various elements in artful renditions and imitations, his basic contribution to the movement lies in his objective psychological realism which manifests itself in the intensely personal, almost confessional tone of his lyrics. In this regard, he serves as the bridge linking the *dolce stil nuovo* and Petrarch.*

In much the same way, the minor members of the *dolce stil nuovo* reflect certain of its aspects, each retaining his own distinct poetic voice and preoccupations. Dino Frescobaldi and Gianni degli Alfani appear to follow the Cavalcantian tragic manner, and Lapo Gianni wrote highly refined and musical *ballate,** which seem to revert to the older tradition and earned the admiration of Dante in *De vulgari eloquentia.*

To return to the passage in *Purgatory,* the *dolce stil nuovo* may now be viewed in the proper perspective vis-à-vis the earlier schools of poetry: the theme of praise (which derived its language and imagery in large part from the cult of Mary) transcends secular adoration of woman; the lady assumes both the appearance and the role of an angel (to lead the poet to spiritual salvation); love is conceived in religious or metaphysical terms and may bestow either supreme happiness (beatitude: Guinizzelli, Dante, Cino) or unbearable anguish (death: Cavalcanti, Gianni degli Alfani). Another major contribution of the *stilnovisti* concerns the forging of a new poetic language, one no longer bound to the conventions and courtly terminology and phrasing of earlier groups. Indeed, they freed poetry thematically from the events of daily life and elevated it linguistically above the common parlance, creating a restricted koine based on those terms central to their new understanding of love and infusing traditional words with new life and meaning: *dolce, spirito, spirare, gentile, salute, virtù, onestà, beltà, mercede, nobiltà, valore, mente, anima, soave, intelletto, sottile,* and so on. While each poet, of course, has his own special language or poetic techniques, with their refined lyricism, richness of poetic techniques, acute awareness of human psychology, and profound spiritual sensitivity, together they represent a major and decisive event in the history of Italian literature.

See also BONAGIUNTA ORBICCIANA DA LUCCA; CAVALCANTI, Guido; CINO DA PISTOIA; DANTE ALIGHIERI; FREDERICK II OF HOHENSTAUFEN; FRESCOBALDI, Dino; GIANNI DEGLI ALFANI; GUINIZZELLI, Guido; GUITTONE D'AREZZO.

Bibliography: Poeti del Duecento, ed. Gianfranco Contini, 2 vols. (Milan: Ricciardi, 1960); *Rimatori del Dolce stil novo,* 2nd ed., ed. Luigi di Benedetto (Bari: Laterza, 1939); *German and Italian Lyrics of the Middle Ages: An Anthology and a History,* trans. Frederick Goldin (Garden City, N.Y.:Doubleday, 1973); D. G. Rossetti, *The Early Italian Poets from Ciullo d'Alcamo to Dante Alighieri [Dante and his Circle]* (London: Ellis & Elvey, 1892); *The Age of Dante: An Anthology of Early Italian Poetry,* trans. Joseph Tusiani (New York: Baroque Press, 1974); Mario Marti, *Storia dello Stil nuovo,* 2 vols. (Lecce: Milella, 1973); Giorgio Petrocchi, "Il Dolce stil nuovo," in *Storia della letteratura italiana,* eds. Emilio Cecchi and Natalino Sapegno, Vol. I, *Le origini e il Duecento* (Milan: Garzanti, 1965); Natalino Sapegno, "Il 'dolce stil nuovo'," in *Il Trecento: Storia letteraria d'Italia,* 2nd ed. (Milan: Vallardi, 1955); Maurice Valency, *In Praise of Love* (New York: Macmillan, 1958).

                                                                          Christopher Kleinhenz

DOMENICO DI GIOVANNI, "Il Burchiello" (1404–1449), Florentine satirical poet, who was called Burchiello because he had the sign of a barge over his barber's shop. Born into a poor family and the eldest of eight children, Burchiello practiced the lowly trade of a barber in a shop on Via Calimala in Florence, where he met most of the outstanding artists and poets of his day, Leon Battista Alberti* in particular. The shop became a regular meeting place for such notables. Drawn into Florentine political conflicts, he supported the Albizzi family against the Medici, and upon the return of Cosimo de' Medici to power in 1434, Burchiello went into exile. Three legal documents report various difficulties with legal authorities in Siena, and after approximately ten years in that city, he moved to Rome where he died in poverty.

Burchiello continues the vernacular poetic tradition of medieval poets like Cecco Angiolieri* and Rustico di Filippo.* Often satirical in intent, his lyrics are characterized by a conscious usage of everyday language and events which most court poets would strive to avoid. For instance, in the sonnet* "La Poesia contende col Rasojo" ("Poetry Argues with the Razor"), he contrasts his artistic vocation with his lowly tonsorial profession. Like so many of Burchiello's poems which only appear unlearned, this one is actually inspired by Lucian's classical dialogue between Sculpture and Liberal Education. Among his noteworthy efforts are "O humil popul" ("Oh humble people"), an attack upon Cosimo de' Medici who is pictured as a hawk disguised as a dove, and his prison poems, the best of which give grotesque descriptions of the prison conditions and his misery, "Lievitomi insu'l come'l pane" ("I lie arising in the trough like bread") and "Cimici e pulci con molti pidocchi" ("Bedbugs and fleas and lots of lice"). Approximately one hundred and fifty poems are attributed to Burchiello, most of which are either sonnets or a variation upon that form—the "tailed" sonnet *(sonetto caudato* or *sonettessa)* formed by the addition of at least one tercet to the usual fourteen lines as a kind of *coda.*

Burchiello was one of the most popular poets in fifteenth- and sixteenth-century Italy. His works were collected by Lorenzo de' Medici* in manuscript, edited by Anton Francesco Grazzini* in 1552, and commented upon by Anton Francesco Doni* in 1553. Burchiello's most famous successor is Francesco Berni,* whose *poesia burlesca* continued many of Burchiello's themes and extended the literary use of the *sonetto caudato.*

See also BERNI, Francesco.

Bibliography: Sonetti inediti, ed. Michele Messina (Florence: Olschki, 1952); Lewis Hall Gordon, "Burchiello inedito," *Italica* 33 (1956), 121–39; Ann West Vivarelli, "On the Nickname Burchiello and Related Questions," *Modern Language Notes* 87 (1972), 123–33; Renée Watkins, "Il Burchiello (1404–1448)— Poverty, Politics, and Poetry," *Italian Quarterly* 14 (1970), 21–57—contains selected translations.

DONI, ANTON FRANCESCO (1513–1574), Florentine writer, journalist, and critic. After entering a monastic order at an early age and being expelled from it (1540), Doni turned to the study of law and then set up a printing press in Florence. He moved to Venice where, along with such writers as Pietro Aretino,* Nicolò Franco (1515–70), and Ortensio Lando (1512–55), he was numbered among the *poligrafi,* a group of versatile and prolific writers in sixteenth-century Venice who made their living by writing vernacular works for a popular audience and who rejected much of humanist learning as pedantic, often proposing plans of social reform which were utopian in nature. Next to the internationally celebrated Aretino, Doni was the most eminent of the *poligrafi*.

Besides an important edition of Burchiello's* poetry (1553) dedicated to Tintoretto and a translation of Sir Thomas More's *Utopia* (1548), Doni produced a vast number of works, most of which remained in vogue until the eighteenth century. In *La zucca* (1551–52, The Gourd), Doni assembled stories, letters, and proverbs. An Italian version of Oriental animal fables, *La moral filosofia* (1552, *The Morall Philosophie*), was very soon translated into English by Thomas North. *I marmi* (1553, The Marble Steps), a series of imaginary conversations overheard on the steps of the Florentine cathedral, one of which defends the Copernican thesis before Galileo,* treats social and political problems of the day in a popular dialect. *I mondi* (1552–53, The Worlds), a series of dialogues describing seven imaginary worlds and seven imaginary hells, one part of which reflects the utopian theories of More, is perhaps the first Italian book influenced by one in English. It is unfortunate that a portrait of Doni by his friend Tintoretto has disappeared.

Bibliography: I marmi, ed. Ezio Chiòrboli, 2 vols. (Bari: Laterza, 1928); *Utopisti e riformati sociali del Cinquecento*, ed. Carlo Curcio (Bologna: Scittori politici italiani, 1941); *The Morall Philosophie of Doni*, trans. Thomas North (London: Denham, 1570); Paul F. Grendler, *Critics of the Italian World 1530–1560: Anton Francesco Doni, Nicolò Franco & Ortensio Lando* (Madison, Wis.: University of Wisconsin Press, 1969).

DOVIZI, BERNARDO, "Il Bibbiena" (1470–1520), churchman, courtier, and playwright. Bibbiena (so named because of his birthplace) was private secretary to Cardinal Giovanni de' Medici. After his patron's elevation to the papacy as Leo X, Bibbiena became first papal treasurer and then cardinal (1513). Regarded by many at the Roman court as the real power behind Leo's policies, Bibbiena was a masterful diplomat and politician. His death, although preceded by a lengthy illness, gave rise to rumors, most likely false, that he had been poisoned by Leo because of his growing influence.

Bibbiena's impact upon the culture of sixteenth-century Italy is impressive. In *The Book of the Courtier*, Castiglione* presents Bibbiena as one of his major interlocutors, and much of the second book of that work contains a lengthy discussion on wit and humor led by Bibbiena. A close friend of Raphael, Bibbiena was painted by the master in one of the finest examples of Renaissance* portraiture, which now hangs in the Palazzo Pitti in Florence. His voluminous correspondence is of great value to the historian of the Italian Renaissance. Bibbiena's literary masterpiece was a learned comedy in Italian prose *La Calandria* (1521, *The Follies of Cal-andro*), which was first performed with a prologue by Castiglione against a stupendous background of sets, musicians, and allegorical *intermezzi* at the court of Urbino in 1513. It was subsequently produced with great success all over Italy and at the court of Catherine de' Medici in France. Bibbiena follows Plautus's *Menaechmi* and modifies the plot involving a pair of twins so that both sexes are represented. The central character of the play, the foolish husband Calandro, is, however, borrowed from several tales in Boccaccio's* *Decameron*. Thus, Bibbiena builds his masterpiece of comic language and humor upon the addition of new characters and new complications to classical plots and themes, a technique typical of learned comedy in sixteenth-century Italy.

Bibliography: Commedie del Cinquecento, ed. Nino Borsellino, Vol. II (Milan: Feltrinelli, 1967); *The Genius of the Italian Theatre,* ed. Eric Bentley (New York: New American Library, 1964); *Epistolario di Bernardo Dovizi da Bibbiena,* ed. Giuseppe L. Moncallero, 2 vols. (Florence: Olschki, 1955, 1965); Giuseppe L. Moncallero, *Il cardinale Bernardo Dovizi da Bibbiena, umanista e diplomatico [1470–1520]* (Florence: Olschki, 1953); Douglas Radcliff-Umstead, *The Birth of Modern Comedy in Renaissance Italy* (Chicago: University of Chicago Press, 1969).

E

EBREO, LEONE (circa 1460–circa 1521), philosopher and physician. Ebreo was born in Lisbon as Jehudah Abarbanel. He was personal physician to Ferdinand and Isabella of Castile, until the expulsion of the Jews from Spain in 1492 brought him to Naples. Earlier, Ebreo had apparently studied at the University of Seville where he had acquired not only medical training but also a knowledge of Latin and Arabic as well as some familiarity with Talmudic and Cabalistic teachings and astrology.

Ebreo's authoritative *Dialoghi d'amore* (1535, *The Philosophy of Love*), composed of three dialogues between Philo, the lover, and Sophia, his beloved (Wisdom), was actually written between 1501 and 1502. It is both a treatise on love and a detailed account of the philosophical position of Neo-Platonism with regard to love. While Ficino's* more famous exposition of Plato's *Symposium* is primarily a commentary, these dialogues are meant to put forward a thorough analysis of love. In the first book, "On Love and Desire," Ebreo distinguishes between love (directed towards things men possess) and desire (directed towards things that are not possessed); this distinction would later become somewhat controversial in philosophical circles. The second book discusses love's universality and its place in human affairs, and the concluding section returns to the definition of love, identifying God with love and treating love's relationship to beauty. Among the most popular of such treatises in its time, the *Dialoghi* was printed in many editions and translated into the major European languages. It influenced many other writers, including Castiglione,* Burton, Montaigne, Bruno,* Bacon, and Spinoza.

See also BEMBO, Pietro; BENIVIENI, Girolamo; CASTIGLIONE, Baldesar; FICINO, Marsilio.

Bibliography: The Philosophy of Love (Dialoghi d'Amore), trans. F. Friedeberg-Seeley and J. H. Barnes (London: Soncino Press, 1937); John Charles Nelson, *Renaissance Theory of Love: The Context of Giordano Bruno's "Eroici furori"* (New York: Columbia University Press, 1958); Anthony T. Perry, "Dialogue and Doctrine in Leone Ebreo's *Dialoghi d'Amore*," *Publications of the Modern Language Association* 88 (1973), 1173–79; Nesca A. Robb, *Neoplatonism of the Italian Renaissance* (1935; rpt. New York: Octagon, 1968).

ECO, UMBERTO (1932–), literary critic and semiotician. Eco's first work, *Il problema estetico in Tommaso d'Aquino* (1956, reissued 1970, The

Aesthetic Problem in Thomas of Aquinas), provides material for his principal critical work, *Opera aperta* (1962, The Open Work). *Opera aperta* gives a key interpretation of contemporary aesthetics which ranges over a wide spectrum of artistic forms (the music of Boulez and Stockhausen, symbolist verse, and the late prose works of James Joyce). It suggests that the "open work" is a form characteristic of contemporary art, that such a work is fundamentally ambiguous in its message, and that open works force the reader, listener, or viewer to participate actively in the creative process itself. The materials in this seminal volume have been revised and published in two separate studies: *Opera aperta, la definizione dell'arte* (1968, The Open Work: The Definition of Art), and *Le poetiche di Joyce: dalla "Summa" al "Finnegans Wake"* (1966, The Poetics of Joyce: From the "Summa Theologica" to "Finnegans Wake").

Eco's interests are catholic. He is a master of a number of foreign languages and is completely conversant with all of the major contemporary critical approaches in aesthetics. Besides having written various extremely interesting studies dealing with popular culture (comic strips, the structure of James Bond novels, the myth of Superman, an analysis of the structure of "bad taste"), Eco has recently emerged as one of the most original figures in semiotic theory since Roland Barthes. A number of his theoretical works develop a vital body of theory in this field, including *La struttura assente* (1968, The Absent Structure), *Le forme del contenuto* (1971, The Forms of Content), and the most recent exposition of his ideas in English, *A Theory of Semiotics.*

See also SEMIOTICS; STRUCTURALISM.

Bibliography: A Theory of Semiotics (Bloomington, Ind.: Indiana University Press, 1976); "The Poetics of the Open Work," *20th Century Studies* 12 (1974), 6–26 (a brief translation of a key section from *Opera aperta*); Teresa de Lauretis, "Semiosis Unlimited," *PTL* 2 (1977), 367–83.

EMBLEM: *See* ALCIATI, ANDREA.

ENEA SILVIO PICCOLOMINI (1405–1464), humanist, writer, and pope. Born in Siena, Aeneas Sylvius, as he called himself in his literary works, was part of a noble but impoverished family which had been excluded from political affairs after 1385. He received an education of sorts, although most of what later humanists considered to be an imposing knowledge of the classics was the result of independent study. He drifted into the service of the church under Domenico Capranica, cardinal of Fermo, with whom he attended the Council of Basel in 1432, when a union of the Greek and Latin churches was being discussed. He then passed into the service of Cardinal Niccolò Albergati, for whom he traveled to Germany and Scotland. Having served the antipope Felix V for a time, Aeneas joined the court of Frederick III of Germany (1442), where he was named poet laureate. After he sent an eloquent letter of apology to Pope Eugenius for his service to Felix V, Eugenius recognized his talents and made him his secretary. Aeneas subsequently became bishop of Trieste (1447) and then of Siena (1450), and was made a cardinal in 1456. His election to the papacy in 1458 was a surprise, and his choice of the name Pius was made as much out of admiration for Virgil's Latin epic* celebrating "pious Aeneas" as for religious reasons. Despite his earlier opposition to the papal authority, Pius II gained renown not only as a great humanist scholar but also as a Christian crusader through his efforts to unite Europe by calling a crusade against the Moslems in the East after the fall of Constantinople, at the Congress of Mantua which he organized in 1459. He opposed the encroachments upon the papal territories by the central Italian barons, particularly Sigismondo Malatesta of Rimini.

Although Aeneas is best known for the commentaries on the Council of Basel and on his life, which describe his election to the papacy, his talents were multifaceted. Two of his most celebrated works were *Historia de duobus amantibus* (1444, *The Tale of the Two Lovers*), a Latin romance in the style of Boccaccio* which was widely translated, and a bawdy Latin play in the manner of Plautus about the life of prostitutes, *Chrysis* (1444, Chrysis). His life was immortalized by the frescoes of Pinturicchio in the Piccolomini Library in the cathedral of Siena, a project initiated by his nephew, Francesco Todeschini Piccolomini, the future Pope Pius III.

Bibliography: De Gestis Concilii Basiliensis Commentariorum Libri II, trans. Denys Hay and W. K. Smith (London: Oxford University Press, 1967); *Memoirs of a Renaissance Pope: The Commentaries of Pius II, An Abridgment,* trans. F. A. Gragg (New York: Putnam's, 1962); *Selected Letters of Aeneas Silvius Piccolomini,* trans. Albert R. Baca (Northridge, Calif.: San Fernando Valley State College, 1969); *The Tale of the Two Lovers,* trans. Flora Grierson (London: Constable, 1929); Cecilia M. Ady, *Pius II* (London: Methuen, 1913); R. J. Mitchell, *The Laurels and the Tiara: Pope Pius II 1458–1464* (London: Harvill, 1962).

ENLIGHTENMENT, a literary movement considered the most prominent feature of the eighteenth century. Its roots are to be found in the European philosophy of the seventeenth and eighteenth centuries, developed by thinkers such as Bacon, Descartes, Gassendi, Newton, Leibniz, Locke, Bayle, and Voltaire, as well as in the scientific tradition created by Galileo.* Although it reached its climax in the second half of the eighteenth century, in the favorable climate that followed the peace of Aix-La-Chapelle (1748), it was already operating in the first half of the century through the best representatives of Arcadia,* particularly in the fields of antiquarian studies and journalism. Thus, both Benedetto Croce* and Mario Fubini (1900–1977) were on solid ground when they stressed the continuity existing between Arcadia and the Enlightenment. But, despite their similarities, the Enlightenment has always appeared to be somewhat different from Arcadia, and the critics have proposed various theories in order to explain this divergence. According to Walter Binni (1913–   ), the second half of the eighteenth century appears to be new because its culture has a strong pre-romantic component. Giuseppe Petronio (1909–   ) has challenged this interpretation as well as the one proposed by Fubini. He has maintained that the Enlightenment cannot be confused with Arcadia because Arcadia shows a tendency to avoid the concrete problems of contemporary life, while the Enlightenment deals exclusively with them. The dispute is still in progress, and no solution appears to be in view, although eighteenth-century studies have achieved considerable results, particularly in the field of social opinions. In any case, it should not be forgotten that a fundamental component of Western civilization, the utopian dream of a perfect society or the Golden Age myth, animated Arcadia as well as the Enlightenment, thus establishing a fundamental affinity between the two movements.

The Enlightenment was nourished by various intellectual centers, among which Milan, Florence, and Naples were prominent. The most brilliant minds of the movement were active in Milan, where they enjoyed the protection of the Austrian monarchy. Here Pietro Verri* created the so-called Accademia dei Pugni (Society of Fists) and established the influential periodical, *Il Caffè* (The Coffee House), which appeared in the years 1764–66. Among the closer collaborators of Pietro Verri, we find his brother Alessandro,* Cesare Beccaria,* the author of the most famous book of the Italian Enlightenment, *Dei delitti e delle pene* (1764), first translated into English as *An Essay on Crimes and Punishments* and published in London by J. Almon in 1767; Alfonso Longo (1738–1804); Giambattista Biffi (1736–1807); Gianrinaldo Carli (1720–1795); and Paolo Frisi (1728–1784), who was a link between the scientific school founded by Galileo and the culture of the new age. Parini* gave poetic expression to this intellectual movement in his *Giorno (The Day)* and in his *Odi* (Odes).

The movement was less vital in other parts of northern Italy. In Piedmont, the Savoy monarchy was against any innovations and therefore thwarted the flourishing of a new, modern, and rationalistic culture. In fact, the outstanding figure of the Piedmontese Enlightenment, Carlo Denina (1731–1813), appears to be more timid and much less original than the Lombard reformers, while the most significant contributions came from writers who had defied the Piedmontese government, such as Alberto Radicati di Passerano (1698–1737), Dalmazzo Francesco Vasco (1732–1794), and his brother Giambattista (1733–1796). As for the Republic of Venice, although the new ideas were unpalatable to its ruling aristocracy, it produced many significant essayists, such as Gianmaria Ortes (1713–1790), Francesco Griselini (1717–1787) who continued the political tradition initiated by Paolo Sarpi,* and Andrea Memmo (1729–1793). It was also the center of important literary activity in the field of journalism, to which *La gazzetta veneta* (The Venetian Gazette) and *L'Osservatore* (The Observer), both edited by Gasparo Gozzi,* attest. Even *La frustra letteraria* (The Literary Whip), an influential magazine started by Giuseppe Baretti* on 1 October 1763, was published in the territory of the Republic, but it was suppressed by order of the Venetian government early in 1765.

The Tuscan Enlightenment coincides with the rule of Pietro Leopoldo (1765–1790), although it was already operating through such figures as Giovanni Lami (1697–1770), editor of the *Novelle letterarie* (Literary News), and the economist Sallustio Antonio Bandini (1677–1760). A disciple of Bandini, Pompeo Neri (1706–1775), is credited with the reforms promoted by Pietro Leopoldo. Other important representatives of the Tuscan Enlightenment were Francesco Maria Gianni (1728–1821), Giovanni Fabbroni (1752–1822), and Filippo Mazzei (1730–1816), a close friend of Thomas Jefferson, who spent many years in America and had an indirect influence upon the drafting of the Declaration of Independence. The Roman scene did not offer any great figures, because all energies were concentrated on the creation of another movement of international scope: neoclassicism.* But the Enlightenment triumphed in the Kingdom of Naples. Here we find the great figure of Pietro Giannone* who fought a memorable battle against the secular power of the church of Rome in his monumental *Istoria civile del regno di Napoli* (translated into English as *The Civil History of the Kingdom of Naples* in London by W. Innys in 1729–31). The new ideas were mainly spread by Ferdinando Galiani,* the author of the *Dialogues sur le commerce des blés* (1770, Dialogues on the Wheat Trade), and Antonio Genovesi (1713–1769) who, both being great admirers of Giambattista Vico,* produced an original brand of Enlightenment, tempered by Vichian insights. The works of his followers, such as Giuseppe Palmieri (1721–1793), Giuseppe Maria Galanti (1743–1806), Gaetano Filangieri,* Francesco Mario Pagano (1748–1799), Vincenzio Russo (1770–1799), and Melchiorre Delfico (1744–1835), attest to the exceptional vitality of Genovesi's propaganda.

The influence of the Enlightenment transcends the chronological limits of the eighteenth century and invests the culture of the mature Risorgimento. Indeed, it appears to be an important component in writers such as Leopardi,* Manzoni,* and Carlo Cattaneo (1801–69).

See also ARCADIA; NEOCLASSICISM.

Bibliography: Illuministi italiani, eds. Franco Venturi, et al., Vols. I–III and V–VII (Milan: Ricciardi, 1965–71); Gianni Scalia, *L'Illuminismo* (Palermo: Palumbo, 1966); Franco Venturi, *Utopia and Reform in the Enlightenment* (Cambridge: Cambridge University Press, 1971), and *Italy and the Enlightenment, Studies in a Cosmopolitan Century* (London: Longman's, 1972).

Gustavo Costa

EPIC, a literary form with a venerable classical heritage held up as the noblest and most important poetic form by Italian writers and critics of the Middle Ages and the Renaissance.* By general agreement, an epic poem is a narrative work of some length which deals with events of a certain grandeur. Modern critics divide epics into two general groups: primary epics such as Homer's *Iliad* and *Odyssey, The Song of Roland,* and *Beowulf;* and secondary or literary epics such as Virgil's *Aeneid,* Petrarch's* *Africa,* Dante's* *Divine Comedy,* and Tasso's* *Jerusalem Delivered.* In the context of Italian literature, a third category must be adduced, that of *poesia cavalleresca* (the chivalric or romance epic). The distinction between a primary and secondary epic derives from cultural and conceptual differences. Originally intended for oral delivery, primary epics are usually written down at a date relatively far removed from the time of their origins, whereas literary epics are consciously composed as poetry to be read, although they may employ many of the features typical of the primary epic (extended similes, catalogues, invocations to the Muses, and the like). In the heroic world of the primary epic, that of Achilles, Beowulf, Roland, and The Cid, the poet's emphasis is most often upon the prowess of the individual warrior who generally dies defending a position of preeminence in his society. In the tradition of secondary epic established by Virgil and imitated by the majority of poets during the Middle Ages and the Renaissance in Italy, the celebration of the hero is transformed into something more compatible with a highly evolved and complex society. With Virgil's Aeneas (no longer the Homeric warrior-hero but the representative of a future Roman Empire), Italian poets and critics discovered a protagonist of epic proportions, with noble goals and religious concerns which more closely resembled their own.

Dante's *Divine Comedy,* Petrarch's *Africa,* and Boccaccio's* *Book of Theseus* provide the earliest examples of epic poetry in Italian literature. Unlike the other nations of Western Europe, Italy can claim no true primary epic poem from its distant past. The most Virgilian work of the three, that of Petrarch, was the least successful, while Dante's poem, which replaced the epic hero with a poet representing humanity on its journey toward Christian redemption, eventually came to be regarded in Italy and abroad as the greatest single narrative work in the Western tradition. Boccaccio's poem is indebted as much to medieval romances as to the classical epic tradition. It pointed the way for future Italian poets with its emphasis upon the theme of love and its relative lack of concern for

what a future generation of Aristotelian critics would hold to be an obligatory sense of epic decorum and narrative unity.

Renaissance poets were offered a wide choice of models upon which to
base their own epic works: the classical Latin poetry of Virgil (Homer
eventually became more important but never so dominant a figure as he
would become in the romantic period), a choice Petrarch's example recommended; the Italian epic of Dante which combined a number of classical
elements with a Christian theme; and the tales or legends from beyond the
Alps concerning the exploits of Roland (the Carolingian cycle) and those
about King Arthur and his noble knights (the Breton cycle). In spite of the
enormous impact the story of Roland (Orlando) had on Italian literature
through the works of Boiardo,* Ariosto,* and other minor writers, the
actual text of *The Song of Roland* as well as those of the primary epics of
medieval England and Spain were to remain unknown until the romantic
era. However, these stories became legendary and provided fertile ground
for Italian writers, who combined them in their own works with various
other literary traditions.

Virgil's impact was most evident in the Latin epics of poets with a
pronounced humanist perspective—Petrarch's *Africa,* Sannazaro's* *De
Partu Virginis* (1526, The Virgin's Childbirth), and Vida's* *Christiados
libri sex* (1535, *The Christiad*). All three works witness the continued
appeal of classical Latin, but those of Sannazaro and Vida reflect a shift of
emphasis from the Roman theme of Petrarch to an epic treatment of
Christian topics. The major current in Italian Renaissance poetry was,
however, the chivalric, inspired by the Breton and Carolingian cycles and
the tradition of romance in Boccaccio's minor works. It was embodied in
widely varying poems, including Boiardo's *Orlando innamorato* (1495,
Orlando in Love); Ariosto's *Orlando furioso* (1532, *The Frenzy of Orlando*), a continuation of Boiardo's poem; Pulci's* *Il Morgante maggiore*
(1483, The Greater Morgante); Folengo's* *Baldus* (1552, Baldus); Bernardo Tasso's* *Amadigi di Gaula,* (1560, Amadigi); and Torquato Tasso's
Rinaldo (1562, Rinaldo). With their common content, all may be grouped
under the general rubric of *poesia cavalleresca,* but their narrative technique, style, and language differ substantially. Trissino's* *La Italia liberata dai Goti* (1548, Italy Liberated from the Goths), Torquato Tasso's
Gerusalemme liberata (1580, *Jerusalem Delivered*), and Tasso's revision
of this same work published under the title *Gerusalemme conquistata*
(1593, Jerusalem Conquered) display an increasingly classical structure
and Christian theme but retain some elements more typical of the chivalric
epic poem.

The issues raised by the composition of epic poetry in these various
modes inspired an animated debate in sixteenth-century Italy. With the
translation and vulgarization of Aristotle's *Poetics,* critics began to assert

its authority over poetic practice and favored epic poems in the classical mode. Other Renaissance critics, in particular Castelvetro* and Giambattista Giraldi,* maintained that Aristotle's remarks on epic poetry should not be applied to contemporary works. The resulting debate touched upon the relative merits of Ariosto, Tasso, and Dante, and engaged many of the best minds of the period, including almost all the important poets, scholars, literary critics, and even Galileo Galilei.* The argument may be said to have culminated (but not to have been definitively resolved) in Tasso's influential *Discorsi del poema eroico* (1594, *Discourses on the Heroic Poem*). Tasso's treatise attempted to reconcile the variety, the interest in the marvelous, and the emphasis on love in the tradition of the chivalric romance with the neoclassical quest for poetic unity and a moral, didactic content.

Italian epic poetry retained its appeal, proving that modern poets could, in fact, imitate and even surpass the ancients. The poems of Ariosto, Boiardo, Tasso, and even of Vida were widely read in Europe through the romantic period, until the impulse to write great epic poetry subsided. Besides serving as the most successful example of a vernacular epic tradition to major European poets (Spenser, Milton, Camoens, D'Aubigné, Saint-Amant, Ronsard, and Voltaire), Italian epic poetry furnished a number of important themes and motifs for the other arts, including operas by Haydn and illustrations from key scenes in the narratives of Ariosto or Tasso by such artists as Rubens, Ingres, Tiepolo, Delacroix, Salvator Rosa, Guercino, Poussin, Luti, Benjamin West, Fragonard, and Carracci.

See also ARIOSTO, Ludovico; BOIARDO, Matteo Maria; CASTEL-VETRO, Ludovico; DANTE ALIGHIERI; GIRALDI, Giambattista; PET-RARCA, Francesco; SANNAZARO, Jacopo; TASSO, Torquato; TRIS-SINO, Gian Georgio; VIDA, Marco Girolamo.

Bibliography: Robert M. Durling, *The Figure of the Poet in Renaissance Epic* (Cambridge, Mass.: Harvard University Press, 1965); A. Bartlett Giamatti, *The Earthly Paradise and the Renaissance Epic* (Princeton, N.J.: Princeton University Press, 1966); Thomas M. Greene, *The Descent from Heaven: A Study in Epic Continuity* (New Haven, Conn.: Yale University Press, 1963); Gilbert Highet, *The Classical Tradition: Greek and Roman Influences on Western Literature* (New York: Oxford University Press, 1967); Rensselaer W. Lee, *Names on Trees: Ariosto into Art* (Princeton, N.J.: Princeton University Press, 1977), and *Ut Pictura Poesis: The Humanistic Theory of Painting* (New York: Norton, 1967); E. M. W. Tillyard, *The English Epic and Its Background* (New York: Oxford University Press, 1966); Bernard Weinberg, *A History of Literary Criticism in the Italian Renaissance,* 2 vols. (Chicago: University of Chicago Press, 1961).

F

FABBRI, DIEGO (1911–), playwright. Fabbri was born in Forlì, received a law degree in 1936, worked with a Catholic publishing house in Rome, and was secretary general of the Catholic Cinematographic Center from 1940 to 1950. Co-director of *La Fiera letteraria* from 1949 to 1959, Fabbri directed the publication until 1967 and also served as president of the Ente Teatrale Italiano. After Ugo Betti,* Fabbri is considered the most important Catholic dramatist in Italy and one of the most widely represented playwrights in the years since 1945. Influenced not only by Ibsen, Chekhov, and Betti but also by Pirandello,* Fabbri has examined the relationship between literature and religion in a collection of essays entitled *Ambiguità cristiana* (1954, Christian Ambiguity), which may be compared in some respects to Betti's famous pronouncement on religion and the theatre.

Inquisizione (1950, Inquisition) is his first significant dramatic work, a penetrating analysis of the torturous psychological and spiritual dilemmas of three characters and a priest which implies the need for Divine grace. Other plays of note include *Processo di famiglia* (1953, Family Trial), an examination of familial responsibilities; *Processo a Gesù* (1955, The Trial of Jesus), a Pirandellian drama which retries Jesus of Nazareth before a modern audience; and *Veglia d'armi* (1957, Armed Vigil), a consideration of the place of the Catholic church in contemporary society. Moral themes predominate in Fabbri's theatre, although his interest in testing various opinions occasionally leads him to adopt the structure of a trial as a dramatic form. What really matters to him is, of course, the destiny of his characters—whether they are guilty or innocent, whether they will save themselves. For this reason, Fabbri has declared that he could well label all his works "trials."

Fabbri has also composed comedies in a lighter vein, such as *La bugiarda* (1954, The Liar), *Lo scoiattolo* (1961, The Squirrel), and *Non è per scherzo che ti ho amato* (1971, It's Not a Joke That I Loved You). In addition, he has adapted a number of narrative works for the stage, including novels by Dostoevsky and Mauriac, and has completed a number of film scripts.

See also BETTI, Ugo.

Bibliography: Ambiguità cristiana (Bologna: Cappelli, 1954); *Processo a Gesù* (Florence: Vallecchi, 1963); *Teatro*, 3 vols. (Florence: Vallecchi, 1959–64); *Tre commedie d'amore* (Milan: Mursia, 1972); Antonio Alessio, *Il teatro di Diego Fabbri* (Rome: Sabatelli, 1970); Giovanni Marchi, "Il teatro di Diego Fabbri," *Nuova Antologia* 507 (1969), 228–51; Giorgio Pullini, *Cinquant'anni di teatro in Italia* (Bologna: Cappelli, 1960).

FANTONI, GIOVANNI (1755–1807), nobleman and lyric poet. Born in Fivizzano and educated in Rome, Fantoni joined the government of the Duchy of Tuscany in 1773 and entered the Accademia dell'Arcadia* three years later as Labindo. After being arrested for bad debts, he returned home and began a serious study of the classics of Latin poetry, in particular Ovid and Horace. An ardent partisan of Jacobin political schemes and an advocate of a confederation of Italian republics, he fought with Masséna in the campaign of Marengo, became a professor at the University of Pisa (1800), and served as secretary (1805) and president (1807) of the Accademia Carrarese.

Fantoni's collection of Horatian odes, *Odi* (1782, Odes) earned him the rather pretentious title of the "Tuscan Horace" from his academic friends. These odes express pre-Risorgimento themes, such as the love of country and a burning faith in and enthusiasm for new political ideas. The figure of Benjamin Franklin appears quite frequently in his patriotic works as a "new Brutus" in the free and independent American nation. Other poems are also democratic in tone, and one in particular—"A Napoleone Bonaparte presidente della Republica italiana" (1803, To Napoleon Bonaparte, President of the Italian Republic)—proposes the formation of a unified Italian state. Of some interest are his *Notti* (Nights), poems modeled after Edward Young's *Night Thoughts,* a work in vogue all over Europe at this time. Fantoni's works manifest not only the neoclassical style typical of the Settecento, but also a new and potentially revolutionary political content imported from abroad.

See also NEOCLASSICISM.

Bibliography: Poesie, ed. Gerolamo Lazzeri (Bari: Laterza, 1913).

FAZIO DEGLI UBERTI (circa 1305–circa 1367), poet. Fazio was a member of the illustrious Ghibelline family driven from Florence in 1267 and immortalized through the figure of Farinata degli Uberti in Dante's* *Inferno* (X). Probably born in Pisa, Fazio was forced to spend his life in exile, wandering among northern Italian courts seeking the sometimes meager patronage of the Visconti in Milan, the Scaligeri in Verona, and the rulers of Bologna. Around 1347 he began his major work, the *Dittamondo* (The Book of the World), a vast compendium of didactic verse and geographical information modeled upon the *terza rima** of Dante. The poem describes the poet's journey through Europe, Asia, and Africa, and remains incomplete after six books of one hundred and fifty-four chapters. During the voyage, the poet encounters various allegorical, mythical, and historical figures (Virtue, Ptolemy, Pliny). Its attack upon church corruption and its invectives against the emperors who have abandoned Italy, the poetic form, and the motif of a journey undertaken by a poet-protagonist—all invite comparison with Dante's masterpiece and with other minor didactic works of the Trecento, such as the *Acerba* (Sour or Unripened Remarks) of Cecco d'Ascoli (circa 1269–1327), a sharp and often bitter didactic poem on the heavens and their influence which includes a famous attack upon poetry and upon Dante specifically; the *Dottrinale* (Textbook) of Dante's own son Iacopo (died 1348), an arid compendium in sixty chapters of unoriginal notions on science and morals; and the allegorical poem *Documenti d'Amore* (1310, Teaching of Love) as well as the treatise *Del reggimento e costumi di donna* (On the Conduct and Manners of Women) of Francesco da Barberino (1264–1348). In addition, Fazio is the author of fourteen *canzoni,** twelve sonnets,* a *frottola,* and two hymns of praise to the Virgin. Because many of these shorter poems contain encomiastic elements directed to his courtly patrons, some critics view Fazio as one of the first Italian poet-courtiers, a role which was to become more common and ofttimes crucial in the Quattrocento and Cinquecento.

Bibliography: Il Dittamondo e le Rime, ed. Giuseppe Corsi, 2 vols. (Bari: Laterza, 1952); *Liriche edite ed inedite,* ed. Rodolfo Renier (Florence: Sansoni, 1883); Giorgio Petrocchi, "Cultura e poesia del Trecento," in *Storia della letteratura italiana,* eds. Emilio Cecchi and Natalino Sapegno, Vol. II (Milan: Garzanti, 1965).

FENOGLIO, BEPPE (1922–1963), novelist. Fenoglio was born in Alba, but apart from his military service and his participation in the partisan resistance, he spent most of his life in Turin. Fenoglio's literary debut took place within a series directed by Elio Vittorini* for promising young writers. This first work, *I ventitré giorni della città di Alba* (1952, The Twenty-Three Days of the City of Alba), was a collection of twelve short stories dealing with the activities of partisans in his native town of Alba. Critics tend to place these stories within the tradition of Italian neorealism* in view of their obvious indebtedness to the narrative styles of such American writers as Dos Passos and Hemingway. His passion for English and American literature is evident in all of his works (he even dreamed of being in Cromwell's army as a young boy). Fenoglio's first novel, *La Malora* (1954, Ruin), which also appeared in Vittorini's collection, depicts the harsh life of the peasants in the Langhe region in a manner which recalls not only Verga* but also Pavese* and Fenoglio's favorite American narrators. Subsequent works returned to the partisan experience, the subject for which Fenoglio is best known. *Primavera di bellezza* (1959, Spring of Beauty), a tale of a young man's encounter with the partisans which the author claims originally to have been written in English and then "translated" into Italian, was the last work to appear during his lifetime.

With his posthumous writings, Fenoglio's critical reputation grew prodigiously. They include *Una giornata di fuoco* (1963, A Day of Fire), containing the brief *Una questione privata* ("A Private Question"), a beautiful story which intertwines the activities of the resistance and the love of a partisan (Milton) for a young girl; a translation of Coleridge's *Rime of the Ancient Mariner* (1964); and his best-known work, *Il partigiano Johnny* (1968, Johnny the Partisan), edited by Lorenzo Mondo after being discovered among the author's papers. Although critical problems concerning the novel's chronology and final form remain unresolved, critics immediately recognized its literary merit. The protagonist, a partisan named Johnny because of the common practice of using a foreign name as a nom-de-guerre, reflects both the author's Anglomania and his searching doubts about the violence of war. The narrative is told in the first person and centers around the tragic events of the winter of 1943. Its language is an interesting combination of literary Italian, dialect, and an amalgam of Anglicisms. Combining subjective lyricism with realistic descriptions of the war, this novel may well be considered the most original of all the many Italian stories of the last decade devoted to this traumatic experience.

See also NEOREALISM.

Bibliography: La malora (Turin: Einaudi, 1954); *Il partigiano Johnny* (Turin: Einaudi, 1968); "A Private Question," in *Italian Writing Today,* ed. Raleigh Trevelyan (Baltimore: Penguin, 1967); Gina Lagorio, *Fenoglio* (Florence: La Nuova Italia, 1970); Walter Mauro, *Invito alla lettura di Beppe Fenoglio* (Milan: Mursia, 1972); Bruce Merry, "Fenoglio e la letteratura anglo-americana," *Nuovi Argomenti* 35–36 (1973), 245–88, "The Thaumaturgy of Violence in Fenoglio's *Partigiano Johnny,*" *Books* 13 (1973), 11–19, and "Thomas Hardy and T. E. Lawrence: Two English Sources for Beppe Fenoglio?," *Romance Notes* 14 (1972), 230–35.

FERRARI, PAOLO (1822–1889), playwright. Born in Modena, Ferrari received a degree in law (1843) and set up a private practice in that city while he composed his first dramatic work in dialect in 1847. Although his father was a highly placed officer in the military service of Modena's ruler, Ferrari took part in the democratic uprisings of both 1849 and 1859. He wrote several of his best plays at this time, including *Un ballo in provincia* (1848, A Provincial Ball), *Un'anima debole* (1848, A Weak Soul), *Un'anima forte* (1848, A Strong Soul), and his masterpiece, *Goldoni e le sue sedici commedie nuove* (1851, Goldoni* and His Sixteen New Comedies). Ferrari was prompted to write this play by a passage in Goldoni's autobiography describing the period in his life when the playwright had agreed to compose sixteen new plays in a single year. Similarly inspired, *La satira e Parini* (1856, Satire and Parini*) was also quite successful.

After Italian unification had been achieved, Ferrari became a teacher of history in Modena and then professor of Italian literature at an academy in Milan. Freed from the earlier constraints of political censorship, he could employ more contemporary themes and social criticism in his plays and set forth the ideals and aspirations of the newly ascendant bourgeois class of post-Risorgimento Italy in such works as *Il duello* (1869, The Duel), *Il suicidio* (1875, Suicide) and *Il ridicolo* (1872, The Ridiculous).

Bibliography: Opere drammatiche, 15 vols. (Milan: Treves, 1877–84); *Il teatro del secondo Ottocento,* ed. Cesare Bozzetti (Turin: UTET, 1960).

FICINO, MARSILIO (1433–1499), Florentine humanist, philosopher, and scholar. Son of the physician to Cosimo de' Medici, Ficino studied at the universities of Bologna and Florence without completing a degree. Because of his connections with the Medici family and his training in classical languages and philosophies, Cosimo gave him a villa in Careggi near Florence in 1462, where he was provided with Greek manuscripts. Ficino first translated from Greek into Latin the *Corpus Hermeticum,* a group of works attributed to Hermes Trismegistus which had a considerable influence upon occult thought and magic in Western Europe. The date of 1462 is also considered the time of the founding of the Florentine Platonic Academy. Having received Plato's complete dialogues and the *Enneads* of Plotinus from Cosimo, Ficino completed his Latin version of the complete collection of Plato's works, the first such translation in any language, in 1469; revised, they were finally printed in 1484. Plato was not, of course, completely unknown in the medieval period. Petrarch* had owned a manuscript in Greek, but he had not been able to read it. The first copy of Plato's complete works arrived in Florence as early as 1423. Florentine Neo-Platonism can be said to date from the church council of 1438 in Ferrara and the visit of the Greek scholar Gemistus Pletho to Florence in 1439.

Ficino's influential commentary on Plato's *Symposium* was completed in 1469 and was included in the first edition of the complete works. A translation and commentary upon Plotinus's works appeared in 1492. His major philosophical work, *Theologica Platonica de Immortalitate Animarum* (1485, Platonic Theology—On the Immortality of the Soul) and other minor works set forth a philosophy intended to reconcile the ideas of Plato, Neo-Platonism, and Christianity. At the heart of this complex of ideas was the view that the human soul was immortal. Taking from earlier medieval thinkers the picture of the universe as a vast hierarchical structure, a great chain of being, Ficino placed the soul in the center of this edifice.

The Platonic Academy which flourished around Ficino was actually a loosely organized group of friends, not the kind of structured literary, scientific, or philosophical academy which Florence was later to create and to pass on to Western Europe in the sixteenth century. It was closer to a religious community where informal conversations, readings of philosophical texts, lectures, and banquets to celebrate Plato's birthday took place. Ficino was able to attract the continued support of the Medici family after the death of Cosimo, especially that of his former student Lorenzo "Il Magnifico,"* and the many invaluable manuscripts at his disposal were obtained through their generosity.

Ficino's views on human love were highly influential in its subsequent treatment in Western literature. In the commentary on the *Symposium,* Ficino developed the doctrine known as "Platonic" or "Socratic" love. Formed by a reading not only of Plato but also of St. Paul, Aristotle, Cicero, Plotinus, and the lyric poets of Tuscany, Ficino's view of "Platonic" love—for him, the love which Plato described in his works— was a love bordering on the Divine and a preparation for experiencing the love of God, the end of all proper human desire. Such a doctrine was easily and enthusiastically incorporated into prevailing literary views of love. The belief that love for another person might be the first step in a search for the Divine ideal as reflected in imperfect, corporal forms quite naturally appealed to the legions of Petrarchan poets who saw their ladies as the embodiment of this ideal. Since Ficino's commentary on Plato was the major source of knowledge about Plato for more than a century after its publication, countless poets turned to Ficino's commentary for inspiration, among them Lorenzo de' Medici, Edmund Spenser, Marguerite de Navarre, the entire French Pléiade, Maurice Scève, Sir Philip Sidney, and John Milton. The more essentially philosophical concepts of Ficino influenced Leone Ebreo,* Giordano Bruno,* and Francesco Patrizi (1529–97) in Italy, as well as many of the trans-Alpine humanists, including John Colet, Johannes Reuchlin, Lefèvre d'Étaples, and Thomas More. Although the lack of adequate translations has inhibited a true understanding of Ficino's works, the Cambridge Platonists revived his reputation to a certain extent in the eighteenth century.

Bibliography: The Letters of Marsilio Ficino, Vols. I and II (London: Shepheard-Walwyn, 1975, 1978)—other volumes to follow; *Marsilio Ficino's Commentary on Plato's Symposium,* ed. Sears Jayne (Columbia, Mo.: University of Missouri Press, 1944); *The Renaissance Philosophy of Man,* eds. Ernst Cassirer, et al. (Chicago: University of Chicago Press, 1948); *Renaissance Philosophy: The Italian Philosophers,* eds. Arturo B. Fallico and Herman Shapiro (New York: Random House, 1967); Paul O. Kristeller, *The Philosophy of Marsilio Ficino* (New York: Columbia University Press, 1943); Nesca Robb, *Neoplatonism of the Italian Renaissance* (1935; rpt. New York: Octagon, 1968).

FILANGIERI, GAETANO (1752–1788), political thinker and social reformer. Born of a noble family, Filangieri was destined for a military career
but chose to study law and received his degree in 1774. As a young man, he
wrote two political tracts—*Della pubblica e privata educazione* (1771, On
Public and Private Education) and *Riflessioni politiche* (1774, Political
Reflections). He served as a courtier to King Ferdinando IV of Naples
from 1777 until 1783, when he retired to a villa at Cava dei Tirreni near
Naples to devote all his time to writing.

Filangieri's major work was a treatise of encyclopedic scope entitled
Scienza della legislazione (1780–83, *The Science of Legislation*). This
treatise was to appear in seven books and to have treated all the chief issues
of human government (population, legislation, wealth, education, religion,
property, and the family), but it remained incomplete at the time of Filangieri's death. Of four sections published, the third was placed on the
Index because it attacked feudal institutions. The last sections of the
unpublished manuscript were apparently destroyed in the political upheavals of 1799 in Naples. The treatise reflects a typical Enlightenment*
program of political and social reform, placing faith in the power of human
reason to change society through new laws and positing happiness as the
goal of all legal institutions. Like many reformers of his day, Filangieri
trusted a benevolent despot, divorced from his former feudal privileges and
motivated by a sense of social obligation, to achieve many of his reforms.
In particular, he supported the abolishment of the many reactionary feudal
privileges and a system of secular education administered by the state. His
treatise was extremely well received all over Europe, although its scope
limited its appeal to some extent. It was translated into many languages,
including two English versions in 1792 and 1806. Because of it, a friendship
grew up between Filangieri and Benjamin Franklin, who first read the work
when it appeared in Paris. The two men began a warm correspondence,
much of which has unfortunately been lost to posterity, and Filangieri at
one time apparently planned to settle in Philadelphia. Franklin not only
publicized his treatise in America but also sent him copies of the American
Constitution which was translated into Italian shortly thereafter. Filangieri
thus represents not only one of the finest expressions of the Italian Neapolitan Enlightenment, but also one of the earliest and most essential links
between Italian culture and Colonial America.

See also ENLIGHTENMENT.

Bibliography: Illuministi italiani: riformatori napoletani, ed. Franco Venturi, Vol.
5 (Milan: Ricciardi, 1962); Marcello Maestro, *Gaetano Filangieri and His Science
of Legislation* (Philadelphia: American Philosophical Society, 1976); Antonio
Pace, *Benjamin Franklin and Italy* (Philadelphia: American Philosophical Society,
1958).

FIRENZUOLA, ANGELO (1493–1543), writer, poet, and lawyer. Born Michelangelo Girolamo in Florence, Firenzuola studied law at both Siena and Perugia, where he met Pietro Aretino.* Although Firenzuola became a cloistered monk in 1517, he was released from his vows of solitude in 1526 after his interests became more worldly during a visit to the Roman court, where he arrived in time to enjoy the splendor of both Leo X and Clement VII and the friendship of many prominent literary figures, including Aretino, Bembo,* Caro,* and Della Casa.* Returning to Florence in 1534, he was made the abbot of a church near Prato; it was here also that he died.

Almost all of Firenzuola's writings were published posthumously, although most circulated widely in manuscript during his lifetime. Besides his Petrarchan lyrics (1549), he published an early treatise on Italian orthography (1524), a very free translation of Apuleius's *Golden Ass* (1550), and a popular collection of *novelle,* * *I ragionamenti d'amore* (1548, *Tales of Firenzuola*), set within a frame in the tradition of Boccaccio* with six storytellers. This project was left unfinished, for Firenzuola completed but eight of the *novelle* told during two of the six possible days of storytelling. He also wrote two prose comedies—*La trinuzia* (1549, The Triple Marriage), which is based partly upon the plot of Bibbiena's* *Calandria, (The Follies of Calandro),* and *I Lucidi* (1549, The Lucidis), which closely follows Plautus's *Menaechmi.* One of Firenzuola's most popular works was *La prima veste dei discorsi degli animali* (1548, The First Version of the Animals' Discourses). These animal stories introduced into Italian literature a famous series of Indian tales, which first appeared in Europe in a Latin version of the thirteenth century and were translated into Spanish in 1493. Firenzuola's timely treatise on feminine beauty, *Dialogo delle bellezze delle donne* (1558, *On the Beauty of Women),* describes in minute detail the perfect features and attributes of the ideal woman who so interested poets and philosophers.

See also NOVELLA.

Bibliography: Opere, ed. Adriano Seroni (Florence: Sansoni, 1958); *On the Beauty of Women,* trans. Clara Bell (London: Osgood, 1892); *Tales of Firenzuola, Benedictine Monk of Vallombrosa* (Paris: Isidore Liseau, 1889).

FLAMINIO, MARCANTONIO (1498–1550), poet, humanist, and reformer. Born at Serravalle, Flaminio came from a well-educated family and moved to Venice to continue his studies. He became a friend of Marcantonio Sabellico (1436–1506), the future Venetian historian, and was quickly accepted into the humanist circle of the city. Upon moving to the papal court of Leo X in 1515, his erudition and skill in writing Latin won him a place among the other humanists and scholars in residence. While in

Rome, and during a visit to Naples, he met such personages as Castiglione,* Sannazaro,* Vittoria Colonna,* Cardinal Reginald Pole, Juan de Valdés, and Cardinal Gaspare Contarini, many of whom saw merit in his Latin poetry. His first book of Latin verse appeared in 1515 and contained Horatian odes, an eclogue, and various other lyric verse. Some years later, he began his pastoral* lyrics, *Lusus pastorales* (1515, Pastoral Trifles), a series of brief lyrical works in elegiac couplets following a new literary form popularized by Andrea Navagero.* He was in the service of Cardinal Alessandro Farnese for a time and later became the secretary of Bishop Giberti of Verona. For a brief period, Flaminio served as secretary to Cardinal Pole, who took him to the Council of Trent where he was offered a post as secretary, which he declined because of poor health.

Besides these bucolics Flaminio published Latin paraphrases of thirty-two Psalms translated from the original Hebrew (1538) and some additional pastoral lyrics. Several of the Horatian odes Flaminio had written in Latin stimulated the development of this genre in Italy and in France. Perhaps most influential was his widely read devotional work, *Beneficio di Cristo* (1543, *The Benefit of Christ's Death*), which sold over forty thousand copies before his friendships with church reformers and his own religious beliefs caused the Inquisition to condemn it, place it on the Index (1559), and destroy all available copies. This work was translated into English several times, and an edition in 1638 was published on the advice of George Herbert. It was the favorite reading of King Edward VI. Flaminio's Latin compositions were greatly esteemed both in Italy and in England. Alexander Pope edited a selection of them, and his Latin poetry was often used in English schools along with the eclogues of Mantuan.*

See also NAVAGERO, Andrea.

Bibliography: Opuscoli e lettere di riformatori italiani del '500, ed. G. Paladino (Bari: Laterza, 1913); *The Benefit of Christ's Death,* trans. Edward Courtenay (Cambridge, Mass: Deighton, 1855); *Fifty Select Poems of Marco Antonio Flaminio,* trans. E. W. Barnard (Chester, Pa., 1829); Carol Maddison, *Marcantonio Flaminio: Poet, Humanist and Reformer* (Chapel Hill, N.C.: University of North Carolina Press, 1965).

FO, DARIO (1926–   ), dramatist and theatrical activist. Fo began his career by acting and writing for small cabarets and theatres, such as the well-known Piccolo Teatro of Milan, and by working for the Italian national radio and television networks. Beginning in social satire, Fo's writing passed rapidly into more obviously political issues. In 1959, he and his wife Franca Rame founded a theatrical group, the Compagnia Dario Fo-Franca Rame, which produced a number of his very popular satirical dramas, including *Gli arcangeli non giocano a flipper* (1959, Archangels

Don't Play Pinball) and *Aveva due pistole con gli occhi bianchi e neri* (1960, He Had Two Pistols With White and Black Eyes). By performing their comic sketches on the television program *Canzonissima,* which attracted enormous audiences of Italians from all social classes, the couple became famous all over Italy. When some of their polemical sketches were censored, they left *Canzonissima* and set up a new company, Nuova Scena, with connections to the Italian Communist party. The most original play from this period, *Mistero buffo* (1969, Comic Mystery), consists of a number of monologues taken from religious works of the Middle Ages which show forth the genius of popular culture. Drawing large crowds, Fo's theatre began to attract criticism within the party for its iconoclastic views on the party's own bureaucracy. Eventually, Fo broke his ties with the party's cultural organization and with Rame formed Il Collettivo Teatrale La Comune in 1970.

Fo's theatrical pieces are written hurriedly and often depend upon improvisation and extensive revisions after every performance. Moving as rapidly as the course of contemporary Italian history itself, the content of these provocative works varies widely. *Morte accidentale di un anarchico* (1970, Accidental Death of an Anarchist) examines the death of Giuseppe Pinelli, who allegedly committed suicide during a police interrogation in 1969. *Pum pum, Chi è? La polizia!* (1972, Knock, Knock—Who's There? The Police!) presents the case of Pietro Valpreda and two other anarchists arrested for planting bombs in a downtown Milan bank in 1969 and eventually blames the prime minister himself for the crime (a "state massacre" as Fo calls it). Other plays deal with specific problems: the rise of the Italian workers' movement, the popular revolt in Chile, and the Palestinian question. Fo's dramas often conclude with a discussion of the issues, involving both the actors and the audience. As a bridge between popular culture and radical intellectuals, Fo's collective theatre occupies a central place in contemporary Italian culture and is the most vital element in Italian theatre today.

Bibliography: Ballate e canzoni (Verona: Bertani, 1974); *Le commedie di Dario Fo* (Turin: Einaudi, 1974); *Morte accidentale di un anarchico* (Turin: Einaudi, 1974); *Mistero buffo* (Verona: Bertani, 1974); *Pum, pum! Chiè? La polizia!* (Verona: Bertani, 1974); *Teatro comico di Dario Fo* (Milan: Garzanti, 1962); Lanfranco Binni, *Attento te. . . .!: il teatro politico di Dario Fo* (Verona: Bertani, 1975) and *Dario Fo* (Florence: La Nuova Italia, 1977); Suzanne Cowan, "The Throw-Away Theatre of Dario Fo," *Drama Review* 19 (1975), 102–13.

FOGAZZARO, ANTONIO (1842–1911), novelist. Born in Vicenza, Fogazzaro studied in the *liceo* under Giacomo Zanella,* who introduced him to many foreign writers and to the problem of reconciling accepted religious beliefs with modern ideas. Fogazzaro devoted several critical essays to his

former professor in later life. After receiving his degree in 1864, he moved
to Milan and married Margherita Valmarana in 1866, by whom he had three
children. Until the publication of a romance in blank verse, *Miranda*
(1874, Miranda), Fogazzaro led a quiet family life, but thereafter he
devoted all of his energies to literature. His first novel, *Malombra* (1881,
The Woman), appeared in the same year as Verga's* *I Malavoglia (The
House by the Medlar Tree)*. No two works could be more representative of
the diverse literary currents that then coexisted within Italian culture,
*decadentismo** and *verismo.** *Malombra* portrays a highly neurotic and
exotic woman of the upper classes named Marina who lives with her older
relative, Count Cesare Ormengo. Believing herself to be the reincarnation
of an ancestor named Cecilia Varrega, who was tortured and killed by one
of the count's ancestors, Marina is driven to avenge the dead woman and
eventually causes the count to die of a stroke. When her own lover,
Corrado Silla, fails to fulfill the role she assigns him as the reincarnation of
Cecilia's lover Renato, she shoots him and disappears.

His second novel, *Daniele Cortis* (1885, *Daniele Cortis*), pictures an
unrequited love between a rising young politician and a woman named
Elena, who is married to an older man. The novel analyzes their tortured
relationship and shows them finally sacrificing their love for higher ideals.
Unlike his first work, *Daniele Cortis* was a tremendous popular success
and established a market for Fogazzaro's novels among northern Italy's
large middle-class audience, many of whom had no taste for the *verismo* of
Verga or the sensuality of D'Annunzio.*

Fogazzaro was deeply interested in modern science, especially
Darwin's views on evolution and the origins of man. Unlike other devout
Catholics, he saw in these revolutionary ideas not a threat to his faith but a
confirmation of a positive and progressive development in man. Several of
his nonfictional works at this time deal with a comparison of the creation
theories of St. Augustine and Darwin (1891) and a consideration of the
origin of man in relation to religious sentiment (1893).

With *Piccolo mondo antico* (1896, *The Little World of the Past*), Fogazzaro established himself as the leading writer of his day, second only, in the
opinions of many, to Manzoni.* Largely as a result of its spectacular
success, he was appointed to the Italian Senate in the same year. The novel
is set against the background of Risorgimento Italy during the 1850s. The
protagonist, Franco Maironi, is the son of a pro-Austrian nobleman who
opposes his marriage to a village girl, Luisa Rigey, and disinherits him.
Franco is a weak character possessed of a sincere religious faith in contrast
to his wife, who is strong-willed and disinterested in religion. The crucial
test of their respective moral positions comes at the sudden death of their
first child, Maria. Franco's faith gives him the courage to bear the loss and
to join the cause of Italian liberation in which he eventually loses his life;
Luisa denounces God for her loss and attempts to contact Maria through

occult practices. At the rather ambiguous end of this novel, Luisa is expecting a second child, perhaps a reincarnation of Maria, while Franco leaves for the army.

Fogazzaro's subsequent novels develop ideas and characters from *Piccolo mondo antico* and reflect his growing interest in modernist or neo-Catholic ideas which sought to liberalize and modernize Catholic dogma. The hero of *Piccolo mondo moderno* (1901, *The Sinner*) is Piero Maironi, the son of Franco and Luisa. Piero is torn by the conflict between his religious beliefs and his love for Jeanne Dessalle. Eventually he disappears, leaving with a priest a letter describing a vision which has led him to the service of God. In the third novel of what many critics term a trilogy, *Il santo* (1905, *The Saint*), Piero reappears as a religious ascetic renamed Benedetto, who is interested in the reform and the spiritual renewal of the faith. Jeanne Dessalle now appears as a temptation to turn him away from his vocation, but she is finally won over to his beliefs and ministers to him until his death. Most memorable is the interview granted to Benedetto in the Vatican by the pope, during which the ascetic urges the pontiff to reform the church and to purge it of the evils of falsehood, clerical administration, greed, and conservatism. The novel and its modernist principles were soundly condemned by the church, and the work was placed on the Index. In Fogazzaro's last novel, *Leila* (1910, *Leila*), the narrative of Piero Maironi is continued through the story of Alberti, one of his followers. This novel, too, was placed on the Index, even though Fogazzaro, as an obedient son of the church, had sincerely accepted the church's condemnation of *Il santo*.

Fogazzaro's works reflect a deep crisis in the values of Italian society at the turn of the century. It would be impossible to understand the meaning of *decadentismo,* the critical term usually employed to describe his literary milieu, without an understanding of his works. In spite of their historical importance, contemporary readers of Fogazzaro may find his popularity at the turn of the century as puzzling as that of D'Annunzio, but the many translations of the writings of both men give ample testimony to their universal approval in the English-speaking world as well.

See also DECADENTISMO; VERISMO; ZANELLA, Giacomo.

Bibliography: Tutte le opere, ed. Piero Nardi, 15 vols. (Milan: Mondadori, 1931–45); *Daniele Cortis,* trans. J. R. Tilton (New York: Holt, 1887); *Leila,* trans. Mary Prichard-Agnetti (London: Hodder & Stoughton, 1911); *The Little World of the Past,* trans. W. J. Strachan (London: Oxford University Press, 1962); *The Saint,* trans. Mary Prichard-Agnetti (New York: Putnam's, 1906); *The Sinner,* trans. Mary Prichard-Agnetti (New York: Putnam's, 1907); *The Woman,* trans. F. T. Dickson (Philadelphia: Lippincott, 1907); Tommaso Gallarati-Scotti, *The Life of Antonio Fogazzaro* (1922; rpt. Port Washington, N.Y.: Kennikat Press, 1972); Donatella and Leone Piccioni, *Fogazzaro* (Turin: UTET, 1970).

FOLENGO, TEOFILO (1491–1544), macaronic poet. Born near Mantua into a family of the minor nobility, all of whose sons were destined for an ecclesiastical career, Folengo entered the Benedictine order in 1509 and remained in it until 1525, when he and his brother Giambattista were granted a dispensation from their vows after another brother, Ludovico, had been expelled from the order.

Folengo's major poetic works had already appeared by this time in an edition of 1517, which contained two eclogues (the basis of *Zanitonella*–Poems About Zanina—a series of poems on rustic life) as well as seventeen books of the *Baldus* (Baldus). The poems had been issued under the pseudonym of Merlin Cocai or Cocaio, and after two printings, a second revised and enlarged edition appeared in 1521, including the complete *Zanitonella*, the twenty-five books of *Baldus*, the *Moscheide* (The Battle of the Flies), an imitation of the pseudo-Homeric *Batrachomyomachia*, and a brief collection of epigrams and poetic letters. This miscellany is often referred to as *Le maccheronee* (The Macaronic Works), a title which describes the special language Folengo used in these poems—a mixture of Italian and Latin which employs Latin inflections, syntax, and vocabulary but which also imposes Latin endings upon many Italian words. Macaronic verse had been written earlier by university students with comic intent, but no true poet before Folengo had employed it in serious literature. In addition, Folengo composed several works in Italian, including a burlesque version of the Roland story in *ottava rima** entitled *Orlandino* (1526, Little Orlando); the *Umanità del Figliuolo di Dio* (1534, The Humanity of the Son of God), a religious poem composed in order to atone for the frivolity of his other secular works; and the *Caos del Triperuno* (1526, The Chaos of the Tripartite Man), a mixture of Italian, Latin, and macaronic prose and poetry, which tells of an allegorical journey.

In spite of his later reputation for loose living and ribald ways, much of which was derived by extrapolation from his poetic works rather than from his personal habits and character, Folengo later decided to return to the church. After a penance of four years living as hermits, he and his brother were readmitted to the order in 1534. Although his *Umanità del Figliuolo di Dio* was part of this penance and the poet was warned against writing further secular poetry, at his death Folengo left a corrected and rewritten version of his *Baldus* which was printed in 1552.

The *Baldus* is unanimously considered to be Folengo's masterpiece. A comic continuation of the Carolingian legends, it tells the story of Baldus, the grandson of a king of France, who is abandoned by his father into the care of a peasant named Berto. Thus, the main character, a potential knight with chivalrous manners, is reduced to a ruffian with rustic ways and questionable companions. The poem is picaresque in form, and most of it traces the adventures of Baldus and his friends as they journey together. Its memorable characters, the giant Fracasso, Cingar, and the dog-man Fal-chetto, owe a great debt to Luigi Pulci's* Morgante and Margutte. On the whole, the poem can be characterized as an anticlassical work, much of which satirizes aristocrats and clergy, courts and courtiers, philosophers and poets. Like so many other comic works of the Renaissance,* Folengo's poem reflects a variety of influences, learned, classical, and popular in origin. His work was well known to François Rabelais, many of whose characters seem related to those in *Baldus* and whose comic use of language may also have been influenced by the Italian poet's macaronic Latin. Folengo's poem helped to liberate Italian literature from the confines of the courtly ambience and the Tuscan dialect. It combined poetic realism and ribald humor with a sense of explosive freedom that was not to be equaled in Italy for some time to come.

See also PULCI, Luigi.

Bibliography: Il Baldo, trans. Giuseppe Tonna, 2 vols. (Milan: Feltrinelli, 1958)—original text with facing Italian translation; *Le Maccheronee,* ed. Alessandro Luzio, 2 vols. (Bari: Laterza, 1927); *Zanitonella,* trans. Giorgio Perini (Turin: Einaudi, 1961)—original text with facing Italian translation; *Italian Poets of the Renaissance,* trans. Joseph Tusiani (Long Island City, N. Y.: Baroque Press, 1971); Ettore Bonora, *Le Maccheronee di Teofilo Folengo* (Venice: Neri Pozza Editore, 1956); Alan Soons, "The Celebration of the Rustic Virtues in the Works of Teofilo Folengo," *The Journal of Medieval and Renaissance Studies* 1 (1971), 119–29.

FOLGORE DA SAN GIMIGNANO (fourteenth century), poet and courtly entertainer. Little is known of the life of this poet, Giacomo da Michele by name, who was recognized for his military exploits in 1305 and 1306 and knighted in 1332. This father of two children is still known to us as Folgore, a nickname meaning "splendor" and no doubt referring to the quality of his life. As an active public servant, Folgore was a determined Guelph partisan. Four of his extant sonnets* give expression to his Guelph ideals and to his disappointment at the defeat of his party by the Ghibellines. One bitter sonnet verges on blasphemy: "Eo no ti lodo, Dio, e non ti adoro" ("I praise Thee not, O God, nor adore Thee").

The thirty-two sonnets which have come down to us were apparently composed between 1309 and 1317. Two finished series of sonnets and an incomplete third reveal Folgore as an enthusiastic participant in the life of the polite society of his time with its gay customs and colorful chivalric ceremonies. A series of fourteen sonnets, now called *The Garland of the Months,* was perhaps written to instruct a "brigata nobile e cortese" (a noble and courtly company of people), who probably should not be identified with the group censured by Dante* in *Inferno* XXIX. After a prefatory sonnet, he guides his audience through the suitable pursuits and pleasures for each month of the year. He portrays a refined existence inspired by an ideal of happiness tempered by good taste, an exquisite sense of worldly elegance, and a deep sense of natural harmony. In their use of the themes of the months and seasons and in their sometimes nostalgic portrayal of the life of leisure, these poems have a peculiarly medieval flavor. Along with an analogous series of eight sonnets on the days of the week, these poems provide a brief glimpse into the social customs of the rich bourgeoisie of Tuscany. This social realism is modified by the idealistic picture of knights and ladies, who are "More gallant and more courteous than Lancelot" and who "shall be so amorous, shall do each other so much courtesy, that they shall be held gracious by all the world" (*The Garland of the Months,* one and seven). Another five sonnets, survivors of a projected group of seventeen, are dedicated to a youth who is to be knighted and describe allegorically the virtues of knighthood. Although this ideal of luxurious and elegant living is quite in contrast to the religious sentiment in St. Francis* and the mystical love of woman expressed by Dante, it may be derived from the Provençal tradition, which was not entirely neglected in the poetry of Dante and his contemporaries.

Bibliography: Sonetti, ed. Giovanni Caravaggi (Turin: Einaudi, 1965); Richard Aldington, trans., *A Wreath for Saint Gemignano* (New York: Duell, Sloan & Pearce, 1945).

FORTINI, FRANCO, pen-name of Franco Lattes (1917–   ), Florentine poet and critic. Fortini received his training in law and literature and participated in the antifascist resistance during World War II. His wartime experiences were decisive in turning his works toward political and ideological concerns and in moving him to see a form of humanistic socialism as a remedy for many of Italy's problems. His collaboration on Vittorini's* journal, *Il Politecnico,* reflects his political involvement. Fortini has continued to contribute poetry, criticism, and essays to a number of major journals, including *Quaderni piacentini, Paragone,* and *Nuovi argomenti.* Notable among his several volumes of criticism is the collection *Dieci inverni 1947–1957* (1957, Ten Winters 1947–1957), which presents an analysis of postwar culture, its aspirations and its shortcomings. In general, Fortini avoids obfuscation and critical fads, and defines the aim of criticism as the moral one of clarifying the relationship between literature and life. The author of several volumes of poetry, he is a distinguished translator who has written Italian versions of authors as diverse as Einstein, Eluard, Proust, Goethe, Kierkegaard, Brecht, and Döblin.

Bibliography: Dieci inverni 1947–1957 (Milan: Mondadori, 1957); *Italian Writing Today,* ed. Raleigh Trevelyan (Baltimore: Penguin, 1967); Giorgio Ferretti, *La letteratura del rifiuto* (Milan: Mursia, 1968); Pier Paolo Pasolini, *Passione e ideologia* (Milan: Garzanti, 1960).

FOSCOLO, UGO (1778–1827), poet. Foscolo, the son of a Greek mother and a ship's surgeon from Venice, was born on the Ionian island of Zante and never forgot his origins. The island is doxologized in his poetry and in his correspondence. In a letter to J. S. Bartholdy (29 September 1808), he declared: "Although Italian by education and origin . . . I shall never forget that I was born of a Greek mother, that I was nursed by a Greek and that I saw the first ray of sun in the clear and woodsy Zante, still resounding with the verses with which Homer and Theocritus celebrated her." In 1784, the family moved to the Dalmatian city of Split, but at his father's death (1788) he followed his mother to Zante and in 1793 to Venice, where the family settled. Foscolo thus set foot on Italy proper when the Italian romantic generation was born and when the country, experiencing the troubled politics of the Napoleonic period, was entering the decisive shift that was to lead to its Risorgimento. Although poor and, as he claimed, with little knowledge of the classics and "entirely ignorant of Tuscan," he obtained access to the most enlightened circles, thanks to his own drive, to the solicitude of his teachers, and to the favors of Isabella Teotochi Albrizzi (1760–1836), in whose salon he met noted artists and writers. His literary reputation began to emerge in 1797 with the publication of lyric poems and the performance of his first tragedy, *Tieste* (Thyestes). Suspected of revolutionary ideas, he left for Milan, launching a long politico-military activism that made him one of the foremost patriot-poets. He volunteered for the National Guard and as an officer fought valiantly, was wounded in the defense of Genoa, and spent two years (1804–06) in northern France, in the Italian division of Napoleon's expeditionary force. In Normandy, he had an amorous relationship with Sophia Saint John Hamilton; it was their daughter, Floriana, who was to provide for him so generously in his later years. Returning to Italy, he held for a brief time the chair of rhetoric at the University of Pavia, but lost it because of his antityrannical, anti-Napoleonic stand. In 1813, after Napoleon's defeat at Leipzig, he joined the defenders of Milan against the Austrians. When the city fell, he was given some blandishments by the victors until he was asked to pledge his allegiance to Austria. He fled to Switzerland and, then, fearing extradition, to England, where he soon struck up warm friendships with several luminaries, entered London's high society, and wrote for prestigious publications. Despite his sizable earnings and his access to Floriana's inheritance, unwise investments and his inflated style of living caused his financial ruin. He incurred substantial debts, and, to avoid arrest for defaulting, lived, often under aliases, in the slums. He died on 10 September 1827 in Turnham-Green and was buried in Chiswick Cemetery.

No epitaph to his battered existence and to the woes of his final days is more apposite than his own prediction, made when still in Italy, that "fate ordained an unwept burial" for him. It was only in 1871 that his remains were transferred to the Florentine church of Santa Croce, among the other great Italians whom he panegyrized.

Despite his early death, his long patriotic and military involvements, his many and turbulent love affiars, and his roving life, Foscolo was a prolific author. Besides *Tieste,* he wrote two other plays, *Aiace* (1811, Ajax) and *Ricciarda* (1813, Ricciarda). He translated Callimachus's *The Locks of Berenice* (1803) and Sterne's *Sentimental Journey* (begun in 1804). But his *magnum opus* as a translator, a version of the *Iliad* more faithful to the original than that of Vincenzo Monti,* remained incomplete. He edited the military works of Raimondo Montecuccoli (1808–09) and composed a satirical poem in Latin, the *Hypercalypseos Liber* (1810, Super-Revelation), with biblical fulminations against the critic Urbano Lampredi (1761–1838). His various orations and his *Discorsi sulla servitù d'Italia* (1814, Discourses on Italy's Servitude) reveal his pessimistic view of Italy in the first decades of the century. He engaged in scholarly and critical pursuits up to the time of his death. His oration *Dell'origine e dell'ufficio della letteratura* (1809, On the Origin and Function of Literature) is justly famous, and his essays on Dante's* *Divine Comedy,* on Petrarch,* and on Boccaccio's* *Decameron* are still of critical consequence. What informs his criticism in these and other essays is his estimate of literature as an educating force and of the writer's commitment to man's sociopolitical and aesthetic betterment. It follows that the authors in whose works he quarried are appraised with his own poetic and vatic norms.

Foscolo is recognized as one of the great authors of Italy on the basis of a slim epistolary novel and his poetry. *Le ultime lettere di Jacopo Ortis (Last Letters of Jacopo Ortis)* began to appear in 1798 and was completed in 1802. The letters chronicle Jacopo's feelings on two major themes: the amatory and the patriotic. Both are impassioned and interrelated. Jacopo's love for Teresa rekindled the anger that had shaken him at Napoleon's cession of Venice to the Austrians at Campoformio. The betrayal of his ideals, the enslavement of his fatherland, the enervation of his countrymen, and his own impotence made him seek respite from his despair in the Arcadian setting of the Euganean Hills, where he had first met Teresa. The sociopolitical conditions of his country and his own feeling of powerlessness do not permit him to effect the breakup of Teresa's engagement to Odoardo, her vacuous but wealthy fiancé, selected by her father and unloved by her. The marriage of Teresa to Odoardo and the sad state of Italy bring him to total despair and finally to suicide. In its effusiveness and sentimentality, the novel recalls Goethe's *Sorrows of Young Werther,* Richardson's *Pamela,* and Rousseau's *La Nouvelle Héloise,* works that

Foscolo knew well and whose protagonists he made "solitude's companions" for his own hero and heroine.

Foscolo wrote hymns, elegies, and several odes, two of which, "A
Luigia Pallavicini caduta da cavallo" (1800, "To Luigia Pallavicini Who
Fell from Her Horse") and "All'amica risanata" (1803, "To His Friend
Restored to Health"), are perfect examples of neoclassic form. His twelve
sonnets are among the most felicitous and moving of the romantic period.
The foreboding of a life buffeted by adversities and destined to incessant
wanderings is given a most personal and, at the same time, cosmic
significance in such justly celebrated sonnets as "A Zacinto" (1803, "To
Zante"), "In morte del fratello Giovanni" (1803, "On the Death of His
Brother Giovanni"), and "Alla sera" (1803, "To Evening"). His longest
poem, *Le Grazie* ("The Graces"), occupied him for years and remained
unfinished. Conceived as a one-hymn counterpart to Antonio Canova's
(1757–1822) *Venus* (1805–07), the project grew with the years to three. The
first, *Venus*, takes place in prehistoric Greece and, in Foscolo's own
prefatory summary, narrates "the divine origin of the Graces and the
progressive civilization of the human race." The second, *Vesta*, is set in
the "Italy of our own days," while the third, *Pallas*, has neither temporal
nor spatial boundaries, taking place "in the middle of the Ocean, in a divine
land and with such divine arts that ours would appear imitations." In the
primitive past, in the historical present, and in a visionary future, the poet
apprehends and extols the beneficent influence of what the Graces symbolize: music, poetry, dance, and all other forms of harmony. From harmony derive beauty and goodness; from it flows the aesthetic and moral
betterment of mankind, and in it resides the salubrity of the physical and
moral universe. For all its thematic nobility, its formal polish, and its
positive reappraisal by recent critics, the poem has never gained the
public's favor, perhaps because of its excessive use of mythology and its
pristine symbolism.

Foscolo's *Dei Sepolcri* (1807, *On Sepulchres*), on the other hand, has
always enjoyed public acclaim. Its two hundred and ninety-five hendecasyllables of blank verse express Foscolo's indignation at Napoleon's
edict of Saint Cloud, which in an exaggerated outburst of sanitation and
egalitarianism forbade burial within the city, prescribed uniformity in
graves, and prohibited all distinguishing features and inscribed epitaphs.
The son of the Age of Reason, Foscolo readily concedes that no urn, no
tears shed on it, no verdant cypress, no epitaph however eloquent can
make death less cruel. As an agnostic, he holds no belief in life after death.
However, although tombs are of no comfort to the departed, he maintains
they have a multiple, useful function for those left behind. On the personal
level, they generate the illusion (a key word in Foscolo's poetics) that the
dead continue to live and thus establish a "heavenly . . . correspondence

of loving feelings," through which "we often live with the deceased friend and the deceased with us." On the national level, at the tombs of Italy's great men, future generations of Italians will be inspired to undertake their country's deliverance from its present wretchedness. Even in terms of the cycles of civilization, they are indispensable because they bridge the past and the present and foster the illusion of man's immortality. To such a reasoned formulation of ideas, Foscolo gave appropriate poetic expression. Others before him—particularly such eighteenth-century English writers as Edward Young, James Hervey, Robert Blair, and Thomas Gray—had cultivated the sepulchral genre in prose or poetry. But Foscolo's composition is its best utterance. The poem is something between a threnody and a short epic.* Of the threnody, it has the quality of rendering mythical the historical events (e.g., Nelson's victory and fate) and personalities (Dante, Petrarch, Machiavelli,* Michelangelo,* Galileo,* Parini,* Alfieri*), and of describing in a fable-like manner sites of life (the Tuscan landscape) or death (the medieval burials in the pavements of churches and the British suburban cemeteries). It is also a most moving expression of the author's microscopic and macroscopic concept of existence and of his view that poetry, a divinely inspired afflatus, "overcomes the silence of a thousand centuries."

Foscolo's correspondence documents major and minor biographical incidents, mirrors his every mood, and allows us to gauge the temper of the man. His letters are seldom void of the reflective and the poetic. Moreover, they reveal those conflicting impulses and attitudes which, in the classification of writers into literary movements, make Foscolo both an opponent and a practitioner of romanticism.* As all classicists, he too considered man to be indivisible and longed for harmony and quietude. Yet, from his earliest years, in words and deeds, he appeared as a man divided against himself, seeking freedom from the tyranny of foreign rule over his fatherland and from the despotism of reason over his own passions. In sum, although his stated literary credo was anti-romantic, in temperament, in his life's vicissitudes, and in his best creative works, Foscolo appears as one of the fathers of Italian romanticism.

Bibliography: Edizione nazionale delle opere di Ugo Foscolo, eds. Mario Fubini, et al., 21 vols. (Florence: Le Monnier, 1933–74); *Last Letters of Jacopo Ortis,* trans. Douglas Radcliff-Umstead (Chapel Hill, N.C.: University of North Carolina Press, 1970); *On Sepulchres,* trans. Thomas G. Bergin (Bethany, Conn.: Bethany Press, 1971); *From Marino to Marinetti,* trans. Joseph Tusiani (New York: Baroque Press, 1974); Eugenio Donadoni, *Ugo Foscolo, pensatore, critico, poeta* (Florence: Remo Sandron Edizioni, 1964); Mario Fubini, *Ugo Foscolo* (Florence: La Nuova Italia, 1962); Karl Kroeber, *The Artifice of Reality: Poetic Style in Wordsworth, Foscolo, Keats and Leopardi* (Madison, Wis: University of Wisconsin Press, 1969); Douglas Radcliff-Umstead, *Ugo Foscolo* (New York: Twayne,

1970); E. R. Vincent, *Ugo Foscolo: An Italian in Regency England* (1953; rpt. Folcroft, Pa.: Folcroft Library Editions, 1973).

Emmanuel Hatzantonis

FRACASTORO, GIROLAMO (1478–1553), poet, humanist, and physician. Born in Verona, Fracastoro studied at the nearby University of Padua, where he apparently knew Copernicus and had access to the lectures of Pomponazzi.* He was a lecturer in logic at Padua from 1501 to 1506, and he was most probably engaged in the active practice of medicine from 1509 until 1530. Fracastoro was appointed medical advisor to the Council of Trent by Pope Paul III in 1545.

Fracastoro is a most unusual figure, even in the Italian Renaissance,* and his talents were to make him famous not only in literature but also in the applied science of medicine. His most famous work was a Latin poem in hexameters, *Syphilis sive Morbus Gallicus* (1530, *Syphilis or the French Disease*), from which the term syphilis originated; this work in three books was dedicated to his friend Pietro Bembo.* In a consistently Virgilian style, frequently mixing classical allusions with his subject matter, Fracastoro discusses in book one the American origins of the malady, a theory which was very popular at the time, and rejects the idea; book two deals with possible remedies and presents the fabricated pseudoclassical myth of a hunter Ilceus who is punished by the gods with the disease and is cured with mercury by a nymph; book three continues remedies, discussing the use of guaiac by American Indians and presenting the story of the shepherd Syphilus whose offense to Apollo caused him to be the first to have been stricken by the disease. The poem was extremely popular and was read and translated all over Europe, including a version by the English poet laureate Nahum Tate in 1686. In 1546, Fracastoro published his important *De Contagione et Contagiosis Morbis (On Contagion and Pestilent Fevers)*, the scientific treatise which argues for the microbic origins of many contagious diseases.

A literary theorist as well as a poet and scientist, Fracastoro also wrote a Latin dialogue on poetics in memory of his friend Andrea Navagero* entitled *Naugerius, sive de Poetica Dialogus* (1555, *Navagero, or A Dialogue on the Art of Poetry*). In this attempt to modify the various theories of poetry popular in Italy at the time, which derived from Horace, Aristotle, or Plato, he concludes that poetry should aim at both pleasure and instruction through imitation of the noblest and most beautiful aspects of its object in a beautiful and suitable style.

See also BEMBO, Pietro; NAVAGERO, Andrea.

Bibliography: De Contagione et Contagiosis Morbis et eorum Curatione, trans.

W. C. Wright (New York: Putnam's 1930); *Naugerius, sive de Poetica Dialogus,*
trans. Ruth Kelso (Urbana, Ill.: University of Illinois Studies in Language and
Literature, 1924); *Sifilide ossia del mal francese,* ed. and trans. Fabrizio Winspeare
(Florence: Olschki, 1955)—contains the Latin text with Italian translation; Leona
Baumgartner and John F. Fulton, *A Bibliography of the Poem Syphilis sive Morbus
Gallicus* (New Haven, Conn.: Yale University Press, 1935).

FRANCESCO D'ASSISI, SAN (1181 or 1182–1226), religious writer and
poet. Born in Assisi to Pietro Bernadone and his French wife Pica, Francesco received the name Giovanni at baptism but acquired the name
Francesco either because of his mother's origins or because he emulated
the French styles of the day. In his youth, Francesco had a definite
inclination towards worldly pleasures and dreamed of a successful military
career, but in his first campaign he was taken prisoner. Released in 1204, he
experienced a physical and spiritual crisis and thereafter devoted himself to
a life of prayer, poverty, and charity. In 1207, he formally renounced his
claims to the family fortune, stripping himself naked to demonstrate that he
had truly abandoned the worldly existence of his family. In 1209, a passage
from Matthew inspired him to imitate Christ and the apostles by preaching;
he gained converts and in 1210 obtained temporary sanction for his new
order from Pope Innocent III through a personal appeal.

As the order grew, many of the legends associated with Francesco
appeared. The popular miracle stories of the *Fioretti (Little Flowers)*
related such incidents as the preaching to the birds, the conversion of the
hare, and the taming of the wolf of Gubbio. After 1216, Francesco gradually relinquished control of his growing order, and in 1219 he fulfilled a
lifelong dream by preaching to the Sultan al-Malik al-Kamil during a
crusade. Definitive approval for the order came in 1223 from Pope Honorius III, and the stories of his stigmatization date from this period.

At a time when the church was not favorably disposed towards reformers, the survival of the Franciscan order is a testament to Francesco's
personal appeal. Although his views on poverty and the imitation of Christ
were not novel, his personality, his emphasis upon peace, his view that
religion was meant for all men from every station, and his belief in the
goodness of the natural world set him apart. He managed to initiate one of
the most decisive spiritual revolutions in the history of Christianity. It is
not by accident that Dante* refers to Francesco in the *Paradiso* (XI) as a
"sun born into the world." Francesco was canonized in 1228 and has
remained one of the most popular of medieval figures.

Francesco preached not only in Latin but also in his own Umbrian
dialect. He was one of the first to use the vulgar tongue and to appreciate
literary and musical texts not written in Latin. Nevertheless, the bulk of his
writings are in Latin and are collected under the title *Opuscula* (Brief
Works). One section contains several Rules of Life to be used by the

Franciscans, as well as a collection of admonitions and instructions to regulate the behavior of the members of the order. A second part is composed of six letters. A third includes a complete Office of the Passion in five forms for the different church seasons. No Latin text, however, presents Francesco's essential message so gracefully and appealingly as the Italian poem *Cantico di Frate Sole (Canticle of Brother Sun),* sometimes referred to by its Latin title, the *Laudes creaturarum.* This poem is one of the oldest literary documents in Italian, and with it, Italian literature begins on a high, noble note.

Because of its resemblance to Psalm 148 and to the song of the children in the fiery furnace (Daniel 3: 57–88), the *Canticle* might be called a vernacular psalm. Like this poetry in the Vulgate, it is composed of stanzas of two to five verses, themselves metrically irregular and unrhymed but rhythmic and rich in assonance. A basic order and balance is established through the anaphoric arrangement of stanzas and the use of four- and five-line stanzas at both the beginning and the end of the work. Its musical setting was probably plain-chant or possibly a tune of Francesco's own composition. The first twenty-two lines portray the majesty of the Creator and His relations with His creations. Francesco elaborates upon the biblical passages in which created things are called upon to praise God, suggesting that the Lord should be praised by all natural things. Recent critics have noted that Francesco deviates from the biblical passages by having his God praised on account of or through his creations. Where the biblical texts contain lengthy enumerations of God's works, Francesco selects the sun, moon, stars, the four elements, and death, curiously neglecting the flora and fauna. Going well beyond Genesis, these parts of the natural world are individualized and pictured as the brothers and sisters of man. In language both biblical and feudal, Francesco establishes that hierarchical relationship between God and his creatures in which the "Signore" (Lord) is the superior of "messer lo frate Sole" ("Sir Brother Sun"). With this one phrase, Francesco makes the sun part of the universal hierarchy and a member of his own religious order, a brother.

Never simply a song of praise and joy, Francesco's *Canticle* portrays the human condition with touching realism. God is not praised through mankind in general but only through those who practice forgiveness, endure their hardships, and live peacefully, obediently, and humbly. Francesco personifies and adopts "Sister Bodily Death" into his order because death is part of the natural order of things in God's universe. The scope of the poem is finally broadened to include the warning that those who die in mortal sin will suffer the "second death" of the spirit. Both the joyful psalmist and the preacher are present in the latter portion of the poem to convey both the beauty and the reality of life, the happiness and the burdens of mankind. In the last two lines, Francesco urges man to "Praise and bless my Lord/ And render thanks, and serve him with great humility."

While the tightly organized poem begins upon a note of exultation it ends upon a note of caution. The Lord is "most high" but mankind, His opposite, must live humbly and peacefully, aware of its debt to the Creator.

Bibliography: Opuscula Sancti Patris Francisci Assisiensis (Rome: Quarrachi, 1941); *The Writings of Saint Francis of Assisi* (Chicago: Franciscan Herald Press, 1964); Lawrence Cunningham, ed., *Brother Francis: An Anthology of Writings by and about St. Francis of Assisi* (New York: Harper, 1972); Edward A. Armstrong, *St. Francis: Nature Mystic–The Derivation and Significance of the Nature Stories in the Franciscan Legend* (Berkeley, Calif.: University of California Press, 1976); Susannah Peters Coy, "The Problem of 'Per' in the Cantico di Frate Sole of Saint Francis," *Modern Language Notes* 91 (1976), 1–11; Paul Sabatier, *The Life of Saint Francis of Assisi* (New York: Scribner's, 1916); John H. Smith, *Francis of Assisi* (New York: Scribner's, 1972).

FREDERICK II OF HOHENSTAUFEN (1194–1250), emperor of the Holy Roman Empire (1220–50). Frederick was born at Jesi near Ancona and died at Castel Fiorentino. The son of Henry VI and Constance, heiress of the Two Sicilies, he was left an orphan in 1198, brought up the ward of the pope, and assumed the government of the Two Sicilies in 1208. With the support of the pope, he established his authority in Germany and was crowned in Aachen (Aix) in 1215 after defeating King Otto IV at Bouvines in the previous year. He had grown up in Palermo where he received a fine education. Crowned emperor by Pope Honorius III in 1220, he continued his efforts to unify Italy and Germany into one empire. However, he was opposed in these efforts by the pope and by the Lombard League. Belatedly fulfilling a pledge to the pope, he led a Crusade to the Holy Land in 1228–29 and procured Jerusalem, Bethlehem, and Nazareth from the Saracens. However, his participation in the fifth Crusade only involved him in another imbroglio with the pope, because he signed a treaty with the Sultan al-Malik al-Kamil instead of pursuing a military victory. In the course of Frederick's prolonged conflict with the cities of northern Italy, the terms *Ghibelline* and *Guelph* came to refer, respectively, to the emperor's supporters and to his antagonists. Often at odds with the papacy, Frederick was excommunicated several times. However, the intensity of the animosity between the parties grew, and, in 1245, the pope declared him deposed, diminishing his power irreparably.

Although Frederick's efforts to centralize political power in southern Italy were ultimately unsuccessful, he was instrumental in the reawakening of Italian letters. A man of considerable versatility, he was an able administrator, legislator, and general, who was personally interested in agriculture, hunting, architecture, and writing. Attempting to destroy the feudal system and centralize authority in the monarchy, he ruled with an iron hand. He enacted legislation and juridical reforms, reorganized the economy, made commerce in oil, wine, and salt an imperial monopoly and imposed excise taxes. Single-minded and cruel in pursuing his aims, he was wise and enlightened in some of his reforms, seemingly the forerunner of the cultivated, enlightened, autocratic Renaissance* princes.

A cultivated man, Frederick was said to have spoken Latin, Italian, German, French, Provençal, Greek, and Arabic. He surrounded himself with cultured men, proved an energetic patron of the arts, science, and philosophy, worked to reorganize the school of medicine at Salerno, and founded the University of Naples in 1224. One project which he promoted was the translation of Aristotle's works into Latin. His endeavors were in that secular spirit which prevailed in the rebirth of art and letters in the centuries to come. The so-called Sicilian School of poetry, the first such group of writers to undertake the writing of love poetry in Italy, consisted of approximately thirty men from various regions of Italy who were attached to his court. The most notable members included Giacomo da Lentino,* Pier della Vigna,* and Rinaldo d'Aquino.* While the Sicilians might have been influenced by Arab and Norman traditions, it is most certain that they were acquainted with the popular traditions as well as with the Provençal lyric, the northern French lyric, and the German *minne-song*. Frederick's four *canzoni* * and one sonnet* written in the Provençal mode exhibit the traditional declarations of love, the expressions of homage to the lady, and the lamentations over the suffering experienced when the poet is deprived of the lady's presence, but none of the stylistic complexities of the troubadours. Unlike his poetry, Frederick's treatise on falconry, *De arte venandi cum avibus* (circa 1229, *The Art of Falconry*), displays the temperament of an innovator. In this study of hawking, which also discusses the anatomy and habits of birds, he reveals himself to be a student of the classics as well as an avid hunter and a careful observer. Rather than relying upon the accounts of authorities such as Aristotle, Frederick stresses the need for independent observation and analysis. This rationalism is complemented by his descriptive powers and his understanding of the essential harmony of nature.

See also DA LENTINO, Giacomo; PIER DELLA VIGNA; RINALDO D'AQUINO.

Bibliography: The Age of Dante: An Anthology of Early Italian Poetry, trans. Joseph Tusiani (New York: Baroque Press, 1974); *The Art of Falconry*, trans. Casey A. Wood and F. Marjorie Fyfe (Stanford, Calif.: Stanford University Press, 1961).

FRESCOBALDI, DINO (circa 1271–circa 1316), poet. Frescobaldi, who worked in the ambience of the *dolce stil nuovo*,* was the son of the poet and Florentine banker and merchant Lambertuccio di Ghino, who had written in the manner of Guittone d'Arezzo,* and the father of a poet, Matteo (circa 1300–1348), who was a late exponent of the new style. Politically, the family aligned themselves with the Blacks. Donato Velluti (1313–1370) in his *Cronica domestica* (begun 1367, Domestic Chronicle), wrote that Dino was a handsome man, a great lover, and the husband of a woman named Giovanna. In the *Trattatello in laude di Dante* (1373, *In Praise of Dante*), Boccaccio* refers to him as a man of considerable intellect and a very famous poet, and tells an anecdote about his involvement in rediscovering the first seven *canti* of Dante's* *Inferno*. Frescobaldi subsequently sent the *canti* to Moroello Malaspino (died circa 1315) with whom Dante had been living during his exile from Florence, so that the entire poem could be completed.

Frescobaldi's *canzoniere* tells of the poet's love for a woman who first brings him joy through her kindness but then, through her reluctance, despair. This tormented love is the source of the tone of anguish and melancholy particularly evident in his noted *canzone** on death, "Morte avversara" (Come, death my enemy). Apparently aware of the limits of the language of the *dolce stil nuovo,* he uses it primarily in the most conventional passages in his poetry, which deal with the torments of love and the proud, disdainful beauty of the lady. He attempts to expand and to renew this poetic language by going back to Cavalcanti,* Dante's *rime petrose* ("stoney" poems), and the first *canti* of the *Divine Comedy*. Some fresh motifs, images, and phrases go beyond the bounds of *stilnovisti* propriety (i.e., the images of the lady as a wolf, the forest of martyrs, the lion, and death's embrace).

In some respects, Frescobaldi cannot be called a true innovator. His work attests to the dangers of sterility in closely adhering to a tradition and to the need to break away from the rather high-minded aims of the *stilnovisti,* a need which becomes even more evident in the poetry of Cino da Pistoia.*

See also DOLCE STIL NUOVO.

Bibliography: Poeti del Dolce stil nuovo, ed. Mario Marti (Florence: Le Monnier, 1969); *German and Italian Lyrics of the Middle Ages,* trans. Frederick Goldin (Garden City, N.Y.: Doubleday, 1973).

FRUGONI, FRANCESCO FULVIO (circa 1620–circa 1686), Baroque* poet and prose stylist. Born in Genoa, Frugoni spent his youth in Spain, where he attended the university and met several of the foremost Spanish Baroque writers, apparently including Luis De Góngora and Francesco De Quevedo. Upon his return to Genoa (the exact date is difficult to determine), he entered a religious order and later joined the household of the ambassador of the Republic of Genoa in Spain. After a second sojourn in Spain, Frugoni traveled throughout Europe, visiting Holland, England, and France. In 1652, he became advisor to the widow of Ercole II Grimaldi, prince of Monaco (Duchess Aurelia). While he traveled with her through France and Italy, he continued to cultivate his literary interests and gained the friendship of Emanuele Tesauro,* the foremost Italian theorist of the Baroque style, during a three-year stay in Turin. At the death of the duchess in 1670, Frugoni moved to Venice, where he completed the notable *Del cane di Diogene* (1689, The Dog of Diogenes), which was published posthumously.

Frugoni's earliest effort is a comic poem in *ottave* entitled *La Guardinfanteide* (1643, The Hoop-Skirtiad), a humorous description of a novel fashion in women's wear which had been imported into Italy from Spain. He then wrote a number of musical dramas, lyrics, and orations, but his most important works were those in prose, including a novel entitled *La vergine parigina* (1660–61, The Parisian Maiden) and a romanticized life of his patroness, the duchess, entitled *L'heroina intrepida* (1673, The Intrepid Heroine). In *L'heroina* Frugoni claimed to have reconciled the conflicting demands of truth and fiction in literature. His fame, today, however, rests upon the encyclopedic sweep of his principal work, *Del cane di Diogene,* which consists of twelve stories in seven volumes. Like Boccalini's* *Ragguagli di Parnaso (Advertisements from Parnassus)*, Frugoni's masterpiece is structured upon a highly unlikely situation. The content is not a journalistic report from Mount Parnassus but rather the wanderings of the philosopher's dog whose "barkings," as Frugoni calls them, are against the customs and characters of both past and present. As in Boccalini, this wily animal manages to visit Parnassus, and his observations there touching upon literary questions constitute the core of the twelve sections of the book. This passage, known as *Il tribunal della critica* (The Tribunal of Criticism), describes the vices of various writers. Frugoni here reveals himself to be a "modern" in his preference for the poetry of Torquato Tasso* over even the acknowledged masters of the Florentine Trecento—Dante,* Petrarch,* and Boccaccio.*

In lyric poetry, Frugoni admired Marino* and the Baroque lyric in general, including the poetry of the great Spanish writers he had encountered abroad. His own prose provides an excellent example of Italian Baroque style, with its emphasis upon the extravagant conceits and ingenious metaphors prescribed in the theories of his friend Tesauro. In spite of the recent interest in the Baroque period, the encyclopedic length of *Del cane di Diogene* has kept it from receiving the critical attention it certainly deserves. Many of his works are not yet available in reliable or complete modern critical editions.

See also BAROQUE; MARINO, Giambattista; TESAURO, Emanuele.

Bibliography: Trattatisti e narratori del Seicento, ed. Ezio Raimondi (Milan: Ricciardi, 1960)—selections of major works; U. Cosmo, *Con Dante attraverso il Seicento* (Bari: Laterza, 1946); Benedetto Croce, *Storia dell'età barocca in Italia* (Bari: Laterza, 1946); Ezio Raimondi, *Letteratura barocca; studi sul Seicento italiano* (Florence: Olschki, 1961).

FUCINI, RENATO (1843–1921), poet and novelist. Fucini, born near Pisa and educated at the University of Pisa, first worked in Florence as an assistant engineer for the city. There, his early interest in literature bore fruit with the publication (under the pseudonym Neri Tanfucio) of a group of sonnets* in the Pisan dialect, *Cento sonetti in vernacolo pisano* (1872, One Hundred Sonnets in Pisan Dialect) which was favorably received by the Florentine literary community and praised by Mazzini* and Guerrazzi.* It was followed a few years later by another collection of fifty similar poems, *Cinquanta nuovi sonetti* (1879, Fifty New Sonnets). Although Fucini's dialect poetry is often witty and ingenious and gives the reader a pleasant view of scenes from Pisan life, it is not really worthy of comparison to the greater literary creations of Porta* or Belli.*

Fucini eventually gave up his post with the city to become a school inspector for the Tuscan district, and he lived most of his life in its rural areas. He also turned from poetry in dialect to narrative prose in Italian. In 1878, he published a fictional work in a journalistic style, entitled *Napoli a occhio nudo* (Naples to the Naked Eye). It was written in the form of nine imaginary letters to a friend, and includes engaging sketches of Neapolitan life and vignettes from Sorrento, Pompei, Vesuvius, and Capri. This interest in regional fiction led Fucini to turn his attention to an area of Italy he knew well, Tuscany and the surrounding countryside. His best known collection of short stories, *Le veglie di Neri* (1884, rev. ed. 1890, Evenings with Neri), placed him in the forefront of Tuscan *bozzettisti* (sketch writers) and *veristi* who, like the Tuscan *Macchiaioli* (Impressionist) painters, concentrated upon rural Tuscan scenes, figures, and themes. Although Fucini seldom struck the tragic note found in the best works of Verga,* Capuana,* or De Roberto* (*veristi* who concentrated upon the region of Sicily), his talents for catching the humorous and pleasant aspects of life in the country were considerable. He continued his regional stories with a Tuscan setting in *All'aria aperta* (1897, In the Open Air), a book of twenty-one tales. Perhaps the most famous and representative of the collection is "Il monumento" ("The Monument"), a comic picture of a small-town committee trying to provide a statue for their town square with only thirty-five lire to spend. During his last years, Fucini became concerned with the quality of public education and wrote a number of works for young children and the schools. Two posthumous collections of stories—*Acqua passata* (1921, Water Under the Dam) and *Foglie al vento* (1922, Leaves in the Wind)—completed his many brief portraits of country life.

See also VERISMO.

Bibliography: Tutti gli scritti (Milan: Trevisini, 1946); *Italian Regional Tales of the Nineteenth Century,* eds. Archibald Colquhoun and Neville Rogers (London: Oxford University Press, 1961)—contains two stories from *All'aria aperta;* Benedetto Croce, *La Letteratura della Nuova Italia* (Bari: Laterza, 1915); Giorgio Varanini, *Renato Fucini* (Pisa: Goliardica, 1955).

FUTURISM, a literary movement, founded by Filippo Tommaso Marinetti* in 1909, which later expanded to include painting, sculpture, architecture, music, theatre, photography, cinema, and politics. Futurism made its appearance on the literary scene with the publication of Marinetti's manifesto "Fondazione e manifesto del Futurismo" ("The Founding and Manifesto of Futurism") on 20 February 1909 in *Le Figaro.* This bombastic declaration, characterized by its aggressive tone and defiant self-confidence, started a trend of manifesto writing that expanded beyond the Italian movement to the whole European avant-garde. The text of the manifesto sounds more like an outburst of romantic exuberance than a systematic program for a new movement. Nevertheless, the main themes of futurism are already clearly outlined: anarchical vitalism, rebellion against *passéisme* (love of the past), destruction of academies and museums, confidence in the achievements of the technological civilization, celebration of the machine as a symbol of the new aesthetics, and "the beauty of speed." According to Marinetti, the development of the technological civilization has produced profound changes both in the physical world and in the human psyche. The world has acquired a new dimension, speed—trains, automobiles, aeroplanes, telegraph, telephone—which has revolutionized the traditional way of life as well as the poetic perception of it. Marinetti effectively captures the new aesthetic principle, "the beauty of speed," when he declares that "a roaring automobile is more beautiful than the Victory of Samothrace." The antecedents of this theme are found in the nineteenth century, in the works of the *poetès maudits* ("damned poets") and some decadents, especially Jules Laforgue and Emile Verhaeren. However, although these poets felt the fascination of the big city as well as the anguish of its dehumanizing power, Marinetti raised technology to a symbol of positive vitalism.

The futurist aesthetics has its roots in the irrationalism that permeated literature and the arts (symbolism, impressionism, cubism) as well as philosophy (Nietzsche, Bergson, Croce*) at the turn of the century, and in the new developments in science and technology. After Einstein's concept of relativity was recognized as a legitimate principle of scientific research, it was no longer possible to believe in a world regulated by strictly logical axioms. The traditional Newtonian architecture of the universe collapsed, the spatial and temporal dimensions overlapped, and the philosophers introduced new cognitive principles in their systems. The futurist aesthetics of speed reflected the poetic perception of a chaotic universe; and it allowed the poet to express the complexity of the whole simultaneously, by means of verbal syntheses. Chaos was elevated to the status of a poetic principle and paradoxically incorporated into a carefully thought-out system based on the Bergsonian concept of simultaneity.

The "Manifesto tecnico della letteratura futurista" (11 May 1912, "Technical Manifesto of Futurist Literature") was the first precise formulation of the futurist aesthetic system. It was followed by several other "technical" declarations; among them were "Risposte alle obiezioni" (11 August 1912, "Answers to the Objections"), "Distruzione della sintassi—Immaginazione senza fili—Parole in libertà" (11 May 1913, "Destruction of Syntax—Wireless Imagination—Liberated Words"), and "Lo splendore geometrico e meccanico e la sensibilità numerica" (18 March 1914, "Geometric and Mechanical Splendor and the Numerical Sensibility"). The futurists advocated the destruction of the traditional poetic language regulated by the laws of causality in favor of a new language based on intuition. The elements superimposed on the language by the logical structure (conjunctions, adverbs, adjectives, verbal conjugations, and punctuation) were eliminated. The reduction of the language to its essential parts (substantives and verbs in the infinitive) provided the poet with a medium suitable to fill the gap between perception and expression. The new poetic language consisted of "liberated words" which were related to each other by analogy, according to the principle of "wireless imagination," that is, without the aid of syntactical conducting wires. The direct juxtaposition of the "liberated words" generated a "chain of analogies." The analogy, therefore, took over the function which until then was proper to syntax, and it connected by simultaneous intuition what was once connected by means of a logical process. The "destruction of syntax" was followed by the "typographical revolution"; the freedom of the "liberated words" was visually emphasized by the use of different types and inks. The next step was the creation of "tables of liberated words," where the words were no longer arranged in a linear succession, but were composed figuratively in order to form a picture. They constitute the first specimens of concrete poetry.

The headquarters of futurism was in Milan, where Marinetti established a publishing house, Poesia, dedicated to the publication of futurist works and manifestoes, and largely financed by Marinetti himself. *Poesia* was also the title of Marinetti's futurist magazine. However, the magazine appeared in 1905, several years before the birth of futurism, and its aim at that time was to acquaint the Italian public with contemporary foreign poetry, especially symbolism. Some of the poets who subscribed to futurism in the years of its flowering (1909–15) were Luciano Folgore (1888–1966), Corrado Govoni,* Paolo Buzzi (1874–1956), Francesco Cangiullo (1888–   ), Enrico Cavacchioli (1885–1954), and Auro D'Alba (1888–1965). Most of them were represented in the first anthology of futurist poetry, *I poeti futuristi* (1912, The Futurist Poets). Three other poet/writers, Giovanni Papini,* Ardengo Soffici,* and Aldo Palazzeschi,* associated with the Florentine magazine *Lacerba,* gave their support to futurism for about two years (1913–15) and then disavowed it.

If it is easy to establish the birth date of futurism, it is rather difficult to establish the date of its death. It is certain that the decline of the first phase of futurism, the truly revolutionary phase, coincided with the futurists' involvement in the interventionist movement and their participation in World War I. After the war, the original group disintegrated, and a new generation of poets assembled around Marinetti. The names that appeared in the anthology *I nuovi poeti futuristi* (1925, New Futurist Poets) are those of epigones. Although futurist works continued to appear until the early 1940s (notable among them were the theatrical texts, the futurist "syntheses"), the movement was coopted by the fascist regime and lost its function as a countercultural force. The impact of futurism in its epic stage was felt not only in Europe, but also in such distant areas as Latin America, Japan, and China; outside Italy it maintained its anarchistic-revolutionary character. Subsequent avant-garde movements, up to the most recent experiments with concrete poetry, are indebted to futurism.

See also MARINETTI, Filippo Tommaso; PALAZZESCHI, Aldo; PAPINI, Giovanni; SOFFICI, Ardengo.

Bibliography: Archivi del futurismo, eds. M. Drudi Gambillo and Teresa Fiore, 2 vols. (Rome: De Luca, 1958–62); *I nuovi poeti futuristi* (Rome: Poesia, 1925); *I poeti futuristi* (Milan: Poesia, 1912); *Teatro italiano d'avanguardia: drammi e sintesi futuriste,* ed. Mario Verdone (Rome: Officina Edizioni, 1970); *Futurist Manifestos,* ed. Umbro Apollonio (New York: Viking, 1973); Raffaele Carrieri, *Futurism* (Milan: Edizioni del Milione, 1963); C. De Michelis, *Il futurismo italiano in Russia: 1909–1929* (Bari: De Donato, 1973); Francesco Flora, *Dal romanticismo al futurismo* (Piacenza: Saggiatore, 1921); Michael Kirby, *Futurist Performances* (New York: Dutton, 1971); Anna Lawton, "Russian and Italian Futurist Manifestos," *Slavic and East European Journal* 2 (1976), 405–20; Marianne Martin, *Futurist Art and Theory 1909–1915* (Oxford: Clarendon Press, 1969); Mario Verdone, *Che cosa è il futurismo* (Rome: Ubaldini, 1970), *Prosa e critica futurista* (Milan: Feltrinelli, 1973), and *Teatro del tempo futurista* (Rome: Lerici, 1969).

Anna Lawton

G

GADDA, CARLO EMILIO (1893–1973), engineer and novelist. Gadda, born in Milan, began writing poetry inspired by Walt Whitman in 1915 just before he joined the Alpine troops at the front in World War I. Captured after Caporetto, he shared a prison barracks with Ugo Betti;* his experiences during the war are related in a journal published in 1955 and 1965. The profound shock of his brother Enrico's death during the war is apparent in his later writings. After the war, he completed his industrial engineering degree (1920) and pursued a career in this field, spending several years in Argentina before returning to Italy. His first work, *La meccanica* (Mechanics) was completed in 1928 but was not published until 1970. During this period, Gadda came into contact with many of the intellectuals associated with the Florentine avant-garde periodical, *Solaria*.

By 1940, Gadda had decided to abandon engineering and moved to Florence where he met Montale,* Vittorini,* and other prominent writers and critics. He published a number of fragments of what would eventually become *La cognizione del dolore (Acquainted with Grief)* between 1938 and 1941 in the journal *Letteratura*. The first chapters of *Quer pasticciaccio brutto de via Merulana (That Awful Mess on Via Merulana)* appeared in the same journal during 1946, and the complete novel in 1957. The year 1950 found Gadda in Rome, where he worked with the Italian national radio network until 1955. After completing a number of minor fictional works, he finally published a version of *La cognizione del dolore* (1963) which he revised in 1970. *Eros e Priapo (Da furore a cenere)* (Eros and Priapus [From Frenzy to Ashes]), a psychoanalytic indictment of Italian fascism as a mass movement based upon exhibitionistic narcissism, appeared in 1967.

Gadda's critical reputation has steadily increased in Italy and abroad. His unique literary language, often compared to that of James Joyce, is considered to be a model for much of contemporary Italian experimental fiction. While some critics have accused Gadda of possessing an intentionally obscure baroque sensibility, Gadda has replied that reality itself is baroque. Although well known to a limited circle of critics and writers, the announcement that *La cognizione del dolore* had won the Prix International de Littérature in 1963 still came as a surprise to many Italians. Gadda's importance as an innovator in fictional narrative stems from two novels, both of which he left unfinished and fragmentary but not necessarily incomplete. *Quer pasticciaccio brutto de via Merulana* is a detective novel set in the Rome of 1927, which describes the murder of a Signora Liliana Balducci and the failure of the investigating officer, Francesco Ingravallo (Don Ciccio), to solve the crime. The plot and its detective form conceal a philosophical intent. As Ingravallo remarks, a crime may indeed have a single immediate motive, but it is ultimately the effect of many elements and is "rather like a whirlpool, a cyclonic point of depression in the consciousness of the world, towards which a whole multitude of converging causes have contributed." Gadda's imaginative and innovative use of various dialects makes a close, textual reading difficult but enormously rewarding. One of the masterpieces of postwar Italian fiction, *Quer pasticciaccio* appeals to the avant-garde novelist or critic as well as to the average reader; it is successful as a simple detective story even in translation, where the author's linguistic virtuosity is less apparent.

The second novel, *La cognizione del dolore,* lacks the reassuring convention of a traditional plot structure and is set in the imaginary South American country of Maradagàl between 1925 and 1933. Actually, the setting is recognizable as Lombardy, and its main city, Pastrufazio, clearly resembles Milan. The central character, Gonzalo Pirobutirro d'Eltino, an engineer who has lost a brother in a war and who suffers from a mysterious malady, is similar in some respects to Gadda himself. Even the Italian fascist movement is transformed into a sinister but satirically presented organization of war veterans named *Nistitúos*. Don Gonzalo himself personifies the Seven Deadly Sins. A most memorable section of the first of the novel's two parts pictures the protagonist gluttonously devouring a lobster in a manner reminiscent of Rabelais's grotesque descriptions of human functions. The novel's second part concentrates upon Gonzalo's mother, and the tortured relationship between mother and son provides ample evidence that the grief mentioned in the title is the essence of the human condition.

Gadda's reputation among contemporary critics rests largely upon his eclectic, literary language, described by Pier Paolo Pasolini* as *plurilinguismo,* a combination of the language of the traditional Italian intelligentsia, the kind of koine typical of the petty bourgeoisie, and dialects from the lower social strata. Gadda himself has argued that any words which improve the expressive power of a language or literature should be acceptable in fiction. A number of Gadda's essays on his language and method of writing, most helpful in any reading of his major works, have been collected in *I viaggi la morte* (1958, Voyages Death).

Bibliography: I viaggi la morte (Milan: Garzanti, 1958); *Acquainted with Grief,* trans. William Weaver (New York: Braziller, 1969); *That Awful Mess on Via Merulana,* trans. William Weaver (New York: Braziller, 1965); Robert Martin Adams, *After Joyce: Studies in Fiction after Ulysses* (New York: Oxford University Press, 1977); Robert S. Dombroski, *Introduzione allo studio di Carlo Emilio Gadda* (Florence: Vallecchi, 1975); Joan McConnell, *A Vocabulary Analysis of Gadda's "Pasticciaccio"* (University, Miss.: Romance Monographs, no. 2, 1973); *From Verismo to Experimentalism: Essays on the Modern Italian Novel,* ed. Sergio Pacifici (Bloomington, Ind.: Indiana University Press, 1969); Gian Carlo Roscioni, *La disarmonia prestabilita: studio su Gadda* (Turin: Einaudi, 1969).

GALIANI, FERDINANDO (1728–1787), diplomat and economic theorist. Galiani was born in Chieti, was educated for a career in the church, and as an abbot traveled to Paris in 1759 to become secretary to the ambassador of Naples. During his ten-year stay in France, he became a social success in the most fashionable salons and a friend of the leading intellectuals and literary figures of the time—Grimm, Diderot, Madame Necker, Madame d'Épinay, d'Alembert, and others. The letters he exchanged with these figures after his return to Naples in 1769 would later constitute one of the most important epistolary collections linking the cultures of France and Italy during the Enlightenment.

A dialogue on women, an incomplete scholarly study of Horace, a treatise on the dialect of Naples, and a partial translation of one of John Locke's minor writings are among Galiani's many minor works. His essay *Della moneta* (1751, *Money*) presents a theory of value based upon utility and scarcity and is cited several times by Karl Marx in his own economic analyses. His major treatise, one which played a significant role in the economic debates of the times, was written in French and published in London as *Dialogues sur le commerce des blés* (1770, Dialogues on the Wheat Trade). In this work, Galiani attacks the doctrines of the Physiocrats and their concept of economic freedom and argues for the necessity of economic regulation.

See also ENLIGHTENMENT.

Bibliography: Dialogues sur le commerce des blés, ed. Fausto Nicolini (Milan: Ricciardi, 1959); *Early Economic Thought,* ed. Arthur E. Monroe (Cambridge, Mass.: Harvard University Press, 1924)—contains an English version of *Della moneta;* Franco Venturi, *Italy in the Enlightenment* (New York: New York University Press, 1972).

GALILEI, GALILEO (1564–1642), mathematician and physicist, universal "man of science." Son of the Florentine musicologist Vincenzo, Galileo taught at the universities of Pisa (his birthplace) and Padua (1592–1610). His early treatise *De motu* (1590, *On Motion*) is regarded as the basis of modern dynamics. His discovery of the isochronism of the pendulum (1583) and the laws of free fall (1604); his theorems on the center of gravity (1587); his *On Mechanics* (1593), Ptolemaic *Cosmography* (1597), and *Military Architecture* (1593); his notes on the nova of 1604; and his vast correspondence on mathematical, physical, and astronomical principles attest to the versatility of Galileo's scientific genius. After his fortunate discovery of Jupiter's satellites, with the help of a rudimentary telescope which he reinvented in 1609 upon learning of the existence of such an instrument in Holland, he became the chief mathematician and philosopher-in-residence to the grand duke of Tuscany. His telescopic observations, published in 1610 with the title *Nuncius sidereus (The Starry Messenger)*, gained him worldwide fame and attention, as well as the hostility of Aristotelian and Neo-Platonic scientists backed by the church of Rome. Galileo's daring plan to force an official acceptance of Copernicus's heliocentric cosmology—which clearly inspired, in the years 1610–15, his work on floating bodies, sunspots, and the famous letters to Benedetto Castelli and to the Grand Duchess Christina on the interpretation of the Scriptures and the autonomy of science—met with a first failure in 1616, when he was summoned to Rome and ordered to abandon the theory. His controversy with the Jesuit Oratio Grassi on the nature of the 1618 comets and the resulting great work *Il saggiatore* (1623, *The Assayer*) show some prudence in this respect. However, after the election of his friend Urban VIII to the papal throne, Galileo renewed his attack on backward science, publishing his masterwork, the *Dialogo sopra i due massimi sistemi del mondo* (1632, *Dialogue Concerning the Two Chief World Systems*). This dialogue is a subtle but scorching indictment of benighted geocentrism and a clear endorsement (notwithstanding his prefatory claims to dispassionate comparison) of Copernicanism. The Florentine Inquisition impounded the work. Again Galileo was ordered to Rome and was forced to confess his "errors" and publicly to abjure his doctrine. Sentenced to indefinite imprisonment, ill and broken by public and private trials (his beloved daughter died in 1634, and he became completely blind in 1637), he lived his last years under house arrest at Arcetri, near Florence, completing and publishing abroad his last great work on modern physics, *Dialoghi delle nuove scienze* (1638, *Two New Sciences*).

Galileo's scientific importance is immense. In the annals of Italian literature, his name appears chiefly on two accounts: as a shaper and modernizer of linguistic usage, and as a gifted dabbler in several literary genres. The choice of Italian (and not Latin) as the medium of his best scientific work is in itself an act of vast cultural importance and influence. It is a direct result of his lifelong concern with the diffusion of knowledge and universal enlightenment, and of his penchant for the empirical and immediate as opposed to the codified and academic. Embodying the best prose tradition of the Florentine Renaissance,* Galileo's style is characterized by vigor, clarity, and elegance; conciseness, plasticity, evidence; an almost "rhythmic" enthusiasm in the description and explanation of natural marvels; a cutting irony in the excited polemics; and an inborn sense for the spoken word in the dialogues. Galileo is a reader of the book of nature, written in mathematical symbols, but in the background of his prose one perceives another kind of reader also—the lifelong enthusiast of Ariosto,* Berni,* Ruzzante,* and the Latin classics.

Of minor importance are Galileo's excursions into the literary genres proper. His verses are hardly more than a curiosity: a series of occasional sonnets,* two *canzoni** in the Petrarchan manner, and a lively *capitolo** entitled "Contro il portar la toga" (1591, "Against the Custom of Wearing an Academic Gown"). His two youthful lectures (which earned him membership in the Florentine Academy) on the "physical dimensions" of the *Inferno* merely show (apart from the ingenuity and ingenuousness of a rigorous land-surveyor lost in a dream) the depth of his readings of Dante.* But his critical annotations to the *Gerusalemme liberata (Jerusalem Delivered)* are still of interest to Tasso's* readers. The *Considerazioni al Tasso* (Considerations on Tasso), together with the fragmentary and private *Postille* (Annotations) to Ariosto and Petrarch,* are a record of Galileo's critical acumen as a reader of poetry. Notwithstanding the harsh and almost total condemnation of Tasso's pre-Baroque sensibility and style, these notes (written, at least in part, during Galileo's years of maturity) gave Francesco De Sanctis,* as he himself admits, "a healthier and more precise idea of poetic creation."

Bibliography: Opere, eds. A. Favaro, A. Garbasso, and G. Abetti (Florence: Barbéra, 1968)—the monumental "edizione nazionale" in 20 vols., of which the ninth comprises Galileo's literary works; *Dialogue Concerning the Two Chief World Systems—Ptolemaic and Copernican,* trans. Stillman Drake, foreword by Albert Einstein (Berkeley, Calif.: University of California Press, 1970); *Discoveries and Opinions of Galileo,* ed. and trans. Stillman Drake (Garden City, N.Y.: Doubleday, 1957)—includes the *Starry Messenger,* the *Letter to the Grand Duchess Christina,* and excerpts from the *Assayer;* Antonio Banfi, *Vita di Galileo Galilei* (Milan: Feltrinelli, 1962); Ludovico Geymonat, *Galileo Galilei: A Biography and Inquiry into His Philosophy of Science,* trans. Stillman Drake (New York: McGraw-Hill, 1965); Erwin Panofsky, *Galileo as a Critic of the Arts* (The Hague: Nijhoff, 1954); Tibor Wlassics, *Galilei critico letterario* (Ravenna: Longo, 1974)—with comprehensive bibliography.

Tibor Wlassics

GALLINA, GIACINTO (1852–1897), actor and playwright. Born in Venice of a family of moderate means, Gallina turned to a musical career after failing in his academic work, playing the cello for an orchestra and giving private lessons on the piano. After two early Italian comedies failed, he was asked to write a play in the Venetian dialect; in order to accomplish this task, Gallina turned to the study of the theatre of Carlo Goldoni,* Venice's greatest playwright. From these efforts issued a work in dialect,

Le barufe in famegia (1872, Family Quarrels), which was a free adaptation of Goldoni's *La famiglia dell'antiquario* (1750, The Antique Dealer's Family). Its success resulted in the composition of many plays in dialect over the next seven years, each set in the Venice of Gallina's time and each following Goldoni's example. Some of the best known plays from this period include *I oci del cuor* (1879, The Eyes of the Heart) and *Una famegia in rovina* (1872, A Family in Ruins).

Having ceased writing for eight years during a personal crisis and illness, Gallina returned to the theatre with plays that reflect a more solemn purpose and increased social concern. A major theme in the works of this period, the power of money, inspired *La base de tuto* (1894, The Basis of Everything), as well as a play entitled *Senza bussola* (Without a Compass), left unfinished at his death. The masterpiece of these later years is usually considered to be *La famegia del santolo* (1892, The Family of the God-father). Gallina's dramas, along with those in Neapolitan dialect by Salvatore Di Giacomo,* are numbered among the masterpieces of dialect literature during the nineteenth century.

Bibliography: Teatro completo di Giacinto Gallina, ed. D. Varagnolo, 18 vols. (Milan: Treves, 1922–30).

GARETH, BENEDETTO: *See* CARITEO, BENEDETTO.

GARIBALDI, GIUSEPPE (1807–1882), soldier, revolutionary, and writer. Garibaldi was born in Nice and was raised a simple sailor. A mutiny aboard a Piedmontese ship in 1834 forced him to flee a death sentence, and he sailed to Brazil as a soldier of fortune to begin his illustrious career as the nineteenth century's most celebrated patriot-soldier. This career culminated in his successful invasion of Sicily, the unification of Italy, and his eventual disillusionment with the outcome of his long struggle. Although his political and military activities are generally known and even prompted Abraham Lincoln to offer him a command during the Civil War, Garibaldi's literary works have often been overlooked.

Garibaldi's *Memorie* (1888, *Autobiography*) is one of the most memorable autobiographies of nineteenth-century Italian literature. Written in an unpretentious style and lacking in erudition, the narrative nevertheless accurately reflects its author's passion for liberty and his engaging personality. A French version (1860) by Alexandre Dumas père helped to popularize the work abroad, and the English version of 1889 contains an interesting supplement to the autobiography by Garibaldi's English friend, Jessie White Mario. Garibaldi had begun writing fiction when he was a prisoner of the Savoy government after his defeat at Mentana in 1876. Much of his bitterness, frustration, and anticlericalism colors the pages of his three historical novels: *Clelia o il governo del monaco* (1870, *The Rule of the Monk*). *Cantoni, il volontario* (1873, Cantoni, The Volunteer); and *I Mille* (1870–71, The Thousand). Each novel portrays one of the author's three major attempts to influence Italian politics. The first describes the period preceding Mentana; the second is set in 1848–49 and describes Garibaldi's Italian Legion and the defense of Rome; and the third narrates the famous invasion of Sicily by his Redshirts. With their avowedly political intent, these books were written to preserve the memory of fallen heroes, to attack the priests and other reactionary forces in Italy, and to arouse Italians to complete the unfinished business of the political Risorgimento.

Bibliography: Edizione nazionale degli scritti di Giuseppe Garibaldi, eds. S. E. Di Marzo, et al., 6 vols. (Bologna: Cappelli, 1932); *Autobiography of Giuseppe Garibaldi*, trans. A. Warner, 3 vols. (1889; rpt. New York: Howard Fertig, 1971); *The Rule of the Monk* (New York: Harper, 1870); C. E. Griffiths, "The Novels of Garibaldi," *Italian Studies* 30 (1975), 86–98.

GATTO, ALFONSO (1909–1976), lyric poet. Gatto, born in Salerno, failed to complete a university degree and moved to Milan in 1934 to begin a journalistic career. His first collections of verse appeared in 1932 and 1937 and were reworked into a more definitive edition entitled *Poesie* (1941, Poems), which included all the verse he had composed since 1929. The influence of the so-called hermetic poets on this work is clearly evident in Gatto's difficult and sometimes obscure style. His poems reveal an obsession with death; in contrast to the world of mutability and change inhabited by the solitary individual, the universe of poetry is seen to be incorruptible and immutably fixed in time. Typical of this phase of his writing are some of Gatto's best lyrics, including "Erba e latte" ("Grass and Milk"), "Morto ai paesi" ("Dead in the Villages"), and "Elegia notturna" ("Evening Elegy").

In 1938, Gatto joined his friend Vasco Pratolini* to direct the literary review *Campo di Marte*. By this time antifascist in his politics and having already served a prison term of six months in Milan for his views, Gatto eventually took an active part in the resistance and belonged to the Communist party for a period (1945–51). These experiences helped to direct him away from strictly hermetic style and themes to a more engaged and socially responsive poetry. With *Il capo della neve* (1949, The Head on the Snow), Gatto collected the lyrics he had written between 1943 and 1947 and came to grips with the tragic reality of the war, attempting to discover positive human values in the simple elements of life. Among these poems is one many critics believe to be his best, "Anniversario" ("Anniversary"), the poet's homage to the dead of the war.

After several collections of verse in 1950 and 1953, *Osteria flegrea*

(Phlegraean Inn) appeared in 1962, containing what he had written since 1954. The poet himself defined this book as a "serene contemplation of death." *La storia delle vittime* (1966, The History of the Victims), poetry with a clearly social intent, was awarded the prestigious Viareggio Prize in 1966 and contains "Sei agosto" ("August 6"), a remarkable treatment of the bombing of Hiroshima. In addition to his poetry, Gatto has written a number of essays on contemporary art and was an accomplished painter.

See also HERMETICISM.

Bibliography: Poesie (1929–1969), ed. Luigi Baldacci (Milan: Mondadori, 1972); *Contemporary Italian Poetry*, ed. Carlo L. Golino (Berkeley, Calif.: University of California Press, 1962); *Twentieth-Century Italian Poetry*, ed. L. R. Lind (Indianapolis, Ind.: Bobbs-Merrill, 1974); Bortolo Pento, *Alfonso Gatto* (Florence: La Nuova Italia, 1972).

GELLI, GIOVAN BATTISTA (1498–1563), Florentine thinker, critic, playwright, and poet. Born into a modest family and trained as a shoemaker, Gelli was self-taught, although he benefited from the learned conversations at the Orti Oricellari. His desire to share with common people like himself the vast storehouse of knowledge accumulated by the intellectuals of his day led him not only to compose many original works but also to translate others, including Euripides's *Hecuba* (circa 1551) and some selections from the philosophical works of his friend Simone Porzio (1496–1554). His lifelong desire to advance the fortunes of the Italian vernacular against those of Latin began with his participation in the Orti and was extended and broadened in both scope and effectiveness when he became one of the earliest members of the Accademia degli Umidi in 1540 (which became the Accademia Fiorentina in 1541). Besides his major works—*La Circe* (1549, *Circe*) and *I capricci del bottaio* (1546, *The Fearful Fansies of the Florentine Cooper*)—and his knowledgeable commentaries on the works of both Dante* and Petrarch,* Gelli composed two prose comedies, *La sporta* (1543, The Bucket) and *L'errore* (1556, The Error). The first was based upon Plautus's *Aulularia* and, according to Grazzini,* was stolen from Machiavelli,* and the second was influenced by Machiavelli's *Clizia* and a minor work of Lorenzo Strozzi (1483–1541).

I capricci del bottaio consists of ten conversations between Giusto the Cooper and his own soul, and treats various subjects (old age, immortality, the sale of indulgences, the papal court, the translation of the Bible). While it enjoyed immediate success because of its satiric wit and its moralistic purpose, it also attracted the opposition of suspicious churchmen and was placed on the Index in 1562. Its most prominent idea is that wisdom does not guarantee moral virtue. During the Renaissance,* the work was translated into French, Spanish, and English.

Gelli's masterpiece, *La Circe,* employs the Homeric legend of the enchantress Circe in its portrayal of eleven men who have been transformed into animals. Ulysses persuades Circe to change the animals back into human beings, but only one of the men, now an elephant, formerly a philosopher, agrees to return to his former state. For a self-taught man, the range of classical and modern sources in the work is remarkable—Homer, Ovid, Plutarch, Pliny, and Aristotle, in addition to the humanist theories of Ficino,* Pomponazzi,* and Pico della Mirandola.* The refusal of the ten animals to return to their human form is a humorous illustration of Pico's famous description of man's potential to become either animal or angel, while the elephant's decision to return to his former condition is celebrated in terms reminiscent of Ficino's Neo-Platonism. Translated three times into English between the sixteenth and eighteenth centuries, *La Circe* may have influenced Jonathan Swift's *Gulliver's Travels* (1726).

Much of Gelli's literary and critical activity was motivated by a constant desire to spread the knowledge contained in the learned works of his day, which too often, in his opinion, were jealously guarded by pedants and academics from the mass of people who might benefit from reading them in the vernacular. His interest in translating sacred writings was the ultimate cause of his difficulty with the church censors. As a popularizer and educator, Gelli felt that the classical languages and their humanist defenders were slowing down the progress of knowledge by limiting access to information. He was one of the earliest thinkers to consider Latin a dead language. Much of the work of the Accademia degli Umidi and, later, of the Accademia Fiorentina was devoted to supplanting Latin with the vernacular by rendering into Tuscan all the knowledge recorded in classical languages. Gelli was one of the major exponents of the theory that the standard literary language should be Tuscan, specifically the language of Florence, but should not be limited to the language of the great Trecento poets Petrarch and Boccaccio,* as some Tuscan purists proposed. Instead, he condidered contemporary language worthy of respect and imitation. Many of his ideas on contemporary Florentine as a standard literary language for Italy can be found in his *Ragionamento sopra le difficoltà di mettere in regole la nostra lingua* (1551, Treatise on the Difficulties of Regulating Our Language).

Because of this feeling in the academy, one of its major undertakings was the revival of the study of Dante and his language, a subject encouraged by Trissino's* discovery of the *De vulgari eloquentia* and the appearance of the first edition of the *Vita nuova* in 1576. Contrary to purists like Bembo* who elevated Petrarch and Boccaccio to the rank of a norm, Gelli and his fellow academicians were more sympathetic to Dante's poetry and language. The group held *lezioni* (public lectures) on Dante and Petrarch each Sunday and Thursday, alternating between each writer each month. These lectures were given by a number of Florentine intellectuals including Benedetto Varchi,* Cosimo Bartoli (1503–1572), and Francesco Verino (1524–1591). Gelli himself was appointed official commentator on Dante in 1553, but his first Dante lecture had taken place as early as 1541. In spite of Gelli's efforts, Petrarch remained more popular than Dante, and after Gelli's death, no one could be found to replace him as a lecturer on Dante. Gelli's commentaries on both writers reflect a more essentially aesthetic point of view than that of other more learned scholars, but Gelli himself was primarily interested in the conceptual aspects of verse and was one of the first commentators to study the doctrinal character of Petrarch's lyrics.

See also GRAZZINI, Anton Francesco; QUESTIONE DELLA LINGUA.

Bibliography: Opere, ed. Amelia C. Alesina (Naples: Fulvio Rossi, 1969); *Letture edite ed inedite di Giovan Battista Gelli sopra la Commedia di Dante,* ed. Carlo Negroni, 2 vols. (Florence: Bocca, 1887); *Lezioni petrarchesche di Giovan Battista Gelli,* ed. Carlo Negroni (Bologna: Romagnoli, 1884); *Circe,* ed. Robert Adams (Ithaca, N.Y.: Cornell University Press, 1963); Armand L. De Gaetano, *Giambattista Gelli and the Florentine Academy: The Rebellion Against Latin* (Florence: Olschki, 1976).

GENTILE, GIOVANNI (1875–1944), scholar, critic, and philosopher. Born in Castelvetrano, Sicily, Gentile studied at the University of Pisa under Donato Jaja (1839–1914), a disciple of the Hegelian scholar, Bertrando Spaventa (1817–1883). In 1896, he became friendly with Benedetto Croce.* The two men, with their mutual distaste for positivism or materialism, and their desire to restore idealist philosophy in Italy to a place of preeminence, were to dominate Italian intellectual life for half a century. In 1914, Gentile succeeded to the chair of philosophy held by Jaja, and a few years later he published his major philosophical treatise, *Teoria generale dello spirito come atto puro* (1916, *The Theory of Mind as Pure Act*). After moving to the chair of philosophy at the University of Rome in 1917, Gentile founded, in 1920, the influential philosophical review, *Giornale critico della filosofia italiana*. Although he continued to contribute his work to Croce's review, *La critica*, which had been established in 1903, Gentile's new periodical marked the beginning of a break with his old friend.

When Mussolini came to power, Gentile was appointed minister of education and served from 1922 until 1924. During this time, he carried out an extensive reform of the Italian educational system which still bears his name. This reform was based upon ideas he set forth in *La riforma dell'educazione* (1920, *The Reform of Education*), and its goals attracted worldwide attention. Gentile joined the Fascist party in 1923. His signature on the "Manifesto of Fascist Intellectuals" in 1925 sparked a bitter reply from Croce and signaled the definitive split between the two men. Gentile became the official philosopher of the regime, lending it legitimacy with his reputation and even co-authoring Mussolini's widely publicized explanation of fascist dogma, while Croce became the regime's most influential opponent, restricted but never silenced. In 1922 Gentile was made a senator and a member of the Grand Council of Fascism.

Gentile never became a party hack, however, and his scholarly achievements under fascism were impressive. He planned and edited the monumental *Enciclopedia italiana,* better known as the *Enciclopedia Treccani,* named after the rich senator he persuaded to finance the project. He also became director of the prestigious Scuola Normale Superiore of Pisa and then president of the Italian Academy. His principal work on aesthetics, *La filosofia dell'arte* (1931, *The Philosophy of Art*), failed to equal the impact of Croce's earlier treatments of the subject, although Gentile's own formulation of an idealist aesthetics had solved many of the critical problems Croce left unanswered. Feeling loyalty to the short-lived Republic of Salò, organized by the Germans with Mussolini as a puppet ruler after the Allied invasion, Gentile continued to call for Italian unity against the invaders. He was assassinated by antifascist partisans in 1944, while he was returning home from interceding on behalf of antifascist university professors who had just been arrested by the authorities. His primary political treatise, *Genesi e struttura della società* (1946, *Genesis and Structure of Society*), was published posthumously.

Although Gentile published numerous monographs, articles, and reviews dealing with literature and literary criticism, his skill at practical criticism was always overshadowed by Croce's. This lack explains, in some measure, why Gentile's theoretical works on aesthetics have not been given the attention they deserve. Nevertheless, Gentile's contributions to the philosophy of what was termed "actual idealism" were substantial. In his view, actual idealism rejected the possibility of any reality outside of or unconnected to the act of thought. The thinking subject was paramount in his system, and its thought shaped and remade reality in a creative act of mind. In *La filosofia dell'arte,* Gentile attempts to apply this philosophy, first systematically explained in *Teoria generale,* to aesthetics. His key concept is the idea of art as self-translation *(autotradursi).* The feeling or sentiment at the basis of a work of art is first denied by the poet by being objectified; the poet then struggles to make this objectification equal to the original sentiment. Every new part of a work is, therefore, a "translation" of this original feeling. Literary criticism would involve three stages: an analysis of the objective elements of a work; an appreciation of the moment of subjectivity at its origin; and an exposition or reconstruction of the work's content. Although Gentile's influence abroad was diminished by his ties to fascism, the works of the English philosopher R. G. Collingwood are greatly indebted to him.

See also CROCE, Benedetto.

Bibliography: Genesis and Structure of Society, trans. H. S. Harris (Urbana, Ill.: University of Illinois Press, 1960); *The Philosophy of Art,* trans. Giovanni Gullace (Ithaca, N.Y.: Cornell University Press, 1972); *The Theory of Mind as Pure Act,* trans. H. Wildon Carr (London: Macmillan, 1922); Merle E. Brown, *Neo-Idealistic Aesthetics: Croce-Gentile-Collingwood* (Detroit, Mich.: Wayne State University Press, 1966); H. S. Harris, *The Social Philosophy of Giovanni Gentile* (Urbana, Ill.: University of Illinois Press, 1960).

GIACOMINO PUGLIESE (thirteenth century), poet. Giacomino, a poet of the Sicilian School esteemed by the romantics, lived in the first half of the thirteenth century. Nothing is known of his life. Various theories about his identity have derived from his poetry, and official records are problematic at best.

According to some critics, the eight *canzoni** attributed to him should be ordered in such a way that they constitute a brief tale of love: the passions, the parting of the lovers, the lady's death. While his originality is somewhat circumscribed by the courtly requirements, Giacomino's poetry is refreshing in its fusion of courtly, personal, and popular elements. This technique stands out in the *canzone* "Morte, perchè m'ài fatta sì gran guerra" ("Death, why have you made so great a war against me?"), a poem echoed in Dante,* which seems to depict a moment of authentic personal inspiration, his lady's death. Although it might be misleading to insist upon a popular, realistic element in Giacomino's poetry, his verse has a certain freshness of language and emotion and a musicality, despite a certain looseness in structure. One pervasive element in his *canzoni* is the theme of memory which Petrarch* later developed with the greatest subtlety. A notable example of the power of memory over the emotions is in the last stanza of "Morte, perchè," where the lover remembers the dead lady's voice and her kind words.

Bibliography: Le Rime della scuola siciliana, ed. Bruno Panvini (Florence: Olschki, 1962); *The Age of Dante: An Anthology of Early Italian Poetry,* trans. Joseph Tusiani (New York: Baroque Press, 1974).

GIACOSA, GIUSEPPE (1847–1906), dramatist and writer of *libretti*. Giacosa was born in Colleretto Parella near Turin, where he studied law and came into contact with representatives of the *scapigliatura** movement. Based upon a romance from medieval legend, his first comedy, *Una partita a scacchi* (1873, A Game of Chess), established him as a fixture of nineteenth-century Italian theatre and put him into contact with important literary figures, including Giovanni Verga* and D'Annunzio.* Among his subsequent dramatic works were *Il Conte rosso* (1880, The Red Count), *La Contessa di Challant* (1891, The Countess of Challant) featuring Sarah Bernhardt, and the series of plays considered his best—*Tristi amori* (1887, Sad Loves); *Diritti dell'anima* (1894, *Sacred Ground*); *Come le foglie* (1900, *Like Falling Leaves*); and *Il più forte* (1905, *The Stronger*). Although today *Tristi amori* may seem no more than a banal bourgeois salon drama of adultery, *Come le foglie* and *Diritti dell'anima* show the influence of Ibsen and deal with more substantial problems—respectively, a psychological study of a female character and a detailed delineation of the disintegration of a wealthy family.

Besides a collection of *novelle** praised by as knowledgeable a critic as Croce,* Giacosa completed an engaging account of his journey to America entitled *Impressioni d'America* (1889, Impressions of America), which describes the lives of Italian-Americans in various parts of the country and reveals his fascination with drinking habits in the New World. While Giacosa's dramas have lost critical favor, his contribution to music is strategic. In collaboration with Luigi Illica (1857–1919), he produced three magnificent *libretti* for Puccini, those of *La Bohème* (1896), *Tosca* (1900), and *Madama Butterfly* (1904), which embody many of his characteristic dramatic themes.

Bibliography: Impressioni d'America (Milan: Cogliati, 1889); *Teatro,* ed. Piero Nardi, 2 vols. (Milan: Mondadori, 1948); *The Stronger: Like Falling Leaves: Sacred Ground–Three Plays by Giuseppe Giacosa,* trans. Edith and Allan Updegraff (Boston: Little, Brown, 1916); *Puccini Librettos,* trans. William Weaver (Garden City, N.Y.: Doubleday, 1966)—contains original *libretti* and translations of *La Bohème, Tosca,* and *Madama Butterfly;* Anna Barsotti, *Giuseppe Giacosa* (Florence: La Nuova Italia, 1973); Benjamin Lawton, "Giuseppe Giacosa 1847–1906 and Giacomo Puccini 1858–1924," pp. 247–59, in *Abroad in America: Visitors to the New Nation, 1776–1914,* eds. Marc Pachter and Frances Wein (Reading, Mass.: Addison-Wesley, 1976); Piero Nardi, *Vita e tempo di Giacosa* (Milan: Mondadori, 1949).

GIANNI DEGLI ALFANI (circa 1271 to 1283–?), Florentine poet and, perhaps, a silk merchant. Very little is known of Alfani except that he was exiled from Florence and traveled widely abroad. He is usually associated with the *stilnovisti* as a minor member of the group. Alfani has left seven lyrics, all of which are *ballate** except for a single sonnet* addressed to Guido Cavalcanti.* Perhaps his most interesting poem is his "Ballatetta dolente" ("Grieving *ballatetta,* go forth, show my sorrow"), which was written in exile and which reveals his debt to similar poetry by Cavalcanti. Alfani has often been dismissed as a minor follower of Cavalcanti with little originality of his own; indeed, his emphasis on love as a painful experience is reminiscent of his model. Whereas for Cavalcanti the pain of love often results in ecstatic visions of beauty and moments of psychological introspection, in Alfani it more often gives rise to detailed descriptions of the moment of pain itself, as in "Guato una donna dov'io la scontrai" ("I am gazing on a lady, standing where I saw her"). In general, his lyrics analyze a moment of anguish in the remote past caused by a sorrowful encounter which, in the present and future, leads to the tormented contemplation of the source of suffering, the lady. Recent scholarship on Alfani views him less as a pale reflection of the great *stilnovisti* than as a poet whose works look forward to Petrarch* and Poliziano.*

See also DOLCE STIL NUOVO.

Bibliography: I poeti del Duecento, 2 vols., ed. Gianfranco Contini (Milan: Ricciardi, 1960); *The Age of Dante: An Anthology of Early Italian Poetry,* trans. Joseph Tusiani (New York: Baroque Press, 1974); *German and Italian Lyrics of the Middle Ages,* trans. Frederick Goldin (Garden City, N.Y.: Doubleday, 1973); Marga Cottino-Jones, "Profilo stilistico di Gianni degli Alfani," *Lettere italiane* 23 (1971), 457–72.

GIANNONE, PIETRO (1676–1748), lawyer and historian. While a practicing lawyer in Naples, Giannone cultivated a lively interest in history which culminated twenty years later in his *Istoria civile del regno di Napoli* (1723, *The Civil History of the Kingdom of Naples*). This work received an almost immediate English translation in 1729 by James Ogilvie. Giannone turned the normal narrative of a city's history from an interest in battles or conquests toward the study of more substantive institutional changes over a period of time. The major thrust of his account was to identify the church with the retrogressive forces of history and to oppose this institution with a free and independent lay state which would oppose ecclesiastical interference in civil affairs and leave religion a private matter of conscience. Although the work thus continues a literary tradition dating back to Dante,* Machiavelli,* and Sarpi,* it combines this tradition with an anticlericalism typical of the Enlightenment.* As such, it must be considered more as a treatise proposing social reform than as a dispassionate work of historiography. Its polemical thesis displeased the authorities and caused Giannone to flee Naples for Vienna and Venice and eventually to move to Geneva, before he was tricked into returning to Italian soil. Giannone was arrested and was forced to abjure his ideas; he died in prison in Turin. His treatise *Triregno* (Three Kingdoms), finally published in 1895, treats three successive stages of human history distinguished by three stages in religious development from the Hebrews to Christ and then to the popes.

Bibliography: Istoria civile del regno di Napoli, 5 vols. (Milan: Borroni e Scotti, 1844–47); *Il Triregno,* ed. Alfredo Parente (Bari: Laterza, 1940); Brunello Vigezzi, *Pietro Giannone, riformatore e storico* (Milan: Feltrinelli, 1961).

GIANNOTTI, DONATO (1492–1573), political official, writer, and political theorist. Born of a moderately wealthy family of artisans in Florence, Giannotti received a degree in law after studying the classics with Marcello Adriani, an important figure in the Florentine Chancellery. He also became a participant in the meetings at the Orti Oricellari of the Rucellai family, where he met distinguished Florentines like Niccolò Machiavelli,* Jacopo Nardi,* and Luigi Almanni.* Sometime during this period of his life, he composed two Italian comedies based upon Latin models, one of which—*Il vecchio amoroso* (The Amorous Old Man)—is considered among the period's best plays. He taught at the university in Pisa (1525–27) and spent some time in Padua and Venice, where he wrote most of his first political treatise, *Della repubblica de' viniziani* (1540, On the Venetian Republic). Recalled to Florence after the Medici fell in 1527, he held Machiavelli's old post as secretary to the Ten of War until their return. He was exiled from his native city in 1530 and devoted the rest of his life to the cause of republicanism. His second major treatise, *Della repubblica fiorentina* (On the Florentine Republic), was completed during his years in exile but was not published until 1721. Some of his other writings include a notable collection of Latin letters, Latin and Italian verse, various political dialogues, Latin translations of Ptolemy and Xenophon, and a dialogue on Dante's* journey through the afterlife.

Giannotti's works continue the Machiavellian republican tradition of Florentine political thought and raise an issue central to Guicciardini's* political thought, the matter of constitutional reform. His study of Venice, utilized by James Harrington in *Oceana* some years later (1656), was an influential interpretation in dialogue form of the Venetian government as a mixed state, recalling the theories of Aristotle and Polybius. In the second work, which concerns Florence, he endeavors to demonstrate how only a mixed government, embodying some of the features of the Venetian model, could serve as the foundation of a stable republic in Florence.

See also GUICCIARDINI, Francesco; MACHIAVELLI, Niccolò.

Bibliography: Opere politiche, ed. Furio Diaz, 2 vols. (Milan: Marzorati, 1974); Rudolf von Albertini, *Firenze dalla repubblica al principato: storia e coscienza politica* (Turin: Einaudi, 1970), J. G. A. Pocock, *The Machiavellian Moment: Florentine Political Thought and the Atlantic Republican Tradition* (Princeton, N. J.: Princeton University Press, 1975); Randolph Starn, *Donato Giannotti and his "Epistolae"* (Geneva: Droz, 1968).

GINZBURG, NATALIA (1916–   ), novelist. Ginzburg was born in Palermo but spent her childhood in Turin. Her first stories appeared in the avant-garde Florentine journal *Solaria* in 1934, shortly before her marriage to Leone Ginzburg, a professor who later died as a prisoner of the Germans in

1944. Her first novel, *La strada che va in città* (1943, *The Road to the City*), appeared under the name Alessandra Torimparte and was published by Einaudi, a firm for which she began to work after her husband's death and where she met and befriended Cesare Pavese.* *È stato così* (1946, *The Dry Heart*), with its moving portrayal of the disintegration of a marriage, established Ginzburg's popular and critical reputation. In both of these early novels, her typical and deceptively simple, antirhetorical style is already apparent, as are her frequent dependence upon autobiographical themes and her great attention to seemingly unimportant details of life which are used subtly to develop characterization.

In *Tutti i nostri ieri* (1952, *A Light for Fools*), Ginzburg attempts to reconstruct the story of her generation and the experiences of fascism, the war, and the resistance. *Le voci della sera* (1961, *Voices in the Evening*) continues this theme, focusing upon a family of leftist factory owners in Piedmont. This novel was followed by *Lessico famigliare* (1963, *Family Sayings*), an autobiographical narrative treating her own family, which hovers between fiction and nonfiction, and for which she earned the prestigious Strega Prize in 1964. Since that date, Ginzburg has published an edition of her major novels, a collection of critical essays entitled *Mai devi domandarmi* (1970, *Never Must You Ask Me*), and another novel, *Caro Michele* (1973, *No Way*). One of her several plays, *L'inserzione* (1968, *The Advertisement*), was translated into English and performed by the BBC. She also translated one of Marcel Proust's works into Italian (1946). Along with Elsa Morante,* Ginzburg is one of the most popular modern Italian female writers and has enjoyed many translations into English. Her poetic, yet simple, narrative with its conversational tone represents one of the most distinctive contemporary literary styles.

Bibliography: Dead Yesterdays, trans. Angus Davidson (London: Secker, 1956); *Family Sayings,* trans. D. M. Low (New York: Dutton, 1963); *A Light for Fools,* trans. Angus Davidson (New York: Dutton, 1957); *Never Must You Ask Me,* trans. Isabel Quigly (London: Michael Joseph, 1973); *No Way,* trans. Sheila Cudahy (New York: Harcourt, 1974); *The Road to the City* (includes *The Dry Heart*), trans. Frances Frenaye (Garden City, N.Y.: Doubleday, 1949); *Voices in the Evening,* trans. D. M. Low (New York: Dutton, 1963); Clotilde S. Bowe, "The Narrative Strategy of Natalia Ginzburg," *Modern Language Review* 68 (1973), 788–95.

GIOBERTI, VINCENZO (1801–1852), theologian and writer from Turin. Although he received a degree in theology, Gioberti was a liberal thinker whose espousal of Mazzini's* ideas forced him to live in exile, first in Paris (1834) and finally in Brussels, where he remained until 1845. Under the influence of Alfieri,* Rousseau, and Kant, Gioberti published his first book in 1838, *Teorica del sovrannaturale* (A Theory of the Supernatural). This was followed by three more important treatises, *Introduzione allo studio* *della filosofia* (1840, Introduction to the Study of Philosophy), *Primato morale e civile degli Italiani* (1843, The Moral and Civic Preeminence of the Italians), and *Rinnovamento civile d'Italia* (1851, The Civic Renewal of Italy). An active participant in the momentous political events in Italy of 1848–49, Gioberti was elected a deputy from Piedmont and was chosen by Victor Emmanuel II to serve as an envoy to France. The failures of the republican forces, however, disillusioned him, and he abandoned an active political career, only to die in Paris shortly thereafter.

Gioberti's works reflect a faith in the Catholic religion and define Italy, the center of Catholic civilization, as the bearer of a civilizing mission in human affairs, which ideally should reconcile tradition and progress, the church and the state. His political treatises were extremely popular in the early stages of the Italian Risorgimento. Gioberti proposed a federation of Italian states headed by the pope with the armies of the Kingdom of Sardinia as their military arm. He links political reform (freedom of the press and religion, concord among social classes) with a moral renaissance in Italy. In a section of the *Primato* where he discusses the evolution of Italian literature from Dante* to the seventeenth century, he reflects a point of view which seems to anticipate the literary historiography of De Sanctis.*

Bibliography: Scritti letterari, ed. Ernesto Travi (Milan: Marzorati, 1971); *Scritti scelti,* ed. August Guzzo (Turin: UTET, 1966).

GIOVANNI FIORENTINO (fourteenth century), writer of *novelle.** We know almost nothing about Giovanni Fiorentino. The only certain biographical detail is furnished by the text of his major work, the *Pecorone* (best rendered as "Numbskull," referring to the many foolish characters in it), which mentions that the author began his stories in the town of Davadola around 1378. The collection employs a framework indebted to Boccaccio's* *Decameron,* and two storytellers, Auretto and Saturnina, are presented in the prologue. Because Saturnina has become a nun, Auretto becomes a monk and the chaplain of her convent in Forlì in order to see her more frequently. The two lovers meet daily, and each tells a story for twenty-five days providing a total of fifty stories. Each day closes with a *canzonetta a ballo,* or dance song. Of these tales, fully thirty-two are taken more or less literally from sections in Giovanni Villani's* *Cronica;* three concern historical figures of the times, and fifteen others derive from various oral or written literary sources.

Giovanni Fiorentino and his contemporary from Lucca, Giovanni Sercambi,* may be considered the two central figures in the development of the *novella* tradition immediately following Boccaccio, although their artistic talents are considerably less than those of their master. Giovanni's themes are typical of the Trecento: love, misfortune, adventure, and the comic portrayal of foolish people. The most famous of these tales, that of Giannetto and the Donna di Belmonte (IV, 1), eventually reached Shakespeare and influenced the memorable "pound of flesh" episode and the character of Shylock in *The Merchant of Venice* (1596). It is still unclear how Shakespeare came to know this story, since it is not one of the two stories (I, 1; IX, 1) from the *Pecorone* translated in William Painter's *Palace of Pleasure* (1566).

See also BOCCACCIO, Giovanni; NOVELLA; SERCAMBI, Giovanni; VILLANI, Giovanni.

Bibliography: Il Pecorone, ed. Enzo Esposito (Ravenna: Longo Editore, 1974); *The Pecorone of Ser Giovanni,* trans. W. G. Waters (London: Lawrence & Bullen, 1897); Salvatore Battaglia, *La coscienza letteraria del Medioevo* (Naples: Liguori, 1965); John K. Hale, *"The Merchant of Venice* and *Il Pecorone,* or Can Course-Study Resolve the Problem of Shylock?" *Journal of the Australasian Universities Language and Literature Association* 40 (1973), 271–83; Luigi Russo, "Ser Giovanni Fiorentino e Giovanni Sercambi," *Belfagor* 11 (1956), 489–504.

GIOVIO, PAOLO (1483–1552), scholar and historian. Born at Como and first educated as a physician, Giovio joined the Roman court of Pope Leo X in 1513, witnessed the Sack of Rome from the Castel Sant'Angelo with his patron Pope Clement VII (who made him bishop of Nocera in 1528), and traveled throughout Italy, France, and Germany in connection with his ties to the Medici family. The year 1549 marked his departure from the papal court in disgust, after Pope Paul III denied him the post of cardinal at Como. From 1551 until his death, he resided in Florence under the protection of Cosimo I.

Giovio's chief contribution is his *Historiae sui temporis* (1551–52, History of His Own Times), a Latin history of the then known world during the period from 1494 to 1544, written in forty-five books. It was almost immediately translated into Italian by Lodovico Domenichi (1515–1564), a proofreader and editor at the important Torrentino Press in Florence. Domenichi eventually translated many of Giovio's Latin works and thereby brought them to an extremely wide European audience during the sixteenth century. Many were also translated into English. Among these other compositions are lives of the Visconti family, Alfonso d'Este, Leo X, and Hadrian VI; a treatise on the Turks; a work on heraldry; and a series of biographical portraits, *Elogia doctorum virorum ad avorum memoria* (1548, *An Italian Portrait Gallery*). The *Elogia* consists of a paragraph of prose and some verse supposedly written to explain the many portraits of famous men he kept hanging in his villa. Many of these portraits were frescoes done by his friend Giorgio Vasari,* whom Giovio apparently encouraged to complete his celebrated biographical study of Italian artists.

See also VASARI, Giorgio.

Bibliography: An Italian Portrait Gallery, trans. Florence Gragg (Boston: Chapman & Grimes, 1935); Benedetto Croce, *Poeti e scrittori del pieno e del tardo Rinascimento* (Bari: Laterza, 1958).

GIRALDI, GIAMBATTISTA, "Il Cinzio" (1504–1573), literary critic, dramatist, and writer of *novelle.** Giraldi was born in Ferrara, where he received the education of a humanist physician and philosopher, and succeeded Celio Calcagnini (1479–1541) as professor of rhetoric at the local university in 1541. After publishing a volume of Latin works earlier, in 1537, he devoted himself exclusively to writing in the vernacular. In some of this verse, Giraldi referred to himself as Cynthius, and he was often known as Giraldi Cinzio or "Il Cinzio" in Italy and as Cynthio in Elizabethan England. From 1541 until 1562, Giraldi held his university chair in Ferrara while he drafted a number of weighty critical and literary works.

The presentation of Giraldi's most important drama, the *Orbecche* (Orbecche), in 1541 was the first performance of an Italian tragedy. By 1543, he had already composed three other tragedies—*Didone* (Dido), *Cleopatra* (Cleopatra), and *Altile* (Altile)—and a pastoral* entitled *Egle* (1545, Egle). Other tragedies followed, the composition dates of which are somewhat obscure—*Gli antivalomeni* (1548, The Changelings); *Arrenopia* (1563?, Arrenopia); *Epitia* (?, Epitia); *Euphimia* (1560?, Euphimia); and *Selene* (1554?, Selene)—as well as a comedy entitled *Eudemoni* (1543, Happy Endings), which was published after his death but never performed. In addition, Giraldi turned out the two important theoretical introductions to the *Orbecche* and *Didone* and two major critical treatises, *Discorso ovvero lettera intorno al comporre delle comedie e delle tragedie (On the Composition of Comedies and Tragedies)* and *Discorso intorno al comporre dei romanzi (On the Composition of Romances),* both of which were read widely in manuscript form before being published together in 1554. Giraldi began writing *novelle* in 1528 and continued throughout his life until the publication of *Gli Hecatommithi* (1565, The Hundred Stories). The stories in this noteworthy collection provided the basis for eight of his own plays—*Orbecche* (II, 2); *Altile* (II, 3); *Selene* (V, 1); *Gli antivalomeni* (II, 9); *Arrenopia* (III, 1), *Epitia* (VIII, 5); *Euphimia* (VIII, 10); and *Eudemoni* (V, 8)—as well as the ultimate source for many important French and Elizabethan works, in particular Shakespeare's *Measure for Measure* (*Epitia* and *Gli Hecatommithi* VIII, 5) and *Othello* (*Gli Hecatommithi* III, 7). The year 1554 was the beginning of a bitter, prolonged argument between Giraldi and his pupil and protégé, Giambattista Pigna (1530–1575), over the origin of the theories expressed in Giraldi's treatise on romances. This feud eventually led to Giraldi's departure from Ferrara in 1562 and Pigna's succession to his teacher's university chair and the duke of Ferrara's favor. After living for some time in Turin and Pavia, Giraldi returned to Ferrara in 1571, where he remained until his death.

Giraldi's most lasting influence was in his dramatic theory and practice. Almost all the main issues in Renaissance* dramatic criticism are examined somewhere in his various works and prefaces. He rejected the Greek arrangement of plays into prologue, episodes, and choral odes and returned to the five acts of the Roman theatre. He reasoned that a good play should first present the argument, direct the argument toward its end, present obstacles to its resolution, offer a means of removing the obstacles, and end with a resolution, all arranged in five acts. In contrast to only three or four speaking parts in some Greek drama, he increased the number of actors used in a play to as many as twenty. Following Seneca, he emphasized the function of the messenger, whose arrivals and reports cause the audience to experience "all the horror and compassion which are the pith of the plot"; consequently, he used soliloquies freely. In drama he preferred verse, rhymed or unrhymed, to prose and favored the separation of stylistic levels between comedy and tragedy. He believed that the proper function of tragedy was both to teach and to delight as well as to induce wonder, pity, and horror. Although he used historical plots in several of his tragedies, he was willing to expand the traditional themes of Italian tragedy to nonhistorical and fictitious plots; the seven plays taken from his own *novelle* all fall into this category. While he never used the term *tragicomedy,* his concept of *tragedia mista* or "mixed tragedy"—tragedy with a happy ending—combines the goal of arousing emotions of horror and pity with the more pleasant satisfaction of seeing good characters rewarded at the end of the play for their virtue. The *Orbecche,* his most influential work, was a Senecan horror tragedy dealing with Sulmone, king of Persia, and his daughter Orbecche. It presented both Orbecche's murder of her father and her subsequent suicide directly upon the stage, a practice imitated in scores of gory scenes in the theatres of Renaissance Italy, France, and England. Thus, his dramatic practice was in this instance more influential than his theoretical preference for tragedy with a happy ending.

Giraldi's treatise on romances reflected his belief that the classical epic* was not the only proper form for narrative poetry, and it defended Ariosto's* *Orlando furioso (The Frenzy of Orlando)* against its detractors. In such matters, Giraldi stands on the side of progressive critics in the early literary quarrels which came to be known as the "Battle of the Books" between the ancients and the moderns. Thus, while he admits the necessity of poetic unity, he denies that it is only of the kind Aristotle observed in Homer. In effect, he defines the poem of Ariosto as evolving from a different source (the *romanzi*) than its classical antecedents, although he believed that all forms of the epic, both ancient and modern, belonged to the same genre.

Published during a period of religious tension, Giraldi's *Gli Hecatommithi* contains references to the moral edification readers may derive from his tales which, he believes, support papal authority and Christianity. Similar to Boccaccio's* *Decameron,* his work contains a prologue set against the background of the Sack of Rome in 1527, from which ten men and women escape by sailing to Marseilles. Love within marriage, for example, is set forth as the only kind of earthly love which can bring true happiness. A measure of the distance the *novella* had traveled since Boccaccio is the absence in *Gli Hecatommithi* of satirical stories about clergymen which were once so typical of this narrative form. A second, non-narrative section of the 1565 edition, entitled *Tre dialoghi della vita civile,* is a three-day discussion of the active moral virtues required for the civic life. This part of the book received an Elizabethan translation as *A Discourse of Civill Life* in 1606 by Lodowick Bryskett, a naturalized Italian and friend of Sidney and Spenser. In England, the most influential of the *novelle* were read in the original Italian or in French translation during the Renaissance.

Bibliography: Raccolta di novellieri italiani (Turin: Pomba, 1853); *Scritti critici,* ed. Camillo Crocetti (Milan: Marzorati, 1973); *Le tragedie,* 2 vols. (Venice: Cagnacini, 1583); Lodowick Bryskett, *A Discourse of Civill Life,* ed. Thomas E. Wright (Northridge, Calif.: San Fernando Valley State College, 1970); *Elizabethan Love Stories,* ed. T. J. B. Spencer (Baltimore: Penguin, 1968); *Literary Criticism: Plato to Dryden,* ed. Allan H. Gilbert (Detroit, Mich.: Wayne State University Press, 1962)—excerpts from prefaces and discourses; *On Romances,* trans. Henry L. Snuggs (Lexington, Ky.: University of Kentucky Press, 1968); Marvin T. Herrick, *Italian Tragedy in the Renaissance* (Urbana, Ill.: University of Illinois Press, 1965), and *Tragicomedy* (Urbana, Ill.: University of Illinois Press, 1962); P. R. Horne, *The Tragedies of Giambattista Cinthio Giraldi* (London: Oxford University Press, 1962).

GIUSTI, GIUSEPPE (1808–1850), satirical poet. Giusti, the son of a well-to-do landowner, was born at Monsummano near Pistoia. He attended a number of schools in Montecatini, Florence, Pistoia, and Lucca before beginning the study of law at the university in Pisa in 1826. He finally obtained his degree in 1834, after briefly delaying his graduation with the circulation of one of his most famous political satires, "La guigliottina a vapore" (1833, "The Steam-powered Guillotine"). He moved to Florence to practice law, and many of his greatest works were written there during the late 1830s and early 1840s. After many of his poems had finally been published in 1844–45, Giusti became interested in traveling outside Tuscany. In 1844, he went to Rome and Naples; in the following year, he visited Milan and made the acquaintance of Manzoni* and Grossi.* Although he often attacked the Tuscan government and its grand duke in his works, Giusti was essentially a political moderate and even became a major in the Tuscan Civic Guard in 1847. In 1848, he narrowly missed being elected to the revolutionary democratic government in Florence headed by Guerrazzi.* When the old regimes were reinstated throughout Italy during 1849, Giusti completely abandoned politics and lived as a recluse, dying of consumption the following year.

Giusti was a brilliant satirical poet, a worthy descendant of Giuseppe Parini,* whose works he edited. Because of the political overtones of his verses, they became extremely popular in nineteenth-century Italy. Their frequent political allusions may make some of them seem difficult or obscure to the contemporary reader. "La guigliottina a vapore" is a witty and well-known description of a new discovery in China—a mechanized means of increasing the number of decapitations which will not only "civilize" that Oriental nation but will also be adopted profitably by the European rulers. Many similar poems followed. In *"Dies irae"* (1835, "The Day of Wrath"), Giusti celebrates the death of the reactionary emperor of Austria, subtly employing a meter derived from the church liturgy (as does the title) to attack his memory. In "Lo stivale" (1836, The Boot), the poet personifies the geographical shape of the peninsula, and the boot discusses its long history and its dire need both of mending and of a new owner. "L'incoronazione" (1838, The Coronation) describes the event officially naming Ferdinand I of Austria king of Italy. Giusti pictures the Italian princes abjectly throwing themselves at the emperor's feet, brings Pope Gregory XVI to task for allowing the church to forget its spiritual mission, and derides the fawning Milanese nobility for scrambling after imperial favors. Giusti assails political opportunism in "Il brindisi di Girella" (1835–40, The Whirligig's Toast), which he ironically dedicates to that arch-opportunist Talleyrand. In "Il Re Travicello" (1841, King Log), Giusti pokes fun at Leopoldo II, grand duke of Tuscany; the poem is based on one of the most famous of Aesop's fables, that of the frogs who, upon requesting a king of Jupiter, are first sent a log and finally a snake which devours them.

When one of Lamartine's Byronic heroes disparaged Italians of the day as "human dust" in comparing them unfavorably to the brave Greeks then fighting for their political freedom, Giusti replied in one of his greatest poems, "La terra dei morti" (1842, "The Land of the Dead"), by affirming the possibility of an eventual spiritual and political Risorgimento in Italy. In one of his later works, "Sant'Ambrogio" (1846, "In Sant'Ambrogio's"), Giusti strikes a middle ground between patriotic pride and a deeper and less nationalistic understanding of human folly. As he visits the church of Milan's patron saint, he is first insulted by the intrusive presence of Bohemian and Croatian soldiers "placed," as he puts it, "in our vineyard here to serve as poles." After a Verdi chorus is followed by a German hymn, however, the poet recognizes a bond between himself and these lonely and despised men, and he understands that Lombards and Germans would naturally be brothers if it were not for this foreign power which separates them. One of Giusti's finest satires without any particular political message is "La chiocciola" (1840–41, "The Snail"), an ode to this humble creature intended to teach men the exemplary virtues of modesty, love for homeland, temperance, pride and intelligence. Giusti's satirical poetry is characterized by a sharp, ready wit, the brilliant use of brief stanzaic forms, and his biting portraits of the vices of his age. Although many of his barbs are directed at Italy's foreign oppressors, he never ignores the defects of his own countrymen.

Bibliography: Epistolario di Giuseppe Giusti, eds. Ferdinando Martini and Quinto Santoli, 5 vols. (Florence: Le Monnier, 1932, 1952); *Poesie,* ed. Nunzio Sabbatucci, 2 vols. (Milan: Feltrinelli, 1962); *From Marino to Marinetti,* ed. and trans. Joseph Tusiani (New York: Baroque Press, 1974); Luigi Baldacci, "Giuseppe Giusti e la società fiorentina," *Paragone* 126 (1960), 3–26.

GOLDONI, CARLO (1707–1793), dramatist. Born in Venice on 25 February 1707, Carlo Goldoni experienced most of the changing attitudes of a complex century that evolved from the classicizing traditions of the Arcadia* and Metastasio's* melodramas* to a new awareness of the social realities of the Italian bourgeoisie and the reformist ideas of the French Enlightenment.* After he completed his studies of law at Pavia and Padua by 1731, Goldoni moved to Venice, where he practiced law until 1747. At the same time, however, the young Goldoni upheld—and even intensified—the paternal love for theatrical performances, which had already caused financial problems to the family since the time of his grandfather Carlo, who used to organize private spectacles. This active interest in the literary and theatrical aspects of comedy led Goldoni to a reading of English, Spanish, and French comedies, especially those of his favorite, Molière. The sixteenth-century Spanish influence on the Italian theatre was therefore superseded by that of French authors. Among classical and Italian writers, Goldoni read Plautus, Terence, Aristophanes, Della Porta,* Machiavelli,* Apostolo Zeno (1668–1750), and Metastasio, in addition to the theoretical writings of Castelvetro* and Gravina.* Goldoni's first literary efforts followed the eclectic tradition of the time, including tragedies for music (*Amalasunta* [1732, Amalasunta]), *intermezzi* (*La birba* [1735, *The Shrewd Young Lady*]), melodramas (*Pisistrato* [1736, Pisistratus]), and occasional poetry. These literary interests were soon sorted out and channeled toward his lasting commitment to comedy and the reform of the Italian theatre. These goals are already apparent in *Momolo cortesan* (1738, Momolo the Courtesan), and *Donna di garbo* (1743, A Lady of Charm), which were praised by Pietro Verri,* Voltaire, and Diderot.

Goldoni's reform of the Italian theatre stems from his renovation of, rather than reaction to, the *commedia dell'arte,** of which he preserved the inventive characters, spirited dialogues, and intriguing plots. More decisive was Goldoni's attack upon the scandalous productions of the literary comedies of the time, which Giovanni Battista Fagiuoli (1660–1742), Girolamo Gigli (1660–1722), and Iacopo Angelo Nelli (1673–1767) had already rejected, by emphasizing a greater sense of austerity and adherence to verisimilitude. With regard to the *commedia dell'arte,* Goldoni corrected its triviality as well as the standard situations and outlines of the *canovacci* (sketches, rough drafts) upon which the actor improvised. Slowly, Goldoni proceeded to give a literary structure to his comedies. In *Momolo cortesan,* the part of the protagonist was completely written out, and *Donna di garbo* became the first written comedy in which the author clearly predominated over the actor. Especially in terms of their written form and didactic purpose, the comedies of Goldoni mark the beginning of modern Italian theatre.

Goldoni's prolific talent reached a peak in 1750, when he wrote seventeen comedies, in a total body of over one hundred works. Among his best comedies are *I Rusteghi,* (1760, *The Boors*), *Casa nova* (1760, *The Superior Residence*), *Sior Todero brontolon* (1762, Mr. Todero the Grouch), and *Baruffe chiozzotte* (1762, *The Squabbles of Chioggia*). Expressive of Goldoni's inspiration at its best, these works generally condition characters to milieu, that of the Venetian bourgeoisie. Detached and sympathetic, Goldoni veils his criticism of social values with a benevolent acceptance of the regenerative tensions between the forces of tradition and those of progress. In *I Rusteghi,* the clash between the young and the old seeks continuity rather than separation. Yet, the notion that a respect for tradition should not stop the development of an inventive, healthy, and independent youth seems to foreshadow the new generations of more progressive Italians. This poetic and moral equilibrium represents the kernel of Goldoni's outlook on life and art.

Having relinquished abstract ideologies and academic conventions, Goldoni centered his theatre on the everyday life of common people, whether merchants or gondoliers from Venice and Chioggia, whom he portrayed in their loves and altercations. Perhaps not insensitive to the contemporaneous emphasis on humanitarian concerns, Goldoni juxtaposed a rather unprejudiced acceptance of life to the historical visions of Vico* and Alfieri,* so much so that Voltaire called him the child and painter of nature. Goldoni was closer to the moderate views of Pietro Verri and Beccaria,* believing that society could be reformed without any recourse to revolutionary measures. Consequently, a subtle and indulgent irony characterizes his critical perspective on society, well short of the more sophisticated and irreverent approach of Baretti,* Alfieri, and Parini.* Nevertheless, Goldoni's adherence to bourgeois values certainly helped shift the focus of literary interest from the academic environment of the Arcadia to a new consciousness of the artistic context of life itself, which Goldoni represented through the spontaneous and anti-academic brilliance of the Venetian dialect. Among his works written in Italian, *La locandiera* (1753, *Mirandolina*) is probably the most successful.

   Disappointed by the relentless criticism waged against him by academicians and critics alike (Pietro Chiari, 1711–1785; Carlo Gozzi*), Goldoni left Italy in 1762, becoming the director of the Comédie italienne in Paris. This period marked a rather unhappy phase in his life. On the one hand, he was forced to resuscitate the *canovacci* of the *commedia dell'arte* and the *commedie a soggetto*, (improvised comedy), which were still quite popular in France. On the other hand, he attempted—and with some success—to gain public acclaim by writing comedies like *Le bourru bienfaisant* (1771, *The Well-Meaning Grouch*) and *L'avare fastueux* (1772, The Ostentatious Miser), which reflected the more decorous canons of French classicism. From 1783 to 1787, Goldoni wrote his *Mémoires (Memoirs)* in French. Like his comedies, the *Mémoires* present a faithful document of the times. Written in a simple and colloquial style, they provide a portrait of a humane individual interested in humanity at large and ready to accept life with a healthy sense of humor. As a private diary suffused with melancholic reminiscences, Goldoni's *Mémoires* counterbalanced the eruptive and exceptional personalities of Casanova* and Alfieri.

   Goldoni spent the last years of his life as a teacher of Italian at court. Among his friends were Favart, De la Place, Diderot, and Rousseau. He died on 6 February 1793.

See also COMMEDIA DELL'ARTE.

Bibliography: Opere, ed. Filippo Zampieri (Milan: Ricciardi, 1954); *Tutte le opere di Carlo Goldoni,* ed. Giuseppe Ortolani, 14 vols. (Milan: Rizzoli, 1935–56); *The Comic Theatre: A Comedy in Three Acts,* trans. John W. Miller (Lincoln, Neb.: University of Nebraska Press, 1969); *The Fan,* trans. Frederick Davies (London: Heinemann, 1968); *Four Comedies,* trans. Frederick Davies (Baltimore: Penguin, 1968); *The Liar,* trans. Frederick Davies (London: Heinemann, 1963); *Memoirs of Carlo Goldoni,* trans. John Black (1926; rpt. Westport, Conn.: Greenwood Press, 1976); *The Servant of Two Masters,* trans. Frederick Davies (London: Heinemann, 1961); *Three Comedies,* trans. Clifford Bax, et al. (Oxford: Oxford University Press, 1961); A. Della Corte, *L'opera comica italiana nel '700* (Bari: Laterza, 1923); Riccardo Bacchelli, *Confessioni letterarie* (Milan: Vallardi, 1932); Heinz Riedt, *Carlo Goldoni* (New York: Ungar, 1974).

                                                        Giancarlo Maiorino

GOVONI, CORRADO (1884–1965), writer and lyric poet. Govoni was born in Tàmara in the province of Ferrara, and was a close friend of Corazzini.* Govoni's first collection of verse, *Le fiale* (1903, The Phials), shows D'Annunzio's* influence, but he soon experimented with other poetic styles. Much of his early poetry in *Armonie in grigio et in silenzio* (1903, Harmonies in Gray and Silence) and *Fuochi d'artifizio* (1905, Fireworks) embodies the *crepuscolari* interest in simple objects and landscapes, reminiscent of impressionist paintings. Collaborating on the reviews *Poesia, La Voce,* and *Lacerba,* Govoni joined the futurist movement for a period with *Poesie elettriche* (1911, Electric Poems) and *Rarefazione e parole in libertà* (1915, Rarefactions and Words in Liberty). These two works contain some of the best examples of "parole in libertà," often accompanied by the poet's own sketches or designs that were an integral part of the verse. After serving in World War I, Govoni moved to Rome and continued a prolific poetic production, including the volume *Il quaderno dei sogni e delle stelle* (1924, Notebook of Dreams and Stars) that contains the frequently anthologized poem, "La trombettina" ("The Little Trumpet"). The brutal experience of the Nazi occupation of Rome, during which his son was murdered in 1944 at the Fosse Ardeatine, inspired *Aladino: lamento su mio figlio morto* (1946, Aladino: Lament for My Dead Son), which contains the moving "Dialogo dell'angelo e del giovine morto" ("Dialogue of the Angel and the Dead Boy"). Although Govoni wrote a great many poems during the rest of his career, such as those in *Preghiera al trifoglio* (1953, Prayer to the Clover) and *Stradario della primavera* (1958, Roadmap of Spring), his earlier poetry contains his most inventive imagery and his most authentic evocations of landscapes, country scenes, and pensive moods.

See also CORAZZINI, Sergio; FUTURISM; GOZZANO, Guido.

Bibliography: Poesie (1903–1959), ed. Giuseppe Ravegnani (Milan: Mondadori, 1961); *Contemporary Italian Poetry,* ed. Carlo L. Golino (Berkeley, Calif.: University of California Press, 1962); *Twentieth-Century Italian Poetry,* ed. L. R. Lind (Indianapolis, Ind.: Bobbs-Merrill, 1974); Fausto Curi, *Corrado Govoni* (Milan: Mursia, 1964).

GOZZANO, GUIDO (1883–1916), lyric poet and writer. Gozzano came from Turin. Although he enrolled at the faculty of law in Turin, he never completed his degree, preferring to attend lectures on literature. During his university years, Gozzano suffered the first serious attacks of the tuberculosis which killed him at the beginning of a brilliant poetic career. His first volume of verse appeared in 1907 as *La via del rifugio* (Road of the Shelter). In an illuminating critical article written in 1910, Giuseppe Antonio Borgese* described a group of young poets, at whose head he placed Gozzano, as a "twilight school" *(scuola crepuscolare),* and the term twilight poet has since that time been applied to Gozzano and others of his generation (Corazzini* and Govoni*). Recent criticism, however, has tended to focus upon Gozzano's individuality rather than upon his leadership of a poetic school. His next work, the important *Colloqui* (1911, Conversations), contains his most famous poems. Besides the influence of such foreign poets as Jammes, Verlaine, Laforgue, and Rodenbach, this verse owes a particular debt to D'Annunzio* and Pascoli* (especially Pascoli's concept of the "poetica del fanciullino" or the "poetics of the small child"). *Colloqui* was both a critical and a commercial success, which gained for its author a reputation as a major new poet and the opportunity to contribute to the important literary reviews. For reasons of health, he embarked from Genoa in 1912 on a three-month voyage to India which resulted in a posthumous volume of essays entitled *Verso la cuna del mondo* (1917, Towards the Cradle of the World). On his return, he began a collection of poems about butterflies, based upon Virgil's *Georgics* and the didactic verse of the Italian Cinquecento. Written in blank verse, these works were to be illustrated by the poet's own drawings but were never completed. In 1915, shortly before his death from tuberculosis, Gozzano was hired by a film company to write the script for a cinematic version of the life of St. Francis of Assisi.* In an essay on the art of the cinema completed in 1916, he declared that the cinema was not an art form but rather an industry which had need of the artists' contributions.

Gozzano's place in Italian literary history rests upon the lyrics in *Colloqui*. As Eugenio Montale* remarked in a preface to one edition of these poems, Gozzano was among the first twentieth-century Italian poets successfully to overcome the influence of D'Annunzio and to stake out a territory of his own, thereby laying the foundations for a new kind of contemporary poetry. Luciano Anceschi's (1911–   ) fundamental study of twentieth-century Italian poetics traces the lyrics of the "twilight poets" back to the poems of Pascoli and sets them apart both from a poetics of form (Carducci,* the poets around the review *La Ronda*) and a poetics of analogy (the futurists and Ungaretti*). As a middle ground between formalism and avant-garde experimentation, *crepuscolare* poetry seeks to express what Gozzano called poetry of "non-serious things" and reflects a regard for what he termed the "good things in the worst taste." An excellent example of such verse is Gozzano's masterpiece, "La signorina Felicità, ovvero La Felicità" ("Signorina Felicita alias Felicity"), wherein the poet examines in great detail the objects, furnishings, bric-a-brac, smells, the atmosphere of a *fin de siècle* home, and praises the "simple life" opposed to his own poetic and intellectual pretensions. He defines the outside world as "that place/ full of hectic traffic and struggles,/ that place full of those pitiful/ 'Things with two legs'. . ./," and he compares the race of men, motivated by the false and empty illusions in which he can no longer believe, to strings of red and black ants, their graves already numbered by Death the Leveller. Only the simple pleasures of the moment and a stoic acceptance of the inevitable extinction of the self in death are offered to the reader as the truths of poetry. Another of his best poems, "Totò Merumeni" ("Totò Merumeni"), may be regarded as an autobiographical portrait in narrative verse. Totò is a man of twenty-five, very learned but with little sense—a perfect son of the modern age according to the poet. Life has taken away from him all its promises; he no longer holds any illusions (especially that of love); he can experience no deep emotions and has a "burnt spirit." Yet, he is almost happy with his poetry and his daily diversions. The conclusion of the poem summarizes Totò's life and the crepuscular mood: "Totò was born one day. Totò one day will die." Gozzano's "twilight poetry" is melancholy, yet never morbid. His best works reflect a pensive attitude of sadness but are, on the whole, relatively cheerful and sympathetic, employing an extremely well-wrought, musical narrative verse.

See also CORAZZINI, Sergio; FUTURISM; GOVONI, Corrado; PASCOLI, Giovanni.

Bibliography: Poesie e prose, ed. Alberto De Marchi (Milan: Garzanti, 1961); *From Marino to Marinetti,* ed. and trans. Joseph Tusiani (New York: Baroque Press, 1974); *Twentieth-Century Italian Poetry,* ed. L. R. Lind (Indianapolis, Ind.: Bobbs-Merrill, 1974); Luciano Anceschi, *Le poetiche del Novecento in Italia* (Turin: Paravia, 1973); Henriette Martin, *Guido Gozzano (1883–1916)* (Paris: Presses Universitaires, 1968); Edoardo Sanguineti, *Guido Gozzano: indagini e letture* (Turin: Einaudi, 1966) and *Tra Liberty e crepuscolarismo* (Milan: Mursia, 1970); Aldo Vallone, *I crepuscolari* (Palermo: Palumbo, 1970).

GOZZI, CARLO (1720–1806), Venetian aristocrat, dramatist, and memorialist. Born in Venice, the sixth of eleven sons in a noble family from Bergamo that had fallen upon hard times, Gozzi could not afford much formal education because of his family's financial reverses and was, therefore, largely self-taught. After three years of service in Dalmatia with the Venetian army, he returned to Venice where he participated in the foundation of the Accademia dei Granelleschi (1747). He soon became that academy's foremost conservative voice in opposing various Enlightenment* ideas and, most notably, the theatrical reforms of Venice's most famous dramatist, Carlo Goldoni.* Rejecting Goldoni's realistic vision of contemporary Venetian society and his desire to modify the traditional *commedia dell'arte,* Gozzi proposed instead a theatre of fantasy and imagination.

In response to a challenge from Goldoni, Gozzi set out to prove that the fickle Venetian theatre audience would desert Goldoni's bourgeois realism for dramatized fairy tales presented in the style of *commedia dell'arte*. Working from a tale in Basile's* *Pentameron,* Gozzi presented his first *fiaba* (theatrical fable or fantasy) in 1761—*L'amore delle tre melarance (The Love of Three Oranges).* After its astounding public success, he prepared nine other *fiabe* for the theatre between 1761 and 1765, including such influential works as *Il re cervo (The King Stag), Turandot (Turandot), Il mostro turchino (The Blue Monster), La donna serpente* (The Snake Woman), *L'augelin belverde* (The Pretty Green Bird), and *I pitocchi fortunati* (The Fortunate Beggars). These plays bring out the traditional *commedia dell'arte* figures—Pantalone, Tartaglia, Brighella, and Truffaldino—and combine a light sense of humor with a satirical purpose and a fairy-tale atmosphere derived from such sources as Basile, Oriental romances, *The Thousand and One Nights,* and popular oral tradition. Gozzi's attacks on Goldoni were so successful that he eventually drove his rival out of Venice to Paris. When the public began to tire of Gozzi's *fiabe,* just as it had briefly turned away from Goldoni's theatre, Gozzi began a series of plays based on Spanish models in which he hoped to reestablish a concern for the now outmoded courtly morality of his patrician class ignored by the bourgeois theatre of Goldoni. Perhaps his most familiar drama of this period is *Droghe d'amore* (1777, Love Potions), which was taken from a play by Tirso de Molina (1571–1648), and in which Gozzi's mistress, Teodora Ricci, played the leading female role. Of related interest is a poem in twelve cantos with affinities to the heroic-comic epic* tradition of Luigi Pulci* and Folengo,* *La Marfisa bizzarra* (1772, Bizarre Marfisa), a work which expresses Gozzi's nostalgia for a lost age of courtly values and his comic contempt for his contemporaries.

Gozzi's last achievement was his *Memorie inutili* (1797–98, *Useless Memoirs*), an absorbing autobiography which clarifies many of his opinions on the function of dramatic art and which elucidates many of his arguments with Goldoni. It may still be read with profit in conjunction with the other important autobiographies of the period by Goldoni,* Da Ponte,* Casanova,* Vico,* and Alfieri.* Although Gozzi's critical reputation in Italy waned considerably after his death, his works were well received beyond the Alps in romantic circles. His *Fiabe,* for example, were translated into German only a few years after they appeared in Italy and won high praise from Goethe, Lessing, the Schlegels, and Schiller (who created a dramatic version of *Turandot*); in France, Madame de Staël and De Musset recognized Gozzi's talents. Wagner based an early opera on *La donna serpente,* and in later years, the operatic versions of *Turandot* and *The Love of Three Oranges* by Busoni, Puccini, and Prokofiev have sustained critical interest in Gozzi's works.

See also COMMEDIA DELL'ARTE.

Bibliography: *La Marfisa bizzarra,* ed. Cornelia Ortiz (Bari: Laterza, 1911); *Memorie inutili,* ed. Giuseppe Prezzolini (Bari: Laterza, 1934); *Opere: teatro e polemiche teatrali,* ed. Giuseppe Petronio (Milan: Rizzoli, 1962); *The Classic Theatre,* ed. Eric Bentley (New York: Doubleday, 1958); *The Genius of the Italian Theatre,* ed. Eric Bentley (New York: Mentor, 1964); *Useless Memoirs,* trans. J. A. Symonds (New York: Oxford University Press, 1962).

GOZZI, GASPARO (1713–1786), journalist and writer. Gasparo was born into a noble but impoverished family and was the older brother of the dramatist Carlo Gozzi.* His early works include *Favole esopiane* (1748, Fables After Aesop), a collection of lyric poetry, and *Lettere diverse* (1750, Miscellaneous Letters), a series of character sketches after the manner of Theophrastus. Like so many other writers of his day, Gozzi attempted to compose drama but he was never successful. He did, however, contribute translations of many works from foreign literature, including plays by Molière, Plautus, and Voltaire. From 1760 until 1761, he was in charge of a periodical, the *Gazzetta veneta,* sponsored as a commercial venture by a group of Venetian merchants. Gozzi added fables, dialogues, essays, *novelle,** and other journalistic pieces to the commercial news. When this magazine was canceled, Gozzi began *L'Osservatore veneto.* During its year-long existence (1761–62), Gozzi continued his encyclopaedic writings on a number of topics and in a number of genres. Both journals owe something to the popularity of Addison and Steele and *The Spectator* and *The Tattler,* which were apparently known to Gozzi through French translations, but Gozzi's journalism relies most heavily upon his native Venice and upon the classics for its inspiration.

Besides this substantive contribution to Enlightenment* journalism, Gozzi composed the *Sermoni* (1763–93, Sermons), a series of satires in verse dealing with contemporary literature and its ignorant critics, autobiographical topics, and contemporary customs. His *Difesa di Dante* (1758, Defense of Dante), one of the earliest Enlightenment documents to display an emerging pre-romantic admiration for Dante's* poetry, also included an Italian version of Alexander Pope's *Essay on Criticism* which Gozzi had translated from the French.

See also ENLIGHTENMENT; GOZZI, Carlo.

Bibliography: *Scritti scelti,* ed. Nicola Mangini (Turin: UTET, 1960); Mario Fubini, *Dal Muratori al Baretti* (Bari: Laterza, 1954).

GRAMSCI, ANTONIO (1891–1937), Sardinian political theorist, intellectual, and critic. Of humble origins, Gramsci managed to win a fellowship to study at the University of Turin in 1910, where he met Palmiro Togliatti (1893–1964, Secretary General of the Italian Communist Party

from 1947 until his death) and became acquainted with the works of Croce*
and De Sanctis* as well as the classical Marxist theorists. Very soon, the
young revolutionary came to the forefront of political activity in the city; he
founded the journal *Ordine nuovo* (New Order) in 1919 and was the regular
drama critic for the socialist paper *Avanti!*. After the Communist party in
Italy was formed following a split with the socialists in 1921, Gramsci was
named party secretary in 1924. From that time until the present day, his
ideas have constituted the major force in Italian Marxism. When *Ordine
nuovo* ceased publication in 1922, Gramsci founded another newspaper,
L'Unità, and was eventually elected to Parliament. Shortly after the Matteotti crisis, the fascist regime passed a series of security laws which
enabled it to suppress all political opposition. Gramsci was arrested in
1926, convicted of political crimes, and sent to prison at Turi di Bari, a
journey which almost killed him and permanently destroyed his health. He
was released from prison in 1937 but died only a week later.

Gramsci's major works were composed in prison and constitute almost
three thousand pages in thirty-two notebooks. They finally appeared in
print between 1948 and 1951 as *Quaderni del carcere (Prison Notebooks)*
and immediately became a best seller in Italy. Earlier, in 1947, his *Lettere
dal carcere (Letters from Prison)* was awarded the Viareggio Prize for
Literature. Most historians consider Gramsci to be the most innovative
European Marxist thinker since Lenin. His works touch upon a number of
cultural and literary problems which have influenced the thinking of many
contemporary Italian intellectuals, Marxist and non-Marxist alike. His
keen insights into the nature and conception of the modern political party
and the role of intellectuals in contemporary society are of fundamental
importance. In the first instance, his analysis of the modern political party
led him to devote an original section of the notebooks to Machiavelli,*
translated into English as *The Modern Prince,* which defined Machiavelli's
treatise as an example of the Sorellian "myth" and suggested that the
political party fulfill the role Machiavelli assigned to his Renaissance*
condottiere.

In his treatment of Italian intellectuals, Gramsci rejected a simplistic
dichotomy between workers and intellectuals, and proposed other categories based upon economic functions (the specialists versus the directors),
geographical and class origin (the urban intellectual versus the rural intellectual), and social status (the "traditional" intellectuals, the creative
artists, and learned men versus the "organic" intellectuals, a group more
directly related to the rise of new economic institutions). Gramsci believed
that, in Italy, the traditional intellectuals were usually from rural areas and
often became state bureaucrats and members of the various professions,
while urban intellectuals were usually of the organic type. He then distinguished between "political" and "civil" society, the first made up of

public institutions and coercive institutions (the army, the courts, and the bureaucracy), and the second of private institutions (the church, the schools, and political parties). Gramsci asserted that, in Italy, organic intellectuals tended to work in the institutions of political society, while the traditional intellectuals were clustered in those of civil society and were less likely to rely upon force in establishing their intellectual control over the rest of society. This analysis gave rise to his important concept of hegemony. Gramsci believed that the hegemony of one social class over the rest of society was first exercised through private institutions of civil society and was obtained more through common consent than by force. Thus, he believed that in order to become an authentic ruling class, the working class first had to establish its claim to be a valid ruling class in the realm of civil society through the hegemony of its own intellectuals. Only then could it move to a successful political victory with the dictatorship of the proletariat in political society. Because Gramsci assigns such a crucial role to the intellectual, he also avoids the rigid economic determinism of some traditional Marxist theory and retains a creative role for the individual's own actions. Gramsci's views on the intellectual's creative role in the political process were indebted to the idealist philosophical tradition, so important in modern Italy, to Vico,* De Sanctis, and Croce, and to Marx and Lenin, a fact which enabled his revolutionary political views to win wider acceptance in Italian society. An excellent critic, Gramsci also produced a number of discerning drama reviews (particularly of Pirandello's* works) and articles on Italian literature and its relationship to Italian culture. Both his theoretical ideas and his practical criticism have been a primary influence upon several generations of Marxist literary scholars in Italy.

Bibliography: Quaderni del carcere, ed. Valentino Gerratana, 4 vols. (Turin: Einaudi, 1975); *Letters from Prison,* ed. Lynne Lawner (New York: Harper, 1973); *Selections from the Prison Notebooks,* trans. Quintin Hoare and Geoffrey Nowell Smith (New York: International Publishers, 1971); Guido Davico Bonino, *Gramsci e il teatro* (Turin: Einaudi, 1974); John M. Cammett, *Antonio Gramsci and the Origins of Italian Communism* (Stanford, Calif.: Stanford University Press, 1967); Martin Clark, *Antonio Gramsci and the Revolution That Failed* (New Haven, Conn.: Yale University Press, 1977); Giuseppe Fiori, *Antonio Gramsci: Life of a Revolutionary* (New York: Schocken, 1973); *Gramsci e la cultura contemporanea,* ed. Pietro Rossi, 2 vols. (Rome: Editori riuniti, 1969); Nikša Stipčević, *Gramsci e i problemi letterari* (Milan: Mursia, 1968).

GRAVINA, GIAN VINCENZO (1664–1718), literary theorist and academician. Born in Calabria and educated in Naples in law and the classics, Gravina came to Rome in 1689 as secretary to Cardinal Pignatelli and soon met most of the important literary figures of the time. One of the founders of the Accademia dell'Arcadia,* Gravina composed the Latin laws for the group which were promulgated in 1696 in the manner of the Twelve Tables of ancient Roman law. His academic title was Opico Erimanteo. Gravina's participation in this literary group did not impede his legal scholarship, and in 1699 he procured a chair of canon and civil law. Many of his Latin works are serious, scholarly studies of the evolution of jurisprudence which attest to an acute historical perception and a classical erudition. In 1711, after a quarrel with another Arcadian, Giovan Mario Crescimbeni (1663–1728), Gravina withdrew from the academy and helped to found a rival group, the Accademia dei Quirini.

Gravina's principal contributions are theoretical. Although he ultimately rejected what he considered to be the banality of Arcadian pastoral* poetry, an early work, *Discorso sull'Endimione* (1692, Discourse on Endymion), defends a pastoral drama by Alessandro Guidi (1650–1712). His impressive treatise *Della ragion poetica* (1708, On the Nature of Poetry) is one of the first rationalist poetics. It defines poetry as a form of rational knowledge based upon imagery and asserts that poetry possesses a civilizing power, akin to that of fables employed by poets to civilize primitive peoples. Another work, *Della tragedia* (1715, On the Nature of Tragedy), attacks the tragic theatre of France as well as the pastoral drama of Tasso* and Guarini,* elevates tragedy over epic* poetry, and proposes a civic purpose for the dramatic genre. Gravina's five classical tragedies illustrate his theoretical ideas but lack true dramatic inspiration.

See also ARCADIA; NEOCLASSICISM.

Bibliography: Scritti critici e teorici, ed. Amedeo Quondam (Bari: Laterza, 1973); Domenico Consoli, *Realtà e fantasia nel classicismo di Gian Vincenzo Gravina* (Milan: Bietti, 1970); Benedetto Croce, *Problemi di estetica* (Bari: Laterza, 1910); Amedeo Quondam, *Cultura e ideologia di Gian Vincenzo Gravina* (Milan: Mursia, 1968).

GRAZZINI, ANTON FRANCESCO, "Il Lasca" (1503–1584), poet, dramatist, and *novelliere*. Grazzini was born in Florence of an ancient Florentine family. His early life and education are not well documented, but apparently, instead of the traditional humanist training in the classics, he received a thorough grounding in vernacular literature. Grazzini cooperated in the foundation of the Florentine Accademia degli Umidi (1540) and took the academic nàme "Il Lasca" or "The Roach," by which he is often known. The Umidi, the first literary gathering in the city of any importance since Ficino's* Platonic Academy and the Orti Oricellari, departed from the goals of these earlier humanist academic circles in their hope to restore the *volgare* to a place of equality with classical languages and literatures. Increasing tension between Grazzini and other members of the group culminated in his expulsion from the organization in 1547, and he remained outside it for many years. The difficulties arose from his refusal to submit to the criticism of fellow academicians and to abide by those pedantic academic rules and ceremonies which the academy had been formed to combat. Through the efforts of Lionardo Salviati,* Grazzini was finally reinstated after he submitted some of his writing to the group's literary censor.

Between the time Grazzini was expelled and his reinstatement in 1566, he published several of his own works, published all of the editions of poetry he had prepared, and had two of his comedies performed. During this period, his editorial work is perhaps most worthy of notice. In an effort to preserve modern Italian poetry, Grazzini edited the writings of Francesco Berni* in 1548. The second of the first two volumes of this collection contained the works of other lesser known burlesque poets. He then undertook an edition of the poetry of Domenico di Giovanni,* "Il Burchiello," which appeared in 1552. He also edited a collection of Florentine carnival songs and the lyrics of Angelo Firenzuola,* Benedetto Varchi,* and many lesser known poets. Little is known of Grazzini's life during the years from 1566 until 1582 when the Accademia della Crusca was established.

Grazzini's collected works give a vivid portrait of life in sixteenth-century Florence and have journalistic and historical merit as well as literary import. He wrote a total of seven comedies, much burlesque poetry, numerous Petrarchan lyrics, and a significant collection of some thirty *novelle* * entitled *Le cene* (The Suppers) which was begun by 1549 but remained incomplete at his death. It was not published until the eighteenth century. Although modern critics prefer the *novelle* and the comedies, Grazzini was known primarily as a poet to his contemporaries. Within the traditions of both burlesque poetry and the serious Petrarchan lyric, Grazzini employed a wide range of poetic forms—sonnets,* *canzoni,* * carnival songs, *ottave,* madrigals,* and *capitoli* *—but his name was always connected with the humorous burlesque tradition established by Berni, his predecessor. In spite of his academic connections, much of his best poetry deals with the freedom of the creative process and the condemnation of pedantry—in particular his "In lode del pensiero" (In Praise of Thought), "Contro al pensiero" (Against Thought), and "In lode della pazzia" (In Praise of Madness). Like other burlesque poets before him, Grazzini often wrote extended forms of traditional verse, using not only the familiar *sonetto caudato* that Berni made famous but also extended madrigals, which he termed *madrigalesse* and *madrigaloni.* He often criticized Petrarch* in these works and praised Berni, Ariosto,* and Pulci,* but his own Petrarchan lyrics and pastoral* eclogues reflect a profound acquaintance with the *Canzoniere* and with the poetry of Benedetto Varchi, Pietro Bembo,* and other Cinquecento Petrarchan writers.

Six of Grazzini's comedies were published together in 1582: *La gelosia* (Jealousy); *La spiritata* (The Possessed); *La strega* (The Witch); *La pinzochera* (The Go-Between); *La Sibilla* (Sibyl); and *I parentadi* (The Kinships). Two other plays currently attributed to him—*L'Arzigogolo* (Arzigogolo) and a farce, once thought to be from the pen of Machiavelli,* entitled *Il frate* (The Friar)—were finally published in the eighteenth century. Several of Grazzini's spiritual dramas and other comedies were either lost or destroyed. His works retain the five-act structure of the erudite comedy of the period but reflect the Florentine tendency to combine classical with farcical or popular elements, producing a decidedly local flavor quite comparable to that of the *novella* tradition. The characters are most often recognizable as stereotypes from the classical theatre or the emerging *commedia dell'arte.**

Grazzini's *novelle* owe an obvious debt to Boccaccio* and are placed within a frame. Ten young storytellers decide to tell their own stories rather than to read from *The Decameron* for evening entertainment. Thus, the historical background of the Florentine plague is replaced by a pleasant company of leisure-loving young people with no loftier purpose in mind than amusing themselves. The tone of the stories often seems at one with that of Grazzini's burlesque poetry, and his narrative is best when it aims at brief, uncomplicated comedy. It employs extensive dialogue and furnishes extremely detailed depictions of the physical world and the human body. D. H. Lawrence rendered one of these *novelle* into English.

See also BERNI, Francesco; DOMENICO DI GIOVANNI; NOVELLA; SALVIATI, Lionardo.

Bibliography: Le cene, ed. Carlo Verzone (Florence: Sansoni, 1882); *Le rime,* ed. Carlo Verzone (Bari: Laterza, 1953); *The Story of Doctor Manente Being the Tenth and Last Story from the Suppers of A. F. Grazzini Called Il Lasca,* trans. D. H. Lawrence (Florence: Orioli, 1929); Robert J. Rodini, *Antonfrancesco Grazzini: Poet, Dramatist and Novelliere 1503–1584* (Madison, Wis.: University of Wisconsin Press, 1970).

GROSSI, TOMMASO (1790–1853), poet and novelist. Born in Bellano, Grossi studied law in Pavia and worked as a notary in Milan, where he became a close friend of Alessandro Manzoni* (whom he served as a secretary from 1822 until 1838) and Carlo Porta.* Both writers, central to the development of Italian romanticism,* were major influences upon Grossi's work. In 1820, Grossi published *Ildegonda* (Ildegonda), his first *novella* in *ottava*. Later, inspired by the examples of Tasso's* *Geru-*

salemme liberata (Jerusalem Delivered) and Sir Walter Scott's *Ivanhoe,* he composed an heroic epic* poem in fifteen cantos entitled *I lombardi alla prima crociata* (1826, The Lombards in the First Crusade), which served as the basis of an opera by Giuseppe Verdi. A line from the then unpublished poem was cited by Manzoni in his *Promessi sposi* (Chapter XI).

Grossi's chief historical novel, *Marco Visconti (Marco Visconti, A Romance of the Fourteenth Century),* appeared in 1834; an English translation of the work went into at least five nineteenth-century American editions. It remains the most important historical novel in the tradition of Scott and Manzoni that Italy produced during the romantic period. The plot concerns a *condottiere* from the fourteenth century, Marco Visconti, who courts Bice del Balzo, a woman in love with Ottorino Visconti, Marco's cousin. Although the link between fiction and history is not as aptly sustained as in Manzoni's masterpiece, several chapters of the work rank among the best descriptive passages in romantic prose. The novel also contains a prisoner's song, "Rondinella pellegrina" ("The Little Swallow") which became popular among Italian prisoners in Austria and during the Risorgimento.

See also MANZONI, Alessandro; ROMANTICISM.

Bibliography: Opere poetiche, ed. Raffaele Sirri (Naples: Fulvio Rossi, 1972); *Marco Visconti, A Romance of the Fourteenth Century* (New York: National Alumni, 1907); *From Marino to Marinetti,* trans. Joseph Tusiani (New York: Baroque Press, 1974).

GROTESQUE THEATRE: *See* TEATRO GROTTESCO.

GUARINI, BATTISTA (1538–1612), poet, courtier, and diplomat. Guarini was born in Ferrara into the illustrious Veronese family that produced the great humanist Guarino de' Guarini (1374–1460). It is likely that Battista studied at Padua. In 1557, he was professor of rhetoric at Ferrara, and in 1564, he went to Padua where he remained as a member of the Accademia degli Eterei until he was called into the service of Alfonso II (d'Este) at Ferrara in 1567. Engaged in ambassadorial and secretarial functions under the duke until 1588, Guarini later served the rulers of Mantua, Tuscany, and Urbino. He was an ambitious and apparently cantankerous man, and his last twenty-five years were particularly embittered by quarrels and litigation with his own children, Venice, and Marfisa d'Este. At the same time, however, he enjoyed enormous prestige as a poet.

Guarini's literary production includes lyric poetry (his madrigals* were much admired and frequently set to music by composers); a comedy entitled *La Idropica* (1583, The Dropsical Lady); a didactic dialogue on the duties of a secretary and the art of letter-writing (*Il Segretario,* The Secretary); some noteworthy letters; and a political treatise (*Trattato della politica libertà,* Treatise on Political Freedom), which was not published until 1818 when it was duly execrated by Italian patriots because of its thesis that the republican form of government was inferior to the tyranny of a benign single ruler. Guarini's name has survived exclusively because of one single but astonishing work—*Il Pastor fido* (1590, *The Faithful Shepherd*)—and the important literary polemic (including his own treatises) that arose from it. Following its publication Guarini's pastoral* drama (or "pastoral tragicomedy" as he pointedly defined it) remained the most popular work of secular literature in Europe for almost two hundred years. Of the many editions and translations, we need mention only the translation by Sir Richard Fanshawe, *The Faithful Shepherd* (1647), an influential literary work in its own right that has received much attention of late. An Oxford edition of Fanshawe's translation was published by W. F. Staton and W. E. Simeone in 1964, followed by J. H. Whitfield's edition in 1976.

Almost certainly written in emulation of *Aminta,* the *Pastor fido* is anything but an imitation of Tasso's* classically structured and elegiacally sensual masterwork. Guarini's play is three times as long (some six thousand verses) as his predecessor's pastoral, and it makes use of a complex, triple-interlocking line of action involving a content and poetic style that mark a vision that is highly manneristic if not typical of the full-blown Baroque.* Moreover, it is too richly ambivalent to be dismissed as a mere example of sensually idyllic escape literature. Along with love, sensual and sentimental, the themes that pervade this tragicomedy are blindness, illusion, *engaño* (deceit), and heroic virtue. These in turn are played against the backdrop of the motif of fate that is fully vindicated in the play's context as a meaningful, dramatic, and cohesive element. While remaining escapist literature of a sort, the *Pastor fido* at the same time reveals an epistemological crisis that reflects the crisis of values characteristic of the Counter-Reformation age.

The most frequently recurring image in the play is concerned with the eye, and at one time or another, the metaphor of blindness is attributed to all the main characters. The most important episodes and situations are almost allegories of blindness and illusion. The play opens with the inhabitants of Arcadia following a mistaken path in seeking to fulfill one part of the Oracle's decree (meant to save them from a cruel law imposed by the outraged goddess of chastity, Diana) and declaring their inability to foresee how the second part can be realized. In the *gioco de la cieca* (a sort of blindman's bluff game), the chief female protagonist, Amarilli, is blindfolded, and soon thereafter the cave scene leads to a tragicomedy of errors that brilliantly develops while further complicating the plot (the dark cave is itself a clear symbol of blindness). Finally, the happy resolution of the knot comes in a recognition scene in which it is literally a blind seer (Tireneo) who finally "sees" the truth and correctly interprets the intention of fate. In this context, the theatrically intriguing figure of Corisca, the chief manipulator of the play's events in an attempt to achieve her personal ends, takes on a new dimension and interest. The significance of this liberated female libertine cannot be limited to her espousal of free (unsentimental) and promiscuous love. In her role as the wily *ingannatrice* (deceiver), she is a veritable creator of illusions that ironically (because contrary to her aim) lead to truth. Thus, even she is "blind" and as much an *ingannata* (deceived) as *ingannatrice,* the blind instrument of that mysterious fate that guides men to foreordained and benign ends. Hence, in the *Pastor fido* we are face to face with the problem of knowledge and the role of the senses in the cognitive process. And, contrary to what one might expect, the senses are not faithful guides to knowledge—at least not those senses we most often rely on to form our concept of reality. Reason, moreover, rather than setting things straight, further confuses them. Thus, Guarini effects a transposition of values which is in direct conflict with Renaissance* Neo-Platonism* whose hierarchy of the senses placed sight and hearing at the top as the only noble senses, worthy of working in conjunction with reason in order to reach ever higher stages of knowledge. This order is reversed in the *Pastor fido* where sight and hearing have a dubious value and their relationship to reason is one of reciprocal deception. On the other hand, taste, smell, and touch are exalted as the only senses having a positive, tangible value leading to the fruition of beauty and even to truth.

In the world of Guarini's pastoral, the will of fate turns out to be in accord with the law of nature (or better, instinct softened by sentiment). But nothing within the power of reason can make us see that; indeed, it is the meddling intellect that brings us close to tragedy in the play. In this connection, the sense of irony which is woven into the dramatic structure is of the utmost importance. The author's imitation of the Sophoclean recognition scene *(Oedipus)* and his use of the fate motif have been judged harshly (and hastily) as a heavy-handed superimposition out of keeping with the spirit of the play—in short, a vulgar parody tolerable only if there were an ironic intention. While the ironic design is, in fact, there, to perceive it, one must be aware of the insistence, from beginning to end, on the themes discussed above. Then the whole last act, which brings in the blind seer and the recognition scene, fits in nicely as a crowning scene of benignly ironic intent. We know that Greek tragedy is often the story of human blindness and error leading to effects opposite from those intended, the truth of which is ironically revealed. Guarini purposefully traces this pattern throughout his pastoral. Greek tragedy was surely his chief model, but he converted the impending catastrophe into one more peripety and his play into a tragicomedy.

It would appear, then, that the *Pastor fido* suggests that the only stable and trustworthy value is the life of the instincts, although, as the play makes clear, even the instincts are not by themselves enough. What is exalted and what really leads to happiness is a sensually grounded love, but it is also accompanied (this too almost instinctively, as it were) by profound affection (sentimentality, if one likes) and heroic virtue. Indeed, the extraordinary attempt to integrate the heroic into the pastoral mode is another of the Baroque (some may say "manneristic") features of the *Pastor fido*. Where Tasso's *Aminta* put shepherds in love on a par with heroes (knights or courtiers) in the matter of refined sentiments and speech, Guarini went one step further and merged the *pastori* (the idyllic) and *eroi* (the heroic) in order to create a new type of pastoral hero and heroine (Amarilli is no less heroic than her suitor, Mirtillo, the male protagonist), just as he has mixed the tragic and the comic to make a new genre. This effort to give his pastoral a heroic cast brought the poet close to writing an allegory or parable. Especially in the case of Mirtillo, the figure of the faithful shepherd with his heroic constancy bringing him to choose martyrdom in the cause of salvation for others, there is a striking parallel with the figure of Christ—the *Pastor fido* and scapegoat par excellence. Yet, the fortunate fact is that in the play (though not in the *ex post facto* exegesis Guarini later wrote on it) neither Mirtillo nor Amarilli is idealized to such a degree that they lose their humanity and become mere aggregates of abstract moral or heroic virtues. It is love as a sentiment lived in its various manifestations—sensual, sentimental, and heroico-spiritual impulse—and with all its accompanying torments and its promise of ecstasy that saves them from that pitfall.

In his verse, Guarini's natural bent is towards a lyrico-pathetic vein. Yet, here too tone and lexicon, as well as the main plot, are often solemn or aulic and bespeak a connection with the heroic. Guarini himself theorized that the lofty style *(forma magnifica)* could be blended with a sweet or tender vein *(forma polita o dolce)* to create the tone suitable for a tragicomedy. This, in fact, is the "mixed style" he conceived as the ideal for the *Pastor fido*. At times, perhaps, the tender (but not lowly) manner predominates, even to the total exclusion of the lofty style. As an ideal fusion of the two styles, however, it is a perfect stylistic solution for the principal part of the play's *favola* (fable) which is, after all, concerned with a tale of love that partakes of both the pathetic and the heroic.

Bibliography: Opere di Battista Guarini, ed. Marziano Guglielminetti (Turin: UTET, 1971); *A Critical Edition of Sir Richard Fanshawe's 1647 Translation of Giovanni Battista Guarini's Il Pastor Fido,* eds. W. F. Staton, Jr., and W. E. Simeone (Oxford: Oxford University Press, 1964); *Il Pastor Fido,* ed. J. H.

Whitfield, trans. Richard Fanshawe (Austin, Tex.: University of Texas Press, 1976); Louise George Clubb, "The Moralist in Arcadia: England and Italy," *Romance Philology* 19 (1965), 340–52; Nicolas J. Perella, "Fate, Blindness and Illusion in the *Pastor Fido*," *Romanic Review* 49 (1958), 252–68, *The Critical Fortune of Battista Guarini's "Pastor Fido"* (Florence: Olschki, 1973), and "Heroic Virtue and Love in the *Pastor Fido*," *Atti dell'Istituto Veneto di Scienze, Lettere ed Arti* 132 (1974), 653–706; Vittorio Rossi, *Battista Guarini e il Pastor Fido* (Turin: Loescher, 1886).

Nicolas J. Perella

GUAZZO, STEFANO (1530–1593), courtier, ambassador, and writer. Born in Casale Monferrato into a rich and noble family which had always served the dukes of Mantua and Monferrato, Guazzo first studied law and then acted as secretary to the Duchess Margherita and to Duke Guglielmo. He also entered the service of Ludovico Gonzaga, later to become the duke of Nevers, and in that capacity he lived in France for seven years. In 1563, Duke Guglielmo sent Guazzo as ambassador to Charles IX of France; in 1566, he became ambassador to Pope Pius IV. Around 1561, Guazzo helped to found the Accademia degli Illustrati. After his marriage in 1566 to Francesca Da Ponte, he retired from public life and devoted most of his time to his literary pursuits.

Guazzo was the author of some Italian and Latin poetry, two collections of letters, various dialogues, and his masterpiece, *La civil conversatione* (1574, *The Civile Conversation*). Most of his works were known in Renaissance* England as well as in other European countries, although none of his works equaled the European reputation of his dialogue on manners and behavior in society. Like Castiglione's* *Book of the Courtier,* Guazzo's work appeared in four books (three written as dialogues, the fourth more in Castiglione's manner with a number of interlocutors) and discusses the problems of nobility, gentility, the place of women in society, proper language, humor, dress and fashion, the nature of love, and the relationship of the courtier to the prince. However, Guazzo's work is no mere imitation of Castiglione. His real interest lies in social reality rather than in appearances, he lacks Castiglione's nostalgic tone, and his concerns are more practical than theoretical. Throughout Europe, the term *civil conversation* came to encompass a whole range of social behavior far beyond the mere art of conversation. *La civil conversatione* received French, Latin, Dutch, Spanish, German, and English translations. The most influential English translation was done by George Pettie and Bartholomew Young; Pettie published the first three books in 1581 and Young introduced a complete version in 1586, which combined Pettie's work with Young's translation of book four.

See also CASTIGLIONE, Baldesar; DELLA CASA, Giovanni.

Bibliography: The Civile Conversation of M. Steeven Guazzo, trans. George Pettie and Bartholomew Young, 2 vols. (London: Constable, 1925); Thomas F. Crane, *Italian Social Customs of the Sixteenth Century and Their Influences on the Literatures of Europe* (New Haven, Conn.: Yale University Press, 1920); John L. Lievsay, *Stefano Guazzo and the English Renaissance, 1575–1675* (Chapel Hill, N.C.: University of North Carolina Press, 1961).

GUERRAZZI, FRANCESCO DOMENICO (1804–1873), novelist and patriot. Born in Livorno, Guerrazzi received a law degree but turned to literary pursuits. Meeting Lord Byron in Pisa at an early stage in his career influenced several early poems and inspired Guerrazzi to write verse in the Englishman's memory after his death. Having composed several tragedies and various essays, Guerrazzi turned to the historical novel, popularized in Italy by Sir Walter Scott and Alessandro Manzoni.* His early novel, *La battaglia di Benevento* (1828, *Manfred, or the Battle of Benevento*), combines the romantic sensibility for the medieval Italian past with an attack upon the union of temporal and spiritual power which had obvious contemporary implications for Italians living under Austrian or papal rule before Italian unification. His liberal tendencies became more pronounced when he edited a journal in Livorno with Mazzini* (1828–30). Arrested in 1832 and 1833 for his liberal political views, he wrote one of his best historical novels, *L'assedio di Firenze* (1836, The Siege of Florence) while in prison and published it in Paris under the pseudonym Anselmo Gualandi. The plot of this novel was complicated by intertwining several love stories with the story of the heroic republican forces resisting the invading Medici tyrants backed by their foreign troops. His other notable historical novels include *Isabella Orsini* (1844, *Isabella Orsini*), *Beatrice Cenci* (1854, *Beatrice Cenci*), and *Il buco nel muro* (1862, The Hole in the Wall). After Italian unification was assured, Guerrazzi was elected to Parliament, a post he held until 1870.

See also MANZONI, Alessandro; ROMANTICISM.

Bibliography: Beatrice Cenci, trans. Luigi Monti (New York: Rudd & Carleton, 1858); *Isabella Orsini*, trans. Luigi Monti (New York: Rudd & Carleton, 1859); *Manfred, or the Battle of Benevento*, trans. Luigi Monti (New York: Carleton, 1875); Madeleine Constable, "Anti-Heroic and Mock-Heroic Elements in the Later Novels of F. D. Guerrazzi," *Forum Italicum* 3 (1969), 213–31.

GUICCIARDINI, FRANCESCO (1483–1540), Florentine statesman, political thinker, essayist, and historian. Born into one of the most distinguished families of Florence and allied to another patrician family, the Salviati, by marriage in 1508, Guicciardini began his illustrious political career in 1511 when he was elected ambassador to King Ferdinand of Spain. After the fall of the republic and the return of the Medici to Florence in 1512–13,

Guicciardini was named governor of Modena by Pope Leo X. When the governorship of Reggio was added to this post in 1517, Guicciardini became one of the most important officials within the Papal States, at that time controlled by a Medici pope. A meeting with Niccolò Machiavelli* in Modena in 1521 gave birth to a close friendship between the two men, despite their different backgrounds and temperaments. After the death of Pope Leo X, Guicciardini was named president of Romagna by another Medici pope, Clement VII. In 1527, he became lieutenant general of the papal forces in the League of Cognac, formed against Emperor Charles V, only to result in the Sack of Rome the same year, the second expulsion of the Medici from Florence, and the reestablishment of a republic in that city. Pope Clement charged Guicciardini with the task of reforming Florence after the republic's fall in 1530 and named him governor of Bologna. When Clement died in 1534, Guicciardini became the political advisor to Duke Alessandro de' Medici who was assassinated in 1537. Although Guicciardini was instrumental in the ascension of Cosimo de' Medici to succeed Alessandro, the new ruler resented his prestige, and Guicciardini retired from politics. This retirement gave him the opportunity to complete his major political and historical works, a task which occupied him until his death.

Guicciardini's various treatises, histories, and political essays represent one of the most significant bodies of such literature to be written during the Italian Renaissance,* comparable in scope, if not in influence, to those of his better known friend Machiavelli. His importance has been continually underrated because many of his works were left unpublished at his death and did not appear in print until the nineteenth century. His first major work, left unfinished and untitled after 1509, is now known as *Storie fiorentine (The History of Florence)*. It presents an interpretation of Florentine history from 1378 until 1509 based on the patrician point of view, as well as a critique of Medici hegemony and the subsequent loss of Florentine liberty. Its relative independence from classical or Renaissance Latin models gives this work a freshness of style which still makes it interesting reading. Guicciardini defines 1494 as a turning point in Florentine history and begins to formulate the theoretical concept of the balance of power implicit in his analysis of how Florence became the fulcrum of Italy under Lorenzo de' Medici's* policies. The most interesting literary passages in the history are Guicciardini's character sketches of three historical figures: Cosimo and Lorenzo de' Medici and Girolamo Savonarola.*

Guicciardini's minor political treatises are crucial to understanding the intellectual debate which resulted from the political upheavals in Florence as republican government alternated with Medici rule between 1494 and 1530. Two essays, the *Discorso di Logrogno* (1512, Discourse of Logrogno) and the *Dialogo del Reggimento di Firenze* (1521–25, Dialogue on the Government of Florence), deal with the proper organization of a Florentine state. Of more interest, however, are Guicciardini's *Considerazioni sui Discorsi del Machiavelli (Considerations on the 'Discourses' of Machiavelli)* and his *Ricordi (Maxims and Reflections)*, neither of which was published in its entirety during his lifetime. Only with the appearance of his complete works in 1857–67 did scholars appreciate their importance. The first work, composed in 1529–30, is a commentary upon thirty-eight chapters of Machiavelli's *Discourses* which Guicciardini saw in manuscript form. It is the first incisive theoretical response to Machiavelli's political theory in Western Europe. Guicciardini attacks central tenets of Machiavelli's political philosophy—that social conflict can be productive in a society and that the people are important guardians of a state's liberty. His pessimistic, sometimes cynical approach to the possibilities of human action, as opposed to Machiavelli's optimistic faith in man's capacity for change, continues in the *Ricordi,* a collection of maxims and observations begun in 1513, revised several times, and finally completed in 1530. Besides rejecting Machiavelli's belief in the imitation of the ancients and in the didactic purpose of history, Guicciardini's two hundred and twenty-one maxims assert his view that self-interest is the guiding force in human history. In such a universe, experience is a better guide for conduct than lessons from the past or abstract theory, and discretion serves man better than virtue. As a practical statesman with a businessman's preference for conciseness, Guicciardini was naturally drawn to the form of the maxim. Its structure and terseness perfectly suited a mind which rejected the grand speculative designs of political philosophy.

The only work by Guicciardini which appeared in the sixteenth century and which alone sufficed to establish his reputation among his contemporaries was his monumental *Storia d'Italia* (1561–64, *The History of Italy*), a book of European scope dealing with the events in Italy between 1490 and 1534. A masterpiece of humanist historiography and a forerunner of modern methods of research in its concern for accuracy, its adherence to critical standards, and its use of primary sources, the work is still used as a sourcebook for Renaissance history. Of greatest interest for world literature are the extremely influential descriptions of the Borgias (descriptions which are responsible for many of the false rumors about their evil deeds), as well as the brilliant literary portraits of the two Medici popes Leo X and Clement VII.

See also MACHIAVELLI, Niccolò.

Bibliography: The History of Florence, trans. Mario Domandi (New York: Harper, 1970); *The History of Italy,* trans. Sidney Alexander (New York: Macmillan, 1973); *Maxims and Reflections [Ricordi],* trans. Mario Domandi (Philadelphia: University of Pennsylvania Press, 1972); *Selected Writings,* ed.

Cecil Grayson (London: Oxford University Press, 1965); Peter E. Bondanella, *Francesco Guicciardini* (Boston: Twayne, 1976); Felix Gilbert, *Machiavelli and Guicciardini: Politics and History in Sixteenth-Century Florence* (Princeton, N.J.: Princeton University Press, 1965); Mark Phillips, *Francesco Guicciardini: The Historian's Craft* (Toronto: University of Toronto Press, 1977); J. G. A. Pocock, *The Machiavellian Moment: Florentine Political Thought and the Atlantic Republican Tradition* (Princeton, N.J.: Princeton University Press, 1975); Roberto Ridolfi, *The Life of Francesco Guicciardini* (New York: Knopf, 1968).

GUIDO DELLE COLONNE (circa 1210–after 1287), poet of the Sicilian School. Guido was probably a jurist by profession; fifteen judicial decisions between 1243 and 1280 are attributed to him. It cannot be determined if he belonged to the Roman family. A small *canzoniere* of five poems, one whose authorship is uncertain, is extant and shows the influence of the Provençal poets as well as his fellow Sicilians. In *De vulgari eloquentia,* Dante honors him as one of the *doctores indigenas* (native teachers) of Sicily (II,v) and quotes two of his *canzoni** as examples of the eloquence possible in the vernacular. "Amor, che lungiamente m'hai menato" ("O Love, who all this while hast urged me on"), twice cited by Dante and translated by Rossetti,* celebrates not the beauty of the lady but the lover's pain. The conventional lover addresses the god of love, who, he says, is driving him on, mercilessly never slackening the reins. Love is a "dolze pena," a "sweet sorrow," and the lover, certain of death, pleads with the lady to temper her pride with compassion. He complains that loving in silence is an additional burden for a troubled heart. In "Ancor che l'aigua per lo foco lassi" ("Though water relinquishes through fire"), also cited by Dante, Guido draws elaborate parallels between natural phenomena and the experiences of love, increasing the complexity of poetry conventional in its expression of the lover's joys and torments. Differing from the earlier poetry of the Sicilian School, Guido's *canzoni* are characterized by a more refined diction and a more polished style. The subtlety of language, the conceptual complexity, and the imagery presage Guittone d'Arezzo* and Guido Cavalcanti.*

Guido is also considered the author of the *Historia destructionis Troiae (History of the Destruction of Troy)*. It was completed in November 1287, according to the epilogue, and played a significant role in popularizing the legends of Troy throughout Europe. Guido claims that his version, his only extant prose work, is an authentic historical account of the Trojan War based upon the eyewitness accounts of Dictys of Crete and Dares the Phrygian. Actually, it is a freely reworked and condensed adaptation in Latin prose of the French romance in verse, the *Roman de Troie* (circa 1160) of Benôit de Sainte-Maure. Composed at the behest of the bishop of Salerno, the *Historia* is a synthesis of all the legends of Troy which interested Europeans who believed that Aeneas and other Trojan refugees had colonized Europe. Guido's *Historia,* believed to be authentic until the eighteenth century, exemplifies traditional medieval notions of historiography which held that poets could be cited as authorities, that all other sources must be referred to, that history must be written in a dignified and rhetorical style, preferably in Latin, and that it must have a Christian moral and philosophical content. Consequently, it contains scholarly as well as moralistic digressions on human failing, pride, and folly. Guido probably believed that he was restoring the romanticized version of Benôit to its original historical mode. His skepticism about the benefits of the Trojan War, a war fought for questionable reasons, no doubt reflected certain contemporary problems.

The *Historia* had a widely successful reception abroad and was rendered into French, German, English, Spanish, Flemish, Bohemian, Czech, and Italian. Raoul le Fèvre included it in his *Recueil des Histoires de Troie,* and Caxton's prose translation (1474–75) of Raoul's version, the first book he printed and the first book printed in England, served as a source for Shakespeare's *Troilus and Cressida* (1601–02). Lydgate's *Troy Book* (1412–21) provided a metrical paraphrase of the work, sometimes showing Benôit's influence. Chaucer commemorates Guido in the *Hous of Fame* (III.379) and probably made some use of the *Historia* in *Troilus and Criseyde* (circa 1385), as had his primary source, Boccaccio,* in his *Filostrato* (1335–36, Prostrated by Love).

Bibliography: Historia Destructionis Troiae, trans. Mary Elizabeth Meek (Bloomington, Ind.: Indiana University Press, 1974); *Le rime della scuola siciliana,* ed. Bruno Panvini (Florence: Olschki, 1962); Frederick Goldin, *German and Italian Lyrics of the Middle Ages* (Garden City, N.Y.: Doubleday, 1973); Raffaele Chiantera, *Guido delle Colonne* (Naples: Le Monnier, 1955).

GUINIZZELLI, GUIDO (circa 1240–circa 1276), poet. From a document in which his widow, Beatrice della Fratta, is given custody of a minor child, Guiduccio, it can be deduced that Guinizzelli died before 1276. The date of Guinizzelli's birth is uncertain, some scholars placing it around 1230, but this would mean that Guido was the same age as Guittone d'Arezzo,* whom Guido calls "padre." It is probable that he died very young. Because of a remark of Benvenuto da Imola (1330–90) in his commentary upon the *Divine Comedy,* this poet was long thought to be a son of Guinizzello da Bartolomeo, descendant from a family of princes and *podestà* of Castelfranco. Modern investigation proves, however, that Guido was the son of Guinizzello da Magnano and Guglielmina di Ugolino Chisleri. His name, as that of a judge, appears in some legal documents in Bologna, beginning from 1266. Guinizzelli took an active part in the political life of the Ghibelline party, controlled by the powerful Lambertazzi family. When the Guelph party defeated the opposing faction (1274), Guinizzelli went into exile at Monselice.

Of Guinizzelli's poetic production, a slim corpus of fifteen sonnets* and five *canzoni** has come down to us. Two short fragments of two songs, otherwise unknown, are found in the *Reggimento e costumi di donna* (circa 1309–13, Behavior and Habits of Women) by Francesco da Barberino (1264–1348). Three other songs—"In quanto la natura," ("Since nature / and instruction"), "Con gran disio" (With great desire), and "Donna, lo fino amore" (Lady, true love)—are doubtfully attributed to him.

Guinizzelli's fame rests mainly on the fact that he is considered a precursor, if not exactly a member, of the school of the *dolce stil nuovo.** Dante* seems to consider him as such both in the *De vulgari eloquentia* (I, ix, 3; II, v, 4) and in the famous episode of *Purgatory* XXVI. There is no doubt, however, that Guinizzelli's first poetical steps moved within the well-established "maniera guittoniana" (Guittonian manner): some themes (the torment of love, the nobility of pure love, the lady's pride) as well as some stylistic features depend strictly on the Guittonian teaching (see, for instance, the songs "Tegno de folle 'mpresa,"—I hold his conduct foolish—or "Madonna, il fino amore"—Lady, true love). But with the song "Al cor gentil rempaira sempre amore" ("Love seeks its dwelling always in the gentle heart"), Guinizzelli seems to deviate from the themes prescribed by the Guittonian school. In this poem, generally considered the manifesto of the *dolce stil nuovo,* Guinizzelli maintains that only a virtuous heart can be brought to perfection by a love for a woman who participates in the nature of divinity since she has the appearance of an angel. Some famous sonnets, like "Vedut'ho la lucente stella diana ("I have seen the shining morning star"), "I' voglio del ver la mia donna laudare" ("My Lady I most truly want to praise"), and "Lo vostro bel saluto" ("The handsome greeting and gentle look"), accentuate even further the departure from the old modes: new stylistic achievements and new themes, like the "saluto-salutifero" and the "loda." Both Bonagiunta degli Orbicciani* ("Voi ch'avete mutato la mainera," "You who have changed the manner") and Guittone* himself ("S'eo tale fosse," If I were such) denounced this intent to deviate from tradition.

This heterodoxy should not be understood as a systematic and coherent new program, but rather as an occasional and casual introduction of some new themes, a lightening of style, and a set of new images which were later programmatically absorbed and developed by the *dolce stil nuovo* whose poets had a much stronger awareness of their distance from the old school. Without operating a full revolution, Guinizzelli was able to infuse the old worn-out language with a fresh vein of sentiment and doctrine. The beauty of his compositions, which are almost classical, as well as the serene rigor of interpreting a psychological complexity, make him worthy of the high praise Dante bestowed upon him.

See also DOLCE STIL NUOVO; GUITTONE D'AREZZO.

Bibliography: Poeti del Duecento, ed. Gianfranco Contini, Vol. 2 (Milan: Ricciardi, 1960); *German and Italian Lyrics of the Middle Ages,* trans. Frederick Goldin (Garden City, N.Y.: Doubleday, 1973); *The Age of Dante: An Anthology of Early Italian Poetry,* trans. Joseph Tusiani (New York: Baroque Press, 1974).

Paolo Cherchi

GUITTONE D'AREZZO (circa 1230–1294), lyric and didactic poet. There is little biographical information on Guittone other than what can be gleaned from his writings. He was born near Arezzo, and his father, Viva di Michele, is mentioned in a letter as a public official, a receiver of public monies. Evidently involved in some commercial enterprise, Guittone traveled widely. Troubled by the discord within Arezzo and having taken the part of the Guelphs, he remained in exile after 1256 because he opposed those who controlled Arezzo. Accordingly, he laments the defeat of the Florentine Guelphs at Montaperti in 1260 in one of the earliest political lyrics before Dante,* "Ahi lasso, or è stagion de doler tanto," ("Alas, This is the time when everyone/ must sorely grieve"). In 1266, a spiritual crisis led him to abandon his wife and three sons and to join the Cavalieri di Santa Maria (Knights of the Blessed Virgin Mary), also called the *frati gaudenti* (merry friars), an allusion to their wordly interests, of which Guittone actively disapproved. During his restless travels to cities such as Pisa, Bologna, and Florence, Guittone became an intimate of important politicians and men of letters. In 1293, he made a substantial donation to the construction in Florence of the monastery of the Camaldosian friars, with the stipulation that the brothers care for him until his death.

The central figure of the second important school of Italian poetry, the Tuscan, Guittone attracted a group of followers including Meo Abbracciavacca (died circa 1313), Panuccio del Bagno* and la Compiuta Donzella,* who called themselves *guittoniani* and who emulated his style and techniques with varying degrees of success. As the most prominent lyricist of his time, he became a target for the rebellion of the new generation. In *De vulgari eloquentia* (I,xiii; II,vi) and in *Purgatory* (XXIV:55, 57 and XXVI:124–26), Dante disparages the language of Guittone and the other Tuscans as plebeian and prone to excess, a style appreciated only by the vulgar or the ignorant. Despite such disclaimers, Dante began by imitating Guittone's style and only later renounced it for the simpler and more graceful diction of the best Sicilians. In searching for his own stylistic mode, Dante no doubt found it profitable to break away from the dominant poetic influence of the time.

Although Dante's opinions colored the judgments of following generations, it is no longer possible to ignore Guittone's efforts in continuing the Italian lyric tradition and in developing the vernacular. At the decline of the

Sicilian School, he rejuvenated the art of writing poetry. The language of his early love poetry is characterized by a more extensive use of Provençal and Latin terms than that of the Sicilians. It is richer in the rhetorical figures and more complex periods characteristic of the traditions of the Latin and medieval rhetorics. Bound by political, economic, social, and religious conventions which differed from those of Provence or Sicily, Guittone adapted the older forms and styles, which originally reflected the ideals of courtly service, to an ethos which reflected the values of the citizenry of the Italian cities who lauded ambition, self-sufficiency, energy, and achievement based upon merit rather than upon inheritance and the privileges of rank.

A prolific writer, Guittone has left some fifty *canzoni,* * two hundred and fifty-one sonnets,* eight poetic epistles, and thirty-six letters. His poetry can be divided into two parts to distinguish the poetry written before his conversion from that following it. The earlier half of his *canzoniere* shows the influence of courtly poetry. His style is learned and obscure, perhaps reflecting his temperament, his cultural formation, and the problems besetting a writer of a still new poetic language. However, his horizons were not restricted to the ideals of *fin'amor,* for sensual and worldly motifs and a group of poems dealing with the art of love broaden the scope of his *canzoniere.* Unlike the courtly poets, Guittone seldom neglects the natural and sensual aspects of human love, and he permits realistic elements to intrude upon the ideals of *fin'amor.* On one hand, this distortion of the courtly inspiration may account for Dante's harsh reaction; on the other, it clarifies the historical importance of a poet who explores more complex reactions than his earlier counterparts. The second half of his *canzoniere* reflects his spiritual experiences and presents religious, moral, and political arguments. He writes of political events, his vocation as a brother, his repudiation of youthful pleasures, his hope for political harmony, and his desire to direct others to lives of virtue.

Guittone's letters, also inspired by biographical situations, were directed to friends and disciples. In general, Guittone's style is related to the attitudes of his poems and letters; it is ardent, tortuous, rhetorical, full of exhortations and moral counsel, and is often marked by logical progression. His contemporaries and the poets of later generations constantly reworked the moralistic and political themes he developed.

Bibliography: Le Rime di Guittone d'Arezzo, ed. Francesco Egidi (Bari: Laterza, 1940); *German and Italian Lyrics of the Middle Ages,* trans. Frederick Goldin (Garden City, N.Y.: Doubleday, 1973); *The Age of Dante: An Anthology of Early Italian Poetry,* trans. Joseph Tusiani (New York: Baroque Press, 1974); Claude Margueron, *Recherches sur Guittone d'Arezzo: sa vie, son époque, sa culture* (Paris: Presses Universitaires, 1966); Vincent Moleta, *The Early Poetry of Guittone D'Arezzo* (London: Modern Humanities Research Association, 1976).

H

HERMETICISM *(Ermetismo),* a critical term used to describe a central tendency in modern Italian poetry which derived from Hermes Trismegistus, supposedly the author of occult works which were "closed" in their meaning to all but the initiated. Francesco Flora (1891–1962) popularized the term in reference to certain major twentieth-century poets, chiefly Ungaretti,* Montale,* and the young Quasimodo,* in *La poesia ermetica* (1936, Hermetic Poetry). Its origins were traced to the French symbolists (particularly Mallarmé) as well as to the native poets Arturo Onofri (1885–1928) and Dino Campana.* The poetry thus described tends to rely upon a nonrhetorical or antirhetorical language, an essentially poetic idiom stressing analogies rather than similarities between ideas and images, an intuitional rather than a strictly logical or narrative form of discourse. Sometimes called "pure" or "naked" poetry, *poesia ermetica* reflects a desire to exploit the word's entire potential, its suggestive power and its musicality as well as its traditional meanings and symbolism. Because of its complicated poetics, hermetic poetry came to be associated with the merely intricate or obscure, since the analogical language employed in a subjective manner by the individual poets seemed totally unlike traditional verse. The passage of time has proved this common notion of hermeticism superficial, for the works which seemed so difficult when they first appeared in print now seem more accessible.

Although some critics view hermeticism's "closed" nature as a response to the censorship of the fascist regime, recent criticism tends to define the hermetic current in contemporary verse as a positive and authentic response to a general crisis of philosophical and literary values in our times which is not necessarily related to a specific political setting. Besides Montale, Ungaretti, and Quasimodo, the poets often associated with this type of verse include Gatto,* Luzi,* Penna,* Sinisgalli,* and Betocchi,* to mention only the most prominent.

Bibliography: Luciano Anceschi, *Le poetiche del Novecento in Italia* (Turin: Paravia, 1973); Giovanni Cecchetti, "The Poetry of the Past and the Poetry of the Present," *Forum Italicum* 10 (1976), 159–77; Francesco Flora, *La poesia ermetica* (Bari: Laterza, 1936); Silvio Ramat, *L'ermetismo* (Florence: La Nuova Italia, 1969).

HUMANISM. Like every major movement in the history of Western thought, humanism is susceptible to various interpretations and definitions. It is perhaps best to begin, as P. O. Kristeller does, by stating that the humanist believed that an education based on the reading of classical literature had the power to "liberate" man and to form him spiritually. This optimistic view of the educability of man and the efficacy of letters constitutes the single factor that united all humanists. It also enables us to think of humanism as a period which began approximately with Petrarch* who is usually considered to be its first great exponent. This belief in education is related to the idea that man is free to make of himself what he desires. This view is powerfully presented by Pico della Mirandola* in his *Oratio de hominis dignitate (Oration on the Dignity of Man),* where man's chief characteristic, the freedom to rise towards heaven or descend towards the beast, is coupled with the responsibility for the choice and its results. It is in this context that the *studia humanitatis* are formulated and that faith in their capacity to liberate man grows. Man must be given an education which will permit him to make the proper choice, a human choice. The great accomplishments of man as contained in literature provide the individual with both a model and an inspiration for his own spiritual growth.

The concept of a model of greatness to be found in antiquity brings us to a second often debated and misunderstood belief of the humanists, their faith in imitation, and to their equally controversial classicism, often debated as either a static or dynamic process. Some critics state that the humanists' faith in imitation led to a sterile, unimaginative production, that their assumption that the ancients had reached an unsurpassable greatness in all things resulted in slavish imitation in the hope of approaching their heights through repetition. In condemning humanism for lack of creativity, such critics seem to forget that it was one of the most fecund movements in Western intellectual history and that the achievements of the later Renaissance* in all fields were a direct consequence of the labors and imagination of the humanists. In a beautiful and precise discussion of style and imitation in his *Familiarium rerum libri,* I, 8; XX, 2 *(Letters on Familiar Matters),* Petrarch stressed that imitation was the father of creativity and originality. He did not advocate, nor did most later humanists, the slavish reproduction of models, but rather the recovery of our spiritual heritage as the foundation for growth. The humanist concept is one of an ever-growing and -changing culture and civilization. It is only when we have mastered the past and taken possession of our heritage that we can continue the process of culture and be ourselves, that is, original. Imitation means assimilation, the recreation of man's history, the reliving of human experience so that from the encounter of past and present the future may spring forth new and old at the same time. We do not reproduce the ancients,

Petrarch states, but re-create. The resemblance is that of a child to his father: the old may be seen in the new, but it is transformed.

Far from being slavish imitators of the ancients, the humanists were responsible for dethroning the ancients from their exalted position. While some medieval thinkers looked upon certain ancient philosophers as the possessors of a truth which they had found and established for all time, the humanists insisted on placing the works of these same philosophers in an historical context, thus abolishing any claim to a universal definitive truth. Through the use of philology, which supplied the means for historical reconstruction, it came to be seen that all philosophers responded to the problems of their own times and that Aristotle, "the master of those who know," was tied to his period rather than being the philosopher for all time who had left to his successors the interpretation of his "truth" as the only possible task. It was because he could not accept this "truth" that Petrarch took up arms against Aristotle, not to destroy his achievements, but to affirm his own intellectual freedom and his concept of truth as a continuous conquest and challenge to human thought. From Petrarch's first steps, the humanists proceeded to a point where they could propose a new logic to supplant the old. Aristotle was dead, thought alive.

It is in this sense that the humanists rediscovered antiquity, but not in the way Jacob Burckhardt thought. It was not a question of discovering or recovering ancient tracts and learning ancient truths which the Middle Ages had ignored, thus bringing the ancients back to life and supplanting a Christian view with theirs. The discovery consisted in insisting on the necessity for the philological reconstruction of these texts and placing them in their proper historical context. It was not the physical discovery of codices, but the discovery of history which redimensioned human life and thought. It was philology which dared question not only Aristotle, but also the Scriptures.

The new sense of history, which opened such broad vistas to the humanists, could logically be expected to bring about many fundamental changes in attitude. It led to the concept of *homo faber,* of man as the maker of history. Man's activities on earth were seen as a glorious opportunity and duty, not as punishment for an original sin and consequent fall. Man's attention should not be directed to the explanation of a Divine design and will which, at best, would remain unfathomable. Was it not presumptuous for man to attempt to understand and explain matters which, being Divine, were not susceptible to penetration by the human mind? He should operate within the realm of his own nature and attempt to understand those matters which fell within its province. Thus, the focus of attention shifted to man and his actions and creations here on earth, chief among which were the state and society.

Every aspect of human experience on this earth came under the scrutiny of the humanists, who were anxious to understand man's world. As a result, there came into being an entire literature comprising treatises on every phase of man's activities: the family, civic government, the art of painting, marriage, and so forth. These treatises have a common outlook in that they concentrate not on the nature of things, but on how to do them. In Alberti's* *Libri della Famiglia (The Albertis of Florence: Leon Battista Alberti's Della Famiglia),* we see how a well-run family operates, the dangers it may encounter, and how they are to be avoided. In Machiavelli's* *Prince,* we do not find a justification for the state, but rather guidelines on how a prince must act if he wishes to preserve his domain. It is not the nature of friendship that interests Alberti, as it had Cicero, but how to make friends and use them. It is the art of a successful life on this earth that is under discussion.

Two fundamental themes concerning life on this earth are usually prominent in the works of these humanists: the social aspect of life and the question of *vita activa* versus *vita contemplativa.* These aspects are amply discussed in Alberti's *Libri della Famiglia.* It is inconceivable to him that a man could live for himself without considering his relationship and obligations to other men to be of paramount importance. It is man's purpose to be as useful as possible to the greatest number of men possible. In the design of nature, everything exists for the good of the whole. Can man fall outside this scheme and break nature's harmony? Not if he wishes to consider himself a man. Should he fail in these obligations, he gives up all claims to the name of man. And of course these obligations fully imply participation in the *vita activa.* As Alberti says, man was not born to rust in idleness, but to be active and useful to others. Over and over again, Alberti and other humanists point to the inventors and great practitioners of the arts as the heroes of mankind, for they have given man the means to live a good life. It is the duty of the strong to help the weak, to form the state so that everyone has the possibility of leading a full, useful life; man cannot live for himself alone.

Petrarch, too, had been concerned with the question. It has been said, erroneously, that Petrarch championed the *vita contemplativa,* because of the poet's insistent call for solitude, a call which has been interpreted as being the equivalent, more or less, of a monastic withdrawal from the world. Nothing is less true. The call to solitude and contemplation is the invitation to look within ourselves and find the true essence of humanity, but only because that knowledge will enable us to understand and reach out to our fellow man. It is not an invitation to isolation, but the most effective way of making contact, regardless of any limitations of time and place.

Humanism, then, was an education for life, the building of a new society and a new world through the recovery of man's sense of obligation towards his fellow man. Most of all, it was the recognition of man's nature, the limitations of that nature, and the effort to overcome them through the sacred office of letters which enabled him to break the bonds of time and place and converse, as Eugenio Garin puts it, with his predecessors as well as with posterity.

See also ALBERTI, Leon Battista; BEMBO, Pietro; BOCCACCIO, Giovanni; BRACCIOLINI, Poggio; BRUNI, Leonardo; DELLA MIRANDOLA, Giovanni Pico; ENEA SILVIO PICCOLOMINI; FICINO, Marsilio; GUICCIARDINI, Francesco; LANDINO, Cristoforo; LORENZO DE' MEDICI; MACHIAVELLI, Niccolò; PETRARCA, Francesco; POLIZIANO, Angelo; PONTANO, Giovanni; RENAISSANCE; SALUTATI, Coluccio; VALLA, Lorenzo; VITTORINO DA FELTRE.

Bibliography: Jacob Burckhardt, *The Civilization of the Renaissance in Italy* (New York: New American Library, 1960); Eugenio Garin, *Italian Humanism*, trans. Peter Munz (1955; rpt. Westport, Conn.: Greenwood Press, 1975), *Medioevo e Rinascimento* (Bari: Laterza, 1954), and *L'educazione in Europa: 1400–1600* (Bari: Laterza, 1957); Myron P. Gilmore, *The World of Humanism: 1453–1517* (New York: Harper & Row, 1952); Paul Oskar Kristeller, *Renaissance Thought II: Papers on Humanism and the Arts* (New York: Harper & Row, 1965); Giuseppe Saitta, *L'Umanesimo* (Firenze: Sansoni, 1961); Charles Trinkaus, *Adversity's Noblemen* (New York: Octagon Books, 1965).

Guido Guarino

J

JACOBUS DE VARAGINE: *See* JACOPO DA VARAZZE.

JACOPO DA VARAZZE or **DA VARAGINE** (circa 1230–1298), Dominican monk, archbishop of Genoa, and author of saints' lives and religious texts. By 1244, Jacopo had become a member of the Dominican order. Having been appointed archbishop of Genoa, he managed to make peace between the warring Guelph and Ghibelline factions of the city, although his talents were primarily those of the scholar and priest. Among his writings are several Latin sermons, a discussion of the historical and religious backgrounds of Genoa, and his masterpiece, the *Legenda Aurea (The Golden Legend),* a collection of one hundred and eighty-two stories, of which one hundred and forty-nine are saints' lives and the rest, treatments of the lives of Christ and the Virgin Mary. Apparently written some time before 1267, the book quickly became the most renowned of such pious collections and had an enormous impact throughout Western Europe. In the fifteenth century alone, shortly after the diffusion of printing, more than one hundred and fifty editions appeared, making it the most popular printed book after the Bible. As a result of the English version based upon an earlier French translation published by William Caxton in 1483, it has a central place in the history of English literature and printing. Numerous artists were inspired by its pages, possibly including Giotto, Fra Angelico, Piero della Francesca, Carpaccio, and countless others. Even today, popular notions of the Christian saints are significantly indebted to Jacopo's vivid descriptions of their actions. Learned poets (such as Boccaccio* in his *Filocolo,* 1336?, Love's Labor) as well as more humble and devout readers turned to the work for inspiration. Rarely has a single book exerted so much influence as this compendium, whose author was canonized at the beginning of the nineteenth century.

Bibliography: Jacobi a Voragine Legenda aurea vulgo Historia lombardica dicta, ed. J. G. Theodor Grasse (1890; rpt. Osnabruck: O. Zeller, 1965); *The Golden Legend of Jacobus de Voragine,* trans. Granger Ryant and Helmut Ripperger (New York: Longmans, 1948); *The Golden Legend; or, Lives of the Saints, as Englished by William Caxton,* 7 vols. (London: Dent, 1928–39).

JAHIER, PIERO (1884–1966), novelist and poet. Jahier was born in Genoa and was of Waldensian extraction. When his father, an evangelical minister

employed by Count Piero Guicciardini in Florence as his librarian, committed suicide, Jahier fell into dire economic straits but managed to attend
the *liceo* and a seminary in Florence. After he obtained a post with the state
railroads which enabled him to pursue his literary interests, he became an
important contributor to and, eventually, the director of *La Voce*. With his
religious background, Jahier was strongly attracted by the works of the
French writers Péguy and Claudel (whom he was first in Italy to translate).
He also translated a number of other writers, including Julien Green,
Joseph Conrad, Graham Greene, Robert Louis Stevenson, and Molière.
Some of his early poetry appeared in the futurist review *Lacerba* and
favored intervention in the war against Germany and Austria, a conflict
Jahier envisioned as a struggle between a mechanical, bureaucratic German culture and a more individualistic Italian way of life. This hatred for
bureaucracy and its leveling effects permeates his first novel, *Resultanze
in merito alla vita e al carattere di Gino Bianchi* (1915, The Outcome
Concerning the Life and Character of Gino Bianchi), a work which presents a bitter satire of the dehumanizing effects of bureaucracy. A lieutenant in the Alpine troops from 1915 until the end of the war, Jahier wrote
a perceptive account of his life in the trenches (partly in prose and partly in
verse) entitled *Con me e con gli alpini* (1919, With Me and the Alpine
Troops), which was followed by another novel, *Ragazzo* (1919, Boy), an
autobiographical work also in verse and prose which evokes the author's
adolescence and family life. With the advent of fascism, Jahier's political
ideals obliged him to cease writing, but he continued to work for the
railroad and turned primarily to the task of translation. He took an active
part in the struggles of the partisans against the Nazis and fascists in 1945.
At the war's end, he returned to writing poetry, essays, and prose for
several literary periodicals, although his works never reached the level of
his early achievements.

Bibliography: Poesie (Florence: Vallecchi, 1965); *Ragazzo–Con me e con gli alpini*
(Florence: Vallecchi, 1967); *Resultanze in merito alla vita e al carattere di Gino
Bianchi* (Florence: Vallecchi, 1966); Paolo Briganti, *Piero Jahier* (Florence: La
Nuova Italia, 1976); Alberto Giordano, *Invito alla lettura di Piero Jahier* (Milan:
Mursia, 1973); Antonio Testa, *Piero Jahier* (Milan: Mursia, 1970).

JOVINE, FRANCESCO (1902–1950), novelist and writer of short stories.
Jovine was born in Guardialfiera, Campobasso. Despite the poverty of his
origins, he obtained a teacher's certificate and a degree in philosophy,
eventually becoming a university *assistente* and a headmaster (a post he
held until his untimely death in the prime of his career). His first work was a
novel entitled *Un uomo provvisorio* (1934, A Temporary Man), but he
attracted the greatest popular and critical attention with a later work,
Signora Ava (1942, *Seeds in the Wind*), a title which refers not to the

novel's protagonist but to a figure in a popular southern Italian song. The novel treats the end of Bourbon rule and the beginnings of unified Italy in the Molise region; its negative judgment of the aftermath of the Risorgimento was unanticipated during the fascist epoch. During this period of his life, Jovine had the opportunity to meet some notable Roman writers and intellectuals (Renato Guttuso, 1912– ; Carlo Levi*; and Giacomo Debenedetti, 1901–67), many of whom were antifascist. He took part in the resistance, and later, in 1948, joined the Communist party. His best known novel, *Le terre del Sacramento* (1950, *The Estate in Abruzzi*), appeared posthumously and was awarded the Viareggio Prize in 1950. The book is set in southern Italy at the time of the march on Rome; its title refers to lands taken from the church in 1867 and now avoided by the superstitious peasants. The protagonist of the book, Luca Marano, resembles Jovine in some respects, for he has managed to rise above his penurious estate and to earn a university education. Although killed in a fight with the fascist authorities, Marano embodies Jovine's ideals for social reform in the countryside and the possibility of moral regeneration in Italy after the fascist debacle.

Bibliography: Racconti (Turin: Einaudi, 1960); *Signora Ava* (Turin: Einaudi, 1966); *Le terre del Sacramento* (Turin: Einaudi, 1962); *The Estate in Abruzzi,* trans. Archibald Colquhoun (London: Macgibbon & Key, 1952); *Seeds in the Wind,* trans. Adrienne Foulke (New York: Roy, 1946); Massimo Grillandi, *Francesco Jovine* (Milan: Mursia, 1971); Eugenio Ragni, *Francesco Jovine* (Florence: La Nuova Italia, 1972).

L

LANDINO, CRISTOFORO (1424–1498), humanist and poet. After studying law at Volterra, Landino came to Florence in 1439 and held the chair of poetry and rhetoric at the university (Studio fiorentino) after 1458. One of the most eminent poets and intellectuals who gathered in Lorenzo de' Medici's* court and a member of the Platonic Academy, he became chancellor of the Florentine Republic in 1467.

Most of Landino's notable philosophical and literary compositions are in Latin. An early work, a collection of Latin elegies entitled *Xandra* (1443–44, Xandra), was named after the woman celebrated in the poetry and dedicated to Leon Battista Alberti.* Of most consequence, besides several philosophical treatises in the Neo-Platonic tradition, was the Latin *Disputationes Camaldulenses,* (1480, Debates at Camaldoli), written in four books and depicting an imaginary gathering at the monastery of Camaldoli which lasted for four days during 1468. Lorenzo de' Medici, Ficino,* and Alberti are among the members of the group whose conversation probes the relative merits of the active and the contemplative life. The argument concludes that each is equally necessary but that contemplation should precede action. Landino's commentaries on Virgil and Petrarch,* as well as a commentary and biography on Dante,* are worthy of note. The 1481 edition of the *Commedia* and the accompanying commentary is Landino's principal work in Italian; its preface provides an interesting treatment of the origin and ends of poetry. The work was initially designed to contain an engraving by Botticelli for each *canto,* although only nineteen engravings were ever completed. Landino defended the vernacular, although he usually wrote in Latin himself. He praised the Italian of writers like Alberti and Matteo Palmieri,* and he believed that a thorough knowledge of Latin was necessary to write good Tuscan. He is also remembered through one of Ghirlandaio's frescoes which portrays him in the church of Santa Maria Novella in Florence.

Bibliography: Testi inediti e rari di Cristoforo Landino e Francesco Filelfo, ed. Eugenio Garin (Florence: Fussi, 1949); *The Three Crowns of Florence: Humanist Assessments of Dante, Petrarca, and Boccaccio,* eds. David Thompson and Alan Nagel (New York: Harper, 1972)—contains the preface to the *Commentary;* Frank Fata, "Some Elements in the Genesis of a Renaissance View of *The Divine Comedy,*" *Modern Language Notes* 86 (1972), 20–36; David Thompson, "Landino's Life of Dante," *Dante Studies* 88 (1970), 119–27.

LANDOLFI, TOMMASO (1908–   ), prose writer. Landolfi was born in Pico, but most of his life has been spent in Florence or Rome. The decisive influence upon Landolfi's fiction has been the hermetic poets associated with Florentine verse of the fascist period and, more importantly, many foreign literatures, particularly that of Russia. Landolfi has published distinguished translations of the works of such Russian writers as Gogol, Tolstoy, Pushkin, and Dostoevsky. His public *persona* is that of an eccentric who avoids photographs and literary gatherings. Few contemporary writers take the craft of fiction as seriously as Landolfi. His first collection of stories, entitled *Dialogo dei massimi sistemi* (1937, Dialogue Concerning the Two Chief World Systems), contains several masterpieces in the author's grotesque style: "Dialogo dei massimi sistemi" (rendered into English rather incorrectly as "Dialogue on the Greater Harmonies," obscuring Landolfi's direct reference to Galileo's* scientific treatise), and "La morte del Re di Francia" ("The Death of the King of France"). Other volumes of his fiction include *La spada* (1942, The Sword); *Le due zittelle* (1946, The Two Old Maids, which contains a well-known tale of the same title); and *Ombre* (1954, Shadows), which includes "La moglie di Gogol" ("Gogol's Wife"), perhaps his most famous story. Landolfi has also written science fiction, such as his *Cancroregina* (1950, Cancerqueen), and poetry, including a group of some three hundred lyrics entitled *Viola di morte* (1972, Death Violet). One of the most original living writers, whose style is often compared to that of Kafka, Borges, or the recent Calvino,* Landolfi continues to produce outstanding fictional narratives without being distracted by passing literary fashions. His most valuable work of late is *A caso* (1975, Inadvertently), a collection of short stories.

Bibliography: Racconti (Florence: Vallecchi, 1961); *Cancerqueen and Other Stories,* trans. Raymond Rosenthal (New York: Dial, 1971); *Gogol's Wife & Other Stories,* trans. Raymond Rosenthal, et al. (New York: New Directions, 1961); Claude Brew, "The 'Caterpillar Nature' of Imaginative Experience: A Reading of Tommaso Landolfi's 'Wedding Night'," *Modern Language Notes* 89 (1974), 110–15; Giancarlo Pandini, *Tommaso Landolfi* (Florence: La Nuova Italia, 1975).

LAPO GIANNI (circa 1270–circa 1332), Florentine lyric poet. Lapo may have been the same person as a notary of the Ricevuti family whose official acts date from 1298 to 1328. Dante* names Lapo alone of the minor *stilnovisti* as a poet who achieved eloquence in *De vulqari eloquentia* (I, xiii, 3), and he also speaks of his friendship with Lapo and Guido Cavalcanti* in a sonnet,* "Guido, i' vorrei che tu e Lapo ed io" ("Guido, I wish that you and Lapo and I"). Although he wrote in the style which has become known as the *dolce stil nuovo,* the idealism in Lapo's poetry is attenuated, and we see the influence of the new style primarily in the formal aspects of his poetry. Generally, he avoids serious ethical problems and endows his poetry with a lighthearted grace and freshness. The lover's suffering has the joyous quality of that of certain Sicilian and Provençal poets. In "Amor, eo chero mia donna in domino" ("Love, I would like my lady in my power"), Lapo's portrait of a lush and peaceful courtly world in which love could thrive resembles the tone and texture of the poetry of Folgore da San Gimignano.*

See also DOLCE STIL NUOVO.

Bibliography: Poeti del Dolce stil nuovo, ed. Mario Marti (Florence: Le Monnier, 1969); German and Italian Lyrics of the Middle Ages, trans. Frederick Goldin (Garden City, N.Y.: Doubleday, 1973).

LASCA: See GRAZZINI, ANTON FRANCESCO.

LAUDA ("Song of Praise"), a religious song in honor of God, the Virgin, Christ, or certain religious concepts (suffering, honor, virtue, charity), which owes its origins to popular adaptations of church liturgy, the earliest examples of which date from the thirteenth century. Early *laude* seemed to follow no fixed metrical scheme, but as the form gained popularity through the activities of the Flagellants, who practiced confraternal singing of *laude* in Umbria, it tended to assume a dramatic form with actual dialogue spoken or sung by different characters. Moreover, the meter of the *ballata** was eventually adopted by these Umbrian composers, chief among whom was Jacopone da Todi,* the greatest poet to work in this genre. Lines of eight syllables were most commonly used by Jacopone and others, although those of seven and eleven syllables were not infrequent. After the flourishing of the *lauda* in Umbria with Jacopone, it spread throughout the Italian peninsula, attracting the attention of such writers as Lorenzo de' Medici* and Girolamo Savonarola.*

See also BALLATA; DA TODI, Jacopone.

Bibliography: W. T. Elwert, Versificazione italiana dalle origini ai giorni nostri (Florence: Le Monnier, 1973); Arnoldo Fortini, La lauda in Assisi e le origini del teatro italiano (Assisi: Edizioni Assisi, 1961); Fernando Liuzzi, La lauda e i primordi della melodia italiana (Rome: Libreria dello stato, 1935).

LEOPARDI, GIACOMO (1798–1837), poet. Italy's greatest modern poet was born in Recanati, a backward provincial town within the Papal States. The religious and political conservatism of his father, Count Monaldo, was matched by the austerity of a mother not given to shows of affection. Despite his reactionary views, Count Monaldo's passion for books and writing resulted in a family library that was surprisingly rich for its time and place. Here Giacomo as a precocious adolescent spent endless hours, soon outstripping his tutors in erudition and teaching himself ancient and modern languages. In the process, his body was forever weakened, even somewhat deformed, and his eyes were so impaired that throughout his life he was forced into periods of inactivity without reading. His juvenile literary endeavors include verse in Italian, translations from Greek and Latin, philological disquisitions, a compilation on the *Storia dell'astronomia (1813, History of Astronomy)* and, more significantly, the *Saggio sopra gli errori popolari degli antichi*, (1815, *Essay on the Popular Superstitions of the Ancients*). Although the *Saggio* is written from the point of view of one who seemed secure both in the revealed truths of Christianity and in the righteousness of reason's war against error, it is not without a secret attraction towards the "illusions" and fables of the past. In 1818, he wrote the *Discorso d'un italiano intorno alla poesia romantica (Discourse of an Italian Concerning Romantic Poetry),* claiming the superiority of the ancients over the moderns (the "romantics") on the grounds that the ancients enjoyed a more spontaneous relationship with nature and were therefore more genuine in their use of the imagination as well as in depth of feeling. From this time on, one of Leopardi's central "myths"— the conflict between nature and reason—takes root along with the theme of the need for "illusions" if there is to be greatness and any chance for happiness. He also began to record his fertile ideas on all subjects (poetry, society, philological questions, philosophical and psychological inquiries) in his private notebooks—*Zibaldone di pensieri* (Notebook of Thoughts)— whose thousands of pages (the last entry was made in 1832) allow us to follow the poet's teeming thought in progress, as it were.

The civic *canzoni** "All'Italia" ("To Italy") and "Sopra il monumento di Dante" (1818, "On the Monument to Dante") made Leopardi's name known in literary circles. Although in the "eloquent" style and "generous" in their patriotic fervor, they also have a suggestion of melancholy and are built on the contrast between the greatness of antiquity and the mediocrity of the present. But it is in the *canzone* "Ad Angelo Mai" (January 1820, "To Angelo Mai") that the pessimism of Leopardi begins to be expressed in radical terms and in connection with another of his major themes—the *noia* or moral *ennui* that besets man when truth or reality is known for what it is and reason reveals the essential vanity of all things. Leopardi early lost his traditional religious faith and a belief in personal immortality, and he moved steadily toward a materialistic position that denied the reality of spirit in a metaphysical sense and insisted that the universe was ultimately finite. Even the astonishing masterpiece of fifteen unrhymed hendecasyllables—"L'infinito" (1819, "The Infinite")—was written from this philosophical position. Yet just here, in his yearning for a release from the finite, the skeptical Leopardi shares an important psychological characteristic with certain German and English romantics, even though his idea of the infinite is grounded in the most extreme doctrines of eighteenth-century sensationalism and associationism, just as his philosophical "myth" of man's right to happiness derives mainly from the French writers of the Enlightenment.*

Basic to the greater part of Leopardi's creative production is his theory that man, who has no innate ideas, nonetheless has an innate desire for an infinite pleasure, but that this desire must be forever frustrated because of the finiteness of reality. Because reason has supplanted the imagination as the guiding faculty in the life of man, poetry, in its truest sense (i.e., as it was for the ancients in whom the imagination reigned), is no longer possible. All that is left for modern man is a "philosophical" or reflective poetry whose proper tone will be melancholy, for, explicitly or implicitly, it will lament the loss of an Eden, or it will suggest the painful contrast between the illusory hopes of man and the revelation of the terrible truth of his metaphysical aloneness. At the same time, in the absence of the possibility of a metaphysics of infinity, Leopardi developed a poetics of the "indefinite" and the "vast" which is a highly personalized and existential version of the aesthetic of the sublime on which eighteenth-century thinkers had tended to theorize in a theological key. It should be noted, moreover, that his theory of the relationship between the indefinite and poetry has nothing of the obscurantism that characterizes the thinking of someone like Edgar Allan Poe on the same subject, and that he insisted on clarity as a fundamental tenet of poetic expression. Thus, Leopardi's poetry and his philosophy derive from a profoundly lived existential crisis which between 1819 and 1822 was expressed in such *canzoni* as "Bruto Minore" ("Brutus the Younger"), "Alla primavera" ("To Spring"), "Ultimo canto di Saffo" ("Sappho's Last Song"), "Inno ai Patriarchi" ("Hymn to the Patriarchs"), and "Ad Angelo Mai," and in a group of highly subjective idylls that include the gems "L'infinito," "Alla luna" ("To the Moon") and "La sera del dì di festa" ("Sunday Evening"). All of these poems reveal some degree of a characteristically Leopardian tension arising from a dynamics of desire that operates even in the heart of disenchantment. In the last two of them, memory—vital to much of Leopardi's poetics and poetry—has a key role. But whereas in "Alla luna" (as in much of his speculation on poetry and the yearning for happiness) memory appears only as a positive value which is inherently sweet even when it evokes past experiences of sorrow, "La sera del dì di festa" presents a more complex psychological situation where, in a remarkable case of involuntary memory accompanied by reflection on the *ubi sunt* theme, it functions to make the self painfully aware of being a prisoner in time, moving no less inexorably towards death and nothingness than the once great civilizations of the past.

Not until late 1822 was Leopardi able to leave the stifling town of his birth. But Rome seemed to him no more than an intellectual and spiritual "desert" (a frequent metaphor for the aridity of life in his poetry), and he returned to Recanati in May 1823. In September, he wrote the *canzone* "Alla sua donna" ("To His Lady"), a unique and profoundly moving version of the romantic themes of the inferiority of the real to the ideal and the awareness that the splendor of the imagination's vision (and so the possibility of happiness) has receded into an unattainable distance which, paradoxically, is also its guarantee of inviolability. In 1824, Leopardi wrote the major part of his *Operette morali (Little Moral Exercises).* Although they are sometimes irritatingly peremptory and derisive, these compositions (most of them in the form of a dialogue), written in a highly personal and rarefied prose, are nonetheless masterpieces of satire and irony. Among the most significant matters recorded in *Operette morali* is Leopardi's reconciliation of poetry and philosophy (but not science), even though the "Dialogo di Timandro e di Eleandro" ("Dialogue Between Timandro and Eleandro"), the piece he chose to close the first edition of the book, is directed "against the modern philosophers" and ironically argues that the ultimate conclusion that true philosophy teaches us is that we are better off not philosophizing. It may be best to consider the author's position as still ambivalent at this time, but what is certain to us now is that the book reveals, more resolutely than perhaps any other European work of the time, a profound crisis (going beyond the romantic dissatisfaction with the real and the historical disillusionment accompanying the Restoration) in the humanistic and bourgeois values of the Western world—a crisis that was to become clear only much later. Along with all semblance of traditional religious metaphysics and teleological explanations, both the classical myth of a Golden Age and the Rousseauistic myth of a happy relationship between uncorrupted man and nature are rejected. Now man's unhappiness is attributed not to the dethronement of the imagination by reason (much less to the Judaeo-Christian concept of original sin), but to real and inevitable calamities that existence necessarily reserves for him (see especially the "Storia del genere umano," "The History of Mankind," which is the introductory fable in the *Operette*). Nature, which in 1821 could still be invoked as a benign mother, is now portrayed as an indifferent stepmother whose sole purpose for perpetuating existence is necessarily at odds with the desire for happiness in her "children" (individuals) who serve only as her pawns ("Dialogo della Natura e di un Islandese," "Dialogue Between Nature and an Icelánder"). A number of other typical Leopardian themes (*ennui* and the experience of nothingness, the role of the imagination, the impossibility of happiness, the vanity of things, the superiority of the ideal over the real, the rarity and solace of love, the appeal to mutual compassion, the decadence of modern man, suicide, the desire for extinction) are treated in the various pieces in a variety of tones ranging from the jocular to the sardonic, from the aggressively polemic to the serenely heroic. Primarily, however, through the whole there breathes a profound but noble melancholy.

In July 1825, Leopardi left Recanati to which he was to return only twice —for the winter of 1826–27 and from November 1828 to June 1830. His search for economic independence brought him to Milan and Bologna where he was intermittently connected with editorial projects. June 1827 saw him in Florence where he was well received by the leading *literati*. But it was in Pisa, where he had gone for the winter and spring of 1828 in the hope of finding milder weather, that he again quickened to nature and poetry (the occasion is recorded in the poem "Il risorgimento," "The Revival"). There he wrote "A Silvia" ("To Sylvia"), perhaps the most poignant elegy in the Italian language, lamenting the dual loss of the life of a girl at the portal of life's promise and of the poet's own childhood hopes and illusions. A series of other lyrical masterpieces followed (written in Recanati), chief of which are "Le ricordanze" ("Remembrances"), a magnificent lyrical compendium of the poet's affective life where memory, which has value as a saving grace in recovery of the past, becomes the vehicle for a bitterly exacerbated awareness of the nullity of the present; and the "Canto notturno d'un pastore errante dell'Asia" ("Night Song of a Nomadic Shepherd in Asia"), one of the supreme modern songs of existential anguish with its vision of man's aloneness in a meaningless universe. Having returned to Florence in June 1830, Leopardi dedicated the first edition of his collected lyrics under the title *Canti* (1831, *Songs*) to the *literati* who befriended him there. He now became the close friend of Antonio Ranieri, a young Neapolitan whom he had assisted and upon whom he was to become greatly dependent emotionally. Late in 1833, the two companions went to live together in Naples where Ranieri was able to enjoy a certain economic stability, although Leopardi, finally receiving some financial aid from home, contributed his share. Here the poet spent his last years, death coming to him in June 1837. Meanwhile, during his last stay in Florence, Leopardi had fallen in love with Fanny Targioni Tozzetti, who, however, was more interested in other suitors. Whatever the details of this somewhat obscure episode may be, it brought first rapture and then the most bitter disillusionment. Of the five poems written out of this experience, "Il pensiero dominante" ("The Ascendant Thought") and "Amore e morte" ("Love and Death") are exalted statements of the power and value of love as a rich source of illusions and sublime sentiments, but also, paradoxically, of its effect of causing one to desire death. The paradox is partially explained by the fact that the celebration of love is coupled with a polemic against the insipidness and vainglory of the modern age and with the idea that only love or death is worthy of truly generous spirits. The poems, in fact, are a strong affirmation of the self, no less so than the epitaphic "A se stesso" ("To Himself"), which even as it bids a stark farewell to a life that had betrayed the poet once too often yet reveals a heart whose truest inclination was to beat fervently; and "Aspasia" ("Aspasia"), which expresses the poet's disenchantment not with love but with the real person (unworthy in herself) who had aroused the dreams and generous feelings that belonged only to himself.

Rarely descriptive in the traditional sense, Leopardi is a poet of evocation who depends not so much on startling metaphors and similes as on vast archetypal symbols and primordial images (though not of the kind of a Blake or Shelley), an unerring, profound musical sense, and intense yet controlled utterance. Even when touching the most poignant chords of pathos in lamenting or protesting nature's betrayal, he is never maudlin or whimpering. Indeed, a heroic or Promethean strain is present in his verse from his earliest endeavors. Thus, he could move (without real contradiction) from the declaration that truth is pain and that life without illusions is meaningless, to the assertion that man's real nobility consists in unmasking the face of truth and in recognizing that existence is inherently evil—a disfiguring birthmark on the face of nothingness. This latter image occurs in the entry in the *Zibaldone* for 19–22 April 1826, a significant page of prose-poetry in which the theme of the evil and suffering that are inherent in the very order of things culminates in the description of the garden-as-hospital. It is this agonistic pessimism that especially dominates the poet's later writings and the polemic against what he took to be the shallow optimism of the Catholic spiritualists and liberals of Florence and Naples. It brought him to the point of being ungenerous at times in the otherwise admirable comico-satirical poem in octaves—*Paralipomeni della Batracomiomachia* (1837, *The War of the Mice and the Crabs*). But it also led to "La ginestra, o il fiore del deserto" ("The Genista, or Flower of the Wasteland"), his last great poetic utterance (save for "Il tramonto della luna," "The Setting of the Moon," which returns to an idyllico-elegiac tone in expressing a calm despair).

In an "ideal" sense, Leopardi's poetry reveals two tendencies: one towards the "pure" expression of sentiment and one towards the impassioned expression of thought. In fact, however, thought and sentiment are co-present in varying degrees in most of the poems. In two famous lyrics—"La quiete dopo la tempesta" ("The Calm after the Storm") and "Il sabato del villaggio" (1829, "The Village Saturday Eve")—idyllico-descriptive elements are even joined with a gnomic manner, although an affective quality is present here too. But it is "La ginestra" that is the poet's most complex lyrical composite; in it philosophy, polemic, contemplation of the universe, and idyllico-elegiac sentiment combine in a summing-up of many of the chief motifs that figure in Leopardi's poetry as a whole. It is a statement that, even as it is the most virile affirmation of the poet's self, reaches out beyond the self in a deep impulse of compassion for the human predicament. The recognition of the nothingness that is man in the scheme of the vast universe that crushes him is now made to serve as the necessary and only valid ground on which mankind may affirm itself by joining together in a struggle against the common and sole enemy that is called nature (understood as the force that is responsible for existence). It would be wrong to judge this poem negatively because of a presumed lack of historical perspective, and equally wrong to try to read into it an anticipation of a sociopolitical message or solution. Its great force and universal appeal depend precisely on the fact that, in the final analysis, the poet's vision and message transcend all historical and political contingencies. For the vision and the appeal are rooted, as is all of Leopardi's major poetry, in an existential anguish that the poet lived with awesome lucidity. This is why the attempt (renewed from time to time since the poet's own lifetime, and against which he rightly protested) to reduce Leopardi's too often misunderstood "pessimism" to an expression of his own personal unhappiness and physical maladies has no more eloquent rebuttal than the fact that no other Italian writer, past or present, seems more our contemporary than he.

Bibliography: Tutte le opere di Giacomo Leopardi, ed. Francesco Flora, 5 vols. (Milan: Mondadori, 1949); *Tutte le opere,* eds. Walter Binni and Enrico Ghidetti, 2 vols. (Florence: Sansoni, 1969, rev. ed., 1977); *Scritti filologici: 1817–1832,* eds. Giuseppe Pacella and Sebastiano Timpanaro (Florence: Le Monnier, 1969); *Tutti gli scritti inediti, rari e editi 1809–1810,* ed. Maria Corti (Milan: Bompiani, 1972); *The Poems of Leopardi,* ed. Geoffrey L. Bickersteth (1923; rpt. New York: Russell & Russell, 1973); *Canti,* trans. John Humphrey Whitfield (Naples: G. Scalabrini, 1962); *Poems,* trans. Jean-Pierre Barricelli (New York: Las Americas, 1963); *Selected Prose and Poetry,* trans. Iris Origo and John Heath-Stubbs (New York: New American Library, 1967); *Poems and Prose,* ed. Angel Flores (Bloomington, Ind.: Indiana University Press, 1966); *Essays, Dialogues and Thoughts of Giacomo Leopardi,* trans. James Thomson (New York: Dutton, 1905); *The War of the Mice and the Crabs,* trans. Ernesto Caserta (Chapel Hill, N.C.: University of North Carolina Press, 1974); Walter Binni, *La Protesta di Leopardi* (Florence: Sansoni, 1973); Cesare Galimberti, *Linguaggio del vero in Leopardi* (Florence: Olschki, 1959); *Leopardi e il Settecento: Atti del I Convegno internazionale di studi leopardiani* (Florence: Olschki, 1964); Iris Origo, *Leopardi: A Study in Solitude* (London: Hamish Hamilton, 1953); Nicolas J. Perella, *Night and the Sublime in Giacomo Leopardi* (Berkeley, Calif.: University of California Press, 1970); G. Singh, *Leopardi and the Theory of Poetry* (Lexington, Ky.: University of Kentucky Press, 1964); J. H. Whitfield, *Giacomo Leopardi* (Oxford: Blackwell, 1954).

Nicolas J. Perella

LEVI, CARLO (1902–1975), journalist, physician, painter, and writer. Levi was born in Turin. After receiving his medical degree in 1923, he turned toward a career in literature and art and also became an active antifascist, for which he was confined in Lucania between 1935 and 1936. This experience was later to give birth to his major novel, *Cristo si è fermato a Eboli* (1945, *Christ Stopped at Eboli*). After his release, he fled to France and eventually took part in the resistance, working for a number of Italian newspapers after the fall of fascism. After 1963, Levi served as a senator elected on the communist ticket. Throughout his life, Levi continued to write journalistic pieces based upon his far-ranging experience in the resistance (*L'Orologio*—1950, *The Watch*), his views on poverty and the Mafia in Sicily (*Le parole sono pietre*—1955, *Words Are Stones*), his travels in Russia (*Il futuro ha un cuore antico*—1956, The Future Has an Ancient Heart), and his visit to the remains of a German concentration camp (*Doppia notte dei tigli*—1959, *The Linden Tree*).

With *Cristo si è fermato a Eboli*, Levi produced a masterpiece, one of the greatest of the many good novels inspired by the Italian experience of fascism and the war. With its highly personal and subjective portrait of poverty and superstition in the south where Christ (the symbol of civilization, history, and the modern world) had yet to penetrate, the book presents a masterful study of the beliefs, customs, folklore, and behavior in pre-industrial agrarian societies. While Levi offered his work as a strictly factual report of conditions as they were, the narrative (like so many neorealist films which seem realistic prior to a close analysis of their structure) is closer to fiction than reportage in its poetic use of metaphor and myth and its highly effective and stylized characterizations. Levi's presentation of the myth of America as it existed among the southern peasants may fruitfully be compared to the same topic in the works of Silone,* Pavese,* Soldati,* and Moravia.*

See also NEOREALISM.

Bibliography: Christ Stopped at Eboli, trans. Frances Frenaye (New York: Farrar, Straus & Giroux, 1947); *The Watch*, trans. John Farrar (New York: Farrar, Straus & Giroux, 1951); *Words Are Stones*, trans. Angus Davidson (New York: Farrar, Straus & Giroux, 1958); Donald Heiney, *America in Modern Italian Literature* (New Brunswick, N.J.: Rutgers University Press, 1964); Gigliola De Donato, *Saggio su Carlo Levi* (Bari: De Donato Editore, 1974).

LORENZINI, CARLO (1826–1890), journalist and writer of children's stories. Lorenzini is better known by his pseudonym Carlo Collodi, a name taken from that of the Tuscan village where his mother was born. He was born in Florence and studied for several years in a nearby seminary before leaving school to work on his own. An ardent Italian patriot, he fought in several campaigns against the Austrians. In 1848, he founded a humor magazine in Florence, *Il Lampione,* and in 1860, he became part of a commission charged by the city with censoring dramatic works. Later, he became secretary to the prefecture. After the publication of his version of Perrault's *Fables* in 1875, he turned chiefly to writing stories for children, such as the successful *Giannettino* (1875, Giannettino) and *Minuzzolo* (1877, Minuzzolo), which helped to develop the kind of child-protagonist that would later become famous in his *Le avventure di Pinocchio: storia di un burattino* (1883, *The Adventures of Pinocchio*). Lorenzini's immortal tale of the mischievous wooden puppet with his memorable nose who finally becomes a real boy, and all its unforgettable secondary characters, found an immediate and nearly universal audience. Its success as a story for the young has hindered the appreciation of its literary merit as a narrative which employs the children's fable as a means of expressing serious human concerns. It has undergone such divergent adaptations as an American film version by Walt Disney and a Marxist interpretation on film in Russia. It continues to attract the attention of serious literary critics with various approaches, including the psychoanalytic, the sociological, and the structuralist.

Bibliography: Tutto Collodi per i piccoli e per i grandi, ed. Pietro Pancrazi (Florence: Le Monnier, 1948); *Pinocchio,* ed. Fernando Tempesti (Milan: Feltrinelli, 1972)—contains two essays on Collodi and the composition of *Pinocchio; The Adventures of Pinocchio,* trans. Carol Della Chiesa (New York: Macmillan, 1972); Renato Bertacchini, *Collodi narratore* (Pisa: Nistri-Lischi, 1961); Gérard Génot, *Analyse structurelle de Pinocchio* (Florence: Industria Tipografica Fiorentina, 1970).

LUCINI, GIAN PIETRO (1867–1914), Milanese poet, writer, and critic. Lucini received a degree in law before turning to literature. Haunted by tuberculosis of the bone which first cost him a leg and finally killed him, he nevertheless sustained a lively interest in current events and cultivated a number of writers as friends, including Marinetti* (with whom he eventually had a falling out because of the futurist movement's support for warfare and colonialism). Despite the discord that developed between them, Marinetti called Lucini a "powerful genius balanced on crutches." His key fictional work, a novel entitled *Gian Pietro da Core* (1895, Gian Pietro from Core), tells of peasant revolt and governmental repression. Reflecting the diverse cultural currents of his epoch (*scapigliatura,* * futurism,* and symbolism), his poetry has recently become the object of serious study by several avant-garde critics, Edoardo Sanguineti* in particular. Lucini, who is usually identified with the increased use of free verse *(verso libero)* which marked the first two decades of this century in

Italian poetry, published an influential defense of this metrical form in 1908.

Bibliography: Prose e canzoni amare, ed. Isabella Ghidetti (Florence: Vallecchi, 1971); *Scritti critici,* ed. Luciana Martinelli (Bari: De Donato, 1971); Rita Baldassarri, *Gian Pietro Lucini* (Florence: La Nuova Italia, 1974).

LUZI, MARIO (1914–   ), poet and scholar. Luzi completed his literary studies at the university in Florence, his birthplace, graduating with a thesis on Mauriac. He has continued teaching French literature while writing and contributing to literary periodicals. His first book of verse, *La barca* (The Ship), appeared in 1935. At approximately the same time, Luzi began his collaboration with *Frontespizio* and *Letteratura* as well as with *Campo di Marte,* a journal noted for its advocacy of hermetic poetry. With Luzi's scholarly background in modern French literature, it is only natural that his poetry would reflect the hermetic emphasis on the purity of the word which the masters of a previous generation had established as the focal point of a new Italian poetry. His next two volumes, *Avvento notturno* (1940, Nocturnal Advent) and *Un brindisi* (1946, A Toast), typify the Florentine hermetic poetry which flourished during the 1940s. After this time, Luzi's works became somewhat simpler in language and more concerned with the existential themes of solitude and alienation.

Besides a brief collection of love poems entitled *Quaderno gotico* (1947, Gothic Notebook), Luzi has composed several other volumes of poetry, including *Primizie del deserto* (1952, First Fruits of the Desert); *Onore del vero* (1957, Respect for the Truth), which shared the Marzotto Prize for 1957 with Saba's* *Canzoniere; Nel Magma* (1963, In the Magma); *Dal fondo delle campagne* (1965, From the Bottom of the Fields); and *Su fondamenti invisibili* (1971, On Invisible Foundations). He has also translated Coleridge, Shakespeare's *Richard III,* and Racine's *Andromache,* and has authored a number of critical essays on Mallarmé, Constant, and symbolism. A difficult poet, Luzi is one of the outstanding writers of the generation after Montale* and Ungaretti.* His devotion to the purity of his craft and his own unmistakable poetic style within the hermetic tradition have made him one of contemporary Italy's influential voices.

See also HERMETICISM.

Bibliography: Il giusto della vita (Milan: Garzanti, 1960)—a collection of works published until that date; *Nel magma* (Milan: Scheiwiller, 1963); *In the Dark Body of Metamorphosis and Other Poems,* trans. I. L. Salomon (New York: Norton, 1975); Bruce Merry, "The Anti-Oracle in Mario Luzi's Recent Poetry," *Modern Language Review* 68 (1973), 333–43; Claudio Scarpati, *Mario Luzi* (Milan: Mursia, 1970).

M

MACHIAVELLI, NICCOLÒ (1469–1527), diplomat, poet, and political theorist. Machiavelli was born in Florence on 3 May 1469. From his father's records we learn that the family was impecunious, although of good descent. Niccolò, the third of four children, was taught Latin and was acquainted with a copy of Livy which Bernardo, the father, was indexing. No further information is available on his studies or his activity until he reaches his late twenties. Among the very first documents of his presence in public life is a letter dated 9 March 1498, which concerns the preaching of Savonarola,* who after the fall of the Medici in 1494 was the dominating figure on the Florentine political scene. It is probable that Machiavelli belonged to the lay faction that would soon (May 1498) overthrow the Savonarolist government of the new popular republic: he was appointed head of the new government's Second Chancery (designated 28 May 1498, elected 19 June), while a few months before, under the old regime, he had been refused a modest clerical job. Soon, a sensitive agency of the government, the Ten of Liberty and Peace (currently designated "Dieci di Balìa"), which was charged with warfare and diplomatic affairs, appointed the new chancellor to function as its secretary (14 July). Working for the Ten was to provide Machiavelli with an invaluable wealth of experiences, contacts, and traveling opportunities.

Machiavelli's unceasing activity as chancellor from 14 July 1498 to 7 November 1512 is recorded in more than six thousand autograph dispatches, minutes, drafts, and reports. This material presents the author's daily encounters with historical events, his reactions and reflections, his development in thought and language. The microcosm of the Florentine Republic displayed a whole spectrum of political life: the pressures from an exiled institutional party, the clashes of patrician and popular classes, the factions of monarchic and oligarchic tendencies within a class, the trends toward corruption or control of civic liberties, centralization or subdivision of power, distinction between urban and nonurban organizations, regulation of associate, allied, and conquered political entities, taxation and economic problems. As for foreign policy, frequent wars and Machiavelli's frequent involvement in the confrontations among major powers incessantly offered serious matters of meditation about the forces that condition the survival of a republic.

We like to think of the fourteen years that Machiavelli spent in active government as a massive period of study and of original instruction. They were integrated by several diplomatic missions abroad, which were recorded in the dispatches known as *Legazioni e commissarie* (Legations and Commissions). These missions provided opportunities to confront impressive contemporary characters (Caterina Sforza or Cesare Borgia), to compare institutional systems (the organization of the realm of France, of Swiss city-republics, of the imperial pyramid), and to observe national and civic attitudes. After the first mission to Caterina Sforza (July 1499), Machiavelli was at the Florentine camp besieging Pisa in June 1500. The Swiss and French troops broke into a mutiny that probably catalyzed his hostility to the mercenary system and his later campaigning for national recruiting. The affair's aftereffects were diplomatic. Machiavelli had to join a mission to France to clear up the matter of the mutiny, which had had not only military but economic and political repercussions as well. While he spent six full months there in vain attempts to solve the problem, he did learn French and made a vast collection of useful observations. The year 1502 marks the encounter with Cesare Borgia—briefly in June and then from October to January when Borgia performed the complex maneuver that checked the rebellion of his *condottieri*. Other foreign missions of high formative importance included Rome (October–December 1503; fall 1506), France (early 1504; summer and fall 1510), and Germany (December 1507–June 1508), as well as several shorter ones in central and northern Italy.

Parallel to the writings which document, day by day, his manifold governmental experiences is a series of eighteen short texts attesting to the beginning of his theoretical activity. Scattered over the period of his active participation in the republic (1498–1512), these texts deal with economic, institutional, and political problems, as well as with observations on the nature of the French and the Germans. They are characterized by a synthesizing spirit, excessively schematic in the early ones, but soon enriched by a unique blend of powerful reasoning, burning passion, and brilliant imagery. The urge to shape historical material into explanatory, critical, and ultimately didactic language appears also in five hundred and fifty Dantesque verses that Machiavelli wrote in the fall of 1504 to summarize the first ten years of the republic, the *Decennale Primo (The First Decade),* covering 1494 to 1504. In his last years in office (1506–12), Machiavelli undertook the project of establishing a Florentine army based on a system of regular military service. He drafted legal projects, personally supervised recruiting all over the state, and directed the organization of ranks, equipment, supplies, armaments, drills, and even parades. The *Discorso dell'ordinare lo stato di Firenze alle armi* (early 1507, Discourse on Florentine Military Preparation) sets forth the theoretical basis of this ambitious enterprise. The conquest of Pisa (June 1509), after fifteen years of vain attempts, was a realistic test of the value of the new army.

No direct evidence helps to place the young Machiavelli in relation to the cultural activity flourishing in post-Laurentian Florence or to the contrasting political tendencies. That he was in contact with the cultural circles is certain from the evidence provided by the highly cultivated humanistic prose and the Dantesque influence manifest in the *Decennali* (a *Decennale secundo, Second Decade,* was interrupted in 1509). For the years after the fall of the republic, we have evidence of his participation in the learned discussions of the Orti Oricellari group. His political position may be assessed as definitely republican, notwithstanding later opportunistic gestures toward the restored autocracy of the Medici. Within the republican institutional faith, Machiavelli seems to have instinctively leaned against the oligarchic supremacy and toward a large representation of popular power—unlike Guicciardini,* for instance,—which explains both the theoretical disagreements between these two and their divergent practical choices of behavior after the return of the Medici. The republic was wiped out when Piero dei Medici, taking advantage both of the prejudice brought against Florence by its pro-French policy and of the success of the papal and Spanish armies in Italy, reaped the fruits of a persistent underground lobbying among the Florentine magnates and succeeded in overthrowing the government. On 16 September 1512, the liberty of Florence ended. Soon after, Machiavelli was fired, jailed, questioned, and finally exiled to his country place of Sant'Andrea in Percussina (March 1513). The moment had come for him to face adverse fortune ("volgere il viso alla fortuna").

Machiavelli's fourteen years in government were to be followed by another fourteen of unwilling retirement and intense writing. An unspoken but steady attitude of veto on the part of the Medici frustrated efforts by Machiavelli and his friends to regain a role in Florentine public life. A few odd jobs began to come his way in 1518, when a group of merchants sent him to Genoa to settle a bankruptcy. In 1520, the university ("Studio fiorentino") commissioned him to write a history of Florence. This was a tragically ironical task for a staunch republican, as the commission was authorized by the ruling autocrats, and the history had to be in substance the chronicle of their success in conquering the democracy. In 1521, a very minor charge brought him to Carpi, where he had to negotiate the separation of the Minorite convents from the other convents of Tuscany. In 1525, he was sent to Venice to handle a complaint filed by Florentine merchants. In 1526, he finally obtained a small office, in the new agency established to reinforce the city's walls. When the ruin of Clement VII, the Medici pope (brought about by the Spanish Sack of Rome in May 1527), caused the new, although temporary, exile of the Medici from Florence, Machiavelli was a finished man. The improvised republican government was a late offshoot of the Savonarolian faction, more suspicious of its lay opponents than of the oligarchic party, and even of the Medicean one. In fact, it confirmed as chancellor (his former post) a member of the Medicean government. Broken in spirit as well as in health, Machiavelli died on 21 June 1527 and was buried in Santa Croce. *Tanto nomini nullum par elogium.*

It was, however, the span between exile and death (1513–27) that would project Machiavelli's existence into immortality. His disgrace brought about the surge of a most incisive theoretical and literary vocation. In the forced retirement of Sant'Andrea, he was led to convey in writing the image of his lifelong dedication—that republic which had absorbed all of his energies, his attention, and his passion. The burning disappointment of defeat focused his mind upon searching for the laws commanding the stability or instability of a given republican regime. This stability had to be founded entirely on secular terms, since the conventional principles, such as the theological ones, appeared unsatisfactory to the powerfully original Machiavellian mind: the "verità effettuale delle cose" (the effectual truth of the matter) is the formula which expresses the strikingly innovative level of inquiry that he adopted. He started expounding his thinking on the biology of the republican organism in the form of a commentary on Livy, but he followed his own general design, supplementing Livy constantly with contemporary evidence. The "esempi freschi" (fresh examples) were supplied to him by his direct observation and concrete governmental experience. This work, begun in 1513, was completed in about 1517, when he agreed to present it in expository form to the intellectuals of the Orti Oricellari. It was published posthumously in 1531 by Blado under the title *Discorsi sopra la prima Deca di Tito Livio (Discourses on the First Decade of Titus Livius)*. It is Machiavelli's major opus, inasmuch as it represents his authentic political position and contains a summa of his knowledge and of his most original thinking. All of his other works, in political science, in military theory, in literature, in drama, and even in history, gravitate around this central core. The *Discorsi* are articulated in three books. The first, subdivided into sixty chapters, deals with the embryology of a state, in the phases of its foundation and constitution; then with the problems of stabilization in succession to power, in armament policy, and in legal arrangements; and then with general modes of instability ("corruption"). The book presents in recurring instances the basic concepts which gave Machiavelli the tools for handling the matter by means of secular principles: knowledge of constants in human nature, individual as well as collective, and analysis of historical events in the timeless perspective of political behavior. The second and third books, encompassing respectively, thirty-three and forty-nine chapters, maintain the energetic intellectual thrust and the impressive style of the first. The second examines the drive for expansion inherent in the growth of a state, and the related policies of arms, neutrality and warfare, alliances, and occupation systems. The third treats concrete ways of securing durability in the typically unstable course of events and deals with single instances of the pathology of stability in war and in peace.

While working on the first book, Machiavelli was led to handle separately a limited case, concerning one of the major threats against the stability of a republic: the seizure of power by an individual. The opuscule, *Il Principe (The Prince);* took the form of a special treatise on monarchy and soon gained an immense and controversial reputation. Completed at the end of 1513 (according to Machiavelli's letter to Francesco Vettori on 10 December), it was dedicated to Giuliano de' Medici, perhaps to show the author's ability to counsel the new rulers and perhaps out of a deeper concern for preserving Florence even under a nonrepublican regime. The little work was probably revised later. It reached a final form with a dedication to Lorenzo de' Medici (probably before 8 October 1516, when Lorenzo took the title of duke of Urbino, which is absent in the book). Like the *Discorsi,* it was published posthumously in 1532 by Blado.

Il Principe encompasses in twenty-five chapters (the twenty-sixth is an exhortation to free Italy from the barbarians) a typology of acquired sovereignties and an evaluation of the forces available for acquiring them, on the military as well as the political and behavioristic levels. Since its surface appearance was normative (in accordance with the widespread Renaissance* fashion), it was open to savage misinterpretation and misquotation, particularly from traditionally moralistic quarters. The author's concern for operating on secular principles (e.g., the constant trends of human nature in political associations) and the technicality of his approach are masked by a beautifully passionate style. Centuries had to elapse before the distinction between moral moment and political moment, between technical approach and moralistic generalities, and even between the subject matter of the book and the author's person were finally achieved.

Once he had resumed work on the *Discorsi,* Machiavelli went on corresponding with Vettori, pursuing vain attempts to regain employment and seeking expression in varied literary compositions. A satirical poem in tercets, the *Asino (The Ass),* where the author imagines himself transformed into an ass in order to be able to attack other "animals," is mentioned as being in progress on 17 December 1517, but was never finished. Probably in 1518 he composed *La Mandragola (The Mandrake Root),* a marvelous play in which knowledge of human nature, dry awareness of people's behavior under the stress of passions and of engaging themselves in the fabric of society, brilliant imagination, and incisive style, all combine to create an amazing blend of narrative, self–expression, comicality, and tragedy. The play had immediate success. Printed first in Florence, probably in 1519, it was reprinted in Venice in 1522 (when it was also played to great crowds) and then in Rome in 1524. Two autograph versions of a translation from Terrence's *Andria* can also be dated around this period (between 1517 and 1520).

Probably between 1515 and 1516, when Machiavelli began taking part in the meetings of Florentine intellectuals at the Orti Oricellari (the gardens of Cosimo Rucellai, 1495–1519), he conceived the idea of a military treatise. The dialogues composing the seven books of the *Arte della Guerra (The Art of War)* are fictionally located at the Orti in 1516, but were actually written later. Although the *Arte della Guerra* is a military treatise, a vast amount of general theory and of historical exemplification (taken as usual in parallel lines from ancient and modern instances) is skillfully wrought into its framework. Again, this work is connected, as a development of a specific subject, to the major theories and methods which characterize the *Discorsi* and was printed in 1521 by Giunti. Around March 1520, the friends of the Orti managed to arrange a meeting between Machiavelli and Giulio de' Medici, who was Lorenzo's successor (died May 1519) in the government of Florence. In the late summer of the same year, Machiavelli had finished a biography, *La vita di Castruccio Castracani (The Life of Castruccio Castracani)*, and a few pages on the government of Lucca, both inspired by a trip to this town in July 1520. It is likely that his one story, *Novella di Belfagor arcidiavolo (The Novella of Belfagor Archdevil)*, was written and known by then, and it is certain that Machiavelli had sent to Rome at the end of 1520 his *Discorso delle cose fiorentine dopo la morte di Lorenzo (Discourse on Florentine Affairs after the Death of Lorenzo)*.

While writing the *Istorie fiorentine (The History of Florence)*, Machiavelli had to face the problem of reconciling his fundamentally republican stand and the Medicean bias that the commissioners expected from an official history. On 30 August 1524, having practically finished the eight books leading up to 1492 (the death of Lorenzo il Magnifico), he wrote to Guicciardini that he was working in the country and that he missed the advice of his friend on how to present certain details without offending the persons concerned. The Orti Oricellari conversations had been over for some time, and his company at the moment was hardly at that cultural level, since he was having a love affair with an actress. He spent the last months of 1524 hastily composing another play, *La Clizia (Clizia)*. Modeled upon Plautus's *Casina*, the work was staged in January 1525. The following May, Machiavelli obtained the authorization to present the *Istorie fiorentine* in eight books to Pope Clement VII, who rewarded him not only with a gift of one hundred and twenty gold ducats, but also with a rather vague commission of reviving the idea of a national militia. This had to be carried out with Francesco Guicciardini, who at that time was in charge of the papal government in Romagna. Accordingly, in the middle of June 1525, Machiavelli proceeded to Faenza to begin talks with Guicciardini. However, it soon became apparent that the skepticism of the top officials and the pope's lack of resolution were bound to doom the initiative. The legal business of a group of Florentine merchants which led Machiavelli to Venice in August 1525 provided an important journey, as it was his first visit to that great center of culture. There he arranged a new staging of the *Mandragola* for the carnival and possibly became acquainted with Bembo's* *Prose della volgar lingua* (Writings in the Vernacular Language, partially known long before, finished in 1524, and printed in 1525). It appears that his *Discorso o Dialogo intorno a la nostra lingua (Discourse or Dialogue on Language)* was written in the fall of 1525 in reaction to Bembo's dismissal of Dante* as a model of classical language.

Since Machiavelli's salary as official historian had been increased, he probably intended to continue the *Istorie* beyond 1492. In fact, toward the end of October 1525 he wrote Guicciardini that he had resumed writing. However, only about fifty pages of fragmentary notes covering the years 1494–98 are extant. War had flared again in Italy, and his efforts to follow the events (and to pursue his dream of the militia) absorbed most of his time. The events were precipitous; the last forces of a tired, disillusioned man were spent. The words "I love my country more than my own soul" appear in a letter of 16 April 1527, written two months before his death. Their halo envelopes a course of action, of thought, of fighting, of writing: they preserve the unity and the pulse of life in those texts that civilization has inherited.

Bibliography: Legazioni, commissarie, scritti di governo, ed. Fredi Chiappelli, 2 vols. to date (Bari: Laterza, 1971–   ); *Tutte le opere*, ed. Mario Martelli (Florence: Sansoni, 1971); *Machiavelli: The Chief Works and Others*, trans. Allan Gilbert, 3 vols. (Durham, N.C.: Duke University Press, 1965); *The Portable Machiavelli*, trans. Peter Bondanella and Mark Musa (New York: Viking Penguin, 1979); Peter E. Bondanella, *Machiavelli and the Art of Renaissance History* (Detroit, Mich.: Wayne State University Press, 1974); Federico Chabod, *Scritti su Machiavelli* (Turin: Einaudi, 1964); Fredi Chiappelli, *Machiavelli e la lingua fiorentina* (Bologna: Boni, 1974), *Nuovi studi sul linguaggio del Machiavelli* (Florence: Le Monnier, 1969), and *Studi sul linguaggio del Machiavelli* (Florence: Il Saggiatore, 1952); Felix Gilbert, *Machiavelli and Guicciardini: Politics and History in Sixteenth-Century Florence* (Princeton, N.J.: Princeton University Press, 1965); Myron P. Gilmore, ed., *Studies on Machiavelli* (Florence: Sansoni, 1972); J. H. Hexter, *The Vision of Politics on the Eve of the Reformation* (New York: Basic Books, 1972); Friedrich Meinecke, *Machiavellism: The Doctrine of Raison D'Etat and Its Place in Modern History* (London: Routledge & Kegan Paul, 1957); J. G. A. Pocock, *The Machiavellian Moment: Florentine Political Thought and the Atlantic Republican Tradition* (Princeton, N.J.: Princeton University Press,

1975); Mario Praz, *The Flaming Heart* (New York: Norton, 1973); Roberto Ridolfi, *The Life of Niccolò Machiavelli* (Chicago: University of Chicago Press, 1963); Leo Strauss, *Thoughts on Machiavelli* (Seattle, Wash.: University of Washington Press, 1969); J. H. Whitfield, *Discourses on Machiavelli* (Cambridge, Eng.: Heffer, 1969).

Fredi Chiappelli

MADRIGAL or **MADRIGALE** (*madriale* and *marigale* are variant forms), a brief lyric poem composed of from eight to eleven lines (usually of eleven syllables or a mixture of eleven and seven syllables). The madrigal is commonly divided into *terzine* employing various rhyme schemes and closes with a couplet. Among the most popular rhyme schemes are the following arrangements:(1) *abc abc dd;* (2) *aba bcb cc;* (3) *abb acc dd;* (4) *abb cdd ee;* (5) *abb acc cdd;* (6) *aba cbc de;* (7) *abb cdd ee ff;* and (8) *abb cdd eff gg.* In its classic form, the madrigal is an elegant poetic genre (not of popular derivation) frequently set to music for a number of voices. The vogue of the madrigal reached its peak in the sixteenth century, particularly in Italy and England. Madrigals usually treat pastoral and amorous themes and are less likely to be used for satire or political topics. A variant of the classical madrigal, called the *madrigalessa* or *madrigalone* and invented by Antonio Francesco Grazzini ("Il Lasca"),* is a longer version of the genre which takes up satirical topics. Among the most important composers of Italian madrigals are Sacchetti,* Petrarch,* Stampa,* Tasso,* Guarini,* and Marino.* Because of its role in music history, the madrigal has remained a popular lyrical form among singers of the twentieth century.

Bibliography: Alfred Einstein, *The Italian Madrigal,* 3 vols. (Princeton, N.J.: Princeton University Press, 1971); Ulrich Schulz-Buschhaus, *Das Madrigal: Zur Stilgeschichte der italienischen Lyrik zwischen Renaissance und Barock* (Hamburg: Verlag Gehlen, 1969); Raffaele Spongano, *Nozioni ed esempi di metrica italiana* (Bologna: Pàtron, 1966).

MAFFEI, SCIPIONE (1675–1755), historian, philologist, moral philosopher, and poet. Maffei was born into the Veronese nobility, completed his education at Jesuit colleges in Parma and Rome, and fought in the battle of Donauworth (1704) with his brother Alessandro, a general in the Bavarian army. Returning to Italy, he entered the Accademia dell'Arcadia* and took the academic name Orildo Berenteatico. One of the founders of the *Giornale dei letterati* in 1710, he continued to pursue varied literary and journalistic interests recorded in six volumes of *Osservazioni letterarie* (Literary Observations) which appeared between 1737 and 1740. Maffei's diverse interests and talents make him one of the most representative figures of early Enlightenment* Italy. His published works cover far-ranging topics. He prepared a scientific treatise, *Della formazione dei fulmini* (1747, On the Formation of Lightning), and studied electricity, phosphorescent insects, and fossils. A political treatise, *Il consiglio politico alla repubblica veneta* (1736, Political Counsel for the Venetian Republic), contains a perceptive description of the English constitution which may foreshadow some of Montesquieu's ideas. Maffei's literary output encompasses a collection of verse (1719); several critical works on the theatre—*Osservazioni* (1700, Observations) on Corneille's *Rodogune, Dei teatri antichi e moderni* (1753, On Ancient and Modern Theatre), and *Discorso storico sul teatro* (1723, A Historical Discourse on Italian Theatre); two comedies; and a melodrama,* *La fida ninfa* (1730, The Faithful Nymph) with music by Antonio Vivaldi.

Of particular note are a tragedy, *La Merope* (1713, *Merope*), and a four-volume inquiry into Verona's history, literature, and culture entitled *Verona illustrata* (1731–32, Verona Rendered Illustrious). The tragedy attracted a wide European audience and was translated into many languages. It provoked a sharp polemic between Maffei and Voltaire, who had originally agreed to translate the work but instead wrote an imitation of the play, claiming that the Italian work was unsuitable for the French public. Subsequent negative judgments by Gotthold Ephraim Lessing and Alfieri* lessened the drama's appeal, but it is still regarded as the best neoclassical tragedy written by an Italian before Alfieri.

See also ARCADIA.

Bibliography: *Opere drammatiche e poesie varie*, ed. Antonio Avena (Bari: Laterza, 1928); Kurt Ringger,"*La Merope* e il 'furor d'affetto': la tragedia di Scipione Maffei rivisitata," *Modern Language Notes* 92 (1977), 38–62; Giuseppe Silvestri, *Scipione Maffei europeo del Settecento* (Verona: Neri Pozza Editore, 1968).

MAGALOTTI, LORENZO (1637–1712), diplomat, scientist, and poet. Born in Rome of a noble Florentine family and educated at the University of Pisa, Magalotti studied under such famous scientists as Vincenzo Viviani (1622–1703), Giovanni Alfonso Borelli (1608–79), and Marcello Malpighi (1628–94), all of whom supported Galileo's* experimental methods. At an early age, he became secretary to the Accademia del Cimento in Florence (1660) and was also a member of the Accademia dell'Arcadia* and the Accademia della Crusca. As a courtier of Grand Duke Ferdinando II, Magalotti traveled in France, England, and Spain with his patron's son Cosimo. When Cosimo succeeded his father, he named his old traveling companion ambassador to Vienna (1675–78) and one of his counselors of state (1689).

Magalotti has left a number of *novelle** in the style of Boccaccio,* a collection of Petrarchan lyrics entitled *La donna immaginaria* (1762, The

Imaginary Lady), a commentary on the first five cantos of Dante's* *Inferno,* and Italian translations of Greek lyric poetry and passages from the Old Testament. Magalotti's travels and his facility in languages also encouraged him to attempt the first Italian version of Milton's *Paradise Lost* (never completed) as well as a version of John Philip's *On Cider.* His most important work is a scientific treatise entitled *Saggi di naturali esperienze* (1667, *Essayes of Natural Experiments*), which collected and explained the various scientific projects of the Accademia del Cimento. The treatise was rendered into English in 1684 and was widely read in the European scientific community. Of far less import, but perhaps more typical of Magalotti's often pedantic proclivities and those of his epoch, is a rather popular essay on *buccheri*—earthenware vases from Peru, Chile, or Portugal which emit an odor when dampened and which were then very fashionable—entitled *Lettere sopra le terre odorose d'Europa e d'America dette volgarmente buccheri* (1695, Letters on Buccheri). Some of his writings describe his foreign travels and are still a rich source of European social customs during that period.

Bibliography: Le più belle pagine di Lorenzo Magalotti, ed. Lorenzo Montano (Milan: Treves, 1924); *Relazioni di viaggio in Inghilterra, Francia e Svezia,* ed. Walter Moretti (Bari: Laterza, 1968); Eric Cochrane, *Florence in the ₁Forgotten Centuries: 1527–1800* (Chicago: University of Chicago Press, 1973); Georges Güntert, *Un Poeta scienziato del Seicento: Lorenzo Magalotti* (Florence: Olschki, 1966).

MAGGI, CARLO MARIA (1630–1699), poet, translator, and dramatist. A native of Milan, Maggi finished his studies in civil and canon law at the University of Bologna in 1650, traveled extensively around Italy, and married in 1656. In 1661, he was named to the Secretariat of the Milanese Senate and later became superintendent of the University of Pavia and a member of both the Accademia della Crusca and the Accademia dell'Arcadia.* A collection of lyrics, *Rime varie* (1688, Miscellaneous Verse), won for Maggi the friendship of Ludovico Muratori* and the admiration of many writers who opposed the excess and sensuality of Marino* and his followers, but Maggi also composed tragedies, *intermezzi,* and melodramas.* In fact, he is best known for his comedies in Milanese dialect: *Il Manco male* (1695, All the Better), *Il Barone di Birbanza* (1696, The Baron of Birbanza), *I consigli di Meneghino* (1697, The Counsels of Meneghino), and *Il falso filosofo* (1698, The False Philosopher). Maggi introduced the character of Meneghino to Italian theatre, who was always thereafter identified as a comic character from Milan.

Maggi opposed the Marinistic tendencies in the Baroque* literature of his day. His dramatic scenario *Il Concorso de' Meneghini* (1698–99, The Competition of the Meneghinis)—a theoretical work on poetics—attacks Marino's concept of the marvelous: "The poet who tries to astonish/

succeeds this way;/ that his comedies are so stupid/ that they cannot stand up.'' In like manner, Maggi opposed what he considered a degenerate form of *commedia dell'arte,* * a type of comedy seemingly devoid of social purpose. Further, his use of dialect stemmed from a belief that dialect represented a world of sound values and good sense still possessed by the common people. As he put it, the Milanese dialect seemed to have evolved expressly to tell the truth. Another dialect poet from Milan, Carlo Porta,* later claimed Maggi as a primary influence upon his own poetry.

See also BAROQUE; MARINO, Giambattista; PORTA, Carlo.

Bibliography: Il teatro milanese, ed. Dante Isella, 2 vols. (Turin: Einaudi, 1964); Antonio Petrella, ''Carlo Maria Maggi's Theory of Comedy,'' *Italian Quarterly* 12 (1969), 223–37.

MALAPARTE, CURZIO (1898–1957), political activist, journalist, and essayist. Malaparte was born Kurt Erich Suckert in Prato. An enthusiastic volunteer for military duty in 1914, Malaparte was wounded and decorated for bravery. He served as the Italian cultural attaché in Warsaw for a time (1919–20), and then aligned himself with fascism, taking part in the March on Rome and in several ''punitive expeditions'' with the Florentine black-shirts. He adopted the name Curzio Malaparte in 1925. After publishing a number of minor works (essays and fiction), he assumed the direction of the *La Fiera letteraria* from 1928 to 1932 and traveled widely around the world. With the publication of *Technique du coup d'état* (1931, *Coup D'État: The Technique of Revolution*), Malaparte was accused of antifascist activities, sentenced to five years in prison (1933–37), and was later released through the intercession of Galeazzo Ciano. Returning to work as a journalist in 1937, he witnessed much of the bitter fighting on the French, Finnish, and Russian fronts, events which are vividly portrayed in *Kaputt* (1944, *Kaputt*), the macabre masterpiece based upon his first-hand experiences. In postfascist Italy, Malaparte became a liaison officer between the newly reconstituted Italian army and the Allies and took part in the battle for Montecassino. *La pelle* (1950, *The Skin*) presents an imaginative portrait of Naples under the American occupation and in its narrative style reflects the influence of American literature. Turning to the cinema and theatre, he wrote several unsuccessful plays (one based upon Marx's *Das Kapital*) and completed an interesting film entitled *Cristo proibito* (1951, *The Forbidden Christ*). His *Maledetti toscani* (1956, *Those Cursed Tuscans*), a portrait of his Tuscan compatriots, was a great commercial success. Malaparte was invited to visit Mao's China in 1957, fell gravely ill during his travels, and returned to die in Rome, converting to Catholicism shortly before he died. This politically ambiguous chain of events ended the life of one of Italy's most charming and contradictory figures. Malaparte had espoused various radical (and diametrically opposed) philosophical and political doctrines during his lifetime, and he had been on intimate terms with such diverse figures as Hitler, Mao, Mussolini, Goering, and a number of antifascists from all over the world. His sense of the absurdity of warfare and his skillful portrayal of its grotesque and essentially ridiculous aspects in *Kaputt* make Malaparte one of the most unique narrators of his generation.

Bibliography: Opere complete di Curzio Malaparte, ed. Enrico Falqui, 9 vols. to date (Florence: Vallecchi, 1957–71); *Coup D'État: The Technique of Revolution,* trans. Sylvia Saunders (New York: Dutton, 1932); *Kaputt,* trans. Cesare Foligno (New York: Dutton, 1946); *The Skin,* trans. David Moore (Boston: Houghton-Mifflin, 1952); *Those Cursed Tuscans,* trans. Rex Benedict (Athens, Ohio: Ohio University Press, 1964); A. J. De Grand, "Curzio Malaparte: The Illusion of the Fascist Revolution," *Journal of Contemporary History* 7 (1972), 73–89; Gianni Grana, *Malaparte* (Florence: La Nuova Italia, 1968).

MANETTI, GIANNOZZO (1396–1459), Florentine humanist and diplomat. Manetti was a disciple of the humanist scholar Ambrogio Traversari (1386–circa 1439) and a close friend of Leonardo Bruni* (whose funeral oration he delivered). He served as Florentine ambassador to Venice, Naples, Rome, Siena, and Rimini. Exiled from Florence in 1453 because of his opposition to Cosimo de' Medici, Manetti lived in Rome for two years before settling in Naples. There, he was befriended by King Alfonso, at whose suggestion he wrote his well-known discussion of the dignity of man.

Manetti was one of the most learned men of his time. He knew Latin and Greek thoroughly and enough Hebrew to attempt a translation of the Psalms from the original text rather than from the Vulgate. His translations of Aristotle's moral writings were widely read. He completed several biographical and historical works, the most significant of which were *Vitae Nicolai V pontificis libri II* (The Life of Pope Nicholas V), and a description of the lives of Florence's greatest poets—Dante,* Petrarch,* and Boccaccio*—which was not published until 1747. This latter work, *Vitae Dantis, Petrarcae, Boccacci* (Lives of Dante, Petrarch, and Boccaccio), contains an influential comparative assessment of these poets. Unlike many of his contemporaries, Manetti valued their vernacular writings almost as highly as those in Latin, a critical perspective which eluded other scholars until the sixteenth century. His major treatise was *De dignitate et excellentia hominis (On the Dignity of Man),* completed in 1452 and printed in 1532. Condemned by the Inquisition in 1584, Manetti's treatise countered the arguments of Innocent III's *On the Misery of Man* and presented the most optimistic view of the human condition prior to that expressed by Giovanni Pico della Mirandola* in his more famous oration.

See also DELLA MIRANDOLA, Giovanni Pico.

Bibliography: Giannozzo Manetti and Innocent III, *Two Views of Man: On the Misery of Man, On the Dignity of Man* (New York: Ungar, 1956); *The Three Crowns of Florence: Humanist Assessments of Dante, Petrarca, and Boccaccio,* trans. David Thompson and Alan Nagel (New York: Harper, 1972); Eugenio Garin, *Italian Humanism,* trans. Peter Munz (1955; rpt. Westport, Conn.: Greenwood Press, 1975); Angelo Solerti, ed., *Le vite di Dante, Petrarca, e Boccaccio scritte fino al secolo decimosesto* (Milan: Vallardi, 1904).

MANTUAN: *See* SPAGNOLI, BATTISTA.

MANUZIO, ALDO, "Aldus Manutius" (1449–1515), publisher, typographer, and humanist. Very little is known of the first part of Manuzio's life except that he studied Greek and Latin in Rome and Ferrara and that he went in 1482 to live with his friend Giovanni Pico della Mirandola,* to whose nephews he became tutor while he continued studying Greek. At that time, he conceived the idea of establishing a printing press to make the whole of Greek literature available. Moving to Venice to be nearer the Greek scholars who had arrived there after the fall of Constantinople, Manuzio had begun his establishment by 1494. By 1515, he had published thirty-three first editions of Greek texts in the original, including all of Aristotle's writings, Aristophanes, Sophocles, Plato, Thucydides, and many others. At the same time, Manuzio invented his own special Greek type-face modeled on the handwriting of a Cretan scholar Marcus Musurus. Although his original plan was to concentrate upon works in Greek, Manuzio published important editions of Latin and Italian authors including Dante,* Petrarch,* Bembo,* Poliziano,* Pontano,* and Erasmus (who visited the press in 1508). Manuzio invented another type-face for the Latin and Italian works which became known as italic.

The colophon of the Aldine Press was a dolphin curled about an anchor, symbolizing the rapidity of its publishing and the stability of its scholarship. Although Manuzio's press won a European reputation for the reliability and scholarly integrity of its texts rather than for the beauty of its illustrations, many historians of printing consider the Aldine edition of Francesco Colonna's* *Hypnerotomachia Poliphili* (1499, *The Strife of Love in a Dreame),* the most beautiful book printed during the entire Renaissance.* Aldo was succeeded by his third son Paolo (1512–1574), a Latin scholar who turned the press's interest to Latin classics, and by his grandson Aldo (1547–1597), who carried on the family tradition in Rome.

See also COLONNA, Francesco.

Bibliography: Horatio F. Brown, *The Venetian Printing Press* (London: Nimmo, 1891); Carlo Castellani, *La stampa in Venezia dalle sue origini alla morte di Aldo* (Venice: Ongania, 1889); W. Theodor Elwert, *Studi di letteratura veneziana* (Venice: Istituto per la collaborazione culturale, 1958); Mario Ferrigni, *Aldo Manuzio* (Milan: La Grafica Moderna, 1925).

MANZINI, GIANNA (1896–1974), novelist. Born in Pistoia into a poor family, with a father whose political beliefs led to his death in a fascist prison, Manzini graduated from the University of Florence with a degree in literature. She married a Florentine journalist and was an active contributor to the important Florentine periodicals, *Solaria* and *Letteratura,* both of which opened up Italian culture to influences from abroad. Her first novel, *Tempo innamorato* (Time of Love), appeared in 1928 and received high praise from critics, many of whom compared her style to that of Tozzi.* In 1936, she moved to Rome where she remained until her death.

Manzini has been appreciated by only a small group of readers outside of Italy. Even within her own country, she failed to gain any of Italy's many literary prizes until the appearance of *Lettera all'editore* (1945, Letter to the Editor). Most highly regarded is her novel *La sparviera* (1956, The Sparrow-Hawk), which depicts the relationship between its male protagonist, Giovanni Sermonti, and the bronchial illness from which he has suffered since childhood; it lurks behind him constantly like the bird of prey in the book's title. Her last works include several novels—*Un'altra cosa* (1961, Another Thing); *Il cielo addosso* (1963, The Nearby Sky); *Allegro con disperazione* (1965, Happy with Despair); and *Sulla soglia* (1973, On the Threshold)—and a series of essays entitled *Album di ritratti* (1964, Album of Portraits), dealing with Ungaretti,* Sartre, Kafka, Virginia Woolf (to whom Manzini has often been compared in Italy), Gide, and Anne Frank. Although one of Italy's most perceptive female novelists, Manzini most often created male protagonists through whom she presented many personal and autobiographical themes. She never achieved the commercial success of other women like Ginzburg,* Morante,* or De Céspedes* and has been largely neglected by translators abroad.

Bibliography: Album di ritratti (Milan: Mondadori, 1964); *Lettera all'editore* (Florence: Sansoni, 1945); *La sparviera* (Milan: Mondadori, 1956); Lia Fava Guzzetta, *Gianna Manzini* (Florence: La Nuova Italia, 1974).

MANZONI, ALESSANDRO (1785–1873), novelist, dramatist, poet, and theorist on literature and Italian language. Manzoni was the son of Giulia Beccaria and Pietro Manzoni, who separated in 1792. His early poems range from an attack on tyranny and ecclesiastical suppression of free thought to neoclassical compositions and to four *Sermoni* (1803–04, Sermons) satirizing morality and culture in the Cisalpine Republic. In 1805, when Manzoni joined his mother in Paris on the death of Carlo Imbonati, her companion for ten years, he encountered the Idéologues, followers of Condillac's sensationist philosophy, and noted their close analysis of individual psychology. He became a close friend and correspondent of Claude Fauriel. The *carme,* or song, "In morte di Carlo Imbonati" (1806, On the Death of Carlo Imbonati), shows a high sense of poetic mission, although Manzoni remains the "giusto solitario" (just but solitary man). The coupling of feeling and meditation recalls his view that the finest contemporary literature stemmed from the bitter conflict resulting from meditation on what is and what ought to be.

In 1808, Manzoni married Henriette Blondel, a devout Calvinist whose example undoubtedly assisted his search for a basis for his own moral position. His accumulating religious crisis broke in 1810 with his "conversion," and Henriette followed him into the Catholic church after instruction from a priest of Jansenist tendencies. The content and form of Manzoni's work now became his own, as he sought to apply Christian teaching to history and life. The first four *Inni sacri (Sacred Hymns),* of 1812–15, describe the historical events of the Incarnation, stressing their enduring significance through the ritual of church festivals. Manzoni sometimes assumed a popular tone and language as he spoke for humanity. He attempted, as he put it, "to bring back to religion the noble, great, human feelings deriving naturally from it." The political hopes and disillusionments of 1814–15 mark the poems "Aprile 1814" (April 1814) and "Il Proclama di Rimini" (The Proclamation of Rimini) in which Murat makes an ineffectual appeal to Italians against Austria. In both, Manzoni identifies the Italian cause with Divine justice. These disappointments and the church's failure to support Italian claims and to oppose reactionary policies led to his religious and political "crisis" of 1817, when Manzoni proposed a journey to Paris for discussions with Fauriel in the hope of resolving his philosophical dilemmas. The logically argued *Osservazioni sulla morale cattolica* (1819, Observations on Catholic Morality) had related Christian teaching to the life of the individual. In this work, Manzoni stresses individual moral responsibility, the rational ability to distinguish right and wrong and the convergence of morality and truth in God. The Christian ethic, he states, is independent of changing historical conditions. As reflected in the *Osservazioni,* Manzoni had read deeply in French seventeenth-century religious writers.

The tragedy *Il conte di Carmagnola* (The Count of Carmagnola), begun in January 1816, was completed only in August 1819. Carmagnola, a fifteenth–century *condottiere* commanding Venetian forces against his former master the duke of Milan, having sustained defeats after initial success, was executed for treason. Manzoni, however, portrays him as the innocent victim of the state and of inevitable injustice in history, who, after his sentence, abruptly turns to God, despairing of earthly justice. The chorus condemns civil war as encouraging foreign intervention. Manzoni had read Shakespeare, Schiller, and A. W. Schlegel and was in touch with romantic thought in Milan. As a result, this work reflects the general rejection of neoclassical dramatic principles that German romantics were advocating, based upon the example of Shakespeare. In the preface to his tragedy, he asserts as criteria of judgment not traditional rules, but the author's intention, its reasonableness and whether he has achieved it. He attacks the unities of time and place as falsely involving the spectator in the time of the action and justifies his introduction of the chorus for his comments on the action. Manzoni's second tragedy, *Adelchi* (1882, Adelchi), deals with Charlemagne's (Carlo's) invasion of 773–74 against the Lombard King Desiderio, at the request of the pope. A crafty politician, Carlo ascribes his victory to Divine support, a view accepted by Desiderio. Adelchi, son of Desiderio, the just man in an unjust age in which glory is impossible, is mortally wounded and regards death and God as the only consolation for the monstrous force controlling history. His sister Ermengarda, the rejected wife of Carlo, is also a victim, even though she was born to a race of oppressors; her only consolation is death, as a celebrated chorus conveys.

Manzoni's patriotism dominates the ode "Marzo 1821" (March 1821). Written when the Piedmontese were expected to unite with Lombard patriots against Austria, it moves with a rapid popular rhythm as it urges Italians to fight together, with Old Testament references to God's vengeance. "Il Cinque Maggio" ("The Fifth of May") depicts the stupor of the world on Napoleon's death, Napoleon's spiritual anguish in exile, and his final turning to God who receives him into eternal peace. The close organization and striking images, the varied movement, and Manzoni's deep commitment produced a masterpiece which Goethe translated in 1822. The fifth sacred hymn, "La Pentecoste" ("Pentecost") of 1822, solves the problem of the tragedies by making the Holy Spirit active in all spheres of life in direct relationship with the individual. It expresses joyful certainty and is the apex of Manzoni's poetic achievement.

Manzoni was now pondering the relationship between literature and history. In 1819–20, he had met the historians Augustin Thierry and François Guizot and the philosopher Victor Cousin in Paris. In the *Lettre à M. Chauvet* (1820, Letter to M. Chauvet), he argues against the unities of time and place and refers to the examples of Racine, Voltaire, Spanish literature, Goethe, and an analysis of Shakespeare's *Richard II*. Manzoni states that, unlike the historian, the tragic poet selects a detached series of events and completes it by restoring its lost parts—not only actions, but especially thoughts, feelings, and speeches. Invention must agree with, and enhance, reality. Facts must not be invented in order to adapt feelings to them. By revealing the moral effect of a historical action, the poet develops in his readers a moral force capable of overcoming their passions. The *Lettera sul romanticismo* (1823, Letter on Romanticism), repeats the romantic opposition to the use of mythology, imitation, and arbitrary rules. Manzoni conceived the historical novel as the representation of a given state of society through actions and characters so like reality as to seem a true history. He acknowledged Scott's example. In the

Lombardy of 1628–31, he found a society, events, impressive characters, and the text of an interesting legal document as a starting point. In a novel, he could present ordinary people as individuals, facing the problems of life and sometimes achieving a relative happiness. Given the unsuitability of traditional literary Italian for such characters, Manzoni used a "Tuscan-Milanese" language for the first edition of *I promessi sposi (The Betrothed)* of 1825–27 and contemporary Tuscan for the edition of 1840–42. Later, he became the champion of Tuscan as the common language of united Italy.

In *I promessi sposi,* Don Rodrigo, a local lord in a Lombard village, coerces the priest Don Abbondio, a man dominated by fear, into not marrying Renzo and Lucia. Don Rodrigo then attempts to kidnap Lucia. The couple, with Lucia's mother Agnese, flee with the help of the Capuchin Father Cristoforo. Renzo goes to Milan where he is arrested during food riots but escapes to his cousin at Bergamo, and the women seek the protection of the nun Gertrude in a convent at Monza. There Lucia is kidnapped by *bravi* of the Unnamed, the leading criminal lord of the whole region, and is taken to his castle. She is released the next day after a night in which his existential uncertainties, heightened by her presence, lead the Unnamed to seek Cardinal Federigo Borromeo, who is visiting a nearby parish, and to repent of his crimes. Lucia goes to Milan and, convalescent from the plague, is found by Renzo, who has also recovered from the plague. Urged by Father Cristoforo, Renzo forgives the dying Don Rodrigo, thereby becoming worthy of Lucia. They are married in their village and move to the Bergamo area with Agnese, where Renzo continues his weaver's trade.

The historical background for the novel is carefully prepared, with analyses of, for example, the Thirty Years' War in Italy, the famine, and the plague. An anonymous manuscript is postulated to support the story of Renzo and Lucia. Manzoni presents a Spanish-dominated Lombardy where "honor" is vital, government inefficient, and the people, collectively, irrational. Gertrude is forced into the convent to save a dowry and her family's status. Only a few characters are motivated by religion. Guided by her faith, Lucia exercises a beneficent effect, especially on the Unnamed. With her, Renzo realizes that troubles visit us inevitably and that Christian acceptance can make them useful for a better life. The turning point, the Unnamed's conversion, is observed psychologically and is no mere Divine intervention. Everyone in the novel must face a moral choice. Characters are closely analyzed and are sometimes presented through their past development. Manzoni contemplates everything from a Christian, rather than historical, viewpoint. The narrative is skillfully organized, with Manzoni ranging from omniscient to speculative or speaking directly to the reader and moving easily from the dramatic to the comic.

Later, Manzoni asserted the incompatibility of history and fiction, although maintaining for art the beauty of the *verosimile* (resemblance to truth). In the later 1820s, he came under the influence of the Christian philosopher Antonio Rosmini from whom his theories on aesthetics and the origin of language developed. Manzoni also wrote the *Storia della colonna infame* (1842, *The Column of Infamy*) against the judges who tortured and falsely condemned some men accused of spreading the plague. Elsewhere, he attacked the concept of utilitarianism in a revised edition of his *Osservazioni sulla morale cattolica* (1855).

Manzoni's novels and poetry have exercised negligible influence in English-speaking countries. Nor have his literary views received adequate notice. Critics have proposed various explanations of this omission, but if *I promessi sposi* had expressed a spiritual quest rather than an achieved certainty, an existential dilemma rather than a theological solution, perhaps the book would have attained the critical reputation its artistic qualities deserve.

See also ROMANTICISM.

Bibliography: The Betrothed, trans. Archibald Colquhoun (New York: Dutton, 1952); *The Column of Infamy*, trans. Kenelm Foster and Jane Grigson (London: Oxford University Press, 1964); *The Sacred Hymns and The Napoleonic Ode*, trans. Joel Bingham (London: Henry Frowde, 1904); Jean-Pierre Barricelli, *Alessandro Manzoni* (Boston: Twayne, 1976); S. B. Chandler, *Alessandro Manzoni* (Edinburgh: Edinburgh University Press, 1974); Archibald Colquhoun, *Manzoni and His Times: A Biography of the Author of 'The Betrothed'* (London: Dent, 1954); Barbara Reynolds, *The Linguistic Writings of Alessandro Manzoni* (Cambridge: Cambridge University Press, 1950); Ferruccio Ulivi, *Il romanticismo e Alessandro Manzoni* (Bologna: Cappelli, 1965); Bernard Wall, *Alessandro Manzoni* (Cambridge: Cambridge University Press, 1954).

S. B. Chandler

MARINETTI, FILIPPO TOMMASO (1875–1944), novelist, leader, and founder of the futurist movement. Born in Alexandria, Egypt, of Italian parents, Marinetti was educated there in a French Jesuit school from which he was expelled for introducing Zola's novels to his classmates. He moved to Paris in 1893, enrolling at the university, while his father (who had by that time amassed a considerable fortune) returned the family to Milan. After obtaining his degree in Paris, he enrolled at the faculty of law in Pavia and then in Genoa, graduating in 1899 with a thesis on parliamentary government. Marinetti was destined never to practice law, for in 1898 he published a free-verse poem in French entitled "Les Vieux Marins" (The Old Sailors). The poem received first prize in a contest conducted by Gustave Kahn and Catulle Mendès at the *Samedis populaires* given by the famous actress Sarah Bernhardt, who herself declaimed the young poet's work.

After this auspicious beginning, Marinetti dedicated himself entirely to a literary career. In France he collaborated on a number of periodicals, while in Italy he helped to popularize the poetry of the symbolists (whom he would later reject in a futurist manifesto of 1911–15, entitled "We Abjure Our Symbolist Masters, the Last Lovers of the Moon"). Most of what he wrote before the foundation of the futurist movement in 1909 was written in French and grew out of the free-verse tradition already popular abroad. Later Marinetti expanded free verse to what he called the futurist "parole in libertà" ("words in liberty"), abolishing all restrictions of syntax or grammar. In 1905, with Sem Benelli* and Vitaliano Ponti, he founded the international journal *Poesia,* which soon became an eloquent voice for the European avant-garde. Some of his French works from this prefuturist period include poems entitled *La Conquête des Étoiles* (1902, The Conquest of the Stars), *Destruction* (1904, Destruction), *La Ville Charnelle* (1908, The Carnal Village), and a satirical tragedy entitled *Le Roi Bombance* (1905, King Carousing), which echoes Alfred Jarry's *Ubu Roi.*

With the publication of the first futurist manifesto in *Le Figaro* on 20 February 1909, Marinetti became one of Europe's strongest voices for revolution and innovation in the arts and established the most vital Italian literary movement of the twentieth century. Initially, his ideas were received enthusiastically by most of the principal writers and artists of the times (although many later claimed the contrary or disavowed his influence). Writers whose works show Marinetti's influence to some degree include Wyndham Lewis, Guillaume Apollinaire, Ezra Pound, Vladimir Mayakovsky, Umberto Boccioni (1882–1916), D. H. Lawrence, Aldo Palazzeschi,* and Ardengo Soffici.* Although he always associated himself and the futurist movement with many other poets, artists, and intellectuals, there was never any doubt that futurism* was closely identified with and dependent upon the tireless efforts and the protean imagination of its founder. In contrast to the limited aims of other avant-garde.movements, Marinetti's futurism aspired to affect every aspect of human life, including politics, literature, aesthetics, art, women's rights, marriage and the family, theatre, cinema, music, dance, and even fashion.

It was inevitable that Marinetti would be remembered longer for his often shocking manifestos than for his purely literary works, which demonstrate the practical applications of his futurist theories. Nonetheless, Marinetti made the writing of a manifesto an art in its own right. He was without rival in combining a felicitous and polemical style with novel ideas guaranteed to outrage the average man, for whose opinions he had nothing but contempt and whose ridicule, he believed, was proof of his genius (see "The Pleasure of Being Booed," a manifesto written between 1911 and

1915). His manifestoes urged poets to embrace a completely modern subject matter (war, the machine, a racing motor car) and to abandon traditional subjects (the moon, the past, love), syntax, verb forms, and language. He hoped to open poetry to new realms of the imagination or the senses, and he was especially interested in the possibilities of onomatopoeia in radically free verse. A typical example of such futurist poetry is "Zang tumb tumb" (1914), which depicts the Turkish siege of Adrianopolis (now Adrianople) in 1911. It relies heavily upon the reproduction of the sounds of battle and clearly exemplifies what Marinetti means by "words in liberty."

Marinetti also wrote several novels, among which are *Mafarka le Futuriste* (1910, Mafarka the Futurist—in French) and a pessimistic futurist allegory entitled *Gli indomabili* (1922, *The Untamables*), but it is his innovations in the theatre which are of paramount importance. In a number of brief dramatic works—*sintesi* or "syntheses" as he called them—he succeeded in expanding the traditional concept of realism in the theatre by breaking down the barriers between the stage and the audience in a most radical manner even before Pirandello.* Moreover, he encouraged revolutionary new stage sets, costumes, and themes. He proclaimed the variety theatre to be the model for new futurist drama, since the variety theatre encouraged audience participation, rejected dramatic conventions or traditions, and was anti–academic by nature (see the manifesto of 1913, "The Variety Theatre," or that of 1915, "The Futurist Synthetic Theatre"). Earlier than most directors, Marinetti recognized the innovative possibilities of film and urged film-makers to avoid transferring the conventions of the stage to this new art based on motion (1916, "The Futurist Cinema"). He also advocated reforms in musical performances and radio broadcasts along futurist lines.

Marinetti's futurism was strongly fused with Italian nationalism. This aspect of the movement he founded eventually hindered its growth abroad where it was initially greeted with enthusiasm. Moreover, Marinetti's reputation was later to be severely compromised by his links to Mussolini and fascism. He praised war as "the world's only hygiene," and he believed that foreign expansion and imperialism were an excellent means of testing a nation's courage and vigor. These ideas were shared with fascists and nonfuturist conservatives. He and his followers were among the first to urge Italy to join the war against Austria and Germany, nations which Marinetti identified with a nonfuturist mentality and a love for the past. Besides influential visits to England (where he met Wyndham Lewis and members of what would become the vorticism movement) and to Russia (where he would play a role in the development of Russian futurism), Marinetti joined the Italian army when war was declared in 1915. Many of his fellow futurist volunteers were wounded (as was Marinetti himself), and others (Boccioni, Sant'Elia, 1888–1916) died valiantly in battle, following their futurist principles to the death.

Before the war's outbreak, Marinetti had been arrested in 1915 (along with Mussolini) as a result of an interventionist demonstration in Rome. After the war was over, Marinetti and Mussolini joined forces in the destruction of the office of *Avanti!*, the socialist daily newspaper of which the younger, socialist Mussolini had once been the editor. This memorable event on 15 April 1919 marked the beginning of the association between futurism and fascism, although Marinetti left the Fascist party in 1920 in anger. He came to an accommodation with the political movement some years later, and Mussolini finally named him (in 1929) to the Italian Academy. However, his earlier hopes that Italian fascism might embody futurist political principles were doomed to disappointment, and his subsequent loyalty to the fascist regime (including the short-lived Republic of Salò) was based more upon his nationalism than upon any real belief in fascist ideology. Nonetheless, he participated in the Ethiopian war and was on the Russian front for a period in 1942–43. Because of his ties to Mussolini and fascism, he was for many years denied adequate scholarly attention or an honest assessment of the considerable contributions of the futurist movement which he founded. Only in recent years have his works been edited, translated, and studied with a modicum of objectivity in Italy and elsewhere.

See also FUTURISM.

Bibliography: La grande Milano tradizionale e futurista, ed. Luciano De Maria (Milan: Mondadori, 1969); *Per conoscere Marinetti e il futurismo,* ed. Luciano De Maria (Milan: Mondadori, 1973); *Teatro,* ed. Giovanni Calendoli, 3 vols. (Rome: Vito Bianco, 1960); *Teoria e invenzione futurista,* ed. Luciano De Maria, 2 vols. (Milan: Mondadori, 1968); *Marinetti: Selected Writings,* ed. R. W. Flint (New York: Noonday, 1972); "Marinetti's Short Plays," trans. Virginia Kirby, *Tulane Drama Review* 17 (1973), 113–25; Sandro Briosi, *Marinetti* (Florence: La Nuova Italia, 1969); Julie R. Dashwood, "Futurism and Fascism," *Italian Studies* 27 (1972), 91–103; Michael Kirby, *Futurist Performances* (New York: Dutton, 1971).

MARINO, GIAMBATTISTA (1569–1625), poet and prosewriter. The son of a successful lawyer, Giambattista was soon expelled from home for abandoning his legal studies, but found no difficulty in being elected to the prestigious Academy of the Svegliati and accepted in several aristocratic houses of his native Naples. Thoroughly immersed in the turbulent life of his times, the exuberant young poet managed to get into scrapes with the law and was imprisoned twice. Although freed, either through lack of evidence or through the pressures exerted by influential patrons, Marino was forced to flee to Rome in 1600. During his residence there, he made a

wide circle of literary acquaintances and was employed by high ecclesiastical dignitaries. In 1605, he accompanied Cardinal Aldobrandini to
his seat at Ravenna and traveled on various missions to Venice, Mantua,
Modena, and Ferrara, and, in 1608, to Turin where he was finally permitted
to remain. In Turin, Marino enjoyed a notable success, but he also became
involved in various quarrels. The fiercest of these polemics, fought with
sonnets,* invectives, and pistol shots, was with Gaspare Murtola
(?–1624), a fellow courtier and poet. In recognition of his poetic merits and
services, the duke of Savoy conferred upon him the cross of a knight of the
order of Saints Maurice and Lazarus. In 1611, however, Marino abruptly
fell into disfavor and found himself jailed for fourteen months, despite the
intercession of powerful defenders. Not until 1615 was he allowed to move
to Paris where he was treated with the highest regard in French literary
circles as well as at the court, which at the time was under strong Italian
influence. Marino's eight-year stay in Paris was a period of intense activity;
he was able to complete his chief work, *L'Adone,* which he dedicated to
Louis XIII. In the year of its publication, 1623, Marino left France. He
died soon after his return to Naples at the height of his popularity as the
most celebrated of living poets.

Marino's early collections of verse were gathered under the title *La Lira*
(The Lyre) and published in three parts in 1614. Part one consists of
sonnets arranged under different headings: *Amorose, Boscherecce, Hero-
iche, Lugubri, Morali, Sacre,* and *Varie;* part two, of madrigals* and
canzoni;* and part three, of about four hundred poems of various forms
grouped under the titles *Amorose, Lodi, Lagrime, Divotioni,* and *Capricci.*
Whereas Marino's earlier lyrics can be related to the late Cinquecento
Italian poetic culture, in part three *La Lira* reveals the full emergence of the
highly mannered style that established his prodigious reputation. The term
Marinism was coined to describe this poetic style characterized by auditory smoothness, sensuous imagery, diffuse metaphorical patterns, and
ostentatious technical and linguistic virtuosity. The *Epitalami* (1616, Epithalamia) contains ten panegyrics composed of unrhymed strophes of lines
varied in length written for the nuptials of various nobles. While given to
the composition of elaborate compliments, Marino is here essentially a
poet of profane love. It is well known that Marino was passionately
interested in the visual arts and derived much inspiration from them. In *La
Galeria* (1619, The Gallery), he gathered some six hundred madrigals and
sonnets, plus a few longer poems describing real or imaginary paintings
(*Favole, Istorie, Ritratti,* and *Capricci*) and sculptures (*Statue, Rilievi,
Modelli,* and *Medaglie*). In 1620 appeared *La Sampogna* (The Shepherd's
Pipes) in which Marino collected his poems of bucolic and mythological
content. It divides into eight *idilli favolosi* (mythological idylls) and four
idilli pastorali (pastoral idylls) and represents the poet's mature art. As a

satirist, Marino is, if not outstanding, at least very able and plentifully inventive. The Bernesque sonnets and *capitoli** against the poet Murtola entitled *Murtoleide* (1626, The Murtoliad) are the best known of his humorous and satirical efforts.

The poet was less successful in his attempts to compose heroic poetry: the *Gerusalemme distrutta* (1633, Jerusalem Destroyed) and *L'Anversa liberata* (Antwerp Delivered, published only in 1956), both of which were left unfinished. Yet, Marino's major work *L'Adone* (1623, *Adonis*) takes the form of a narrative poem in the manner of the Renaissance* epic.* Written over a period of thirty years and consisting of twenty cantos of nearly forty-one thousand lines, *L'Adone* is founded on the classical myth. Cupid, chastised by his mother, resolves to take revenge; he brings Adonis to the shores of Cyprus and causes Venus to fall in love with him. The goddess leads the beautiful youth to her palace, where Cupid relates the story of his love with Psyche, while Mercury recounts the tales of Narcissus, Hylas, Actaeon, and other victims of love. Adonis is then escorted through the gardens of pleasure into the tower of delight. But Mars opposes the love of Venus and Adonis and the youth is forced to flee; he falls into the hands of the witch Falsirena who imprisons and tries to seduce him. He manages to escape and, after many wanderings, returns to Venus, but, during a hunting expedition, Mars and the wicked fairy contrive to send against him the boar which brings on the catastrophe. Adonis's death, his interment, and funeral games conclude the poem. In addition to narrative digressions, the bulk of the work is composed of interpolations of varied subjects (a game of chess, a theatrical performance, panegyrics, a flight into the heavens, and a musical duel between a lute player and a nightingale) and elaborate descriptions (pastoral scenes, festivities, pictures of palaces, fountains, and gardens). The famous account of the gardens of the five senses comprises three cantos of about five thousand lines.

The main characters, the setting, and the time of *L'Adone* are ancient, but Marino attains considerable success in wedding antiquity to contemporary life and culture. Typical of his practice is the conscious use of a multitude of models and sources, both classical and modern, written and visual. Marino is thus seeking to outdo all other poets by reworking their themes and improving on them. In addition, he felt that poetry was obliged to compete with the art and music which were flourishing in his age. To the historian, *L'Adone* may appear an anomalous poem, a compendium of previous poetry which from time to time is brought to new life by Marino's mastery of rhetorical devices and consummate ingenuity in the deployment of images and words. *L'Adone*, in fact, is a richly orchestrated poem which emphasizes the musical effect of sound patterns such as alliteration, assonance, or repetition. The poet's technique and thematic material remain of compelling interest to students of Marinism and the literary Baroque,* but there are signs of a fresh reassessment of the poem as an individual artistic work. Yet, the current reevaluation of *L'Adone's* obvious qualities and its appeal to professional exegetes as an important literary document cannot obscure the fact that as a narrative the poem is weak.

Marino's weakness as a narrative poet is also seen in his other major epic work based on one of the most popular devotional themes of post-Tridentine art. Published posthumously, *La Strage degli Innocenti* (1632, *The Slaughter of the Innocents*) is usually divided into four books: "Sospetto d' Erode" ("Herod's Suspicion"), "Consiglio de' Satrapi" ("The Satraps' Counsel"), "Essecuzione della strage" ("Execution of the Slaughter"), and "Il Limbo" ("Limbo"). Planned as early as 1605, it still occupied Marino's last productive hours. He was very pleased with the poem and hoped to make his final reputation with this contribution to the growing tradition of the Christian epic. The great number of editions and translations into Latin, English, German, French, Dutch, Serbo-Croatian, and Russian testify to the enduring success of the poem in the seventeenth and eighteenth centuries.

Prose accounts for a small part of Marino's large output. His most extensive prose work is the *Dicerie sacre* (1614, Sacred Discourses), which contains three long discourses on the subjects of the shroud of Christ, the seven last words and the order of Saints Maurice and Lazarus, based on elaborate metaphors worked around the themes of painting, music, and heaven, respectively. The *Dicerie* are offered both as sermons and as didactic treatises, but their virtues lie largely in their style. The single central metaphor is elaborated by use of witty analogies, sustained conceits, subtle patterns of clauses and phrases, and the resources of a difficult, lush vocabulary.

Both Marino's historical position and his intrinsic worth as a poet are still being debated. In the history of Italian letters, only Petrarch* exerted as much appeal and attracted as many imitators in Italy and abroad. But whereas Petrarchism* continued to stimulate new poetry for centuries, Marino's fame and Marinism had waned by the end of the seventeenth century. Despite a dazzling technical mastery of rhetorical devices and phonic value, he was usually held up as an example of how not to succeed in being a poet of the first rank, and he was condemned for being the poet of the senses and failing to devote his art to the service of an ideal, whether ethical, religious, or political. Critical rehabilitation of Marino and his style was not to come until recent years in the wake of the revival of interest in Baroque art and the emergence of common features in much twentieth-century poetry and poetic theory. As modern readers and critics are coming to recognize, Marino is not only a brilliant craftsman and a master exploiter of language, but also a significant poetic sensibility responding to and interpreting the values or, better, the crisis of values of his time. Marino is also becoming increasingly important for any attempt to understand the late Renaissance poetic culture. Accordingly, the need for careful study of his work has become more urgent.

See also BAROQUE.

Bibliography: The Slaughter of the Innocents by Herod (London: Andrew Clark, 1675); Adonis: Selections from L'Adone of Giambattista Marino, trans. Harold Priest (Ithaca, N.Y.; Cornell University Press, 1967); Marziano Guglielminetti, Tecnica e invenzione nell'opera di Giambattista Marino (Messina-Florence: D'Anna, 1964); James V. Mirollo, The Poet of the Marvelous: Giambattista Marino (New York: Columbia University Press, 1963); Marzio Pieri, Per Marino (Padua: Liviana Editrice, 1976); Giovanni Pozzi, "Guida alla lettura," in L'Adone (Milan: Mondadori, 1976), II, 7–140, and "Ludicra mariniana," Studi e problemi di critica testuale 6 (1972), 132–62; Stephen Warman, "The Subject-Matter and Treatment of Marino's Images," Studi secenteschi 10 (1969), 56–131.

                                                                   Albert N. Mancini

MASCHERONI, LORENZO (1750–1800), scientist and poet. A native of Castagneta, Mascheroni underwent a scientific education and taught physics and mathematics in Bergamo until his professional reputation gained him a post in mathematics at the University of Pavia in 1785. He took an active role in the political events leading to the formation of the Cisapline Republic. One of his scientific works, the *Geometria del compasso* (1797, The Geometry of the Compass), was dedicated to Napoleon. His literary fame springs from a single work, "Invito di Dafni Orobiano a Lesbia Cidonia" (1793, The Invitation of Dafni Orobiano to Lesbia Cidonia). Written in blank verse, this didactic poem narrates the visit of the Arcadian countess Lesbia (in reality, Paolina Secco Suardi) to the University of Pavia guided by the Arcadian Dafni Orobiano (Mascheroni). The University of Pavia is celebrated in the work as a new Athens of erudition. Lesbia is welcomed by the learned faculty and is given a tour of the university's famous museum of natural history, its scientific laboratories, its library, and its botanical gardens, all of which are described in some detail. Extremely popular in its time, the poem appeared in some fifty editions. It may be considered the best example of a particular kind of "scientific" poetry of the neoclassical period which attempted the union of poetic and scientific themes.

Bibliography: I lirici del Seicento e dell'Arcadia, ed. Carlo Calcaterra (Milan: Rizzoli, 1936).

MASUCCIO SALERNITANO (circa 1410–1475), writer of *novelle.** Born Tommaso Guardati into a noble family from Salerno (the origin of his pen-name), Masuccio became secretary to Roberto Sanseverino, the prince of Salerno, whom he served until his death in 1475. Masuccio also became acquainted with many of the leading writers and intellectuals of the Neapolitan court, Giovanni Pontano* in particular.

Masuccio's single literary work is the extremely notable collection of *novelle* entitled the *Novellino* (1475, *The Novellino*). Continuing the narrative tradition of Boccaccio* and others, Masuccio's collection is disposed according to five themes, each of which contains ten stories: the misdeeds of churchmen; tricks and injuries caused by jealousy; the "defective" female sex; tearful matters; and stories of the magnanimity of princes. Prefaced by a dedication, the *Novellino* closes by recalling the memory of his former patron. Each of the stories is addressed to a member of the Aragonese court; an exordium introduces the story and the narrator ends it with a comment. Unlike Boccaccio or many other writers in this genre, there are no storytellers; all the stories are narrated by Masuccio. The language is a southern Italian dialect rather than a literary Tuscan. Perhaps the most influential *novella* in the collection (XXXIV) provides the first general framework for the story of Romeo and Juliet. In Masuccio's version, the story is set in Siena and the characters are Mariotto Mignanelli and a girl named Ganozza. In the next century, Luigi Da Porto* based another *novella* upon this tale, and his version influenced Shakespeare.

See also DA PORTO, Luigi; NOVELLA.

Bibliography: Il Novellino, ed. Alfredo Mauro (Bari: Laterza, 1940); *The Novellino,* trans. W. G. Waters, 2 vols. (London: Lawrence & Bullen, 1895); Letterato Di Francia, *Novellistica,* 2 vols. (Milan: Vallardi, 1924); Giorgio Petrocchi, *Masuccio Guardati e la narrativa napoletana del Quattrocento* (Florence: Le Monnier, 1953), and *Stile e lingua nel Novellino di Masuccio* (Messina: Editrice Universitaria, 1960); D. P. Rotunda, *Motif-Index of the Italian Novella in Prose* (Bloomington, Ind.: Indiana University Press, 1942).

MAZZINI, GIUSEPPE (1805–1872), patriot, political thinker, and critic. Born in Genoa the year of Napoleon's coronation as king of Italy, Mazzini received a university law degree in 1827, the same year he became a *Carbonaro*. He also began to author articles on literary topics for publication in reviews in Livorno and Genoa. Arrested in 1830 and imprisoned, he was allowed to go into exile in the following year. In Marseilles during that same year, he founded *Giovine Italia* (Young Italy), an organization that worked for Italian unification under a republican form of government with Rome as its capital. When Carlo Alberto became king in Piedmont, Mazzini urged him to assume the leadership in the struggle for Italian independence. By 1832, Mazzini's revolutionary ideas had flooded Italy. Driven from France in 1833, Mazzini moved to Switzerland, where he founded Young Switzerland and Young Europe, counterparts to *Giovine Italia*. The aim of Young Europe was to establish a union of European republican nation-states, all espousing the principles of equality and brotherhood. Again forced into exile, Mazzini moved to London in 1837 and remained there until 1848.

In England, Mazzini wrote several astute literary analyses of Dante,* Byron, Goethe, Carlyle, Foscolo,* and romanticism,* in addition to numerous letters and political treatises. When the revolts of 1848 erupted all over Europe, he returned to Italy, witnessing the eventual abandonment of Lombardy by the Piedmontese and the fall of the short-lived Roman Republic (of which he was one of the Triumvirs). Returning to England upon the triumph of the reactionary forces throughout Italy, Mazzini continued his prolific publication of literary and political writings, and helped to arouse the sympathy of the British and American public for the cause of Italian liberty. He also helped to organize unsuccessful uprisings in Milan (1853) and Genoa (1857), but he opposed Cavour's policy of linking Italian unification to the fortunes of the House of Savoy. Although his revolutionary ideas helped to inspire the most memorable events of the Italian Risorgimento, including the bold actions of Garibaldi* and his followers, Mazzini was always regarded with suspicion by the ruling classes, and he suffered much the same fate as Thomas Paine had experienced after the American Revolution. In 1860, he published *I doveri dell'uomo (The Duties of Man)*, a political tract addressed to the workingmen of Italy. He urged them to fulfill their obligations to God, humanity, and their families, and to reject the doctrines of materialism then being spread among them by non-Christian, Marxist thinkers.

In London from 1860 until 1868, Mazzini became a close personal friend of George Meredith and the poet Swinburne. The last four years of his life were spent in Italy, primarily in Lugano. During this time, Mazzini founded a new journal and an association for Italian workers. He was also imprisoned for a brief time for his part in a conspiracy to liberate Rome, and he continued to write countless articles. His life was a testament to the highest ideals of the Italian Risorgimento, and his political ideas moved patriots all over the world, winning over public opinion to the cause of Italian unification.

While Mazzini is best known for his political activities, his critical writings represent an essential contribution to Italian romanticism. Furthermore, they are an excellent reflection of the close connection that often existed in nineteenth-century Italy between new literary ideas and social and political change. An early essay on Italian literature, for example, asserted that the character of Italian poetry reflected Italy's failure to produce strong and independent political organizations, and called for the creation of a new Italian literature with "social man in action" as its theme.

Mazzini also attacked Italy's writers for their habitual servile admiration of the powerful, their imitation of alien literary schools or movements, and their tragic separation of literature from Italian national life.

Mazzini's important essay on Dante reveals him as a prophet of Italian unity, but this essentially political interpretation of Dante's works is based upon a fresh reading of the poetry itself, rather than upon a scholarly analysis of Dante's annotators or "rummaging," as he puts it, "through the archives of monasteries." It echoes Foscolo's earlier appeal for a "new criticism" of Italy's greatest literary figure. In his study of Byron and Goethe, Mazzini views the two men as contrasting figures, each representing divergent intellectual positions: "Goethe better expresses lives; Byron life. The one is more vast; the other more deep. The first searches everywhere for the beautiful, and loves, above all things, harmony and response; the other seeks the sublime, and adores action and force." Mazzini defines poetry as an undertaking with a religious, popular, and visionary mission. Although he praised much of the new romantic literature of his generation, he rejected the romantic cult of the individual, the idea of art as a mere imitation of nature, or the formula "art for art's sake." As he put it, "Nature, reality, and form, should, all of them, be so rendered and expressed by art, as to reveal to mankind some ray of the truth—a vaster and profounder sentiment of life."

See also ROMANTICISM.

Bibliography: Scritti editi ed inediti di Giuseppe Mazzini, 100 vols. (Imola: Galeati, 1906–43); *Selected Writings,* ed. N. Gangulee (1945; rpt. Westport, Conn.: Greenwood Press, 1974); Gwilym O. Griffith, *Mazzini: Prophet of Modern Europe* (London: Hodder & Stoughton, 1932); Emilia Morelli, *L'Inghilterra di Mazzini* (Rome: Istituto per la storia del Risorgimento italiano, 1965); Joseph Rossi, *The Image of America in Mazzini's Writings* (Madison, Wis.: University of Wisconsin Press, 1954); Gaetano Salvemini, *Mazzini* (London: Jonathan Cape, 1956).

MEDICI, LORENZO DE', "Il Magnifico" (1449–1492), Florentine poet, patron, and statesman. The son and grandson of Florentine rulers, Lorenzo became head of the Florentine state in 1469 and remained a dominant figure in Italian diplomacy until his death. He assumed an active role as both participant and patron in the cultural and intellectual life of Florence, which attracted many of the most eminent scholars and gifted writers and artists of the age. His defense of the vernacular as a literary language was a lasting contribution to Italian letters in a period of linguistic crisis. His own literary production reflects the range of his interests and includes realistic observations of Tuscan life, courtly love poetry in the Italian tradition, long poems on classical themes, carnival and dance songs, and works of philosophical and religious inspiration.

The precise chronology of Lorenzo's literary works has not been established. From his early period date three poems: the *Uccellagione* (Falcon-Hunt); *Simposio* (Symposium); and *Nencia da Barberino* (Nencia from Barberino), all probably composed before or during 1474. Each poem recreates some aspect of Lorenzo's participation in or observation of everyday life in his native Tuscany, and all reflect the diversions of the poet's youthful *brigata* or group of friends. The *Nencia*, perhaps Lorenzo's masterpiece, is a poem of twenty octaves which presents the shepherd Vallera's musing about his love for Nencia, a village girl. Amused but sympathetic observation of country life and a fine rendering of rustic speech combine with thinly veiled allusions to both popular and literary tradition to create an artful effect of apparent spontaneity.

Lorenzo's collection of lyric poems is extensive, including one hundred and eight sonnets,* eight *canzoni,* * five *sestine,* * and a single ballad. With a few important exceptions they are highly derivative, reflecting both the Petrarchan manner and the influence of earlier *stilnovisti* poets and treating the subject of love almost exclusively. Forty-one of the sonnets are combined with lengthy prose presentations in the ambitious *Comento ad alcuni dei suoi sonetti* (Commentary to Some of his own Sonnets—dates various and uncertain), in a sequence illustrating moments of an individual love experience and relating these to a psychology and philosophy of love reflecting both the early Italian poetic tradition and the contemporary interpretation of Platonic doctrine as elaborated by Marsilio Ficino.* The pattern for the structure of the work is provided by the *Vita nuova* and the *Convivio* of Dante.* Its important *proemio* includes not only a justification of the poet's choice of love as subject, but also a defense of the vernacular for literary composition.

Perhaps the best known of Lorenzo's works are his carnival songs which, like his two brief short stories *Giacoppo* and *Ginevra,* defend the claims of youth to enjoy present pleasure. These exuberant poems, celebrating the delight and occasionally the sadness of love, are best illustrated by the famed *Canzone di Bacco* (Song of Bacchus). While most of the poem presents the revelry of a mythological cast including Bacchus, Ariadne, nymphs, and satyrs, the final two stanzas suggest the more serious side of Lorenzo's use of the *carpe diem* theme. The melancholy sense of the limitations which time imposes on human happiness is expressed in the famous refrain: "Let him who wishes to, be merry: there's no certainty about tomorrow."

Always responsive to the literary trends of his time, Lorenzo was increasingly influenced by classical sources during the later period of his life. His mythological poems undoubtedly reflect his contact with the more famous and learned poet Poliziano.* He composed five works on mythological subjects: *Corinto* (circa 1486, Corinto), *Ambra* (?, Ambra), the

Selve d'Amore (?, Forest of Love), and the incomplete poems *Apollo e Pan* (?, Apollo and Pan) and *Amori di Venere e Marte* (?, Loves of Venus and Mars). The most successful are the *Corinto* and *Ambra,* remarkable for their fusion of personal and classical inspiration in which the mythological material is naturalized into the contemporary Tuscan setting. The brief eclogue *Corinto* consists largely of the shepherd's lament about the disdain of his love by the nymph Galatea, and his fantasies of an encounter with her. In *Ambra,* the title celebrates both a nymph who is saved through metamorphosis from a pursuing river god, and Lorenzo's villa by that name at Poggio a Caiano which was surrounded by a river. In general outline, Lorenzo's version follows Ovid's story of Arethusa, but the landscape and the vivid description of country life in winter are identifiably Tuscan. The mythological theme is successfully integrated into a new pattern of the struggle of living creatures against the hostile forces of nature.

Philosophical and religious questions recur insistently in the works of Lorenzo's maturity. *L'Altercazione* (after 1473, The Dispute) presents a debate concerning the relative merits of city and country life; the debate is resolved in the Neo-Platonic explanation that true happiness consists only in the good of the spirit, the contemplation of God. The poem also reveals the longing for tranquility which is a dominant note in the few poems of personal inspiration among Lorenzo's religious poetry. In general, however, both his orations and his *laudi** (songs of praise) are largely derivative, the former as studied renderings of hermetic and Neo-Platonic texts and the latter as versions of popular poetry.

Also on a religious theme is Lorenzo's single dramatic work, the *Sacra Rappresentazione di San Giovanni e Paolo* (Sacred Play about Saints John and Paul), composed during the last years of his life. While he draws on learned sources for the story of the martyrs, Lorenzo emphasizes psychology of character in his portrayal of the two emperors, Constantine and Julian the Apostate, and he focuses on the possession and use of power in a debate which reveals the preoccupations of the statesman-poet.

See also BUONARROTI, Michelangelo; FICINO, Marsilio; POLIZIANO, Angelo; PULCI, Luigi.

Bibliography: Italian Poets of the Renaissance, trans. Joseph Tusiani (Long Island City, N.Y.: Baroque Press, 1971); *Renaissance and Baroque Lyrics,* ed. Harold Priest (Evanston, Ill.; Northwestern University Press, 1962); Cecilia Ady, *Lorenzo dei Medici and Renaissance Italy* (New York: Collier, 1966); Angelo Lipari, *The Dolce Stil Novo According to Lorenzo de' Medici* (New Haven, Conn.: Yale University Press, 1936); Sara Sturm, *Lorenzo de' Medici* (New York: Twayne, 1974).

Sara Sturm-Maddox.

MELI, GIOVANNI (1740–1815), Sicilian chemist, physician, and poet. After studying with the Jesuits in Palermo, Meli turned to educating himself by thoroughly reading the Latin and Italian classics and the French *philosophes* whose progressive ideas were beginning to make inroads into Sicily. Largely to please his mother, Meli took up the study of medicine, but his first love was lyric poetry. His early compositions, often based upon the Arcadian poets, earned him an invitation to join the Accademia del Buon Gusto (1760) and the Galante Conversazione (1761), a group formed by the prince of Campofranco. His reputation in both courtly and popular circles grew as his pastoral* and anacreontic verses, lyrics written in both Italian and dialect, found an audience in Palermo's high society as well as among commoner folk.

After obtaining the license to practice medicine in 1764, Meli moved to Cinisi, a small town near Palermo, where he lived from 1767 until 1772. There, he wrote many of his most notable works, including most of his *Elegii* (Elegies), part of the *Buccolica* (The Bucolics), a number of minor lyrics, and the first draft of *Riflessioni sul meccanismo della natura* (Reflections on the Mechanism of Nature), a treatise embodying Enlightenment* ideas, which was suppressed by the censor when it appeared in Naples in 1777. Most critics judge his *Buccolica* superior to his other works. Written in dialect, it is divided into an introduction of two sonnets* and four groups of poems (eclogues and idylls), each treating one of the seasons—*La primavera* (Spring), *L'està* (Summer), *L'Autunnu* (Autumn), and *L'Invernu* (Winter). Many of these poems are worthy of comparison to the pastoral lyrics of the classical tradition which inspired them. Meli's use of the Sicilian dialect lends greater authenticity to his vignettes of Sicilian country life, which recall the poetry of the first pastoral poet, Theocritus.

In 1772, Meli returned to Palermo where he lived for the rest of his life. Although part of the smart society of that city, Meli found time to become a professor of chemistry at the Accademia degli Studi in 1787 and to compose a heroic-comic poem in dialect entitled *Don Chisciotti e Sanciu Panza* (Don Quijote and Sancho Panza). All his poetry was assembled in a five-volume edition printed in 1787. After helping to found the Accademia Siciliana in 1790, Meli took part in the famous debate over the forgeries of Giuseppe Vella (1740–1814) in 1790–93 (an event which provided Leonardo Sciascia* with the plot for his novel, *Il Consiglio d'Egitto, The Council of Egypt*). In 1808, he received an official university degree in medicine *honoris causa*. His later poetic works often explored political issues (Admiral Nelson, Napoleon's Russian campaign, Sicilian constitutional problems). In 1813, Meli edited a seven-volume edition of his own complete works, including the *Favuli morali* (Moral Fables) which he had been compiling since 1787. Told in dialect, these stories reveal a basic Enlightenment faith in human progress, but their theme that men are less wise than the beasts because they refuse to lead a life according to nature anticipates romanticism.*

Meli's works reflect the influence of such varied figures as Anacreon, Petrarch,* Rousseau, Sannazaro,* Thomson (in *The Seasons*), Paolo Rolli,* and minor lyric poets of the pastoral tradition. His verses were much admired by poets like Foscolo,* Herder, and Goethe, all of whom translated selections. His critical reputation was assured in 1875 when Francesco De Sanctis's* critical essay illuminated his original contributions to the Italian lyric tradition.

Bibliography: *Opere*, ed. Giorgio Santangelo, 2 vols. (Milan: Rizzoli, 1965-68); *From Marino to Marinetti*, trans. Joseph Tusiani (New York: Baroque Press, 1974); Francesco De Sanctis, *Saggi critici*, Vol. 3 (Bari: Laterza, 1957); Giacomo Etna, *Giovanni Meli* (Rome: Editrice La Navicella, 1963); Alessio Di Giovanni, *La vita e l'opera di Giovanni Meli* (Florence: Le Monnier, 1938).

MELODRAMA. A fervent desire to recreate the dramatic art of ancient Greece impelled Italian poets and musicians at the close of the sixteenth century to produce an entirely new theatrical form: opera, or "melodrama" where song *(melos)* and drama are fused into an aesthetic unity. Throughout the sixteenth century, the attempt to unite poetry, song, dance, and drama had been evident in the often quite spectacular *intermezzi* inserted between the acts of tragedies or learned comedies with their elaborate stage machinery and allegorical ballets. Another example of the endeavor to set a story to music, drawing character types from the *commedia dell'arte*,* was the madrigal* comedy *(commedia armonica) l'Amfiparnaso (The Lower Slopes of Parnassus)* by Orazio Vecchi (1550–1605), who published his work in 1597. In Florence, a group of scholars and musicians gathered in the homes of such wealthy patrons as Count Giovanni Bardi (1534–1612) and Jacopo Corsi (1560–1604) to constitute the informal "Camerata," where they discussed the nature of ancient Greek drama and the need to fashion an individual melodic line which would underscore dramatic verse. One of the Camerata's members, Vincenzo Galilei (1533–91), the scientist's father, had already published his *Dialogo della Musica antica e moderna* (circa 1582, *Dialogue of Ancient and Modern Music*). He maintained that to unite words and melody the accompaniment should be restricted to as few instruments as possible, words should be sung in a natural and unaffected declamation, and melody should express without superfluous embellishments the sentiments of the dramatic speeches. The feeling that music had accompanied the entire performance of ancient Greek tragedies led the members of the Florentine Camerata to develop the monodic recitative of early opera.

During the carnival of 1597, opera was born with the production of *Dafne (Daphne)*, with text by Ottavio Rinuccini (1562–1621) and music by Jacopo Peri (1561–1633), in Corsi's home. As a dramatic poet, Rinuccini continued the Italian pastoral* tradition of Poliziano* and Tasso,* concentrating on a sudden change in events which threatens to disturb the serenity of an idyllic setting but which finally resolves itself without causing tragedy. Rinuccini's other melodramas include *Euridice* (1600, *Eurydice,* with music by Peri and Giulio Caccini [1550–1618]); *Arianna* (1608, *Ariadne,* music by Claudio Monteverdi [1567–1643]); and *Narciso (Narcissus)* dating from the final years of the poet's life. In all of Rinuccini's melodramas, the poetry is intended to prevail over the music, with the solo voice dominating while a small chorus comments on events and assists in overcoming the menace of tragedy by closing the drama with a ballet of reconciliation. These early Florentine operas all dealt with mythological subjects as they were composed for humanistic and aristocratic audiences.

Opera reached its first artistic height in the works of the composer Monteverdi whose *Orfeo (Orpheus)* of 1607 with a text by Alessandro Striggio (1573–1630) attained a balance between passionate music and poetic expression. Monteverdi's musical fable is in five acts with prologue, but the underlying act structure falls into a symmetrical arrangement of prelude, three central acts, and epilogue. Rather than follow the traditional myth of Orpheus's dismemberment, the composer chose to celebrate the death of Orpheus (the universal musician) as a glorious ascension to heaven in the company of Apollo. After moving from Mantua in 1613 to become choirmaster of St. Mark's in Venice, Monteverdi continued his innovations in creating the *stile concitato* ("agitated style") in musical composition. This style is evident in some of the final works of his career such as the operas *Il Ritorno d'Ulisse in Patria* (1641, *The Return of Ulysses to His Country*) and *L'Incoronazione di Poppea* (1642, *The Coronation of Poppea*), where he displayed a Baroque* love for juxtaposition by having the expository recitative pass into emotional arias and comic scenes contrast with serious ones. In *L'Incoronazione di Poppea,* set to a *libretto* by Francesco Busenello (1598–1659), the composer's fully mature manner explores the themes of erotic obsession and political intrigue, resorting to a florid style for pathetic laments and tense duets. Poetic text, musical notation, and carefully controlled orchestration with a *tremolo* of strings all unite in Monteverdi's poignant melodramas.

Monteverdi's career reflected the major changes which were taking place in opera production during the second quarter of the seventeenth century. Whereas the earliest operas had premieres at courtly ceremonies such as state weddings, after 1637 Monteverdi and other composers in Venice saw their works performed in public theatres. To please the tastes of the paying public, composers and librettists emphasized scenic display achieved through stage machinery and comic relief from tragic intensity. In addition to mythological subjects, operas presented dramas derived from the chivalric romances of Ariosto* and Tasso, famous episodes from Oriental, Greek, or Roman history, and tales of religious martyrs. Magical transformation, effected through frequent disguises and plots of mistaken identity, mirrored the period's delight in the marvelous. By midcentury, the chorus largely gave way to the ballet, and the supreme figure of opera ceased to be either the composer or the librettist but became the virtuoso soloist who exploited the aria to astound audiences with vocal fireworks. The *libretto* was no longer the clearly declaimed poetic drama aspired to by the Florentine Camerata but a versified pastiche intended only for performance and not for publication. Some of the composers of the Venetian school were Pier Francesco Cavalli (1602–1676) and Pietro Antonio Cesti (1623–1669), whose works carried Italian opera abroad to France and Germany.

Opera also radiated from Venice and Florence to other Italian urban centers like Rome and Naples. At Rome, the powerful Barberini family (including Pope Urban VIII) had their own theatre for private productions before a select audience of ecclesiastical dignitaries and foreign diplomats. Some of the finest singers of the century came from Rome, where they received their training in musical ensembles to sing at festive occasions. Around 1626, the opera *Catena d'Adone (The Chain of Adonis)*, with music by Domenico Mazzocchi (1592–1655) and text by Ottavio Tronsarelli after episodes from Marino's* long poem *Adone,* presented Roman audiences with a melodrama portraying the liberation of humankind from sensual domination. This allegorical, edifying tendency became typical of Roman operas. Doubtless the most important librettist to appear in the eternal city was Giulio Rospigliosi (1600–1669), who eventually rose in the clerical hierarchy to be Pope Clement IX from 1667 to 1669. Working with the composer Stefano Landi (1590–1655), Rospigliosi opened the Barberini Theatre in 1632 with the opera *Sant'Alessio (St. Alexis),* which was a musical version in the *sacra rappresentazione** tradition which combines a tale of temptation and sacrifice with a representation of everyday life. Other texts by Rospigliosi include *Erminia sul Giordano* (1633, *Erminia by the Jordan,* based on Tasso's *Jerusalem Delivered*), the story of martyrs *Didimo e Teodora (Didymus and Theodora),* the romantic comedy *Dal Male il Bene* (1653, *Good from Evil*), and the comedy of manners *Chi soffre, speri* (1637, *Who Suffers May Hope*). While melodrama in Rome appealed to a rather restricted audience, in Naples opera reached a wide public comparable to that of Venice. There Neapolitan composers brought comic opera (*opera buffa* as compared to *opera seria*) to perfection, as in Giovanni Battista Pergolesi's (1710–1736) *La Serva Padrona (The Maid Mistress)* of 1733. Alessandro Scarlatti (1659–1725), in operas like *Griselda* of 1721, joined folk elements of popular melodies to realistic dialogues.

By the close of the seventeenth century, Italian melodrama had extended its influence throughout Europe. But the excesses of composing music to insipid *libretti* as a display vehicle for coloratura sopranos and castrati singers led to reform in Italy, first by Apostolo Zeno (1668–1750) and then by Pietro Metastasio* who sought to restore to melodrama the refinement and purity of poetic expression and the musical intensity once envisioned by the Florentine Camerata.

See also ARIOSTO, Ludovico; BAROQUE; COMMEDIA DELL' ARTE; HUMANISM; MARINO, Giambattista; POLIZIANO, Angelo; TASSO, Torquato.

Bibliography: Drammi per Musica da Rinuccini allo Zeno, ed. Andrea Della Corte (Turin: UTET, 1958). *Teatro del Seicento,* ed. Luigi Fassò (Milan: Ricciardi, 1956); Antonio Belloni, "Le Origini del Melodramma," in *Storia letteraria d'Italia: Il Seicento,* Vol. VII (Milan: Vallardi, 1943), 402–44; David J. Grout, *A Short History of Opera* (1947; rpt. New York: Columbia University Press, 1965); Claudio Varese, "Il Teatro per Musica," in *Storia della letteratura italiana: Il Seicento,* eds. Emilio Cecchi and Natalino Sapegno, Vol. V (Milan: Garzanti, 1967), 531–43.

Douglas Radcliff-Umstead

METASTASIO, PIETRO (1698–1782), librettist and lyric poet. Metastasio, born Pietro Armando Dominico Trapassi, was the fourth child of a relatively poor Roman family. He had the good fortune to be discovered in 1708 by Gian Vincenzo Gravina,* a principal Arcadian, who adopted him and saw to it that he received a sound classical education. Gravina changed his name to Metastasio, a poetic title based upon the Greek word *metastasis* that rendered the Italian *trapasso* ("changing from one place to another"). By the age of fourteen, Metastasio had already completed a tragedy. Shortly after Gravina's death in 1718, he entered Arcadia* under the name Artino Corasio and published a one-act melodrama or *cantata* entitled *Gli orti esperidi* (1721, The Gardens of the Hesperides), set to the music of Niccolò Porpora whom he had met during a visit to Naples in 1719. During that journey, Metastasio fell in love with a beautiful actress, Marianna Benti Bulgarelli ("La Romanina"), who sang the role of Venus in his *cantata* and inspired the composition of his famous *Didone abbandonata* (1724, *Dido Forsaken*).

After the success of *Didone,* Metastasio moved from Naples to Rome (1727–30) where he was invited to fill the position of *poeta cesareo,* or court poet, at the Viennese court of Emperor Charles VI upon the recommendation of Apostolo Zeno (1668–1750), an Italian poet in that post who longed to return to his native Venice. There Metastasio remained until his death, serving both Charles and Maria Theresa. His abilities as a brilliant improviser and as a swift composer of pleasing *libretti* enabled him to produce a great quantity of literature which amused the court. His fame grew and moved along with the vogue of the melodrama.*

Praised as the greatest of writers during his lifetime, Metastasio was certainly one of the most talented lyric poets in a century noted primarily for its drama and prose. But after the melodrama had become less fashionable, Metastasio was eventually abandoned by popular taste and literary historians, much as Baroque* literature had been eclipsed. Although his talents were primarily poetic in nature, his lyric inspiration was firmly wedded to dramatic forms and music. His *libretti* were often published independently of their musical scores, but their dramatic effects were considerably diminished in the process. Metastasio's subjects derive primarily from classical sources. Typically, he employs blank verse or a freely rhymed combination of hendecasyllable and seven-syllable verse. Classical in style, his texts exhibit a three-act structure wherein the unities and the rules of decorum are normally respected. The frequent use of two pairs of characters allows him to exploit not only the full range of the human voice but also his favorite thematic preoccupation, the conflict of strong ideas, especially love and duty. Perhaps the most memorable passages in his works are his famous *ariette* ("little arias")—brief, intense stanzas which reflect a moment of great passion in the plot and which became so popular that they were often memorized by his audiences.

Metastasio composed over seventy melodramas, the most important of which, *Didone abbandonata, Artaserse* (1729, *Artaxerxes*), *Attilio Regolo* (1732, *Attilius Regulus*), *La clemenza di Tito* (1732, *The Clemency of Titus*), and *Temistocle* (1736, *Themistocles*), were composed during his early years at the Austrian court. With *Didone*, Metastasio recast Virgil's well-known story of Aeneas and Dido in a Settecento setting and produced a melodrama closer in spirit to Tasso* than to the Latin epic.* Metastasio, whose plays often traced dramatic conflicts between love and duty, found a sympathetic model in the drama of Pierre Corneille, and many of his best works show the direct or indirect influence of the French dramatist. Voltaire compared *La clemenza di Tito,* which owes a debt to both Corneille and Suetonius, to the best plays of Corneille and Racine. *Temistocle* portrays the famous Athenian exile torn between love for his native city and his obligations to his patron, the king of Persia. In order to remain true to both of these moral imperatives, Themistocles decides to commit suicide, but just as he is about to drink from a poisoned goblet, his moral conflict is resolved and the play ends with a note of praise for Metastasio's patron, Charles VI. The plot of *Attilio Regolo,* in which Metastasio comes the closest to achieving a "tragic" melodrama, follows Livy's account of the Roman hero captured in the First Punic War and sent to Rome to conclude a peace treaty or to face imprisonment or death in Carthage. Regulus speaks against the treaty as a threat to Rome's liberty and then returns to meet his fate in Carthage. In the next century, Italians saw his final words extolling Roman virtue and courage as a prefiguration of Risorgimento patriotism.

Metastasio also completed the *libretti* for a number of oratorios dealing with the sacred stories of Christ's passion, Isaac, and Judith. During his lifetime, his works were put to music by composers such as Mozart, Pergolesi, Domenico Scarlatti, Gluck, and Handel and, after his death, by Rossini, Cimarosa, Cherubini, and Mendelssohn.

See also MELODRAMA.

Bibliography: Tutte le opere di Pietro Metastasio, ed. Bruno Brunelli, 5 vols. (Milan: Mondadori, 1943–54); *Dido Forsaken,* trans. Joseph Fucilla (Florence: Valmartina, 1952); *Dramas and Other Poems of the Abbe Pietro Metastasio,* trans. John Hoole, 3 vols. (London: Otridge, 1800); Marie Henri Beyle (Stendhal), *Haydn, Mozart and Metastasio* (New York: Grossman, 1972; French original 1814); Joseph Spencer Kennard, *The Italian Theatre: From the Close of the Seventeenth Century* (1932; rpt. New York: Benjamin Blom, 1964); Vernon Lee, *Studies of the Eighteenth Century in Italy* (London: Unwin, 1907); Luigi Russo, *Metastasio* (Bari: Laterza, 1943).

MICHELSTAEDTER, CARLO (1887–1910), writer and philosopher. Michelstaedter was born in Gorizia and originally enrolled in the University of Vienna to study mathematics. He visited Florence in 1905, and his academic interests shifted to literature and philosophy. Shortly after completing his thesis, Michelstaedter committed suicide. Entitled *La persuasione e la retorica in Platone e Aristotele* (1913, Persuasion and Rhetoric in Plato and Aristotle), this dissertation was published posthumously along with a volume of verse, *Poesie* (1917, Poems). Together, the two volumes had an impact far greater than they might have had without their author's dramatic suicide. The reputation of his pessimistic theories (indebted to Schopenhauer, Nietzsche, and a number of other nineteenth-century philosophers) grew among those critics who viewed his "case" as evidence of a crisis in middle-class values around the turn of the century. The crux of his thought may be found in his heuristic distinction between "persuasion" and "rhetoric." Michelstaedter sees rhetoric as a byproduct of man's attempt to impose an illusory purpose upon a meaningless universe. Persuasion, or authentic existence, is lived by only a few great minds (Plato, Christ, and Leopardi,* among others), who create their own values by rejecting rhetorical illusion. Because of his belief that reality had no autonomous existence outside the individual's consciousness of it, Michelstaedter is often viewed as a precursor of Italian existentialism.

Bibliography: Opere, ed. Gaetano Chiavacci (Florence: Sansoni, 1958); Marco Cerutti, *Carlo Michelstaedter* (Milan: Mursia, 1965); Antonio Piromalli, *Michelstaedter* (Florence: La Nuova Italia, 1968).

MINTURNO, ANTONIO (1500–1574), churchman and literary critic. Born Antonio Sebastiani, Minturno lived in various Italian cities before coming to Naples in 1526, where he was elected to the local academy. Besides literature, languages, and rhetoric, he was trained in mathematics and Scholastic theology and was considered a disciple of the Aristotelian scholar Agostino Nifo (1473–1538). Named bishop of Ugento in 1559 by Pope Pius IV, he participated in the Council of Trent. He was transferred to the bishopric of Crotone in 1565 and remained there until his death.

Although Minturno was the author of Petrarchan lyrics, poetry based upon the Psalms, eclogues inspired by Virgil, epigrams, a pastoral* novel, and numerous letters, he became best known for two treatises on poetics, the Latin *De poeta* (1559, On the Poet) in six books and the Italian *Arte poetica* (1563, *The Art of Poetry*) in four books. The first treatise discusses most of what was said about poetry in antiquity by the major classical critics and is the first truly comprehensive Renaissance* poetics. Minturno's view is that the poet must imitate life, follow rules of decorum, and respect the integrity of literary genres. Poetry, he claims, has both the power to civilize men and to sway their emotions. The second treatise applies his general principles to literature in the vernacular. Influenced by the Counter-Reformation climate, it is a stronger statement of Aristotelian critical principles and is more concerned with the definition of the various literary genres. In it, Minturno rejects the romantic epic* of Ariosto* as a form equal to that of the classical epic, advocating instead the unified Virgilian epic as a model. His discussion of the Aristotelian theory of cartharsis and purgation in tragedy had an impact upon later neoclassical poetics. Minturno influenced the poetic practice of such poets as Tasso* and Ronsard and the poetics of Sir Philip Sidney.

See also CASTELVETRO, Ludovico; SCALIGERO, Giulio Cesare; TRISSINO, Gian Giorgio; VIDA, Marco Girolamo.

Bibliography: De poeta (Munich: Wilhelm Fink, 1970), and *L'Arte poetica* (Munich: Wilhelm Fink, 1971); Allan H. Gilbert, *Literary Criticism: Plato to Dryden* (Detroit, Mich.: Wayne State University Press, 1970)—contains selections from *Arte poetica;* Bernard Weinberg, *A History of Literary Criticism in the Italian Renaissance,* 2 vols. (Chicago: University of Chicago Press, 1961).

MONTALE, EUGENIO (1896–   ), poet, essayist, critic, and editor. Montale spent his childhood and youth between Genoa, his native city, and the village of Monterosso on the eastern part of the Ligurian seashore. At Monterosso, his middle-class family had a villa that was to provide him with a unique vantage point for the vistas in which his poetry finds its breathing space. After military service in World War I, he freelanced in literary journalism and moved to Florence (1927) to work as editor for Bemporad Publishers. In 1938, his persistent refusal to join the Fascist party cost him the position he had found nine years earlier as curator of the Vieusseux Rare Book Collection. During World War II, still in Florence with his wife, he devoted himself entirely to his writing, which included translation of verse and prose authors, mainly English or American. In 1947, Montale went to Milan as contributing editor for the literary and musical sections of the daily newspaper, *Corriere della sera,* and he still lives there, retired, some thirty years later. His stature as a poet has earned him a permanent seat in the Italian Senate and the 1975 Nobel Prize for Literature.

Montale's first book, *Ossi di seppia* (1925, Cuttlefish Bones), is a mature achievement rivaling Ungaretti's* extraordinary start. A comparison between the two poets who thus far share primacy in the Italian twentieth century is instructive at this early phase of their careers, for *Cuttlefish Bones* sounds in many ways like an antiphon to Ungaretti's *Il porto sepolto* (1916, *The Submerged Seaport).* Thematically, *Cuttlefish Bones* reduces to near invisibility the war experience that stood out in the foreground of *The Submerged Seaport,* as if the younger poet, faced with an ominous postwar world that held little promise for the future, turned all the way back to the temporal and spatial oasis of Liguria where his childhood had thrived between olive-tree studded rocky slopes and sea, before the war and the wound of adulthood came to break the spell. Even if the rift cannot ultimately be healed, there is nothing to do but "go home again," away from history, back to the prelapsarian time of the seething sea. Thus, Liguria becomes an Eden revisited, but because memory the would-be healer cannot really fill the gap between happy childhood and war-tried manhood, that Eden can also be a glaring desert. The Montalian persona would want to "feel rugged and essential/ like the pebbles" the Mediterranean surf tosses around, while the Ungarettian persona, who in "The Rivers" has at least momentarily attained unison with the consecrating elements, *is* "like a pebble" polished into essentialness by the baptismal waters of the Isonzo; the rage of battle is miraculously suspended and for the time being that fateful river is no longer bloodied by slaughter. Montale painfully clings to his roots, an "agave of the cliff," while Ungaretti the nomad remembers his exotic birthplace and the other stations of the pilgrimage that has finally brought him to his ancestral homeland in the midst of war. Accordingly, if Ungaretti writes his first book this side of the formalized prosodic tradition he will then gradually repossess, Montale holds on from the start to traditional verse and elaborate syntax, poles apart from the primitivist (and partly even futurist) leanings of Ungaretti's early style.

At the same time, Montale treats traditional meter with a liberty which occasionally verges on the subversive. Off rhymes set up dissonant chords, and lines often exceed their statutory length or suddenly shrink beyond expectation. In the "Mediterraneo" series, free hexameter-like units alternate with hendecasyllables and shorter lines to evoke a tidal feeling.

Montale's approach to "style and tradition" (to name the programmatic title of an essay he published in 1925 in *Il Baretti*) has nothing to do with supine neoclassicism,* a label which would hardly fit the uniquely resilient phrasing, so lexically variegated to include the colloquial and the courtly in a mixture particularly suitable to the prevalently low-keyed, conversational diction. Word choice tends to punctilious exactitude, thereby sharpening the etching-like quality of imagery. Lowering the tone (after so much grandiloquence or *bel canto* in D'Annunzio's* generation) brought about an intrinsic revaluation of the word, which is now used for cognitive rather than just sensuous purposes. Consequently, the natural world is seen with sober intensity, and without losing its existential concreteness, it can project emblems of the human condition—mostly desolate, like the bottle-shard topped wall of "Meriggiare" ("Nooning"), or the choked brook, crumpled leaf, and fallen horse of "Il male di vivere" ("The Pain of Living"), or the light-maddened sunflower, or the pervasive stony imagery that has elicited from many a critic the recognition of Eliotian affinities, though countervailing signs of vitality and deliverance do rescue the Montalian landscape in *Cuttlefish Bones* from the doom of an unrelieved wasteland.

Certainly, *Le Occasioni* (1939, The Occasions) deepens the somber note already so marked in "Arsenio" of 1928 (a last addition to the first book, thoroughly instinct with a sense of inescapable paralysis) and contracts the language to often elliptical ruggedness. The poet's imagination has entered history, and everywhere it descries omens of apocalypse; the "compass turns crazily at random" ("La casa dei doganieri," "The Shorewatchers' House"), "evil conquers . . . The wheel will never stop" ("Eastbourne"), and the primal dream of justice and happiness is lost ("Barche sulla Marna," Boats on the Marne). Entropy undermines the world and disaster looms over Europe. A dogged private fidelity to the perennial values now threatened or suppressed by aggressive totalitarianism can only sustain a hope against hope, as Dora Markus, Liuba, and Gerti, members of a persecuted community, very well know: "it is late, ever later."

Those memorable portraits of real women caught in the trap of adverse contingency, in the eponymous poems, are offset by the many more poems which address an unspecified lady by the mythical name of Clizia (Ovidian Clytia, the woman changed into a sunflower). Lover, prophetess, and goddess in turn, she takes poetical shape as the inner interlocutor of the poet's anguished persona to denounce a fallen world in the name of the light that shines in darkness. Yet, her Dantesque, Beatrice-like apotheosis cannot obliterate the origin of this personal myth in an actual love experience with an American Jewess whom the poet met in the 1930s. Of the poems inspired by her, the twenty "Motets" form a series unto itself, a book within the book, as if to oppose a redemptive center of vision and love to the darkening framework of the hopeless times. "Elegy" (to say it in the confessional words of *Cuttlefish Bones*) has not become "hymn" but threnody and veiled protest.

The trend partly continues in Montale's third book, *La bufera e altro* (1956, The Storm and Other Things), which collects verse from the World War II years and the first postwar decade. On the other hand, antiphonal hymnic notes do ring out here, either to glorify Clizia the godlike and unheeded seer or to celebrate in the emblematic guise of "the Fox" and "the Eel" another lady who embodies vitality triumphant in the very teeth of rocky sterility. In the two final lyrics, Montale gives us his "little testament" and "dream of a prisoner"—respectively, an outspoken rejection of the two contrasting mass ideologies (Stalinism and conformist Christianity) and a disclaimer of faith in the future of our civilization. These Stoic poems set the theme, if not the tone, for the subsequent books of verse, *Satura,* (1971, Satura), and *Diario del '71 e del '72* (1973, Diary of 1971 and 1972), where style purposely descends from lyrical pitch to satirical prosiness (with some exceptions, the most conspicuous being "Xenia"—a series of affectionate epigrams commemorating Montale's deceased wife). On the whole, in these late collections Montale's intonation has radically changed from the sustained song of *La bufera e altro* and of the partly coeval *Quaderno di traduzioni* (1948, A Notebook of Translations) which includes masterly Italian renditions of such poets as Shakespeare, Hopkins, Hardy, and Dickinson. Meanwhile, Montale's prose works come to the fore: *La farfalla di Dinard* (1956, Butterfly of Dinard) revisits the landscapes of *Cuttlefish Bones* and *The Occasions* to compose a thinly disguised autobiography from short stories previously published by the *Corriere della sera; Auto da Fè* (1966, Act of Faith) collects articles of literary, cultural, and political import; and *Fuori di Casa* (1968, Away from Home) amounts to such a travelogue as we can expect from a man of Montale's culture and observant sensitivity. Two more volumes of essays are in the works, and they will document in a more complete fashion the rare insight of the critic who was the first to champion, over four decades ago, the curiously neglected novelist Italo Svevo.*

Bibliography: Quaderno (Milan: Mondadori, 1977); *Butterfly of Dinard*, trans. G. Singh (London: London Magazine Editions, 1970); *New Poems*, trans. G. Singh (New York: New Directions, 1976); *Poesie/ Poems*, trans. G. Kay (Edinburgh: Edinburgh University Press, 1964); *Provisional Conclusions*, trans. E. Farnsworth (Chicago: Regnery, 1970); *Selected Poems*, with an introduction by G. Cambon (New York: New Directions, 1966); *Xenia*, trans. G. Singh (Los Angeles: Black Sparrow Press, 1970); Glauco Cambon, *Eugenio Montale* (New York: Columbia University Press, 1972); Joseph Cary, *Three Modern Italian Poets–Saba, Ungaretti, Montale* (New York: New York University Press, 1969); Claire Huffman, "T. S. Eliot, Eugenio Montale, and Vagaries of Influence," *Comparative Litera-*

ture 27 (1975), 193–207; Angelo Jacomuzzi, *Sulla poesia di Montale* (Bologna: Cappelli, 1968); *Omaggio a Montale,* ed. Silvio Ramat (Milan: Mondadori, 1966).

Glauco Cambon

MONTI, VINCENZO (1754–1828), poet, translator, and dramatist. Monti, the eighth of ten brothers, was born near Fusignano in the province of Ravenna. He attended the seminary of Faenza in 1766 before moving to the University of Ferrara to study medicine. But his major interests were literary ones, and after he entered Arcadia* with the name Autonide Saturniano in 1775, Monti won the patronage of Cardinal Scipione Borghese (then papal legate in Ferrara) with a poem entitled "Visione di Ezechiello" (Vision of Ezekiel). In 1778, he moved with his patron to Rome where he also gained the favor of Cardinal De Bernis, the French ambassador. An early Pindaric ode, "Prosopopea di Pericle" (The Prosopopoeia of Pericles) reflects his neoclassical taste; in the poem, Pericles himself praises the age of Pope Pius VI. His fortune was assured in 1781, when at the wedding of the pope's nephew, he recited "La Bellezza dell'universo" (The Beauty of the Universe). This poem in *terzine* attempts to reconcile the classical Platonic tradition with that of the Bible and shows the influence of Tasso,* Milton, Ovid, and other minor Latin poets. Because of the poem's success, the pope's nephew hired Monti as his secretary.

In 1783, Monti read Goethe's *Sorrows of Young Werther.* Inspired by the German poet, Monti wrote one of his most famous compositions, a poem in blank verse entitled "Dunque fu di natura ordine e fato" ("Was It Then Fate or Nature's High Decree"), which he dedicated to Prince Don Sigismondo Chigi, as well as his *Pensieri d'amore* (Thoughts of Love), also in blank verse. Another noted ode of the same period, "Al Signor di Montgolfier" (To Signor Montgolfier), celebrates the historic ascent of Montgolfier's balloon in 1783 in neoclassical language, likening the event to the voyage of Jason and his Argonauts and manifesting an attitude favorable to scientific progress. Between 1786 and 1787, Monti turned to neoclassical drama and completed the *Aristodemo (Aristodemus),* a treatment of the ancient ruler of Messina which was intended to surpass the examples of Alfieri.* Moreover, he completed a minor tragedy, *Galeotto Manfredi* (Galeotto Manfredi), based upon a brief reference in Machiavelli's* *History of Florence,* but it failed to attract much attention. He also began both his translation of Homer's *Iliad* from a Latin version and his most important tragedy, *Caio Gracco (Caius Gracchus).* Derived from Livy's account of the Gracchi, the play was finally completed in 1800. By that time, Monti had lived through the tumultuous period of the French Revolution and had also encountered Chénier's French version of the story. The fully developed drama thus gives expression to a new republican perspective and a patriotic sentiment that would have been impossible had the play been completed in 1788.

Earlier, Monti had married Teresa Pikler (1791) and published a violently antirepublican work entitled *In morte di Ugo Bassville (The Penance of Hugo)*, usually known as the *Bassvilliana*, a long poem occasioned by an imaginary penance imposed upon a French republican official murdered by a Roman mob in 1793. Appropriately enough for a visionary picture of the afterlife, the work is in five cantos of *terza rima** modeled after Dante's* *Comedy*. Its most memorable sections portray the terrible scenes from the Revolution, particularly the Terror and the execution of Louis XVI. By 1797, however, Monti had repudiated his earlier political views and had passed to the other side, even becoming for a short time an official of the Cisalpine Republic. During the brief period when Austrian forces had again seized control of northern Italy (1799–1801), Monti went into exile in Paris, but after the battle of Marengo and Napoleon's liberation of northern Italy, Monti responded with one of his most famous poetic works, the *canzonetta* "Bella Italia, amate sponde" (1801, "Beautiful Italy, beloved shores"). In the same year, he was named to the chair of rhetoric at Pavia and held it until 1804, when he became the official poet of the Italian government established upon the return of Napoleonic rule in Italy. During his French exile, he had translated Voltaire's *Pucelle d'Orléans*, and in 1804 he published a version of Persius's *Satires*. However, his major translation, and perhaps his finest poetic work, was his influential version of the *Iliad*, a blank-verse translation which finally appeared in 1810.

After the collapse of the French-backed regimes in Italy in 1814, northern Italy passed back under Austrian control. In spite of his earlier republican works, Monti eventually came to terms with the new rulers of Italy and wrote poetry favorable to their government. His many changes of position prompted Francesco De Sanctis* to remark that for Monti, ideas were "less a conviction than a fashion." Judged from the limited perspective of Italian patriotism, Monti does, indeed, seem less admirable than poets such as Parini,* Foscolo,* or Alfieri* who were guided by constant ideals. One minor work of interest from his later, less productive years is his "Sermone sulla mitologia" (1825, Sermon on Mythology), a composition in blank verse which defends the neoclassical taste for mythology against the attacks of the romantic poets.

See also NEOCLASSICISM.

Bibliography: Opere scelte, ed. Cesare Angelini (Milan: Rizzoli, 1940); *Poesie*, ed. Guido Bezzola (Turin: UTET, 1969); *Aristodemus, A Tragedy*, trans. J. A. Favalli (Dublin: Mahon, 1809); *Caius Gracchus, A Tragedy*, trans. Lord George Russell (London: Moyes, 1830); *The Penance of Hugo, a Vision on the French Revolution*, trans. Rev. Henry Boyd (London: Longman, 1805); *From Marino to Marinetti,* trans. Joseph Tusiani (New York: Baroque Press, 1974); Donata Chiomenti Vassalli, *Vincenzo Monti nel dramma dei suoi tempi* (Milan: Ceschina, 1968).

MORANTE, ELSA (1918–), novelist, poet, short-story writer, and essayist. Morante has spent most of her life in Rome, her birthplace. She is the ex-wife of Alberto Moravia.*

In 1941, Morante published *Il gioco segreto* (The Secret Game), a collection of essays separately contributed to periodicals. In 1942, the children's book *Le bellissime avventure di Cateri dalla trecciolina* (The Marvelous Adventures of Kathy Pigtail) appeared with illustrations by the author (revised and expanded as *Le straordinarie avventure di Caterina,* The Extraordinary Adventures of Katherine, in 1959). *Menzogna e sortilegio* (1948, *House of Liars*), her first novel, won the Viareggio Prize in 1948. It is the lengthy family saga of a southern Italian petty bourgeois family, narrated by Elisa, its only survivor. For three generations, Elisa's people have created fantasy worlds as a rebellion against impossible historical and social conditions. All were ruined by trying to live out their fantasies. The language in the novel is highly poetic and unrealistic. The emphasis on memory, intensity, and musical lyricism (influenced by Katherine Mansfield, whom Morante has translated) is typical of the Italian literary scene of the 1930s, dominated by the periodical *Solaria* and by Bacchelli's* saga *The Mill on the Po.* Nevertheless, the novel has an ideological thrust: it is a tragic epic meant to express the current crisis of the Western middle class.

The following novel, *L'Isola di Arturo* (1957, *Arthur's Island*), which won the Strega Prize in 1957, narrates an adolescent's rude awakening from a bejewelled and gossamer dream world. Arturo, lost in visions of his lovely, dead mother and of the fabulous voyages his adored father recounts to him, becomes suddenly aware of his love for his young stepmother, who is horrified at this near incest. Then, his homosexual father betrays his son's love for the sake of a petty criminal, and the fabulous voyages turn out to range no further than the gay circuit in Naples. Arturo is saved from despair by the return of his male childhood nurse, with whom he leaves the island-womb to enlist. Morante's bitter vision of reality tends to be submerged in her allusive, poetic style and her iridescent, fabulous, and lyrical imagery. Her greatest gift is a magical realism, and her style constantly re-expresses the theme of her first novel. *Alibi* (1958, Alibi) is a collection of poetry that serves as a choral commentary on her novels. *Lo scialle andaluso* (1963, The Andalusian Shawl), a book of short stories, is an impressive affirmation of her psychological and lyric gifts. Her second collection of poetry, *Il mondo salvato dai ragazzini* (1968, The World Saved by Children), is a mixture of poetic forms written in the ambiguously Marxist and pseudo-Christian vein made popular by Pasolini* among others. Morante's vision of the world is bitter and apocalyptic, but the book ends in a generic expression of hope, because the very young it depicts are still capable of love, honesty, and salvation.

La Storia (1974, *History: A Novel*), a recent, lengthy narrative, reaffirms the Christian and Marxist ideology but seems to deny the hope. Real history (as Manzoni* showed) is the suffering of the poor and oppressed, an idea Morante makes manifest by the capsule narration of events dealing with war, repression, oppression, and weapons development preceding and following each of the eight sections of the work. The novel's reputation as one of the greatest of the century stems partly from the appeal of its theme and partly from the popular editorial policy of the publisher, reinforced by the extreme political tension between right and left in Italy. Set between 1941 and 1947, it is the story of the childlike Iduzza, a half-Jewish elementary school teacher, and of her son 'Useppe, born of a rape by a German soldier. 'Useppe, in his six years, experiences air raids, deportations, and deaths (including that of his older brother Nino, fascist, then partisan, finally black marketeer and gun runner, killed fleeing from police). He develops epilepsy and dies of an attack, which destroys his two maternal protectors, Iduzza and Bella, his brother's sheep dog, who has had long conversations with him, assuring him that the weak and the suffering in this world are really the loveliest people. Iduzza goes insane at his death, and Bella is shot by the authorities while guarding his body. A host of minor characters includes the memorable Davide Segre, a Jewish intellectual turned partisan and factory worker, who dies of an overdose of heroin. Jewishness is obsessively symbolic of the sacrifice of humanity throughout the book. Morante's intense feeling and desire to speak directly to the poor and humble of this world have affected her style in this work, which has lost its magic lyricism and borders on the simplistic. The point of view of the narrator (who is omniscient, with occasional interjections by a reportorial "I") is geared to the mentality of Iduzza and of 'Useppe, much of whose baby talk is reproduced verbatim. The novel's literary worth is, therefore, minimal. Its interest lies in the passionate ideology of the author, a recent development typical of a whole generation including poets like Sereni* and novelists like Vittorini,* who also shifted from a "literary" world view to a position of *engagement*.

Bibliography: Arthur's Island, trans. Isabel Quigly (New York: Knopf, 1959); *History: A Novel*, trans. William Weaver (New York: Knopf, 1977); *House of Liars*, trans. Adrienne Foulke (New York: Harcourt, 1951); E. A. McCormick, "Utopia and Point of View," *Symposium* 15 (1961), 114–30; Julian Mitchell, "Absolute Beginner," *Italian Quarterly* 3 (1960), 70–74; A. R. Puppino, *Struttura e stile nella narrativa di Elsa Morante* (Ravenna: Longo, 1968).

Joy Hambuechen Potter

MORAVIA, ALBERTO (1907–   ), novelist, playwright, journalist, editor, and literary and film critic. Moravia, born in Rome as Alberto Pincherle, was the son of a prosperous Jewish architect and a Catholic mother. Tuberculosis of the bone interrupted his education in 1916, and he was forced to spend most of the next nine years in bed. His intellectual formation is to be attributed principally to his readings of that period: Dostoevsky, Rimbaud, Goldoni,* Manzoni,* Shakespeare, Molière, and Joyce. After the publication of his first novel in 1929, Moravia began to contribute to various Italian periodicals. During the 1930's, he traveled to England, France, the United States, Mexico, China, and Greece. After his return to Italy, the growing mistrust of the fascist regime and the racial laws of 1938 obliged him to take the pen-name of "Pseudo." In 1943, Moravia was warned that his name was on a list of subversives who were about to be arrested. Hoping to reach the advancing Allied lines in the south, Moravia fled Rome with his wife, Elsa Morante,* whom he had married two years earlier. They failed to reach their destination and were forced to spend a harsh winter in the hills near Fondi. After the war, Moravia collaborated on a number of newspapers and periodicals, and in 1953, he founded with Alberto Carocci (1904–1972) the journal *Nuovi Argomenti*. Moravia became the film critic for *L'Espresso* (Rome) in 1957. His intense journalistic activity did not, however, diminish his creative production; he continued to publish a succession of novels, short stories, and plays, as well as essays and travelogues. Soon after his separation from Morante in 1962, he began a new relation with Dacia Maraini (1936–   ), also a writer, with whom he and Enzo Siciliano organized in 1966 a short-lived theater group called the Porcospino (Porcupine). Moravia now lives in Rome.

Moravia's first and most significant novel, *Gli indifferenti* (1929, *The Time of Indifference*), brought him instant fame and even notoriety in Italy. Although he had intended it as a literary experiment in which theatrical techniques were applied to fiction, the public interpreted it as an attack on the Italian middle class. More recently, critics have viewed it as a pre-Sartrian existentialist novel. The themes of this story are those characteristic of Moravia's future works: the superficiality of the bourgeoisie, the importance of sex and money in human affairs, and the lack of rapport between men and reality (alienation). Although he wrote some of his best short stories during the 1930's, his next novel in this period was disappointing: *Le ambizioni sbagliate* (1935, *The Wheel of Fortune*) is verbose and confused. A protest against fascism, *La mascherata* (1941, *The Fancy Dress Party*) is a thinly veiled satire of Mussolini's regime; Moravia later (1954) rewrote it as a play. The novelist's most artistic work, *Agostino* (1944, *Agostino*), is the sympathetic and psychologically penetrating study of a middle-class adolescent's growing awareness of sexuality and his first steps toward adulthood. The journey is completed in *La disubbidienza*

(1948, *Luca*), which may be read as a sequel to *Agostino*. Sexuality is also a principal theme in *L'amore coniugale* (1949, *Conjugal Love*), *Il conformista* (1951, *The Conformist*), and *Il disprezzo* (1955, *A Ghost at Noon*).

In an important essay on humanism, "L'uomo come fine" (1946, "Man as an End"), Moravia ascribed the ills of the world to the widespread conception of man as a means toward nonhuman ends. The author maintained that only by reversing this notion and by considering man as an end in himself could there be hope for reestablishing an authentic rapport between man and reality. Believing that such a rapport already existed among the people, Moravia wrote a series of works whose characters belong to the working classes: *La romana* (1947, *The Woman of Rome*) describes in somewhat moralistic overtones the life of a prostitute, while the heroine of his best novel, *La ciociara* (1957, *Two Women*), succeeds in adapting herself to life in postwar Italy; two volumes of short stories, *Racconti romani* (1954, *Roman Tales*) and *Nuovi racconti romani* (1959, *More Roman Tales*), offer a panorama of life among the masses of Rome.

Moravia's literary interest in the lower classes faded during the late 1950's, when he turned his attention to the problem of the intellectual in a bourgeois world. Abandoning narration in the third person for the more subjective first-person point of view, he proposed the "essay-novel," which was to be constructed on ideological bases. Strongly influenced by the ideas of Ludwig Wittgenstein, *La noia* (1960, *The Empty Canvas*) investigates the relation of man to reality. The relation of the artist and his material constitutes the main theme of *L'attenzione* (1965, *The Lie*). Concern with intellectual problems characterizes not only Moravia's novels of this period but also his collected short stories—*L'automa* (1962, *The Fetish,*), *Una cosa è una cosa* (1967, *Command and I Will Obey You*)—and his plays—*Il mondo è quello che è* (1967, *The World Is What It is*), *Il dio Kurt* (1968, *The God Kurt*), and *La vita è gioco* (1969, *Life Is a Game*). The comic novel *Io e lui* (1971, *Two, A Phallic Novel*), which mocks the intellectual pretensions of the protagonist, signals perhaps the end of Moravia's "intellectualizing" period. The author's most recent short stories explore contemporary civilization from a feminist point of view and have been collected in three volumes: *Il paradiso* (1970, *Paradise*); *Un'altra vita* (1973, *Lady Godiva*); and *Boh* (1976, *Who Knows?*).

Moravia's long career and his voluminous production have made him the dean of contemporary Italian fiction. Although his works have always stirred critical debate, even the author's detractors recognize his narrative gifts and his dedication to literature. Aside from his merits as a creative writer, Moravia's cosmopolitan outlook (evinced in his works on the *USSR*, India, China, and Africa), his cultural *engagement*, and his commitment to humanistic ideas have enriched the civilization of Italy.

Bibliography: Man as an End: A Defense of Humanism, trans. Bernard Wall (1966; rpt. Westport, Conn.: Greenwood Press, 1976); *The Time of Indifference*, trans.

Angus Davidson (1953; rpt. Westport, Conn.: Greenwood Press, 1975); *Two Adolescents: The Stories of Agostino and Luca,* trans. Beryl de Zoete and Angus Davidson (1950; rpt. Westport, Conn.: Greenwood Press, 1976); *Two Women,* trans. Angus Davidson (New York: Manor Books, 1974); Jane E. Cottrell, *Alberto Moravia* (New York: Ungar, 1974); Donald Heiney, *Three Italian Novelists* (Ann Arbor, Mich.: University of Michigan Press, 1968); Edoardo Sanguineti, *Alberto Moravia* (Milan: Mursia, 1962).

Louis Kibler

MORETTI, MARINO (1885–), poet and writer. Moretti was born in Cesenatico and became a friend of Tozzi,* Palazzeschi,* Corazzini,* and Govoni.* After service in World War I, Moretti moved to Rome, where he met Federigo Tozzi. In 1922, he began a thirty-year collaboration with the *Corriere della sera* in Milan. His early literary works were published in the milieu of turn-of-the-century Florence. Moretti's first important collection of verse, *Poesie scritte col lapis* (Poems Written with a Pencil), appeared in 1910. His critical reputation was established when Giuseppe Borgese's* seminal essay on "twilight" poetry appeared in 1910, contrasting the verse of Moretti and others to that of the preceding generation dominated by D'Annunzio,* Pascoli,* and Carducci.* Moretti's poetry in this *crepuscolare* vein, like that of other and better known members of this group, rejects the rhetoric of D'Annunzio for simple subjects and a more humble poetic language. The *crepuscolare* experience also colors much of Moretti's prose. His first novel, *Il sole del sabato* (1907, Saturday Sun), is perhaps his best and presents an interesting feminine protagonist named Barberina, the first of many striking women in his fiction. Similar to Moretti's later tragic figures, Barberina endures her misfortunes, never rebels against her lot, and patiently accepts her fate as inevitable. Deledda* and Pirandello* praised the book, seeing in it an antidote to the sensual *femme fatale* typical of D'Annunzio's fiction.

Moretti's adherence to Croce's* antifascist manifesto brought him into disfavor with Mussolini's regime but he never put down his pen. Among some fifty volumes of his writings, the most notable novels include *La voce di Dio* (1921, The Voice of God) and *La vedova Fiorvanti* (1941, The Widow Fiorvanti). His collected short stories received the Viareggio Prize for Literature in 1959. While Moretti's style is essentially conservative and his fiction traditional, his works reveal an admirable devotion to the art of storytelling and painstaking craftsmanship.

Bibliography: Tutte le novelle (Milan: Mondadori, 1959); *Tutte le poesie* (Milan: Mondadori, 1966); Francesco Casnati, *Marino Moretti* (Milan: Istituto di Progaganda Libraria, 1952); Sergio Pacifici, *The Modern Italian Novel from Capuana to Tozzi* (Carbondale, Ill.: Southern Illinois University Press, 1973); Claudio Toscani, *Marino Moretti* (Florence: La Nuova Italia, 1975).

MURATORI, LODOVICO ANTONIO (1672–1750), librarian, historian, and antiquarian. Born in Vigola near Modena, Muratori completed his studies in philosophy and in civil and canon law, but his status as a priest and his scholarly bent prevented him from ever becoming a practicing lawyer. In 1695, he was given charge of the Ambrosiana Library in Milan, where he spent five years. While in Milan, Muratori became a close friend of the poet Carlo Maria Maggi,* whose biography he wrote and whose lyric poetry he edited (1700). Because of his scholarly renown, the duke of Modena entrusted him with the care of the Estense Library in 1700, a post he retained until his death.

Muratori was a member of the Arcadia* with the academic name Leucoto Gateate, and his early works were primarily literary. In a treatise entitled *Della perfetta poesia italiana* (1703, On Perfect Italian Poetry), he discusses the role of the imagination in the creation of verse. By elevating the imagination above the judgment or intellect, while rejecting neither of these two qualities, Muratori's aesthetic theories constituted an influential part of the body of poetics which eventually inspired and justified romantic literature. Other minor works in this literary vein include his *Osservazioni* (1707, Observations) on Petrarch,* his *Riflessioni sul buon gusto* (1708, Reflections on Good Taste), and a critical edition of the works of Castelvetro* (1727). Muratori's wide interests prompted him to compose works on nonliterary subjects, including one on public hygiene, *Del governo della peste* (1714, On the Control of Pestilence), and a political tract, *Della pubblica felicità oggetto de' buoni principi* (1749, On Public Happiness, The Object of Good Princes).

Muratori's chief accomplishments were scholarly. Beginning around 1712, he began to publish the indispensable tomes of Italian history which still form a rich lode of primary sources for contemporary scholars. In the *Antichità estensi* (1717, 1740, Historical Backgrounds of the Este Family), Muratori uncovered the genealogy of his patron's family and sent the first part of the work to Leibnitz, who was also engaged in research on the origins of the Este and Brunswick families at the time. More important for posterity was his monumental *Rerum italicarum scriptores* (1723–50, Historians of Italy), a work of staggering proportions in many volumes which assembled the bulk of Italian historical documents and chronicles from 500 to 1500 A.D. This invaluable tool for research was succeeded by his *Antiquitates italicae medii aevi* (1738–42, Medieval Italian Archaeology) in six volumes, a veritable fount of information concerning the customs, daily life, and institutions of medieval Italy. In order to make this mass of material available to the general reading public, Muratori composed the *Annali d'Italia* (The Annals of Italy). The first nine volumes appeared in 1744 and covered Italian history until 1500; the second twelve volumes were published between 1744 and 1749 and carried the narrative to 1749.

In his historical works, among the foremost of the early Italian En-lightenment,* Muratori exhibits the influence of both Cartesian rationalism and Galileo's* experimental methods. His goal was to return to the most ancient historical sources extant (the equivalent of the return to "nature" in experimental science). Subsequent historical traditions which had ob-scured these primary documents were rejected as the equivalent of "au-thority" in the sciences. What emerges from his lifelong endeavors in research and scholarship is not merely a collection of dry facts or dusty documents. Instead, Muratori's collected historical works assembled the raw materials required for charting the history of the emerging Italian nation and created a new awareness of Italy's past, which cultivated the growth of the romantic and Risorgimento movements in the next century.

Bibliography: Opere, eds. Giorgio Falco and Fiorenzo Forti, 2 vols. (Milan: Ricciardi, 1964); *Rerum italicarum scriptores*, ed. Giosuè Carducci, 34 vols. (Città di Castello: S. Lapi, and Bologna: Zanichelli, 1900–   ); Fiorenzo Forti, *Ludovico Antonio Muratori: fra antichi e moderni* (Bologna: Zuffi, 1953); Mario Fubini, *Dal Muratori al Baretti* (Bari: Laterza, 1954); J. G. Robertson, *Studies in the Genesis of Romantic Theory in the Eighteenth Century* (Cambridge: Cambridge University Press, 1923).

MUSSATO, ALBERTINO (1261–1329), humanist, historian, and play-wright. A notable member of a group of writers and scholars from Padua, Mussato experienced the early influence of his teacher Lovato Lovati (1241–1309), who encouraged him to write poetry in Latin. Mussato en-tered public life in 1296 and served his native city in various capacities, including that of ambassador to Emperor Henry VII, who made him a nobleman in 1311. Although his politics were Guelph, Mussato became Henry's staunch admirer. He was also deeply involved in Paduan politics during the period when Can Grande della Scala, lord of Verona, threatened the city's liberty. Eventually, in 1328, the city fell into Can Grande's hands and Mussato went into exile for the remainder of his life.

Mussato's major Latin compositions are heavily indebted to the histori-ans Livy, Caesar, and Sallust and to the dramatist Seneca; his Latin lyrics also recall the major poets of Roman antiquity. Upon the death of Henry VII, Mussato wrote *De gestis Henrici VII Cesaris* (1314, The Deeds of Emperor Henry VII), usually known as *Historia Augusta*, which recounts Italian history from the emperor's descent into the peninsula (1310) until his death. In 1315, he completed *De gestis Italicorum post Henricum VII Cesarem* (Italian Events After the Death of Emperor Henry VII), a collection of fourteen books which continued his narrative of Italian his-tory to the year 1321. Insofar as it emphasizes the human causes of history as well as the role of fate or providence, this work represents an important advance toward the developments in humanist historiography of the following century. In addition, Mussato's political vision and interest in a revival of the classics animate his own Latin Senecan tragedy entitled *Ecerinis* (1315, *The Tragedy of Ecerinis*). Depicting the tyranny of Ezzelino da Romano (1194–1259), Ghibelline ruler of Verona, the play is a thinly disguised warning to the citizens of Padua against the tyrannical ambitions of Can Grande della Scala. Although not divided into the formal acts and scenes typical of later Renaissance* neoclassical tragedy, there is a less formal organization into five parts, each marked by a choral passage. Dramatically most interesting are the revelation by Ezzelino's mother (Adeleita) of the circumstances surrounding the tyrant's conception—not the consequence of a natural union of father and mother but of his mother's rape by the devil—and the account of Ezzelino's eventual death. Apparently destined by its author for recitation rather than dramatic presentation, the play displays Mussato's mastery of Senecan metrics and his taste for the Roman poet's fascination with horror and grandiloquence.

In honor of his historical and dramatic works, Mussato was crowned poet laureate of the city of Padua in 1315, an event which apparently moved both Dante* and Petrarch* to aspire to the same sort of civic recognition for their more memorable poetic achievements.

See also HUMANISM.

Bibliography: Mussato's Ecerinis and Loschi's Achilles, trans. Joseph R. Berrigan (Munich: Wilhelm Fink, 1975)—contains both Latin text and English translation; *The Tragedy of Ecerinis: Latin Text and English Translation,* trans. Robert W. Carrubba, et al. (University Park, Pa.: Pennsylvania State University, Department of Classics, 1972); Manlio Torquato Dazzi, *Il Mussato preumanista 1261–1329: l'ambiente et l'opera* (Vincenza: Neri Pozza, 1964).

N

NARDI, JACOPO (1476–1563), Florentine historian, humanist, and politician. Nardi, the son of an anti-Medici family and a follower of Girolamo Savonarola* after 1494, held various positions in the Florentine Republic after the expulsion of the Medici under Savonarola. After their return in 1512, he apparently continued to work for his former enemies. He was a frequent visitor to the Orti Oricellari, although he did not take part in the plot organized against the Medici by Luigi Alamanni* and others (1522). After the second expulsion of the Medici (1527) and their return (1530), Nardi was sentenced to exile from Florence and moved to Venice where he lived until his death.

Nardi wrote several political discourses during the polemic struggles in Florence before the Medici family established their hereditary duchy, a collection of carnival songs, and two comedies based on tales from Boccaccio's* *Decameron*. His popular translation of Livy's history (1540) furthered the cause of republicanism by making available to the reader in the vernacular an essential classical text which had been widely studied by republican partisans after the appearance of Machiavelli's* *Discourses* in 1531. Nardi's most important book was *Istorie della città di Firenze* (1582, The History of the City of Florence). Appearing posthumously, this history in ten books analyzes Florentine affairs between 1494 and 1538 from the viewpoint of the defeated Savonarolian republicans.

See also ALAMANNI, Luigi; MACHIAVELLI, Niccolò.

Bibliography: Istorie della città di Firenze, 5 vols. (Florence: Salani, 1925); Rudolf von Albertini, *Firenze dalla repubblica al principato: storia e coscienza politica* (Turin: Einaudi, 1970).

NAVAGERO, ANDREA (1483–1529), Venetian humanist, poet, historian, and diplomat. Navagero was educated at Padua under the philosopher Pompanazzi* and served the Venetian Republic as ambassador to Spain (1516) and to France (1526). A friend of the Venetian printer Aldo Manuzio,* Navagero prepared many of the fine Aldine editions of the classics, including the *Metamorphoses* of Ovid and works of Cicero and Quintilian. He became the custodian of the important library given by Cardinal Bessarion to the city of Venice in 1516. For a time, he served as the official historian for Venice, succeeding Marcantonio Sabellico (1436–1506) and followed in this post by Pietro Bembo.*

Although Navagero's Italian lyrics are rather commonplace, his influence upon Juan Boscán, a Spaniard whom he met during his residence in Madrid, initiated the vogue of Petrarchan lyrics in Spain. Furthermore, his letters from Spain have historical import; in one from Seville (1526), for example, he describes Indians brought from the New World. His collection of Latin poems, *Ludus* (1530, Playful Pieces), a series of poems in the style of Catullus and the Greek Anthology, were occasioned by Navagero's love for a woman named Hyella. Considered to be among the best neo-Latin lyrics composed during the Renaissance,* they were translated and imitated by Thomas Lodge, Joachim Du Bellay, and Pierre de Ronsard as well as by many neo-Latin Italian poets.

See also MANUZIO, Aldo; PETRARCHISM.

Bibliography: Opera omnia (Padua: Comine, 1718); *Ludus* (Haarlem, 1947)—contains selections plus translations and imitations by French poets; W. L. Grant, *Neo-Latin Literature and the Pastoral* (Chapel Hill, N.C.: University of North Carolina Press, 1965); James Hutton, *The Greek Anthology in Italy to the Year 1800* (Ithaca, N.Y.: Cornell University Press, 1935).

NEERA, pen-name of Anna Radius Zuccari (1846–1918), novelist. Neera was born in Milan and lost both of her parents in her youth. Although she often complained of a restricted cultural background, her instincts as a writer were sure, and her tastes in reading other writers were catholic. By 1875, she had begun to publish her first prose under the pseudonym Neera. *Vecchie catene* (1878, Old Chains) and *Un nido* (1880, A Nest), her first novels, attracted the admiring attention of no less a critic than Luigi Capuana.* An influential essay by Benedetto Croce* in 1904 praised her work and insured her critical reputation.

Neera's portrayal of women may be seen as an early manifestation of Italian feminist concerns, but she perceived the prospect of women's emancipation from traditional roles in Italian society in a conservative fashion. Her most memorable novels, *Teresa* (1886, Teresa), *Lydia* (1887, Lydia), *L'indomani* (1890, The Next Day), and *Anima sola* (1894, *The Soul of an Artist*), analyze female protagonists and their struggles to realize their personal goals within a society alien to their possibilities. Her female characters are doomed to failure, and their lives are ultimately dominated by masculine values established without regard to feminine feelings or aspirations for the future.

Bibliography: Neera, ed. Benedetto Croce (Milan: Garzanti, 1943); *The Soul of an Artist,* trans. E. L. Marison (San Francisco: Elder, 1905); Sergio Pacifici, *The Modern Italian Novel from Capuana to Tozzi* (Carbondale, Ill.: Southern Illinois University Press, 1973).

NEGRI, ADA (1870–1945), poet and novelist. Negri was born in Lodi. Her working-class origins and poverty-stricken childhood inform many of her writings. Negri passed quickly from teaching in the public schools to a relatively clamorous success with her first collections of verse, *Fatalità* (1892, *Fate*) and *Tempeste* (1895, Tempests), both of which put into words her early humanitarian themes and social protest. Although largely ignored by contemporary anthologies, Negri's verse attracted a wide critical following in her time and eventually earned a number of literary prizes. She became a member of the Accademia d'Italia in 1940. As her writing moved beyond her early socialist leanings, the poetry in *Il libro di Mara* (1919, Mara's Book) or *Canti dell'isola* (1924, Songs of the Island) began to show the influence of D'Annunzio.* Perhaps most enduring is her auto-biographical *Stella mattutina* (1921, *Morning Star*), a moving portrait of her childhood and early career as a teacher. She also translated Prévost's *Manon Lescaut* (1931). Although Negri continued to enjoy the recognition of the literary establishment until her death, her reputation owed more to her early works than to those from the last two decades of her life.

Bibliography: Poesie (Milan: Mondadori, 1956); *Prose* (Milan: Mondadori, 1954); *Fate and Other Poems*, trans. A. M. von Blomberg (Boston: Copeland & Day, 1898); *From Marino to Marinetti*, trans. Joseph Tusiani (New York: Baroque Press, 1974); *Morning Star*, trans. Anne Day (New York: Macmillan, 1930); Salvatore Comes, *Ada Negri da un tempo all'altro* (Milan: Mondadori, 1970).

NEOCLASSICISM, a literary movement that reached its full development in the second half of the eighteenth and the beginning of the nineteenth century. Its origins are to be found in the plastic arts with which it always maintained strict ties. The incunabula of neoclassicism are to be found in the new style of architecture created by Andrea Palladio (1508–1580) and in the works of painters such as Nicolas Poussin (1594–1665) and Claude Lorraine (1600–1682). As far as art theory is concerned, the first significant manifestations of the new trend were Giovanni Pietro Bellori's (1615–1696) anti-Baroque* books, *Idea del pittore, dello scultore e dell'architetto* (1664, Idea of the Painter, Sculptor, and Architect) and *Vite de' pittori, scultori ed architetti moderni* (1672, Lives of Modern Painters, Sculptors, and Architects). Bellori was the librarian of Christina of Sweden, and came from the same intellectual climate that favored the rise of the Arcadia.* Thus, various aspects of the Arcadia coincided with neoclassicism, because both movements were prompted by the same aversion to Baroque taste. Gian Vincenzo Gravina's* insistence on Greek literary models in his treatise *Della ragion poetica* (1708, On the Nature of Poetry), Johann Joachim Winckelmann's favorite book, was an important contribution to neoclassic taste. Successful Arcadian poets such as Alessandro Guidi (1650–1712), a protégé of Christina of Sweden, Paolo Antonio Rolli,* and Pietro Metastasio,* all of whom were deeply influenced by Gravina, incorporated neoclassic ideals into their works. This trend was also strengthened by the influence of French and English literature, as a consequence of the well-known Francomania and Anglomania of eighteenth-century Italy. The example set by English poets such as Milton and Pope caught the eyes of Italian men of letters and encouraged them to follow in their path. From this point of view, Rolli and Antonio Conti (1677–1749) had an important role as mediators between the English and Italian literatures.

Despite all these pioneering efforts, neoclassicism would never have been able to reach its full bloom, were it not for the intellectual activity deployed in favor of Greek art by the father of modern archaeology, Johann Joachim Winckelmann, a German scholar working in Rome. His theory of ideal beauty was founded on the perfect harmony of ancient masterpieces, showing a clear preference for straight lines, design, flat surfaces, and immobility at the expense of curved lines, color, round surfaces, and movement which characterized Baroque art. His most important followers were Francesco Milizia (1725–1798), a staunch opposer of Baroque architecture, and Luigi Lanzi (1732–1810), author of *Storia pittorica d'Italia* (1795–96, History of Italian Painting), a pioneering work in the field of art history. Winckelmann's aesthetic ideas also guided the activity of contemporary artists who accomplished a radical revolution in plastic arts. It was along these lines that Antonio Canova (1757–1822) and Raphael Mengs (1728–1779), author of the widely acclaimed *Riflessioni su la bellezza e sul gusto della pittura* (1762, Considerations on the Beauty and Taste in Painting), completely renewed sculpture and painting, while Filippo Juvara (1676–1736), Luigi Vanvitelli (1700–1773), and Giuseppe Piermarini (1734–1808) applied neoclassic principles to architecture. This trend was strengthened by the discovery of Herculaneum, the Roman center destroyed along with Pompeii by an eruption of Mount Vesuvius (A.D. 79), and moreover by the publication of *Le antichità di Ercolano* (The Antiquities of Herculaneum) in the years 1755–92.

Under the impact of such artistic developments, literary output acquired a marked neoclassic connotation. The change in taste is apparent in the third and fourth parts of Giuseppe Parini's* *Il Giorno (The Day)*, where figures are immersed in a serene atmosphere and the social commitment is abandoned; in other writings of the same author, particularly in the treatise *De' principii delle belle lettere applicati alle belle arti* (completed circa 1777, On Principles of Belles-Lettres Applied to Fine Arts), sensistic and neoclassic ideas are fused together. But the most significant representatives of this movement were Vincenzo Monti* who produced typically neoclassic poems, such as "Prosopopea di Pericle" (The Prosopopoeia of Pericles), a eulogy of Pius VI that can be considered a manifesto of neoclassicism, and Ugo Foscolo,* a great poet, who combined his romantic sensibility with the cult of Greek literature and art, attaining his highest results in the *Grazie* (The Graces).

Other neoclassic writers enjoyed a considerable reputation during their lifetime. Lodovico Savioli (1729–1804) offered in his *Amori* (1758, Loves) a faithful mirror of the elegant and detached mood of his times, while Carlo Gastone Della Torre di Rezzonico (1742–1796) applied the Longinian idea of the sublime to the principles of ideal beauty. Agostino Paradisi (1736–1783) contributed to the movement not only through his *Rime* (1787, Rhymes) and *Versi sciolti* (1762, Unrhymed Hendecasyllables), but also through his critical writings, such as *Saggio metafisico sopra l'entusiasmo nelle belle arti* (1769, A Metaphysical Essay on Enthusiasm in Fine Arts) and *Saggio politico sull'ultima decadenza d'Italia* (1770, A Political Essay on the Last Decay of Italy). Luigi Cerretti (1738–1808) imitated Savioli in his *Amori giovanili* (Youthful Loves) and Horace in his *Odi* (Odes), both collected and published after 1791. His pupil, Luigi Lamberti (1759–1813), with the help of the great archaeologist Ennio Quirino Visconti (1751–1818), illustrated the sculptures of the Borghese Collection in Rome, and, despite Foscolo's attacks, enjoyed a considerable reputation among his contemporaries. His most successful poems included "Lamento di Dafni" (Lament of Daphne), "Il bagno" (The Bath), and "I cocchi" (The Coaches). Francesco Cassoli (1749–1812), a close friend of Giancarlo Passeroni (1713–1803) and Parini, was a good translator of Latin poetry (Virgil and Horace). He fused his modern sensibility with the imitation of classics in his original works, reaching his highest point in a few noble lyrics, particularly in "Alla lucerna" (To the Lamp) and "Al letto" (To the Bed).

See also ARCADIA; BAROQUE; ENLIGHTENMENT.

Bibliography: Lirici del Settecento, ed. Bruno Maier (Milano: Ricciardi, 1959); Walter Binni, *Classicismo e Neoclassicismo nella letteratura del Settecento* (Firenze: La Nuova Italia, 1967); Bruno Maier, *Il Neoclassicismo* (Palermo: Palumbo, 1964); Mario Praz, *On Neoclassicism* (London: Thames & Hudson, 1969).

Gustavo Costa

NEO-PLATONISM: *See* BEMBO, PIETRO; CASTIGLIONE, BAL-DESAR; DELLA MIRANDOLA, GIOVANNI PICO; EBREO, LE-ONE; FICINO, MARSILIO.

NEOREALISM, a term which, over the years, has been employed to describe what might loosely be defined as a trend or movement in Italian art, literature, and cinema. The term first appeared in 1930 in an essay by

Arnaldo Bocelli (1900–1976) which outlined the literary production of that year. The neorealist works were described as analyzing the human condition in light of the social environment and of objective psychological insights, and as avoiding the then prevalent stylistic and formal hedonism. Foremost among these works, which until then had been generally overlooked or undervalued by the critics, was Alberto Moravia's* *Gli indifferenti* (1929, *The Time of Indifference*).

While neorealism did not reach its zenith until the years immediately following World War II, its roots extend into the nineteenth century. The subject matter and the linguistic experimentation of neorealism, the depiction of the lower classes as protagonists, the regional, provincial settings, and the borrowings, influences, and use of dialectal expressions—all can be traced back to Emile Zola, Giovanni Pascoli,* and Giovanni Verga.* From the realists and the naturalists, the neorealists inherited the depiction of everyday life and the perception that the interests of different social classes did not necessarily coincide. But, while naturalism's sympathy for the worker offered no solution to his plight, neorealism often emulated socialist realism. Although numerous neorealist works revealed a more or less explicit faith in Marxist dialectical conflict, in the inevitability of historical evolution, and in the irresistible power of collective effort, they did not generally share the doctrinaire optimism of socialist realism and the consequent inescapable solution. At the same time, neorealism reflected the Italian fascination with the American dream and its glorification of the limitless potential of the individual.

Over the years, many, if not most, critics have conceived of neorealism as a primarily ideological, leftist movement, and have all too willingly ignored any contradictory data. Italo Calvino,* among the neorealist writers, presents the most explicit rejection of the conventional definitions of neorealism in his 1967 preface to *I sentieri dei nidi di ragno* (1947, *The Path to the Nest of Spiders*). Even though Calvino's statements pertain directly to the literary production of the immediate postwar years—and notwithstanding his repeated assertions that neorealism was not a "school" and that he speaks only for himself—his comments do shed light on much of neorealist literature. Calvino acknowledges the importance of the "extraliterary" elements in the movement—the war, the Italian political situation under Mussolini, the partisan experience. However, on several occasions he reiterates that the neorealists were concerned more with the expression of the stories to be told than with the stories themselves; that, although concerned with content, he and the other neorealists were compulsive formalists; and that they were fully aware that the "musical score is more important than the *libretto*." Time and again, he alludes to the importance of literary sources, including not only Verga, but also Ippolito Nievo,* Ernest Hemingway, Isaac Babel, and Alexander Fadeev.

He then returns to the cornerstone of his reflections: the literary essence of neorealism, its revolutionary rejection of the major trend in the history of Italian literature and of the urge to write elegantly, according to the somewhat artificial canons of the official Italian grammars. Neorealism, he states, represents the single major effort since Dante* to give the Italian spoken language a written form, a process intended both as a liberation from old strictures and as a legitimization of new forms. Given the nature of this linguistic experiment, which in many ways emulated the experiments of the American writers of the 1930s, the subject matter treated and the ideology presented had to reflect a popular, if not proletarian, point of view, and in any case had to come into conflict with the traditional class structure. According to Calvino, the writers who best exemplify the literary range of neorealism are Elio Vittorini,* Cesare Pavese,* and Beppe Fenoglio.* Among the many other writers who have been considered neorealists are Alberto Moravia, Carlo Emilio Gadda,* Carlo Levi,* Carlo Bernari,* Carlo Cassola,* Vasco Pratolini,* Leonardo Sciascia,* Ignazio Silone,* Renata Viganò (1900–   ), and Mario Tobino.*

In addition to neorealist literary works, there is an equally important neorealist current in the films produced in Italy between 1945 and 1951 by directors such as Roberto Rossellini (1906–1977), Vittorio De Sica (1902–1974), and Luchino Visconti (1906–1976). And yet, the attempts to define neorealism in cinema, to establish its chronological, ideological, aesthetic, and human parameters, have only recently met with any degree of success. According to a recent seminal study by Lino Miccichè ("Per una verifica del neorealismo," For a Verification of Neorealism—the first essay of *Il neorealismo cinematografico italiano,* Italian Cinematographic Neorealism), neorealism did not suddenly materialize in the years immediately following World War II, nor was it the major trend in the Italian cinema of the period. Its roots may be found in Nino Martoglio's (1870–1921) *Sperduti nel Buio* (1913–14, *Lost in the Dark*) and in Gustavo Serena's (1882–1970) *Assunta Spina* (1915). From that early date and parallel to the historical spectaculars and frivolous comedies—and often incorporated in them—works containing elements which would later be considered intrinsically neorealistic were produced. Among such antecedents to neorealism are Alessandro Blasetti's (1900–   ) *Sole* (1929, *The Sun*) and *1860* (1932); the documentaries of Francesco De Robertis (1902–1959) (1941, *Uomini sul fondo* [*S.O.S. Submarine*]), and of Rossellini (1941, *La nave bianca* [*The White Ship*]); and the sentimental comedies starring Vittorio De Sica (1932, *Gli uomini che mascalzoni* [*What Rascals Men Are*], and 1942, *Teresa Venerdi* [*Teresa Friday*]). While some critics feel that the 1942-43 season, with Visconti's *Ossessione (Obsession)*, Blasetti's *Quattro passi fra le nuvole (Four Steps in the Clouds)*, De Sica and Cesare Zavattini's (1902–   ) *I bambini ci guardano (The*

Children Are Watching Us), and Michelangelo Antonioni's (1912–)
Gente del Po (People of the Po), marks the beginning of neorealism,
Miccichè disagrees. He points out that the films cited above represent at
best only a rejection of the past, of the Italian cinema's glorification of
imperialistic adventures and of upper-middle-class protagonists.

It is with Rossellini's *Roma, città aperta* (1945, *Rome, Open City*) that
we find the first and only critically, as well as financially, successful
neorealist film. Based loosely on the clash between partisans, fascists, and
Nazis, the film's realism was largely the accidental result of a limited
budget, poor film stock, erratic sources of electricity, and the very physical
appearance of the city and its protagonists. Still, it is this work which
establishes the ideological and aesthetic point of departure of filmic neorealism and which is the model against which all subsequent neorealistic
films have been judged. Neorealist films thus generally embody a vague
populist or leftist viewpoint, while also incorporating somewhat mystical
notions of Christian brotherhood. They focus on lower class protagonists,
but they by no means limit themselves to the proletariat. On the contrary,
they include, among others, landowning farmers, technicians, small businessmen, students, priests, policemen, soldiers, and government employ-
ees. They generally possess a documentary-like appearance, even though
it is often achieved through totally contrived means. They are usually
based on purportedly real events portrayed in a romanticized manner,
when they are not linked to willfully distorted literary sources. Finally,
they employ nonprofessional actors to some extent to help reinforce their
aura of realism. But, while these are the major components of filmic
neorealism, they were not adopted programmatically by the various film-
makers, nor were they equally stressed in the different neorealist films.
Rather, the neorealist film-maker, like the neorealist writer, seems to have
found in the reality around him matter which each, according to his own
personal vision, attempted to transform into what De Sica described as the
"poetry of real life."

In the years that followed *Rome, Open City,* only Rossellini's *Paisà*
(1946, *Paisan*), Pietro Germi's (1914–1974) *In nome della legge* (1948, *In
the Name of the Law*), De Sica and Zavattini's *Ladri di biciclette* (1948,
Bicycle Thieves), and Giuseppe De Santis's (1917–) *Riso amaro* (1949,
Bitter Rice) were relatively successful at the box office. Films considered
classics today, such as Visconti's *La terra trema* (1947, *The Earth Will
Shake*), De Sica and Zavattini's *Sciuscià* (1946, *Shoe Shine*), Rossellini's
Germania anno zero (1947, *Germany Year Zero*), De Sica and Zavattini's
Miracolo a Milano (1950, *Miracle in Milan*), and *Umberto D.* (1951, *Um-
berto D.*), were complete economic failures. In fact, of the eight hundred
and twenty-two feature films produced in Italy between 1945 and 1953,
only ninety can be broadly described as neorealist. Still, even if neorealist

films were relatively few in number and not always well received, their importance in the history of the cinema is unquestionable. In their concern for and study of the everyday world around them, they expanded the narrative and aesthetic potential of the cinema and provided a focal point for the polemical debate over the function and nature of the arts which has raged for the last thirty years in Italy.

See also BERNARI, Carlo; CALVINO, Italo; CASSOLA, Carlo; LEVI, Carlo; MORAVIA, Alberto; PAVESE, Cesare; PRATOLINI, Vasco; SILONE, Ignazio; VERGA, Giovanni; VERISMO; VITTORINI, Elio.

Bibliography: Roy Armes, *Patterns of Realism: A Study of Italian Neo-Realist Cinema* (New York: A. S. Barnes, 1971); *Teorie e prassi del cinema italiano, 1950–1970,* ed. Edoardo Bruno (Milan: Mazzotta, 1972); Ernesto Guidorizzi, *La narrativa e il cinema italiano* (Florence: Sansoni, 1973); Donald Heiney, *Three Italian Novelists: Moravia, Pavese, Vittorini* (Ann Arbor, Mich.: University of Michigan Press, 1968); Giuliano Manacorda, *Storia della letteratura italiana contemporanea: 1940–1965* (Rome: Editori Riuniti, 1974); Lino Miccichè, ed., *Il neorealismo cinematografico italiano* (Venice: Marsilio, 1975); Sergio Pacifici, ed., *From Verismo to Experimentalism: Essays on the Modern Italian Novel* (Bloomington, Ind.: Indiana University Press, 1969), and *A Guide to Contemporary Italian Literature: From Futurism to Neorealism* (Carbondale, Ill.: Southern Illinois University Press, 1962); Giorgio Pullini, *Il romanzo italiano del dopoguerra* (Padua: Marsilio, 1970).

Ben Lawton

NICCOLINI, GIOVANNI BATTISTA (1782–1861), Tuscan tragedian. Having studied the classics and earned a degree in law, Niccolini taught history and mythology at the Accademia di Belle Arti in Florence after 1807. Although he was a staunch anticlerical republican and a friend of Ugo Foscolo,* to whom he dedicated a translation, he was never active in politics. Niccolini's dramatic works combine the neoclassicism* of the eighteenth century and the pre-romantics with the emerging romanticism* of his own century. Between 1810 and 1814, Niccolini produced a series of tragedies inspired by classical models and by the example of Alfieri,* including *Polissena* (1810, Polyxena), which was awarded a prize by the Accademia della Crusca, *Medea* (1816, Medea), and *Nabucco* (1819, Nebuchadnezzar). In *Nabucco,* Niccolini attacks Napoleonic tyranny, using the figure of the ancient despot as a thinly veiled symbol for a contemporary Italian problem.

Niccolini's eight subsequent tragedies treat medieval and modern subjects in the style of the emergent romantic theatre which was under the influence of Shakespeare, Schiller, Byron, and Manzoni.* Works of this period include *Antonio Foscarini* (1827, Antonio Foscarini); *Ludovico Sforza* (1833, Ludovico Sforza); *Beatrice Cenci* (1838, Beatrice Cenci), a work based upon Shelley's *The Cenci;* and his masterpiece, *Arnoldo da Brescia* (1843, *Arnold of Brescia*), a play whose central character (a medieval monk) reflects a liberal belief in Italian freedom and unification as opposed to the tyranny of emperor or pope. Taken together as a group, these later works depict the heroic Italian struggles against the tyranny of several epochs. Niccolini also wrote scholarly treatises on mythology, Greek tragedy, and a commentary on Dante's* *Divine Comedy*.

See also ALFIERI, Vittorio; MANZONI, Alessandro; ROMANTICISM.

Bibliography: *Opere edite e inedite,* ed. Corrado Gargiolli, 8 vols. (Milan: Guigoni, 1862–71); *Arnold of Brescia, A Tragedy,* trans. Theodosia Garrow (London: Longmans, 1846).

NIEVO, IPPOLITO (1831–1861), poet, patriot, and novelist. Born in Padua where he received a law degree in 1855, Nievo began his literary career as a poet under the influence of Parini* and Giusti* with two early collections entitled *Versi* (1854, 1855, Verse). Shortly thereafter, he completed two novels—*Angelo di bontà* (1856, Angel of Goodness) and *Il conte pecoraio* (1857, The Shepherd Count)—as well as a number of short stories with rustic settings and a novelette entitled *Il Varmo* (1856, The Varmo River). From 1857 until 1859, Nievo lived in Milan, where he frequented various intellectual and patriotic circles. During this time, he composed a comedy, two tragedies in verse, a long satirical tale entitled *Il barone di Nicastro* (1859, The Baron of Nicastro), and another collection of poetry, *Le lucciole* (1858, Fireflies).

Between December 1857 and August 1858, he completed the single work for which he is best remembered, a novel entitled *Le confessioni d' un italiano* (1867, *The Castle of Fratta*), the title of which was changed by the editor in the posthumous first edition of 1867 to *Le confessioni di un ottuagenario* (The Confessions of an Octogenarian). A fervent patriot, Nievo participated in the campaign of 1859 with Garibaldi* and was one of Garibaldi's Thousand in Sicily in 1860. Some of his minor works reflect these experiences, including a collection of poetry, *Amori garibaldini* (1860, Garibaldinian Love Affairs); a political tract, *Venezia e la libertà d'Italia* (1859, Venice and the Freedom of Italy); and the unfinished fragment of another novel, *Il pescatore d'anime* (The Fisher of Souls).

Nievo died in a tragic shipwreck between Sicily and the mainland while on military service. At the time of his death, he was not particularly well known, and his reputation grew only posthumously with the recognition of his major novel. The rousing success of *Le confessioni* upon its publication after the author's death can be partially attributed to its patriotic, Risorgimento tone. Indeed, its famous first sentence caught the imagination of an entire generation of Italians who lived through the events Nievo narrates: "I was born a Venetian 18 September 1775, the Day of St. Luke the Evangelist and I shall die, by the Grace of God, an Italian, whenever the Providence that mysteriously controls our world shall so ordain." Nievo's first person narrator is Carlino Altoviti, an old man whose confessions come to a close in 1855, just a few years before Nievo actually began writing the story. It presents a panorama of the crucial period in Italian history encompassing the fall of the ancient Venetian Republic, the Napoleonic invasions, the restoration of the old monarchies and the Austrian domination of Italy, the age of romanticism,* and the Risorgimento. It was thus understandable that a nineteenth-century Italian reading public nourished on the historical novels of D'Azeglio,* Grossi,* Guerrazzi,* and Tommaseo* would accept *Le confessioni* as a continuation of this genre.

Only recently have literary critics gone beyond this essentially political preoccupation with the novel's historical milieu to examine and appreciate Nievo's modernity as a novelist. The novel's originality resides in its autobiographical protagonist whose subjective narrative combines aspects of Nievo's own personality with those typical of his generation. Within the framework of the traditional historical novel, Nievo's narrator analyzes the psychology of his characters with consummate skill, disclosing his own nostalgia for the dead world of the past and expressing his hopes for the future. The most memorable parts of the book concern Altoviti's lifelong passion for his cousin Pisana, a singular creature whom critics have compared to Proust's Albertine. In addition to his exceptional characterizations, Nievo has a pronounced talent for describing landscapes as well as a sharp wit. While he makes use of an exciting historical background in the novel, Nievo deflates the typical heroic protagonist of the nineteenth-century historical novel and replaces him with a quite ordinary man who examines his past in a memoir. As such, the main character has closer affinities to the protagonists in novels of the next generation than to his counterparts in the traditional historical romances. Benedetto Croce,* among others, reproached the novel's lack of unity, a result of what he saw as an unnatural mixture of Nievo's autobiography and Italian history. However, this "contamination" of life and art, once thought to be a defect, is considered admirable by contemporary readers, trained as they are to appreciate the works of Proust or Svevo.* It is this aspect of Nievo's art which makes him more acceptable to the twentieth-century reader than the many historical novels of the period which have long been forgotten.

Bibliography: Tutte le opere di I. Nievo: Poesie, ed. Marcella Gorra (Milan: Mondadori, 1970); *Tutte le opere narrative di I. Nievo,* ed. Folco Portinari, 2 vols. (Milan: Mursia, 1967); *Opere,* ed. Sandro Romagnoli (Milan: Mondadori, 1952); *The Castle of Fratta,* trans. Lovett F. Edwards (London: Oxford University Press,

1957); Nicolae Iliescu, "The Position of Ippolito Nievo in the Nineteenth-Century Italian Novel," *Publications of the Modern Language Association* 75 (1960), 272–82; Emilia Mirmina, *La poetica sociale del Nievo* (Ravenna: Longo, 1972); Olga Ragusa, "Nievo the Writer: Tendencies in Criticism," *Italian Quarterly* 2 (1958), 20–34.

NOVELLA, a prose form whose origins have been traced to richly varied sources ranging from literary tradition (fables, chivalric romance, and fabliaux), to folk tradition (folk tales, fairy tales), and to religious writings, including the Bible, hagiography, and exempla. Tales were collected from far and wide and recounted in a written form which was brief, adhered to the notions of unity of time and action, and had a single plot and direct style of narration, and whose avowed purpose was the entertainment or edification of its readers. A variety of personages from all walks of life, although predominantly from the merchant class or from the ruling class, was represented in scenes of everyday dramas. Throughout the period from the thirteenth to the seventeenth century, these basic characteristics identified the Italian *novella.*

Whether given the name of *conto* or *novella,* the earliest examples of short prose writing began to appear in Italy during the thirteenth century. The most noted collection from the last half of the century was the *Novellino,** or *Cento novelle antiche,* written by an anonymous Tuscan author. The rubric added to the collection in the fourteenth century aptly indicates the subjects and themes of the individual *novelle:* "Questo libro tratta d'alquanti fiori di parlare, di belle cortesie e di be' risposi e di belle valentie e doni, secondo che per lo tempo passato hanno fatti molti valenti uomini" ("This book treats of several flowers of elegant speech, of noble courtesies and of quick answers and of worthy deeds and gifts which in times past were done by many valorous men"). Often the intent of these brief tales was to offer an example of virtuous life or of an individual who was master of the witty statement. Scenes of encounters with personages from past and present give a glimpse into medieval life.

It is with Boccaccio* that the *novella* reached its most sophisticated stage of development. His collection of one hundred *novelle, The Decameron,* was the principal model upon which centuries of short-story writing were based and judged. Every aspect of his style and language had a bearing on his successors: his manner of drawing freely upon both established literary tradition and popular oral tradition to collect the stories which he then wove into compact, intricate narratives; the economy of detail by which the superfluous or merely decorative was excluded; the thematic topics which probed into a wide range of human experience, from lowest to highest according to three categories of fortune, love, and intellect; and the enduring characters who inhabited the *novelle:* the shrewd knave Ser Cepparello, the quick-witted cook Chichibio, the noble lover

Federigo degli Alberighi, the less-than-noble lover Peronella, and the saintly Griselda. Another major feature of *The Decameron* is the arrangement of its *novelle* within a *cornice* or framework: ten storytellers are brought together by external circumstances (the plague and its effects on living conditions in Florence) and within the specified period of ten days they recount stories to one another according to themes chosen by the group.

Of the numerous fourteenth-century imitators of Boccaccio, Ser Giovanni Fiorentino* and Giovanni Sercambi* deserve mention. Giovanni Fiorentino, in his collection of fifty tales entitled *Il Pecorone*, adopted the *cornice* to encase his *novelle* whose material derived variously from a contemporary chronicler of Florence, from Livy, from Apuleius, and from Boccaccio himself. One of his *novelle* (that of Giannetto and the Donna di Belmonte) influenced Shakespeare's *The Merchant of Venice*. More prolific (approximately one hundred and fifty *novelle*) and more deeply set in the Boccaccian mold, Giovanni Sercambi showed a keen interest in the fantasy and fairy-tale elements from popular tradition. The most distinguished *novelliere* of the century was Franco Sacchetti* (*Trecento novelle*, of which only two hundred and twenty-three survive). Unlike many of his contemporaries, he rarely drew his subject material from either literary or oral tradition; the main source of his inspiration was life in the *piazze*, the human experiences of city life, the daily happenings, anecdotes, practical jokes, curious stories, and local customs. Sacchetti accordingly abandoned the restrictive arrangement of material by theme and the *cornice*. His style is simple and direct, as are the moralistic considerations which he appends to the *novelle*.

A number of religious *novelle* and legends appeared in the fourteenth century in Italy, especially those of Domenico Cavalca (1270–1342) (*Vite dei Santi Padri*, Lives of the Holy Fathers), Jacopo Passavanti* (*Specchio di vera penitenza*, circa 1354, The Mirror of True Penitence), and the ever-popular though anonymous *Fioretti di San Francesco (Flowers of St. Francis)*. Their general purpose was to edify the reader, but the intent to entertain with a pleasant narrative was not forgotten.

Particular to the humanistic atmosphere of the fifteenth century were examples of *novelle* in Latin, the most original being the *Historia de duobus amantibus* (1444, *The Tale of the Two Lovers*) by Enea Silvio Piccolomini* (later Pope Pius II). In the hands of Poggio Bracciolini,* the Latin *novella* assumed the form of a *facetia* (a tale based on a practical joke or witty statement). Bracciolini collected his works in his *Liber facetiarum* (1438–52, *The Facetiae*, also known as *Confabulationes*). Vernacular *facezie* also appeared, which were usually anonymous or of doubtful authorship. In Florence, there were the *facezie* of the Piovano Arlotto (1396–1484), collected anonymously. A number of versions suggest the widespread popularity of the long *novella* of the "Grasso legnaiuolo" or "fat cabinet-maker" (attributed to Antonio Manetti, 1423–1497), which is a representative example of the *facezia* extended into a long narrative. Among the century's imitators of Boccaccio were Giovanni Gherardi da Prato (circa 1367—circa 1446), who intermingled *novelle* in his *Paradiso degli Alberti* (The Albertis' Paradise Villa); the Sienese Gentile Sermini (dates uncertain), author of many rather obscene *novelle* of dubious literary merit collected around 1424; and Giovanni Sabbadino degli Arienti (1450–1510) (1483, *Le Porrettane*, The Ladies of Porretta), who was quick to represent comic scenes from the city of Florence. Closer to the vivid and colorful world of oral tradition was the satirical and polemical Masuccio Salernitano* *(Novellino).* His tale of two young lovers, Mariotto and Ganozza, was handed down through different versions from Luigi da Porto* in the sixteenth century to Bandello* and through French and English translations until it was transformed by Shakespeare into *Romeo and Juliet.* The fifteenth century was not without its representative of religious storytelling; San Bernardino of Siena (1380–1444) did not hesitate to insert vivid realistic tales in his sermons.

From the outset, the city of Florence and Tuscany in general played an important role in the development of the *novella,* producing writers, thematic episodes and characters, and the standard for language and style. The sixteenth century was a particularly fertile period for the *novella.* Although formally linked to Boccaccio, two Tuscan writers—Pietro Fortini (1500–1562) and Anton Francesco Grazzini ("Il Lasca")*—were more closely identified with another Florentine, Franco Sacchetti.* They shared the same curiosity for daily happenings in the city and for the expressiveness of the spoken tongue. The twenty-two *novelle* of Grazzini's *Le Cene* (The Suppers) are comical and realistic; Fortini's are about comical encounters, questions of love, and social games, arranged in the complicated *cornice* of *Novelle de' Novizi* (circa 1560, The Novices' Tales). A counterpoint to the popularizing tendencies of Grazzini and Fortini is provided by Angelo Firenzuola,* who disregarded content and focused his attention on form and style. The ten *novelle* of his incomplete work, *I ragionamenti d'amore (Tales of Firenzuola)* show his efforts to achieve a distinctive prose style based on spoken Florentine as opposed to the language of the Boccaccian model.

A non-Tuscan, Matteo Bandello stands out from the many *novellieri* of the sixteenth century. Bandello wrote two hundred and fourteen *novelle* and, in lieu of the *cornice,* preceded each of the *novelle* with a dedicatory letter which reflected the occasion of the telling of the story. It is through these letters, which at times are mini-*novelle,* that insight is gained into the social customs of the courtly life of which Bandello was a participant. Based primarily on sensual and erotic themes, though not without a note of tragic drama, (e.g., the *novella* of Giulia da Garzuolo, the victim of a rape who commits suicide), Bandello's *novelle* gained a wide audience throughout Europe and were translated into many languages. Similar to other non-Tuscans (Gian Francesco Straparola* and Girolamo Parabosco, 1524–1557), Bandello generally exercised more freedom in his choice of themes, and he had a keen interest in tales of adventure. He had less concern for style than his Tuscan counterparts, and his penchant for complex plots led to the lengthening of his *novelle* beyond the traditional standard. A contemporary of Bandello, Giambattista Giraldi (Il Cinzio),* possessed a similar interest in tales of romance and adventure, although he was much more influenced by the Counter-Reformation. Cinzio infuses his one hundred and thirteen *novelle (Gli Hecatommithi,* The Hundred Stories) with a strong sense of morality. Shakespeare is indebted to Cinzio for one such *novella* about a Moorish captain who takes a Venetian wife—the source for his tragedy *Othello.* In the hands of Straparola, the interest in adventure is complemented by an equal fascination with the world of fantasy. His collection of seventy-three *novelle* in *Le piacevoli notti* (1550–53, *The Nights of Straparola)* constitutes an important link in the development of the *novella* based on oral tradition and folklore. Within this fervent atmosphere of *novella* writing, the imposing figure of Niccolò Machiavelli* is felt with his single tale, *Novella di Belfagor arcidiavolo (The Novella of Belfagor Archdevil).* The work, also known as the *Favola,* is an amusing account of the misfortunes of a devil who takes a wife to investigate the accusation of the damned that their wives lead them to their ruin.

By the beginning of the seventeenth century, the *novella* had assumed its characteristic form and its three basic types: *novelle* drawn from a literary source modeled on Boccaccio's *Decameron;* the *facetia,* or *novella* which revolves around a practical joke or witticism and which reflects everyday life in terms of both language and style; and the *novella* taken from an oral tradition in which the fairy tale and the world of fantasy and magic play a dominant role. There are, of course, overlappings and variations which in turn enrich this expressive short prose form. The major representatives of these three main types of *novelle* during the seventeenth century were Giovanni Sagredo (1617–1682) (*Arcadia in Brenta,* Arcadia in Brenta) and Anton G. Brignole Sale (1605–1655), who was strongly influenced by the Baroque style of the contemporary Boccaccian *novella;* Carlo Roberto Dati (1619–1676), Francesco Redi,* and Lorenzo Magalotti* of the *facetia;* and Giambattista Basile* with his *Pentamerone, lo cunto de li cunti,* of the fairy tale. Judged to be a model collection of fairy tales by the brothers Grimm, the *Pentamerone,* written in Neapolitan dialect, is a storehouse of memorable tales.

The *novella* reached a definite plateau during the seventeenth century, and in the following years it assumed new forms with authors such as Giovanni Verga* and Luigi Pirandello.* Its foundation was firmly set on Italian soil, and it enjoyed an extended period of vitality and popularity for over five centuries. The form has not completely exhausted its potential in the twentieth century, as is seen in the modern *novelle* of Carlo Emilio Gadda,* Alberto Moravia,* and Italo Calvino.*

See also BANDELLO, Matteo; BASILE, Giambattista; BOCCACCIO, Giovanni; GIOVANNI FIORENTINO; GIRALDI, Giambattista; GRAZZINI, Anton Francesco; NOVELLINO; SACCHETTI, Franco; SERCAMBI, Giovanni.

Bibliography: Italian Short Stories from the 13th to the 20th Centuries, ed. Ernest Rhys (New York: Dutton, 1932); *Penguin Book of Italian Short Stories,* ed. Guido Waldman (Harmondsworth: Penguin, 1969); Thomas Roscoe, *The Italian Novelists* (London: W. Simpkin & R. Marshall, 1836); Robert J. Clements and Joseph Gibaldi, *Anatomy of the Novella: The European Tale Collection from Boccaccio and Chaucer to Cervantes* (New York: New York University Press, 1977); Yvonne Rodax, *The Real and the Ideal in the Novella of Italy, France and England: Four Centuries of Change in Boccaccian Tale* (Chapel Hill, N.C.: University of North Carolina Press, 1968); Dominic P. Rotunda, *Motif-index of the Italian Novella in Prose* (Bloomington, Ind.: Indiana University Press, 1942).

Dennis Dutschke

NOVELLINO *(The Hundred Old Tales),* a collection of brief *novelle** from the late fourteenth century by an anonymous author or authors. Although the extant manuscript mentions the title *Libro di novelle et di bel parlar gentile* (The Book of Novelle and of Comely Gentle Speech), a letter by Giovanni della Casa* dubbed it *Novellino,* a title by which it has been commonly known ever since. A concise prologue, in which the author reveals his preoccupation with speech and courtly manners, introduces the one hundred anecdotal tales, some no longer than several sentences. It has also been suggested that certain dominant thematic concerns divide the collection into ten groups, each consisting of ten *novelle.* If true, this may account for Boccaccio's* interest in the work. The stories show the influence of a great many popular and learned sources, ranging from the Bible to Oriental, classical, French, and medieval Latin literature. The characters involved in the stories range from the most obscure to such famous figures as Hector, David, Solomon, Saladin, Richard the Lion-Hearted, Prester John, and Alexander the Great. The terse, often didactic nature of many of the tales in this collection, the first truly Italian fictional work, reflects its close relationship to the medieval exemplum and its origins in a tradition which was not exclusively literary in nature.

See also BOCCACCIO, Giovanni; NOVELLA.

Bibliography: Il Novellino, ed. Guido Favati (Genoa: Fratelli Bozzi, 1970); *Il Novellino: The Hundred Old Tales,* trans. Edward Storer (New York: Dutton, 1925).

O

ORIANI, ALFREDO (1852–1909), novelist and social thinker. Oriani was born in Faenza and was the son of a well-to-do property owner. Although he studied law in Rome and Naples, he passed most of his life as a lonely recluse on his country estate. His early writings such as *Memorie inutili* (1876, Useless Memoirs), *Al di là* (1877, Beyond), and *Matrimonio e divorzio* (1886, Marriage and Divorce), were practically ignored by the critics, a neglect that caused him no small amount of bitterness. Oriani's finest literary works are considered to be three novels—*Gelosia* (1894, Jealousy), *La disfatta* (1896, The Defeat), and *Vortice* (1899, Vortex). The first of these, *Gelosia,* describes the love affair between a young man and the wife of a lawyer, who forgives her faithlessness after her lover, in a state of vindictiveness, has revealed their illicit passion to him. Oriani's fervent belief in the eventual victory of the spirit over the flesh looms large in this ending. The second novel, regarded as his masterpiece, describes the struggles of a certain Professor De Nittis to unite thought and action; his moral defeat lies in his failure to participate in life's onward movement. *Vortice* analyzes the last day of a suicide, an obsessive gambler who wages both his fortune and his honor.

Oriani's reputation was almost entirely posthumous and was created by the fascists' belief that his ideas foreshadowed their own theories and the new era ushered in by Il Duce, a view made official in 1924, when a national edition of Oriani's works was commissioned, edited by Benito Mussolini himself. Three political essays by Oriani were largely responsible for this belated and unbesought status: *Fino a Dogali* (1889, All the Way to Dogali); *La lotta politica in Italia* (1892, The Political Struggle in Italy); and *La rivolta ideale* (1908, The Ideal Revolt). They reflect the influence not only of Hegel but also of Vico,* Nietzsche, and Angelo Camillo De Meis (1817–1891), the Italian Hegelian professor at the university in Bologna. Dogali was the scene of one of Italy's major colonial defeats in Africa, and *Fino a Dogali* sketches in rather grandiloquent terms Oriani's views on Italy's mission in Africa and the nation's new destiny in the modern world after unification. The second volume sets forth a stirring discussion of Italian history from the fall of the Roman Empire to the Risorgimento and also debates the greatness of Italy, its future destiny as a world power, and the role of spiritual struggle in this historical development. Both works thus furnished the view of *italianità* and the heroic concept of life that fascist theorists later repeated in their own ideology and rhetoric. *La rivolta ideale* condemns the materialism and positivism of the nineteenth century and asserts the necessity of idealism, spiritual faith, and human struggle. It calls for a new aristocracy to lead the people in a revolutionary upheaval which will carry them and their nation to fulfill their historical and spiritual destiny.

Because Oriani's posthumous fame rested on his link to Italian fascism, postfascist criticism of Oriani has too often been colored by the critics' opposition to this political movement. However, Oriani's true place in Italian literature has not yet been settled. An unbiased analysis of his works would probably place them within the framework of Italian *decadentismo.**

See also DECADENTISMO.

Bibliography: Opera omnia, ed. Benito Mussolini (Bologna: Cappelli, 1923–33); Francis Authier, "État présent des études sur Alfred Oriani," *Revue des Études Italiennes* 7 (1960), 250–69; Benedetto Croce, *La letteratura della nuova Italia,* Vol. 3 (Bari: Laterza, 1964); Robert S. Dombroski, "Oriani's *Vortice* as a Political Metaphor," *Forum Italicum* 6 (1972), 488–96.

ORTESE, ANNA MARIA (1915–   ), Roman journalist and writer. Ortese's first collection of stories, *Angelici dolori* (Angelic Sorrows), appeared in 1937 and won the praise of Massimo Bontempelli.* Her next important work, *Il mare non bagna Napoli* (1953, *The Bay Is Not Naples*), was discovered by Elio Vittorini* through a story which he read in *Il Mondo.* It received the Viareggio Prize for fiction and established her as a successful regional realist with Naples as her typical subject matter. After several lesser works, Ortese moved her fiction to Milan with *Poveri e semplici* (1967, Poor and Simple People), a revealing portrait of life in her neighborhood. Often compared to the best work of her mentor Vittorini for its lyrical qualities, the book received the Strega Prize for 1968. In addition to her fiction, Ortese regularly contributes articles to various periodicals and has composed a perceptive account of a visit to the Soviet Union.

Bibliography: The Bay Is Not Naples, trans. Frances Frenaye (London: Collins, 1955); Ines Scaramucci, "Anna Maria Ortese," in *I contemporanei* (Milan: Marzorati, 1974), V, 887–902.

OTTAVA RIMA, a stanza composed of eight lines of eleven-syllable verse. Its origins date back to thirteenth-century Sicily and fourteenth-century Florence. In its Sicilian form, the eight lines were rhymed alternately *(abababab)*, while its Tuscan variation, the *strambotto** or *rispetto*, employed slightly different rhyme schemes *(ababababcc, ababcccc, ababccdd)*. These early folk forms, often sung in dialect, were modified as the influence of romances sung in verse was felt by the minstrels who began to transfer French metrical forms and French themes into Italian narrative poetry. Eventually, the octave with the metrical arrangement *abababcc* became the standard for narrative poetry in Italy, especially that which treated themes from Arthurian or Carolingian legend.

Giovanni Boccaccio* was the first major Italian poet to adopt *ottava rima* for serious narrative verse, using it in the *Filostrato* (Prostrated by Love), the first Italian romance in octaves, and the *Teseida* (*The Book of Theseus*), an early Tuscan epic,* as well as in the *Ninfale fiesolano* (*The Nymph of Fiesole*), the first Italian idyll. Following Boccaccio's example, *ottava rima* became most popular among the major epic poets of the fifteenth and sixteenth centuries and was used in Luigi Pulci's* *Morgante* (Morgante), Angelo Poliziano's* *Le Stanze per la giostra* (Stanzas for the Tournament), Matteo Maria Boiardo's* *Orlando innamorato* (Orlando in Love), Ludovico Ariosto's* *Orlando furioso* (*The Frenzy of Orlando*) and Torquato Tasso's* *Gerusalemme liberata* (*Jerusalem Delivered*). Spanish and Portuguese epic poets of the Renaissance* also had recourse to the form. Its English equivalent utilizes the same rhyme scheme (*abababcc*) but substitutes iambic pentameter for the standard eleven-syllable line in Italian. It has served such diverse poets as Spenser, Byron, Shelley, and Yeats. The nine-line Spenserian stanza with its rhyme scheme of *ababbcbcc*, which unites eight lines of iambic pentameter and a final alexandrine, is often erroneously taken to be a version of *ottava rima*. More probably Spenser invented this particular stanzaic form for *The Faerie Queene* by adding an alexandrine to an eight-line ballade form, already employed by Chaucer.

Bibliography: Alex Preminger, ed., *Princeton Encyclopedia of Poetry and Poetics* (Princeton, N.J.: Princeton University Press, 1965); Raffaele Spongano, *Nozioni ed esempi di metrica italiana* (Bologna: Pàtron, 1966).

P

PALAZZESCHI, ALDO, pen-name of Aldo Giurlani (1885–1974), poet and novelist. Born in Florence of a middle-class family, Palazzeschi spent part of his youth in Paris where he was introduced into avant-garde cultural circles. His first literary efforts were the collections of verse *I cavalli bianchi* (1905, White Horses); *Lanterna* (1907, Lantern); and *Poemi* (1909, Poems). A first novel was initially entitled *Riflessi* (1908, Reflections) but changed in 1943 to *Allegoria di novembre* (November Allegory). Written under the obvious influence of D'Annunzio* and Oscar Wilde, the novel describes the love of a Roman prince (Valentino Core) for John More, a young Englishman, and the prince's eventual suicide. Palazzeschi's literary reputation was destined not to turn upon works in the mode of D'Annunzio or poetry written in the *crepuscolare* ("twilight") style of the *fin de siècle*, for in 1909 he became associated with Marinetti* and the futurist movement.

Palazzeschi's association with the futurists lasted only until 28 April 1914, when he broke with the movement in a letter addressed to Giuseppe Prezzolini,* editor of *La Voce*. Still, this brief association was responsible for most of his finest poetry. He never wrote poetry of any significance after 1914, when most of his efforts were confined to revisions of his youthful works. Essential to anthologies of twentieth-century Italian verse, these poems include the famous "La fontana malata" ("The Ailing Fountain"), a telling example of futurist humor and its attention to the importance of sound in poetry; "Chi sono?" (Who Am I?), a definition of his poetic identity; "Rio Bo" ("Rio Bo"); and "Lasciatemi divertire" (Let Me Enjoy Myself), a zestful expression of the exhilaration futurists experienced in the act of artistic creation. Of equal importance is his futurist novel, first entitled *Il codice di Perelà* (1911, Perelà's Code) but changed in 1954 after revisions to *Perelà, uomo di fumo (Perelà, The Man of Smoke)*. This innovative allegory on freedom constitutes a radical stylistic change from the decadent atmosphere of his first novel. It is based upon the fantastic account of a man of smoke who has lived in a chimney for thirty-two years and who suddenly ventures forth into the world. Initially, he is greeted favorably and is charged with establishing a new code, but people eventually turn against him and condemn him to prison, causing him to dissolve in a puff of smoke.

After his break with futurism,* Palazzeschi published several prose works worthy of note. First appeared a novel entitled *La piramide* (1926, The Pyramid) and then *Due imperi . . . mancati* (1920, Two Empires . . . That Came to Nought), a series of memoirs attacking war and imperialism which contains a pseudo-Marxist ethic based upon Christian principles. In 1934 came *Le sorelle Materassi (The Sisters Materassi),* the novel which most critics acknowledge as his prose masterpiece. It is the tale of two older, unmarried sisters whose perverse infatuation for their profligate nephew Remo leads them to economic ruin and shame. Eventually, Remo abandons them for an American millionairess named Peggy. The minute description of this strange relationship based upon egotism, suppressed sexual desires, and masochistic affection is one of the most subtle psychological dissections in midcentury Italian fiction.

Palazzeschi continued to produce some outstanding narratives after the appearance of *Le sorelle Materassi,* although none surpasses this masterful novel. In *I fratelli Cuccoli* (1948, The Cuccoli Brothers), he explores the theme of paternity through the life of a man who adopts four orphans. In *Roma* (1953, *Roma*), he employs a rather conventional form to analyze a religious Roman family, tracing their lives from 1940 until 1950. *Il doge* (1967, The Doge) and *Stefanino* (1969, Stefanino), two of his last novels, return to the fantastic spirit of *Perelà. Il doge* creates a surrealistic picture of Venice where, on three separate mornings, it is announced that the doge will appear at the Loggia of the Ducal Palace at precisely noon. Although these appearances never transpire, the Basilica of St. Mark disappears for a brief moment during the night, as Palazzeschi's imagination triumphs over mundane reality. In *Stefanino,* Palazzeschi fashions a grotesque fantasy about an orphan whose physique is extraordinary—his sexual organs and his head are interchanged, although both function perfectly. In addition to these imaginative tales, which aroused a good deal of critical attention when they appeared, Palazzeschi published several short-story collections during his lifetime—including *Il re bello* (1921, The Handsome King) and *Bestie del '900* (1951, Animals of the Twentieth Century)—as well as collections of memoirs or recollections such as *Stampe dell'800* (1932, Nineteenth-Century Prints). His final novel was *Storia di un'amicizia* (1971, History of a Friendship).

Palazzeschi's literary career spanned several generations, various movements, and shifting period styles. His constant adaptability and consistent inventiveness are, in many respects, unique in the history of twentieth-century Italian literature.

See also FUTURISM.

Bibliography: Tutte le opere, 3 vols. (Milan: Mondadori, 1957–60); *Contemporary Italian Poetry: An Anthology,* ed. Carlo L. Golino (Berkeley, Calif.: University of

California Press, 1962); *Perelà, The Man of Smoke,* trans. Peter Riccio (New York: Vanni, 1936); *Roma,* trans. Mihaly Csikszentmihalyi (Chicago: Regnery, 1965); *The Sisters Materassi,* trans. Angus Davidson (New York: Doubleday, 1953); Thomas G. Bergin, "The Enjoyable Horrendous World of Aldo Palazzeschi," *Books Abroad* 46 (1972), 55–60; *From Verismo to Experimentalism: Essays on the Modern Italian Novel,* ed. Sergio Pacifici (Bloomington, Ind.: Indiana University Press, 1969); Giorgio Pullini, *Palazzeschi* (Milan: Mursia: 1972).

PALLAVICINO, SFORZA (1607–1667), churchman, critic, and historian. The son of a nobleman from Parma, Pallavicino received an education in law and theology in Rome before entering the priesthood in 1630 and joining the Roman Curia. Because of his support for one among the party of cardinals that favored Galileo* in his dispute with the church, he fell into disfavor with Pope Urban VIII for a period of time. In 1636, Pallavicino joined the Jesuit order, and in 1659, he was elevated to the rank of cardinal.

Pallavicino's *Istoria del Concilio di Trento* (1656–57, The History of the Council of Trent) was intended to counter the impact of Paolo Sarpi's* more important history of the same name which was widely read abroad and had become a fertile source for anti-Catholic propaganda. An abridged version eventually received several English translations, one under the title *The New Politick Lights of Modern Romes Church-Government* (1677) and another as *The Policy of Rome* (1681). Pallavicino's style was praised by the influential Accademia della Crusca. His historical research was clearly enriched by his access to secret Vatican archives, which enabled him to correct some of Sarpi's mistakes. This history is, nevertheless, more a Catholic apology than a genuine contribution to the art of historiography, which might have rivaled Sarpi's achievement.

Pallavicino also wrote a moral dialogue entitled *Del bene* (1644, On the Good) and several treatises on style or grammar, the most important of which was *Considerazioni sopra l'arte dello stile* (1646, Considerations on the Art of Style). Both deal with that crucial Baroque* issue, the relationship of verisimilitude and the marvelous in literature. For Pallavicino, the truth of poetry—a truth distinguished from philosophical truth—is reflected in the force of well-expressed metaphors which themselves guarantee the presence of the marvelous in poetry. For him, poetry is born from the intellect's apprehension of an object without regard to its truth or falsity; the only goal of poetic fables is to "adorn" the intellect with images and with new and miraculous apprehensions.

See also BAROQUE; SARPI, Paolo.

Bibliography: Storia del Concilio di Trento, ed. Mario Scotti (Turin: UTET, 1968); *Trattatisti e narratori del Seicento,* ed. Ezio Raimondi (Milan: Ricciardi, 1960);

Mario Costanzo, "Note sulla poetica del Pallavicino," *Giornale storico della letteratura italiana* 136 (1959), 517–55; Giovanni Ghilli, "Strutture ritmico-sintattiche nella prosa del Pallavicino," *Giornale storico della letteratura italiana* 143 (1966), 518–56; Ludovico Pallavicino-Mossi, *Sforza Pallavicino* (Bologna: I grandi cardinali nella storia, 1933).

PALMIERI, MATTEO (1406–1475), humanist and public official. Although of humble Florentine origins, Palmieri was taught by some of the city's greatest humanist teachers, including Carlo Marsuppini, and was a friend of Leonardo Bruni.* He rose to hold many important political and diplomatic posts with the Florentine Republic. In spite of his humanist background, Palmieri wrote both in Italian and in Latin. Among his numerous writings are a biography of Niccolò Acciaiuoli; a funeral oration for Marsuppini; *Liber de temporibus* (The Book of Epochs), a Latin chronicle of the history of the world from the creation to 1449; a Latin history of Florence, *Historia florentina* (History of Florence); and *De captivitate Pisarum liber* (The Capture of Pisa), an account of a war with Pisa. These historical works were first published by Muratori* in his *Rerum italicarum scriptores* (1723–50, Historians of Italy). One of his most curious compositions is a poem entitled *La città di vita* (The City of Life), which contains three books divided into one hundred *capitoli** in *terza rima.** Like its model, Dante's* *Commedia,* this poem describes a visit to the afterworld where the poet is guided by the Cumaean Sibyl and observes the souls of the angels who had refused to choose between God and Satan and who are about to be reborn as men so that they must choose good or evil. *La città di vita* was not published until this century, perhaps partly because the sealed manuscript he sent to the Guild of the Notaries upon his death sufficed to have the poem condemned as heretical and his remains removed from holy soil. Palmieri's principal work is *Della vita civile* (1528, On Civic Life), an Italian dialogue in four books on the qualities of the ideal citizen, which defines the good life as the virtuous fulfillment of those public offices for which one is suited. The dialogue has affinities to Alberti's* treatise on the family, and both works are among the most interesting expressions of Florentine civic humanism during the Quattrocento.

See also ALBERTI, Leon Battista; HUMANISM.

Bibliography: La Vita Civile di Matteo Palmieri e il De Optimo cive di Bartolomeo Sacchi, ed. Felice Battaglia (Bologna: Scrittori politici italiani, 1944); *Libro del Poema Chiamato Città di Vita,* ed. Margaret Rooke, 2 vols. (Northampton, Mass.: Smith College Studies, Nos. 8–9, 1927–28); Hans Baron, *The Crisis of the Early Italian Renaissance: Civic Humanism and Republican Liberty in an Age of Classicism and Tyranny* (Princeton, N.J.: Princeton University Press, 1955); George Holmes, *The Florentine Enlightenment 1400–50* (New York: Pegasus, 1969).

PANZINI, ALFREDO (1863–1939), novelist and teacher. Panzini was born in Senigallia and received a degree in literature from the University of Bologna with a thesis on macaronic Latin. In 1887, he commenced his long teaching career, eventually moving to a *liceo* in Milan upon the recommendation of his university professor (Carducci*), where he remained until 1917. Panzini's first novel, *Il libro dei morti* (1893, The Book of the Dead), elaborates his characteristic theme, the feeling of rootlessness which precipitates a search for meaning in the past to contend with the emptiness of modern existence. After a number of novels, classroom texts, and a dictionary of the contemporary Italian language (1905) which was highly successful, Panzini published what many critics consider his best work, *La lanterna di Diogene* (1907, The Lantern of Diogenes). Based upon the author's bicycle trip through Italy, it presents a panoramic view of modern Italian life in which the author pursues authentic human relationships, learns about himself through his contacts with people he meets on his journey, and establishes a rapport with nature. Similarly, *Il viaggio di un povero letterato* (1919, The Voyage of a Poor Man of Letters), recounts another trip, this time on a train. According to some critics, Panzini's literary output was too great to sustain a consistently high narrative style, but he achieved a measure of excellence in *Io cerco moglie!* (1920, *Wanted —A Wife*); *Il mondo è rotondo* (1921, The World Is Round); and *Il padrone sono me* (1922, The Boss Is Me). Named to the Accademia d'Italia by Mussolini in 1929, Panzini continued to produce amusing, pleasant fare for his middle-class reading public until his death.

Bibliography: Sei romanzi fra due secoli (Milan: Mondadori, 1954); *Wanted—A Wife,* trans. F. T. Cooper (New York: Brown, 1922); Giorgio De Rienzo, *Alfredo Panzini* (Milan: Mursia, 1968); Sergio Pacifici, *The Modern Italian Novel from Capuana to Tozzi* (Carbondale, Ill.: Southern Illinois University Press, 1973).

PAPINI, GIOVANNI (1881–1956), Florentine poet, editor, and essayist. Papini's formal education was relatively limited (he received no university degree), but through his assiduous reading and attendance at university lectures as an auditor, he acquired an impressive culture and knowledge of literature and philosophy.

Papini joined Giuseppe Prezzolini,* a close friend from his early school days, helping to found the periodical *Leonardo,* which from its appearance in 1903 until its demise in 1907 was an important intellectual force in Italian culture. Papini became its director, as well as chief editor of *Regno,* a nationalist publication directed by Enrico Corradini (1865–1931). While in Geneva in 1904 to deliver a paper at an international philosophical conference, Papini met Henri Bergson, who later introduced him to a number of major artistic and literary figures in Paris during his visit to the city in 1906. Papini's first important book, *Il crespuscolo dei filosofi* (1906,

The Twilight of the Philosophers), represents a precocious reassessment of the ideas of the major nineteenth-century thinkers and concludes by rejecting their oppressive influence upon contemporary thought because of their lack of philosophical certainty. After *Leonardo* ceased publication, Papini became associated with another important Florentine journal, *La Voce,* which had been launched by Prezzolini. Although Papini actually directed the journal for a time in 1912, the two friends differed in their goals. Papini eventually left the group around *La Voce* and, along with Ardengo Soffici,* founded an even more avant-garde publication called *Lacerba.* This lively journal became the influential mouthpiece for the Italian futurist movement soon after its birth in 1913, but Papini eventually broke away from the futurist movement to pursue his own intellectual interests as he had done so many times previously.

Among the dozens of books Papini published during his lifetime, his greatest achievement is unanimously considered to be *Un uomo finito* (1912, *The Failure*), an autobiographical work which documents what Papini calls his failure to interrelate his intellectual activity with his practical and political affairs. The book concludes on an optimistic note with its author assuming a Promethean stance in keeping with his indefatigable energies and interests: "If, after you have listened to me, you still believe, in spite of what I have said, that I really am through, that I really am a failure, you will at least have to admit that I failed because I started too many things, that I am nothing because I tried to be everything!"

Papini's most characteristic opinions and narrative techniques appear in a number of his collected essays—*24 cervelli* (1912, *Four and Twenty Minds*); *Stroncature* (1916, Savage Reviews); *Testimonianze* (1918, Testimonies); and *Gli operai della vigna* (1930, *Laborers in the Vineyard*). His use of the genre of the essay is most personal; his essays are impassioned, subjective, even lyrical, but never pedantic or academic. They are most typically about writers, artists, or philosophers (Croce,* Alberti,* Michelangelo,* Spencer, Hegel, Kwang-Tse, and many others). Although a confirmed atheist in his youth, Papini experienced a religious conversion later in life which resulted in a popular biography, *La storia di Cristo* (1921, *The Life of Christ*), which was translated and read all over the world. His portrayal of Christ is idiosyncratic, and hostile critics have accused him of reducing Christ to his own petit bourgeois level. This charge was later repeated against his equally individualistic interpretations of Dante and Michelangelo in *Dante vivo* (1933, The Living Dante) and *Vita di Michelangelo* (1949, The Life of Michelangelo).

During the fascist era, Papini's religious conservatism and nationalist politics met with the approval of the regime. However, he was forced to relinquish the chair of Italian literature at the University of Bologna, to which he was named in 1935, because of an eye illness. He became a member of the fascist Accademia dell'Italia and was president of the Istituto per gli Studi sul Rinascimento. With *Italia mia* (1939, My Italy), Papini aligned himself with the foreign policy of the fascist government. The youthful futurist iconoclast had finally come full circle and was now a part of the cultural establishment he once so cheerfully attacked. After the war, Papini continued to write, but none of these later works equaled the original contributions of his youth. Although striken by an illness in 1952 which progressively paralyzed his hands and voice, he continued to pursue his literary career until the day of his death.

Papini was a genuine man of letters who loved the controversy which always swirled about his writings. His interests were closer to those of the cosmopolitan culture of the Enlightenment* than to the narrower interests of some professional academics. His contribution to twentieth-century Italian culture was multifarious and substantial.

See also FUTURISM; PREZZOLINI, Giuseppe.

Bibliography: Tutte le opere di Giovanni Papini, 11 vols. (Milan: Mondadori, 1958–66); *The Failure,* trans. Virginia Pope (1924; rpt. Westport, Conn.: Greenwood Press, 1972); *Four and Twenty Minds,* trans. E. H. Wilkins (1922; rpt. Freeport, N.Y.: Books for Libraries, 1970); *Laborers in the Vineyard,* trans. Alice Curtayne (1930; rpt. Port Washington, N.Y.: Kennikat Press, 1970); *The Life of Christ,* trans. Dorothy Fisher (New York: Harcourt, 1923); Mario Isnenghi, *Papini* (Florence: La Nuova Italia, 1972); Janvier Lovreglio, *Une odyssée intellectuelle entre Dieu et Satan: Giovanni Papini (1881–1956),* 2 vols. (Paris: Editions P. Lethielleux, 1973–75); Roberto Ridolfi, *Vita di Giovanni Papini* (Milan: Mondadori, 1957).

PARINI, GIUSEPPE (1729–1799), poet and satirist. A contemporary of the major representatives of the Italian Enlightenment,* Parini was born in Bosisio, a small town in Lombardy, of a modest family (his father was a silk merchant). At the age of nine, he was sent to an aunt in Milan, where he was educated by the Barnabites and would spend most of his life. In 1752, he published *Alcune poesie di Ripano Eupilino* (Some Poems of Ripano Eupilino), a collection of ninety-two poems whose basic Arcadian inspiration is given form by a meticulous care for classical precision and simplicity of expression. The work was favorably received and won the young poet acceptance in the Accademia dei Trasformati, a literary academy with a program of moderate cultural reforms, and in other literary circles and associations. In 1754, with a legacy from his aunt whose modest income he was to inherit if he decided to become a priest, Parini was ordained and shortly after entered the household of the duke of Serbelloni as a tutor to his son. This position, which he held for eight years, gave him the opportunity to observe the corruption and decadence of a class he was soon to reproach and satirize.

In 1757, Parini wrote the *Dialogo sopra la nobiltà* (Dialogue on Nobility), a dialogue on human equality and on the rights and privileges of nobility between a nobleman and a poet, who find themselves neighbors in the grave. The poet's argument eventually convinces the nobleman that nobility without virtue is worthless and becomes the object of laughter rather than admiration. The situation of the dialogue is somewhat contrived—two representatives of distant social classes buried side by side—but extremely revealing as to the author's human and social concerns prior to the composition of his major works. The same fundamental concerns and values—honesty, health, and intelligence placed high above wealth and nobility, together with a profound faith in justice and human solidarity, expressed long before the great revolutions—inspired most of the lyrical odes written between 1756 and 1769. But it was *Il mattino* (1763, The Morning), the first part of a longer projected poem in hendecasyllables, that rightly established Parini not only as the relentless scourge of the decaying upper classes, but also as an exemplary moralist and as a citizen and patriot of adamant integrity.

After serving one year (1768–69) as editor of the Milan *Gazzetta,* Parini was named humanities professor in the Palatine schools and dedicated most of his later years to teaching. When the French entered Milan in 1796, the poet was appointed to the city council but was soon dismissed because, in spite of his age and failing health, he did not hesitate to denounce the abuses and extortions perpetrated by the new demagogues.

The nineteen *Odi,* written over a period of about forty years, are the positive expression of Parini's own vision and sentiment. Often they are quietly Horatian in temper, and some of the later odes attain a notable sophistication in their elegantly controlled treatment of love. But Parini's major contribution to eighteenth-century literature is in the poignant satire of *Il giorno (The Day).* The poem was originally conceived in three parts: *Il mattino* (Morning); *Il mezzogiorno* (Noon); and *La sera* (Evening), later divided into *Il vespro* (Vespers) and *La notte* (Night). The first two parts appeared in 1763 and 1765, while the other two were published posthumously in the first complete edition of the poet's *Opere* (Milan, 1801–04). Parini sets himself up as *precettor d'amabil rito* (tutor and instructor in the worldly art of living) for a young peer of the Milanese aristocracy and, in that capacity, purports to guide him through all the frivolous activities of his daily life. The obvious intention of this device is systematically to unmask and ridicule the useless and worthless existence of the pupil, from his late awakening (followed by various ceremonies such as the lengthy toilette and the morning interviews with the teachers of dance, music, and French) to his nightly society games and very late return home. Through this satirical portrayal and its serious historical implications, *Il giorno* expresses the indignant protest of moral conscience against a perverse system that allows extravagant privileges to the very few while neglecting the basic needs of the people. The style is elaborate and rich in heightened images and allusions to classical and contemporary culture. But this causes no serious imbalance between form and content, for its principal motivation is precisely to enhance the irony and satire in all contexts and situations.

Bibliography: Opere, ed. Giuseppe Petronio (Milan: Rizzoli, 1957); *The Day: Morning, Midday, Evening, Night,* trans. Herbert M. Bower (London: G. Rutledge & Sons, 1927); William D. Howells, *Modern Italian Poets: Essays and Versions* (1887; rpt. New York: Russell & Russell, 1973); Sergio Antonielli, *Giuseppe Parini* (Florence: La Nuova Italia, 1973); Francesco De Sanctis, *History of Italian Literature* (New York: Barnes & Noble, 1968); *Questioni di critica letteraria,* ed. Giorgio Petrocchi (Naples: Loffredo, 1973).

Antonio Illiano

PARISE, GOFFREDO (1929–   ), novelist and journalist. Parise, born in Vicenza, abandoned his university studies in philosophy for literature. His first work, *Il ragazzo morto e le comete* (1951, *The Dead Boy and the Comets*), was a critical success and is still considered by some to be his highest achievement. Within a typical neorealist setting, Parise abandoned realistic description for mysterious occurrences and a surrealist style. Then followed *La grande vacanza* (1953, The Great Vacancy), which continues the technique of intertwining reality and fantasy. *Il prete bello* (1954, *Don Gastone and the Ladies*), a humorous story of an unworthy priest, is perhaps his most popular novel. Parise returned to his early fantastic style in *Il padrone* (1965, *The Boss*), a grotesque allegorical representation of consumer society, the factory, and capitalism. In addition to his fiction, Parise has both worked in the cinema and contributed articles to several newspapers. He has written about his many travels, treating China, Biafra, and Vietnam.

Bibliography: The Boss, trans. William Weaver (New York: Knopf, 1966); *The Dead Boy and the Comets,* trans. Marianne Ceconi (New York: Farrar, Straus & Young, 1953); *Don Gastone and the Ladies,* trans. Stuart Hood (New York: Knopf, 1955); Claudio Altarocca, *Goffredo Parise* (Florence: La Nuova Italia, 1972).

PARUTA, PAOLO (1540–1598), historian and political theorist. Born in Venice of a noble family from Lucca, Paruta studied in Padua before returning to Venice in 1561, where he held many important diplomatic and political positions for the republic, including the post of city historian after the death of Pietro Bembo* in 1579. Paruta continued this ongoing civic project but wrote his own contribution to the history in Italian rather than Latin. His *Istorie veneziane* (1605, *The History of Venice*) treats the events which occurred between 1513 and 1552 in twelve books. It received an English translation in 1658 by Henry Carey, Earl of Monmouth, an important English interpreter of the works of Paruta, Campanella,* and Boccalini.* Another brief history, *Storia della guerra di Cipro (History of the Cyprian War)*, was composed around 1573, and a translation of this work was usually included in the English editions of the history of Venice.

It is Paruta's political treatises which are most influential. In *Discorsi politici* (1599, *Politick Discourses*)—also translated by Carey in 1657—Paruta continues the debate opened by Machiavelli's* *Discorsi* on the causes for Roman greatness, offers explanations of his own which often take issue with Machiavelli's and accentuates the importance of the mixed form of government he believed Venice to possess. Unlike Machiavelli, who emphasized a state's establishment, the more conservative Paruta was most interested in its preservation. This book was an important source for Montesquieu's *Considérations sur les causes de la grandeur des Romains et de leur décadence* (1734). Paruta's masterpiece is his *Della perfezione della vita politica* (1579, On the Perfection of Political Life), a dialogue in three books which treats the ideals of the citizen, the statesman, and the perfect form of government. Here, Paruta argues that the active or political life is not inferior to the contemplative life as long as it is guided by moral values. The end of government, he states, is a life which is both virtuous and comfortable, one endowed with both spiritual and material benefits, and the best means of achieving this end is a mixed government like that of the Venetian Republic.

Bibliography: Degli'istorici delle cose veneziane, 10 vols. (Venice: Lovisa, 1718–22); *Opere politiche di Paolo Paruta*, ed. C. Monzani, 2 vols. (Florence: Le Monnier, 1852); *Scrittori politici del '500 e '600*, ed. Bruno Widmar (Milan: Rizzoli, 1964); William J. Bouwsma, *Venice and the Defense of Republican Liberty* (Berkeley, Calif: University of California Press, 1968).

PASCARELLA, CESARE (1858–1940), Roman poet. Pascarella's education began in a seminary. His early interests in painting subsided after his success with his first published sonnets* in Roman dialect in 1881. In 1885, he began a series of voyages through Europe, the United States, Latin America, Africa, and the Orient, the first of which was a journey to India which he announced to his friends through a humorous note left on his door —"I'm going to India for a moment and will return shortly." Praised highly by Carducci* when it appeared in 1886, the collection of twenty sonnets entitled *Villa Gloria* (Villa Gloria) marks a departure from his earlier reliance on Belli's* example in dialect verse. The fifty sonnets which followed, called the *Scoperta dell'America* (1894, The Discovery of America), focused upon the exploits of Christopher Columbus. Pascarella's talent for recitation and the patriotic content of much of his poetry guaranteed him enthusiastic audiences wherever he traveled. In 1905, he recited the first poems from his *Storia nostra* (Our History), a projected collection of three hundred and fifty sonnets which was to treat Italian history from Rome's foundation until the successful conclusion of the fight for independence in 1870. By working on this project for the rest of his life and by renouncing his public recitations after 1911, he completed two hundred and sixty-seven poems, which appeared posthumously in 1941. In addition to his verse, some sixteen notebooks of his travels provide insights into Italian emigration abroad, the administration of government in Italian colonies, and a variety of interesting regions, landscapes, and people. He was made a member of the Accademia d'Italia in 1930.

Bibliography: I sonetti, Storia nostra, Le prose, ed. Emilio Cecchi (Milan: Mondadori, 1962); *Taccuini,* ed. Emilio Cecchi (Milan: Mondadori, 1961); Emilio Cecchi, *Letteratura italiana del Novecento,* 2 vols. (Milan: Mondadori, 1971); Gaetano Mariani, *Ottocento romantico e verista* (Naples: Giannini, 1972).

PASCOLI, GIOVANNI (1855–1912), poet born in San Mauro di Romagna. Family deaths during Pascoli's childhood and early youth left in the sensitive boy a sense of awe before the irrational devastating force within man and beyond man's control. In 1867, his father, an administrator of a large land estate, was murdered by undiscovered assassins. Within a year, his mother and a sister died, and a short time later, two other brothers. In 1873, he won a scholarship to the University of Bologna, from where he was graduated in 1882, after a hiatus which included active membership in the *Internazionale* and several months of incarceration for participating in a socialist demonstration. Upon his graduation, he held a number of teaching positions in various Italian cities. In 1906, he succeeded Carducci* as professor of Italian literature at the University of Bologna, a position which he held until his death. His finest and most representative poems are to be found in the volumes, *Myricae* (1891, Tamerisks), and *Canti di Castelvecchio* (1903, Songs of Castelvecchio), while his Latin poems, for which he won several prizes at Amsterdam, are gathered in two volumes bearing the title *Carmina* (1914, Songs). His criticism, which included studies on Leopardi* and three volumes on Dante,* tended to be personal; hence, it was a reflection of his own poetics.

As a result of his incarceration in 1879, Pascoli's views of society and the universe were significantly modified. All forms of violence, including the class struggle, were rejected, and he even assumed a conciliatory tone toward the immediate political and social conditions. The existential dilemmas which enveloped all human beings in brotherhood before their common enemies, i.e., death, violence, and grief, became a source of speculation. Much of his poetic inspiration arose from the impenetrable mystery which engulfed life. Scientific discoveries had shown that all living organisms, including the heavenly spheres, seemed embarked on an apocalyptic course. Beyond the apparent timeless and peaceful vision of the celestial spheres, there was constant change which in due time could bring total destruction. In the poem "Il ciocco" (Blockhead), the earth and the other planets are compared to gnats flying around a lamp. In "La vertigine" (Dizziness), men are seen suspended upside down in a boundless space in which the earth is merely an atom. It was perhaps this apocalyptic view of the universe that prompted Pascoli to reject the findings which science offered as valid forces for coping with life, and to dwell instead on the mystery which enfolded the universe and human actions. The evil which was threatening nations with imperial and ethnic wars and which had brought about the death of an "innocent man," his father ("X agosto" [August X] and "La Cavalla storna" [The Grey Mare]), is also seen in an inexplicable light. Christianity had failed in its inability to eradicate evil from society in nearly two thousand years. Man is an ephemeral creature wandering in darkness, ignorant of his origin or his future. A return to the primordial aspects of life becomes an important theme in his poetry as a refuge from science and the evil seed that one finds among men.

· The theme of the home as a nest where man can find tranquility became a reality for Pascoli when he purchased a house in Castelvecchio, a rustic place nestled in the mountains, where he went whenever his working schedule permitted. Plants, domestic and wild animals, fields, peasants' toils, and folkloric ways are important themes in his poetry. For the sake of precision and to satisfy his pantheistic concept of the world, he developed a poetic device of naming. Objects and animals, along with humans, are treated as equals and as individual entities, each with its peculiar characteristics. A tree is not simply a tree, but it is an oak, a poplar, a chestnut, a peach. A bird is not simply a bird, but it is a sparrow, a swallow, a finch, a blackcap. The communion which binds men, animals, and objects, and their interdependence among themselves can be noted in "La quercia caduta" ("The Fallen Oak"). In "X agosto," an analogy is drawn between the senseless killing of a swallow on its way to the nest to feed its little ones and the death of his father who was also murdered on his way home. The stars join in unison with the earth to weep at the wretchedness of violence. A pacifist most of his life, Pascoli frequently called on men to stop their quarrels and to unite in brotherhood before the mystery which encompasses and permeates the very essence of life ("I due fanciulli" [The Two Children]).

The ordinary and elementary themes which Pascoli treated in his poetry called for the use of an everyday language. This need to communicate directly with nature led to the use of a rich and varied vocabulary which established immediate adherence to the objects discussed, including the use of onomatopoeia, dialectal and technical terms, and baby talk. The results were quite extraordinary. The refined scholar of classical erudition became antiliterary in his poetic compositions by breaking with the Italian literary tradition. The lofty tones and complex verse structures were rejected by him as being artifical and intellectual. His poetry became a strict reflection of the beating of his own heart, that is, the translating into words of sensations rich in affective nuances which are by their very nature fleeting and inexpressible. An original poetic rhythm which communicated by suggesting through symbols replaced the concrete expression, as in "Gelsomino notturno" ("The Jasmine at Night") and "Scalpitìo" ("Horses' Hoofs"). The stress was not on developing a logical philosophical argument but rather on capturing several sensations within a poem and, often, within a single line. The apparent lack of purpose and meaning in the world refuted a priori the development of a coherent discourse on its functioning. Man could only hope to gain insights into the nature of things in a very fragmentary manner. It is in these poems that Pascoli revealed his finest qualities as a poet.

In a fifty-page essay, *Il fanciullino* (The Child), which first appeared in *Il Marzocco* (1897), Pascoli articulated his concept of life and poetry. According to the poet, there is a child that remains within all adults. This child of unblemished innocence is free from the influences of a systematized society and is all sensitive to the essence of life and the workings of nature. In a certain sense, this child is the primitive man of Vico* who sees everything with wonder and astonishment. Man is no longer the protagonist of nature but a figure who listens, observes, and seeks understanding. By listening to the "pure voice" within him, the poet feels that he captures a deeper truth of reality. The poet is put on a pedestal for his higher sensitivity to the workings of nature. This romantic reaction to positivism which perceives reality imaginatively through the eye of innocence (the child), coupled with Pascoli's sensuous feeling for the evocative power of words, puts him in the camp of *decadentismo,** a cultural movement which dominated the literary scene at the turn of the century. Pascoli's poetics as uttered in *Il fanciullino* shows its weaknesses when it is carried to extremes. The primitive and childish disposition in the poet is abused, and it gives way to complacency and false perplexities.

See also DECADENTISMO.

Bibliography: Poems of Giovanni Pascoli, trans. Arletta M. Abbott (New York: Vinal, 1927); *Poems*, trans. Evaleen Stein (New Haven, Conn.: Yale University Press, 1923); Emilio Cecchi, *La poesia di Giovanni Pascoli* (Naples: Ricciardi, 1912); Francesco Flora, *La poesia di Giovanni Pascoli* (Bologna: Zanichelli, 1959); Michael Ukas, "Nature in the Poetry of Giovanni Pascoli," *Kentucky Foreign Language Quarterly* 13 (1966), 51–59.

Silvano Garofalo

PASOLINI, PIER PAOLO (1922–1975), poet, novelist, critic, film director, and one of the most original figures in twentieth-century Italian culutre. A native of Bologna, Pasolini published his first volume of poetry in Friulian dialect in 1942, one of the first indications of a fascination with language and dialect which endured throughout his lifetime. In subsequent years, he published several important and scholarly anthologies of popular or dialect poetry—*La poesia dialettale del '900* (1952, Dialect Poetry of the Twentieth Century) and *Canzoniere italiano* (1955, Italian Songbook). The decisive formative influence upon the young Pasolini was Antonio Gramsci.* His interest in dialect and the folklore of the lower classes led Pasolini to collaborate on a number of films with several noted directors and screenwriters (including Federico Fellini, Mario Soldati,* and Giorgio Bassani*). At the same time, he began to play an active role in the intellectual life of the times, publishing stories and articles in *Paragone* and *Officina,* a journal based upon a new awareness of Gramsci's views on culture and intellectuals that Pasolini helped to establish.

In his novels, Pasolini employs Roman dialect as well as his own peculiar literary language. Pasolini's first novel, *Ragazzi di vita* (1955, *The Ragazzi*), depicts a milieu dear to the author—the Roman slums and the lower classes living in them—and traces the lives of these young slum dwellers from Rome's liberation by the Americans until the beginnings of the so-called Italian economic miracle which leaves the lives of the poor relatively unchanged. The sordid side of existence in the Eternal City, the reverse of the *dolce vita* atmosphere made famous by Fellini's film, is also treated in *Una vita violenta* (1959, *A Violent Life*), a novel whose protagonist, Tommaso Puzzilli, embodies Pasolini's growing awareness that social reform may be possible through the action of a revolutionary party of the lower classes. The key to Pasolini's views on Marxism and Gramsci may be found in his collection of poetry entitled *Le ceneri di Gramsci* (1957, The Ashes of Gramsci), especially in the poem "Lo scandalo del contraddirmi" ("The Scandal of My Self-contradiction"). In this seminal collection, Pasolini engages Gramsci in an imaginary dialogue, accepting Gramsci's praise of the proletariat not because of its presumed role as the vanguard of the revolution but, instead, because of its retention of a preindustrial mythical consciousness.

Pasolini's interest in linguistics and poetics finally led him to the cinema, which he defined as an essentially poetic language of signs expressing reality not with symbols but with reality itself. The dream-like quality (*oniricità*) of film enabled the artist to portray the mystery and ambiguity inherent in reality without resorting to a naturalism he abhorred, and it allowed him to reach a mass audience for whom his prose or poetry had little appeal. Pasolini's first film, *Accattone* (1961, *Beggar*), returns to the Roman slums of his novels and explores the pre-bourgeois, pre-industrial, and mythical elements of this social class. In this film and many others to follow, Pasolini followed his earlier style in poetry or narrative and employed what he termed a "pastiche" construction, juxtaposing the basest images, objects, or themes with those representing the highest expression of official culture—for example, beggars and the music of Bach; garbage and images from the paintings of Renato Guttuso; peasants with the costumes and expressions of figures from the paintings of Piero della Francesca. He embodied his ideas on the poetic nature of cinema in a number of films, most of which were taken from literary sources and all of which constitute major developments in the search for a contemporary cinematic language—*Il Vangelo secondo Matteo* (1964, *The Gospel According to St. Matthew*); *Uccellacci e uccellini* (1966, *Hawks and Sparrows*); *Edipo re* (1967, *Oedipus Rex*); *Teorema* (1968, *Teorema*); *Porcile* (1969, *Pigsty*); and *Medea* (1969, *Medea*). His original interpretations of classical and biblical myths, or contemporary stories of his own invention, reflect his personal ideology and his belief in the mythical qualities of pre-industrial societies. Pasolini's somewhat sentimental view of the lower classes of southern Italy and the Third World finds its ultimate expression in *Medea* and his medieval "trilogy of life"—*Il Decameron* (1971, *The Decameron*); *I racconti di Canterbury* (1972, *The Canterbury Tales*); and *Il fiore delle mille e una notte* (1973, *The Arabian Nights*). Together, these last three films employ widely different classics from medieval literature to celebrate the guiltless sexuality of a pre-industrial era.

This happy moment in Pasolini's career was a brief one, for only a few years later the director published an abjuration of both the trilogy and its view of the past, now regarding his beloved subproletariat as a class rapidly losing its mythical features in a process of being assimilated by the petit-bourgeois mentality characteristic of industrial society everywhere. Having employed the metaphor of sex in the trilogy (and in his many other poetic and narrative works) as a means of expressing the zest for life of an ancient culture, Pasolini now turned to sex as a metaphor for power politics and class struggle in a filmed version of De Sade's infamous novel entitled *Salò o le 120 giornate di Sodoma* (1975, *Salò or The 120 Days of Sodom*). Pasolini set the story not in the Age of Reason but in the fascist Republic of Salò in 1944. The frank portrayals of the many scatological perversions catalogued in the original novel guaranteed that the film would be censored or never released in many countries, but Pasolini used such scenes metaphorically to portray the modern world's obsession with the consumption of worthless products ("excrement," as Pasolini termed them). Shortly after the release of the film, Pasolini was murdered in a bizarre manner, reminiscent of the many violent scenes and homosexual encounters in his films and stories.

With Pasolini's death, one of Italy's most original and controversial voices was silenced. Pasolini made fundamental contributions to several art forms (cinema, the novel, and poetry) and was a major critic and theorist in the fields of semiotics* and film theory. Many of his best critical essays, including the fundamental discussion of the poetic nature of cinema, are reprinted in *Empirismo eretico* (1972, Heretical Empiricism).

See also GRAMSCI, Antonio; SEMIOTICS.

Bibliography: Empirismo eretico (Milan: Garzanti, 1972); *The Ragazzi*, trans. Emile Capouya (New York: Grove, 1968); *A Violent Life*, trans. William Weaver (1968; rpt. New York: Garland, 1977); Vittoria Bradshaw, *From Pure Silence to Impure Dialogue: A Survey of Post-War Italian Poetry* (New York: Las Americas, 1971)—contains bilingual translations of selected lyrics and abridged criticism; *Pier Paolo Pasolini*, eds. Alfredo Luzi and Luigi Martellini (Urbino: Argalia Editore, 1973); René Predal, "Pier Paolo Pasolini," *L'Avant Scène du Cinéma* 175 (1976), 27–42, and 176 (1976), 16–36; Oswald Stack, *Pasolini on Pasolini* (Bloomington, Ind.: Indiana University Press, 1970); *Bianco e nero* 37, No. 1 (1976)— Pasolini memorial issue with complete bibliography and filmography.

PASSAVANTI, JACOPO (circa 1302–1357), preacher and theologian. Passavanti was born of a noble Florentine family and entered the Dominican order in 1317. He studied for three years (1330–33) in Paris before he became a preacher at the church of Santa Maria Novella in Florence in 1340 and, eventually, its prior. During the disastrous plague of 1348, he served as librarian for the church and helped to increase its holdings of important manuscripts by acquiring works from owners who perished from the disease. Apparently, he was also a major force behind the building and decoration of parts of Santa Maria Novella, including the famous frescoes in the Chapel of St. Thomas depicting Hell and Paradise as Dante* described them in the *Divine Comedy*.

Passavanti's major work, *Lo specchio di vera penitenza* (The Mirror of True Penitence), was born out of his Lenten sermons of 1354 in Santa Maria Novella. Its central concept is an awareness of human corruption and the inevitable but just Divine retribution for this sinful condition. It was written in the vernacular rather than Latin because Passavanti hoped its message would be widely disseminated. Its literary interest lies in its importance in the history of the Italian language and in its frequent use of exempla, many similar to secular *novelle,* * which illustrate in concrete and vivid terms the theological views discussed in the book. Passavanti employed a number of literary sources in *Lo specchio,* ranging from classical texts (Terence, Ovid, and Apuleius) to anonymous medieval devotional works. Critics have been drawn to Passavanti's work because it so sharply contrasts in tone and content with Boccaccio's* *Decameron.* Boccaccio's ten storytellers meet and depart from Passavanti's own cathedral, but their stories and reactions to the plague clearly differ from those of this Dominican contemporary.

Bibliography: Lo specchio di vera penitenza, ed. Maria Lenardon (Florence: Libreria Editrice Fiorentina, 1925); Ginetta Auzzas, "Per il testo dello *Specchio della vera penitenza:* due nuove fonti manoscritte," *Lettere italiane* 26 (1974), 261–87; Marcello Aurigemma, "La fortuna critica dello *Specchio di vera penitenza* di Jacopo Passavanti,'' in *Studi in onore di Angelo Monteverdi,* Vol. I (Modena: Società tipografica editrice modenese, 1959), and *Saggio sul Passavanti* (Florence: Le Monnier, 1957).

PASTORAL. If one accepts the broadly inclusive definition that the critics of our own age have applied to the pastoral, then a full treatment of this most variable of literary modes would have to include discussions on almost every major Italian author from Dante* to the present. While it is legitimate and valuable (and even necessary) to consider the presence of pastoral attitudes and modes in such writers as Leopardi* and Verga,* or D'Annunzio* and Pavese,* it is best here to restrict our attention primarily to the conscious efforts to create the pastoral during the fifteenth and sixteenth centuries. Even within the limits of this period which is traditionally associated with the flowering of the pastoral in Italy, the Italian experience is a rich one, chiefly, though not solely, because of the masterpieces created by Sannazaro,* Tasso,* and Guarini.* Few works have been so immensely popular or have exercised as much influence on other writers and on the development of sentimental attitudes at home and abroad as the *Arcadia,* the *Aminta,* and the *Pastor fido.*

The history of the pastoral in Italy, however, is almost as difficult to state precisely as the question of the nature of the pastoral is vexatious, for the pastoral is seldom, if ever, found to be independent of other modes or themes. Perhaps nothing is more elusive, if not chimerical, than the idea of pure pastoral. Some of the most effective uses of pastoral occur when it is employed as an interlude in a contrasting context, as the episode of Erminia among the shepherds in Tasso's *Jerusalem Delivered,* or as a foil, such as in the case of the destruction of the pastoral peace as a fiction in the episode of Orlando's madness in Ariosto's* *Orlando furioso (The Frenzy of Orlando).* And as for the pastoral drama in particular, it may be said that no other genre in Italian literature has given rise to so much research and debate in connection with the question of origins.

Popular and learned traditions alike are factors in the rise of the pastoral, although its characteristic themes and attitudes are the product of a refined literary taste. In the many imitations of Virgil's *Eclogues* during the Middle Ages, the allegorical intent became fundamental, as in the Latin eclogues of Dante, Petrarch,* and Boccaccio,* where the pastoral fiction was a thin veil for a statement on historical, political, or even personal matters. Into and during the Renaissance,* the eclogue continued to be used for making comments on contemporary historical or personal events both directly and allegorically (for example, Boiardo's* Italian eclogues and, soon afterwards, those of Ariosto, Trissino,* and Alamanni*). Meanwhile, other motifs were being introduced into the form along with the representation of courtly figures. Mention should also be made of the medieval erotic *pastourelle* which also had its worthy Italian examples, the best known of which are Guido Cavalcanti's* "In un boschetto trova' pasturella" ("In a little grove I found a shepherdess") and several lyrics by Franco Sacchetti.* The humanistic impulse spawned a vast amount of Latin idylls in the Graeco-Roman manner, but in the vernacular other vaguely "pastoral" elements found expression in compositions suggestive of popular rhythms and forms such as *contrasti, canzonette, rispetti,* and *ballate.** It is from this tradition that there ultimately came such fifteenth-century poems as Lorenzo de' Medici's* *Nencia da Barberino,* Luigi Pulci's* *Beca da Dicomano,* and certain lyrics of Poliziano* in a manner sometimes referred to as *poesia rusticale* (rustic poetry). For all the "popular" elements it assumes or exploits, this production reflects the cultural and sentimental detachment of the cultivated man of letters from the world of country and hills. It lies somewhere between a burlesque of rural crudity and sophisticated awareness of the dangers of idealization. (It may, in this sense, perhaps be considered as antipastoral.) A more idyllic but also exquisitely humanistic contemplation of nature is found in Poliziano's *Stanze.* To characterize it as "pastoral," however, is perhaps even more misleading than is the application of the term to the author's mythological drama (or *favola*) *Orfeo.* The *Orfeo* does, however, have pastoral elements and owes something to the dialogued eclogues that were becoming more and more popular, but even more to the *sacra rappresentazione** which the lyrico-dramatic eclogues themselves seem to reflect to a degree in their dialogue. In many of the writings referred to hitherto, amid a variety of styles (popular and aulic), tones (sentimental and parodistic), and pluralistic linguistic elements, one of the chief recurring motifs is that of a desire for "escape" into an idyllic or hedonistic world, but it is not the only motif.

The first work which truly satisfied the Renaissance taste and needs for pastoral was Sannazaro's *Arcadia* which presents a vision of serenity and beauty that is one side of humanism's* spiritual aspiration. But the work is not without its secret tension, especially in connection with love which was to become the most important single motif of Italian pastoral in general. As a pastoral romance, Sannazaro's *Arcadia* has no equal in Italian literature, but the development of pastoral drama was to result in two works surpassing it in poetic and psychological depth: Tasso's *Aminta* and Guarini's *Pastor fido.* A confluence of diverse traditions, including the contemporaneous development of comedy and tragedy, was responsible for the eventual realization of the genre as we know it in these two masterpieces. Its beginnings, however, are almost certainly connected with the preexisting tradition of dramatic eclogues, especially those playing on the theme of a contrast between the corruption and cares of life at the court or in the city and the simpler life of the country and the "shepherd." Nor must we forget the abundance of other dialogued and representational pieces in which one or more pastoral elements may have been a constant without being the central motif. Such compositions were meant either for courtly society or for a wealthy middle-class and academic audience. Here we may mention Castiglione's* *Tirsi,* (1506, Tirsi), written in octaves, in which three "shepherds" engage in simple dialogue, with allusions to figures and matters of the court at Urbino. In fact, Castiglione's piece uses the "pastoral" mode in order to expound the courtly ideal of *grazia* ("grace") and *sprezzatura* ("nonchalance") that is better known through the author's famous *Book of the Courtier.* Two other works that may be recalled in this context derive from Naples: Marcantonio Epicuro's (1472–1555) *Cecaria* (before 1525, Cecaria) and Luigi Tansillo's* *I due pellegrini* (1523, The Two Pilgrims). Although they do not make use of pastoral settings and characters as such, they do center on themes and sentiments that are intimately associated with the pastoral.

It was the court of Ferrara that was the scene of the development of the pastoral drama proper. Here were produced the first two compositions that are unequivocally specimens of the genre: Giambattista Giraldi's* *Egle* (1545, Egle) and Agostino de' Beccari's (1510–1590) *Sacrificio* (1554, The Sacrifice); and here *Aminta* and *Pastor Fido* were conceived and created. Giraldi's *Egle* is divided into five acts, and its dialogue is in unrhymed *endecasillabi* and *settenari.* The characters are satyrs, fauns, and nymphs. There is a mixing of the comic and the pathetic, and the naturalistic hedonism that was already present in the theatrical tradition to a greater or lesser degree is now taken as the central value. Beccari's *Sacrificio* does without enamored satyrs and fauns (it is the shepherds who are in love with nymphs) and reveals even more of the influence of Sannazaro's *Arcadia.* Hedonism is here intoned in a more idyllic key than is true of *Egle,* although again adventurous and farcical elements are not absent. The five acts are without chorus, and the "plot" is based on a comic intrigue of three loves with a happy ending. Until Tasso's *Aminta* (1573), this type of complicated intrigue, which also allowed for the implementation of comic elements as well as lyrical and "rustic" movements, dominated the pastoral drama: the *Aretusa* (1563, Aretusa) of Alberto Lollio (1508–1568), and the *Sfortunato* (1567, The Unlucky) of Agostino Argenti (?–1576), both of which were done at Ferrara.

Experimentation and plurality of intention and technique in pastoral dramas did not end with *Aminta,* nor were they restricted to the *Pastor fido* as the most conspicuous example of success of this kind. It may be said that, following the *Aminta,* there was in general a return to the freer type of construction in the manner of Beccari's *Sacrificio,* but also, in the wake of Tasso's play, a greater stress on the musical value of the word and verse. Of the plethora of pastoral plays that were written at the end of the sixteenth century and in the first decade of the seventeenth century, we need recall but one—the *Filli di Sciro* (1607, Phyllis of Sciro) by Guidobaldo Bonarelli (1563–1608). This work with a complicated intrigue includes, among other things, the situation (unusual for the literature of the time) of a maid equally in love with two men. Bonarelli's vein is in the tender and pathetic, the elegiaco-idyllic mode that runs through much of the pastorals of Tasso and Guarini. Like his greater predecessors, the author reveals an exquisite psychological insight into the sentiment of love.

It may be true that the most fundamental characteristic of the pastoral is the sense of a lost Golden Age, but that, of course, is a profound and many-faceted motif; only a simplistic attitude can dismiss the pastoral in general as a literature of evasion pure and simple. The Italian pastoral drama in particular is seldom so entirely devoid of social or religio-philosophical concerns as to be unambiguously escapist. In Tasso's *Aminta,* for example, hedonism is evoked as an unattainable ideal or aspiration and really serves as a foil for the expression of a profoundly elegiac, if not tragic, vision of life. Besides being, in the Counter-Reformation age, the genre par excellence for the exposition of the psychology and philosophy of love as both a sentimental and biological need, it was, at its best, the vehicle for the representation of values and questions of the utmost importance to civilized man—matters such as the conflict between instinct and law, nature versus art, love, death, and, not of least importance, poetry itself. The famous contrasting choruses on the Golden Age motif in *Aminta* and *Pastor fido* are only the most conspicuous evidence of this fact.

See also GUARINI, Battista; POLIZIANO, Angelo; SANNAZARO, Jacopo; TASSO, Torquato.

Bibliography: Emilio Bigi, "Il dramma pastorale del Cinquecento," in *Il teatro classico italiano nel '500* (Rome: Accademia Nazionale dei Lincei, 1971), pp. 101–20; Enrico Carrara, *La poesia pastorale* (Milan: Vallardi, 1909); Louise George Clubb, "The Making of the Pastoral Play: Some Italian Experiments between 1573 and 1590," in *Italian Criticism and Theatre: From Petrarch to Pirandello,* ed. J. A. Molinaro (Toronto: University of Toronto Press, 1973), pp. 45–72; W. W. Greg, *Pastoral Poetry and Pastoral Drama: A Literary Inquiry with Special Reference to the Pre-Restoration Stage in England* (1906; rpt. New York: Russell & Russell, 1959); Peter V. Marinelli, *Pastoral* (London: Methuen, 1971); Nicolas J. Perella, *The Critical Fortune of Battista Guarini's "Pastor Fido"* (Florence: Olschki, 1974).

Nicolas J. Perella

PAVESE, CESARE (1908–1950), novelist, poet, essayist, translator, and editor. Pavese was born into a lower-middle-class family at Santo Stefano Belbo in the hilly Langhe region of Piedmont. He spent his youth between the country, where he had his summer vacations, and the city of Turin, where he got his education and graduated in 1930 with a thesis on Walt

Whitman. In 1935, he was arrested and "confined" by fascist authorities in the southern village of Brancaleone Calabro for ten months. When he returned, the woman he loved had married someone else; this was perhaps the first of a long series of "failures" in his life. From 1933 until his death, Pavese worked for the publishing house of Einaudi, first as editor of the review *La cultura* and as reader; then as translator from the American (together with Vittorini* and, to a lesser degree, Cecchi* and Montale,* Pavese brought about the modern discovery of America in Italian letters, and his version of Melville's *Moby Dick* remains memorable); and finally as director of an ethnology series through which he made such authors as Lévy-Bruhl and Fraser known in Italy. Although he was an antifascist, he did not take an active part in the Resistance, but he wrote cultural articles for the communist paper *L'Unità*. In 1950, he was awarded the coveted Strega Prize, but in despair and solitude he killed himself in a Turin hotel room that year.

Pavese's first published work was a collection of poems entitled *Lavorare stanca* (1936, *Hard Labor*), in which he tried to go beyond the predominant, hermetic tone of the period and to write a sort of epic poetry after the example of Whitman (long, free verses, social considerations, the poet as the voice of the people). However, his interest in mythology and his lyrical sensitivity are also present in many poems, giving the book a complex structure and making it a milestone in contemporary Italian poetry.

The first novel Pavese published, *Paesi tuoi* (1941, *The Harvesters*), was innovative in style and content. Erroneously hailed as neorealist by critics, it actually achieved the rendering of a symbolic reality which fused mythological archetypes with the powerful sociological figures of Piedmontese peasants. His next book, *La spiaggia* (1942, *The Beach*), is the subtle portrayal of a bourgeois milieu on the Italian Riviera, reminiscent of F. Scott Fitzgerald.

Feria d'agosto (1946, *August Holiday*) is a remarkable collection of short stories and essays dealing with Pavese's childhood experiences in the country, his discovery of the world, and his theories of myth and symbol. *La terra e la morte* (1947, Earth and Death) is a collection of poems in which landscapes are charged with erotic and symbolic meaning. Both of these works were preparations for *Dialoghi con Leucò* (1947, *Dialogues with Leucò*), one of Pavese's masterpieces made up of dialogues between mythological characters chosen by the author for their affinities with his own personal problems, interests, or ideas. These mythological characters become Jungian archetypes as well as lyrical spokesmen for Pavese. The model for the book was Leopardi's* *Operette morali (Little Moral Exercises)*, but its emphasis is on mythology rather than philosophy.

Il compagno (1947, *The Comrade*) is Pavese's most deliberately political novel, but the didactic tale of the protagonist Pablo who overcomes his contemplativeness to embrace political action is paradigmatic rather than convincing. *Prima che il gallo canti* (1949, Before the Cock Crows, containing *Il carcere* [*The Political Prisoner*], written in 1938–39, and *La casa in collina* [*The House on the Hill*], written in 1947–48) is a moving testimony to Pavese's predicament as an intellectual who did not act (hence his "betrayal") in order to contemplate and to understand the movement of history and the timeless humanity of all men, including his enemies.

La bella estate (1949, *The Beautiful Summer,* including also *Il diavolo sulle colline* [*The Devil in the Hills*] and *Tra donne sole* [*Among Women Only*]) develops Pavese's fascination for both the urban upper classes and the wild life of the countryside, played against each other as representations of incommunicability and as externalizations of inner complexes. *La luna e i falò* (1950, *The Moon and the Bonfires*) is Pavese's best novel, the summa of all his themes and his stylistic as well as gnosiological research. In narrating the impossible return of the emblematically bastard narrator Anguilla ("Eel") to the *paese* in quest of his roots and identity, he is able to provide a sensitive portrayal of historical facts (the Resistance, the class struggle); to give a lyrical account of childhood memories; and to judge and at the same time to mythicize his land and his people, cast between the immanence of the moon (the seasons, cyclical time) and the transcendence of the bonfires (human endeavors, linear time). Paraphrasing Pavese, it can be said that *La luna e i falò* is indeed "the maturity of a great lyric writer."

Many other works by Pavese were published posthumously: *Verrà la morte e avrà i tuoi occhi* (1951, Death Will Come and Its Eyes Will Be Yours), lyric poems written in 1950; *La letteratura americana e altri saggi* (1951, *American Literature: Essays and Opinions*), essays from 1930 to 1950, dealing also with culture, myth, and symbol; *Il mestiere di vivere* (1952, *The Burning Brand*), a diary covering the years 1935–50, an unusually important book for understanding the inner life of the author as well as the development of his poetics and his critical self-awareness; *Notte di festa* (1953, *Festival Night*), short stories written in 1936–38; *Fuoco grande* (1959, *A Great Fire*), a novel written in 1946 with Bianca Garufi; *Lettere 1924–44* and *Lettere 1945–50* (1966, *Selected Letters*); *Ciau Masino* (1969, Hi, Masino), short stories written in the early 1930s. Various poems, film scripts, and short pieces scattered in journals are not yet collected in book form.

Pavese's work stands out as the most perceptive rendering of an age divided between the archaic heritage of the rural, local, Italian civilization and the onrushing demands of an urban, technological, European culture— with all the anguish and the unresolved problems inherent in such a situation. His writings constitute a tremendous body of stylistic experimentation which achieves a uniquely personal character by combining the best of classicism, *verismo,** American influences, and *decadentismo** with artistic self-awareness. The "intellectual rhythm" and the mythologizing power of his work are perhaps the most valuable and stimulating heritage Pavese left for the writers of the younger generation.

See also DECADENTISMO; LEOPARDI, Giacomo; NEOREALISM; VERISMO; VITTORINI, Elio.

Bibliography: American Literature: Essays and Opinions, trans. Edwin Fussell (Berkeley, Calif.: University of California Press, 1970); *The Burning Brand: Diaries 1935–1950,* trans. A. E. Murch (New York: Walker, 1961); *Dialogues with Leucò,* trans. W. Arrowsmith and D. S. Carne-Ross (Ann Arbor, Mich.: University of Michigan Press, 1965); *Hard Labor,* trans. W. Arrowsmith (New York: Viking, 1977); *The Harvesters,* trans. A. E. Murch (London: Peter Owen, 1961); *The Moon and the Bonfires,* trans. Marianne Ceconi (1953; rpt. Westport, Conn.: Greenwood Press, 1975); *The Selected Works of Cesare Pavese,* trans. R. W. Flint (New York: Farrar, Straus & Giroux, 1968)—includes *The Beach, The House on the Hill, Among Women Only,* and *The Devil in the Hills;* Gian-Paolo Biasin, *The Smile of the Gods: A Thematic Study of Cesare Pavese's Works* (Ithaca, N.Y.: Cornell University Press, 1968); Armanda Guiducci, *Il mito Pavese* (Florence: Vallecchi, 1967); Philippe Renard, *Pavese: prison de l'imaginaire, lieu de l'écriture* (Paris: Larousse, 1972).

                                                                    Gian-Paolo Biasin

PELLICO, SILVIO (1789–1854), patriot, poet, and memorialist. Pellico was born in Saluzzo at the outbreak of the French Revolution, and most of his life was directly connected to the political and literary upheavals resulting from this event. His family was apparently of French extraction, and throughout his life, Pellico was especially open to the force of French culture and displayed a thorough knowledge of its literature and language. During his formative years, he lived for a time in Lyon, returning to Milan with his family after his father found employment there. In France, he encountered the works of the liberal thinkers and *philosophes,* and upon his return to Italy, he came under the influence of Ugo Foscolo* and Vittorio Alfieri.* Together, these liberal thinkers helped to forge his own anti-Austrian, pro-nationalist views. Furthermore, his friendship in Milan with Foscolo, Manzoni,* Berchet,* Monti,* and Ludovico di Breme* placed Pellico in the mainstream of the Italian romantic movement.

    Pellico's first important literary work was a tragedy, *Francesca da Rimini* (1815, *Francesca da Rimini*), a five-act play after the neoclassical models of Alfieri. Its plot, known to every educated Italian from its famous source in Dante's *Inferno* V, insured for the play an enthusiastic audience in Italy, and the growing popularity of the legend of Francesca and Paolo in the romantic period made it appeal to a larger, European audience. Lord Byron admired it a great deal and apparently collaborated on one English translation with John C. Hobhouse Broughton. A single patriotic speech in the play only increased its appeal in an era of rising nationalistic sentiment. After the play's success, Pellico became secretary to Count Luigi Porro Lambertenghi (1780–1860), who, in 1818, helped to establish the Milanese periodical *Il Conciliatore*, a vital outlet for romantic ideas in northern Italy. Pellico eventually became its compiler and worked closely on the journal with many of his friends. Several perceptive articles bear his signature, including reviews of literary works by Lord Byron, Schiller, Chénier, and Alfieri.

In 1820, after *Il Conciliatore* had ceased publication, Pellico's friendship with a young patriot named Piero Maroncelli (1795–1846) led him, along with many other Milanese of the period, to join the Carbonari movement. Through an indiscretion on Maroncelli's part, Pellico's membership was discovered by the Austrian authorities. He was arrested and imprisoned first in Santa Margherita Prison in Milan and then in the infamous Piombi Prison in Venice (from which Casanova* made his notable escape), where he received the death sentence. This was commuted to fifteen years in the Spielberg Prison in Moravia, eight years of which Pellico served before he was released in 1830 and escorted to the border of Piedmont. Most of his remaining years were spent in Turin.

Pellico's experience in prison produced one of the most influential works of the Italian romantic movement or the Risorgimento era, *Le mie prigioni* (1832, *My Prisons*). This autobiography was so widely read in the nineteenth century that it rivaled and even surpassed the recognition received by Manzoni's* greatest novel. Although its author was a fervent Italian patriot, the message of the memoirs is one of patient suffering without rancor for the narrator's Austrian captors. As the book opens, Pellico declares in retrospect that all his years of incarceration have not proved humanity to be so evil, intolerable, or unworthy as he had once imagined. Like Beethoven's *Fidelio,* that other great romantic hymn to the imprisoned human spirit, Pellico's story of his life was first and foremost a literary masterpiece and only secondly a political document. In fact, the very Christian tone of forgiveness in the work did more damage to the Austrian cause than any of the more violent documents written by the political firebrands of the time. Among its most memorable episodes are the sections devoted to the kindly jailer, Schiller, and the moving description of the operation performed on Pellico's friend Maroncelli in the Spielberg.

Pellico wrote a large number of dramatic works, many of which appeared after his release from prison. None of them enjoyed the critical or popular success of *Francesca,* and he finally abandoned writing for the theatre because of the extremely hostile reception accorded one of his tragedies.

These plays portrayed various historical personalities, including *Ester d'Engaddi* (1830, *Esther of Engaddi*), *Tommaso Moro* (1833, Thomas More), and *Boezio* (1834, Boethius). Besides a prose translation of Lord Byron's *Manfred* and an historically crucial body of correspondence, Pellico wrote a number of minor poetic works, the most important of which is the *Cantiche* (1830, 1834, 1837, Canticles), a collection of songs in blank verse that are imagined to be sung by a troubadour of the thirteenth century. A political tract, *Dei doveri degli uomini* (1834, *The Duties of Men*), may be compared to Mazzini's* *Il dovere dell'uomo (The Duties of Man)* for its essentially Christian politcal message of human brotherhood and high moral ideals.

See also ROMANTICISM.

Bibliography: Opere scelte di Silvio Pellico, ed. Carlo Curto (Turin: UTET, 1964); *My Prisons,* trans. I. G. Capaldi (London: Oxford University Press, 1963); *Francesca da Rimini,* trans. J. F. Bingham (Cambridge, Mass.: Seaver, 1897); Marino Parenti, *Bibliografia delle opere di Silvio Pellico* (Florence: Sansoni, 1952).

PENNA, SANDRO (1906–1977), poet. Penna was born in Perugia and, after an irregular education, received a degree in accounting. He lived in Milan for a time, working as a clerk in a bookstore, before moving to Rome where he remained until his death. During his lifetime, he contributed to literary periodicals such as *Letteratura, Poesia, Botteghe oscure,* and *Paragone.* His first collection of verse appeared in 1938. Critical opinion unanimously cites Umberto Saba* as Penna's first and principal model; and the poet in fact began by sending his early works to Saba. One of his first poems, written on the margins of a newspaper in a single evening, has always been singled out as one of his best by Saba and the critics. In the poem, "La vita è ricordarsi di un risveglio" (Life Is Remembering an Awakening), Penna employs a simple structure (two stanzas of five hendecasyllables without rhyme) to describe two moments of an awakening on a train which is then compared to life. Penna's skill at fixing such simple moments of insight in verse can also be traced in another of his best poems, "La veneta piazzetta" ("The Little Venetian Square"). On the basis of this poem, one noted critic has compared Penna to the post-impressionistic Filippo De Pisis (1896–1956) and has asserted that his poetry consists primarily of the evocation of a mood, a moment, or a fleeting image. If Penna's verse embodies a simplicity characteristic of Saba's work, the hermetic experience and its impact upon contemporary Italian verse are also apparent in his rapid and allusive imagery. Penna's collected works were awarded a Viareggio Prize in 1957; two major collections of his verse appeared in 1957 and 1970, respectively.

Bibliography: Tutte le poesie (Milan: Garzanti, 1970); *Contemporary Italian Poetry,* ed. Carlo L. Golino (Berkeley, Calif.: University of California Press, 1962);

Twentieth-Century Italian Poetry: A Bilingual Anthology, ed. L. R. Lind (Indianapolis, Ind.: Bobbs-Merrill, 1974); Robert S. Dombroski, "The Undisciplined Eros of Sandro Penna," *Books Abroad* 47 (1973), 304–06; Gianni Pozzi, *La poesia italiana del Novecento* (Turin: Einaudi, 1969).

PETRARCA, FRANCESCO (1304–1374), Italy's greatest lyric stylist and poet, literary arbiter of his time, precursor of the humanist movement, noted especially for his worldwide influence on the love lyric down to the nineteenth century and for his role in the recovery of classical texts. Brought up in Provence where his father, a Florentine notary, had fled as a political exile, Petrarch, as he is commonly called in English, studied law at Montpellier and Bologna until the death of his father in 1326 when he returned to Avignon (the temporary location of the Holy See) where he turned to literary studies. The initial inspiration for his love lyric presumably came to him on Good Friday of 1327 in a church in Avignon where he first beheld his hauntingly beautiful Laura whose exact identity has never been established. Her reticence to return his love served as the overpowering motivation for Petrarch's greatest lyrics. Legal complications regarding the settlement of his father's estate compelled Petrarch to consider the priesthood. While he is known to have received the tonsure, it is doubtful that he ever took minor orders. In 1330, he entered the services of the powerful Colonna family which led to the assumption of several canonries starting in 1335. The purchase in 1337 of a modest property in Vaucluse, just outside Avignon, marks the beginning of Petrarch's extraordinary career as poet and man of letters par excellence. This "trans-Alpine Helicon" became headquarters for the most varied activities which eventually led to his becoming not only a kind of literary and cultural czar for European writers and thinkers, but also a consultant to emperors, popes, and kings. By 1340, his reputation was such that he received two invitations to be crowned poet laureate, one from Rome and the other from Paris. On 8 April 1341, he received the crown from the Roman Senate in an elaborate ceremony on the Capitoline. From this moment began his seemingly ceaseless journeys between France and Italy, as well as to other parts of Europe. Major periods of residency occurred in Milan, Venice, and Padua where he spent considerable time as the invited guest of rulers. In 1370, he purchased a house which still stands in Arquà near Padua, where he spent the happiest moments of his last years and where his tomb is still standing today.

Although Petrarch's Latin works far outnumber his Italian ones, he is best known for his *Canzoniere (Lyric Poems)* and his *Trionfi (Triumphs),* both begun in Vaucluse in 1342–43 and both dedicated primarily to the glorification of Laura. Among his more than a dozen Latin works, perhaps the most important are the *Africa* (begun 1338–39, *Africa*), an unfinished epic* glorifying Scipio Africanus and primarily responsible for his coveted laurel crown; the *Secretum (My Secret)* (started in 1342–43), modeled on the *Confessions* of St. Augustine and defining the essence of Petrarch's moral concerns; his two revealing collections of letters modeled on Cicero and Seneca, the *Rerum familiarium libri* (Books on Personal Matters) in twenty-four books consisting of three hundred and fifty letters written during his youth and middle life (1325–66); and the *Epistolae Seniles (Letters of Old Age)* written for the most part between 1361 and 1374, and containing one hundred and twenty-five letters divided into seventeen books. These works shed invaluable light on Petrarch's basic artistic and literary perspective as reflected ultimately in his incomparable poetry to Laura.

Other Latin works that provide additional insights into Petrarch's complex personality and thought may be divided into those with a strong classical orientation and those showing deep Christian and moral concerns. Among the former are the *De viris illustribus (On Illustrious Men)*, begun in early 1337; the *Rerum memorandarum libri (Books on Matters to Be Remembered)*, an unfinished treatise on the cardinal virtues, begun in 1342–43 and having the form of anecdotes and biographies; twelve highly allegorical *Eclogues*, begun in 1345–47; a collection of letters in verse, the *Epistolae metricae (Metrical Letters)*, also begun at that time; another collection of antipapal letters in prose carefully organized in a separate work entitled *Liber sine nomine (Book Without a Name)*, started in 1351–53; and several invectives or attacks against a variety of critics or detractors: *Invective contra medicum* (1355, *Invective Against a Doctor*), *Invective contra quendam Gallum* (after 1373, *Invective Against a Certain Frenchman*), *De sui ipsius et multorum ignorantia* (1367, *Concerning His Own Ignorance and That of Many Others*), and *Apologia contra cuiusdam Galli calumnias* (after 1373, *Defense Against the False Accusations of a Certain Frenchman*).

Works reflecting serious moral or spiritual concerns include, in addition to the *Secretum (The Secret)*, *Psalmi poenitentiales (Penitential Psalms)*, started in 1342–43; the *De vita solitaria (On the Solitary Life)* and the *De otio religioso (On Religious Idleness)*, written in 1345–47; and the ponderous but highly popular *De remediis contra utriusque fortune (On Remedies Against Both Kinds of Fortune)*, begun in 1353. The coronation oration provides invaluable insights into Petrarch's poetics.

The classical and Christian dimensions of Petrarch's thought and works have only recently been recognized as being clearly reflected and recapitulated in the two works which have been viewed as the primary source of Petrarch's greatness: the *Rerum vulgarium fragmenta (Poetic Fragments in the Vernacular)* or *Canzoniere*, and the *Trionfi*, the only two written in Italian to have come down to us. Each evinces the deep inner conflict between Petrarch's innermost convictions and aspirations and the demands of Christian salvation. However, only through some knowledge of his more significant Latin works can one arrive at a recognition of the unity of the entire corpus of his works, both Latin and Italian. Through such knowledge one can see how the essence of Petrarch's artistic and humanistic greatness is summarized in his two highly poetic figures: Laura and Scipio Africanus. The works in which these two inspirations were to be ultimately extolled remain unfinished: the *Triumphs* in the case of Laura and the *Africa* in the case of Scipio. While Petrarch regarded the *Africa* as his crowning achievement, his most polished and enduring monument remains his *Canzoniere,* consisting of three hundred and sixty-six Italian poems in various forms and on many subjects, but primarily on his love for the beautiful Laura.

Petrarch's Latin works contain a virile and noble view of mankind deriving from a literary-historical study of its pagan and Christian past. They exalt the achievements of ancient heroes and thinkers as indications of the heights that man can attain. By transmitting such accomplishments in the form of a grieving and transient humanity searching for a timeless happiness, Petrarch projects on the screen of eternity the profound need for man's moral regeneration and redemption. Viewed within the Christian framework, all past achievements and knowledge are made to mirror both man's greatness and his limitations. The Christian is therefore capable of a fuller and richer life since he can grasp how, through the light of God, all past knowledge can become true wisdom. Without such insight man will continue to suffer the error, melancholy, and dejection of Adam.

Petrarch's Italian poetry, on the other hand, with its lofty lyricism goes far beyond the usually cited influence of the Provençal troubadours, Dante's* *dolce stil nuovo,** Ovid, or Virgil. By identifying his passion for Laura with the myth of Daphne in its symbolic connotation not only of fleeting love but also of the eternal beauty and fragility of human creativity, Petrarch endows his "book of songs" (intended, like the *Breviary,* to be read over three hundred and sixty-six days) with a tone of perennial sadness. By superimposing a Christian awareness of the pagan myth, Petrarch produced lingering echoes of the disturbing conflict between what might be called a pagan Parnassus and a Christian Calvary. Laura as simply beauty, poetry, and earthly love degenerates into an idol if not viewed within the context of Christian salvation. When viewed thusly Laura can be justified either by recanting or by extension. The apparent recantations of poems No. 1 and No. 366 are mere *tours de force.* Laura's meaning by extension should have produced either a Beatrice or a Medusa. Fortunately, Petrarch's actual extension speaks most clearly. The process of eliminating time in the *Triumphs* leads to a Laura who is a truly *nova figura.* As Laura reaches the pinnacle of the *Triumph of Eternity,* she is defined by her entourage: leaders, led by Scipio, who had created a safe "nest" for mankind; or thinkers, led by Plato, who had created master-pieces of truth through intellect or art. In his human power of creativity, man truly reflects the image of God. Thus, we move from the powerful love lyrics of a sensitive, restless, and perennially grieving artist, who, in the *Canzoniere,* tries bravely to find redemption in the very contemplation of the forbidden fruit, to an epic-like poem in which we behold the anguish of a new man who no longer knows how to rest in the peace of a transcendent heaven and bravely labors all his life to bring that heaven on this earth. This may be seen even in those poems in either Latin or Italian dealing with public affairs or with moral and religious issues.

One may say, in sum, that in both his Latin and Italian works Petrarch strives valiantly to depict humanity's eternal struggle for love and peace, but the struggle remains unresolved because of the haunting realization of the limitations and tribulations of life on earth and a lingering unwillingness to forsake totally a human ideal for a Divine one. Fifteenth-century human-ism* had clearly dawned.

See also PETRARCHISM.

Bibliography: The Life of Solitude, trans. Jacob Zeitlin (Urbana, Ill.: University of Illinois Press, 1924); *Petrarch: Four Dialogues for Scholars,* trans. Conrad Rawski (Cleveland, Ohio: Western Reserve University Press, 1967); *Petrarch's "Africa,"* trans. Thomas G. Bergin and Alice S. Wilson (New Haven, Conn.: Yale Univer-sity Press, 1977); *Petrarch's Book Without a Name,* trans. Norman Zacour (Tor-onto: Pontifical Institute, 1973); *Petrarch's Bucolicum Carmen,* trans. Thomas G. Bergin (New Haven, Conn.: Yale University Press, 1974); *Petrarch's Lyric Poems,* trans. Robert M. Durling (Cambridge, Mass.: Harvard University Press, 1976); *Petrarch's Secret,* trans. W. Draper (1911; rpt. Norwood, Pa.: Norwood, 1976); *Rerum Familiarium libri I-VIII,* trans. Aldo S. Bernardo (Albany, N.Y.: State University of New York Press, 1975); *The Triumphs,* trans. Ernest H. Wilkins (Chicago: University of Chicago Press, 1962); Thomas G. Bergin, *Pe-trarch* (New York: Twayne, 1970); Aldo S. Bernardo, *A Concordance to the "Familiari" of Francesco Petrarca* (Albany, N.Y.: State University of New York Press, 1977), *Petrarch, Laura and the "Triumphs"* (Albany, N.Y.: State Univer-sity of New York Press, 1974), and *Petrarch, Scipio and the "Africa"* (Baltimore: Johns Hopkins University Press, 1962); Morris Bishop, *Petrarch and His World* (Bloomington, Ind.: Indiana University Press, 1963); Umberto Bosco, *Francesco Petrarca* (Bari: Laterza, 1961); *Francis Petrarch, Six Centuries Later: A Sym-posium,* ed. Aldo Scaglione (Chapel Hill, N.C.: University of North Carolina Press, 1975); Ernest H. Wilkins, *The Life of Petrarch* (Chicago: University of Chicago Press, 1961), *The Making of the "Canzoniere" and Other Petrarchan Studies* (Rome: Edizioni di storia e letteratura, 1951), *Petrarch's Eight Years in Milan* (Cambridge, Mass.: Mediaeval Academy, 1958), and *Studies in the Life and Works of Petrarch* (Cambridge, Mass.: Mediaeval Academy, 1955).

Aldo S. Bernardo

PETRARCHISM, the overall impact of Petrarch's* Italian poetry in Italy and abroad from the late fourteenth to the mid-seventeenth century. The term has often been used pejoratively to refer to the more artificial and hackneyed devices of the Renaissance* imitators of Petrarch. In its best sense, it denominates the most far-flung and long-lived productivity in the literary history of Western Europe. It was a powerful factor in the great educational process that was the Renaissance, and it stimulated the finest songs and sonnets* of the period. Its principal instrument, but not its only one, was the sonnet. Its fountainhead was Petrarch's two Italian works: the *Trionfi (Triumphs),* a typically medieval poem in *terza rima* * with passages of great beauty, and especially the *Canzoniere* or Song Book *(Lyric Poems),* which is mainly a sonnet book and the most influential one ever written.

The European vogue of the *Triumphs* reached its height in the late fifteenth and early sixteenth centuries and faded in the late sixteenth. It was first printed, with the *Canzoniere,* in 1470; the two works appeared often thereafter in print accompanied by commentaries. The *Triumphs* was translated into French, English, Spanish, Portuguese, and German. It was often interpreted as an allegory of the growth and progress of the human soul, as set forth by the commentator Bernardo Illicino (no sure dates) in 1475. It was first admired as a storehouse of encyclopedic learning and then gradually appreciated as poetry, and translated and imitated as such. Its language, technique, and psychology presented a useful challenge to European poets. What success the *terza rima* achieved outside Italy during the Renaissance can be attributed to the *Triumphs* rather than to the *Divine Comedy.* The *Triumphs* also had an impressive impact on paintings, frescoes, tapestries, enamels, medals, emblems, as well as on pageants, progresses, ballets de cour, theatricals, and other noble entertainments.

The *Canzoniere* (as it is usually called even in English) delighted the love poets of all Europe. Already, the romance and the lyric had provided a long education in the ways of the heart and had transformed love itself. Love was both more complex and more stylized than in Catullus or Ovid. It involved the mind and the soul to an extent the ancients never dreamed of. No ancient lyric poet was therefore considered adequate as an inspiration and guide for modern poets. None had suffered enough or been introspective enough to suit Renaissance taste. Thus it came to pass that Petrarch, who enjoyed these painful advantages and was a great singer as well, took his place as a classic model for the poetry of feeling.

Petrarch's lyrics present a kind of sentimental biography. His lady, Laura, is both idealized and real, unattainable and familiar, retaining the charm of her gestures, her voice, her eyes, the way she walked and talked, her special smile, her restrained, not-quite-approving acceptance of his adoration. She was long remembered as Petrarch had once seen her among the blossoms, gracious and golden, womanly and wise, with a goddess-like majesty now become angelic, a living sun. She was a new feminine presence in European literature, and her somewhat enigmatic figure furnished a powerful attraction for generations of readers and an enduring model of a muse. She flourished for several centuries. Eventually, some Petrarchists celebrated the individual features of her beauty in catalogued hyperboles: her hair gold wires, her teeth pearls, etc. She occasionally degenerated into a dehumanized, composite mistress, soon parodied by the Petrarchists themselves (for example, by Berni,* Du Bellay, and Quevedo). The parody does not mean that they thereupon gave up the fashion; it usually meant merely that they knew what they were about and that in their jovial moments they could make fun of it or even turn the parody itself into an affectionate compliment, as Shakespeare did. But this was likely only within the convention. This parody has been called Anti-Petrarchism, which is hardly an accurate term since it suggests two groups of poets speaking different poetic languages.

Many aspects of Petrarch's technique were readily imitable. He had himself borrowed from various sources an arsenal of devices which he employed brilliantly and which other poets could borrow and adapt to their own languages, temperaments, and talents. This led to innumerable literary exercises and produced much bric-à-brac along with true poetry. Petrarch's style had a classical precision, a pleasing and varied diction, and, to express his inner tensions, a characteristic use of antithesis, oxymoron, hyperbole, the imagery of stormy seas and lovely landscapes, apt metaphor and conceit, and other figures of rhetoric. Its haunting musicality, its eloquence and elegance, and its ability to project mood and feeling made it the best available instrument for introspection and self-analysis. Throughout the Renaissance it remained the universal model for the language of poetry. It was also involved in the theoretical debate on the question of Italy's standard speech. Outside Italy, it greatly influenced matters of language, scansion, and diction during a period of rapid linguistic change.

Petrarchism indeed became a true period style, a cultural phenomenon enveloping most of Europe. It had proved to be a vital process that was always growing beyond itself, accommodating itself to all tastes and talents, and inviting the most powerful individual geniuses. It offered its practitioners an intense training in elegance and taste, in the shaping of a number of poetic forms, and in gathering sequences, garlands, or entire volumes of occasional poems purporting to be segments of sentimental biography, or glorifications of a lady, or of famous sites, or of God and his saints. Petrarchism was an arduous education in the poetic uses of rhetorical figures, in diction, in variations on themes, in versification, in the fresh (or not so fresh) presentation of the eternal commonplaces, in the uses of wit, conceits, and imagery, in the tight organization of a work, in the patterning of sound, in the arts of translation, adaptation, transplantation, and finally in how to be one's own sensitive and cultivated self in one's own lyric creations. It was a patrician art which, when the time was right, crossed frontiers with ease.

In Italy, its impact began modestly with Boccaccio,* increased gradually through a number of minor poets, and was reflected in Boiardo* and Lorenzo de' Medici.* In the late fifteenth century, it entered a more popular and rather flamboyant phase with Cariteo* and his followers Tebaldeo,* Serafino,* Panfilo Sassi (1455–1527), and Marcello Filosseno (1450–1520). This group aroused much enthusiasm at home and was the first to be influential abroad. Pietro Bembo* prepared an Aldine edition of the *Triumphs* and the *Canzoniere* (1501) and made himself a sort of literary dictator encouraging, by precept and uninspired example, the imitation of Petrarch. His numerous followers included the best poets of the Renaissance from Alamanni* and Ariosto* to Michelangelo* and Marino.* Meanwhile, important anthologies of Petrarchist verse and many editions of the *Canzoniere* were printed and exported to the rest of Europe where they were eagerly studied.

The first English adaptation of a sonnet of Petrarch's was made by Chaucer (but not as a sonnet) in *Troilus and Criseyde* (circa 1385). This remained an isolated case. Petrarchism did not take firm root in England until the sixteenth century with Wyatt and Surrey, in the first English sonnets and in other forms. These were followed after a brief pause by a brilliant period of lyric production—Shakespeare, Spenser, Sidney, Donne, Milton, and their lesser contemporaries—all students of Petrarch and the Italian and French Petrarchists.

In France, King Francis I, who was something of a poet, made *rondeaux* of two of Petrarch's sonnets. Marot, Saint-Gelais, the Lyons group, the Pléiade poets, and scores of others soon naturalized in France both Petrarchism and the sonnet, and in their turn they became models. Philippe Desportes became a sort of international broker in poetical wares, importing from Italy and exporting his French imitations to England, Scotland, the Netherlands, and Germany.

In Spain, the Marqués de Santillana wrote sonnets "in the Italian manner" around 1440, but failed to start a vogue. In 1526, Boscán began experiments with Italian forms in Spanish verse. His sonnets and *canciones,* seconded immediately by the sonnets of Garcilaso de la Vega, began a tremendously successful Petrarchist tradition in Spain (Diego Hurtado de Mendoza, Acuña, Herrera, Cetina, Aldana, etc.) and in Portugal (Sá de Miranda and Camões).

Late in the sixteenth century, the new poetry appeared in the Netherlands with Jan van der Noot and, after 1600, Pieter Hooft and Constantijn Huygens. In Germany, it began in the seventeenth century with Weckherlin, Opitz, and Gryphius. Before 1600, it had spread to Poland,

Hungary, Dalmatia, and Cyprus. Everywhere the success of Petrarchism meant a vast expansion of sensibility, a stimulus to creativity, and a renewal of the art of poetry.

Bibliography: Carlo Calcaterra, "Petrarca e il petrarchismo," in *Problemi ed orientamenti critici di lingua e di letteratura italiana,* Vol. 3 (Milan: Marzorati, 1949)—gives copious bibliography; D. D. Carnicelli, ed., *Lord Morley's Tryumphes of Fraunces Petrarcke* (Cambridge, Mass.: Harvard University Press, 1971); Leonard Forster, *The Icy Fire: Five Studies in European Petrarchism* (Cambridge: Cambridge University Press, 1969); Joseph G. Fucilla, *Estudios sobre el petrarquismo en España* (Madrid: Revista de Filologìa Española, 1960); Henri Hauvette, *Les Poésies lyriques de Pétrarque* (Paris: Malfère, 1931), Part II, "La Fortune des poésies de Pétrarque"; Hans Pyritz, "Petrarca und die deutsche Liebeslyrik des 17. Jahrhunderts," in his *Schriften zur deutschen Literaturgeschichte* (Cologne: Böhlau, 1962); Ernest H. Wilkins. "A General Survey of Renaissance Petrarchism," *Comparative Literature* 2 (1950), 327–42.

Chandler B. Beall

PICCOLO, LUCIO (1903–1969), lyric poet. Piccolo, born in Palermo, led an uneventful life on his Sicilian property at Capo d'Orlando far from the main centers of Italian cultural and intellectual activity. Piccolo thus resembles his famous cousin Tomasi di Lampedusa* in his diffident attitude towards the outside literary world. He owes his critical discovery in large measure to Eugenio Montale's* favorable reaction to his first volume of poetry, *Canti barocchi* (1956, *Baroque Songs*). In a letter accompanying the gift of his verse, Piccolo told Montale that his purpose was to re-evoke and fix for all time in poetry a unique Sicilian world, particularly that of Palermo, which was about to disappear. Elsewhere, Piccolo spoke of poetry as an absolute mode of expression outside of time and articulated his basic theme, the fleeting quality of the self. In general, Piccolo worked to explore all the musical qualities of his words ("All my poems are composed like symphonies"). Before his death, he completed two additional collections: *Gioco a nascondere* (1960, *Hide and Seek*) and *Plumelia* (1967, *Plumelia*). Perhaps his most widely cited poem is the title poem of his second collection, "Gioco a nascondere," a long work which embraces all his essential themes.

Bibliography: Collected Poems of Lucio Piccolo, trans. Brian Swann and Ruth Feldman (Princeton, N.J.: Princeton University Press, 1972)—contains a translation of Montale's preface to *Canti barocchi;* Vittoria Bradshaw, *From Pure Silence to Impure Dialogue* (New York: Las Americas, 1971).

PIER DELLA VIGNA, (circa 1190–1249), influential minister of Frederick II* and poet of the Sicilian School. Born in Capua of an obscure and probably humble family, Piero had to make sacrifices to study at Bologna. Introduced to Frederick in 1220 by the archbishop of Palermo, he joined the emperor's court at Naples, where he was appointed a notary in 1220 and a judge in 1225. Piero eventually conducted several highly sensitive diplomatic missions. By the time he added the offices of logothete and protonotary of the Kingdom of Sicily and imperial chancellor (1247 and 1249) to his titles, he had become one of the most noted statesmen of his time. Unfortunately, his brilliant political successes and his intimacy with the emperor aroused the jealousy of other courtiers. They implicated him in a plot against Frederick, who, prone to deal cruelly with his opposition, was persuaded to condemn his confidant and friend, possibly without justification. Piero was imprisoned and subjected to torture. Utterly disgraced, he was carried in chains from city to city as an example and blinded with a red-hot iron at San Miniato. It is not certain if he died as a result of the torture or by committing suicide in Pisa in 1249.

Dante* immortalizes Piero in *Inferno* XIII, where this tortured soul is imprisoned in the trunk of a tree eternally ripped apart by the Harpies. Dante's moral judgment of suicide is harsh, but his historical judgment vindicates Piero, whose shade is made to swear his loyalty to the emperor. No doubt Dante admired his efforts in Frederick's struggles against the pope as well as his culture and eloquence. Piero's official letters, written in Latin in a style both eloquent and obscure, were famous in their day and remain important primary sources for the history of Frederick's era. Among his unofficial letters are a love letter coupling his own thoughts on love with quotations from the Latin poets and a letter addressed to the empress on the respective merits of roses and violets. Three *canzoni** and one sonnet,* part of the poetic debate or *tenzone* between Jacopo Mostacci (died after 1277), Giacomo da Lentino,* and himself, are extant. His often-cited *canzone* "Amore, in cui disio ed ò speranza" ("Love, in whom I have my hope and desire,") expresses an unfulfilled love which remains always full of hope like the sailor who never ceases to have faith in the winds which move his ship. Artful in its conceits, allusions, and language, Piero's poetry shows the Provençal influence.

See also FREDERICK II.

Bibliography: Le rime della scuola siciliana, ed. Bruno Panvini (Florence: Olschki, 1962); *German and Italian Lyrics of the Middle Ages,* trans. Frederick Goldin (Garden City, N.Y.: Doubleday, 1973).

PINDEMONTE, IPPOLITO (1753–1828), poet and translator. Born in Verona of a noble family, Pindemonte was given a classical education and turned to a literary career with an early translation of Racine's *Bérénice* which he published in 1777 together with an ode on tragedy. Two years later, he wrote a tragedy entitled *Ulisse* (Ulysses) which he published anonymously in the following year. In 1770, he traveled to Florence and Rome, where he entered Arcadia* under the name Polidete Melpomenio; he continued on this journey to visit Naples, Sicily, and Malta. Upon his return to Verona, he dedicated his life entirely to letters, publishing a series of minor works, including a poem in praise of the English General Elliot who had defended Gibraltar from a Franco-Spanish Army, *Gibilterra salvata* (1782, Gibraltar Rescued). During these early formative years, he also attempted writing in several poetic genres, including a number of tragedies (some of which he burned when they were not successful) and several projects for epic* poems which remained unfinished.

By 1783, Pindemonte had met Parini* in Milan. From 1788 to 1790, he completed the obligatory grand tour of Europe, during the course of which he spent considerable time in England and France and met both Alfieri* and Monti.* Retiring to the solitude of his country villa, he published his significant *Poesie campestri* (Rustic Poetry) in 1788, which was followed in 1796 by *Prose campestri* (Rustic Prose). The sensibility of the poetry in this volume mirrors that of many English poets of the period, including Gray, Young, Pope, Thomson, and Collins. The ode entitled "La melanconia" (Melancholy), perhaps the most famous of these poems, describes the simple pleasures of country life; Melancholy is personified as a gentle nymph in a pleasant pastoral landscape. After his return from traveling abroad, Pindemonte composed a treatise on the then fashionable English gardens (1792, published in 1817); an autobiographical novel entitled *Abaritte* (1790, Abaritte); and a tragedy entitled *Arminio* (1804, Arminius), based upon a Germanic hero described in Tacitus and also treated by the German poet Klopstock, whom Pindemonte imitated. A year later, he published his *Epistole in versi* (Letters in Verse), a collection of blank verse. During the same year, he began his translation of Homer's *Odyssey* which was finally completed in 1818 and published in 1822. Like Vincenzo Monti's *Iliad,* this *Odyssey* became the standard translation for successive generations of Italians and, during his lifetime, made Pindemonte as famous as the more talented Ugo Foscolo.*

After completing a number of lines on a work entitled *I cimiteri* (The Cemeteries), Pindemonte learned of the publication of Foscolo's masterpiece, *Dei Sepolcri* (1807, *Of Sepulchres*), dedicated to Pindemonte. Pindemonte responded by writing a poem of his own with the same title, but it never quite measured up to its model. Late in life, Pindemonte wrote a series of moralizing *Sermoni* (1819, Sermons) in blank verse and a number of minor poems, none of which helped to rescue his name from oblivion after his death or to modify the generally accepted critical opinion that his translation of Homer was his chief literary contribution.

Bibliography: Lirici del Settecento, ed. Bruno Maier (Milan: Ricciardi, 1959); *L'Odissea d'Omero,* ed. Giulio Reichenback (Turin: UTET, 1944); Nicola Francesco Cimmino, *Ippolito Pindemonte e il suo tempo,* 2 vols. (Rome: Edizioni Abete, 1968).

PIOVENE, GUIDO (1907–1975), novelist, journalist, and critic. Piovene was born to a noble family of Vicenza and was educated in philosophy. He wrote a thesis on Vico,* which strongly opposed Crocean views, and turned to journalism. While he served as a correspondent in Germany, he wrote for several prominent periodicals. Piovene was an ardent fascist in his youth, but his political ideas gradually shifted until he became sympathetic to Marxism. With *Lettere di una novizia* (1941, *Confession of a Novice*), the study of a young woman who is forced against her will into a convent from which she eventually escapes, Piovene produced what many critics consider a masterpiece. Written as a series of letters, it was made into a film in 1960 and has remained his most popular work. After a number of minor novels published during and immediately after the war, Piovene turned almost exclusively to journalism for a time, writing a significant account of life in America, *De America* (1953, On America) and establishing a brilliant reputation as a writer for the newspaper *La Stampa* of Turin. A series of essays entitled *La coda di paglia* (1962, The Tail of Straw) recounts the years of his youth and his former link to fascism. His past apparently cost him an important literary prize for his next novel *Le furie* (1963, The Furies), a strange autobiographical work filled with visions and meditations of a metaphysical nature. Piovene's philosophical bent again comes to bear upon his fiction in his last significant novel, *Le stelle fredde* (1970, The Cold Stars), which received the Strega Prize in 1970. Its most intriguing passage concerns a visit to the protagonist by the novelist Dostoevsky, who has returned from the afterlife to carry on a series of visionary conversations.

Piovene also served as a key figure in UNESCO's Division of Arts and Letters and worked for the RAI, the Italian radio service.

Bibliography: Le furie (Milan: Mondadori, 1963); *Lettere di una novizia* (Milan: Bompiani, 1974); *Le stelle fredde* (Milan: Mondadori, 1970); *Confession of a Novice,* trans. Eithne Wilkins (London: Kimber, 1951); Maria Luise Caputo-Mayr, "La funzione della natura e del paesaggio nei romanzi di Guido Piovene," *Italica* 50 (1973), 53–65; Jacques Goudet, "Piovene, la morale et la métaphysique," *Revue des Études Italiennes* 15 (1969), 148–97; Giuseppe Marchetti, *Invito alla lettura di Guido Piovene* (Milan: Mursia, 1973).

PIRANDELLO, LUIGI (1867–1936), playwright, novelist, short-story writer, essayist, critic, and poet. Pirandello was born on the southern, Arabic coast of Sicily near Agrigento, where (in his own words) "taciturn apathy, suspicious mistrust, and jealousy had remained indelible in the souls and customs of the people." He studied law at the University of Palermo but changed to romance philology when he transferred in 1887 to the University of Rome and, in 1889, to the University of Bonn in Germany. His earliest publications were two verse collections and his dissertation on the dialect of his home town. Upon his return to Italy, he settled in Rome (1893) and devoted himself to writing. In 1894, having turned from lyric poetry to narrative, he published the first of many collections of short stories which would eventually form the two volumes of *Novelle per un anno* (1937–38, Stories for a Year), a pendant to the two volumes of *Maschere nude* (1958, Naked Masks), the collection of his plays. In 1903, a disaster in his father's sulphur mines in Sicily cut off his income and forced him to turn to teaching. Two volumes of essays, *Arte e scienza* (Art and Science) and *L'umorismo (On Humor),* both published in 1908, won him a tenured post as professor of Italian at the Girls' Normal School in Rome. For the rest of his life he carried a heavy work load, while family problems added a special burden.

There is evidence that Pirandello showed an early interest in the theatre, but it was not until the years of World War I that he was actually drawn to the stage. This occurred both under the influence of the Sicilian dialect theatre and in the context of what was then known as "the new Italian school," that disquieting, ironic, subverting *teatro grottesco** (theatre of the grotesque) which in so many respects was a forerunner of the theatre of the absurd. Often deriving his plots from his earlier short stories, Pirandello wrote or translated into dialect *Lumíe di Sicilia* (1915, *Sicilian Limes*), *Liolà* (1916, *Liolà*), *La giara* (1917, *The Jar*), *La patente* (1918, *The License*), and other plays for the great Sicilian actor Angelo Musco (1872–1937). In a number of other plays, he was co-author with the playwright and producer Nino Martoglio (1870–1921), famous for the hit *L'aria del continente* (1915, A Breath of Continental Air). Of the plays written in Italian and performed, unlike the Sicilian ones, by major acting companies in the leading theatres of Italy, some critics consider the parable *Così è (se vi pare)* (1917, *It Is So [If You Think It So]*) his absolute masterpiece. But there were many others in that period, of which *Il piacere dell'onestà* (1917, *The Pleasure of Honesty*) and *Il giuoco delle parti* (1918, *The Rules of the Game*) are particularly worthy of note. The latter was singled out by Pirandello himself as emblematic of his work when he chose it as the play being rehearsed on the unset stage of *Sei personaggi in cerca d'autore* (1921, *Six Characters in Search of an Author*), surely one of the single most influential works in the history of twentieth-century drama and aesthetics.

With *Sei personaggi,* at first a spectacular failure and then an international success, began Pirandello's total involvement in the world of theatre. His plays, which no doubt owe much of their remarkable dramatic energy, the rapid and apparently completely spontaneous thrust of the action, and their "spoken" quality to the regional dialect theatre—a modern version of *commedia dell'arte**—now explored and exploited every conceivable "conflict in the complex of elements that constitutes theatre: characters and actors, author and director, drama critics and assenting or contrary spectators." Such were Pirandello's own words in the 1933 introduction to the volume that brought together his trilogy of "the theatre in the theatre": *Ciascuno a suo modo* (1924, *Each in His Own Way*) and *Questa sera si recita a soggetto* (1930, *Tonight We Improvise*) in addition to *Sei personaggi*.

Pirandello's interest in the theatre went beyond writing plays. He became a director and producer, and in 1925, he founded his own company, the Teatro d'Arte di Roma, with its own specially designed theatre and a repertoire that included works by other contemporary authors as well as his own. With this company he toured the principal theatrical centers of Europe and America. Although a partisan of the legitimate stage in the struggle between stage and screen then taking place, Pirandello did not disdain the motion picture medium altogether. If in his novel *Si gira* (1915, later known as *Quaderni di Serafino Gubbio operatore* [*Shoot!*]) he had expressed horror at the mechanization of modern life and had seen the cameraman reduced to the status of "a hand that turns a crank," this did not keep him from visiting Germany in 1928 to discuss the projected filming of *Sei personaggi*, nor Hollywood in 1930 for the filming of *Come tu mi vuoi* (*As You Desire Me*) with Greta Garbo, nor from trying his hand at scriptwriting, which he did for Walter Rüttman's *Acciaio* (1932, Steel).

In a period of extraordinary theatrical experimentation (the names of Adolphe Appia, E. Gordon Craig, and Max Reinhardt come to mind, the discovery of the Russian ballet in the West, and the vibrant theatrical life of the Paris of the 1920s), Pirandello's genius was recognized (in the words of Georges Pitoëff) as that of "the Theatre made man." In 1934, when he was awarded the Nobel Prize for Literature, it was for "his bold and brilliant renovation of the drama and the stage." The very abundance of Pirandello's production, the variety of genres, the disciplines straddled, the constant reuse of his own materials, the as yet incomplete documentation of his activity, the apparent abstruseness and controversial nature of his "philosophy"—all have made a definitive critical assessment of his work difficult. The partisanship that divided his audiences in his lifetime continues today between those who accept his "radical pessimism" (as Croce* called it) and those who reject it, those who recognize in him an uncompromising censor of all established values and those who see him instead as politically acquiescent and even reactionary, and between those who judge him not only a great theatrical innovator but a great writer—one of the prime poetic imaginations of the age of Proust and Joyce, Kafka, Musil, and Thomas Mann—and those who claim on the contrary that he has no style and but a handful of worn ideas repeated over and over again, ideas that are variations on the metaphysical problem of reality and illusion or being and seeming, and on its analogues in psychology and drama, the self and the role, the face and the mask.

In tracing Pirandello's development, it is customary to skim over the naturalistic beginnings reflected (although already muddied by his view of man's uncontrollable urge to "reason") in the Sicilian stories, in the historical novel *I vecchi e i giovani* (1908, *The Old and the Young*), and still present in the "inner story" of *Sei personaggi,* in the family tale of adultery and sibling rivalry for which the six are seeking an author. The more characteristic works, those that have turned his name into an adjective, are understandably the ones that continue to attract the most attention. First, the funny and serious *Il fu Mattia Pascal* (1904, *The Late Mattia Pascal*), the confession-narrative of a bungling everyman who lives the initially exhilarating and eventually suffocating adventure of the man who has escaped his juridical identity to become a "stranger in life." Then, *L'umorismo,* basic for placing Pirandello's ideas on the comic, or irony or the grotesque or whatever else one may wish to call what he himself defined as that "exceptional and most specious form of art," within the whole European tradition from the Renaissance* to Bergson. Third, *Così è (se vi pare),* which has lost none of its effectiveness as a direct, if somewhat didactic, statement of one of the ideas that has become most closely identified with Pirandello: the belief that all truth is relative. And finally, *Sei personaggi,* which in transcending representationalism or *mimesis* takes the group of small-town gossips who in *Così è* are intent on uncovering the objective, verifiable facts of the lives of a family of newcomers in their midst and turns them into a company of run-of-the-mill actors startled one day to find fully alive characters (whom they mistake for persons) demanding from them the immortal life of art. With *Sei personaggi,* as Pirandello shows in the preface he added to the play in 1925, the stage is no longer the traditional living room of nineteenth-century drama nor yet the "two boards and a passion" of which Fergusson speaks, but the concretization of the space in the playwright's mind where the act of artistic creation takes place.

The plays that fall under the rubric of "the theatre in the theatre" and such related ones as *Sagra del Signore della nave* (1925, *Our Lord of the Ship*) and *I giganti della montagna* (*The Mountain Giants,* left unfinished) are in line with one of the aspects of *Sei personaggi.* Others instead reach back beyond that play and pursue another aspect of it, that concern with the anguish of existence that had been a hallmark of Pirandello's work from the beginning and led to the creation of an unparalleled group of suffering *raisonneurs.* In spite of their problematic identities, their unheroic circumstances, and their humiliated status of puppets in a godless universe, Pirandello's protagonists, men and women, are the very opposite of anonymous ciphers. Two can be cited: the nameless madman in *Enrico IV* (1922,

Henry IV), who returns from the abyss of incommunicability which is insanity to heap his disdain and deadly aggression on the corrupt and foolish people around him; and Ersilia Drei, the victimized governess of *Vestire gli ignudi* (1922, *To Clothe the Naked*), who rises to tragic heights when she forgives those who have prevented her from dying in her "decent little dress" by recognizing that they too need to "construct" themselves, to cover their paltry and ugly nakedness with a beautiful fiction. These two join others, too numerous to mention—a unique gallery of characters who more than anything else in Pirandello's work point to the concreteness, the "living images" rather than philosophical concepts, of his art.

Sartre, Camus, Beckett, Ionesco, O'Neill, Pinter, Albee, Wilder, Gelber, Anouilh, and Genet are among the many dramatists whose work in one way or another reveals the presence of Pirandello.

See also TEATRO GROTTESCO.

Bibliography: Naked Masks, trans. Eric Bentley, et al. (New York: Dutton, 1958); *One-Act Plays,* trans. William Murray (New York: Anchor, 1964); *On Humor,* trans. Antonio Illiano and Daniel Testa (Chapel Hill, N.C.: University of North Carolina Press, 1974); *The Late Mattia Pascal,* trans. William Weaver (New York: Doubleday, 1964); *Short Stories,* trans. Frederick May (London: Oxford University Press, 1965); *Pirandello. A Collection of Critical Essays,* ed. Glauco Cambon (Englewood Cliffs, N.J.: Prentice-Hall, 1967); Gaspare Giudice, *Pirandello: A Biography* (London: Oxford University Press, 1975); Jørn Moestrup, *The Structural Patterns of Pirandello's Work* (Odense: Odense University Press, 1972); Olga Ragusa, *Luigi Pirandello* (New York: Columbia University Press, 1968); Domenico Vittorini, *The Drama of Luigi Pirandello* (New York: Dover, 1957).

Olga Ragusa

PIUS II: *See* ENEA SILVIO PICCOLOMINI.

POLIDORO VERGILIO, "Polydore Vergil" (circa 1470–1555), cleric, diplomat, and historian. A native of Urbino, Vergil entered the service of Pope Alexander VI and was appointed to assist the collector of Peter's Pence in England, an office which brought him to that country in 1502. Earlier, Vergil had published an edition of a commentary on Martial; the *Adagia* (1498, Adages), an extremely fashionable collection of proverbs which, at one time, rivaled the better known work of Erasmus; and the *De Inventoribus Rerum* (1499–1521, *History of Inventions*), a voluminous study of inventors which became something of a best seller. It appeared in more than one hundred editions in various languages and was later put on the Index because of its remarks about the origins of religion.

Vergil became acquainted with King Henry VII in England, who had close ties to the court of Urbino and a taste for Italianate culture, and most of his life was spent in the English court. After a brief sojourn in Italy during 1513–14, Vergil became involved in the religious conflict between Henry VIII and Cardinal Wolsey and was imprisoned for a short time. His greatest achievement was the *Historiae Anglicae* written in twenty-six books (1534, book twenty-seven added in 1555, *English History*), a study of England from its origins to 1538. Besides the standard classical sources, Vergil employed oral tradition, the recollections of older colleagues still alive during the composition of the work, and philological evidence from surviving ruins and documents. From a philological standpoint, his most important contribution was to have demonstrated that the traditional legend of Brutus and the Trojan origin of England was without foundation. One of the first and finest English examples of humanist historiography, this history is in many respects comparable to works produced in fifteenth-century Florence and was to influence later historians and, to some extent, Shakespeare's historical plays.

See also BRACCIOLINI, Poggio; BRUNI, Leonardo; HUMANISM.

Bibliography: Polydore Vergil's English History from an Early Translation, ed. Sir H. Ellis (London: Camden Society, 1846), Books 1–8; *Three Books of Polydore Vergil's English History Comprising the Reigns of Henry VI, Edward IV and Richard III from an Early Translation,* ed. Sir H. Ellis (London: Camden Society, 1844), Books 23–25; *The Anglica Historia of Polydore Vergil A. D. 1485–1537,* ed. Denys Hay (London: Royal Historical Society, 1950); Denys Hay, *Polydore Vergil: Renaissance Historian and Man of Letters* (London: Oxford University Press, 1952).

POLIZIANO, ANGELO (1454–1494), Renaissance* humanist, teacher, and poet, sometimes known in the English-speaking world as Politian. The short but productive life of Poliziano is closely tied to the city of Florence and to the Medici family. On 14 July 1454, Agnolo Ambrogini (later he assumed the humanistic appellation Politianus) was born in the Tuscan village of Montepulciano. His father led an active political life by holding various public offices in Montepulciano and was a staunch Medici supporter. Between the time of his father's death (1464) and 1469, Poliziano moved to Florence where he quickly showed himself to be a promising young scholar, both in Greek and Latin studies. Having translated Books II and III of the *Iliad,* he dedicated them to Lorenzo il Magnifico,* a gesture which was to give him access to the powerful Medici family. In 1473, by invitation from Lorenzo, Poliziano became a permanent member of the Medici household while assuming such responsibilities as tutor to Lorenzo's son Piero and the priory of San Paolo. Six years of relative tranquility followed during which Poliziano was left free to continue his studies in the Medici library and with the various scholars residing in or passing through Florence (Bartolomeo della Fonte, 1445–1513; Marsilio

Ficino;* Giovanni Argiropulo, 1415–1487; Andronico Callisto, died after 1476; and Cristoforo Landino*). In 1475, he became Lorenzo's personal secretary *(cancelliere)*. For reasons unknown, in 1478, Poliziano fell into disfavor with Lorenzo's wife, Clarice, and with Lorenzo himself; as a result, Poliziano left Florence and sought the protection of Cardinal Francesco Gonzaga in Mantua. His absence from Florence was of short duration. In 1480, Poliziano wrote to Lorenzo seeking permission to return, and a few months later, Lorenzo granted him his wish. Although he did not return to his former post as Lorenzo's secretary, he was given the chair of *eloquenza greca e latina* (Greek and Latin eloquence) in the Florentine Study and a small villa in nearby Fiesole. The solace of his country living was disrupted only occasionally by literary polemics, principally with Michele Marullo (1453–1499), Bartolomeo Scala (1428–1497), and Giorgio Merula (1430–1494). Between September 28 and 29 in the year 1494 Poliziano succumbed to a severe attack of fever.

Although Poliziano wrote poetry throughout his life, the years 1471–80 constitute his most prolific period. During this time, Poliziano wrote various types of poems, in Latin and Greek (1473–78; elegies, odes, epigrams) and in Italian *(canzoni a ballo, rispetti)*. His fame, however, rests principally on the *Stanze di messere Angelo Poliziano cominciate per la giostra di Giuliano de' Medici* (1475–78, The Stanzas of Angelo Poliziano for the Tournament of Giuliano de' Medici). Written in the popular narrative octave form, it was begun in 1475 in honor of Giuliano de' Medici and was abruptly left unfinished when Giuliano was killed (26 April 1478) in the Pazzi conspiracy. The *Stanze* allegorically depicts Giuliano, Lorenzo's younger brother, as a heroic youth who is free from the concerns of love and who is dedicated to the pleasures of hunting and adventure. Venus overhears his bold criticism of love and lovers and vows to capture him. A hunting scene follows in which Giuliano is attracted to the image of a beautiful deer or *cervia*. He follows, and as the *cervia* disappears a beautiful nymph appears, his future loved one, Simonetta Vespucci Cattaneo. Attention then shifts to Venus and to an elaborate description of her realm; thus ends Book I. In Book II, Venus incites Giuliano, in a dream, to do battle in the next joust in Florence so that he may win glory and the love of Simonetta. The celebration of this joust was never to be written and the *Stanze* remains truncated at Book II, St. 46. In terms of characters and situations, the *Stanze* represents a composite of Latin encomiastic poetry and vernacular (Italian) narrative octaves. This syncretic tendency is also reflected in the language and style which are derived from both literary (Greek and Latin as well as Italian) and popular traditions; any given stanza contains echoes from Homer, Propertius, Seneca, Horace, Ovid, Dante,* and Petrarch.* In terms of theme, the *Stanze* is an exaltation of Renaissance humanistic ideals—the virtues of love, war, beauty, poetry, and fame; all are expressed in an elegant and flowing style. The richly descriptive scenes of nature, art, and man are interrupted only infrequently by melancholic interludes which dwell on the contemplation of the fragile, fleeting nature of the idyllic world.

It is in the *Orfeo* (1480, *Orpheus*), a *favola pastorale* (variously termed a ballad play, verse tragedy, or lyric pastoral in dramatic form), that the melancholic undercurrent of the *Stanze* surfaces as a central part of the thematic inspiration. The myth of Orpheus and Eurydice becomes a contemplation of the human experience dominated by the forces of death and destiny. While in Mantua (1480), Poliziano was requested to provide an entertainment for the reception of Duke Galeozzo Maria Sforza; within the short span of two days he produced the *Orfeo*. Because the work possesses elements of both the *sacra rappresentazione** (with a distinctly dramatic intent and rudimentary scenery) and the eclogue in dialogue form, it is considered to be a prototype of Renaissance secular theatre.

Although Poliziano displayed open disregard for his vernacular poetry in favor of his Greek and Latin writings, the *Stanze* and the *Orfeo* became models (the *Orfeo* for the pastoral *fabula*) of poetry which were emulated and read by Ariosto* and Tasso* as well as by successive generations.

Poliziano's return to Florence in 1480 signals a return to his philological and critical investigations of Greek and Latin authors. His most demanding efforts were directed to exegetical and textual studies on Aristotle, the *Pandette* and the *Miscellanea*. The open lectures contained in the two extant collections of the *Miscellanea* also attest to Poliziano's wideranging and profound capabilities as a teacher. Of the Greek and Latin poetry which Poliziano wrote during this time (Greek epigrams, Latin elegies), the four *Sylvae* in Latin hexameters were also incorporated into his opening lectures.

Throughout his life, Poliziano sought individual freedom and thrived in the culturally and intellectually fecund atmosphere of fifteenth-century Florence. Although in the company of Neo-Platonic scholars of the stature of Ficino* and Pico della Mirandola,* Poliziano maintained his own particular identity as poet, philologist, and teacher. His writings show an insatiable curiosity for minute detail and a profound knowledge of ancient and contemporary literature. His Italian works, the *Stanze* and the *Orfeo*, mark him as one of the most representative poets of fifteenth-century Italy.

See also DELLA MIRANDOLA, Giovanni Pico; FICINO, Marsilio.

Bibliography: Stanze di messere Angelo Poliziano cominciate per la giostra di Giuliano de' Medici, ed. Vincenzo Pernicone (Turin: Loescher-Chiantore, 1954); Harry M. Ayres, "A Translation of Poliziano's *Orfeo*," *Romantic Review* 20 (1929), 13–24; Guy Davenport, *"The Tournament:* Poliziano," *Delos* 4 (1970), 82–97 (English version of Book I, st. 1–28); Eugenio Donato, "Death and History in Poliziano's *Stanze*," *Modern Language Notes* 80 (1965), 27–40; Arnolfo Ferruolo, "A Trend in Renaissance Thought and Art: Poliziano's *Stanze per la*

Giostra," *Romanic Review* 44 (1953), 246–56; Ida Maïer, *Les Manuscripts d'Ange Politien: Catalogue descriptif* (Geneva: Librairie Droz, 1965); Leo Spitzer, "The Problem of Latin Renaissance Poetry," *Studies in the Renaissance* 2 (1955), 118–38.

Dennis Dutschke

POLO, MARCO (1254–1324), Venetian adventurer, merchant, and writer. In 1260, Marco's father Niccolò and his uncle Maffeo began a rather common journey from Constantinople to the Crimean port city of Suday. For a number of reasons, their trip concluded with a visit to the court of Kublai Khan in far-off Peking. Departing for the West, they arrived at Acre, the eastern outpost of Latin Christendom in 1269, where they secured the permission of the papal legate for a return journey to fulfill the request of the ruler of the Mongol Empire, who had asked them to bring back a number of men versed in the Christian religion. When the legate, Tedaldo Visconti, was elected Pope Gregory X, they received further support. During their second journey, Niccolò brought along his son Marco (then seventeen), and after four years the group reached their destination. They remained there for approximately seventeen years, finally returning to Venice by sea in 1295 after a three-year voyage.

Polo's account of his adventures struck a responsive chord in the European imagination, and literally hundreds of editions of his travelogue in a variety of languages have appeared since the fourteenth century. Although his descriptions were often questioned by his contemporaries, the gradual increase of interest in cartography among Europeans, along with the demands of commercial travel to the East, eventually made his work extremely popular. Even when political changes in the lands he visited again divided Europe from the Orient, his book was seen in a romantic light as an imaginative portrait of another, remote but exciting world. Those who still sought ways to reach this region examined the book in great detail, and it was fitting that a Latin edition of the book owned by Christopher Columbus, with copious notes in his own hand, accompanied Columbus on his first voyage to what turned out to be a New World.

The circumstances surrounding the composition of the book are somewhat obscure. According to the most plausible account, Polo was captured in 1298 by the Genoese along with a romance writer named Rustichello da Pisa (uncertain dates); together, the two men produced the story of his travels. But even its title is mysterious. The oldest codices carry a French title, *Le divisament dou monde* (The Description of the World), while the title commonly used today—*Il Milione*—derives either from Polo's great personal wealth or from a form of "Emilio" that was apparently part of the author's full name. The original manuscript, no longer in existence, was no doubt written in French. The problem of establishing a reliable text is gargantuan, given the fact that some one hundred manuscripts of differing reliability remain. It is now commonly accepted that a manuscript from the early fourteenth century preserved in Paris, supplemented by others in Latin and Venetian dialect, together with an influential but sometimes questionable Italian edition published posthumously by Giovanni Battista Ramusio (1485–1557) in 1559, has produced an account of Polo's adventures that is as close to the original as will ever be available to the modern reader.

Bibliography: Il Milione, ed. Luigi F. Benedetto (Florence: Olschki, 1928); *The Travels of Marco Polo,* trans. Ronald Latham (Baltimore: Penguin, 1958); Henry H. Hart, *Marco Polo: Venetian Adventurer* (Norman, Okla.: University of Oklahoma Press, 1967).

POMPONAZZI, PIETRO (1462–1525), philosopher. A Mantuan by birth, Pomponazzi received his education at the University of Padua, afterwards holding a post there as professor of natural philosophy for some years (1488–96, 1499–1509). From 1511 until his death, he taught moral and natural philosophy at the University of Bologna and became identified with the most brilliant phase of Renaissance* Aristotelianism which flourished in the northern Italian universities, particularly in Padua, and which is often termed Paduan Averroism.

Only a few of Pomponazzi's writings were published during his lifetime. The most controversial was the Latin treatise *De immortalitate animae* (1516, *On the Immortality of the Soul*), which grew out of a remark in a lecture that Aquinas's views on immortality did not agree with those of Aristotle. Pomponazzi's conclusion is that the question of the soul's mortality or immortality cannot be determined through natural reason; the question must therefore be resolved by God Himself, who has made the doctrine of the soul's immortality an article of faith in the Holy Scriptures. The book was publicly burned, and a rebuttal was commissioned by Pope Leo X. Pomponazzi also wrote two other treatises in Latin, both of some importance and published posthumously in Basel: *De incantationibus* (1556, On Incantation) and *De fato* (1557, *On God's Foreknowledge and Human Freedom*). The first offers natural explanations for various phenomena popularly explained by the presence of demons or spirits; Pomponazzi boldly proposes that effects of the stars studied by astrologers stem from natural causes. This book alone among Pomponazzi's works was placed on the Index for a time. The second and longest of the two treatises deals with the questions of fate, free will, and predestination. As he had earlier in his study of the soul's immortality, Pomponazzi notes that rational explanations fail to reconcile the problems of free will and predestination, but he declares himself willing to submit to the church's teachings that free will, fate, and divine predestination are compatible. Pomponazzi's style represented a marked turn from the normal humanist search for elegance of expression. His rationalist approach to such issues as the immortality of the soul would later be viewed by free thinkers of the Enlightenment* as an early example of their own approach to these questions.

Bibliography: Renaissance Philosophy: The Italian Philosophers, eds. Arturo B. Fallico and Herman Shapiro (New York: Modern Library, 1967); Ernst Cassirer, et al., *The Renaissance Philosophy of Man* (Chicago: University of Chicago Press, 1948); Paul Oskar Kristeller, *Eight Philosophers of the Italian Renaissance* (Stanford, Calif.: Stanford University Press, 1964).

PONTANO, GIOVANNI (1429–1503), humanist, diplomat, scholar, and poet. Born and educated in Umbria, Pontano moved to Naples when it was still ruled by the House of Aragon and entered the service of the royal family, fulfilling many important political and diplomatic functions. He was named secretary of state in 1486. Pontano had already become the driving force behind the Neapolitan Academy and was its official leader after 1471. Within that group, he was known by the Latin title Jovianus Pontanus, following the Academy's custom of adopting classical names.

Pontano's voluminous literary production is almost entirely in Latin, but it displays an elegant, polished style considered in its time the equal of its Roman models. Besides many dialogues on the nature of the prince, prudence, obedience, fortune, generosity, and other moral subjects, Pontano also wrote about astrology and philology. The source of his most lasting influence is, however, his Latin poetry. A collection of familiar poetry, *De amore coniugali* (1480–84, Conjugal Love), represents his best efforts and contains poems depicting the joys of family life—the birth of children, the pleasures of domestic life, and several epithalamia on the occasion of a daughter's marriage. Three pastoral* eclogues and three idylls stimulated the Neapolitan revival of the classical bucolic tradition which later produced Sannazaro's* masterpiece, *Arcadia.* All six of these Latin works ("Acon," "Quinquennius," "Maeon," "Meliseus," "Lepidina," and "Coryle") had appeared in Aldine editions by 1518. Although Pontano followed both Theocritus and Virgil in some respects, he created pastoral poetry that was considered by many Renaissance* writers and critics as equal or superior to his classical models.

See also PASTORAL; SANNAZARO, Jacopo; SPAGNOLI, Battista.

Bibliography: Carmina: ecloghe, elegie, liriche, ed. Johannes Oeschger (Bari: Laterza, 1948); Eliane Jeanette Harper, *The Eclogues of Giovanni Pontano* (Ph.D. Dissertation, Indiana University, 1957)—contains complete English translations; Erasmo Percopo, *Vita di Giovanni Pontano* (Naples: ITEA, 1938).

PORTA, CARLO (1775–1821), satirical poet who wrote in the Milanese dialect. A native of Milan, Porta studied in Monza and a seminary in Milan before his father removed him from school and sent him to Venice to prepare for a bureaucratic career. His earliest compositions in dialect date back to 1792 and include a translation of a poem by Parini.* After returning to Milan, Porta became a popular dialect actor at the Teatro Patriottico and a member of the city's literary academy (1800). Inspired by the example of Domenico Balestrieri (1714–1780), who had already rendered Tasso's* *Gerusalemme liberata* into Milanese in 1772, Porta attempted to duplicate this feat with Dante's* *Inferno* between 1802 and 1805. In the meanwhile, he began working in a government agency, a position which he held for most of his life, married Vincenzina Prevosti in 1806, and had three children by her. His life was brief and uneventful, with no trace of the heroic or tragic incidents usually associated with Italian poets of the period.

Porta's dialect poetry portrays a cross-section of everyday life in the city, subjects often ignored by more respectable neoclassical writers. Furthermore, his roots in Enlightenment* thought and his debt to Voltaire and Parini led him to employ his realistic and humorous descriptions of Milanese life for biting social satire and political commentary. Several of the best early poems, "Desgrazzi de Giovannin Bongee" (1812, The Misadventures of Giovannino Bongeri) and "Olter desgrazzi de Giovannin Bongee" (1813, Further Misadventures of Giovannino Bongeri), describe the antics of a Milanese of the lower classes during the French occupation of Milan. After the return of the Austrians in 1814, Porta became more directly involved in the great political and literary debates which had sprung up around the journal *Il Conciliatore,* many of whose collaborators were his close friends.

In 1816, Porta wrote one of his longest poems, "Lament del Marchionn di gamb avert" (The Lament of Bow-Legged Melchior), the humorous portrait of a bow-legged mandolin player who is tricked into marriage. He also became involved in a dispute over the aesthetic value of dialect literature occasioned by the attack of Pietro Giordani (1774–1848) against an anthology of such verse which included samples of Porta's own works. During that same year, a clandestine anti-Austrian satire was commonly attributed to Porta. Although the work was actually written by Grossi,* the incident nevertheless led Porta to renounce writing for almost two years. He returned to his artistic vocation and his dialect poetry in 1818, now more conscious than ever of the moral responsibility of the poet to his audience, with "Il Romanticismo" (1818, Romanticism), a poem which placed Porta squarely in the camp of the literary movement spearheaded by his Milanese friends. In the work, addressed to Madame Bibin, a typically superficial society lady of the poet's own invention, Porta defines poetry as the art of pleasing through moving all the reader's hidden passions. He notes that poetic themes and style must vary from era to era and that the neoclassical preoccupation with dramatic rules and unities or classical motifs must be abandoned.

Porta's best known poem, and the one which most strongly attacks the society of his day, is "La nomina del cappellan" (1819, "The Selection of the Chaplain"). It describes how the Marchioness Paola Cangiasa, one of the "first ladies of all Lombardy," chooses a chaplain to replace the one who had died of pneumonia while walking her dog Lilla. A crowd of some thirty aspiring priests gathers at the woman's home, attracted more by the table she sets and the free lodging and laundry the job provides than by any spiritual vocation. As the butler lists the requirements for the position— saying Mass only when the marchioness wishes, making the service as brief as possible, playing at Tarot cards, running errands, and, most importantly, walking the dog—the field is rapidly reduced to only six men. One priest is dismissed for kicking the dog, and two more leave because they cannot suppress their laughter when the woman sits on her pet. The final choice, made by the dog itself, falls upon Don Ventura—the most ignorant and unworthy priest of the entire group. Only at the end of the poem does the reader learn how this wily priest has hidden several slices of salami beneath his cassock to attract Lilla's interest and favor and to secure the post for himself. No more damaging portrait of Italy's northern nobility had appeared in print since Parini's satirical masterpiece, *Il giorno (The Day)*.

Although less bitter or cynical in tone than the works of the great Roman dialect poet Belli,* Porta's best verse reflects his heartfelt denunciation of a reactionary and anachronistic world which was blind to new ideas and his belief that moral, political, and literary reform was inevitable. With the renewed interest in dialect among contemporary Italian writers and the publication of critical editions of his works with accompanying Italian translations, Porta's place in Italian literary history as Milan's greatest dialect poet seems secure.

Bibliography: Le lettere di Carlo Porta, ed. Dante Isella (Milan: Ricciardi, 1967); *Le poesie*, ed. Carla Guarisco, 2 vols. (Milan: Feltrinelli, 1964); *From Marino to Marinetti*, trans. Joseph Tusiani (New York: Baroque Press, 1974); *Concordanze delle poesie milanesi di Carlo Porta*, ed. Silvio Cipriani (Milan: Ricciardi, 1970); Attilio Momigliano, *L'opera di Carlo Porta* (Città di Castello, 1909).

PRAGA, EMILIO (1839–1875), bohemian painter and poet. Praga was born near Milan. Between 1857 and 1859, he traveled extensively in Europe and, while in Paris, he discovered Baudelaire's *Les fleurs du mal* which had a decisive influence upon his future literary works. He seems to have preferred foreign poets, such as Baudelaire, Poe, Heine, or Hugo, to the Italians. In 1859, he exhibited four oil paintings in his first exhibition, at Brera, and in 1862, he published his first volume of verse, *Tavolozza* (Palette). In the same year, he married Anna Maria Benfereri, and a son Marco* (the future playwright) was born to them. In 1863, Praga collaborated with Arrigo Boito* in the writing of a comedy, *Le madri galanti* (The Gallant Mothers), which was greeted by whistles and jeers when it opened in Turin. Two other books of verse soon followed— *Penombre* (1864, Penumbrae) and *Fiabe e leggende* (1869, Fables and Legends).

His father's death in 1864 forced the poet to support himself, a task to which he soon proved unequal. Although he was engaged to teach Italian literature at the music conservatory in Milan, he turned to drink and this dissolute existence destroyed his fragile health. Eventually, his wife abandoned him and took their son with her. He died a premature death. Several of his works appeared posthumously—a collection of verse entitled *Trasparenze* (1878, Transparencies) and an incomplete novel, *Memorie del presbiterio* (1881, Memoirs of the Presbytery).

Praga was recognized as the foremost poet of the *scapigliatura** movement, a bohemian reaction to bourgeois society and its culture that sprang up in Milan, Italy's most advanced urban center. As a poet, Praga rejects the sentimentality of the romantic lyric without, however, completely abandoning its forms or syntax, and he often exploits the relationships he sees between poetry and the visual arts. Heavily influenced by Baudelaire and other *poètes maudits,* Praga had a taste for the exotic and the bizarre typical of *scapigliatura* literature.

See also SCAPIGLIATURA.

Bibliography: Opere, ed. Gabriele Catalano (Naples: Fulvio Rossi, 1969); Gaetano Mariani, *Storia della scapigliatura* (Rome: Salvatore Sciascia Editore, 1967); Piero Nardi, *Scapigliatura da Giuseppe Rovani a Carlo Dossi* (Milan: Mondadori, 1968).

PRAGA, MARCO (1862–1929), Milanese playwright and drama critic. The son of the bohemian poet Emilio Praga,* Marco was educated as an accountant but was soon attracted to the theatre after he had obtained a position which allowed him the leisure to write. He may be considered one of the most typical representatives of the bourgeois theatre which thrived around the turn of the century and included the dramas of Praga, Giuseppe Giacosa,* Gerolamo Rovetta,* and Roberto Bracco.* Not only did he write a number of successful plays, but he also directed theatrical performances after 1913 at the Manzoni Theatre in Milan. He was one of the first men in Italy to stage Pirandello's* works. Later Praga became president of the Italian Society of Editors and Writers. He served as theatre critic for *L'Illustrazione italiana* from 1919 until his death.

Praga published a single novel in 1889 but is best remembered for his dramatic works. Of note are the plays *Le vergini* (1889, The Virgins) and

La moglie ideale (1891, The Ideal Wife). His favorite themes include the social pretensions of the bourgeois world and the bourgeois institution of marriage with its hypocritical role-playing and subterfuges. In *Le vergini,* he portrays women who, although technically virgins, are nevertheless ready to sell their charms to the highest bidder. In *La moglie ideale,* usually considered his masterpiece, he depicts the perfect middle-class housewife and mother (Giulia) who, in reality, lives a secret life which she conceals with matchless hypocrisy and simulation. Although Praga's works debunk, in an ironic fashion, the hallowed bourgeois institutions of marriage and the family, they never expand these themes in a fundamentally philosophical manner as would later be the case in the *teatro grottesco** or the early works of Pirandello. Praga's theatrical criticism, collected from his many articles, is an excellent guide to the theatrical life of early twentieth-century Italy.

Bibliography: Cronache teatrali, 11 vols. (Milan: Treves, 1920–29); *La moglie ideale* (Milan: Galli, 1891); *Le vergini* (Milan: Chiesa, 1890); Lander MacClintock, *The Age of Pirandello* (Bloomington, Ind.: Indiana University Press, 1951); Giorgio Pullini, *Marco Praga* (Bologna: Cappelli, 1960).

PRATI, GIOVANNI (1814–1884), poet from Campomaggiore. After studying law at Padua, Prati turned to literature. Imprisoned by the Austrians in 1840, he was released in the following year and went to Milan. There he became friends with Manzoni* and Grossi* and published his most famous work, *Edmenegarda* (1841, Edmenegarda), a long poetic *novella** of Byronic inspiration treating the love affair of a young woman ultimately betrayed by her lover. Three collections of romantic lyrics followed: *Canti lirici* (1844, Lyric Songs), reflecting the influence of Manzoni's hymns and Lamartine; *Canti per il popolo* (1843, Songs for the People), containing poems in a patriotic vein; and the *Ballate* (1843, Ballads). After another brief period of confinement in 1848, Prati moved to Turin and remained there until 1865. Made court historian of the House of Savoy for his work, he subsequently declined the offer of the chair in Italian literature at Bologna and became a senator. He worked as the director of Rome's Magistero until his death.

Prati's early works were written in a typically romantic poetic style. In his later years, under the influence of Leopardi,* poets from abroad, and the classics, Prati's lyrics tended to be more restrained in their style and showed an increased use of classical allusions. One major collection entitled *Psiche* (1876, Psyche) contains several hundred sonnets* on a myriad of personal, often idyllic, topics. Similar in tone is his final work, *Iside* (1878, Isis), which seems to embody the fantasies and dreams of the poet's old age. An able poet both in the variety of his subject matter and the musicality of his language, Prati's chief failing was a tendency towards prolixity, a common characteristic of much late romantic verse.

Bibliography: Poeti minori dell'Ottocento, ed. Luigi Baldacci, 2 vols. (Milan: Ricciardi, 1958); *From Marino to Marinetti,* trans. Joseph Tusiani (New York: Baroque Press, 1974).

PRATOLINI, VASCO (1913–), Florentine novelist and neorealist. Largely self-taught and the product of a working-class background, Pratolini was raised in Santa Croce, the workers' district of Florence which figures prominently in his later novels. Before he became a professional writer, he held various jobs (waiter, workman, printer). In 1936, he met Elio Vittorini,* another autodidact, who encouraged him to write and to shake off the influence of fascism. (Earlier he had contributed articles to a fascist periodical entitled *Il Bargello.*) In 1938, he joined the poet Alfonso Gatto* in founding a literary review entitled *Campo di Marte,* which was suppressed by the government after only twelve issues. Although short-lived, it had attracted contributions from such major figures as Montale,* Landolfi,* Quasimodo,* Gadda,* and Vittorini. Pratolini joined the resistance (1943–44) not long after publishing his first fictional works— *Il tappeto verde* (1941, The Green Carpet); *Via de' Magazzini* (1942, Magazzini Street); and *Le amiche* (1943, The Girl Friends).

His first important novel is *Il quartiere* (1945, *A Tale of Santa Croce*). It was followed closely by a series of works which immerse the reader in the atmosphere of fascist Italy, the resistance, and the working-class sections of his native Florence which figure in his neorealist fiction: *Cronaca familiare* (1947, *Two Brothers*); *Cronache di poveri amanti* (1947, *A Tale of Poor Lovers*); *Un eroe del nostro tempo* (1949, *A Hero of Our Time*); and *Le ragazze di San Frediano* (1949, The Girls of San Frediano). *Il quartiere* depicts life in the Santa Croce district between 1932 and 1937. Although written in the first person, its narrator (Valerio) probably mirrors Pratolini's own experiences. With considerable skill for a young writer, Pratolini traces the lives of a group of young people from the district, intertwining their personal experiences with larger, historical events (the African war, the rise of class consciousness among the workers). Pratolini describes *Cronaca familiare,* inspired by the death of his own brother in 1945, as an intimate dialogue with this dead brother written to seek consolation for having failed to understand him while he was still alive.

Cronache di poveri amanti, the masterpiece of Pratolini's neorealist phase, returns to an historical analysis of Florence from the year 1925 with a group of over fifty characters. It reveals the complex social and personal relationships of the inhabitants of the Via del Corno, a poor street near the Palazzo Vecchio. Among its major protagonists are its hero, a blacksmith named Corrado (called Maciste); Ugo Poggioli, a fruit vendor who eventually inherits Maciste's antifascist ideas and becomes a key member of the Communist party; and Carlino Bencini and Osvaldo Liverani, two fascists. The description of Maciste's death during one of the fascist "punitive expeditions'' in the city is perhaps the most memorable incident. Maciste is typical of Pratolini's proletarian heroes; his actions are guided not merely by Marxist rhetoric but, rather, by love and friendship for the members of his class. Pratolini uses the word *cronaca* in his title deliberately and with reference to the work of the medieval historian Dino Compagni*: he believes that fascism imposed its grip upon the people of the Via del Corno just as the Guelphs gained power over the Ghibellines centuries earlier— by terror and violence.

The last two products of this phase of Pratolini's writing—*Un eroe del nostro tempo* and *Le ragazze di San Frediano*—are less successful than *Cronache di poveri amanti*. The first portrays a sado-masochistic relationship between Sandrino Vergesi and his mistress, Virginia Aloisi. Pratolini borrows the title from the Russian novelist Mikhail Lermontov, for Sandrino is a protagonist who symbolizes a world in which violence and sadism are the norms. The novel ends with Sandrino's grotesque murder of Virginia by impaling her on an iron gate near the site of their first meeting. The second novel is more lighthearted and sketches the portraits of five girlfriends of Aldo, a mediocre Don Juan (nicknamed Bob) from the working-class district in Florence called San Frediano. In the book, Pratolini admirably captures the sense of class solidarity and neighborhood pride the young women share, which, he believes, represent the best virtues of the working class.

In 1950, Pratolini began work on an ambitious trilogy entitled *Una storia italiana* (An Italian Story) under the influence of such diverse writers as Balzac, Zola, Martin du Gard, Dreiser, and Sholokhov. A landmark of social realism in modern Italian prose, the trilogy covers various facets of Italian life from 1875 until 1945, thus dealing with the major historical events of modern Italy—the development of capitalism, fascism, and socialism—within the now familiar working-class environment of Florence. *Metello* (1955, *Metello*), perhaps the best of the three parts, describes the early development of class consciousness among the Florentine working class during the first strikes by construction workers in the nineteenth century. Its protagonist Metello is one of Pratolini's most successful fictional creations. Over thirteen hundred pages in length, the second work, *Lo scialo* (1960, The Waste), examines life in Florence between 1910 and 1930, with particular attention given to the middle class and its eventual domination by fascism. For evident historical and ideological reasons, this novel moves away from Pratolini's earlier emphasis upon the proletariat.

Pratolini interrupted the trilogy in 1963 with the publication of a first-person narrative entitled *La costanza della ragione (Bruno Santini)*, the story of a young worker born in 1941. It reveals the problems of moral and political commitment during the postwar era and ends with Bruno's decision to join the Communist party, a decision he comes to more for personal than ideological reasons. Pratolini's sensitive portrayal emphasizes the individual rather than the sociological motivations underlying Bruno's commitment. The cycle was finally completed in 1966 with *Allegoria e derisione* (Allegory and Derision); this work returns to the period from 1915 until 1945 and concludes with a postscript dated 1965. Written as the first-person narrative of its protagonist, Valerio Marsili, the work differs from the first two books of the trilogy in its subjective treatment of historical time.

Pratolini's works create a complex fresco of the Florentine working class. They are infused with the belief that solidarity is the only source of class strength and that brotherhood and love among individuals of the working class serve as a means of combatting those who would exploit the group. Although Pratolini's fiction has an undeniable Marxist tone and is popular in the Soviet Union, his ideology is also infused with the morality of the Sermon on the Mount. *Metello* was awarded the prestigious Viareggio Prize for fiction in 1955; in 1957, the Accademia dei Lincei honored Pratolini for his entire opus.

See also NEOREALISM.

Bibliography: Bruno Santini, trans. Raymond Rosenthal (Boston: Little, Brown, 1964); *A Hero of Our Time,* trans. Eric Masbacher (New York: Prentice-Hall, 1951); *Metello,* trans. Raymond Rosenthal (Boston: Little, Brown, 1968); *A Tale of Poor Lovers,* no trans. (New York: Viking, 1949); *A Tale of Santa Croce,* trans. Peter and Pamela Duncan (London: Peter Owen, 1952); *Two Brothers,* trans. Barbara Kennedy (New York: Orion Press, 1962); Giorgio Pullini, *Il romanzo italiano del dopoguerra,* 4th ed. (Padua: Marsilio Editori, 1972); Frank Rosengarten, *Vasco Pratolini: The Development of a Social Novelist* (Carbondale, Ill.: Southern Illinois University Press, 1965).

PREZZOLINI, GIUSEPPE (1882–   ), self-taught critic, essayist, journalist and teacher. Prezzolini was born in Perugia. Along with his close friend Giovanni Papini,* Prezzolini visited Paris at the turn of the century (1902) and came into contact with the ideas of Henri Bergson and the pragmatists. In 1903, Prezzolini and Papini founded *Leonardo,* a cultural periodical which ceased publication in 1907; both collaborated upon *Il Regno,* a nationalist review headed by Enrico Corradini (1865–1931). Profoundly influenced by Crocean idealism, Prezzolini founded *La Voce,* a review which made a significant impact upon early twentieth-century Italian culture and included such contributors as Papini, Palazzeschi,* Sbarbaro,* Jahier,* Rèbora,* and Campana.* Prezzolini's personality was largely responsible for keeping peace among these diverse figures and for instilling in all of them his own interest in contemporary moral, social, and literary problems. After Prezzolini stepped down from the editorship of *La Voce* in 1914, he was replaced by Giuseppe De Robertis (1888–1963) until the journal's demise in 1916.

During World War I, Prezzolini served at the front, but before the outbreak of the conflict he had collaborated as a correspondent with both Mussolini's *Il Popolo d'Italia* and the *Rivoluzione liberale* of Piero Gobetti (1901–1926). Immediately after the war, he published biographies of Mussolini and Giovanni Amendola, as well as a life of Machiavelli,* and worked in Paris with a cultural service of the League of Nations from 1925 until 1929. In 1930, Prezzolini was invited to Columbia University as professor of Italian and head of the Casa Italiana. A number of discerning essays about his American experiences eventually appeared, and during his years at Columbia his forceful personality was instrumental in guiding the fortunes of the study of Italian in America.

After World War II, Prezzolini returned to journalism and contributed essays to various Italian newspapers (*La Nazione, Il Tempo,* and *Il Borghese*). *L'Italiano inutile* (1953, The Useless Italian), a collection of his autobiographical writings from as far back as 1938, covered his early work on *Leonardo* and *La Voce,* the war, and his experiences abroad in France and America. Much of the writing of his later years has been directed towards assembling an historical record of his early friendships and correspondence, such as the important two-volume collection of his correspondence with Papini between 1900 and 1956 entitled *Storia di un'amicizia* (1966–68, Story of a Friendship). Age has not diminished his energy or productivity. Recent works have included *Dio è un rischio* (1969, God Is a Gamble); an invaluable anthology of writings from *La Voce* (1974); *Manifesto dei conservatori* (1972, Manifesto of Conservatives); and a defense of his years as head of the Casa Italiana against the recent charges that he pursued a profascist policy in that position. Perhaps the most valuable of the postwar books unrelated to his early career is his *Machiavelli anticristo* (1954, Machiavelli), a spirited treatment of the Florentine political theorist and his impact upon social thought which grew out of Prezzolini's lectures at Columbia University.

See also PAPINI, Giovanni.

Bibliography: Il meglio di Giuseppe Prezzolini (Milan: Longanesi, 1971); *La Voce 1908–1913: cronaca, antologia e fortuna di una rivista* (Milan: Rusconi, 1974); *Machiavelli,* trans. Gioconda Savini (New York: Farrar, Straus & Giroux, 1967); Eugenio Garin, *Cronache di filosofia italiana* (Bari: Laterza, 1959); Margherita Marchione, ''Prezzolini Recaptures His Past,'' *Italian Quarterly* 14 (1970), 75–92.

PUCCI, ANTONIO (circa 1310–1388), popular poet, bell-founder and ringer, town-crier for the city of Florence for most of his adult life, and a friend to eminent writers including Boccaccio,* Sercambi,* and Sacchetti.* Pucci's many works encompass a wide variety of influences and sources and a remarkable selection of poetic themes and genres. In his friend Sacchetti's *Trecentonovelle* (CLXXV), he is described as a ''pleasing Florentine''; Pucci's own life provided that writer of *novelle** with a humorous story about how the poet turned the tables on some friends who had made him the butt of a practical joke. Perhaps in response to his official duties, much of Pucci's verse elaborates patriotic themes that would have been of interest to the municipal government. The *Centiloquio* (The Centiloquy) is a rhymed version of Villani's* history of Florence, which contains a well-known section on Dante.* He composed at least five *cantari*, long narrative poems in *ottave* usually intended for public recitation, which generally recount religious or chivalric tales of French origin. One *cantare* entitled *Madonna Lionessa* contains the first version of the "pound of flesh" motif which apparently reached Shakespeare through the *Pecorone* of Giovanni Fiorentino* and reappears in *The Merchant of Venice*. Besides brief lyrics and "tailed" sonnets,* or *sonetti caudati* (a typical mode of expression for popular literature in Florence through the sixteenth century), Pucci wrote several historical *serventesi* (a genre of Provençal origin, usually in praise of a lord or patron); a number of works on Florence's wars with Pisa; the *Contrasto delle donne* (The Dispute over Women), a poetic debate on the virtues and vices of the fairer sex; the *Noie* (The Annoyances), a catalogue of humorous things which bother the poet inspired by the *enueg,* a Provençal genre devoted to nuisances; the *Proprietà di Mercato Vecchio* (The Property of the Old Market), a *capitolo** in *terza rima** offering a memorable description of the old market place of Florence; and the *Libro di varie storie* (Book of Miscellaneous Stories), a collection of miscellaneous stories and notable events derived from a great many other authors, including Marco Polo,* Dante, Villani, and Brunetto Latini.*

Taken as a whole, Pucci's works depict a full range of human experience and present Florentine history in a more popular manner than was acceptable among the many learned writers who were his contemporaries. His poems evince a flourishing popular literary tradition among the lower classes of the city, whose values he shared and for whom he wrote.

See also GIOVANNI FIORENTINO; SACCHETTI, Franco; VILLANI, Giovanni.

Bibliography: Libro di varie storie, ed. Alberto Varvaro (Palermo: L'Accademia, 1957); *Le noie,* ed. Kenneth McKenzie (Princeton, N.J.: Princeton University Press, 1931); *Poeti minori del Trecento,* ed. Natalino Sapegno (Milan: Ricciardi, 1952); *Rimatori del Trecento,* ed. Giuseppe Corsi (Turin: UTET, 1969); Kathleen Speight, "*Vox Populi* in Antonio Pucci," in *Italian Studies Presented to E. R. Vincent,* eds. C. P. Brand, et al. (Cambridge: Heffer, 1962).

PULCI, LUIGI (1432–1484), Florentine poet. By the time Luigi was born in Florence to Brigida di Bernardo de' Bardi and to Iacopo Pulci, the noble and ancient Pulci family, Guelph in tradition and supposedly French in origin, had fallen on hard times. Pulci's father, a former *podestà* and captain, had been barred from public office in his later years because of his failure to pay off his debts to the Commune. He died in 1450 isolated from public life, leaving his heirs a small parcel of farmland and heavy financial burdens. Luigi and his brothers Luca and Bernardo were all poets of some ability, but Luigi was outstanding. His older brother, Luca, eventually went to Rome to work in a bank, but fortune eluded him and he died in prison in 1470 at the age of thirty-nine. His younger brother, Bernardo, also left Florence to clerk in a bank, but Pulci stayed on with the hope of being aided by friends like Francesco Castellani. It was Castellani who employed him as an accountant and made it possible for him to attend the poetry lessons of the humanist Bartolomeo Scala (1428–1497) in the house of Pierfrancesco de' Medici. By 1461, the mediation of Castellani and Scala, Medici intimates, had opened the doors of the Medici palace to Pulci and had brought about his admittance into the inner circle of Lorenzo the Magnificent.* He had undoubtedly begun writing poetry by then and was probably presented as a poet of popular inspiration. The diffident attitude of the humanists toward vernacular literature had been attenuated somewhat (thanks to the efforts of such men as Leon Battista Alberti*), and even the most erudite men found pleasure in works written in the vulgar tongue. Lorenzo himself was enthusiastic about popular poetry, and the popular *cantari* which earlier were performed in the public square infiltrated the rarified heights of the Medicean court. Lorenzo's mother, Lucrezia Tornabuoni, quickly took a liking to Luigi Pulci. It was she who, soon after his introduction into the Medici circle, commissioned him to sing of the deeds of Charlemagne, thereby leading to the creation of his comic epic masterpiece, *Il Morgante* (1483, Morgante).

Although Lorenzo was much younger than Luigi, the two became warm friends. When Lorenzo became head of the Medici family, he looked to the poet not only for amusement and companionship, but also for diplomatic service, assigning him missions to Naples, Bologna, and other cities. Pulci displayed a sense of humor which ranged from gaiety and indiscretion to bitter satire and polemic inspired by jealousy and pessimism. His light treatment of the question of the immortality of the soul (which, with the questions of free will and the dignity of man, lay at the core of humanist polemics) caused Matteo Franco (1447–1494), another Medici intimate much esteemed by Lorenzo, to accuse him of heresy. The polemic was joined by none other than Marsilio Ficino* on the side of Franco. It seems that the exchange was provoked by Franco, who may not have liked the idea of sharing Lorenzo's affection with Pulci. On another occasion, however, when Bartolomeo Scala (a miller's son) was made chancellor, Pulci produced some caustic sonnets* for the occasion which clearly reflected his own envious nature. His feud with Franco earned him the accusation of heresy, partly founded on his interest in magic and on

numerous unorthodox beliefs. Although he wrote a *Confession* (1481) and
was supposedly reconverted by the humanist friar Mariano da Gen-
nazzano (1460–1531), his confession was considered insincere. Thus, the
accusation stuck, and a Christian burial in consecrated ground was denied
him.

Luigi Pulci is best remembered for his imaginative reworking of the
anonymous fourteenth-century *Orlando* in which he uses the details of the
legend of Roland as a frame for the colorful escapades of his characters.
Traditional themes include trials of strength and courage, the avenging of
wrongs, and the punishment of traitors. His lengthy poem acquired the
popular title of *Morgante*, after the giant character who formerly went
about playing pranks such as disrupting the quiet of a convent and whom
Orlando converts to Christianity and makes his squire. Although the
Morgante was probably composed between 1460 and 1470 and may have
been printed before 1480, the earliest known editions are an incomplete
Venetian printing of the twenty-three *cantari* of 1481, another Florentine
edition of 1482 (also of twenty-three *cantari*), and the full twenty-eight
cantari edition of 1483, which bears the title *Morgante maggiore* (The
Greater Morgante), which, in five new books, contains half again as much
material as the shorter version. The *Morgante* reveals Pulci's mastery of
Florentine linguistic expression (Machiavelli* used him as a model). It
presents, in vigorous idiom rich in popular flavor, a world in which Charlemagne is portrayed as an ingenuous and comical simpleton who is failing
in his old age, a world of giants and enchantment, of quick religious con-
versions, and of the likes of Astraroth, a philosophical demon-theologian
who advocates religious tolerance and foretells the discovery of lands
across the Atlantic. Pulci's giant hero Morgante dies of a crab's bite. The
ribald demigiant Margutte, of dubious intentions, son of a Greek nun and a
Moslem priest, whose impudent and ribald profession of faith and other
pronouncements are a constant cause of laughter, dies laughing over a
prank played on him by Morgante. The total result is a poem which reveals
a complex amalgam of fifteenth-century Florentine cultural differences
which link the lowest tavern to the most ethereal academy. Buffoonery
colors every part of the poem, even those moments which were so serious
in the French *chansons de geste*. This fact suggests that Pulci had little
sympathy for the essentially violent and sometimes irrational heroic life.

Pulci's other works include his *Vocabolista* (1465, Lexicon), a collection
of over seven hundred Latinisms adaptable to vernacular usage; *La giostra
di Lorenzo* (1482, Lorenzo's Joust), which celebrates Lorenzo's extravagant tournament of 1469; and the *Beca da Dicomano* (written sometime before 1470, Beca from Dicomano), a parody of Lorenzo's pastoral
Nencia di Barberino (Nencia from Barberino). In addition, Pulci wrote
many poems in the popular lyric manner, including *frottole, rispetti,* and

strambotti,* as well as a number of sonnets attacking Bartolomeo Scala, Matteo Franco, and Marsilio Ficino. Sometime in his later years he wrote the *Novella dello sciocco senese* (Tale of the Sienese Fool).

Pulci's influence abroad was limited but important. The *Morgante* was a major source for Rabelais. During the romantic period in England, an era that witnessed the increased popularity of long narrative poetry from Italy, Pulci again attracted the notice of key critics and poets. Coleridge lectured on his works, and Leigh Hunt summarized parts of his poetry in *Stories from the Italian Poets*. Sir Walter Scott also read Pulci (along with Ariosto,* Boiardo,* and Tasso*) and made these works an integral part of his concept of romance and chivalry. Lord Byron translated the first part of Pulci's *Morgante* ("The Morgante Maggiore of Pulci"), and the Italian poet's style is evident in the mock-heroic tone of his *Don Juan*.

See also ARIOSTO, Ludovico; BOIARDO, Matteo Maria; HUMANISM.

Bibliography: Morgante e lettere, ed. Domenico De Robertis (Florence: Sansoni, 1962); Angelo Gianni, *Pulci uno e due* (Florence: La Nuova Italia, 1967); Giovanni Getto, *Studio sul "Morgante"* (Florence: Olschki, 1967); Leigh Hunt, *Stories from the Italian Poets* (New York: Wiley & Putnam, 1846); Edoardo A. Lebano, "Luigi Pulci and Late Fifteenth-Century Humanism in Florence," *Renaissance Quarterly* 27 (1974), 489–98; Salvatore Nigo, *Pulci e la cultura medicea* (Bari: Laterza, 1972); John Owen, *The Skeptics of the Italian Renaissance* (New York: Macmillan, 1893).

Andrea di Tommaso

QUASIMODO, SALVATORE (1901–1968), poet, translator, and critic. Born in Modica (Sicily), Quasimodo completed his early studies in Palermo at the Technical Lyceum and attended the Polytechnical University in Rome, where he received training as an engineer. In 1928, he began working for the Ministry of Public Works. After a year in Reggio Calabria, which was a formative influence upon his poetry, Quasimodo moved to Florence where, through his brother-in-law Elio Vittorini,* he met Eugenio Montale* and the then editor of *Solaria* Alessandro Bonsanti (1904–   ). His first collection of poems, *Acque e Terra* (Waters and Land), appeared in *Solaria* in 1930. In 1938, Quasimodo formally quit his trade as a technician to work for the Association of Italian Periodicals and, later, to become editor-in-chief of the weekly magazine *Il Tempo.* In 1941, he was nominated minister of public education and made professor of Italian literature at the Conservatory Giuseppe Verdi in Milan. Among the several literary prizes awarded to Quasimodo were the Etna-Taormina Prize for Poetry in 1953 (shared with Dylan Thomas), the Viareggio Prize in 1958, and the Nobel Prize for Literature in 1959.

Typical of Quasimodo's first collection, *Acque e Terra,* is the bringing together of traditional influences (Leopardi,* Pascoli,* and D'Annunzio*) and classical poetic ideals with the creation of an essential, allusive language of analogy and evocation, directed toward the realization of a "poetry of words," characteristic of his early hermeticism.* The dominant theme of this book is the rediscovery of Sicily, the lost Eden of the poet's youth, re-experienced through the nostalgic recollection of places and events associated with the simple life of his people. From the subdued immobility of brilliant images derives a general tone of anguish and despair: the scent of the land, of fruit trees and exotic vegetation, the sight of fish baskets and children awake before dawn ("Terra"), of birds looking for millet ("Antico inverno," "Ancient Winter"), and of the broad hills of Tindari ("Vento a Tindari," "Wind at Tindari") deepen the poet's sorrow of exile from the land of his youth as well as the realization that in the modern world this glorious, primordial civilization is forever lost.

The poems contained in *Oboe sommerso* (1932, Sunken Oboe), *Erato e Apollion* (1936, Aerato and Apollyon), and *Poesie* (1938, Poems) show how Quasimodo, through the conscious assimilation of symbolism, attempts, in a more extreme way than in his previous compositions, to revitalize the poetic word by investing it with a new, suggestive musicality. His abundant use of analogy, elliptical constructions, allusion, and metaphor aims at the perfecting of a pure, skeletal-like verse, often devoid of associative implications, to the point of separating the "essential" word from its surrounding objective images. The isolation of the word in a context evoking vague dreams and nostalgic melancholia verifies both the ultimate mystery of things, as well as the poet's alienation. The temporal universe of a mythical Sicily and the innocence of childhood are the poet's remedies to the disorganic and fragmented historical world.

The collection *Nuove poesie* (1936–42, New Poems), poems written during the period of the Spanish Civil War and the Axis pact, reveals a less private and more ethically inspired poetry reflecting a new commitment to historical reality. It is recognized that Quasimodo's work as a translator of Greek and Latin poetry during these years—*Lirici greci* (1940, Greek Lyric Poets), *Il fiore delle Georgiche* (1942, The Best from the Georgics), and *Catulli veronensis carmina* (1945, The Poetry of Catullus)—notably influenced his poetic form and language. The difficult accommodation of language and style necessitated by the ancient texts called for a greater philological discipline than what was implied in the sometimes verbal arbitrariness of his previous verse. The myths he so greatly coveted in his early collections now became consolations in history, dialectically connected to the political events of servitude and war.

The postwar collections *Giorno dopo giorno* (1947, Day After Day), and *La vita non è sogno* (1949, Life Is Not Dream) mark a further change in Quasimodo's poetic language, in the direction of an easier, more discursive syntax and a simpler vocabulary and diction. He now sees poetry as a committed dialogue with humanity in an attempt to remake man. The verses "Che urli almeno qualcuno nel silenzio/ in questo cerchio di sepolti" ("Let someone at least cry in this silence/ in this circle of buried bodies") exemplify well this new poetry of political and social commitment. In his "Discourse on Poetry," appended to the collection *Il falso e vero verde* (1953, The False and the True Green), Quasimodo writes that the new social poetry aspires to dialogue rather than monologue and is dramatic or epic, rather than gnomic or sociological. History has conditioned a new poetic content: "Poets know that today they cannot write idylls or horoscopes."

But Quasimodo's essentially lyrical vocation was a strong hindrance in the creation of an epic or choral poetry along the lines of Pablo Neruda (translated by Quasimodo in 1952). Instead, the best results of this later phase are reached in compositions in which the grief elicited by the memory of tragedy and the depression brought on by inactivity and frustration are expressed with the elegiac melancholy and allusiveness characteristic of his early poetic manner. Nevertheless, the strength and significance of his postwar production lie essentially in its social rather than individualistic qualities, for which Quasimodo has deservingly received international recognition.

Quasimodo's last two volumes of poetry were *La terra impareggiabile* (1958, The Incomparable Land) and *Dare e avere* (1966, *To Give and to Have*). His complete poetical works were published by Mondadori in 1960 (*Tutte le poesie*). As a translator, Quasimodo has provided excellent Italian versions of Ovid, Shakespeare, Molière, Pound, and Cummings. His critical essays have been collected in the volumes *Il poeta e il politico e altri saggi* (1960, *The Poet and the Politician*) and *Poesie e discorsi sulla poesia* (1971, Poems and Discourses on Poetry).

See also HERMETICISM.

Bibliography: Poesie e discorsi sulla poesia, ed. Gilberto Finzi (Milan: Mondadori, 1971); *The Poet and the Politician and Other Essays,* trans. Thomas Bergin and Sergio Pacifici (Carbondale, Ill.: Southern Illinois University Press, 1964); *Selected Writings,* trans. Alan Mandelbaum (New York: Farrar, Straus & Cudahy, 1960); *To Give and to Have, and Other Poems,* trans. Edith Farnsworth (Chicago: Regnery, 1975); Chandler B. Beall, "Quasimodo and Modern Italian Poetry," *Northwest Review* 4 (1961), 41–48; Glauco Cambon, "Quasimodo," *Chelsea* 6 (1960), 60–67; *Quasimodo e la critica,* ed. Gilberto Finzi (Milan: Mondadori, 1969); Sergio Pacifici, "Salvatore Quasimodo," *Cesare Barbieri Courier* 3 (1960), 10–16; Louis R. Rossi, "Salvatore Quasimodo: A Presentation," *Chicago Review* 14 (1960), 1–23.

Robert S. Dombroski

QUESTIONE DELLA LINGUA, the term used to indicate the centuries-long controversy over the proper definition of the national standard language (often equated with the literary language) of Italy. Three interrelated and mutually dependent elements—political disunity, strong regional dialectalism, and a geographic situation unfavorable to rapid communication —have been largely responsible for the origin, permanence, and vitality of the *questione* in Italy. The roots of this problem are primarily political and may be traced to the anomalous linguistic configuration of pre-Roman Italy, which was the natural consequence of geographically isolated settlements by peoples of diverse language heritages (Osca, Umbrian, Gaulish, Liguric, etc.). The affirmation and expansion of Latin under the Roman Republic, and especially the Empire, hastened the demise of these languages, which were nevertheless important, as linguistic substrata, in determining certain regional phonological and morphological peculiarities. In the half millennium following the fall of the Empire (476), the linguistic and political topography of the Italian peninsula was continually disrupted and altered by numerous foreign invaders (Visigoths, Ostrogoths, Langobards, Franks, etc.). In broad terms, linguistic evolution on the Italian peninsula mirrors the changing political structure: the ancient languages were supplanted by Latin, which yielded to Vulgar Latin, which was eventually overcome by the Italian (Romance) vernacular(s). The Italian *questione* is then the most recent in a long series of struggles for predominance between the written literary language and the common spoken idiom.

The *questione della lingua* may be divided chronologically and ideologically into two distinct phases: first, the competition for preeminence between Latin and the vernacular and, second, the determination of the proper characteristics of the national language. While the earliest record of the Italian vernacular is contained in Latin legal documents dating from 960 (the *placiti cassinesi* or Cassinese decrees), its first appearance in what could be called a "literary" text came some two centuries later in the several *ritmi* or verses (Cassinese, Laurenziano, Sant'Alessio); in the *Laudes creaturarum* by St. Francis*; and finally in the refined lyrics of the Sicilian School. By the first part of the Duecento, the vernacular seems to have won the advantage over Latin. At the same time, however, the numerous and diverse Italian dialects reflect the chaotic political state of the peninsula and attest to its linguistic disunity. In retrospect, it would appear that the first attempt to deal, albeit unconsciously, with this problem was made by the poets at Frederick II's* court, whose extensive lyric production in Sicilian dialect by poets from various regions had a twofold effect. First, it provided Italy with a desperately needed literary heritage in the vernacular; and, second, it raised one dialect to the level of a literary language equal to those of Provence, northern France, and Germany. The poetic language they forged was then "tuscanized" by copyists during its transmission in manuscript, and in this guise their lyrics served as a model to subsequent generations of poets (Bonagiunta da Lucca,* Guittone d'Arezzo,* the *stilnovisti,* Petrarch,* et al.). Dante* was the first to come to grips with the *questione* in modern terms. In *De vulgari eloquentia,* he examines fourteen major Italian dialects in order to determine which one would merit becoming the national literary language, and he concludes that, while none of them possesses in itself all requisite qualities, each has certain excellent features which could be combined to form this perfect idiom. In his treatise, Dante is concerned solely with artistic style in poetic composition, with the speech he describes as "illustrious, cardinal, courtly and curial," and not with the larger issue of a common national language for all Italians. Nevertheless, after the *Convivio* in which Dante demonstrated the capacity of the vernacular to express philosophical concepts, the *Divina Commedia* through its mixture of styles and essentially Florentine basis represents his final statement on and his practical resolution of the problem of language. Although Dante's example had considerable linguistic influence on subsequent ages, the Florentine Trecento furnished two other representatives of vernacular eloquence: Petrarch for poetry *(Canzoniere)* and Boccaccio* for prose *(Decameron)*. Together, these "three crowns" firmly established Florentine as the literary language par excellence and one which should serve as the model for the linguistic unification of Italy.

Despite their success with the vernacular, Petrarch and Boccaccio were constant in their belief that Latin was a more noble language. By using it for all of their "serious" works, they paved the way linguistically and intellectually for the humanistic movement which swept across Italy from the late Trecento through the Quattrocento. During this latter period, there were several attempts (by Leon Battista Alberti,* et al.) to raise Italian to the dignity of the classical tongues. In the last quarter of the fifteenth century, these attempts led to the creation of a sort of vernacular humanism largely through the efforts of Lorenzo de' Medici,* Poliziano,* Boiardo,* and Sannazaro.* Following the triumph of the vernacular over Latin as a valid and worthy vehicle of expression, eminently more adaptable to the needs of contemporary society, and given that the advent of printing necessitated some form of standardization to serve the largest possible reading public, the attention of scholars during the Cinquecento was directed toward determining the character of the national language and the rules of grammar and orthography. Thus begins the second phase of the *questione della lingua.*

In the first part of the sixteenth century, the debate centered on which idiom should be both model and basis for the national language. Each of the following candidates had numerous and prominent supporters: (1) the archaic usage of the Trecento found in Petrarch and Boccaccio (Pietro Bembo,* *Prose della volgar lingua* [1525, Writings in the Vernacular Language]; and Sperone Speroni*); (2) an eclectic (i.e., non-Tuscan and nonarchaic) *lingua cortigiana* based on the language used in the various Italian courts (Vincenzo Calmeta, 1460–1508; Mario Equicola, 1470–1525; Baldassare Castiglione*), or *lingua comune* (Gian Giorgio Trissino;* G. P. Valeriano, 1477–1560; Girolamo Muzio, 1496–1576); and (3) contemporary spoken Florentine or Tuscan (Niccolò Machiavelli;* G. B. Gelli;* Claudio Tolomei, 1492–1557; Benedetto Varchi*). Of these three currents, the one supported by Bembo won the most favor and continued to prevail primarily through the efforts of Lionardo Salviati* and the Accademia della Crusca, whose *Vocabolario* (published in 1612) confirmed this pro-Tuscan, archaistic tendency. The influence of the Accademia (reinforced by subsequent editions of the *Vocabolario* in 1623, 1691, 1729–38) predominated for over two centuries, but not without fierce opposition from individuals such as Bernardo Davanzati (1529–1606),

Alessandro Tassoni,* Paolo Beni (1552–1625), Alessandro Verri* (and other contributors to *Il Caffè*), Giuseppe Baretti* (in *La frustra letteraria*), and finally, toward the end of the eighteenth century, Melchiorre Cesarotti,* who advocated (in his *Saggio sopra la lingua italiana* [1785, Essay on the Philosophy of Language]) the liberal adoption in the standard language of all words (dialectal and foreign, especially French) for which no Italian term existed.

Just as the linguistic purism and archaism fostered by the Cruscans may have fulfilled during those dark centuries of foreign domination a vital cultural need (i.e., as the symbol of *toscanità*, and by extension *italianità*), so by Cesarotti's time there were other social, political, and cultural forces in operation (rationalism, sensism, Arcadia/anti-Arcadia, Frugonianism, and the growth of science), which militated against traditional linguistic conservatism. While the Crusca still had some supporters (Antonio Cesari, 1760–1828), the prevailing attitude was to move away from its extreme provincialism and archaism and to work, on the one hand, toward the realization of a refined, cultured, literary language (classicism: Vincenzo Monti*) or, on the other hand, to transform the linguistic question into a social and political one which would involve all Italy (romanticism*: Alessandro Manzoni*). As the most authoritative voice on these matters in the nineteenth century, Manzoni was firmly convinced of the absolute necessity of approximating the written to the spoken language. This concern is amply demonstrated by his successive revisions of *I promessi sposi,* where he consciously substituted contemporary Florentine equivalents for the original Milanese expressions and altered literary archaisms according to standard Tuscan usage. After the political unification of Italy (1861), Manzoni continued his active role in the linguistic controversy. Indeed, in 1868 he was appointed head of the national commission charged with determining the characteristics of a suitable national idiom and the means of diffusing it among the Italian populace. Among other things, he proposed that Florentine be the basis of the common language and that a dictionary of contemporary Florentine usage be compiled. These recommendations ultimately received the decisive stamp of approval from the government. Nevertheless, for all his theorizing, Manzoni's greatest contribution toward resolving the controversy probably lies in his revisions of *I promessi sposi,* where, by demonstrating the essential unity of the spoken and written word, of language as the bridge between life and literature, he provided a worthy and much imitated model.

In the century since unification, many factors (technological, sociological, ideological, educational, and political) have assisted the spread of the standard language throughout Italy. Radio, television, motion pictures, newspapers, and magazines have brought the standard idiom to millions; rapid train transit and the construction of *autostrade* have increased the mobility of Italians and thus broken down regional linguistic barriers; the centralized government with the capital first at Florence, and then in Rome, together with its program of compulsory education and conscription, has had a strong stabilizing influence on the national language. In Italy today the *questione della lingua,* at least in its traditional historical sense, is dead, and the furor which surrounded it for centuries has long subsided. To be sure, other problems, new questions, different in kind, more restricted in scope and generally less serious, will inevitably arise as a matter of course. However, with appropriate modifications, the national standard language, the excellent and flexible product of this lengthy controversy, will long endure.

Bibliography: Giacomo Devoto, *Il linguaggio d'Italia: storia e strutture linguistiche italiane dalla Preistoria ai nostri giorni* (Milan: Rizzoli, 1974); Robert A. Hall, Jr., *The Italian Questione della Lingua: An Interpretative Essay* (Chapel Hill, N.C.: University of North Carolina Press, 1942); Thérèse Labande-Jeanroy, *La Question de la langue en Italie* (Strasbourg: Publications de la Faculté des Lettres de l'Université de Strasbourg, No. 27, 1925); Bruno Migliorini, "La questione de la lingua," in *Questioni e correnti di storia letteraria* (Milan: Marzorati, 1949), pp. 1–75, and *The Italian Language* (New York: Barnes & Noble, 1966); B. T. Sozzi, *Aspetti e momenti della questione linguistica* (Padua: Liviana, 1955); Maurizio Vitale, *La questione della lingua* (Palermo: Palumbo, 1960).

Christopher Kleinhenz

R

REA, DOMENICO (1921–   ), Neapolitan short-story writer and novelist. Rea's writings reflect varied foreign sources, including Russian and American novels. Of humble origins, Rea educated himself largely through avidly reading books borrowed from the library of a friend and through early contacts with local intellectuals. His first book, *La figlia di Casimiro Clarus* (1945, The Daughter of Casimiro Clarus), the tale of a love affair between a poor school teacher and the daughter of a rich landowner, was favorably reviewed. Succeeding collections of memorable Neapolitan tales included *Spaccanapoli* (1947, The Spaccanapoli Quarter); *Gesù, fate luce* (1950, Jesus, Shed Your Light), which received the Viareggio Prize in 1951; and *Quel che vide Cummeo* (1955, What Cummeo Saw). Although his talents seem best suited to the short story, he has written several novels, including *Una vampata di rossore* (1959, *A Blush of Shame*). Usually linked to the Italian neorealist movement, Rea is one of the more distinguished Neapolitan exemplars of that style.

Bibliography: Gesù, fate luce –Spaccanapoli (Milan: Mondadori, 1972); *A Blush of Shame,* trans. Maureen Duffy (London: Barrie & Rockliff, 1963); Corrado Piancastelli, *Domenico Rea* (Florence: La Nuova Italia, 1975).

RÈBORA, CLEMENTE (1885–1957), Milanese poet. Rèbora's first literary works drew inspiration from the cultural milieu associated with the Florentine periodical *La Voce*. In 1913, *La Voce* published *Frammenti lirici* (Lyrical Fragments), Rèbora's first collection of verse, which makes manifest his desire to understand the world in its entirety and his belief that a spiritual crisis gripped his contemporaries. At the outbreak of World War I, he was enlisted by the military, wounded seriously, and discharged from the army. This experience moved him to oppose war and violence in future writings. In 1919, he abandoned his teaching position in the public schools and supported himself in Milan by giving private lessons and teaching in evening schools, living in the poorest quarter of the city and sharing his meals with the least of its citizens. In 1920, his translation of Tolstoy's *Happy Ever After* appeared, followed by his version of Gogol's *The Overcoat* in 1922. During the same year, he published *Canti anonimi* (Anonymous Songs), containing one of his best poems, "Dall'imagine tesa" ("Tense-faced"). This poem mirrors the hope that guided him to a spiritual conversion in 1929 and, finally, to enter a religious order in 1931. After taking his vows in 1936, Rèbora remained isolated from the mainstream of Italian literature until 1956, when he published *I canti dell'infermità* (Songs of Illness), comprised of lyrical works written after 1946. By this time, he had identified poetry with liturgy; verse had become a concrete means of expressing his love for God and his fellow man.

Bibliography: Le poesie 1913–1957, ed. Vanni Scheiwiller (Milan: Pesce d'oro, 1961); *Twentieth-Century Italian Poetry: A Bilingual Anthology,* trans. Margherita Marchione (Rutherford, N.J.: Fairleigh Dickinson University Press, 1974); *Omaggio a Clemente Rèbora* (Bologna: Boni, 1971)—includes articles by Carlo Betocchi, Mario Luzi, Eugenio Montale, and Vittorio Sereni; Marziano Guglielminetti, *Clemente Rèbora* (Milan: Mursia, 1968); Margherita Marchione, *L'imagine tesa: la vita e l'opera di Clemente Rèbora* (Rome: Edizioni di storia e letteratura, 1960).

REDI, FRANCESCO (1626–1698), physician, scientist, academician, and poet. Redi, born in Arezzo, received a Jesuit education and took a degree in medicine and philosophy in 1647. After brief stays in Naples, Venice, and Rome, he came to Florence in 1654 to become the court physician of Ferdinando II, grand duke of Tuscany. Redi's father had held the position before him, and Redi continued in this capacity under the successive reign of Cosimo III until his death. In 1655, he joined the Accademia della Crusca, where he favored a language without pedantry which would respect the grand linguistic traditions of the Trecento. Besides becoming the public lecturer on the Tuscan language in 1663, Redi joined the Accademia dell'Arcadia* under the name Anicio Traustio. More significantly, he was one of the moving forces behind a group of Italy's foremost scientists, the Accademia del Cimento, which continued the scientific tradition of Galileo.* In this way, Redi achieved a reputation throughout Europe as a scientist.

Redi established himself as one of Europe's most distinguished biologists through several works, the chief among them being *Esperienze intorno alla generazione degli insetti* (1668, *Experiments on the Generation of Insects*), which refuted the then widely held notion of spontaneous generation. As a collector of rare manuscripts, Redi was instrumental in preserving the works of many writers, the most famous of which is the autobiography of Benvenuto Cellini.* Besides a collection of love poetry written in imitation of the great Italian lyric poets from the Duecento until his time, Redi's greatest contribution to literature was a dithyrambic poem *Bacco in Toscana* (1685, *Bacchus in Tuscany*), perhaps the only masterpiece in any modern language of this classical genre which celebrates Bacchus and wine. In the thousand lines of this work, begun in 1666 and finally published in 1685 with copious annotations, Redi describes the arrival of Bacchus in Tuscany accompanied by Ariadne and a host of satyrs and bacchantes. During the course of the poem, a goodly number of local wines are sampled and evaluated, other drinks are condemned, and Bacchus becomes increasingly inebriated. The poem was widely read both because of the originality of its thematic content (which sometimes taxes the imagination with its virtuosity) and because of Redi's artful use of language and his various and unusual combinations of rhymes.

See also ARCADIA; CELLINI, Benvenuto.

Bibliography: Opere, 9 vols. (Milan: Società tipografica, 1809–11); *Bacchus in Tuscany, A Dithyrambic Poem,* trans. Leigh Hunt (London: Privately printed, 1825); *Experiments on the Generation of Insects,* trans. Mab Bigelow (Chicago: Open Court, 1909); Eric Cochrane, *Florence in the Forgotten Centuries: 1527–1800* (Chicago: University of Chicago Press, 1973); C. A. Madrignani, "La poetica di Francesco Redi nella Firenze letteraria di fine Seicento," *Belfagor* 15 (1960), 402–14, and "Il metodo scientifico di Francesco Redi," *Rassegna della letteratura italiana* 65 (1961), 476–500.

RENAISSANCE, the period in the history of Italian civilization running approximately from the middle of the fourteenth century to the close of the sixteenth. Although Renaissance Italians did not use the term itself to identify the historical period in which they lived, they possessed a general awareness of the distinctiveness of their own time, an historical self-consciousness that separated them absolutely from their predecessors in the Middle Ages. From Petrarch* on, they divided history, not according to the Christian scheme of ages before the Law, after the Law, and after Grace, but according to a secular one: classical antiquity, followed by what they dubbed the Dark or Middle Ages, and then the period they hailed as the Rebirth. Moreover, Renaissance thinkers were aware of the uniqueness of those periods—and of subperiods within them—and they discovered the concept of anachronism, a discovery made possible by their recognition that historical periods are unique and that historical change proceeds in ways amenable to rational analysis. By the time Vasari* composed his monumental *Lives of the Artists* (1568) in the mid-sixteenth century, Renaissance men's historical periodization had become a cliché and their historical self-consciousness inescapable.

When Renaissance thinkers identified their own age as the Rebirth, they meant by that the recovery or rediscovery of classical antiquity. Although medieval art, religion, philosophy, and social and political institutions continued to exert a strong influence throughout the period, men in the Renaissance did quite consciously reject much in medieval culture and attempted to resurrect ancient culture within their own. The period saw a tremendous expansion in the knowledge of antiquity, as artists and archaeologists dug up relics of the past, and humanists and philosophers and scientists dug out the manuscripts of classical writers long buried in monasteries. They recovered the texts of Plato, Lucretius, Catullus, Tacitus, and countless other Latin and Greek authors. Yet, the mere recovery of such texts does not really explain the Renaissance, since the writers and works most important— with the major exception of Plato—were well known throughout the Middle Ages. What did produce the Renaissance was a new kind of interest in ancient culture, an awareness of its historical identity and uniqueness, and a desire to preserve and imitate the essential qualities defining its artifacts. Where a medieval Latin poet wrote a hymn to the Virgin in the classical elegiac meter, a Renaissance poet restored that meter to its original purpose, writing a secular love poem to his mistress and employing a classical Latin style based entirely on the writings of ancient poets. Similarly, Renaissance architects studied ancient buildings to rediscover the essential principles of their design; prose writers consciously imitated the style and sentiments of Cicero or Seneca; historians followed Livy or Suetonius; and philosophers developed systems of thought out of Plato or Aristotle or Lucretius. To be sure, Renaissance men's recreations of antiquity always differed from it in some respect, and they were always conscious that an immense gulf lay between their own age and that period before the Christian revelation. Yet antiquity remained the center of their attention, a challenge to artists, a problem for theologians and philosophers, and an invitation to creative adaptation for everyone.

The Italian Renaissance may be conveniently, if simplistically, divided into two phases: an ascending phase stretching from Petrarch and Boccaccio* through the first decades of the sixteenth century, and a descending phase running the length of that century. The ascending phase is generally characterized by a basic optimism about man, social idealism, enthusiasm over the recovery of classical culture, and a belief that it could be harmonized with medieval institutions and particularly Christianity. It was also a time of great prosperity for Italy, the intensive cultivation of all the arts, the soaring growth of city-states from Venice to Florence to Naples and magnificent courts in Milan, Mantua, Urbino, and Rome. A profound optimism characterizes much of the literature of this period and is especially noticeable in the works of the humanists, in their countless dialogues and treatises on ideal princes and teachers and courtiers, families, and cities. This optimism rests on their historical self-consciousness and their vision of man and his culture freed from predetermined theological schemata. If man and his culture are unique, then they must be open to development in new directions, to reach heights well above previous levels of achievement. It became possible for Renaissance men to dream of utopias inhabited by humanistically trained elites. Consequently, the literary and philosophical works of this long period, from Boccaccio's

Decameron (1349–51) through Leon Battista Alberti's* *Libri della famiglia* (1433–43, *The Family in Renaissance Florence*) down to Pico della Mirandola's* *Oratio de hominis dignitate* (1486, *Oration on the Dignity of Man*), and Baldesar Castiglione's* *Il libro del Cortegiano* (1528, *The Book of the Courtier*), all not only offer idealistic visions of man and society, but are based on the optimistic assumption that men are educable, society improvable, and the writer's and reformer's task really possible.

Although there were gloomy and pessimistic exceptions during the ascending phase of the Renaissance (Petrarch himself was hardly a model of self-confidence), from the beginning of the sixteenth century the very freedom of man which before had proved so heady became a source of insecurity and anxiety, and the mood of Italian literature grew increasingly dark. During this century, artistic classicism hardened into rigid dogma and academicism; the Council of Trent (1545–63), called to respond to the Protestant challenge, gave new life to the Index and the Inquisition and ultimately stifled the development of Italian science, philosophy, and culture; and the Sack of Rome (1527) by the troops of Charles V led to the eventual Spanish (and papal) domination of the peninsula and the suppression of republican freedoms everywhere. Denying humanist optimism quite directly, Machiavelli* and Guicciardini* offer pessimistic, cynical views of human nature as unstable, eternally striving, and insatiable. Ariosto* treats all human ideals and aspirations with gentle, but unmistakable skepticism, and a strong nostalgia for a vanished paradise marks the *Arcadia* (1502) of Sannazaro* and the countless pastoral* poems and plays that followed it throughout the century. Although the celebration of the individual self, the God-rivaling artist, can be detected in the works of Cellini* and Vasari, it is more than balanced by the tortured despair of Michelangelo's* poetry, the frustration of Petrarchan imitators like Giovanni della Casa,* and the melancholy sense of human limitation and failure which haunts the works of Torquato Tasso.* This last great Renaissance poet epitomizes the declining culture of the Renaissance; his life was marked by paranoid suspicions, haughty rivalries, and ultimate insanity and incarceration. His epic* poem, *Gerusalemme liberata* (1570–75, *Jerusalem Delivered*), occasioned endless petty academic debates and challenges over its morality and religion.

See also HUMANISM.

Bibliography: Jacob Burckhardt, *The Civilisation of the Renaissance in Italy* (New York: Random House, 1954; original ed. 1860); Wallace K. Ferguson, *The Renaissance in Historical Thought* (Boston: Houghton-Mifflin, 1948); Eugenio Garin, *Italian Humanism*, trans. Peter Munz (1965; rpt. Westport, Conn.: Greenwood Press, 1975); Myron Gilmore, "The Renaissance Conception of the Lessons of History," in *Facets of the Renaissance,* ed. William H. Werkmeister (New York: Harper & Row, 1959), pp. 73–86; Thomas M. Greene, "The Flexibility of the Self in Renaissance Literature," in *The Disciplines of Criticism*, eds. Peter Demetz, Thomas Greene, and Lowry Nelson, Jr. (New Haven, Conn.: Yale University Press, 1968), pp. 241–64; Hiram Haydn, *The Counter-Renaissance* (New York: Harcourt, 1950); Erwin Panofsky, *Renaissance and Renascences in Western Art*, 2 vols. (Stockholm: Almqvist & Wiksell, 1960).

                                                                            Wayne A. Rebhorn

RINALDO D'AQUINO (thirteenth century), poet of the Sicilian School active in the first half of the thirteenth century. Rinaldo's identity has not been ascertained, but he may have been a page and falconer of Frederick II* born in Montella nell'Irpinia (a place mentioned in "Amorosa donna fina,"["Gentle lady bearing love"]), who swore an oath of fidelity to the Angioini in 1266 and who received a benefice from Carlo I in 1270. Others identify him as the Rinaldo d'Aquino described in a document of 1242 with the title of magister who died between 1279 and 1281. The most interesting speculation connects the poet with the illustrious house of Aquino. As the story goes, in 1243 or 1244 Rinaldo, aided by Pier della Vigna,* kidnapped his brother Thomas from the Dominicans and detained him in the family castle of San Giovanni in order to dissuade him from joining that order. However, his efforts were to prove futile; the future St. Thomas escaped and returned to the church.

The extant poetry consists of one sonnet* and a dozen *canzoni* * which sing of a lady of Messina. Dante* twice praises the canzone "Per fin'amore vao sì allegramente" (For true love I go so joyfully) in *De vulgari eloquentia* (I, xii; II, v), which is not now considered among his best. In general, he is faithful to the Provençal heritage in his language and in the treatment of love, the obligations of a servant of love, and the duties of the lady. He transports the *fin'amor* of Provence to the Sicilian court with little innovation in such poems as "Amorosa donna fina," "Ormai quando flore e mostrano verdura" ("Now when meadow and bank"), and "Guiderdone aspetto avire" ("I expect a reward"). Still, his poetry is distinctive because of his skill in handling the traditional forms and themes. His most noted lyric, "Già mai non mi conforto" ("I shall never more take comfort"), is a traditional *chanson de croisade* (crusade song) which also shows the influence of the popular lyric. In the name of a woman who is disconsolate over her lover's departure for the Holy Land, Rinaldo composes a poem which expresses with simplicity and poignancy the distress such separations cause. The lady's state of mind is reflected by the confusion of prayers and laments throughout the poem; she recommends her lover to God's protection while she reproaches the Cross for destroying her happiness. Finally, she asks the jongleur Dolcietto to write a proper sonnet which she can send to Syria. Rinaldo is the most important Sicilian after Giacomino Pugliese* to rejuvenate courtly poetry by adapting themes and techniques from the popular lyric.

Bibliography: Le Rime della scuola siciliana, ed. Bruno Panvini (Florence: Olschki, 1962); *German and Italian Lyrics of the Middle Ages,* trans. Frederick Goldin (Garden City, N.Y.: Doubleday, 1973); *The Penguin Book of Italian Verse,* ed. George R. Kay (Baltimore: Penguin Books, 1965).

RISORGIMENTO: *See* ROMANTICISM.

RISPETTO: *See* STRAMBOTTO.

ROBORTELLO, FRANCESCO (1516–1567), humanist and critic. A native of Udine, Robortello was educated at the University of Bologna and served as a professor at the universities of Lucca, Pisa, Bologna, and, lastly, Padua, where he remained for most of his life. A polemical scholar, he carried on critical debates with many of the great humanists of his day, including Erasmus and Henri Estienne. He contributed the first extensive Renaissance* commentary on Aristotle's *Poetics, In librum Aristotelis de arte poetica explicationes* (Commentary on Aristotle's *Poetics*), which appeared in 1548. Aristotle's treatise had been known during the Middle Ages from a summary by Averroes, but its significance was not realized until a Latin version published by Aldine Press in 1498 made the text readily available. Robortello's version was the first edition of Aristotle's poetics in classical Greek and preceded the first Italian translation of Bernardo Segni (1504–1558) by one year. Even more important, in a sense, than the established text in the original language was Robortello's Latin commentary. Robortello applied his own literary theories to Aristotle's text and clearly turned from Aristotle's emphasis upon poetics and formal considerations in literature to an interest in rhetoric and moral persuasion. For him, poetry had several ends: the Horatian ends of pleasure and usefulness as well as the Aristotelian end of imitation. Pleasure, he stated, may be derived from imitation which becomes an intermediate rather than an ultimate goal, and poetry may imitate any object, not merely human passions and actions, as Aristotle had suggested. Pleasure may also be derived from the solution of a difficult problem or the admiration one feels for the marvelous and the extraordinary. In addition, Robortello wrote several fundamental treatises on satire, comedy, humor, the elegy, and comedy as well as a summary of Horace's *Ars poetica* (The Art of Poetry), all of which were appended to his commentary in a separate section of the volume.

Bibliography: Bernard Weinberg, "Robertello on the *Poetics*," in R. S. Crane, et al., *Critics and Criticism: Ancient and Modern* (Chicago: University of Chicago

Press, 1952), pp. 319–48, and *A History of Literary Criticism in the Italian Renaissance,* 2 vols. (Chicago: University of Chicago Press, 1961).

ROLLI, PAOLO ANTONIO (1687–1765), poet, teacher, translator, editor, and librettist. Rolli was born in Rome. He came under the influence of Gian Vicenza Gravina* and entered the Accademia dell'Arcadia* in 1708 with the academic title Eulibio Brentiatico. When Gravina left Arcadia to form the rival Accademia dei Quirini in 1714, Rolli accompanied his mentor. At the invitation of Thomas Herbert, eighth earl of Pembroke, Rolli moved to England in 1716 and there began a fruitful career in letters, for many years serving as a vital link between Italian and English culture. He immediately disseminated Italian literature in England by producing an edition of the satires and verse of Ariosto* (1716), an Italian translation of *On the Nature of Things* by Lucretius (1717), and a volume of his own poetry (1717). Rolli's lyrics reflect his sound background in classical Greek and Latin literature. His interest in novel verse forms and his taste for pastoral* lyrics and poetry in the manner of Virgil and Anacreon made him a favorite poet of those times in Italy, and in some ways he was as popular as Metastasio*. His own translations of Anacreon appeared in 1739. At least one of his lyrics which appeared in another collection published in 1727—a *canzonetta* entitled "Solitario bosco ombroso" ("Lonely forest, shade-possessed")—was considered so beautiful by the young Goethe that he committed it to memory.

Appointed tutor to the children of the prince of Wales (later George II), Rolli became the Italian secretary to the Royal Academy of Music which was founded in 1719 to encourage the performance of Italian melodrama.* In this position, he became associated with the academy's director Handel and wrote a number of *libretti* for him, including *Floridante* (1721, Floridante), *Scipione* (1726, Scipio), *Alessandro* (1726, Alexander), and *Riccardo I* (1727, Richard I). *Muzio Scevola* (1721, Mutius Scaevola) combines a Rolli *libretto* with music by Handel, Filippo Amadei (born 1683), and Handel's rival Giovanni Bononcini (1672–1748). Rolli apparently considered his collaboration with such composers of less consequence than his editorial and scholarly work. From editions of Guarini's* *Pastor fido* (1718, *The Faithful Shepherd*), Berni's* lyrics (1720, 1724) and Boccaccio's* *Decameron* (1725), he turned to Italian translations of English literature. The most famous is his version in blank verse of Milton's *Paradise Lost* (1729–35), complete except for several brief passages omitted in order to avoid problems of censorship in Italy. The edition included an excellent essay on Milton and his life, the problems of translating English blank verse, and the impact of the Italian classics upon English literature. His analysis of Chaucer's debt to Dante,* Boccaccio, and Petrarch,* as well as the relationship of Shakespeare's *Othello* and its source, a *novella* by Giambattista Giraldi,* is one of the first discussions of specifically comparative problems. Among his other translations are a version of Steele's *The Conscious Lovers* (1724, *Gli amanti interni*) and the first Italian version of any passage from Shakespeare—Hamlet's soliloquy "To be or not to be" (1739). Elected a Fellow of the Royal Society in 1729, Rolli published a single scientific paper on a curious case of two deaths by what he considered to be spontaneous combustion. This paper was translated into French and was even indirectly used as a source by Charles Dickens in *Bleak House* (Chapter XXXIII).

Like so many Italians abroad, Rolli sometimes felt obliged to defend his national culture against its detractors. Even before Baretti's* quarrel with Voltaire, Rolli's *Remarks Upon M. Voltaire's Essay on the Epick Poetry of the European Nations* (1728) answered the Frenchman's rather shallow estimate of the merits of the Italian epic* poets and Milton as well. Apparently, his specific corrections and criticisms were effective, for many of his remarks were incorporated into Voltaire's revision of the essay which was republished in French in 1732. In 1744, Rolli finally returned to Italy and remained there until his death. His later life was somewhat uneventful when compared to his illustrious career in London, but he translated several of Racine's plays into Italian and a posthumous work by Sir Isaac Newton entitled *Chronology of Ancient Kingdoms* (1757), while composing several minor literary works. Rolli's tireless efforts in the cause of Italian culture abroad did much to keep alive an interest in Italy among the learned, upper-class Englishmen whose society he frequented. His death ended the career of one of the century's most gifted Anglophiles.

See also ARCADIA; BARETTI, Giuseppe; ENLIGHTENMENT.

Bibliography: I lirici del Seicento e dell'Arcadia, ed. Carlo Calcaterra (Milan: Rizzoli, 1936); *Lirici del Settecento,* eds. Bruno Maier and Mario Fubini (Milan: Ricciardi, 1959); *From Marino to Marinetti,* trans. Joseph Tusiani (New York: Baroque Press, 1974); G. E. Dorris, *Paolo Rolli and the Italian Circle in London 1715–1744* (The Hague: Mouton, 1967); Franco Fido, "Dall'Arcadia all'Europa e ritorno," *Italica* 45 (1968), 365–76.

ROMANTICISM. As a literary movement, Italian romanticism was born in 1816, when Madame de Staël published in the *Biblioteca italiana* her essay, "Sulla maniera e l'utilità delle traduzioni" (On the Manner and Usefulness of Translations), which invited the Italians to renew their literary tradition by reading and translating works of foreign literatures. Obviously, the reactions to this program were twofold. While many considered it a betrayal of the Italian and classical traditions, others realized the necessity of offering an alternative to the static and imitative culture of the time. This latter camp produced a number of polemical and programmatic statements.

Among them, the most influential were Ludovico Di Breme's* *Intorno all'ingiustizia di alcuni giudizi letterari italiani* (June 1816, Discourse Concerning the Injustice of Some Italian Literary Judgments); Pietro Borsieri's* *Avventure letterarie di un giorno* (September 1816, Literary Adventures of a Day); and Giovanni Berchet's* *Sul Cacciatore feroce e sulla Eleonora di G. A. Bürger: Lettera semiseria di Grisostomo al suo figlio* (December 1816, On the "Fierce Hunter" and "Leonora" of G. A. Bürger: The Semiserious Letter from Chrysostom to His Son). Berchet proposed a more popular and didactic form of literature, which would be possible only when his contemporaries' adherence to the classical tradition was superseded by a more innovative response to the romantic spirit. Voicing the ideas of M. de Staël and A. W. Schlegel, this program inspired the journal *Il Conciliatore* (1818–19) which was suppressed in 1819 by Austrian authorities who feared the libertarian and liberal ideas aired in its columns. Finally, it resulted in Alessandro Manzoni's* letters *Sul romanticismo* (1823, On Romanticism) and the *Lettre à M. Chauvet* (Letter to M. Chauvet), in which the organic and romantic structure of Shakespearean tragedies takes precedence over the classical works of Racine.

The romantic reception of Shakespeare's works can be traced back to Alfieri,* who stopped reading Shakespeare for fear of becoming too much influenced by him. Alfieri's proto-romanticism also identifies the indigenous roots of Italian romanticism. At the time of the *Sturm und Drang,* his study of the growth of the *pianta uomo* (man-tree) brought to light a titanic individualism intolerant of social conventions and political restrictions. His treatises *Della Tirannide* (1789, *On Tyranny*) and *Del principe e delle lettere* (1785–86, *The Prince and Letters*) set up the political character of Italian romanticism. Although theoretical and quite extraneous to the realities of the time, Alfieri's relentless call to freedom acquired a historical and social consciousness in Ugo Foscolo's *Dei sepolcri* (1807, *On Sepulchres*). His spiritual legacy was to spearhead the Risorgimento, which unified Italy under the monarchic leadership of Piedmont after three wars of independence.

Ugo Foscolo's works exemplify typical features of the age. It is the political element that differentiates *Le ultime lettere di Jacopo Ortis* (1798–1802, *Last Letters of Jacopo Ortis*) from its prototype, Goethe's *Sorrows of Young Werther.* On the other hand, his odes and *Le grazie* (after 1812, "The Graces") bring to light the classical component of Italian romanticism that was to lead, later in the century, to Carducci* and D'Annunzio.* This interest in the classics followed the Greek revival of the English romantics in spite of Manzoni's firm opposition to any form of classical imitation. Although romantic at heart, even Leopardi* looked on the "romantic" phenomenon with suspicion in his *Discorso d'un italiano intorno alla poesia romantica* (1818, *Discourse of an Italian Concerning*

Romantic Poetry). Whatever their attitude toward antiquity, the Italian romantics preserved the classical notions of measure, restraint, and a certain objectivity. Even Leopardi's interpretation of the infinite ("L'infinito") remained extraneous to the more visionary, psychological, and ineffable side of romanticism, which would surface later in the century in the poetics of *scapigliatura** and *decadentismo.** At a literary level, therefore, romanticism was not as revolutionary in Italy as in northern cultures. Besides the classical heritage, even the cultural circle of *Il Conciliatore* aimed, as the word implies, at moderation and reconciliation, aware as it was of the reformist heritage of the eighteenth century, from Parini* to the group of *Il Caffé*.

This strict adherence to the sociopolitical realities of the time produced an inflationary literature burdened with oratorical and propagandistic overtones. In its more universal expressions, however, such a consciousness produced a fresh outlook on history and society at large. The concepts of independence and republicanism gave new dimensions to the traditional notions of heroic individualism. Disillusioned by Napoleon's betrayal of his revolutionary ideals, Foscolo turned against all personifications of absolute power. The hero of *Dei sepolcri* is not Achilles, but Hector: the victim overshadows the victor. Likewise, Leopardi celebrates Brutus, not Caesar. In Manzoni's tragedy *Adelchi* (1822), the young prince Adelchi recognizes the guilt and responsibilities of his father and his peers, who have thrived on the exploitation of the people. In this sense, Manzoni seems to introduce the notion of historical nemesis, which reappeared in the works of Carducci. Although often expressed in negative terms, the conception of historical progress gained strength and conviction with Mazzini* and Gioberti.* The more pessimistic Leopardi dissolved contemporary issues into the eternal vicissitudes of life.

At a more social level, this antiheroic attitude precipitated a greater concern with and recognition of the simple and rustic life of common people. The peasants of William Wordsworth found appropriate company in the humanity Leopardi presented in his *Canti*. In *I promessi sposi (The Betrothed)*, not only simple folks but a whole rustic community became the protagonist of a novel that asserted itself as the prototype of the historical novel. Inspired by Walter Scott, Manzoni gave life to a tradition that was to gain highly propagandistic overtones throughout the Risorgimento, when the realistic component was often overshadowed by political considerations. In this context, even Manzoni's thoughtful search for an expressive language accessible to all Italians identified another contribution to the Risorgimento. This linguistic bond represented an alternative to the tyranny of French and the restrictions of the dialect. Under these historical conditions, autobiographical literature also reflected a didactic and political intent, from Pellico's* *Le mie prigioni* (1832, *My*

Prisons) to *Le ricordanze della mia vita* (1879, Remembrances of My Life) of Luigi Settembrini (1813–1876) and *I miei ricordi* (1868, *Things I Remember*) of D'Azeglio.* Giovanni Ruffini* wrote his *Lorenzo Benoni* (1853) and *Dottor Antonio* (1855) in English, so as to win the sympathy of English readers to the Italian cause. National glories were revived in Grossi's* *Marco Visconti* (1834, *Marco Visconti*) and D'Azeglio's *Niccolò dei Lapi* (1841, *Niccolò dei Lapi*), which exemplified the most popular expressions of the historical novel. With *Le confessioni di un italiano* (1857–58, *The Castle of Fratta*) by Ippolito Nievo,* the historical novel found a happy combination of character development, psychological insight, and historical context.

This moral and political commitment did not obscure a critical view of art sensitive to the romantic emphasis on freedom and individualism. In the tradition of Vico,* Gravina,* and Foscolo, Francesco De Sanctis* juxtaposed the social and moral function of art to the notion of artistic creation as an independent and imaginative product free of rules, in anticipation of the aesthetics of Benedetto Croce.*

Bibliography: Mario Fubini, *Romanticismo italiano* (Bari: Laterza, 1971); Robert F. Gleckner and Gerald E. Enscoe, eds., *Romanticism: Points of View,* 2nd ed. (Detroit, Mich.: Wayne State University Press, 1975); Gilbert Highet, *The Classical Tradition* (New York: Oxford University Press, 1957); Karl Kroeber, *The Artifice of Reality: Poetic Style in Wordsworth, Foscolo, Keats, and Leopardi* (Madison, Wis.: University of Wisconsin Press, 1964); Agostino Lombardo, "Shakespeare and Italian Criticism," in *The Disciplines of Criticism,* ed. Peter Demetz, et al. (New Haven, Conn.: Yale University Press, 1968); Mario Puppo, *Il romanticismo* (Rome: Editrice Studium, 1957); Luigi Salvatorelli, *The Risorgimento: Thought and Action* (New York: Harper, 1970); René Wellek, *Concepts of Criticism* (New Haven, Conn.: Yale University Press, 1963).

Giancarlo Maiorino

ROSA, SALVATORE (1615–1673), painter and satirical poet. Born into a poor family of painters near Naples, Rosa was educated in a religious order but had a greater calling to the fine arts than to theology. At the age of twenty, he left Naples for Rome, where he made a name for himself as an able painter of landscapes and battle scenes and as an active performer in the theatre of the period. Most of his productive years were spent in Rome, but during a period between 1641 and 1649 in Florence under the protection of the Medici family, he was introduced to the cultural life of the city and to the ambience of the Accademia della Crusca. It was in Florence that Rosa began the composition of his *Satire* (1694, Satires) in *terza rima,* * a work which is considered the most trenchant and typical example of this genre in a century noted for its satirical literature.

Rosa's seven satires were first recited to his close friends and remained unpublished at his death; the posthumous edition of 1694 was the first edition. The first three satires treat various artistic media from the perspectives of both an artist and a poet and deplore the miserable state of music, poetry, and painting in his day. In *La musica* (1640–41, Music), Rosa rejects the common mixture of sacred and profane elements in music and attacks the corruption of courts, priests, and princes. *La poesia* (Poetry), apparently composed in 1642, presents a critique of the exaggerated aspects of Marinism or Baroque* style and attacks literary pedantry. In *La pittura* (Painting), he assails painters for their ignorance and trivial subjects, which are not informed by abstract ideas or philosophical concepts. He finds fault with the decadent naturalism of their still-life paintings which are devoid of a moral purpose and designed only to flatter their patron's tastelessness. The remaining three satires appearing in the original edition include *L'invidia* (Envy), an attack upon Rosa's detractors and enemies, which was probably the product of his rather difficult and eccentric personality; *La Babilonia* (Babylon), a stinging denunciation of corruption in the Roman Curia in general and in the Chigi family in particular; and *La guerra* (War), an outcry against misgovernment and war, including a celebration of the popular uprising led by Tomaso Aniello (1620–1647) and provoked by the burdensome taxation of greedy rulers. *La guerra* was sufficient to create a legend around Rosa as a pre-Risorgimento patriot. The final satire, *Tirreno* (Tyrenus), an autobiographical work depicting the poet's loneliness and isolation in his later years, was published only in 1876.

Rosa's paintings often depict the wilder and most energetic aspects of nature, scenes of craggy mountains, rocky shorelines, storms, and battles. Many of them found an appreciative audience among the Englishmen of gentle birth and wealth who traveled throughout Italy during the eighteenth century on the Grand Tour. They played a small but significant role in fashioning the emergent romantic taste for natural spectacles in art and poetry. The reputation Rosa enjoyed in subsequent years was enhanced by the admiring but often inaccurate biography written by Lady Sydney Morgan (1783–1859)—a woman who was an important link between Italy and English romanticism—and by the fact that Rosa became the protagonist in one of E. T. A. Hoffmann's popular *Tales* (1814–22). Recent scholarship has only begun to explore the interrelationships between Rosa's poetry and his paintings.

Bibliography: Poesie e lettere inedite, ed. Uberto Limentani (Florence: Olschki, 1950); *La satira nel Seicento,* ed. Uberto Limentani (Milan: Ricciardi, 1961); Benedetto Croce, *Saggi sulla letteratura italiana del Seicento* (Bari: Laterza, 1962); Nancy R. Fabbri, "Salvatore Rosa's Engraving for Carlo de' Rossi and His

Satire, *Invidia*," *Journal of the Warburg and Courtauld Institutes* 33 (1970), 328–30; Lady Sydney Morgan, *The Life and Times of Salvator Rosa*, 2 vols. (London: H. Colburn, 1824).

ROSSETTI, GABRIELE (1783–1854), poet and patriot. Born at Vasto in the Abruzzi, Rossetti moved to Naples, joined the Arcadia,* and became known as a composer of light verse. He took an active part in the Neapolitan revolt of 1820. His best known work is perhaps a patriotic poem of significance to his contemporaries—"La costituzione in Napoli nel 1820" (The Constitution in Naples in 1820). Escaping from Naples and the victorious forces of reaction on an English ship bound for Malta, where he remained for three years, Rossetti finally arrived in England in 1824 to live there for the rest of his life, teaching at King's College and publishing various poetic and critical works. His four children—William Michaele, Maria Francesca, Cristina and, most famous of all, Dante Gabriele— possibly represent his greatest gift to his adopted homeland. Through their poetry and painting and their scholarship, the intellectual and literary relationships between Italy and England were strengthened and nourished in the late nineteenth century.

Rossetti composed a number of essays on Dante,* Beatrice, and the Middle Ages. One of his most eccentric ideas was that a secret society opposed to papal tyranny had existed in the Middle Ages and that Dante was a member of this group. Besides a commentary on Dante's *Inferno* (1826) which interpreted the poem as an antipapal political work, Rossetti composed an autobiography in verse, later translated by his son William. He exerted some influence upon future critics who tried to see a secret revelation or political message in Dante's poem, and he had an obvious influence upon the formation of his son's intellectual heritage and, thus, upon the Pre-Raphaelite Movement in England.

Bibliography: Poeti minori dell'Ottocento, ed. Luigi Baldacci, 2 vols. (Milan: Ricciardi, 1958); *Gabriele Rossetti: A Versified Autobiography,* trans. W. M. Rossetti (London: Sands, 1901); E. R. Vincent, *Gabriele Rossetti in England* (Oxford: Clarendon Press, 1936).

ROSSO DI SAN SECONDO, PIER MARIA (1887–1956), playwright. Rosso di San Secondo was born in Caltanissetta and moved to Rome to study law, where he made the acquaintance of Luigi Pirandello* and became the great dramatist's close friend. After service in World War I, he apparently took Pirandello's advice and transformed one of his *novelle** into a play entitled *Marionette, che passione!* (1917, Marionettes, What Passion!). His theatrical debut was a tremendous success, and this play, his acknowledged masterpiece, was promptly translated into several European languages. His drama was influenced by Pirandello and formed a part of what drama critics came to call the *teatro grottesco*.* Although Rosso di San Secondo's other works never won the acclaim of his first effort, some critics consider the later *La bella addormentata* (1919, Sleeping Beauty) to be his best play.

Marionette, che passione! concerns an absurd encounter between three characters at a telegraph office; they are merely referred to as The Lady with the Blue Fox Scarf, The Gentleman in Gray, and The Gentleman in Mourning. The three characters are puppets, moved by the passion of sensual love. The Gentleman in Gray finally takes poison, while the other two characters represent earlier stages of the same absurd despair. In *La bella addormentata*, Rosso di San Secondo presents what he terms a "colored adventure," the story of a village prostitute (Carmelita) who lives as if in a dream until she discovers herself pregnant and becomes a woman with a sense of dignity.

Rosso di San Secondo completed some thirty plays during his career. He represents a critical link between the turn-of-the-century dramatic style, which was evolving towards a sense of the absurd in the *teatro grottesco*, and the early works of Pirandello.

See also TEATRO GROTTESCO.

Bibliography: Teatro (Rome: Bulzoni, 1976); *Teatro (1911–1925)*, ed. Luigi Ferrante (Bologna: Cappelli, 1962); Luigi Ferrante, *Rosso di San Secondo* (Bologna: Cappelli, 1959); Lander MacClintock, *The Age of Pirandello* (Bloomington, Ind.: Indiana University Press, 1951); Adriano Tilgher, *Studi sul teatro contemporaneo* (Rome: Libreria di scienze e lettere, 1923).

ROVETTA, GEROLAMO (1851–1910), novelist and dramatist. Rovetta was born in Brescia. After his father's death, he took his inheritance and moved to Milan, making his theatrical debut with a comedy entitled *Un volo dal nido* (1875, A Flight from the Nest). He continued writing dramatic works, all of them rather typical of the bourgeois theatre of the period, including *La moglie di Don Giovanni* (1877, The Wife of Don Giovanni), *In sogno* (1878, In a Dream), and *Gli uomini pratici* (1879, Practical Men). After his popularity was assured by a pathetic, lacrimonious novel, *Mater dolorosa* (1882, Sorrowful Mother), Rovetta combined his work in the theatre with writing popular novels, such as *La baraonda* (1894, Babel), and *Il tenente dei lancieri* (1896, The Lieutenant of the Lancers).

Although Rovetta belonged to the fashionable society of Milan, his vision of this aspect of contemporary Italy was by no means optimistic. Influenced by Balzac, he hoped to depict the entire human comedy in his writings and to lay bare crucial economic factors which determine social relationships. Many of his plays reflect the dark underside of the times. For example, *I disonesti* (1892, The Dishonest Men) shows how a cashier's honesty is destroyed by circumstances leading him to embezzle funds from his employer, and *La realtà* (1895, Reality) rejects utopian socialism because of man's innately evil nature and shows successful men in society to be thieves or hypocrites. Rovetta's most popular play, *Romanticismo* (1901, Romanticism), is written in a different vein. It is a melodramatic picture of Italian resistance to Austria during the Risorgimento and has a patriotic, optimistic tone. Rovetta took his own life in 1910, leaving behind an unfinished novel.

Bibliography: Romanticismo (Milan: Baldini & Castoldi, 1903); Giorgio Pullini, *Teatro italiano fra due secoli* (Florence: Parenti, 1958); Cheryl Reimold, " 'A Passing Smile': On Some Plays of Rovetta," *Italica* 51 (1974), 215–35.

RUFFINI, GIOVANNI (1807–1881), novelist and patriot. Ruffini was born in Genoa; he received a law degree and practiced for a time. His two brothers were followers of Mazzini,* and Ruffini soon joined the revolutionary movement. He became a friend of Mazzini and helped to form the group known as the *Giovine Italia*. Having taken part in an uprising during 1833, Ruffini was condemned to death in absentia. Thereafter, he fled first to France and then, in 1837, to England with Mazzini, where he stayed for some time. Ruffini's literary career developed almost entirely in England and France; his major works were originally written in English and then translated into Italian (often by Ruffini himself). The first of these, *Lorenzo Benzoni,* was begun in 1838 and published in Edinburgh in 1853; it is an autobiographical work, treating the adventures of an Italian patriot and the political conditions in the Piedmont of the 1830s. His second and most famous novel, *Doctor Antonio* (1855), is a love story which again pictures Italy in a most favorable light and also has autobiographical elements. Ruffini completed two other novels—*Lavinia* (1860) and *Vincenzo* (1863)— and aided Gaetano Donizetti in composing the *libretti* for two operas, *Don Sebastiano* (1843) and *Don Pasquale* (1843).

Bibliography: Doctor Antonio, A Tale (Edinburgh: Constable, 1855); *Don Pasquale, A Comic Opera,* trans. Edward Dent (London: Oxford, 1946); *Lavinia, A Novel* (New York: Rudd, 1861); *Lorenzo Benzoni* (Edinburgh: Constable, 1853); *Vincenzo, or Sunken Rocks* (Leipzig: Tauchnitz, 1863); Giovanni Faldella, *I fratelli Ruffini* (Turin: Roux, 1895); Sergio Romagnoli, *Ottocento tra letteratura e storia* (Padua: Liviana, 1961).

RUSTICO DI FILIPPO (circa 1240–circa 1300), Florentine lyric poet. Little is known about Rustico except that he was born in the Santa Maria Novella district of the city and was a Ghibelline in his politics. Although Brunetto Latini* dedicated one of his minor works to Rustico, Dante* makes no mention of him in his discussions of contemporary poets, and he was apparently not considered to be a major figure in his own lifetime.

Almost all of his some sixty extant sonnets* are preserved in a single manuscript at the Vatican Library. Rustico is traditionally grouped with the so-called *poeti giocosi* or "realistic" poets along with the better known Cecco Angiolieri* from Siena. However, like that of Cecco Angiolieri, Rustico's poetry is indebted to both the vernacular comic tradition inspired by Goliardic Latin verse and the dominant tradition of courtly love poetry from Provence, Sicily, and Tuscany. Roughly half of Rustico's lyrics belong to the comic tradition, and these have brought him recognition. The remainder of his poetry reveals his knowledge of the courtly conventions, but his lyrics in a comic or realistic vein are clearly wittier. They range from tender vignettes describing the illness of a young country girl ("Su, donna Gemma, con la farina" ["Come, Mona Gemma, come with fresh-made bread"]) to the more famous sarcastic caricatures ("Quando Dïo messer Messerin fece" ["When God created Messer Messèrin"]).

See also ANGIOLIERI, Cecco.

Bibliography: Poeti giocosi del tempo di Dante, ed. Mario Marti (Milan: Rizzoli, 1956); *Sonetti,* ed. Pier Vincenzo Mengaldo (Turin: Einaudi, 1971); *The Age of Dante: An Anthology of Early Italian Poetry,* trans. Joseph Tusiani (New York: Baroque Press, 1974); Mario Marti, *Cultura e stile nei poeti giocosi del tempo di Dante* (Pisa: Nistri-Lischi, 1953).

RUZZANTE (1502?–1542), actor and playwright. Ruzzante was born with the name Angelo Beolco but became famous as the stage character Ruzzante which he created and performed. Without a doubt, Ruzzante was the most important playwright working in the Paduan dialect during the Renaissance.* The illegitimate son of the rector of the faculty of medicine at the University of Padua, he was only eighteen when he founded a dramatic company with several of his friends. Throughout his life he remained close to the countryside near Padua, administering his family's estates and coming to know the peasants intimately. As no other dramatist of his era, Ruzzante united rustic and learned literary traditions in plays that display a perfect classical form and a subject matter drawn from peasant life. Ruzzante's acting company, which consisted not of professionals but of amateurs in the best sense of the word, frequently performed for the wealthy Venetian patrician Luigi Cornaro (1475–1566). Ruzzante's dramas of rustic life appealed to Venetian and Paduan aristocrats, who did not regard the peasants of their region with contempt but smiled with sympathy at their awkwardness and their entangled love affairs.

Early in his career Ruzzante programmed his poetic ideas. The prologue to his comedy *Betìa* (circa 1521 or 1524, Betìa) explains the author's belief that persons should always behave naturally. Ruzzante despised academic affectation, seeing the natural as the basic value of art. For this actor-playwright, the natural effect that an artist should try to achieve came from picturing life at a simple, instinctive level as it was found among peasants. In Ruzzante's view, authors must also be faithful to nature. For that reason, he wrote most of his plays in his native Paduan dialect—a remarkable feat at a time when most Italian writers aspiring to fame across the various regions of the politically divided peninsula wrote either in contemporary Tuscan or the golden-age Tuscan of Boccaccio's* prose in *The Decameron* or Petrarch's* verse. Since the characters of his works were mainly peasants of the Paduan area, Ruzzante felt he would be falsifying his art with Tuscan. It was always to the principle of the natural that this actor-playwright returned to justify his works.

Natural drives like hunger and love dominate Ruzzante's dramas. His literary career started with a verse play *La Pastorale* (circa 1520, The Pastoral Comedy), which comes close to parody with its farcical portrait of a hungry shepherd and a stolid Bergamask physician. The influence of learned comedy is evident in the play *La Moscheta* (1526–28, The Well-Spoken Lady), a prose drama in five acts like regular comedies where the peasant characters are transported to the urban environment of Padua. Here the character Ruzzante and his friend Menato have retained their country outlook, while Ruzzante's wife Betìa has taken on a city sophistication. One of the peasant characters—the soldier Tonin who competes with Menato for Betìa's favors—is a braggart warrior. The play pivots on a scheme of Ruzzante to test his wife's fidelity by assuming a disguise and entreating her affections. After Betìa fails to penetrate the disguise, she takes refuge at Tonin's house. Ruzzante's underlying cowardice prevents him from successfully storming the soldier's home. But as in a tale from *The Decameron,* peace comes with the triumph of intelligence over the desire for vengeance as the wife reconciles husband and lovers without injuring anyone's pride. As this play illustrates, peasant characters possess a sense of dignity that even their awkwardness in a city setting cannot diminish.

Around 1528, Ruzzante produced the works which should be considered his masterpieces: *Parlamento de Ruzzante (Ruzzante Returns from the Wars)* and the *Bìlora* (Bìlora). In the first play, the hero Ruzzante has gone off to war hoping to make a fortune. During Ruzzante's absence, his wife Gnua became a prostitute. Upon his return home after a disastrous battle, Ruzzante not only fails to regain Gnua's love, but he also suffers a humiliating beating by one of her hoodlum protectors. As a dramatic character, the Ruzzante of the *Parlamento* is a peasant braggart warrior who ends more impoverished than before his military service, made a cuckold because of his ambitions and his cowardly inability to pursue them. Both Ruzzante and his wife are dominated by their poverty, which pushed him off to war and her into prostitution. This theme of economic necessity also pervades the *Bìlora,* which displays some of the murderous jealousy of

Othello with the exception that the wife Dina is actually guilty of adultery. Once again the theme concerns the unnatural consequences of peasants' moving to the city. Bìlora resorts to murder to avenge his wife's taking the elderly but well-to-do Messer Andronico for a lover. The author viewed characters like Ruzzante, Gnua, Bìlora, and Dina as fallen in total desperation. Sympathetically portraying their weaknesses, he created dramas of human illusions in the midst of severe economic realities.

Some of the later plays that adapt classical form to peasant material include the *Fiorina* (circa 1529–30, The Comedy of Fiore), *L'Anconitana* (circa 1529–32, The Woman from Ancona), the *Piovana* (circa 1532–33, The Girl from the Piove), and the *Vaccaria* (1533, The Comedy of the Cows). While most critics consider the *Fiorina* to be a refreshing *mariazo* (farce about domestic strife), the final three plays are frequently dismissed as slavish imitations of classical models. But *L'Anconitana* is a vigorous effort at linguistic diversity: peasants speak Paduan, young lovers use a florid Tuscan, and a middle-aged merchant employs Venetian. While the *Piovana* and the *Vaccaria,* respectively, have sources in Plautus's comedies *Rudens* and *Asinaria,* Ruzzante remains true to his ideal of the natural by creating peasant dialectal dramas within a classical frame.

Bibliography: Teatro, ed. Ludovico Zorzi (Turin: Einaudi, 1967)—contains Italian translations of the dramas; *The Classic Theatre: Six Italian Plays,* ed. Eric Bentley (Garden City, N.Y.: Doubleday, 1958)—contains *Ruzzante Returns from the Wars;* Nino Borsellino, "Ruzzante," *Enciclopedia dello Spettacolo* 8 (1961), 1342–50; Franco Fido, "An Introduction to the Theatre of Angelo Beolco," in Alan C. Dessen, ed., *Renaissance Drama: New Series VI 1973* (Evanston, Ill.: Northwestern University Press, 1973), pp. 203–18; Carlo Grabher, *Ruzzante* (Milan: Principato, 1953); Emilio Lovarini, *Studi sul Ruzzante e la letteratura pavana* (Padua: Antenore, 1965); Alfred Mortier, *Un Dramaturge de la Renaissance Italienne: Ruzzante (1502–1542)* (Paris: Peyronnet, 1925–26)—contains French translations of Ruzzante's plays in Vol. 2.

Douglas Radcliff-Umstead

S

SABA, UMBERTO (1883–1957), poet. Saba was born as Umberto Poli in Trieste when the city was still part of the Austro-Hungarian Empire. He was the son of a Jewish mother and a Christian father who abandoned the family while the poet was still an infant. Saba's formal education was severely limited. Although he read voraciously and precociously wrote verse, he was trained in a vocational school as a clerk. He left this position in 1902 to wander about northern Italy, writing poetry and supporting himself as best he could. The first published volumes of his verse appeared in 1911 and 1912 (the second printed by *La Voce* in Florence). Back in Trieste in 1907, he met Lina, the seamstress who was to become the Laura of his *Canzoniere,* whom he married a year later. During World War I, Saba served as an inspector on an airfield. Afterwards, he bought an antiquarian bookstore in Trieste which supported him for the remainder of his life. Saba was a close friend of Italo Svevo,* Trieste's major writer, with whom he shared a deep interest in Freud. Saba even underwent psychoanalytical treatment in 1929 and, for a time, became a doctrinaire Freudian. His Jewish background caused him difficulties with the fascist government in the last years of World War II and eventually forced him to close his store and to live in exile for three years in France and Italy (where he was sheltered in Florence by Montale* and other friends). The last decade of his life brought some of the critical recognition he had so eagerly sought. His resentment over the neglect of the critics early in his career probably brought him to write his own volume of self-criticism.

Saba's complete *Canzoniere* (Songbook), in its definitive form of 1961, was divided into three "volumes" corresponding to his youthful works (1900–20), his mature poems (1921–32), and the compositions of his old age (1933–54). Much of the previously published material was revised for this final edition. This singular poetic achievement is similar to Petrarch's* more famous *Canzoniere* in that it is a lyric autobiography and represents a body of poetry which has been corrected and polished over the years. Unlike Petrarch, however, Saba also composed that fascinating work of self-criticism, the *Storia e cronistoria del Canzoniere* (1948, History and Chronicle of the Songbook). This systematic analysis of his own poetry is written in the third person and describes the *Canzoniere* as the history of or a psychological novel about a life relatively poor in external events but rich in inner feelings and emotions.

Saba's youthful compositions, especially the unusually long "A Mamma" (To Mamma), exhibit Leopardi's* influence and, to a lesser extent, that of the *crepuscolari* or "twilight" poets. Another section of this first volume, five poems grouped under the title *Casa e campagna* (1909–10, Home and Countryside), relate to Saba's marriage and the birth of a daughter; it contains two authentic masterpieces: "La capra" ("The Goat") and "A mia moglie" ("To My Wife"). The first poem, with its famous and enigmatic description of the goat's semitic face, establishes a community of suffering between the beast and humanity. The second is a hymn to his wife, comparing her to a number of domestic animals (a pregnant heifer, a timid rabbit, a pullet, a she-dog, a swallow, a frugal ant, and an industrious bee). Saba himself notes the poem's prayerful tone. Other critics have compared its simplicity of syntax and diction to the *Laudes creaturarum* of St. Francis.* In the largest section of this first volume, entitled *Trieste e una donna* (1910–12, Trieste and a Lady), the poet broadens his scope to depict his urban surroundings in forty-five poems, including several of his best—"Trieste" and "Città vecchia" (The Old Town).

Two major poems appear in *Cuor morituro* (1925–30, Moribund Heart), a section from the second volume of mature works. Reflecting the influence of Freud, "La brama" (Hunger) is devoted to the libido or sexual drive Saba had come to regard as the life force of humanity. "Il borgo" (The Town), on the other hand, is a pessimistic palinode to Saba's earlier hopes for the establishment of a community of human understanding. In the third volume of the *Canzoniere*, Saba moves away from traditional verse forms, patterns, or rhymes and the classical lyric forms of Leopardi to the experimental poetry of Ungaretti.* It contains a number of excellent poems, including "Ceneri" ("Ashes") and "Felicità" ("Happiness"), as well as the work many critics regard as Saba's masterpiece, the brief "Ulisse" ("Ulysses"), a poem in which Saba recapitulates his own personal history as a poet and a man through the myth of Ulysses (primarily the Ulysses of Dante*). Not all of Saba's works are successful, but his extraordinary achievement is to convince the reader that all of his works are worthy of attention, since both his masterpieces and his less appealing works are inseparable elements of a single poetic autobiography.

Bibliography: Il Canzoniere (Turin: Einaudi, 1961); *Prose,* ed. Linuccia Saba (Milan: Mondadori, 1964)—includes the *Storia e cronistoria; Italian Sampler: An Anthology of Italian Verse,* trans. Thomas G. Bergin (Montreal: Casalini, 1964); *Twentieth-Century Italian Poetry: A Bilingual Anthology,* ed. L. R. Lind (Indi-

454 *Saba, Umberto*

anapolis, Ind.: Bobbs-Merrill, 1974); Joseph Cary, *Three Modern Italian Poets: Saba, Ungaretti, Montale* (New York: New York University Press, 1969); Folco Portinari, *Umberto Saba* (Milan: Mursia, 1963).

SACCHETTI, FRANCO (1332?–1400), poet, *novelliere,* and merchant. Born of Florentine parents in Ragusa, Dalmatia (the modern Dubrovnik) and an active participant in the political life of Florence, Sacchetti held a large number of important positions in the city's government. His first poetic work, *La battaglia delle belle donne di Firenze con le vecchie* (1354, The Battle of the Beautiful Florentine Women with the Old Women), is a humorous composition in *ottave* which describes the inevitable victory of beauty and youth over old age and jealousy. A prolific experimenter in various poetic forms, Sacchetti composed many lyrics, including sestinas,* *canzoni,** sonnets,* madrigals,* *caccie,** and *ballate,** and brought them together as the *Libro delle rime* (circa 1362, The Book of Poems). This work, the autograph manuscript of which has been preserved, contains some of the most remarkable lyrics of the fourteenth century, including the beautiful *ballata* "O vaghe montanine pasturelle" ("O lovely shepherdesses of the lea") and "Passando con pensier per un boschetto" ("Pensively walking through the woods one day").

In prose, Sacchetti composed the *Sposizioni di Vangeli* (1381, Expositions on the Gospels), a collection of forty-nine pieces. Each is linked to a Lenten day, the Mass for that day, or a passage from the Scriptures. His masterpiece, however, is of a completely secular nature, the famous *Trecentonovelle* (1392–97?, The Three Hundred Novelle), only two hundred and twenty-three of which remain (plus seven fragments). The codices containing the originals were lost many years ago, and the remaining stories survive because a Cinquecento scholar, Vincenzo Borghini (1515–1580), copied them for posterity. Unlike the stories of his model Boccaccio,* Sacchetti's lack the frame consisting of a group of storytellers gathered together under some pretext suitable to their narration. They are generally brief and sometimes completely anecdotal, and many deal with historical figures (Frederick II,* Pope Boniface, Castruccio Castracani) or contemporary artists and writers (Dante,* Cavalcanti,* Giotto), as well as a number of anonymous men and women from every possible social class and occupation. Certain character types and themes (fortune, love, wit, tricks played upon fools) provide some internal coherence to the collection. Although Sacchetti's narrative occasionally reminds the reader of Boccaccio's realistic depiction of his times, his stories are far more closely connected to the medieval exemplum and ordinarily close with an implicit or explicit moral. In a brief prologue to the collection, Sacchetti describes himself as a man with little culture or erudition, but both his verse and his prose evince a thorough knowledge of Petrarch* and Boccaccio and a more than adequate background in the literature of his times.

See also BOCCACCIO, Giovanni; NOVELLA.

Bibliography: Opere, ed. Aldo Borlenghi (Milan: Rizzoli, 1957); *Italian Poets of the Renaissance,* trans. Joseph Tusiani (Long Island City, N.Y.: Baroque Press, 1971); *Tales from Sacchetti,* trans. Mary Steegman (London: Dent, 1908); Lanfranco Caretti, *Saggio sul Sacchetti* (Bari: Laterza, 1951).

SACRA RAPPRESENTAZIONE, a religious drama of popular origin which developed out of the *lauda*'s* dramatic potential and which was most commonly performed in the churches and public squares of central Italian cities. Its subject matter included scenes from the Old and New Testaments as well as edifying religious stories from Christian legend and the saints' lives. Its most popular verse form was the *ottava rima,** and the works were usually not divided into acts or scenes, although a prologue was often delivered by an angel. In most cases, the authors were anonymous, but some of these dramatizations were composed by notable writers, including Feo Belcari (1410–1484), Jacopo Nardi,* and Lorenzo de' Medici.* Most *sacre rappresentazioni* were composed during the fifteenth century, but at this same time the form also came to be utilized for mythological subjects, as in Angelo Poliziano's* important dramatic fable *Orfeo* (1480, *Orpheus*). The *sacra rappresentazione* gradually lost its appeal in the sixteenth century when Italian critics and poets began to rediscover classical theatre and criticism with its more clearly defined dramatic structures and its more pronounced erudite, literary character.

See also LAUDA; MEDICI, Lorenzo de'.

Bibliography: Laude drammatiche e rappresentazioni sacre, ed. Vincenzo De Bartholomaeis, 3 vols. (Florence: Le Monnier, 1943); Alessandro D'Ancona, *Origini del teatro italiano,* 2 vols. (1891; rpt. Rome: Bardi, 1966); Paul Colomb De Batines, *Bibliografia delle antiche rappresentazioni sacre e profane stampate nei secoli XV e XVI* (1852; rpt. Milan: Gorlich Editore, 1958).

SALIMBENE DA PARMA (1221–after 1288), Franciscan monk and historian. Born Ognibene de Adam into one of the most prominent families of Parma, he joined a religious order by 1238 and changed his name to Salimbene in 1239. Upon completing his novitiate year, he traveled throughout central Italy. In 1247–48, he went to France and met King Louis XI and Giovanni di Pian del Carpine, an Italian who had recently completed a mission to the Far East. After a sojourn in Ferrara (1249–56), during which he began to collect the materials for his future chronicle, the next news of him documents his move to the monastery of Montefalcone in the province of Reggio, where he died sometime after 1288. The *Cronica (Chronicle)*, his only extant work, survives in a single but incomplete autograph manuscript. This history covers the period 1168–1287 in a traditional manner, but its contents treat an amazingly broad range of political, economic, artistic, social, and religious events. It is one of the best eyewitness accounts preserved from the thirteenth century and as such represents an invaluable historical source. His language is a Latin enriched by the influence of the vernacular in various dialects. Perhaps of greatest interest is Salimbene's description of the popular religious upheavals in Italy—the Great Alleluia of 1233 and the Flagellant movement of 1260. His stirring descriptions of the period's warfare, his portrait of Frederick II,* and the prophecies of Gioacchino da Fiore are passages worthy of note.

Bibliography: Cronica, ed. Giuseppe Scalia, 2 vols. (Bari: Laterza, 1966); George G. Coulton, *From St. Francis to Dante: Translations from the Chronicle of the Franciscan Salimbene* (1907; rpt. Philadelphia: University of Pennsylvania Press, 1972); Delno West, "The Present State of Salimbene Studies with a Bibliographic Appendix of the Major Works," *Franciscan Studies* 32 (1972), 271–83.

SALUSTRI, CARLO ALBERTO: *See* TRILUSSA.

SALUTATI, COLUCCIO (1331–1406), humanist, scholar, and statesman. Born at Stignano in the Val di Nievole, Salutati was educated in Bologna under the humanist Pietro da Muglio (died 1382), one of the most famous professors of rhetoric at the time and a friend of both Petrarch* and Boccaccio.* This humanist training not only gave Salutati the solid grounding in the classics which later made him famous, but also drew him into contact with the two greatest writers of his day in either Latin or Italian. Salutati had prepared himself for a career as a notary, and from 1350 until 1367, he practiced his profession in a number of small towns. Moving to Rome in 1368, he finally obtained the post of chancellor of Lucca, a job he held for one year, with the assistance of Pope Urban V. In 1374, however, he was given an important position controlling elections and voting in Florence. In the next year, he finally attained the office his talents merited —chancellor of the Florentine Republic—the powerful position he held until his death.

Salutati's appointment established a tradition of humanist chancellors in the Florentine government which not only produced Poggio Bracciolini* and Leonardo Bruni,* his immediate successors, but also guided later writers in the vernacular such as Machiavelli* and Guicciardini.* In Salutati, the city had found the perfect combination of statesman and scholar. A follower of Petrarch and his humanist principles, Salutati elevated the writing of letters of state and documents in Latin to a new level of style, winning praise for his eloquence and rhetorical skill even from his enemies. It was Salutati, more than any other writer, who helped to establish the basis of what modern scholars call "civic humanism" by his unfaltering belief that Florence was the heir to ancient republican Rome, the bulwark of liberty in Italy, and the opponent of tyrants such as Gian Galeazzo Visconti and papal politicians such as Pope Gregory XI. Besides his voluminous correspondence, which rivals Petrarch's in its bulk if not in its prominence, Salutati helped to collect a magnificent library of classical manuscripts. More importantly, he was instrumental in bringing the Byzantine scholar Manuel Chrysoloras to Florence as professor of Greek, the pivotal event which opened up an entire new area for humanistic studies in Italy.

In spite of his political obligations, Salutati composed many works besides his official correspondence. In his youth, he wrote a series of Latin eclogues in imitation of Petrarch and Boccaccio which are now lost, and he had once hoped to compose a Latin epic* like Petrarch's *Africa,* a project he soon abandoned. His longest work, *De laboribus Herculis* (1405–06, On the Labors of Hercules), began as an allegorical explanation of Seneca's *Hercules furens* but was expanded to include a defense of poetry and an encyclopedic collection of materials pertaining to the myth itself. In spite of its medieval flavor, the new spirit of Italian humanism* is apparent in Salutati's careful citations from the original classical texts. Other minor compositions include *De saeculo et religione* (circa 1381, The World and the Religious Life), a discussion of the relative merits of the secular and religious life; the *De fato et fortuna* (circa 1396–98, On Fate and Fortune), a treatise on free will; and *De nobilitate legum et medicinae* (1399, On the Worth of Law and Medicine), a work which reveals a typical humanistic preference for the legal profession over the scientific pursuit of medicine.

Of Salutati's many writings, the one which has attracted the most attention from modern scholars is *De tyranno* (1400, *A Treatise on Tyrants*), which raises the question of whether the assassination of a tyrant is justified. Basing his discussion upon the opinions of Bartolo da Sassoferrato (1314–1357), the greatest legal mind of his times, Salutati first defines a tyrant as a man who usurps a government or who rules unjustly without regard for the law; he then declares that tyrannicide is, in fact, justified. He extends his deliberations to the question of whether Dante* was correct in condemning the murderers of Caesar to hell for their crime and whether, indeed, Caesar himself was a tyrant. The issue was a vexing one for Quattrocento Florence, since Dante was the city's greatest poet, and the claim that Florence had inherited the tradition of Roman republican liberty might be used to imply that the greatest poet of Florence had praised a tyrant (like the Visconti the city opposed), while he had con-

Salutati, Coluccio

demned his republican murderers to everlasting punishment in the *Inferno*. Salutati's solution to this question was to declare that Caesar had actually achieved power legally and that accordingly his assassination was unjustified, therefore saving Dante's verdict from coming into conflict with the ideology of civic humanism.

Salutati's many works and letters, as well as his own personal example and influence, helped to establish the humanist movement in Florence, bringing the sometimes esoteric scholarship of Petrarch and Boccaccio into contact with the world of practical politics and statesmanship.

See also BRACCIOLINI, Poggio; BRUNI, Leonardo; HUMANISM.

Bibliography: Prosatori latini del Quattrocento, ed. Eugenio Garin (Milan: Ricciardi, 1952); *Humanism and Tyranny: Studies in the Italian Trecento,* ed. Ephraim Emerton (1925; rpt. Gloucester, Mass.: Peter Smith, n.d.)—contains translations of *De tyranno* and two long letters; Hans Baron, *The Crisis of the Early Italian Renaissance: Civic Humanism and Republican Liberty in an Age of Classicism and Tyranny* (Princeton, N.J.: Princeton University Press, 1955); Nancy S. Struever, *The Language of History in the Renaissance: Rhetoric and Historical Consciousness in Florentine Humanism* (Princeton, N.J.: Princeton University Press, 1970); B. L. Ullman, *The Humanism of Coluccio Salutati* (Padua: Antenore, 1963).

SALVIATI, LIONARDO (1539–1589), Florentine scholar, writer, and literary critic. Salviati was born into a branch of one of the most prominent families of Florence. Educated by Pier Vettori (1499–1585), a lecturer in the Studio di Firenze, Salviati acquired sound training in both Latin and Greek and a taste for philological studies. His first work, *Dialogo dell'amicizia* (circa 1560, Dialogue on Friendship), was based in large measure upon Cicero's *De Amicitia.* Both this and a series of funeral orations he composed at about the same time brought about Salviati's acceptance by the literary society of that time in Florence as one of its brighter lights.

When the Accademia degli Umidi became the Accademia Fiorentina in 1542 under the direction of Duke Cosimo I de' Medici (perhaps the first European monarch to realize the political advantages of a centralized institution loyal to the state which was the arbiter in matters of culture and literary taste), the academy began to envision its role as that of a defender of the growing national consciousness which sought to glorify the Florentine language and its literary tradition. The cultural hegemony which earlier Quattrocento humanists had vested in the classics thus passed to literature in the vernacular, especially that written in Tuscan by the greatest of Italian writers—Dante,* Petrarch,* and Boccaccio.* When Salviati's *Orazione in lode della fiorentina favella* (1564, Oration in Praise of the Florentine Tongue) was delivered at a public lecture before the academy, it helped to make him a fixture in the intellectual life of the city.

This work initiated Salviati's lifelong project of transferring the cultural aims of humanism* from the classics to the Italian language and of creating a national tradition transcending that of antiquity. Here, the Italian language is specifically identified with that of Florence. In a funeral oration delivered in 1565 upon the death of Benedetto Varchi,* Salviati expands the original definition of humanist as a teacher of classical literature and languages to include those skilled not only in the classics but in the Florentine language and literature as well.

After he had been elected consul of the Accademia, Salviati composed two comedies which follow Roman models, *Il granchio* (1566, The Crab) and *La spina* (1592, The Thorn), the latter published after his death. Their real signficance lies in his use of language. The first play employs an essentially idiomatic Florentine, and the second attempts to reproduce the language of Boccaccio, a sign of Salviati's devotion to Boccaccio as a literary model. After the Medici family had transformed Florence into an hereditary duchy in 1569, Salviati's position became increasingly that of a courtier who sought his sovereign's favor for advancement and whose works were often written for that purpose. Salviati was most unfortunate in narrowly missing the honor of being the first editor of Aristotle's *Poetics* (his manuscript was never published), and he never succeeded in producing a literary work of the first rank.

Salviati's place in literary history is therefore guaranteed by his work as a critic and scholar. In 1580, he undertook the task of expurgating *The Decameron*, an act often cited to belittle his posthumous reputation. But Salviati was no prudish bowdlerizer. Since the book had already been placed on the Index in 1559, Salviati's attempt to make the work conform to Post-Tridentine tastes was motivated more by his desire to keep the book in circulation than to censor Boccaccio's work, which, to him, represented the apex of Florentine achievement in prose and a model for future writers. This revision of Boccaccio, known as the *rassettatura* ("tidying up") of *The Decameron*, was published in a Venetian edition in 1582. What emerged was a completely new work. Sixty stories were corrected; all derogatory remarks about the church or clergymen were removed; glosses were added to make the book appear to be a series of moral exempla; and the endings of some works were changed to moralize them.

Salviati became a member of the relatively new Accademia della Crusca in 1584 and assumed the academic name of the Infarinato, or the "one covered with flour." At the same time, he published his major linguistic treatise, *Avvertimenti della lingua sopra 'l Decameron* (1583, Remarks on the Language of "The Decameron"). In later years, he took an active part in the disputes among critics over the relative merits of Ariosto* and Tasso.* Salviati defended Ariosto's epic poem as an example of a classic Italian work written under its own set of rules and not subservient to classical models. Salviati passed on to posterity a series of ideas on the vernacular languages and their relationship to antiquity which anticipate the arguments of the moderns against the ancients in the Battle of the Books by at least half a century. The *Vocabolario della Crusca* (1612, Crusca Dictionary) was, perhaps, the most enduring monument to his linguistic principles. The countless generations of Italian writers, like Manzoni,* who came to Florence to "wash their clothes in the Arno" would pay homage to his lasting influence.

Bibliography: Opere complete del cavaliere Lionardo Salviati (Milan: Classici Italiani, 1810); Peter M. Brown, *Lionardo Salviati: A Critical Biography* (Oxford: Oxford University Press, 1974); Baxter Hathaway, *Marvels and Commonplaces: Renaissance Literary Criticism* (New York: Random House, 1968); Joel E. Spingarn, *Literary Criticism in the Renaissance* (1962; rpt. Westport, Conn.: Greenwood Press, 1976); Bernard Weinberg, *A History of Literary Criticism in the Italian Renaissance,* 2 vols. (Chicago: University of Chicago Press, 1961).

SANGUINETI, EDOARDO (1930–   ), avant-garde critic, poet, and prose writer. Sanguineti was born in Genoa and earned a degree at the University of Turin with a thesis on Dante,* later published as *Interpretazione di Malebolge* (1961, Interpretation of Malebolge). His criticism, particularly his study of Guido Gozzano* and a monograph entitled *Tra liberty e crepuscolarismo* (1961, Between Art Nouveau and Crepuscularism), has provided new perspectives on turn-of-the-century Italian poetry and culture. His influential anthology *Poesia italiana del Novecento* (1969, Twentieth-Century Italian Poetry) has transformed the accepted canon of modern texts, encouraging the rehabilitation of some neglected poets (such as Lucini*) while diminishing the relative importance of other writers. In addition to a free translation of Petronius's *Satyricon,* Sanguineti has published a number of plays as well as experimental novels, including *Capriccio italiano* (1963, *An Italian Caprice*) and *Il giuoco dell'oca* (1967, The Goose Game). With a number of other foreign poets (Octavio Paz, Jacques Roubaud, and Charles Tomlinson), he has authored an unusual multilingual poetic work entitled *Renga, A Chain of Poems* (1971), which employs a sequence of linked poems in a metrical form that first flourished in feudal Japan.

Bibliography: Il giuoco dell'oca (Milan: Feltrinelli, 1967); *Tra liberty e crepuscolarismo* (Milan: Mursia, 1961); *Italian Writing Today,* ed. Raleigh Trevelyan (Baltimore: Penguin, 1967)—contains a selection from *Capriccio italiano; Renga, A Chain of Poems* (New York: Braziller, 1971); Renato Barilli, *La barriera del naturalismo* (Milan: Mursia, 1964); Gabriella Sica, *Sanguineti* (Florence: La Nuova Italia, 1974); Tibor Wlassics, "Edoardo Sanguineti," in *I contemporanei* (Milan: Marzorati, 1974), VI, 1917–57.

SANNAZARO, JACOPO (1458?–1530), Renaissance* humanist and pastoralist, in Italian and neo-Latin. An aristocrat of modest fortune, Sannazaro lived virtually his entire life in Naples and its environs, latterly at his Villa Mergellina, deeded to him by King Frederick in 1499. He remained unmarried, and was evidently not robust. He took no part in affairs of state, although all his writings reflect a strong attachment to his native city, and to King Frederick and his predecessors.

Sannazaro was admitted to the literary academy of Naples, under the sponsorship of Giovanni Pontano* and Giuniano Maio (1430–circa 1500), possibly as early as 1478–79. He was given the academic name of Actius Syncerus, a name which is generally taken to suggest some kind of special interest in the sea (*Lat.* acta, seashore), plus moral qualities of sincerity and simplicity. (These academic names were intended to be allusive and evocative, however, and it is fruitless to attempt exact interpretation.) Presumably much of his writing in Italian was done in the 1480s, and thereafter was largely superseded by his intense labor on his excellent Latin poetry. Sannazaro's *Rime* (Rhymes), not published in his own lifetime, consist of about a hundred sonnets* and *canzoni,* competently done in the Petrarchan mode. Naturally, complaints of unrewarded love prevail, but a good many sonnets are directed to the praise of friends or to reflections on general subjects, such as mortality and fortune. Sannazaro's major preoccupation in the 1480s must have been his *Arcadia (Arcadia)*. This work was surely begun, and perhaps even a draft completed, before Sannazaro took up residence in Naples, but it must have been polished and repolished while the poet was surrounded by books and manuscripts in Naples. An extant manuscript of the original version of *Arcadia* is dated 1489. To this version were later added two more eclogues, with connecting prose, apparently reflecting Sannazaro's grief at political events around 1500. Hence, it appears that the poet esteemed the *Arcadia* as more than rejected juvenilia, although he did not officially sanction the publication of the work in 1504, after a pirated edition had appeared in 1502.

By 1490, Sannazaro seems to have been deeply committed to establishing his fame through neo-Latin poetry. The rest of his life was devoted to steady labor at composing, elaborating, and refining Latin poems in various genres. This labor was interrupted badly by an unhappy period (1501–04) when the poet sacrificed the serenity of his comfortable life in Naples in order to follow his king into exile in France, when Frederick was deposed by French and Spanish power politics. Only after Frederick's death did Sannazaro return to Villa Mergellina, and he remained steadfastly aloof from the political and social life of Naples thereafter. Throughout this last period of his life, he maintained a close relationship, hovering between friendship and love, with a certain Cassandra Marchese, a Neapolitan aristocrat whom Sannazaro aided in her prolonged legal struggles with her estranged husband. In his last years, Sannazaro paid daily visits to Cassandra; he died in her residence on 6 August 1530. His elaborate tomb in Santa Maria del Parto, designed by the poet himself and partially built under his supervision, is a splendid example of the deliberate blending of Christian and classical in Renaissance art. In view of the great care expended by the poet on planning this tomb, perhaps we should accept its statement that Sannazaro died at the age of seventy-two, and thus retain the traditional birthdate of 1458.

The *Arcadia* follows Boccaccio's* *Ameto* in alternating pastoral* eclogues with narrative links in prose, but goes far beyond that work in translating, paraphrasing, and adumbrating passages from virtually every Greek or Roman writer who touched on country matters. It precipitated an enthusiasm for the pastoral genre that lasted in Europe for two hundred years. Some fifty editions of *Arcadia* appeared in the sixteenth century alone. Several causes may be suggested for the remarkable popularity of the pastoral during the Renaissance: the age encouraged in its art a function of presenting life not only as it was, but also as it might be, or ought to be, as in a Golden Age or an Arcadia; the growing complexities of capitalist urban and national cultures encouraged a counterview praising rural simplicities, or exploiting the tensions between the complex and simple; the natural decor of the pastoral adapted readily to a growing interest in "landscape," in poetry as well as in painting; and the relatively limited corpus of Graeco-Roman pastoral made it easy for poets to practice, and for audiences to recognize, the much-prized "imitation of classical models."

Sannazaro begins *Arcadia* with idyllic shepherds pasturing their flocks, singing their loves, and practicing religious rituals with simple piety, chiefly in scenes of early morning and noontime tranquility. But gradually the pastoral stasis is disturbed: the songs become songs of funereal grief, melancholy and despairing love, and bitter social protest; the narrative links recount unhappy loves, with threats of suicide; the landscape is a landscape of desert places, forbidding woods, nocturnal shadows, mysterious ravines, and deep romantic chasms—and finally (in a dream-vision) a marvelous underground chamber, the source of all the rivers in the world. At the end, Arcadia has vanished like an insubstantial vision, and the narrator (Sincero) is back at Naples, bitterly grieving for the fate of his beloved city and still praising the virtues and accomplishments of her learned citizens. The Graeco-Roman pastoral of love-songs has been complicated with political and social protest more intrusive than Virgil's, with magic and folklore more pronounced than that of Theocritus, with a melancholy bitterness over mortality and mutability that rivals Petrarch's,* and with a patriotic attachment to a particular city and a particular region that does not appear so vividly in any of Sannazaro's predecessors. In the world of pastoral, one shepherd-poet hands down his reed to another, but the songs of the successor, though sedulously imitative, acquire their own distinctive sound.

Sannazaro's excellent Latin poetry is also recurringly pastoral in subject and in manner, although a collection of nearly one hundred and fifty epigrams (published posthumously in 1535) demonstrates some talent for witty brevity on various subjects, including invective against contemporary political opponents, such as Poliziano* and the Borgias. The three books of *Elegies,* also published in 1535, are pleasant imitations of Propertius and Tibullus, but less monumentally imposing than the *Piscatoria* (1526, *Piscatorial Eclogues*), of which five are extant, plus a fragmentary sixth. These Virgilian eclogues, replacing shepherds and their flocks with fishermen on the sunlit Bay of Naples, are among the finest achievements of neo-Latin poetry, their hexameters rising at times to splendidly sonorous waves of sound and sense that Virgil himself need not have disdained. The magnum opus, *De Partu Virginis* (1526, The Virgin's Childbirth), commands respect for its fine Latinity and careful artistry, but is likely to disappoint literary tastes nurtured by the Anglo-Saxon Protestant tradition. Necessarily devoid of action and dwelling heavily on the Virgin's piety, maternal love, and (through prophecy) maternal grief, the poem will commend itself to most readers for its undeniably sharp pictorial qualities —whether in epic similes, as when the Virgin resembles a Nausicaa-like maiden wading in the surf, or in narrative passages, as when Joseph and Mary thread the crowded streets of Bethlehem, or the shepherds wind in torchlight procession around the mountainside. Combining its Christian subject with a thoroughly classical decor, the *De Partu* is itself a monument to Sannazaro's lifelong dedication to renewing for his time the glories of Greece and Rome.

See also PASTORAL.

Bibliography: Opere di Iacopo Sannazaro, ed. Enrico Carrara (Turin: UTET, 1970); *Arcadia & Piscatorial Eclogues,* trans. Ralph Nash (Detroit, Mich.: Wayne State University Press, 1966); Antonio Altamura, *Jacopo Sannazaro* (Napoli: Silvio Viti, 1951); David Kalstone, *Sidney's Poetry* (New York: Norton, 1965); Renato Poggioli, *The Oaten Flute* (Cambridge, Mass.: Harvard University Press, 1976).

Ralph Nash

SARPI, PAOLO (1552–1623), historian, theologian, and canonist. Born in Venice, Pietro Sarpi was a precocious student who entered the order of the Servites at the age of thirteen and soon became one of its leading figures. Recognized even in his youth as a brilliant scholar, Sarpi (who took the name Paolo when he joined the Servites) won the admiration of contemporaries for his intellectual abilities and wide learning. His interests included Greek and Hebrew, mathematics and medicine, astronomy and biological sciences, ancient and Scholastic philosophy, and civil as well as canon law. When Sarpi was still eighteen, the duke of Mantua named him court theologian. He was ordained a priest in 1574 and moved briefly to Milan in the service of Carlo Borromeo. Sarpi completed his doctorate at Padua in 1578 and taught philosophy and theology at the Servite convent in Venice. He was only twenty-seven when he was elected provincial and thirty-two when he was sent to Rome as procurator-general of his order. Back in Venice in 1588, Fra Paolo carried on his study and teaching while finding time to frequent cultivated circles and to associate with prominent foreigners. This life of studious retirement ended when Pope Paul V laid Venice under interdict and the Senate appointed him, now already fifty-four, its adviser on theological and jurisdictional matters. From 1606 until his death, Fra Paolo was a public figure who authored many legal opinions and directed the pamphlet war between Venice and the papacy. He emerged as one of the ablest polemicists of his age and became a familiar name among educated men of Europe. Sarpi was considered so dangerous to the Roman Curia and its allies that he was excommunicated during the interdict and was the target of a nearly fatal plot against his life late in 1607. To be sure, the suspicion of the ecclesiastical authority had manifested itself long before this dispute: Fra Paolo had been denounced to the Inquisition when in his early twenties, reported several times to his superiors for other reasons, and twice refused the bishopric which Venice sought to obtain for him.

Sarpi's merits as a scientist and philosopher should not be exaggerated. His scientific manuscripts were never published, and his personal papers were destroyed by fire in 1769. And clearly it would be difficult to make out a case for Sarpi on the basis of the six hundred and seventy-five extant *Pensieri* (Thoughts), written between 1578 and 1597, and the short treatise often referred to as *L'Arte di ben pensare* (after 1590, The Art of Thinking Well). Similarly, Sarpi cannot be more properly understood as a church reformer. The discussion has arisen primarily from his important epistles, especially his extensive correspondence with non-Catholics in France, Germany, and England; and it is closely related to the complex issue of his positions on religious issues. For some, the diffident Sarpi chose to conceal his true beliefs to avoid persecution; for others, he was an orthodox Catholic or a solid Protestant. Admittedly, historical evidence gives us a puzzling, ambiguous Sarpi. It ought to be noted, however, that Sarpi could continue to regard himself a Catholic because he thought these theological distinctions had slight foundations. He felt no need to expound his views on theology in a systematic manner. Moreover, he showed a startling dislike for the doctrinal dogmatism of his time.

Sarpi's appointment to the post of adviser to the Republic proved to be a major turning point in his life and career. It was principally his political writings, and especially his polemical writings, which made him famous throughout Europe in his own time. In his *consulti* (legal opinions or counsel) written for the government, as well as in his pamphlets and treatises directed to a wider public, Sarpi addressed himself to concrete problems of church-state relations. The most famous of these polemical writings are the *Trattato dell'Interdetto* (1606, Treatise on the Interdict), signed by five other Venetian theologians; the *Discorso dell'origine, forma, leggi ed uso dell' Ufficio dell'Inquisizione in Venezia* (1638, *The History of the Inquisition*); and the *Trattato delle materie beneficiarie* (1676, *Treatise of Matters Beneficiary*), an historical account and analysis of the church's temporal power and financial resources since antiquity. In these works as well as in others on the right of asylum or the Index of Prohibited Books, Sarpi opposes with all the learning and sagacity at his command the Roman Curia's misuse of powers and its efforts to encroach on the sphere of temporal government. Through them, Fra Paolo became for Protestant Europe a leader against the secular aspirations of Rome. The interest of Sarpi's writings as theologian for the Republic lies not in their theoretical, religious, and political content but rather in their polemical vigor and in the assiduous search for materials which support the writer's case.

Sarpi's current reputation rests primarily on his historical works, which were also written after the controversy surrounding the interdict: the *Istoria dell'Interdetto* (1626, *The History of the Quarrels of Pope Paul V with the State of Venice*), the official account of the event from the point of view of Venice; the *Aggionta* and *Supplimento* to the *Istoria degli Uscochi* (1617, Addition and Supplement to the History of Uskosks); the *Trattato di pace et accomodamento delli moti di guerra eccitati per causa d'Uscochi* (first published in 1965, Treatise on the Peace and Agreement of the Wars Caused by the Uskosks); and, most important of all, the *Istoria del Concilio Tridentino* (1619, *History of the Council of Trent*), the last great monument of Italian Renaissance* historiography and the focal point of Sarpi's work. Circulated first in manuscript and smuggled out of Italy by his English friends, the *Istoria* was published in an unauthorized edition at London in 1619 by the exiled archbishop of Split, Marcantonio de Dominis, who provided the book with a dedication to James I and a polemical subtitle. Within ten years, the *Istoria* was translated in Latin, German, French, and English; it had more than thirty editions in the seventeenth century; and it continued to influence the direction of religious controversy and historical writing in Europe until well into the nineteenth century. As in his polemical treatises, Sarpi treats ecclesiastic history essentially as politics. The *Istoria* is the chronicle of what should not have been; it is intended to show how the Curia played politics with the concerns of Christianity and perverted the primary purpose of the Council, turning it to the aim of strengthening papal control and absolutism. Behind Sarpi's dry and measured account of the debates on dogmatic and liturgical issues reappears the polemical contrast between the post-Tridentine church and the primitive church. This negative view of Trent led Sarpi to underestimate the achievements of the Council, but his animus is seldom allowed to break out in passages of open indictment. The prose style of the *Istoria* is direct, vigorous; the manner of narration calm, impassionate. Indeed, the carefully detailed description of the origin and progress of the Council, and the painfully earnest exploration of the hidden causes of its final outcome, make Sarpi the last great historian and moralist of the Italian Renaissance.

Bibliography: The Histoirie of the Councel of Trent (London: J. Bill, 1620); *The History of the Inquisition* (London: J. Okes, 1639); *The History of the Quarrels of Pope Paul V with the State of Venice* (London: J. Bill, 1626); *History of Benefices and Selections from History of the Council of Trent,* ed. Peter Burke (New York: Washington Square Press, 1967); William J. Bouwsma, *Venice and the Defense of Republican Liberty* (Berkeley, Calif.: University of California Press, 1968); Gaetano Cozzi, "Paolo Sarpi," in *Storia della letteratura italiana: Il Seicento*, eds. Emilio Cecchi and Natalino Sapegno (Milan: Garzanti, 1967), V, 415–70; John Leon Lievsay, *Venetian Phoenix: Paolo Sarpi and Some of His English Friends, 1606–1700* (Lawrence, Kans.: University Press of Kansas, 1973).

Albert N. Mancini

SAVONAROLA, GIROLAMO (1452–1498), church reformer, preacher, and writer. Savonarola was born in Ferrara. He received a sound education in Scholastic theology and gained a thorough knowledge of the Bible. After entering a Dominican monastery as a novice at the age of seventeen, he returned to Ferrara in 1479 and first came to Florence in 1482. After some years of preaching at San Gimignano and Brescia, he was recalled by Lorenzo de' Medici* to Florence in 1490 and became the prior of San Marco, the church traditionally associated with Medici patronage. Savonarola's role in the Florence of his day is a complicated one. Although head of a church under Medici patronage, he did not hesitate to attack his patrons on moral grounds. His basic message was that the corruption of Florence and of the church in general must give way to a moral reformation to avoid God's wrath. His numerous sermons were most frequently based upon Old Testament texts.

At the time of the French invasion of Italy, Savonarola's moral reform took on political overtones. His major political tract, *Trattato circa il reggimento e governo della città di Firenze* (1498, Treatise on the Organization and Government of Florence), looks upon Charles VIII as the scourge of God and identifies him with the Divine wrath Savonarola had prophesied would fall upon Florence. Written at the request of the Florentine Signoria, this work is republican in spirit. Savonarola argues that a republic is the only form of government suitable to the nature of the Florentine people, voices his opposition to an aristocratic or tyrannical form, and advocates an enlarged Grand Council based on his interpretation of that branch of the Venetian government. In 1497, he was excommunicated by Pope Alexander VI on political and religious grounds, and he wrote the *Triumphus Crucis (The Triumph of the Cross)* in defense of his own position. Under papal pressure, the Signoria brought him to trial, the main charges involving his ability to prophesy, and he was condemned to death after being tortured. The sentence was executed in the square before the Palazzo Vecchio. Savonarola's influence was not thereby effaced. His religious and political followers, the *Piagnoni* ("Weepers"), were to remember his vision of a broadly based republic in a subsequent revolt against the Medici in 1527.

Bibliography: Prediche sopra Aggeo con il Trattato circa il reggimento e governo della città di Firenze, ed. Luigi Firpo (Rome: Belardetti, 1965); *The Triumph of the Cross,* trans. J. Procter (London: Sands, 1901); Roberto Ridolfi, *The Life of Girolamo Savonarola* (New York: Knopf, 1959); Ronald M. Steinberg, *Fra Girolamo Savonarola: Florentine Art and Renaissance Historiography* (Athens, Ohio: Ohio University Press, 1976); Donald Weinstein, *Savonarola and Florence: Prophecy and Patriotism in the Renaissance* (Princeton, N.J.: Princeton University Press, 1970).

SBARBARO, CAMILLO (1888–1967), poet. Sbarbaro was born in Santa Margherita Ligure. His early academic interests included a taste for botany which culminated in a study entitled *Licheni* (1967, Lichens) which appeared just after his death. His first poetry appeared in 1911, and soon he began collaborating with two noted periodicals of the time, *La Voce* and *Lacerba,* contributing both verse and essays. In 1914, *La Voce* published his *Pianissimo* (Very Softly), an important book of verse republished twice during his lifetime. It contains Sbarbaro's most frequently anthologized lyric, "Taci, anima stanca di godere" ("Be Still My Soul, Weary of Pleasure"), in which the poet gives voice to his pessimistic view of the world: ". . . and all is/ what it is, only what it is./ Alternating joys and sorrows/ do not touch us. The siren of the world/ has lost its voice, and the world is a vast/ desert." After his military service in the war, he met Montale* (who dedicated several of the lyrics in *Ossi di seppia* to him). During the time of the fascist regime which he openly opposed, Sbarbaro's botanical expertise, as well as his skill as a translator and a teacher, enabled him to support himself. The poetry he wrote during this period was finally published in 1955 under the title *Rimanenze* (Remainders). Among the writers he rendered into Italian are Sophocles, Aeschylus, Euripides, Balzac, Stendhal, Flaubert, and Zola. In 1948, he published *Trucioli* (Shavings), a collection of his prose writings from 1914 to 1940.

468 Sbarbaro, Camillo

Bibliography: Poesia italiana del Novecento, ed. Edoardo Sanguineti, 2 vols. (Turin: Einaudi, 1969); *Contemporary Italian Poetry: An Anthology,* ed. Carlo L. Golino (Berkeley, Calif.: University of California Press, 1962); *Italian Sampler: An Anthology of Italian Verse,* trans. Thomas G. Bergin (Montreal: Casalini, 1964); Giorgio Bàrberi Squarotti, *Camillo Sbarbaro* (Milan: Mursia, 1971); Gina Lagorio, *Sbarbaro controcorrente* (Parma: Guanda, 1973); Lorenzo Polato, *Sbarbaro* (Florence: La Nuova Italia, 1969).

SCALIGERO, GIULIO CESARE (1484–1558), scholar and critic. After participating in the battle of Ravenna in 1512 and studying at the University of Bologna, Scaligero went to Agen in France to serve as personal physician to Bishop Angelo Della Rovere. Scaligero's literary career commenced in 1531 with an oration in Latin attacking a satire of Erasmus written in the Ciceronian style; he published a second polemical oration in 1536. He engaged in literary arguments with other distinguished writers, including François Rabelais, Jerome Cardan, and Étienne Dolet. His Latin works, both those which remain and those that have been lost, are varied and numerous, but his reputation rests primarily upon his *Poetices libri septem* (1561, *Poetics*), one of the most extensive works on the nature of poetry to appear during the Renaissance.* Typically, Scaligero does not hesitate to take issue with Aristotle over the very nature of poetry itself. Rejecting the concept that poetry is imitation *(mimesis),* he accentuates the moral, pedagogical function of poetry and assigns to *mimesis* an intermediary end directed towards a higher moral goal. In practical criticism, Scaligero elevated Virgil above Homer as a poet of the well-ordered aristocratic society he admired. He also maintained a rigid separation of genres based upon subject matter which was to be reflected in the neoclassical movements all over Europe.

See also CASTELVETRO, Ludovico; MINTURNO, Antonio; ROBORTELLO, Francesco.

Bibliography: Julius Caesar Scaliger, *Select Translations from Scaliger's Poetics,* trans. F. M. Padelford (New Haven, Conn.: Yale University Press, 1905); Rose Mary Ferraro, *Giudizi critici e criteri estetici nei Poetices Libri Septem* (Chapel Hill, N.C.: University of North Carolina Studies in Comparative Literature, No. 52, 1971); Vernon Hall, Jr., "Life of Julius Caesar Scaliger (1484–1558)," *Transactions of the American Philosophical Society* 40 (1950), 85–170; Bernard Weinberg, *A History of Literary Criticism in the Italian Renaissance,* 2 vols. (Chicago: University of Chicago Press, 1961).

SCAPIGLIATURA (the Italian counterpart to the French *bohème* from *scapigliato,* meaning "disheveled" or "unkempt"). This name is given to a group of literary artists (some of whom were also painters and composers), active mostly in Milan during the 1860s, who radically opposed bourgeois manners, habits, and aesthetic ideals. Carlo Righetti (1830–1874, pseudonym Cletto Arrighi) was the first to use the term. In his novel *Scapigliatura e il 6 febbraio* (1862, Scapigliatura and February 6), he describes the *scapigliatura* as a kind of mystical consortium uniting a cross-class assemblage of existential companions, each marked by genius, restlessness, eccentricity, and a keen sensitivity to social issues.

The major exponents of the *scapigliatura* were the poet-painters Emilio Praga* and Giovanni Camerana (1845–1905); the poet-composer Arrigo Boito*; Igino Ugo Tarchetti (1830–1869); Righetti himself; and Carlo Dossi (1849–1910), who was famous for his refined linguistic experimentalism. The group's mentor was Giuseppe Rovani (1818–1874), the author of *I Cento Anni* (1859–64, One Hundred Years), a historical novel depicting Lombard society in the eighteenth century. Rovani is also known for his synaesthetic theories, which he expounded—as an example of the *scapigliatura*'s anti-academism—at the table of an inn. Outside of Milan, analogous literary and moral attitudes were found in the Piedmontese Giovanni Faldella (1846–1928), Achille Giovanni Cagna (1841–1904), and Roberto Sacchetti (1847–1881). Alberto Cantoni (1841–1904), from Mantua, a humorist whom Pirandello* considered his forerunner, and the Neapolitan Vittorio Imbriani (1840–1885) can also be said to have belonged to the *scapigliatura*, but in a more general way.

Living in a society characterized by the deflation of the Risorgimento's ideals and expectations, the *scapigliati* as a group are characterized by a feeling of displacement and isolation, which for them meant the loss of true human uniqueness and potential for creativity in mass society. As a response to being cut off from the structures of organized culture (the degradation of their role as artists in society), the *scapigliatura* contemptuously attacked institutionalized morality and the "normality" of middle-class life, mocking the church and religion, to which it opposed the virtues of sexual perversion, alcoholism, and drug addiction. Proof of the authenticity of the *scapigliatura* revolt is the real poverty and degeneracy of its adherents, as well as the fact that Camerana committed suicide and Praga and Tarchetti died prematurely from the effects of the excessive consumption of alcohol and disease.

In contesting the dominance of bourgeois social and economic norms, the *scapigliati* either directly inveighed against the wealth and privileges of high society, heralding its demise, desecrated its idols and ideals, or elaborated, as an alternative to alienation, a romantic nostalgia for primitiveness and mystical communion with nature, conceived as a mysterious unity embracing all forms of life. The group's poetry focuses mainly on penetrating the secret of life, uncontaminated by human reason, which was seen to be manifested in the natural processes of evolution and transformation of matter. What in fact distinguishes the *scapigliati* from other Italian romantics is their sensitivity to *process;* their literature of "maggots" and "coffins" shows an excessive, nearly religious, preoccupation with the mysteries of corrosion and decomposition. For example, in the *scapigliati* the traditional romantic "love-death" motif takes on an aura of sacrilegious morbidity in their obsession with the correspondences between the signs of beauty and pleasure and those of decay—as in Tarchetti's "Memento" (in *Disjecta* [1879, Dispersions]), where the poet conjoins the pleasures of carnal intimacy with the terrifying images of his lover's skeleton.

The *scapigliati*'s aesthetic ideal was to create a nonfinite, "open" art, as opposed to the "fixed" reality of mimetic representation. They rejected canonized literary models and the classification of the arts as separate and autonomous in favor of a mixture of the technical procedures common to poetry, music, and painting, and the contamination of genres and styles. Praga's poetry, in fact, is noted for its attempt to capture impression and "verbal color," while Boito, in *Re Orso* (1902, King Bear), Dossi, in *Desinenza in A* (1878, Ending in A), *Ritratti umani* (1883, Human Portraits), and *Note azzurre* (1912, Blue Notes), and Faldella in *Figurine* (1875, Figurines) begin a tradition of the *pastiche*, which culminates in the works of Carlo Emilio Gadda.*

Notwithstanding its explicit ridicule of the spiritualism and sentimentalism typical of poets such as Giovanni Prati* and Aleardo Aleardi,* the art of the *scapigliati* does not go beyond being much more than an extreme form of romantic sensibility. For in spite of its unconventional subject matter, meant to challenge the propriety of traditional poetic topics, the manner in which the *scapigliato* poet organizes his experience is not substantially different from past romantic visions. Its terms are the negativity of the present world and the authenticity of a new, projected totality. In poetry, the *scapigliati* portray the breakthrough into "Life" of the now displaced artist and objectified art. Boito's poem "A una mummia" (To a Mummy) from *Il libro dei versi* (1877, The Book of Verses) dramatizes this experience in a nearly paradigmatic way: "Ma un dì verrà, novissimo,/ Che in una cupa valle/ cadrem tremanti, pallidi,/ Coi i nostri errori a spalle,/ E senterem la tromba/ Che spezzerà ogni tomba./ Mummia, quella mattina/ Romperai la vetrina" (A most glorious day will come,/ When in a gloomy valley/ Trembling and pale, we will fall,/ Our mistakes behind us,/ We will hear the trumpet's sound/ shattering every tomb./ Mummy, in that morning/ You will break through the glass).

Being unable to propose a real alternative to the social and cultural institutions from which they were estranged, the *scapigliati* envisaged only modes of reintegration into a future society sensitive to creative genius. Nevertheless, the movement's importance lies in the literary and cultural attitudes it originated; its iconoclasm, contempt for bourgeois rationality, and quest for mystical or mythical totalities presaged more distinguished forms of Italian literary modernism, in particular futurism.*

See also DECADENTISMO; ROMANTICISM.

Bibliography: G. B. Carsaniga, "Scapigliatura," in *The Age of Realism,* ed. F. W. J. Hemmings (Baltimore: Penguin, 1974); Giorgio Cusatelli, "La poesia dagli scapigliati ai decadenti," in *Storia della letteratura italiana,* eds. E. Cecchi and N. Sapegno, Vol. 8 (Milan: Garzanti, 1968); Dante Isella, "La Scapigliatura letteraria lombarda: un nome, una definizione," in *Catalogo della Mostra della Scapigliatura* (Milan: Palazzo della Permanente, May–June 1966); Jørn Moestrup, *La Scapigliatura, Un capitolo della storia del Risorgimento* (Copenhagen: Analecta Romana Instituti Danici, III, Supplementum, 1963).

Robert S. Dombroski

SCHMITZ, ETTORE: *See* SVEVO, ITALO.

SCIASCIA, LEONARDO (1921–   ), journalist, playwright, and novelist, generally regarded by critics to be Sicily's finest living writer. A native of Recalmuto (Agrigento), Sciascia enjoyed a number of excellent teachers, including Vitaliano Brancati,* from whom he acquired his hatred of arbitrary power (either that of the fascists or the Mafia) and corruption. His early, formative reading included the French *philosophes,* Manzoni,* Casanova,* and a number of American novelists (Dos Passos, Caldwell, and Steinbeck). In 1949, he began teaching in the elementary schools. His first work of note, *Le parrocchie di Regalpetra* (1956, *Salt in the Wound*), already contained the Sicilian settings and themes which were to be characteristic in all his writings. Later, in his preface to the 1967 edition of *Le parrocchie di Regalpetra,* Sciascia admitted that his works form a unified whole: "All my books taken together form one: a Sicilian book which probes the wounds of past and present and develops as the history of the continuous defeat of reason and of those who have been personally overcome and annihilated in that defeat."

Il giorno della civetta (1961, *Mafia Vendetta*) created Sciascia's critical and popular reputation as a novelist of the Mafia. (The Italian title, literally meaning "the day of the owl," refers to a line in Shakespeare's *Henry VI.*) It is a detective novel dealing with a Mafia execution and the subsequent investigation of the crime by a policeman named Bellodi, a young man from Parma and an ex-partisan who strongly believes in the ideals of democracy and justice. Bellodi's inability to bring the guilty party, Don Mariano Arena, to justice exposes the Mafia's corruption of Sicily's political and legal institutions. Sciascia's next novel, *Il consiglio d'Egitto* (1963, *The Council of Egypt*), abandons the detective genre and takes up that of the historical novel, only to parody some of its conventions. The work is set in eighteenth-century Palermo and describes the invention of a fraudulent Arabic codex by an abbot named Giuseppe Vella, treating the Arabic conquest of Sicily. The "discovery" of Vella's forged document makes him a wealthy celebrity, since the inhabitants of the city hope that the document will prove that their ancestors were granted prestigious positions and benefices by the Arabs. This subplot is intertwined with a political subplot concerning the life of Francesco Paolo Di Blasi, a lawyer who led an unsuccessful Jacobin revolution against the very feudal privileges which Vella's forgery has affected. Eventually, both Vella and Di Blasi are destroyed by the authorities.

The same kind of historical reconstruction within a fictional plot occurs in *Morte dell'inquisitore* (1964, *The Death of the Inquisitor*). Sciascia sets the novel in the seventeenth century and describes how Diego La Matina, an Augustinian father, is eventually burned at the stake in 1658 for heresy and the murder of the chief inquisitor, Giovanni Lopez Cisneros. While popular legend had made of his protagonist a kind of brigand, Sciascia uses his novel to restore to the murderer of the inquisitor the dignity of a heroic lover of justice, and Diego becomes a worthy successor to Di Blasi of *Il consiglio d'Egitto*. Sciascia's subsequent fiction returns to his favorite themes of the Mafia and of justice, set within the framework of the detective novel. In *A ciascuno il suo* (1966, *A Man's Blessing*), he creates another protagonist, Professor Paolo Laurana, whose curiosity and love for justice lead him to investigate the murder of a pharmacist. However, by the time Laurana has solved the mystery of the killer's identity, he has also revealed his knowledge to the murderer and is eventually killed. *Il contesto* (1971, *Equal Danger*) expands Sciascia's typical indictment of the Sicilian Mafia to include all of modern society. The setting, an imaginary and unidentified country in which the initial crime takes place—the murder of a district attorney and three judges—calls attention to the metaphysical dimensions of this narrative. The investigation is entrusted to Inspector Rogas but ends with his own death under mysterious circumstances that reveal the total corruption of the political institutions of the unnamed country. Sciascia defines the work as a "fable about power anywhere in the world" wherein the historical institution of the Mafia is transformed into a universal metaphor of corrupt, absolute power. In the recent *Todo modo* (1974, *One Way or Another*), Sciascia continues his dissection of the links between crime and power, corruption and authority, again employing the detective novel to explore the web of complicity linking a number of important figures who gather at a retreat for "spiritual exercises."

In addition to his novels, Sciascia has written a number of short stories; a play entitled *L'Onorevole* (1965, The Deputy); and an important assessment of Pirandello,* *Pirandello e la Sicilia* (1961, Pirandello and Sicily). His original and imaginative use of the historical novel and detective fiction has expanded the narrative possibilities of both genres. A number of important political films have been made from his works, principally by the directors Francesco Rosi and Elio Petri. His latest works include *La* *scomparsa di Majorana* (1975, The Disappearance of Majorana) and *I pugnalatori* (1976, The Stabbers), both of which combine the techniques of mystery fiction and historical analysis to treat the disappearance of an Italian physicist during the fascist era and a strange series of murders in the Palermo of 1862.

Bibliography: Pirandello e la Sicilia, 2nd ed. (Rome: S. Sciascia Editore, 1968); *The Council of Egypt,* trans. Adrienne Foulke (New York: Knopf, 1966); *Equal Danger,* trans. Adrienne Foulke (New York: Harper, 1973); *Mafia Vendetta,* trans. Archibald Colquhoun and Arthur Oliver (New York: Knopf, 1964); *A Man's Blessing,* trans. Adrienne Foulke (New York: Harper, 1968); *One Way or Another,* trans. Adrienne Foulke (New York: Harper, 1977); *Salt in the Wound/The Death of the Inquisitor,* trans. Judith Green (New York: Orion, 1969); Claude Ambroise, *Invito alla lettura di Sciascia* (Milan: Mursia, 1974); Walter Mauro, *Sciascia* (Florence: La Nuova Italia, 1970).

SEMIOTICS, or semiology, the general science of signs of which linguistics is but a part, has exerted a strong influence upon contemporary Italian literary criticism. Founded upon the insights of Ferdinand de Saussure, C. S. Pierce, and C. W. Morris, semiotics is closely related to structuralism,* for in the analysis of cultural artifacts conceived of as a system of signs, the system of relationships or structures which allows meaning to be produced by the signs must also be carefully considered. The concepts of message and code are fundamental to the semiotic approach, for every act of human communication is conceived as a message sent and received through various types of signs. The rules governing the combination of these messages are prescribed by codes, logical constructs which allow messages to be understood. Viewed in this fashion, all forms of human expression—music, literature, art, film, fashion, food—can be analyzed as a system of signs whose specific codes may generate meaning. Semiotic theory shares, in many respects, the same intellectual heritage as structuralism, but in Italy in recent years semiotics seems to have achieved a greater measure of success, both on the theoretical level and in the practical criticism of literature or film. While most contemporary Italian semioticians are indebted to de Saussure, Pierce, Morris, and a group of recent French critics (Roland Barthes and Christian Metz in particular), a number of them have made their own original contributions in theory (Umberto Eco*), literature (Cesare Segre, 1928– ; Maria Corti, 1915–), linguistics (Paolo Valesio, 1939–), and cinema (Pier Paolo Pasolini;* Emilio Garroni, 1925– ; Gianfranco Bettetini).

See also ECO, Umberto; PASOLINI, Pier Paolo; STRUCTURALISM.

Bibliography: Gianfranco Bettetini, *The Language and Technique of Film* (The Hague: Mouton, 1973); *I metodi attuali della critica in Italia,* eds. Maria Corti and Cesare Segre (Turin: ERI, 1970); Jonathan Culler, *Structuralist Poetics* (Ithaca,

N.Y.: Cornell University Press, 1975); Emilio Garroni, *Semiotica ed estetica* (Bari: Laterza, 1968); *The Tell-Tale Sign: A Survey of Semiotics,* ed. Thomas A. Sebeok (Lisse: De Ridder, 1975); Cesare Segre, *Semiotics and Literary Criticism* (The Hague: Mouton, 1973).

SERAFINO AQUILANO (1466–1500), poet, musician, and courtier. Serafino was born Serafino de' Ciminelli in Aquila in the Abruzzi. After studying music in Naples, he quickly gained recognition for his musical adaptations of Petrarch's* lyrics accompanied upon the lute. Much of his life was spent at various Italian courts (Rome, Urbino, Mantua, Milan, and Naples) in the service of some of the most prominent personalities of the late fifteenth century (Cesare Borgia, Cardinal Ascanio Sforza, Isabella d'Este, Francesco Gonzaga, and Ferrandino of Aragon). At Mantua in 1495, Serafino organized a famous allegorical spectacle, a vogue in courtly entertainment that attracted even the genius of Leonardo da Vinci* at the Sforza court in Milan, in which his own risqué performance as the character of "Voluptuousness" brought him as much renown as his minor musical and poetic talents. A born entertainer, Serafino combined these gifts with a pleasing personality, charm, wit, and skill in games of chance to become one of the period's most celebrated courtly figures.

Serafino's Petrarchan style was considered ornate and affected by a purist like Pietro Bembo,* who attempted to recreate Petrarch's elegant but refined and graceful poetic idiom, and represented the kind of excesses which were the object of Bembo's poetic reforms. Serafino's characteristic literary form was the *strambotto,* * of which he produced over three hundred and fifty, as well as over one hundred sonnets.* His poetry does not constitute a coherent work with an internal development like that of Petrarch's *Canzoniere.* The *strambotto,* an eight-line stanza usually ending in a rhymed couplet, was admirably suited to his particular combination of fantastic poetic conceits (derived, for the most part, from imagery taken out of its context in the *Canzoniere*) and pleasing music befitting the courtly setting. Abroad, his particular form of Petrarchism* with its highly wrought imagery, together with that of his contemporaries Tebaldeo* and Cariteo,* influenced lyric poets at the same time as these poets encountered the works of their master Petrarch and their critic Bembo. Thus, Renaissance* poets in France, England, Spain, and elsewhere, whose object was to develop a new poetic diction in their own languages, had several forms of Petrarchism from which to choose. The influence of Serafino upon Wyatt, Jean Lemaire de Belges, Surrey, and others testifies to his usefulness as a stylistic model, even if his own inspiration never equaled that of Petrarch. In spite of the derogatory judgments of Bembo and literary historians, Serafino was the most popular poet in Italy when he died.

See also CARITEO, Benedetto; PETRARCHISM; STRAMBOTTO; TEBALDEO, Antonio.

Bibliography: Le Rime, ed. Mario Menghini (Bologna: Collezione di opere inedite o rare, 1894); Barbara Bauer-Formiconi, *Die Strambotti Des Serafino Dall'Aquila* (Munich: Wilhelm Fink, 1967); Patricia Thomson, "Wyatt and the School of Serafino," *Comparative Literature* 13 (1961), 289–315.

SERAO, MATILDE (1857–1927), journalist and novelist. The daughter of a Greek mother and a Neapolitan father, Serao was born in Patras, Greece, and entered the Scuola Normale in Naples with rather poor academic preparation (she did not learn the alphabet until she was nine years old). Nonetheless, by the age of seventeen, she earned the diploma necessary for teaching in the public schools. From 1876 until 1878, while she worked in a telegraph office, she began journalistic writing. Some of her best short stories ("Scuola normale femminile," "Telegrafi dello stato"[The Normal School for Women, State Telegraphs]) deal with these early and formative experiences. After the publication of her first novel, *Cuore infermo* (1881, The Sick Heart), Serao gained her first truly permanent position as a journalist on the very successful Roman daily, *Capitan Fracassa,* whose contributors included D'Annunzio,* Carducci,* and Edoardo Scarfoglio (1860–1917), her future husband. Her short stories and bylines appeared in many of the outstanding periodicals of the period.

Serao's second novel, *Fantasia* (1882, *Fantasy*), traces the closely inter-connected lives of two schoolgirls—Caterina, a typical bourgeois girl, and her friend Lucia, her opposite in every respect. After a skillfully drawn introduction to the two characters set in the repressive atmosphere of their boarding school, Serao moves to complicate her plot, as Caterina marries Andrea Lieti and Lucia marries Alberto Sanna. The couples pass a great deal of time together until Andrea and Lucia finally fall in love and elope, leaving Alberto behind with a serious illness and driving Caterina to suicide. The novel was an instant success with a reading public that valued passionate tales of fatal love affairs. Serao's best work moves beyond this essentially upper-middle-class milieu reminiscent of the early novels of D'Annunzio to a more realistic view of contemporary life in Rome or Naples.

Many of the articles on Naples which Serao published in Roman periodicals were collected and reissued in 1884 as *Il ventre di Napoli* (The Belly of Naples). Little reporting from the nineteenth century captures so skillfully the panorama of life in the popular quarters of a large European city—from the picturesque food of the populace, their daily occupations, their mania for the state lottery, to the many striking street scenes and religious festivals still to be seen by the casual tourist. Her practical aim was to obtain government funds from the Depretis government to initiate a program of urban renewal in her city.

In 1885, Serao married Scarfoglio and published *La conquista di Roma* *(The Conquest of Rome).* Familiar in the fiction of the last century, the theme is one of Serao's favorites—the arrival of a provincial type in the capital city, and the story of his or her subsequent failure or success. In this instance, her protagonist is a deputy from a poor region in southern Italy, Don Francesco Sangiorgio, who comes to King Umberto's Rome in the 1880s. The novel paints a brilliant portrait of life at that time—the crowds of shoppers, the Piazza Montecitorio and the political assemblies, the duels among the deputies, the society whirling about the political life. Sangiorgio is eventually overwhelmed in this environment and returns to his provincial home after resigning his seat in Parliament. Similarly, *Vita e avventure di Riccardo Joanna* (1887, The Life and Adventures of Riccardo Joanna) traces the life of another character bent upon conquering Rome, a journalist who builds a daily paper up to a circulation of over one hundred thousand copies, only to end his career in ruin. Serao and Scarfoglio themselves had vainly attempted to conquer Rome, and their ambitious publication, *Il Corriere di Roma,* failed. More fortunate than Riccardo Joanna, however, the couple was aided by a sympathetic banker, Matteo Schilizzi, who paid off their debts so that they could move to Naples to co-edit *Il Corriere di Napoli.*

Matilde Serao completed an extraordinary number of novels and short-story collections (too many, in the opinion of many critics, who feel that her huge literary output contains many pieces of an inferior quality). Among the most notable of them are *All'erta, sentinella* (1889, *On Guard*), *La ballerina* (1899, *The Ballet Dancer*), *Suor Giovanna della Croce* (1901, Sister Giovanna of the Cross), and *Ella non rispose* (1914, *Souls Divided*). There is general agreement that *Il paese di Cuccagna* (1891, *The Land of Cockayne*) is her masterpiece. In this work, Serao returns to the raw material of *Il ventre di Napoli* and provides the reader with both the pageant of Neapolitan life and an analysis of the mania for gambling in the lottery which infects all segments of the city's society like a cancer. One of her greatest short stories, "Terno secco" (a reference to a lottery number), as well as her reporting, had already treated this theme. Her characters are inveterate gamblers—a marquis, a physician, an unfrocked priest, a lottery office manager, and a stockbroker. In a series of vignettes closer to episodic sketches than to separate but completely interrelated sections of a unified novel, Serao projects the grotesque behavior of her characters against the colorful spectacle of Neapolitan festivals, processions in honor of the city's patron, Saint Gennaro, and the weekly ritual of the lottery drawing each Saturday that spells disappointment for so many and good fortune for so very few. Serao's Neapolitan tales and her picture of Umbertian Rome complement the other memorable regional portraits in nineteenth-century Italian literature by Verga,* Capuana,* and Fogazzaro,* although Serao's fiction never surpasses these writers in originality or in craftsmanship. Nevertheless, her works constitute one of the most impressive collections of fiction or journalism by a woman in the literature of turn-of-the-century Italy or elsewhere.

Bibliography: Serao, ed. Pietro Pancrazi, 2 vols. (Milan: Garzanti, 1944–46); *The Conquest of Rome* (New York: Harper, 1902); *Fantasy,* trans. H. Harland (London: Heinemann, 1890); *The Land of Cockayne,* trans. anonymous (1901; rpt. New York: Howard Fertig, 1977); Anna Banti, *Matilde Serao* (Turin: UTET, 1965); Anthony Gisolfi, *The Essential Matilde Serao* (New York: Las Americas, 1968); Judith J. Howard, "The Feminine Vision of Matilde Serao," *Italian Quarterly* 18 (1975), 55–77; M. G. Martin-Gistucci, *L'oeuvre romanesque de Matilde Serao* (Grenoble: Presses Universitaires de Grenoble, 1973).

SERCAMBI, GIOVANNI (1348–1424), historian and *novelliere.* Sercambi, born in Lucca, was an apothecary by profession. He held important governmental posts in Lucca, which was ruled by the Guinigi family, including those of *gonfaloniere* (standardbearer) of justice, ambassador, and member of the general council. His most substantial work, *Croniche* (Chronicles), is a lengthy history of Lucca from 1169 until 1400. Apparently written over a span of many years (1368 until 1423), it was left unfinished because of its author's failing health. Notable for its keen political judgments based upon historical phenomena, it reveals Sercambi as a cultured businessman with a wide knowledge of learned and popular sources.

Sercambi is best known for the *Novelle,* his collection of some one hundred and fifty-five stories. Recalling *The Decameron,* the occasion of the storytelling is the plague of 1374 in Lucca which causes a group of people to leave the city in search of safety. Despite obvious parallels between the works of Sercambi and Boccaccio* (the use of the plague motif and the subsequent flight from the stricken city), there are essential differences. Sercambi is the single narrator of the tales (a fact underlined by an acrostic poem in the prologue), and the *Novelle* therefore lacks the thematic and stylistic variety of *The Decameron* provided by the various storytellers' points of view and the subtle artistic effects of filtering the author's many opinions through the personalities of ten storytellers. While Sercambi's tales speak of the passion, love, violence, and cruelty pervasive in Boccaccio, they usually lack the master's touch. Sercambi relied heavily upon oral tradition for his tales, and on the whole, his style is less pleasing. Often his obvious narrative transitions become repetitious, and he seeks to convince the reader of the story's actuality by frequent shifts from past to present tense. Because of the narrator's presence during the journey from Lucca, the reader's attention is drawn not only to the tales he narrates but to events and sights as well. Furthermore, the irregular insertion into the narrative of poems which are often only tenuously connected to the content can be contrasted to Boccaccio's harmonious synthesis of the narrator, storytellers, framework, and the poems concluding each of the ten days of storytelling. In general, Sercambi's *novelle* are closer to chronicle or history than to an integrated artistic vision of the world such as Boccaccio's. In their attention to detail and concrete particulars, they may be considered an apt reflection of the literary tradition which grew up among Tuscan merchants and businessmen during the Trecento.

See also BOCCACCIO, Giovanni; NOVELLA.

Bibliography: Le Chroniche di Giovanni Sercambi lucchese, ed. Salvatore Bongi (Rome: Fonti per la storia d'Italia, 1892); *Novelle,* ed. Giovanni Sinicropi, 2 vols. (Bari: Laterza, 1972); Christian Bec, "La Fortune du *Décameron* à la fin du Trecento: Plagiat et réinvention dans le *Novelliero* de Sercambi," *Revue des Études Italiennes* 21 (1975), 62–81, and *Les Marchands écrivains: affaires et humanisme à Florence (1375–1434)* (Paris: Mouton, 1967); Ann West Vivarelli, "Giovanni Sercambi's *Novelle* and the Legacy of Boccaccio," *Modern Language Notes* 90 (1975), 109–27.

SERENI, VITTORIO (1913–   ), poet and editor. Sereni was born in Luino in the province of Varese and graduated from the University of Milan with a thesis on Gozzano* (1936). Afterwards, he began to teach while making regular contributions to literary reviews sympathetic to hermetic poetry. Among his friends in Milan could be numbered Quasimodo,* Gatto,* and Sinisgalli.* It was to be expected, therefore, that his first collection of verse, *Frontiera* (1941, The Border)—subsequently revised and republished in both 1942 and 1966—would reflect an affinity to the lyric style and themes already associated by the critics with many of his friends. Of particular significance in this volume are the poems "Terrazza" ("The Terrace") and "3 dicembre" ("December the Third").

The war changed Sereni's life and affected his lyric poetry, moving him toward a less closed and more socially responsive kind of verse. Captured by American troops in Sicily and sent to Algeria for two years as a prisoner of war, Sereni composed the lyrics which would appear in *Diario d'Algeria* (1947, Algerian Diary), poetry whose autobiographical character breaks out of the strictly private hermetic mode and uses the war and Italy's defeat to speak eloquently of universal human problems in a voice accessible to a wide audience. After his repatriation, Sereni returned to teaching and engaged in a series of translations, notable among them the poetry of René Char and William Carlos Williams. After six years in the publicity department of the Pirelli firm, Sereni became an important editor for the Mondadori Publishing House in Milan and continued to contribute essays and poems to a number of literary reviews. The verse written after 1945 is collected in *Gli strumenti umani* (1965, The Human Instruments) and reflects a new postwar Italian society characterized by increased prosperity and political stability but confused values and uncertain prospects for the future. The poet's own troubled search for new ideals is dramatized in "Un sogno" ("A Dream"), where a leaden, faceless apparition confronts him and demands his "papers"; the poet is forced to respond that he possesses only hopes, memories, and a few friends but no documents, and is told that one cannot pass "without a programme." In recent years, Sereni has also turned to narrative with *L'opzione* (1964, The Option), a satirical picture of the Frankfurt Book Fair; and "Ventisei" (1970, Twenty-Six). The latter is an exceptional account of the poet's experiences in his quest to retrace his life during the war twenty-six years later and his discovery that he must come to grips with the vexing problem of how a poet employs the past in his work.

See also HERMETICISM.

Bibliography: Poesie scelte (1935–1965), ed. Lanfranco Caretti (Milan: Mondadori, 1973); "Ventisei," *Forum Italicum* 4 (1970), 576–89; *Contemporary Italian Verse*, trans. G. Singh (London: London Magazines Editions, 1968); Vittoria Bradshaw, *From Pure Silence to Impure Dialogue* (New York: Las Americas, 1971)—contains bilingual selections from *Diario d'Algeria;* Massimo Grillandi, *Sereni* (Florence: La Nuova Italia, 1972); Francesco P. Memmo, *Vittorio Sereni* (Milan: Mursia, 1973); Bruce Merry, "The Poetry of Vittorio Sereni," *Italian Studies* 29 (1974), 88–102.

SERRA, RENATO (1884–1915), literary critic and writer. Serra was born in Cesena. His education at the University of Bologna put him under the formative influence of Giosuè Carducci.* After earning his degree with a thesis on the *Trionfi (Triumphs)* of Petrarch,* Serra published a number of critical essays, including a novel article in *La Voce* entitled "Carducci e Croce." In a later version, expanded and published under the title "Per un catalogo" (1910, For a Catalogue), Serra breaks with many of his contemporaries, pronounces Carducci the master of literary criticism, and rejects many of Croce's* critical principles. In 1914, he admitted Croce's importance, only to wonder if Croce dominated Italian literary life because he had an exceptional mind or, by default, because others lacked perspicacity. In a number of essays, indispensable to an understanding of the culture of the period, Serra traces the contributions of such figures as Pascoli,* Carducci, D'Annunzio,* and Gozzano,* and examines the situation of the publishing industry in Italy and the nature of its literary criticism. On the verge of a brilliant career, Serra was inducted into the army at the outbreak of hostilities in 1915 and died during an attack on Mount Podgora. Had he lived, his example might have successfully opposed the hegemony of

Crocean idealism in Italian literary studies during the period following World War I.

Bibliography: Epistolario di Renato Serra, ed. Luigi Ambrosini, et al. (Florence: Le Monnier, 1953); *Scritti letterari, morali e politici: saggi e articoli dal 1900 al 1915,* ed. Mario Isnenghi (Turin: Einaudi, 1974); Sandro Briosi, *Renato Serra* (Milan: Mursia, 1968); Giovanni Pacchiano, *Serra* (Florence: La Nuova Italia, 1970).

SESTINA, a verse form originally developed by the troubadour poets of medieval Provence. As the Provençal influence spread throughout Italy during the twelfth and thirteenth centuries, medieval Italian poets inherited not only many of their ideas concerning courtly love but also poetic forms such as the sestina. The Italian sestina follows the pattern of its Provençal model and can, in fact, be considered a special variation of the *canzone.** It contains six stanzas of six verses each and concludes with an envoy of three lines, usually called a *commiato* or *congedo* in Italian. Thus, the sestina ordinarily contains thirty-nine lines of eleven syllables each. The difficulty of composing poetry in this form is due to the complex substitute for rhyme. Using no rhymed sounds, the sestina repeats the terminal words of each of the first six lines in a fixed and ordered fashion throughout the entire poem, a process known technically as cruciate retrogradation. Each stanza successively picks up the terminal words of lines 6, 1, 5, 2, 4, and 3 of the preceding stanza until the possible permutations of this progression are exhausted. Finally, the envoy redoubles the intricacy of the sestina by using all six of the terminal words. Since the form demands that a poem be constructed around the poetic possibilities of six single words, used successively in different contexts and in different orders, it has always represented a challenge to those poets who prize formal organization and intellectual skill in composition. The troubadour poet who made the sestina famous was Arnaut Daniel. He was imitated by both Dante* and Petrarch.* The sestina became a poetic form employed by many Italian poets, among them Lorenzo de' Medici,* Cariteo,* Torquato Tasso,* Bembo,* Sannazaro,* Carducci,* and D'Annunzio.* In English, largely because of the influence of Dante and Petrarch, the sestina has been practiced by such poets as Sir Philip Sidney, T. S. Eliot, Ezra Pound, and W. H. Auden.

Bibliography: Peter E. Bondanella, "Arnaut Daniel and Dante's *Rime Petrose:* A Re-Examination," *Studies in Philology* 68 (1971), 416–34; *Princeton Encyclopedia of Poetry and Poetics,* ed. Alex Preminger (Princeton, N.J.: Princeton University Press, 1965); János Riesz, *Die Sestine* (Munich: W. Fink, 1971); Raffaele Spongano, *Nozioni ed esempi di metrica italiana* (Bologna: Pàtron, 1966).

SICILIAN SCHOOL: *See* DA LENTINO, Giacomo; FREDERICK II; PIER DELLA VIGNA.

SILONE, IGNAZIO, pseudonym of Secondo Tranquilli (1900–1978), novelist, political activist, and militant writer. Silone was born in Pescina dei Marsi (L'Aquila), and during the earthquake of the Marsica (1915), he was left an orphan with a younger brother, Romolo (who died in 1932 as a result of fascist tortures in the penitentiary of Procida). These early traumatic experiences and their aftermath left in him deep psychological scars and the seeds of future protest, the genuine desire for greater social justice and solidarity among men. Drawn from his formal education by the political and social problems afflicting Italy during World War I and the years immediately following, he enrolled in the Socialist party in 1918 and began a period of intense political activism while leading a bohemian existence in Rome. In 1921, he was present in Leghorn at the foundation of the Communist party, to which he remained totally committed for a decade. He worked for the party in different functions, carrying out key and risky assignments, serving as editor or staff member of various papers (the Rome weekly *L'Avanguardia,* the Trieste daily *Il Lavoratore,* and *L'Unità*), keeping the lines of communication open inside the party even under the closest fascist surveillance and the constant threat of reprisal, publishing clandestinely, and working closely with the top party leaders, Antonio Gramsci* and Palmiro Togliatti, whom he accompanied on several missions to Moscow. After the promulgation of the fascist "exceptional laws" (1926) and the worsening of the political situation, he was arrested and expelled successively from Spain, France, and Switzerland, where he had sought refuge (1930). Sick and disillusioned, he underwent a spiritual crisis that led to his break with the Communist party (1931) and the beginning of his literary work (*Fontamara* [1930, *Fontamara*]; first published in German, 1933; Italian and English editions, 1934). A self-analysis of this painful experience, and other autobiographical documents, are contained in *Uscita di sicurezza* (1965, *Emergency Exit*). Upon his return to Italy (1944), he resumed for a while his political activity among the ranks of the socialists, edited the paper *Avanti,* and served as Socialist party deputy to the Constituent Assembly (1946–47). He gradually withdrew from the political scene to dedicate himself almost exclusively to writing. He has received several literary prizes (Marzocco, 1965; Campiello, 1968), and from 1956 to 1968, he edited *Tempo presente* with Nicola Chiaromonte (1905–1972).

Silone's works are closely related to his political activity and to the sociopolitical problems of the period in which they were conceived. While they represent the eternal drama of the humble and oppressed, they depict a more particular, more personal human tragedy, that of the *cafoni* (peasants) of the author's native land. The realistic dimension and regional setting of Silone's works call to mind the European naturalistic narrative of the nineteenth century (Verga,* Zola), and their political and social themes can be placed in the current of Italian neorealism (Alvaro,* Pratolini,* Jovine*). However, they follow an essentially autonomous line of development, not only in their stylistic form (antiliterary, in a simple form of dialogue), but also in the unique nature of the themes which have been characterized as a religious love for justice. Socialism and Christianity are, in fact, the poles between which Silone's narrative evolves, from the first novel, *Fontamara,* to the recent play *L'avventura di un povero cristiano* (1968, *The Story of an Humble Christian*). Silone's socialism is an integral Christianity, à la Kierkegaard, free of formalism and translated into socially useful action. His art could be defined as social realism, or as Christian realism. The heroes of Silone's novels (Berardo Viola, Pietro Spina, Rocco, Luca, Daniele, Celestino) are men who "hunger and thirst after righteousness." They are martyrs of a society more pagan than Christian.

The socioreligious inquiry assumes various forms in Silone's novels, essays (*La scuola dei dittatori* [1938, *The School for Dictators*]), and plays (*Ed egli si nascose* [1944, *And He Hid Himself*]). In *Fontamara,* he establishes a fraternal dialogue with the men of his land to give vent to his suffering and to make known to the world the plight of the *cafoni;* Berardo embodies the feelings and the aspirations of the author, who, sick and in exile, would like to shake the tyranny of fascism at its roots, but is himself like an oak felled by man's hatchet. In *Pane e vino* (1937, *Bread and Wine*), he relates the drama of Pietro Spina, a refugee who hopes to find help and understanding among the *cafoni. Il seme sotto la neve* (1942, *The Seed beneath the Snow*) presents the same contrast between good and wicked, heroes and cowards, saints and traitors. Pietro Spina and the venal Sciatap reappear in this novel as they do in *The Story of an Humble Christian.* Although in the later novels, *Una manciata di more* (1952, *A Handful of Blackberries*) and *La volpe e le camelie* (1960, *The Fox and the Camelias*), Silone continues to speak of clandestine communist activities, it is to show the excesses and failures of the party. Accusations, reprisals, and betrayals are no less frequent and ruthless than among the fascists. Only the power of love can defeat the sly foxes of oppression. The myth of communism has been shattered and with it the hope for a new social order. *Il segreto di Luca* (1956, *The Secret of Luke*) continues the personal and social tragedy of this critical postwar period: Silone's return to his native village, and his disappointment before the crumbling of another myth, the change for the worse of that noble world of the *cafoni,* which had sustained his protest and his literary inspiration. In *The Story of an Humble Christian,* the political and social problems of this century are viewed from a vaster historical perspective as problems which have afflicted mankind since the beginning of time and as a result of historical failure: the shrewd politics of a Boniface VIII prevailed over the Christianity of Celestine.

The sincere desire to harmonize the two paths of Christianity and politics is the dream Silone has so eloquently expressed in his works.

Bibliography: A Handful of Blackberries, trans. Darina Silone (New York: Harper, 1953); *Bread and Wine,* trans. Harvey Fergusson (New York: Atheneum, 1962); *Fontamara,* trans. Harvey Fergusson (New York: Atheneum, 1960); *The Story of an Humble Christian,* trans. William Weaver (New York: Harper, 1971); Luce d'Eramo, *L'opera di Ignazio Silone* (Milan: Mondadori, 1971); Richard W. B. Lewis, *The Picaresque Saint* (Philadelphia: Lippincott, 1959), Nathan A. Scott, Jr., *Rehearsals of Discomposure* (New York: King's Crown Press, 1952).

Ernesto G. Caserta

SINISGALLI, LEONARDO (1908–   ), lyric poet. Sinisgalli was born in Montemurro in the province of Potenza. A promising scientist, he was invited by Enrico Fermi (1901–1954) to join his research institute in 1928 but refused, preferring to "follow the painters and poets," as he put it. Although he eventually received a degree in electrical and industrial engineering, Sinisgalli remained closely linked to literary circles in Rome and Milan, was a close friend of the poets Ungaretti,* Quasimodo,* Sereni,* and Gatto* (to mention but a few), and has always retained a most characteristic dual interest in scientific modes of thought and poetic invention. Although his early verse is indebted to the hermetic poets who were his colleagues and friends, like most writers of this generation, he incorporated the lessons of hermeticism* into poetry of a personal nature. Major poets and critics praised his earliest lyrics, which appeared in 1936. Perhaps his best known collections of verse are *Campi elisi* (1939, Elysian Fields) and *La vigna vecchia* (1952, The Old Vineyard). The title of one of his most inventive prose works, *Furor mathematicus* (1944, A Passion for Mathematics), calls attention to his typical combination of geometrical form and intellectual rigor with the richly evocative quality of his poetry. Besides his verse, Sinisgalli has directed documentary films, edited a technical journal called *Civiltà delle macchine,* and contributed to various literary reviews.

See also HERMETICISM.

Bibliography: L'Ellisse: poesie 1932–1972, ed. Giuseppe Pontiggia (Milan: Mondadori, 1974); *Italian Sampler: An Anthology of Italian Verse,* trans. Thomas G. Bergin (Montreal: Mario Casalini, 1964); *Twentieth-Century Italian Poetry,* ed. L. R. Lind (Indianapolis, Ind.: Bobbs-Merrill, 1974); Gianni Pozzi, *La poesia italiana del Novecento* (Turin: Einaudi, 1970).

SLATAPER, SCIPIO (1888–1915), essayist, critic, and writer. Slataper was born in Trieste and received his education in Florence, where he met Prezzolini,* Papini,* and Soffici* and became one of the chief contributors to *La Voce*, providing essays on political affairs and on Trieste. In 1912, he completed his university degree, having prepared a thesis on Ibsen. After a love affair ended in the suicide of his mistress, he married and traveled abroad, worked in Hamburg for several years, and returned to Trieste and Rome in 1913–14 to agitate for Italian intervention against the Austrians. He enlisted in the army when Italy entered the war and was killed at the front near Mount Podgora. *Il mio Carso* (1912, My Carso), his skillful autobiographical novel, has attracted the attention of contemporary critics for its interesting narrative structure and its symbolic and mythical evocation of the Carso region.

Bibliography: *Opera omnia,* ed. Giani Stuparich, 6 vols. (Milan: Mondadori, 1950–58); Carlo Delcorno, "Rassegna di studi su Slataper (1965–1972)," *Lettere italiane* 24 (1972), 532–48; Anco Marzio Mutterle, *Scipio Slataper* (Milan: Mursia, 1965); Giani Stuparich, *Scipio Slataper* (1922; rpt. Milan: Mondadori, 1950).

SOFFICI, ARDENGO (1879–1964), painter, critic, poet, and prose writer. Soffici was born near Florence in Rignano sull'Arno and was forced to move into Florence after his family suffered financial setbacks. His first passion was painting, and he frequently attended lectures at the city's academy where the famous impressionist painter Giovanni Fattori (1825–1908) taught. After his father's death, he traveled to Paris, lived a bohemian existence from 1903 until 1907, and met Picasso, Max Jacob, Apollinaire, Braque, and Giovanni Papini,* for whom he wrote his first critical essays on art for the review *Leonardo* under the pen-name Stefan Cloud. Papini also introduced him to Giuseppe Prezzolini* in Florence. Thus, Soffici became a collaborator on *La Voce* (publishing notable essays on Medardo Rosso [1858–1928] and the impressionists) and eventually on *Lacerba* in its futurist phase. Before joining the futurist movement, however, Soffici wrote a review critical of one of their exhibitions in Milan and was set upon by Umberto Boccioni (1882–1916), Marinetti,* Carlo Carrà (1881–1966), and others at a popular artists' bar in Florence for his impertinence. Once a part of the movement, Soffici wrote several penetrating critical works on futurist poetics and aesthetics, the relationship between cubism and futurism,* and some early lyrics in the futurist mode, published as *Bif₤zf + 18, Simultaneità, Chimismi lirici* (1915, Bif₤zf + 18, Simultaneity, Lyric Chemisms).

The bulk of Soffici's literary output is narrative and autobiographical in character. It comprises an early novel, *Lemmonio Boreo* (1911, Lemmonio Boreo), a picaresque tale with a character whose name Soffici borrowed from Cellini's* *Vita; Arlecchino* (1914, Harlequin), essays depicting Soffici's experiences in his travels between Paris and Florence; *Giornale di bordo* (1915, Logbook), a selection of his polemical opinions on a wide range of cultural matters; and war diaries such as *Kobilek* (1918, Mount

Kobilek) and *La ritirata del Friuli* (1919, The Retreat from Friuli), both of which are traditional in narrative style but are ideologically akin to futurist and fascist glorifications of a warlike Italian spirit. With the advent of fascism, Soffici moved from his youthful iconoclasm to a more conservative and traditional position. His autobiography in four volumes, published under the general title *Autoritratto di un artista italiano nel quadro del suo tempo* (1951-55, Self-portrait of an Italian Artist in the Context of His Time), is an illuminating record of the many decisive political, philosophical, and cultural upheavals which occurred during his lifetime. It gives insight into the movement of Soffici's career from revolutionary positions to conservative opinions, a trajectory typical of many intellectuals in this century.

See also FUTURISM.

Bibliography: *Opere,* 8 vols. (Florence: Vallecchi, 1959-68); Mario Richter, *La formazione francese di Ardengo Soffici 1900-1914* (Milan: Vita e Pensiero, 1969); Edoardo Sanguineti, *Tra liberty e crepuscolarismo* (Milan: Mursia, 1961).

SOLDATI, MARIO (1906-   ), novelist, journalist, film director, and critic. Soldati was born in Turin and studied literature at the university there. He published a play in 1924 and a collection of *novelle** in 1929. Awarded a fellowship to Columbia University in art history, Soldati came to America in 1929. The fruit of this visit and two subsequent trips in 1932-33 was an immensely influential description of the United States entitled *America, primo amore* (1935, America, First Love), the story of a personal encounter which, like many first loves, ends in disenchantment. Although Soldati did not intend a political message, many fascists saw in his writing proof of the American decadence which their propaganda always reported. During this decade, Soldati became more and more involved with cinema, turning to both directing and scriptwriting, often in collaboration with Mario Camerini (1895-   ).

Soldati's first novel, *La verità sul caso Motta* (1941, The Truth About the Motta Case), a surrealistic psychological thriller, was followed by *Fuga in Italia* (1947, Flight into Italy), a diary containing an account of his escape from the Germans in 1943, and *A cena col commendatore* (1950, Dinner with the Commendatore), a collection of three long stories. Perhaps his best known work is *Le lettere da Capri* (1954, *The Capri Letters*), for which he was awarded the Strega Prize in 1954. In this book, Soldati returns to his American experience and constructs a novel that some critics have compared to the Italian novels of Henry James in plot construction, point of view, and the characterization of two American expatriates living in Italy. Soldati's subsequent novels include *La confessione* (1955, *The Confession*), an account of a Jesuit novice's spiritual crisis; *Le due città*

(1964, *The Malacca Cane*), an apparently autobiographical account of life in Turin and Rome with a protagonist (Emilio Viotti) whose attraction to a career in film resembles Soldati's own; *La busta arancione* (1966, *The Orange Envelope*), a continuation of earlier treatments of the ill effects of a rigorous religious education; and *L'attore* (1970, The Actor), a work concerning the life of a television director which became a best seller in Italy and was awarded the Campiello Prize in 1970. Soldati continues to contribute to a number of Italian periodicals as a journalist, commentator, and writer of criticism and fiction.

Bibliography: The Capri Letters, trans. Archibald Colquhoun (New York: Knopf, 1956); *The Confession,* trans. Raymond Rosenthal (New York: Knopf, 1958); *Dinner with the Commendatore,* trans. Gwyn Morris (New York: Knopf, 1953); *The Malacca Cane,* trans. Gwyn Morris (London: André Deutch, 1973); *The Orange Envelope,* trans. Bernard Wall (London: André Deutch, 1969); Donald Heiney, *America in Modern Italian Literature* (New Brunswick, N.J.: Rutgers University Press, 1964).

SONNET, a lyric poem ordinarily of fourteen lines which lends itself to a number of themes and metrical schemes. Despite Dante's* judgment of the sonnet as a less noble form, in its multiple variations, it is perhaps the most prominent and long-lived lyric form in Western literature. It originated at the imperial court of Frederick II* between 1220 and 1250. Some evidence suggests that its inventor was Giacomo da Lentino,* whose "Amore è un desio che ven dal core" ("Love is a longing born within the heart") is considered to be the first sonnet. Considerable study has not divulged an earlier form familiar to the poets in the Frederician court which might have inspired the creation of the sonnet, although it is possible that Giacomo and his group were influenced by local Sicilian tradition. These poets must have been familiar with the *canzuna* sung by Sicilian peasants, composed of eight hendecasyllabic lines and organized by the rhyme scheme *abababab* into distichs. However, this form was not actually recorded until after Frederick's time. The sonnet's inventor, it has been suggested, may simply have been inspired to add a double refrain of six lines to this *canzuna,* or it may have had to do with the accompanying music. Each of the nineteen sonnets known to have been written by Sicilian poets (fourteen by Giacomo alone) have fourteen lines of eleven syllables each. Although differing from what was to become the standard Italian or Petrarchan form, the earliest sonnets open with the rhyme scheme *abababab* and customarily close with *cdecde,* although the sestet varies (*cdcdcd, ccdccd,* for example). Despite the rhyming of the octave, a tendency toward the familiar division into quatrains and tercets is perceptible in these early poems because of the full stop at the end of the octave, as well as the sense and the punctuation, especially in the poetry of Giacomo's contemporaries, the abbot of Tivoli (active around 1240), Jacopo Mostacci (died after 1277), and Pier della Vigna.*

At this time, it is surprising to find a fixed poetic form in Italian literature, since the measure of a poet's originality was his virtuosity. With the exception of the sestina,* no set patterns had been established for such types as the *canzone*,* the *ballata*,* the *contrasto,* and the *discordo*. Still, the poets of the thirteenth and early fourteenth centuries carried on metrical and structural experimentation, producing such variations as the *sonetti minori* and the *sonetti caudati, doppi, doppi caudati, rinterzati,* and *raddoppiati*. The sonnet was also used in poetic debates *(tenzoni),* in longer narratives *(Il fiore),* and in shorter *corone* (Folgore da San Gimignano*; Cenne da la Chitarra [lived circa 1321]; the so-called *casistica amorosa*). The Tuscan poet Guittone D'Arezzo* brought to the sonnet more of the troubadour stylistics, derived from the conceits of the Roman and Greek poets of love. It remained for him also to establish the preferred structure of the Italian sonnet, the configuration adopted by Cavalcanti,* Dante, and Petrarch.* Still a fourteen-line poem in hendecasyllables, the Italian or Petrarchan sonnet, as it is often called, is customarily and formally divided into an octave in closed rhyme *(abba abba)* and a sestet in various schemes such as the interlaced rhyme *(cde cde* or *cde dcc; cdc dcd; cde ced)*.

The disproportion between octave and sestet reflects their functions. The octave presents a problem, a question, a reflection, or a description, which the sestet answers, illuminates, reiterates, or resolves. Structural, thematic, and logical unity is achieved through the conjunction, juxtaposition, or contrast of the concepts, through the use of specialized language or through rhetorical devices. The bipartite structure gives rise to or is a function of the form's logical disposition. Some perceive a relationship between the morphology of the sonnet—in which a proposition is elaborated, examined, or demonstrated, and then confirmed, resolved, or concluded—and the syllogism. Frequently, the division between octave and sestet is marked by a surprising turn in thought or feeling *(volta)* and may culminate in a witty summation. The greater brevity of the sestet has the effect of bringing the sonnet to its conclusion. The compactness and metrical regularity of the form have not hindered the subtlest invention. Rather, the morphology of the Italian sonnet, its structural imbalance between octave and sestet, sustains a logical relationship between form and content which in the hands of a skilled poet lends itself to achieving poetic brilliance. The sonnet encourages the wit, precision, and density of imagery typical of the finest poetry. Rhetorical figures and technical devices provide the necessary variety and sustain the essential unity of structure and thought. Abroad, most poets followed the example of Petrarch and employed the form typical of the Italian sonnet. However, in England the sonnet was modified in several ways. The English or Shakespearean sonnet usually has four divisions: three quatrains (usually rhymed *abab cdcd efef*) and a rhymed couplet *(gg),* which provides a more epigrammatic conclusion than is typical in the Italian form. The Spenserian sonnet has three quatrains and a couplet, but employs linking rhymes between the quatrains *(abab bcbc cdcd ee).*

Although courtly in origin, the sonnet could be adapted to different subjects and ages. Love has been the primary preoccupation of sonnet writers, but various serious personal concerns, matters artistic, moral, philosophical, theological, and historical, have provided their themes. If the sonnet was in the beginning primarily a means of lyrical self-expression, poems on serious topics came to have both a public and private significance. In the hands of some of Petrarch's less gifted imitators, such as Serafino Aquilano,* the sonnet became the victim of empty rhetoric until Pietro Bembo,* along with Michelangelo* and Castiglione,* returned it to its original purpose. In the great sonnet writers such as Petrarch, personal inspiration gives life to empty form. Abroad, the sonnet's appeal and venerable literary tradition compelled every important lyric poet and countless versifiers and lesser talents to test their skill against the formal requirements of its structure. By the seventeenth century, the sonnet had become fairly well codified. Torquato Tasso,* for example, divided his sonnets into love sonnets, heroic sonnets, and sacred and moral sonnets. The nature sonnet, alone absent from Tasso's classification, was a later development.

The many transformations of the sonnet reflect the diversity of the Italian cities and their artists as well as the vitality of the cultural movements of the Renaissance.* The form was afterward used by many writers, including Marino,* Alfieri,* Foscolo,* Carducci,* and D'Annunzio.* Only a literary form with special adaptability could have survived the revolutions in Western thought. Although an unlikely choice in a period which has moved away from the traditional fixed forms, the sonnet continues to be used by contemporary writers of every nationality.

See also BEMBO, Pietro; BUONARROTI, Michelangelo; DA LENTINO, Giacomo; GUITTONE D'AREZZO; PETRARCA, Francesco; PETRARCHISM.

Bibliography: Morfologia e antologia del sonetto, ed. Ada Ruschioni, 2 vols. (Milan: Celuc, 1974); John Fuller, *The Sonnet* (London: Methuen, 1972); Christopher Kleinhenz, ''Petrarch and the Art of the Sonnet,'' pp. 177–91, in *Francis Petrarch, Six Centuries After: A Symposium,* ed. Aldo Scaglione (Chapel Hill, N.C.: University of North Carolina Press, 1975); Walter Monch, *Das Sonett: Gestalt und Geschichte* (Heidelberg: Kerle, 1955); E. H. Wilkins, *The Invention of the Sonnet and Other Studies in Italian Literature* (Rome: Edizioni di storia e letteratura, 1959).

SORDELLO **[SORDEL]** (circa 1200–circa 1270), poet. This Provençal troubadour of Italian birth was born at Goito near Mantua to a family of the minor nobility. Although there is little biographical information on Sordello, some details of his youthful escapades as well as the successes of his maturity have been preserved. He evidently began his career by wandering from castle to castle. He assisted in carrying off the wife of one of his hosts, Riccardo di San Bonifazio, and provoked a second scandal by secretly marrying Otta da Strasso during a stay in one of her family's castles near Treviso. Once the marriage was discovered, he abandoned his wife and fled to Spain around 1228, before arriving in Provence where he secured the patronage and friendship of Lord Blacatz. By 1233, he had joined the court of Raimon Berenger IV, the count of Provence, and remained in the service of that prince and Charles of Anjou the rest of his life. Sordello was knighted prior to joining Charles' expedition into Italy in 1265 which led to a short imprisonment in 1266. Four years afterwards, recognition and recompense came in the form of certain lands and castles in the Abruzzi granted to him by Charles. The circumstances of his death are unknown.

Sordello produced about forty poems written on various themes in a variety of forms. He wrote about twelve *cansos* (songs) but showed a preference for such forms as the *sirventes* (a strophic poem on topics other than love, such as personal abuse and praise) and the *partimen* (a form of *tenzone* or poetic debate). His love lyrics, resembling those of such poets as Guilhem de Montanhagol, exalt chastity and the purity of love. Equally high-minded and serious is his most often quoted poem, a *planh* (funeral lament) written on the death of Blacatz (1236). This poem gives him the opportunity to criticize rather sharply the other sovereigns of the time, inviting, among others, the kings of England, France, Castile, and Aragon and the Emperor Frederick II* to eat of his patron's heart so that they might gain something of his nobility and courage. His "Documentus honoris" (Worthy Example), a courtly and moral treatise, also opposes the corruption of the lords of the time. These works led Dante* to view Sordello as a patriot and reformer, the ideal guide in the valley of negligent princes in *Purgatory* VII. In Canto VI, Sordello appears righteous and majestic, the exemplar of patriotism in the best sense. After Sordello and Virgil, both poets and both Mantuans, embrace, Dante digresses upon the conditions within the Italian peninsula, comparing Italy to a brothel and to a ship in a storm without a pilot, castigating the Emperor Albert and delivering an invective against the city of Florence, inspired by Sordello's lament. Sordello's fame derives as much from Dante's noble characterization as from his own poetry. No doubt his personality and his scorn for political and moral corruption appealed to Robert Browning and Ezra Pound.

Bibliography: Sordello, le poesie, ed. Marco Boni (Bologna: Palmaverde, 1954); *Lyrics of the Troubadours and Trouvères,* trans. Frederick Goldin (Garden City, N.Y.: Doubleday, 1973).

SPAGNOLI, BATTISTA (1448–1516), humanist, cleric, and poet. Spagnoli was born in Mantua, which was the origin of his pen-name, Baptista Mantuanus or Mantuan. Having studied at Padua, he was elected first vicar-general of the Carmelite Congregation of Mantua in 1483 and then in 1513 head of the entire order, a post he apparently held until his death. He was canonized by Pope Leo XIII in 1883. Besides several religious and biographical works, Mantuan's literary reputation rests primarily upon ten pastoral* eclogues in Latin, eight of which were written while he was a student and the other two composed after he joined the Carmelites. After careful revision, they were first printed in 1498, and they were almost immediately reissued all over Europe. Their popularity was assured for the next two centuries, because they became standard Latin texts in the schools of Europe. In these works, Mantuan imitated not only the classical models of Virgil but also the pastoral poetry of Petrarch* and Boccaccio.* Besides being immortalized in a line from Shakespeare's *Love's Labour's Lost* (IV, ii, 95), Mantuan's eclogues were read and imitated by many English poets, especially by Spenser in the *Shepheards Calender* (1579). Nine of the eclogues appeared in English in 1567, the tenth being added when a complete English translation was published in 1656. Less well known but still of note was *Parthenices* (1481, Hymns to the Virgin), a group of seven poems whose treatment of the infernal council theme in a description of hell inspired similar scenes not only in Sannazaro,* Marino,* and Tasso,* but also in Milton's *Paradise Lost.*

See also PASTORAL; PONTANO, Giovanni; SANNAZARO, Jacopo.

Bibliography: The Eclogues of Baptista Mantuanus, ed. Wilfred Mustard (Baltimore: Johns Hopkins University Press, 1911); *The Eclogues of Mantuan,* trans. George Burbervile, ed. Douglas Bush (New York: Scholars' Facsimiles, 1937).

SPERONI, SPERONE (1500–1588), critic, dramatist, and scholar. A native of Padua, Speroni studied under Pomponazzi,* later held the chair of logic at Bologna, and wrote a great many dialogues and treatises in Italian. The *Discorsi sopra Virgilio* (Discourses on Virgil), written around 1563–64 but published posthumously, attacks the critical reputation of Virgil and elevates Homer to a place of pre-eminence with the claim that Virgil invented nothing and only followed Homer. Of greater note, the *Dialogo sulle lingue* (1542, Dialogue on Languages) reiterated Bembo's* program of perfecting the modern languages by imitating works from classical antiquity in the vernacular literatures. This idea strongly influenced Joachim Du Bellay's *Defense et illustration de la langue francoyse* (1549) as well as the poetry of Pierre de Ronsard.

Speroni's tragedy, *Canace e Macareo* (1546, Canace and Macareo), whose subject is the incestuous love of the children of Aeolus, was first read before the Accademia degli Infiammati in Padua and provoked a critical debate over the nature of tragedy which continued throughout the century. It is a work in the tradition of Senecan revenge tragedy, established in Italy by Giambattista Giraldi's* *Orbecche* (1541). In a treatise appearing in 1546, Bartolomeo Cavalcanti (1503–1562) attacked the play because it did not produce the required Aristotelian emotions of pity and fear. In his reply (completed around 1554, although not published until 1597), Speroni maintained that his work was a true tragedy and defended his use of a mixture of seven- and ten-syllable verse with infrequent rhyme. He read a series of six lectures on the same topic in Padua around 1558, which he published with the defense of 1597. Speroni's choice of mythological subject matter and his emphasis upon the Aristotelian principle of *peripeteia* had its effect upon subsequent Italian Renaissance* tragedy.

See also GIRALDI, Giambattista.

Bibliography: Dialogo delle lingue, ed. Helene Harth (Munich: Wilhelm Fink, 1975); *Teatro italiano antico,* Vol. 4 (Milan: Società Tipografica de' Classici italiani, 1808–12); Francesco Cammarosano, *La vita e le opere di Sperone Speroni* (Empoli: Noccioli, 1920); Marvin T. Herrick, *Italian Tragedy in the Renaissance* (Urbana, Ill.: Illinois University Press, 1965); Bernard Weinberg, *A History of Literary Criticism in the Italian Renaissance,* 2 vols. (Chicago: University of Chicago Press, 1961).

STAMPA, GASPARA (1523–1554), poetess. Stampa, born in Padua, was forced to move to Venice in 1531 after the death of her father. There she freqented various literary circles and became a member of the Accademia dei Pellegrini, taking the academic title of Anassilla. She opened her own literary salon and received many of Venice's most distinguished cultural figures. It is uncertain whether she actually became a courtesan, but it was not uncommon for Venetian courtesans to be as gifted or sophisticated in literary matters as she was. During 1549, she fell in love with the lord of Treviso, Count Collatino di Collato, who abandoned her after two years for another woman. Although she had other lovers, she immortalized her first and best love in her verse.

Stampa's literary fame rests upon her *Rime* (1554, Rhymes), some three hundred lyric poems, mostly sonnets,* which depict her love for Collatino. The poetry was published by her sister and dedicated to the noted Petrarchan poet, Giovanni della Casa.* Petrarchan in style, tone, and content, her lyrics are considered today to be the foremost poetic production by any woman of the Renaissance* period. Often with subtlety Stampa uses the

Petrarchan conceits, rhetoric, and themes to portray a burning, passionate love which cannot be denied. One memorable sonnet, "Io non v'invidio punto, angeli santi" ("I, holy angels, envy not at all"), suggests that although angelic beatitude is more extensive than her own amorous pleasure because it is eternal, it is, nevertheless, no greater in intensity. She remarkably managed to infuse her poetry with a deeply personal quality within a tradition that was becoming, at least within Italy, increasingly weary and unimaginative. Furthermore, Stampa sustains a narrative throughout her collection, in contrast to other Petrarchan poets of the time who were content to imitate only Petrarch's* style. Although she was not exceedingly popular as a poet in her own day, one important contemporary critic has compared her to Sappho. Her works were rediscovered in the last century by various romantic critics.

See also COLONNA, Vittoria; DELLA CASA, Giovanni; PETRARCHISM.

Bibliography: Gaspara Stampa and Veronica Franco, *Rime*, ed. A. Salza (Bari: Laterza, 1913); *Poesia del Quattrocento e del Cinquecento,* eds. Carlo Muscetta and Daniele Ponchiroli (Turin: Einaudi, 1959); *Italian Poets of the Renaissance,* trans. Joseph Tusiani (Long Island City, N.Y.: Baroque Press, 1971); Giovanni Cesareo, *Gaspara Stampa, donna e poetessa* (Naples: Perrella, 1920); Justin Vitiello, "Gaspara Stampa: The Ambiguities of Martyrdom," *Modern Language Notes* 90 (1975), 58–71.

STORNELLO, a very brief poetic form of popular origin which became fashionable in the seventeenth century in Tuscany and spread to other southern regions. The word has no English equivalent. Its most typical form is an opening line addressed to a flower (usually of five syllables) and two other eleven-syllable lines. The first and third lines have consonantal or assonant rhyme, while the first and second lines are linked by atonic rhyme. In the nineteenth century, the form came to be employed in patriotic verse, as in Carducci's* "Fior tricolore" (Tricolor flower).

Bibliography: Francesco Manna, *Dolce stile: nozioni di stilistica, di retorica e di metrica italiana* (Milan: Signorelli, 1967); E. H. Wilkins, *A History of Italian Literature,* rev. ed. (Cambridge, Mass.: Harvard University Press, 1974).

STRAMBOTTO, a brief popular poetic form, usually concerned with the theme of love (although it is sometimes used for satire), which occurred as early as the thirteenth century and became most fashionable in Tuscany and Sicily during the Renaissance.* The most popular metrical arrangements of this poetic form consisted of a single stanza of either six or eight eleven-syllable lines: *ababab; ababcc; aabbcc; abababab; ababccdd; abababcc;* or *aabbccdd.* While the so-called *ottava siciliana* or Sicilian octave form *(abababab)* was most popular in the south, the *ottava rima**

form *(ababab cc)* predominated in Tuscany. In Tuscany, the *strambotto* is often confused with the *rispetto,** which may be regarded as a special form of the *strambotto*. It, too, consists of a stanza of eight lines of eleven-syllable verse, most commonly arranged in the following manner: *ababccdd.* The word *rispetto* ("respect") refers to the fact that most of these poems contain the homage of the lover for his lady. Both the *strambotto* and the *rispetto* reached the height of their popularity and artistic perfection during the Quattrocento and Cinquecento in Tuscany and were written by such poets as Leonardo Giustinian (1388–1436), Francesco Galeota (?–1497?); Poliziano,* Lorenzo de' Medici,* Serafino Aquilano,* and a host of minor figures. In the modern era, both Carducci* and Pascoli* composed poems of this type.

See also SERAFINO AQUILANO.

Bibliography: Rispetti e strambotti del Quattrocento, ed. Raffaele Spongano (Bologna: Tamari Editori, 1971); W.T. Elwert, *Versificazione italiana dalle origini ai giorni nostri* (Florence: Le Monnier, 1973); Raffaele Spongano, *Nozioni ed esempi di metrica italiana* (Bologna: Pàtron, 1966).

STRAPAROLA, GIAN FRANCESCO (?–circa 1557), poet and writer of *novelle.** Little is known of Straparola except that he was born in Cara-vaggio. Although he is credited with a volume of poetry, primarily sonnets* and *strambotti,** which was first published in 1508, more significant is a collection of *novelle* entitled *Le piacevoli notti* (1550–53, *The Nights of Straparola*). Like the more famous collection by Boccaccio,* this one has a framework and the *novelle* are narrated by a larger group of storytellers—thirteen ladies and numerous gentlemen. The scene is set on the island of Murano near Venice during the last thirteen days of the Venetian carnival. Each of the seventy-five tales told ends upon a riddle with multiple mean-ings, one usually obscene which is, of course, not the one the storyteller claims to have intended. Apparently as popular as Boccaccio's *Decameron* in its time, *Le piacevoli notti* went into almost twenty editions in the two decades after its appearance and received many European translations. Its originality lies in the inclusion of many Oriental folk tales (also found in Basile's* *Pentamerone*) and the use of animal fables. One *novella* (IX, 1) presents the first version of the classic tale "Puss in Boots," a story evidently created by Straparola. Some of the tales with priests as pro-tagonists were considered offensive to Counter-Reformation sensibilities, and the work was placed on the Index in 1624.

See also BASILE, Giambattista; BOCCACCIO, Giovanni; NO-VELLA.

Bibliography: Le piacevoli notti, ed. Giuseppe Rua, 2 vols. (Bari: Laterza, 1927); *The Nights of Straparola,* trans. W. G. Waters, 2 vols. (London: Lawrence &

Bullen, 1894); Letterato Di Francia, *Novellistica: dalle origini al Bandello* (Milan: Villardi, 1924).

STRUCTURALISM. As a theory of literature and a method of textual analysis and practical criticism, structuralism began to take hold in Italy in the early 1960s. In 1965, under the title "Strutturalismo e critica" (Structuralism and Criticism), published in the General Catalogue of the Milan publisher Il Saggiatore, Cesare Segre (1928–) edited the responses of fourteen scholars to a questionnaire intended to assess the impact of post-Saussurian linguistic structuralism on Italian literary studies. The questionnaire asked if a structural methodology was capable of providing useful "critical instruments," and if it could be integrated with a critical tradition which was primarily historicist (such as the Italian). The responses indicated great interest in the methodological implications of the basic concepts of structuralism as they had developed in Europe from the seminal works of de Saussure in linguistics, Lévi-Strauss in anthropology, and Propp in folklore: (1) the notion of the work of art as a structure or system whose coherence rests on the interrelation of linguistic, thematic, and rhetorical elements *internal* to it; and (2) the idea of an objective critical method aimed at describing (rather than evaluating or explicating) the formal elements of the work and the relations obtaining among them which constitute the process of signification.

One of the reasons for the appeal of structuralism in Italy was the lack of a formalist critical tradition. Its major result was to be the theoretical and interdisciplinary thrust it promoted in literary research. A number of new scholarly journals appeared, specializing in structural theory and analysis of literature, such as *Strumenti critici* published by Einaudi of Turin, and *Lingua e stile* by Il Mulino of Bologna (the titles themselves are revealing). Existing journals, like *Paragone, Lettere italiane, Sigma,* and *Nuova corrente,* also devoted much space to the new critical views. Since 1973, *Strumenti critici* has included in every issue a current bibliography of studies in structuralism and semiotics.*

In Italy, structuralist criticism has favored the analytical study of literary texts. Single works, especially of poetry and narrative, have been analyzed phonologically and syntactically, in relation either to the poetic universe of the author, or to the other works within the genre, or to an entire cultural period. Theoretical inquiry, on the other hand, shifted very early toward semiology, or semiotics as it is called today, extending its field of study far beyond literature to cinema, theatre, architecture, the mass media, and the like.

The sudden success and notoriety of structuralism in the late 1960s, and the ideological attack waged against it by Marxist critics (e.g., Romano Luperini, 1940–), caused many of its supporters and practitioners to think through its theoretical presuppositions, in particular (1) the view of a text as a totally self-contained entity that can be studied in isolation from other social and cultural processes; (2) the possibly idealist implications of positing an a priori structure immanent in the work; and (3) the tautological fallacy of a critical effort directed solely at verifying the existence of formal structures already assumed to be in the object. As a result of the ensuing dialogue, structural criticism in Italy has acquired a greater awareness of its historical function and theoretical limits. Thus, today, the term *structuralist* has come to denote a rather rigid and narrow view of the critical activity, while the innovative charge and the conceptual tools first introduced by structuralism continue to be developed and sharpened by semiotic research and semiotic criticism.

See also ECO, Umberto: SEMIOTICS.

Bibliography: D'Arco Silvio Avalle, *L'analisi letteraria in Italia. Formalismo-Strutturalismo-Semiologia* (Milan: Ricciardi, 1970); Maria Corti, *Principi della comunicazione letteraria* (Milan: Bompiani, 1976); Teresa de Lauretis, "The Shape of the World: Report on Structuralism and Semiotics in Italy," *Books Abroad* (1975), 227–32; Umberto Eco, "The Analysis of Structure," *Times Literary Supplement,* 27 September 1963, pp. 755–56, *La struttura assente* (Milan: Bompiani, 1968), and *A Theory of Semiotics* (Bloomington, Ind.: Indiana University Press, 1976); Cesare Segre, *Semiotics and Literary Criticism* (The Hague: Mouton, 1973).

Teresa de Lauretis

SVEVO, ITALO, pseudonym of Ettore Schmitz (1861–1928), novelist and playwright. Svevo was born in Trieste, an active port-town on the Adriatic coast, then belonging to the Austrian empire, of a well-to-do Jewish family. When, at the time of publishing his first novel, Svevo chose his pen-name "Italus the Swabian," he meant to express his mixed ancestry (his father was of German descent and his mother, Allegra Moravia, came from an Italian Jewish family of Trieste), his dual language background, and his being an Austrian by citizenship but an Italian by culture and political choice. Until the age of seventeen, Svevo attended the Brüssel Institute, a well-known school for the sons of Jewish businessmen near Würzburg in Germany, where he showed a marked inclination toward literature and the German classics—Schiller in particular. Upon his return to Trieste, his mind already set on becoming a writer, he managed to forestall his father's plans for his business career and obtained permission to enroll in the Istituto Superiore Commerciale Revoltella, where he sampled courses in law and medicine without much commitment to seeking a specific degree. His interest in theatre also dates back to this time, when with his brothers he planned scenes and acts of plays that never materialized. In 1880, because of his father's sudden financial and physical collapse, Svevo was forced to abandon his studies and, at the age of nineteen, to take a job as a bank clerk—an alienating experience he was later to describe in his first novel, *Una vita* (1893, *A Life*). It is not unreasonable to assume that two of the major recurrent themes of his writing, senility and neurotic fantasies, had their genesis in this traumatic turn of events. The next personal disaster to find a lasting echo in his works was the death in 1887 of his younger brother Elio, a long-suffering victim of chronic nephritis. Disease, in its physical and emotional symptomatology, was to be Svevo's most obsessive theme and his compelling metaphor of existence. He began seriously to work at his first novel, drawing on both his own and his brother's experience.

By the time *Una vita* was published, at Svevo's expense, his father had died. Three years later, his mother also died, and Svevo found himself alone and a confirmed bachelor at the age of thirty-four, with one totally unsuccessful, indeed forgotten, novel to his credit. In the next four years he published another novel, *Senilità* (1898, *As a Man Grows Older*), and married Livia Veneziani, whose parents owned a manufacturing firm where Svevo was to work all his life, eventually taking over its management and becoming a prosperous and successful businessman. His second novel having been received even less favorably than the first, Svevo devoted himself entirely to his business and his family. Disillusioned and bitter toward the literary establishment which, with few minor exceptions, had taken no notice of his books, he refused to publish anything for the next twenty-five years. He did, however, continue to write plays, fables, short stories, and a diary which he considered primarily a tool of self-analysis.

In 1907, looking for a private tutor in the English language, which he needed for his frequent business transactions with England, Svevo met James Joyce who, still relatively unknown as a writer, was earning his living in Trieste as an English teacher. Although they were very different in their literary styles and interests, their relationship, which lasted after Joyce left Italy and until the end of Svevo's life, was based on mutual respect as men and as writers. They discussed and admired each other's work. Joyce, who was then working on *A Portrait of the Artist* and was discouraged over his failure to publish the manuscript of *Dubliners*, liked *Senilità* very much and even knew its last paragraph by heart; Svevo, for English composition exercises, wrote critiques of Joyce's works. Though it always remained rather formal, their friendship was highly beneficial to both. To Joyce, Svevo gave financial help in the form of loans and job opportunities in Trieste, and possibly encouragement to keep writing; in turn, the Irishman was later to promote Svevo's novel to international acclaim.

Shortly after the end of the war, and having developed great interest in the works of Freud, Svevo abandoned his resolution and, with intense excitement, turned again to writing fiction. He was sixty-two years old when his most famous novel, *La coscienza di Zeno* (1923, *Confessions of*

Zeno), was published; many consider it a masterpiece of modern fiction. Its appearance, like that of the previous two novels by the Triestine writer, went more or less unnoticed in Italy, but was destined to cause a stir in the European literary scene giving rise to what is known as "il caso Svevo" (the Svevo case). Upon the strong recommendation of Joyce, who considered it by far Svevo's best, *La coscienza di Zeno* was translated and published in Paris by Valéry Larbaud and Benjamin Crémieux, who promoted it as a masterpiece and dubbed its author "the Italian Proust." The news of Svevo's success in France, where he was discovered as a major figure in contemporary Italian literature, was quick in crossing the Alps. In Italy, Eugenio Montale's* now famous article in *L'esame* (1925) was the first to recognize Svevo's originality and the high literary value of his novels, which Montale defined as "the poem of our complex modern madness." During the last years of his life, encouraged by the long overdue critical recognition, Svevo wrote many shorter pieces such as *Una burla riuscita (The Hoax), La novella del buon vecchio e della bella fanciulla (The Nice Old Man and the Pretty Girl), Corto viaggio sentimentale (Short Sentimental Journey),* and a few chapters of a projected novel, "Il vecchione" ("The Old Old Man"), which remained unfinished at the time of his death in an automobile accident.

After its belated and uneasy beginning, Svevo's fortune in Italy remained precarious and the object of heated debate. It was not until the 1960s that "the Svevo case" was finally closed. Critics were divided in their assessment of the quality and literary stature of his works. Comparing him with his contemporary D'Annunzio* and with his great predecessor Manzoni,* Svevo's adversaries lamented his "slipshod," dry prose style, which was too close to the Triestine dialect while at the same time too reminiscent of Svevo's formal training in the German language. They also deprecated the lack of organic form and of a sublime vision, and were unable to accept his choice of unattractive, weak, commonplace heroes. In contrast, his supporters, whose numbers grew in time, appreciated his keen sense of humor and subtle irony in portraying the Italian bourgeoisie; they praised his masterful handling of the subjective point of view and of the technique of the interior monologue. In its analytical excavation into the personality in search of the inner reality of the self, they found that his fiction was comparable to that of Kafka, Musil, Mann, and Joyce. Svevo himself acknowledged as his masters the naturalist novelists, Schopenhauer, and Freud; he had discovered Freud's theories around 1912 and had admittedly used them in the writing of *La coscienza di Zeno*.

Svevo's major works, the three novels for which he is best known, are extraordinarily similar in theme and structure. In large part autobiographical, they are centered on an introspective, unheroic hero and his relationship with his parents or parental figures. His efforts to find love, self-determination, and identity constitute a story uneventful but rich in psychological nuances and keen observation of social mores. Recurring Svevian themes are the interrelation of guilt and disease, love and jealousy, death and the passing of time (with the insistent motif of old age), and the yearning for expression and creativity. The three protagonists are but different images of a single obsessive experience seen from successive points of time along the path to self-discovery. Each novel is a journey into the depths of the self, and all three together represent modern man's quest to attain both consciousness and conscience, the two meanings united in the ambiguous title of *La coscienza di Zeno*. As Zeno recounts his life, allegedly in an attempt to find the origin of his smoking habit and thus a cure for his innumerable psychosomatic diseases by means of psychoanalysis, he treads over the emotional footprints of his two predecessors: Alfonso Nitti in *A Life*, a suicide victim at the age of twenty, and Emilio Brentani, whose "senility" at age thirty-five and whose self-contained, unfulfilled existence are also the proof of a failure or inability to live. But from the vantage point of his fifty-seven years of life experience, Zeno reshapes events and characters, turning tables and settling accounts, and emerges the winner. Through Zeno, who lies and distorts, or fictionalizes, the story of his life—as it were recovering his lost time—Svevo shows his faith in the power of language to transform and recreate experience. Like Verga,* whose great and innovative contribution to the language of narrative was also not recognized until after his death, Svevo is responsible for a major stylistic and thematic shift in modern Italian fiction writing. Ironically, the strong contemporary appeal of this writer, of whom people used to say that he could not write well, stands on his commitment to literary experimentation and on his having created a narrative form destined to influence all subsequent Italian fiction from the early novels of Moravia* to the works being written today.

Bibliography: A Life, trans. Archibald Colquhoun (New York: Knopf, 1963); *As a Man Grows Older,* trans. Beryl de Zoete (New York: Bantam, 1968); *Confessions of Zeno,* trans. Beryl de Zoete (New York: Vintage, 1958); *Further Confessions of Zeno,* trans. Ben Johnson and P. N. Furbank (Berkeley, Calif.: University of California Press, 1969); *Short Sentimental Journey,* trans. Beryl de Zoete, et al. (Berkeley, Calif.: University of California Press, 1967); Teresa de Lauretis, *La sintassi del desiderio: struttura e forme del romanzo sveviano* (Ravenna: Longo, 1976); P. N. Furbank, *Italo Svevo: The Man and the Writer* (Berkeley, Calif.: University of California Press, 1966); Naomi Lebowitz, *Italo Svevo* (New Brunswick, N.J.: Rutgers University Press, 1977); Thomas F. Staley, ed., *Essays on Italo Svevo* (Tulsa, Okla.: University of Oklahoma Press, 1969); *Modern Fiction Studies* 18 (1972)—special Svevo issue.

Teresa de Lauretis

SWEET NEW STYLE: *See* DOLCE STIL NUOVO.

T

TANSILLO, LUIGI (1510–1568), courtier poet from Venosa. After 1535, Tansillo was installed at the court of Don Pedro di Toledo, viceroy of Spain in Naples, whose son, Don Garzia, he accompanied on many voyages and on military and naval campaigns. Apparently, he was also acquainted with both Garcilaso de la Vega and Juan Boscán, two gifted literary figures of the Spanish Renaissance who helped to spread Italianate literary forms in their homeland.

Tansillo was very prolific. His early poems in *ottava rima** include *Il vendemmiatore* (1532, The Vintager), which describes the sometimes sensual gaiety of peasants during the grape harvest; *Stanze a Bernardino Martirano* (1540, Stanzas for Bernardino Martirano), which relates the life of a sailor; and *Clorida* (1547, Clorida), a mythological and narrative poem describing the nymph that supposedly resided in his patron's country villa. However, Tansillo's renown stems not from this poetry but from his various Petrarchan sonnets* and a longer poem, *Le lagrime di San Pietro* (1585, The Tears of St. Peter). Tansillo's lyrics were anthologized in a very famous volume published by the Venetian printer Gabriele Giolito (died 1578) in 1552 and carried throughout Europe by foreigners who had visited Italy. Perhaps the most accomplished of these, "Poi che spiegate ho l'ale al bel desio" ("Now that toward beauty I have spread my wings"), a poem also included in Bruno's* *Degli eroici furori* (1585, *The Heroic Frenzies*), contains an elaborate comparison of the lover to Icarus. The longer work on St. Peter established a tradition of lacrimonious literature in Italy as well as in France, England, Portugal, and Spain, where it was continued by such poets as Malherbe and Southwell. Also of interest is a didactic poem in *terza rima,* *La balia* (1566, *The Nurse*), which exhorts young mothers to breastfeed their infants themselves.

See also PETRARCHISM.

Bibliography: *Poemetti,* ed. Carmelo Cappuccio (Florence: Sansoni, 1954); *The Nurse, A Poem,* trans. William Roscoe (London: John Furman, 1800); *Italian Poets of the Renaissance,* trans. Joseph Tusiani (Long Island City, N.Y.: Baroque Press, 1971).

TASSO, BERNARDO (1493–1569), courtier, critic, and poet. Born in Bergamo of a noble family, Tasso studied in Padua and entered the service of

Count Guido Rangone of Modena. Later, he joined Ferrante Sanseverino, prince of Salerno, and when his patron was forced into exile after a political dispute with the Emperor Charles V, Tasso accompanied him abroad for a brief time. After his return to Italy, he spent much of the rest of his life in various Italian courts.

Tasso's initial publication was a collection of lyrics in the Petrarchan tradition (1531), the first of a number of such collections he would compose during his lifetime, most of them marked by an effort to unite Petrarchan themes and techniques with classical ideas in the manner of Benedetto Gareth (Il Cariteo*). Besides various eclogues, songs, elegies, fables, numerous letters, and an essay on poetry, *Ragionamento della poesia* (1562, Discourse on Poetry), Tasso composed original Horatian odes in the Italian vernacular—the first poet to do so. His major undertaking was the epic* *Amadigi di Gaula* (1560, Amadigi), a poem of one hundred cantos in *ottava rima** based upon a Spanish romance by Garci Ordoñez de Montalvo on Amadis of Gaul, whom Tasso mistakenly identifies with France, not Wales. The work describes three separate love stories—the love of Amadigi, son of the king of France, for Oriana, daughter to the king of England; that of Oriana's brother for Amadigi's sister; and that of the prince of Castille for Filidora, a magician's daughter. Tasso tried to avoid the attacks directed against Ariosto's* *Orlando furioso (The Frenzy of Orlando)* by critics who felt it lacked the unity of classical epics; each of the three stories moves along together in almost every canto, and many of the cantos begin and end with a sunrise and sunset, thereby simulating the diurnal timespan of earlier oral narrative. Critics have not treated Tasso's poem kindly since its popularity waned at the close of the Baroque* period. Nevertheless, it is a document central to the critical debate over the nature of the epic poem during the Renaissance* and was a formative influence upon Bernardo's more famous son, Torquato.* In 1563, Bernardo began the composition in *ottava rima* of a sequel to the *Amadigi* entitled *Floridante* (Floridante, Prince of Castile), but his work was never completed.

See also EPIC; TASSO, Torquato.

Bibliography: Giorgio Cerboni Baiardi, *La lirica di Bernardo Tasso* (Urbino: Argalla Editore, 1966); Edward Williamson, *Bernardo Tasso* (Rome: Edizioni di storia e letteratura, 1951).

TASSO, TORQUATO (1544–1595), poet. Born in Sorrento, the son of Porzia de' Rossi and Bernardo,* himself a poet and author of *Amadigi di Gaula* and *Floridante,* Tasso attended a Jesuit school in Naples. After a short period at the court of Urbino, his father sent him to the University of Padua to study law, but since his interests lay in the pursuit of literary studies, he was soon allowed to abandon jurisprudence for philosophy and eloquence. While in Padua, in 1562, he published the *Rinaldo* (Rinaldo), a romantic epic* in twelve cantos that clearly showed his mastery of the hendecasyllabic line and the *ottava** as well as his fondness for themes of epic complexities. In 1572, after eight years spent in the service of Cardinal Luigi d'Este, he obtained the patronage of Duke Alfonso II, thus becoming poet-in-residence at the court of Ferrara where, in the same capacity, Ariosto* had lived and worked. Tasso was highly ambitious and impressionable, hard-working to the point of self-neglect, and abnormally fearful of adverse criticism. He impressed the court, in the summer of the following year, with the *Aminta (Aminta),* a pastoral* play. He himself meticulously directed the performance of the play by the Gelosi actors. At this point, Tasso's life became a succession of tragic events—his partial confinement, his escape to Sorrento (where, unrecognizably emaciated, he brought his sister the news of his own death), his return to Ferrara, his peregrinations to Mantua, Padua, Venice, Pesaro, Turin, and Bergamo, his arrest for vagrancy, his last return to Ferrara and sudden public vituperation of the duke, his seven-year confinement in the prison-like asylum of Sant'Anna, his liberation, and his new wanderings to Bologna, Loreto, Florence, Mantua, and Rome, where he died without seeing the day of his poetic coronation on the Capitol, which had been planned for him at the request of Pope Clement VIII. Earlier, while he languished in Sant'Anna, and utterly without his knowledge, his poem was partially published, in 1580, under the title of *Il Goffredo,* and then in its entirety as *Gerusalemme Liberata (Jerusalem Delivered),* a title seemingly borrowed from Trissino's* *La Italia liberata dai Goti* (Italy Liberated from the Goths).

Tasso's insanity, which was most likely caused by undisciplined work habits, religious scruples, want of affection, insecurity and melancholia, has become one of the most pathetic legends in literature. Some of his lyrics and letters addressed to Leonora, Duke Alfonso's sister, are somewhat responsible for the inception of the rumor of a romantic link between the poet and the duchess—a love "fathomless" and with "no shore," as Lord Byron calls it in his poem *The Lament of Tasso* (1817). The theory that Tasso was imprisoned because of his pure yet presumptuous love was sustained by Goethe in his play, *Torquato Tasso* (1789), and given musical popularity by Gaetano Donizetti in his three-act opera *Torquato Tasso* (1833). Even Milton in one of his epigrams took for granted what modern scholarship has proved to be groundless. No one, however, has yet solved the mystery of Duke Alfonso's obstinate and most inhuman deafness to the poet's countless supplications for pardon, even after his release from Sant'Anna.

Tasso's distinguished place in Italian literature would be firmly established on the basis of his *Aminta* alone. This perfect pastoral play, which revitalizes the world of Virgil, Theocritus, Moschus, and Bion, is as simple in plot as it is pure in lyrical texture. Partly reminiscent of the mythological tale of Vertumnus and Pomona (and also of Boccaccio's* Africo and Mensola in *Ninfale fiesolano* [*The Nymph of Fiesole*]), the story of Aminta's unrequited love for Silvia is so tenderly told from beginning to happy ending, so subtly interwoven with episodes of sheer enchantment, that the line of demarcation between fable and reality is indeed quite negligible.

Based on the final phase of the first Crusade (that is, with a classical beginning *in medias res*), the story of the *Jerusalem Delivered,* which Tasso had most likely begun to write after the battle of Lepanto, is also rather simple, especially if compared with that of Ariosto's *Orlando furioso.* In the spring of 1099, Godfrey of Bouillon, the new commander-in-chief of the Christian army, besieges Jerusalem. In a desperate last attempt to halt the victorious Crusaders, the forces of Hell make themselves felt through temptresses sent to the Christian camp, through haunted forests, through drought and mutiny, and finally, through the onrush of reinforcing troops from Egypt; but Heaven triumphs and Godfrey ultimately leads his knights to the sepulcher of Christ, thus delivering the sacred city from pagan hands. The poetic celebration of a crusade had no literary precedent to which Tasso might have turned for guidance, John of Garland's ponderous *De Triumphis Ecclesiae* (before 1252, The Victory of the Church, a chronicle in hexameters of Saint Louis IX's third Crusade) being unknown to him. Consequently, he resorted to the epics of the past as a basis for his "heroic" poem which, as he envisioned it, had to be "verisimilar" and "marvelous," and therefore historical and Christian, respectively. But, more than the fusion of historic events and religious motivations, Tasso had first to reconcile history with fiction as there was no other alternative for the achievement of epic grandeur. Thus, in his invocation, he begs the forgiveness of his Muse (apparently the Blessed Mother) for his audacious, yet inevitable, mixture of "truth" and "ornaments." True, that is, historical, are such personages as Godfrey, his brother Baldwin, Tancred, Bohemond, Raymond IV of Toulouse, Peter the Hermit, and Solyman, sultan of Nicaea. Ornamental, that is, indispensable to the epic structure of the poem, are such other characters as Armida, Erminia, Clorinda, Argante, and Rinaldo, the young Christian knight who not only has nothing in common with his Carolingian namesake but also is given preeminence (thus, Tasso paid his debt of gratitude to Duke Alfonso) as the founding father of the Este family. We can, of course, most easily conjecture the failure the *Jerusalem Delivered* would have been without these "ornaments," for, whenever Tasso is most intent on maintaining truth, and truth alone, his genius is not deeply involved, and magic disappears. For instance, in the case of Godfrey, who must under all circumstances remain as "pious" as Aeneas, the more the poet strives to make his piety convincing, the less he succeeds in making us love him. Another poignant case is that of Peter the Hermit. Had Tasso drawn his inspiration less from history than from legend, the fiery priest of Amiens would undoubtedly have played a greater role in his poem. But, as Guibert of Nogent says, at the beginning of 1098 Peter was already "a fallen star," so all that Tasso could utilize from the chronicle of William of Tyre was a scanty reference to the detail that he led the supplicatory procession that preceded the battle of Ascalon in August 1099.

The publication of the *Jerusalem Delivered* marked the beginning of a strange, though understandable, literary feud between Tassophiles and Ariostophiles, that is, between admirers of Tasso's uniqueness and advocates of Ariosto's unsurpassable supremacy. The echoes of the war were felt in England and France for almost two centuries. Indeed, Ariosto had so naturally and even elegantly exploited every possible feature of chivalric poetry that there seemed to be nothing left worth repeating about knights-at-arms or magic palaces and gardens. But this Tasso had understood. He knew well that, after Boiardo* and Ariosto, all a poet could do was to treat with feeling rather than with fancy the various wars and warriors already, so to speak, waiting for him to give them new life. This he had done more unconsciously than consciously, heeding his own sentimental nature more than the dictates of his literary education. For it is Tasso's melancholy—a spiritual habit he had inherited from his own father's elegiac ditties—that spreads its veil on heroes and heroines, and transforms an entire poem, of which there is hardly a detail that cannot be traced back to its Homeric or Virgilian source, into a sustained lyrical flight. This is most likely the reason for Tasso's sudden popularity in Italy and, soon afterwards, in the rest of Europe. Especially in England, his influence goes far beyond some particulars of the Bower of Bliss in Spenser's *The Faerie Queene* and of Lucifer's peroration in Milton's *Paradise Lost*. Among the best known Ariostophiles were Galileo* and Voltaire (Voltaire's preference is discussed in Casanova's* *Memoirs*); among the best known Tassophiles were Pope and Rousseau. Dryden, most singularly, shifted from one camp to another. He first called Tasso "the most excellent of modern poets, and whom I reverence next to Virgil." Years later, he recanted in these terms: "His story is not so pleasing as Ariosto's: he is too flatulent sometimes: many times unequal, and almost always forced; and, besides, is full of conceits, points of epigram, and witticisms: all which are not only below the dignity of heroic verse, but contrary to its nature: Virgil and Homer have not one of them." Most assuredly, Tasso's style is at times "full of conceits, points of epigram, and witticisms," but Dryden failed to mention that Ariosto's *Orlando furioso* marked the culmination of the Italian Renaissance,* whereas Tasso's *Jerusalem Delivered* with its first faint prelude of the Baroque* tolled its conclusion.

After his release from Sant'Anna, Tasso completed his *Torrismondo*

(1586, Torrismondo), a tragedy, based on the *Oedipus* of Sophocles, which he had begun to write as *Galealto, re di Norvegia* (Galealto, King of Norway) soon after the performance of the *Aminta*. The play lacks inner fire. We might say that his tragic life had not made a tragedian of him. For five more years he worked on the revision of his major opus. His *Gerusalemme conquistata* (1593, Jerusalem Conquered), which he believed to be far superior to the *Jerusalem Delivered,* is the painful document of a mind hopelessly perturbed by religious, moral, and literary scruples. It is also the unprecedented example of how a poet allows his own cold self-criticism to dissect and destroy the warm inspiration of his youth. Of Tasso's other works, also written after Sant'Anna, the lengthy poem in blank verse *Le sette giornate del mondo creato* (1594, The Creation of the World in Seven Days), inspired by Saint Ambrose's *Hexameron* and, possibly, Du Bartas' *La Sepmaine Sacrée ou Creation du Monde,* is probably the best, notwithstanding its several faults—excessive erudition, lack of proportion, and an obvious desire to write a work in the religious spirit of the Counter-Reformation as well as to please Clement VIII, the reigning pontiff. Worthy of mention are *Le Lagrime di Maria Vergine Santissima* (1593, *The Tears of the Blessed Virgin*) and *Le Lagrime di Giesù Cristo Nostro Signore* (1593, *The Tears of Christ*), two poems of scarce inspiration but of genuine religious sincerity. Finally, standing apart is Tasso's vast *Rime* (Poems), a collection of more than a thousand compositions divided among love poems, panegyrics, and religious poems, the exquisite beauty of some of which found their complement in the music of Gesualdo and Monteverdi. Also vast is Tasso's production in prose. Some of his nearly two thousand letters, particularly those written from Sant'Anna, are extremely moving and beautiful. His *Dialoghi* (various dates, Dialogues) which treat such disparate themes as love, worthy life, idolatry, friendship, beauty, virtue, art, heroism, father-and-son relationships, and Tuscan poetry, are important, but most important for our understanding of the *Jerusalem Delivered* are his *Discorsi del poema eroico* (1594, *Discourses on the Heroic Poem*).

Bibliography: *Jerusalem Delivered,* trans. Joseph Tusiani (Rutherford, N.J.: Fairleigh Dickinson University Press, 1970); *Aminta,* trans. Ernest Grillo (London: Dent, 1924); *Discourses on the Heroic Poem,* trans. Mariella Cavalchini and Irene Samuel (Oxford: Clarendon Press, 1973); C. B. Beall, *La Fortune du Tasse en France* (Eugene, Ore.: University of Oregon Press, 1942); William Boulting, *Tasso and His Times* (London: Methuen, 1907); C. P. Brand, *Torquato Tasso: A Study of the Poet and of His Contribution to English Literature* (Cambridge: Cambridge University Press, 1965); Mario Praz, "Tasso in England," in *The Flaming Heart* (New York: Norton, 1973); Pierantonio Serassi, *La vita di Torquato Tasso* (Bergamo, 1785); Angelo Solerti, *Vita di Torquato Tasso,* 2 vols. (Rome: Loescher, 1895); Alessandro Tortoreto and Joseph Fucilla, *Bibliografica analitica tassiana*

(Milan: Bolaffio, 1935) and *Versi e prose ispirati al Tasso: bibliografia e antologia* (Bergamo: Centro di Studi Tassiani, 1966).

Joseph Tusiani

TASSONI, ALESSANDRO (1565–1635), poet, literary critic, and political writer. Born of noble family in Modena and orphaned in early childhood, Tassoni grew up among hostile relatives and found his inheritance attacked by lawsuits. He undertook his university training at Ferrara, Pisa, and Bologna, obtained a doctorate *utroque iure* (both canon and civil law) in 1585, and acquired some reputation for his learning and exuberant satirical humor. Tassoni was well past thirty when he began his career as a courtier in the service of Cardinal Ascanio Colonna, whom he accompanied to Spain. In 1603, he quit this post and took up residence in Rome, where for the next seven years he attended to writing and study. His passionate interest in politics and his relentless anti-Spanish attitude soon brought him into contact with Carlo Emanuele, Duke of Savoy. From 1618 to 1620 he was employed by Cardinal Maurizio, son of the duke, in Turin and Rome, but court intrigues and perhaps the opposition of Spain caused him to retire to a little villa in Trastevere to enjoy solitude, hunting, and the cultivation of flowers. Tassoni's slender fortunes did not permit him to maintain his independence for long, and in 1626, he was forced back into the service of prominent ecclesiastics, this time Cardinal Ludovisi, the nephew of Pope Gregory XV. Upon his patron's death in 1632, Tassoni finally returned to his native Mantua and spent the last three years of his life at the court of Francesco I of Este.

Tassoni's face in the best known contemporary portrait seems shrewd and quizzical; in his hands he holds a fig symbolizing the benefits gained from his services in the courts. In his correspondence, Tassoni portrays himself as bookish and independent in his conduct and opinions, shy and unhappy in his relations with others. Temperamentally, he was difficult, quarrelsome, and even cantankerous. But it would perhaps be futile to speculate, from the available evidence, on the psychological reasons for Tassoni's pessimism. One cause was no doubt the temper of the age itself, which was one of ferment, change, and contradictions. With the best Italian spirits of his time, Tassoni taught that humanistic learning was sterile, modern letters mediocre, the ruling class corrupt, and government bad.

Of Tassoni's prose works, the *Considerazioni sulle rime del Petrarca* (Reflections on Petrarch's Poetry), written during his second trip to Spain in 1602 but revised until 1611 in four different versions, consist of a series of notes, too fragmentary to amount to a thoroughly complete and serious commentary on the *Canzoniere*. Tassoni's stated purpose is to attack

Petrarch's pedantic imitators rather than their model, but he does not fail to condemn Petrarch himself. His criticism is quite systematic, concrete, and comprehensive, yet it never goes beyond rhetorical formalism; it deals mainly with the vocabulary, grammar, and style of the poems, and it often appears lost in details or given to humorous remarks or irrelevant personal comments. Tassoni is singularly acute in discovering minor defects, and his wit renders his criticism effective. The storm of dispute occasioned by the publication in 1609 of the *Considerazioni* established Tassoni's position as a literary figure and vigorous polemicist. His spirit of rebellion against authority is evident also in the *Filippiche* (1615, Philippics), two anonymously published orations, which are attributed to him.

However, the prose work which Tassoni himself regarded as his major claim to fame is his encyclopedic *Dieci libri di pensieri diversi* (1620, Ten Books of Miscellaneous Thoughts). The original *Pensieri* which appeared in 1608 numbered only one hundred and fifty-one, but by 1627, the date of issue of the final edition, the figure reached two hundred seventy-seven. They are a miscellany of essays which take the form of answers to specific questions. By this device, Tassoni is able to comment on a vast array of topics: primarily science in the first four books, and ethics, literature, and politics in the following five. In the tenth book, Tassoni sets the model for the controversy about ancient and modern learning and art that occupied the intellectuals of Europe through the seventeenth century. The *Pensieri* depict the Modenese writer as a sharp-eyed observer of the contemporary scene as well as a trenchant critic of such established institutions as the Accademia della Crusca, Homer, Aristotle, and other ancients. In the main, Tassoni is in favor of the moderns, but his attitude remains ambivalent: he criticizes both the new science and the still widespread Aristotelianism of his day. The most notable deficiency of the *Pensieri* is that they are too scattered and contradictory to make a full impact on any point. Tassoni's genius is primarily negative, and his observations, sharp and brilliant though they are, do not add up to an organized system of ideas. Tassoni knows satire, parody, caricature, and rebellion, but not critical thinking.

Tassoni is commonly thought of as the originator of the modern mock-epic for his poem *La secchia rapita* (1622, *The Rape of the Bucket*) in *ottava rima.** First written in ten cantos in 1585 and widely circulated in manuscript, it was extended to twelve in 1618, published in Paris with the title *Secchia* in 1622, and revised until the definitive edition of 1630. The basic subject of the poem is the petty war between the Guelph Bologna and the Ghibelline Modena caused by the theft of a wooden bucket. Tassoni imagines that the conflict takes place in the middle of the thirteenth century. The two armies are reviewed and they meet in battle; there is a truce; and finally peace is arranged. This fundamental theme is interwoven with incidents and episodes concerned with love and chivalry. Also, around the Olympian gods and the historical characters are grouped contemporary personages among whom the reader can identify the poet's personal friends or enemies. Tassoni normally employs the mock-heroic, which is both a technique and a tone, but often resorts to the burlesque or makes use of both in combination. More specifically, Tassoni goes further. He varies his tone, style, and language, constantly attaining an effect of irony by mixing fantasy and fact, pathos and vulgarity. The critical problem posed by the *Secchia rapita* at present is not so much the question of whether Tassoni was inspired by personal pique, by patriotism, or by the intent to parody outmoded literary forms or to satirize contemporary society, as the question of whether the poem can be read as an interesting, yet ultimately inconsequential, comic invention without a central motive or a serious meaning. Of course, it must be recognized that there is as much danger in overemphasizing the serious undercurrents of Tassoni's comic inventions and modes as there is in taking them too lightly or disregarding them completely. The *Secchia rapita* was very popular in its time, and it exercised considerable influence on the development of the mock-epic during the seventeenth and early eighteenth centuries. Many of the great European mock-heroic poems belong to the trend inaugurated by Tassoni's masterpiece.

Bibliography: La secchia rapita: rime e prose scelte, ed. Giovanni Ziccardi (Turin: UTET, 1952); *The Rape of the Bucket,* 2 vols. (London: J. M. Richardson, 1825); Roberto Alonge, "Nota sulla *Secchia rapita,*" *Sigma* 5 (1968), 107–20; Bruno A. Arcudi, "The Author of the *Secchia* Does Battle with Pietro Bembo's School," *Italica* 44 (1967), 291–313; Carmine Jannaco, ed., *Studi Tassoniani* (Modena: Aedes Muratoriana, 1966).

Albert N. Mancini

TEATRO GROTTESCO, a theatre created by a group of dramatists, most of whose works were written and produced during the first two decades of the twentieth century. The adjective *grotesque,* however, has a longer history in literary criticism. A term first used by art critics during the Renaissance* to define the ornamental style characteristic of the remains of classical paintings excavated at that time, it eventually came to designate a combination of playfulness and fantasy with sinister overtones. Montaigne's *Essays* transferred the term from art history to literature. Modern literary criticism generally uses *grotesque* to refer to a style which, unlike the classical, Baroque,* or romantic, is not restricted to a particular epoch. The most influential study in recent years, Wolfgang Kayser's *The Grotesque in Art and Literature* (1963), supplies both an historical survey of the term and instances of its application in practical criticism. For Kayser, the fundamental aspect of the grotesque is its power to evoke in the reader a feeling of alienation or estrangement from the world. In the theatre, he sees the destruction of the notion of personality as a central aspect of this estrangement.

Most often connected with this group of modern dramatists are Luigi Chiarelli,* Rosso di San Secondo,* Luigi Antonelli,* Enrico Cavacchioli (1885–1954), and Luigi Pirandello.* Their earliest critics, Silvio D'Amico (1887–1955) and Adriano Tilgher (1887–1941), believed they formed a genuine movement with a coherent philosophy. The term *grottesco* which came to be applied to many of their works derived from a line in Chiarelli's *La maschera e il volto* (1916, *The Mask and the Face*), a play which won worldwide recognition, a success unequaled in contemporary Italian theatre before Pirandello or Betti.* Other major works associated with the *teatro grottesco* include Rosso di San Secondo's *Marionette,che passione!* (1918, Marionettes, What Passion!); Antonelli's *L'Uomo che incontrò se stesso* (1918, The Man Who Met Himself); Cavacchioli's *L'Uccello del paradiso* (1919, The Bird of Paradise); and Pirandello's *Il piacere dell'onestà* (1918, *The Pleasure of Honesty*).

The plays of the *teatro grottesco* characteristically use the traditional triangle of husband-wife-mistress, which was the basic plot for much of nineteenth-century drama. Yet, from a stylistic point of view, few if any of the grotesque works aspire to the naturalism of that period, and most reject the norms of objectivity and impersonality by having the author inject himself and his ideas into the play, usually by means of a "mouthpiece" character. Most significantly, there is a sharp division in the main character between his social personality and his authentic or private personality, the mask and the face of Chiarelli's title. In these plays, the "grotesque" manifests itself in bizarre, fantastic, absurd events or situations. Personalities are actually split on stage so that a person meets himself; a man pretends to kill his wife to avoid the appearance of being ridiculous and is acquitted for it, only to be tried because she has been discovered alive; a wife betrays two husbands at once (who are the same person).

The plays of the *teatro grottesco* are most accurately seen as works which reject the rigidly traditional, middle-class naturalistic theatre. In reality, the futurist plays of the same epoch and the early dramas of Pirandello were the truly revolutionary theatre at the turn of the century. Most critics, however, refused to recognize futurism as a valid approach to drama and even failed to realize that many of the original ideas they attributed to these works, particularly the division between mask and face, were already present in Pirandello's treatise on humor, *L'Umorismo* (1908, *On Humor*), and his early novels *L'Esclusa* (1893, *The Outcast*) and *Il fu Mattia Pascal* (1904, *The Late Mattia Pascal*)—all of which were published before the term *teatro grottesco* became popular. Most of the plays in question, even those of Pirandello, could otherwise be described as tragicomedies.

See also ANTONELLI, Luigi; CHIARELLI, Luigi; PIRANDELLO, Luigi.

Bibliography: Teatro grottesco del Novecento: Antologia, ed. Gigi Livio (Milan: Mursia, 1965); *International Modern Plays,* ed. Anthony Dent (London: Everyman, 1963); Silvio D'Amico, *Il teatro italiano* (Milan: Treves, 1932); Wolfgang Kayser, *The Grotesque in Art and Literature* (Bloomington, Ind.: Indiana University Press, 1963); Adriano Tilgher, *Studi sul teatro contemporaneo* (Rome: Libreria di scienze e lettere, 1928); Mario Verdone, *Teatro del tempo futurista* (Rome: Lerici, 1969).

TEBALDEO, ANTONIO (1463–1537), lyric poet. Tebaldeo (a Latinized form of his family name Tebaldi) was born in Ferrara. He frequented the courts of Ferrara and Mantua, but after the election of the Medici Pope Leo X, he went to Rome, gained Leo's patronage, and lost his library and much of his wealth during the Sack of Rome in 1527. In Rome, Tebaldeo became acquainted with Bembo* and Castiglione.* He appears in one of Raphael's frescoes in the papal apartments.

The first edition of Tebaldeo's Italian lyrics appeared in an unauthorized Milanese volume published by a cousin in 1499; it was popular enough to be reissued eleven times during the first part of the sixteenth century. The most complete version of his *Rime* (Poems), which the poet himself prepared, appeared in 1534. The collection includes not only love sonnets* but also pastoral* eclogues, *strambotti,* * and poems in *ottava* * and *terza rima.* * Like Petrarch's* *Canzoniere,* Tebaldeo's sonnets have their Laura —a young girl from Siena called Flavia who recalls not only her Petrarchan model but also Catullus's Lesbia and women from *The Metamorphoses* of Ovid. Like the lyric poems of Il Cariteo* and Serafino Aquilano,* Tebaldeo's Petrarchan verse was considered defective and exaggerated by Bembist purists. Nonetheless, his poems were included in the important Petrarchan anthologies which foreign travelers took home with them from Italy and which were indispensable to the vogue of the international lyric style of Petrarchism.*

See also BEMBO, Pietro; CARITEO, Benedetto; PETRARCHISM; SERAFINO AQUILANO.

Bibliography: Poesia del Quattrocento e del Cinquecento, eds. Carlo Muscetta and Daniele Ponchiroli (Turin: Einaudi, 1959).

TECCHI, BONAVENTURA (1896–1968), novelist, scholar, and translator. Tecchi was born in Bagnoregio. His active military participation in World War I brought him into contact with German literature and placed him in the same prison camp as Ugo Betti* and Carlo Emilio Gadda.* In the postwar years, he traveled in Germany and Switzerland and directed the Gabinetto Vieusseux in Florence for a time (1925–31). In Florence, he was associated with the group of writers contributing to the avant-garde periodical *Solaria*. After several years abroad in Czechoslovakia as an Italian teacher, Tecchi returned to become professor of German literature in Rome. His first literary work, a collection of stories entitled *Il nome sulla sabbia* (1924, The Name on the Sand), was followed by a number of novels, including *I Villatauri* (1937, The Villatauris); *Giovani amici* (1940, Young Friends); *Valentina Velier* (1950, Valentina Velier); *Gli egoisti* (1959, The Egoists); *Gli onesti* (1965, The Honest Men); and a posthumously published narrative, *La terra abbandonata* (1970, The Abandoned Land). Tecchi's scholarly studies of German culture and literature treat such central figures as Goethe, E.T.A. Hoffmann, and Thomas Mann, and such genres as romantic theatre and fable.

Bibliography: Opere di Bonaventura Tecchi, ed. Arnoldo Bocelli (Milan: Bompiani, 1974); *The Egoists*, trans. Dennis Chamberlin (New York: Appleton-Century, 1964); *Stories of Modern Italy*, ed. Ben Johnson (New York: Random House, 1960); Giuseppe Amoroso, *Itinerari stilistici di Tecchi* (Florence: Le Monnier, 1970); Piero De Tommaso, *Bonaventura Tecchi* (Ravenna: Longo, 1971).

TERZA RIMA, a verse form usually composed of tercets of hendecasyllabic verse in *rima incatenata (aba bcb cdc ded . . . xyx yzy z),* in which the first line rhymes with the third, the second with the first of the following tercet and so forth. The chain is closed with a final line, called the *chiusa*, or "closing." Various theories have been advanced as to the background of this form. Scholars have suggested that it was based upon the tercets of the Provençal *sirventes* or upon those of the classical sonnet,* but there is no doubt that it was first used by Dante* in the *Divina commedia* and was especially appropriate because of the theological suggestiveness of the number three. Because of its particular structure, it is extremely difficult to add or subtract materials from the original, or even to modify the poem during its composition, except at the beginning or the conclusion of the poem. This fact may explain why there are rarely omissions of lines or passages in the extant manuscripts of Dante's masterpiece. Few verse forms have proved to be so capable of expressing numerous tonal or stylistic levels and of treating so great a variety of themes. After Dante, Petrarch* employed it in *I trionfi (The Triumphs)* and Boccaccio* used it in his *Amorosa visione* (Amorous Vision). In Italy, many poets, including those of the present era, have expressed various poetic themes (satire, politics, allegorical and didactic verse) in *terza rima*. Abroad, it was introduced into English literature by Chaucer and served such writers as Wyatt, Daniel, Byron, von Hofmannsthal, Shelley, Auden, and Mac-

Leish, to mention only a few. It is a particularly difficult form for a language less rich in rhymes than Italian.

Bibliography: Raffaele Spongano, *Nozioni ed esempi di metrica italiana* (Bologna: Pàtron, 1966); J. S. P. Tatlock, "Dante's *Terza Rima,*" *Publications of the Modern Language Association* 51 (1936), 895–903.

TESAURO, EMANUELE (1592–1675), literary theorist, poet, and historian. Tesauro was born in Turin. He entered the Jesuit order in 1611 and taught rhetoric in Milan and Cremona, leaving the order in 1634. After that time until his death, he fulfilled a number of duties for his patrons at the court of Savoy, most particularly as court historian and tutor. He was the author of a wide range of works, including three tragedies, a collection of panegyrics, a treatise on moral philosophy, and several histories. His fame rests almost entirely on a single work of literary theory entitled *Il cannocchiale aristotelico* (1655, The Aristotelian Telescope), the best known and most complete treatise on the conceit or metaphor produced during the Italian Baroque* period.

Tesauro's work owes much to an earlier treatise, *Arte de Ingenio* (1642, The Art of Wit) by Baltasar Gracián (1601–1658), a Spanish writer. For both Gracián and Tesauro, the essence of myth was to be found in the rhetorical figure and in anything which transformed and elevated ordinary expression. Tesauro identifies three kinds of figures—those which delight the ear, those which delight the affections by their imagery, and those which delight the intellect by their wit *(ingegno)*. Wit is embodied in metaphor, which Tesauro divides into eight forms. As an unqualified admirer of the Baroque poetry of Marino,* Tesauro discerned an analogy between the poetry of conceits or "metaphysical" poetry and the universe; the world is God's poem which is written in conceits, and God is thus a "witty creator" and an "arguto favellatore" (sharp speaker). Thus, the traditional notion of the world as book or the book of nature is subtly transformed into a Baroque universe of metaphor, analogy, and conceit in Tesauro's poetics. For Tesauro, the conceit is defined as an "urbane enthymeme," an ingenious syllogism in which one of the premises has been suppressed. Unlike other theorists of the time, Tesauro had managed to distinguish the conceit from other rhetorical tropes on the basis of its structure alone, thus providing modern literary critics with a useful tool in the analysis of the Baroque works of such diverse writers as Marino, John Donne, Quevedo, and many others.

See also BAROQUE; MARINO, Giambattista.

Bibliography: Il cannocchiale aristotelico, ed. August Buck (Berlin: Gehlen, 1968); Eugenio Donato, "Tesauro's Poetics: Through the Looking Glass," *Modern Language Notes* 78 (1963), 15–30; Joseph A. Mazzeo, "Metaphysical Poetry and the Poetic of Correspondence," *Journal of the History of Ideas* 14 (1953), 221–34; Robert E. Proctor, "Emanuele Tesauro: A Theory of the Conceit," *Modern Language Notes* 88 (1973), 68–94.

TESTI, FULVIO (1593–1646), poet and political figure. A native of Ferrara, Testi received a Jesuit education and attended the universities of Ferrara and Bologna. He entered the service of Duke Cesare d'Este in Modena and was soon appointed to the important positions of secretary of state (1628) and ambassador to Vienna (1632), Turin (1635), and the court of Spain (1636–38). For his services, he acquired the title of count. Discovered undertaking secret negotiations with the French government in order to obtain a post in Rome, he was arrested and imprisoned in 1646 at the fortress of Modena, where he died just as he was about to receive a ducal pardon.

Testi began several epic* poems—*Costantino* (Constantine) and *L'India conquistata* (The Conquest of India)—neither of which was completed beyond the first canto, and he wrote several plays, among them a tragedy entitled *L'Isola di Alcina* (1626, The Island of Alcina). His voluminous correspondence constitutes one of the most useful collections from the period, both because of the historical value of his letters and their admirable stylistic qualities. The source of Testi's fame, however, was his lyric poetry, which, inspired by the models of Petrarch,* Pindar, and Horace, avoided the excesses of Marino* and similar stylists and represented a moment of classical restraint in the Baroque* period. The first edition of his verse, *Rime* (1613, Rhymes), contained sonnets,* *canzoni,* * and epigrams, and was revised and republished in 1617. In this second edition he placed his most famous work, a patriotic poem in forty-three stanzas of *ottava rima* * usually known as the *Pianto d'Italia* (The Suffering of Italy). The work is in the form of a dream-vision, during which Italy speaks to the poet of her past grandeur, blames Spain for her present decadence, and places her future hopes for a national revival in the person of Carlo Emanuele I of the House of Savoy. It is more notable for its patriotic emotion and its historical significance than for its poetry. Still, Testi was capable of great poetry, as his *canzone* directed to Count Raimondo Montecuccoli, "Ruscelletto orgoglioso" ("O haughty rivulet"), demonstrates.

See also BAROQUE.

Bibliography: I lirici del Seicento e dell'Arcadia, ed. Carlo Calcaterra (Milan: Rizzoli, 1936); *Lettere,* ed. Maria Luisa Doglio, 2 vols. (Bari: Laterza, 1967); *From Marino to Marinetti,* trans. Joseph Tusiani (New York: Baroque Press, 1974); Giovanni Getto, *Il barocco in prosa e in poesia* (Milan: Rizzoli, 1969).

TESTORI, GIOVANNI (1923–   ), art critic and writer. Testori was born in Novate Milanese on the outskirts of Milan, the city that figures so prominently in his fiction. Besides his interpretations of various contemporary artists (Renato Guttuso, Giacomo Manzú, Carlo Carrà), his studies of painting in Piedmont and Lombardy between the sixteenth and eighteenth centuries are well known. Testori began as an author of short stories, the first volume of which was edited by Vittorini* and published in 1954. It was ultimately included in a five-part series of short stories, plays, and a novel he called the "Segreti di Milano" (Secrets of Milan), comprised of two collections of stories, *Il ponte della Ghisolfa* (1958, The Ghisolfa Bridge) and *La Gilda del Mac Mahon* (1959, Gilda of MacMahon Street); two comedies, *La Maria Brasca* (1960, Maria Brasca) and *L'Arialda* (1961, Arialda); and the novel *Il fabbricone* (1961, *The House in Milan*). One of his stories inspired Luchino Visconti's memorable film on a Milanese working-class family, *Rocco and His Brothers* (1960). In addition to the two comedies in his series, Testori has written several other plays, including *La monaca di Monza* (1967, The Nun of Monza), produced in Milan by Luchino Visconti; and *Ambleto* (1972, Hamblet), written in dialect and based on the play by Shakespeare. Because of his interest in the proletarian milieu of Milan and its local dialects, Testori's works have often been compared to those of Gadda* or Pasolini.*

Bibliography: Il ponte della Ghisolfa (Milan: Feltrinelli, 1958); *La Gilda del Mac Mahon* (Milan: Feltrinelli, 1959); *The House in Milan,* trans. Sidney Alexander (New York: Harcourt, 1962); Enrico Ghidetti, "Giovanni Testori," in *I contemporanei* (Milan: Marzorati, 1974), VI, 1565–88.

TIRABOSCHI, GIROLAMO (1731–1794), scholar, librarian, and literary historian. Born in Bergamo, Tiraboschi became a Jesuit at the age of fifteen and taught eloquence in the schools there before being called to Modena by Duke Francesco III to direct the famous library, at one time headed by Lodovico Muratori.* Besides various minor writings in Latin and Italian, Tiraboschi produced a single monumental work entitled *Storia della letteratura italiana* (1772–82, The History of Italian Literature), the most comprehensive history of its type until De Sanctis.* It encompasses the origins and the progress of letters from the time of the Etruscans to 1700. It was closer to a cultural history than what is understood today as a literary history, since it concentrated more upon the biographical details of a poet's life than upon textual analyses of his works, and it defined literature in the broadest of terms to include art, philosophy, medicine, law, science, and many other fields no longer considered by contemporary literary historians. Tiraboschi did, however, view Italian literature as an expression of national consciousness before Italy existed as a political entity. For him, the golden age of Italian letters was the learned age of humanism,* with Petrarch* as its foremost representative. Future generations of critics and scholars would refer to Tiraboschi's work for its copious and indispensable documentation, even when his point of view had long been abandoned.

See also MURATORI, Lodovico Antonio.

Bibliography: Storia della letteratura italiana, 16 vols. (Milan: Classici italiani, 1822–26); Giovanni Getto, *Storia delle storie letterarie* (Florence: Sansoni, 1969).

TOBINO, MARIO (1910–   ), physician, novelist, and poet. Tobino was from Viareggio. He had already published an anthology of poetry by the time he received his medical degree in 1936. During 1939 and 1940, when he was drafted and sent to Africa, Tobino worked in an asylum, a setting recalled in his best and most recent fiction. His first novel, *Il figlio del farmacista* (1942, The Pharmacist's Son), appeared during World War II, which provided the subject matter for another book, *Il deserto della Libia* (1951, *The Deserts of Libya*), which describes the desert campaign. Then followed *Le libere donne di Magliano* (1953, *The Women of Magliano*), a novel animated by Tobino's experiences as a doctor in a mental institution; *Il clandestino* (1962, *The Underground*), a novel describing the resistance following the fall of the fascist regime, which was awarded the Strega Prize for that year; and a number of minor works. Tobino's most recent novel of note, *Per le antiche scale* (1972, Down the Ancient Staircase), returns to the milieu of *Le libere donne di Magliano,* the mental institution, and has inspired an excellent film of the same title by Mauro Bolognini. This book received the Campiello Prize in 1972. Tobino continues to practice psychiatric medicine at a hospital near Lucca and contributes articles and reviews to various Italian periodicals.

Bibliography: The Lost Legions: Three Italian War Novels (New York: Knopf, 1967)—contains a translation of *Il deserto della Libia* by Archibald Colquhoun and Antonia Cowan; *The Women of Magliano,* trans. Archibald Colquhoun (New York: Putnam's, 1954); *The Underground,* trans. Raymond Rosenthal (Garden City, N.Y.: Doubleday, 1966); Felice Del Beccaro, *Mario Tobino* (Florence: La Nuova Italia, 1973).

TOMASI DI LAMPEDUSA, GIUSEPPE (1896–1957), Sicilian aristocrat and novelist. A descendant of one of the most noble Sicilian families, duke of Palma and prince of Lampedusa, Lampedusa (as he is known in the English-speaking world) grew up in the aristocratic environment which his single novel depicts. His facility in five major foreign languages gave him early and continued exposure to the best of modern fiction, especially that from France. As an officer in the Italian army, he took part in both world wars but refused to participate actively in the fascist movement. When his beautiful palace in Palermo was destroyed during an Allied bombardment, he took refuge with his cousin, Luccio Piccolo,* and it was at his home that he first made the literary contacts with Eugenio Montale* and Giorgio Bassani* which encouraged him to set about writing his novel.

Il gattopardo (1958, *The Leopard*) was composed between 1955 and

1956, but Lampedusa never lived to see its publication. The book was the result of a lifetime of reading and thinking. Although it was initially rejected by several leading publishers, Giorgio Bassani recognized its merit and recommended it to Feltrinelli. It was awarded the Strega Prize for 1959, became a memorable film directed by Luchino Visconti in 1963, and has enjoyed an unparalleled success all over the world. Its artistic merits equal its popularity, and it can rightly be called one of the masterpieces of modern Italian literature.

When the novel first appeared, it seemed to be a work in the naturalist tradition of Verga* and De Roberto,* a historical novel about the Risorgimento and its failure to improve the lot of southern Italy. A bitter polemic sprang up in Italy over its political and philosophical content, much of which obscured its literary qualities. In recent years, most serious interpretations of the novel have called attention to its status as both an historical and a psychological novel with a primarily symbolic or poetic structure. The novel concentrates upon one major character, Don Fabrizio Corbera, the prince of Salina, whose family crest bears the leopard of the title. Don Fabrizio and his family are introduced as Garibaldi* invades Sicily in 1860 and overthrows the decadent Bourbon Kingdom of the Two Sicilies. Although the prince declines to take sides in the struggle, his opportunistic nephew, Tancredi Falconeri, sees the need for members of their class to participate in the revolution; as he cynically puts it, "if we want things to stay as they are, things will have to change."

Tancredi marries the beautiful daughter of the unscrupulous bourgeois liberal, Don Calogero Sèdara, and much of the novel's political content is devoted to this union of an ancient family and newly acquired wealth. Don Fabrizio sees the new republic as just another fraud disguised in the name of liberty and predicts that Sicily will receive no more benefit from its new rulers than from other invaders. His death in 1883 thus signals the passing of an entire era, one which Lampedusa compares favorably with the new republic; from the epoch of the noble leopard, Sicily has turned to the rule of jackals. The final chapter moves beyond his death to the fiftieth anniversary of Garibaldi's landing in 1910 to expose the emptiness of the Risorgimento's promises and man's ultimate failure to dominate his universe.

Far from being a simple historical novel of the type common in the nineteenth century, Lampedusa's masterpiece succeeds in presenting a complex plot based upon the conflicts of north and south, Christianity and paganism, order and chaos, all of which is expressed in one of the most complex and beautiful literary languages of this century. The historical theme of the Risorgimento, the revolution that failed, is thus part of a more profound psychological study—an analysis of the human struggle to impose order upon chaos and its inevitable failure.

Besides *Il gattopardo,* Lampedusa composed several short stories, left a second novel unfinished, and completed one impressive theoretical essay on Stendhal and the art of the novel.

See also DE ROBERTO, Federico; VERISMO.

Bibliography: The Leopard, trans. Archibald Colquhoun (New York: Avon, 1975); *Two Stories and a Memory,* trans. Archibald Colquhoun (New York: Grosset, 1968); "Lezione su Stendhal," *Paragone* 9 (1959), 3–49; Richard H. Lansing, "The Structure of Meaning in Lampedusa's *Il Gattopardo,*" *Publications of the Modern Language Association* 93 (1978), 409–22; Olga Ragusa, "Stendhal, Tomasi di Lampedusa, and the Novel," *Comparative Literature Studies* 10 (1973), 195–228; Simonetta Salvestroni, *Tomasi di Lampedusa* (Florence: La Nuova Italia, 1973).

TOMMASEO, NICCOLÒ (1802–1874), poet, patriot, lexicographer, and scholar. Born in Dalmatia, Tommaseo completed his early studies in a seminary and entered the University of Padua to study law in 1817. His first poetic works date from around 1814, and his formative years were more occupied with reading the classics and the Italian masterpieces than with the study of law. As early as 1822, he began to translate works in foreign languages (Homer's *Iliad,* Rousseau's *Nouvelle Héloïse*); this was the initial stage of a lifelong interest in translation. After meeting Manzoni* in 1825, Tommaseo gained a permanent job in Florence on the staff of Gian Pietro Vieusseux's (1779–1863) *Antologia,* where he began various projects which reflected his particular linguistic talents. In 1830, the first edition of his *Dizionario dei sinonimi* (Dictionary of Synonyms) appeared; in addition, he began his commentary on Dante's* *Commedia,* gathered material for his *Dizionario della lingua italiana,* and collected a number of popular Tuscan, Greek, Dalmatian, and Corsican folk songs for future publication. One of his own political articles precipitated the suppression of *Antologia* by the authorities in 1833. Forced into exile in France, Tommaseo met many of the most important writers of the time and published some of his works in Paris, including a book of verse entitled *Confessioni* (1836, Confessions) and a historical narrative, *Il Duca d'Atene* (1837, The Duke of Athens), based upon materials found in the histories of Florence by Villani* and Machiavelli.* He also completed his commentary on Dante, which appeared in Venice in 1837. While in Corsica, he concluded a novel, *Fede e bellezza* (Faith and Beauty), which was published in 1840.

After the Austrians declared an amnesty for exiles, Tommaseo returned to Italy and settled in Venice. He undertook a translation of the *Psalms,* the publication of his *Dizionario estetico* (1840, Aesthetic Dictionary), four volumes of folk songs (1841–42), and numerous critical works. Arrested in 1848 along with Daniele Manin, the future head of the short-lived Venetian Republic, Tommaseo wrote poetry and translated the Gospels until he was liberated from prison by a Venetian mob. As one of the most ardent republicans, he served as minister of public education and ambassador to France until the government's downfall. With the end of the republic in 1849, Tommaseo went into exile to Corfu, where he remained until 1854. There, he married and had two children while he suffered from progressive blindness. Much of his best poetry was written at this time and was later combined with his early compositions and published as *Poesie* (1872, Poems). He also completed *Rome et le monde* (1851, Rome and the World), a plea for the church to abandon its temporal power. Eventually, Tommaseo moved to Turin (where he worked as a teacher) and then to Florence in 1859. In spite of the fact that he was almost totally blind by this time, he continued work on an amazing number of projects—articles on politics, education, criticism, and philology; corrections of his previous scholarly and reference works; and the publication of his monumental *Dizionario della lingua italiana* (Dictionary of the Italian Language) from 1858 to 1879.

It is extremely difficult to characterize fully the activities and writings of such a complex figure. Tommaseo's political deeds or his accomplishments as a lexicographer occupied most critics of his works until recently, for Tommaseo left no single literary work which rivals in importance or originality his great dictionary. His attention to folk songs and his several historical narratives attest to his typically romantic interest in the medieval past or in the popular origins of lyric poetry. Recent critics, however, have turned attention from his reference works or from his prose to his poetry, in which they find evidence of Tommaseo's most individual contributions to nineteenth-century literature. "La poesia" ("Poetry"), a brief poem written between 1845 and 1860 which serves as a preface to *Poesie*, may be considered Tommaseo's statement on poetics. In the work, Tommaseo rejects the primacy of any single element in poetry (thought, imagery, harmony, theme) and asserts that it is their unity in a composition which must define the creative experience. Among his best works are "A una foglia" (1855, "To a Leaf"), a comparison of the death of a leaf to the mutability of the poet, and the moving "D'un quasi cieco e presso a esser vedovo" (1871, "Of One Almost Blind and Soon to Be a Widower"), a poem written during the fatal illness of Tommaseo's wife when the poet was almost totally blind. At its best, Tommaseo's poetry has the confessional, autobiographical tone of a poetic diary, and it reflects the interpenetration of the poet's romantic sensibility with his profoundly classical and humanistic training.

See also ROMANTICISM.

Bibliography: Opere, ed. Mario Puppo, 2 vols. (Florence: Sansoni, 1968); *From Marino to Marinetti,* trans. Joseph Tusiani (New York: Baroque Press, 1974); Raffaele Ciampini, *Studi e ricerche su Niccolò Tommaseo* (Rome: Edizioni di storia e letteratura, 1944) and *Vita di Niccolò Tommaseo* (Florence: Sansoni, 1945);

Giacomo Debenedetti, *Niccolò Tommaseo: quaderni inediti* (Milan: Garzanti, 1972).

TOZZI, FEDERIGO (1883–1920), Sienese novelist. Tozzi's family life was extremely difficult. His mother Annunziata lost eight children before the birth of Federigo, and her early death in 1895 left the young man in the care of a father, who beat him frequently and considered him of little worth. Tozzi did poorly in school and was expelled several times before finally receiving a diploma from a technical institute in Arezzo. Between 1899 and 1903, he had his first love affair with a peasant girl, an experience later recalled in a novel. In 1908, he began working for the state railroad and was eventually assigned a position in Florence. Before his premature death in 1920 from pneumonia, he managed to publish several collections of poetry in the style of D'Annunzio*—*Zampogna verde* (1911, Green Bagpipe) and *La città della Vergine* (1913, The City of the Virgin)—and several novels, among them *Bestie* (1917, Animals) and *Con gli occhi chiusi* (1920, With Closed Eyes). Other important novels, as well as many unproduced dramatic works, appeared posthumously.

Tozzi was relatively unknown in Italy at the time of his death and was almost unheard of abroad. Yet, in the years since the appearance of his major novels, and particularly in the last two decades, many influential Italian writers and critics have compared him to the greatest of this century's novelists. His contribution to twentieth-century Italian literature cannot be ignored. His first major work was the novel *Con gli occhi chiusi*. Containing obvious autobiographical elements, this work describes a man, Pietro Rosi, who (like Tozzi himself) is the child of a couple who manage a *trattoria* in Siena and own a farm outside the town. Eventually, Pietro falls in love with a peasant girl named Ghísola (as had Tozzi in his youth). A central scene in the novel, particularly crucial to a psychoanalytical reading of the work, is that in which the son witnesses the almost indiscriminate castration of the farm animals ordered by his father. Not surprisingly, the work focuses upon the relationship of father and son and how this experience affects the protagonist's interactions with other characters. The title of the novel refers to the effects of the Oedipal relationship—Pietro's closed eyes symbolize his blindness to life and his inability to respond to any meaningful confrontation with reality. His unsuccessful love affair with Ghísola is yet another aspect of his arrested development caused, in large measure, by the conflicts with his father.

Tre croci (1920, *Three Crosses*) describes the lives of three brothers—Giulio, Niccolò, and Enrico Gambi—who operate a Sienese bookstore. Incompetent businessmen but gluttonous eaters and egotists, the three are forced to forge the signature of a generous friend to promissory notes in order to make ends meet. The novel describes their experience of awaiting the inevitable discovery of their misdeeds and the consequences of their dishonesty. When at last the crime is uncovered by a bank teller, Giulio commits suicide. Although his two brothers gain a reprieve when a court erroneously decides they did not share in his guilt, the burden of their consciences proves too much for them, and each eventually succumbs to illnesses brought upon him by his sense of complicity.

In *Il podere* (1921, The Farm), Tozzi portrays the inept Remigio Selmi who inherits a farm from a father whom he had abandoned some years earlier. He immediately becomes the target of financial machinations against his inheritance, and his naïveté makes him unaware of the remedies he might have taken against the dishonest schemes of his father's friends and business associates. Both human and natural disasters conspire to destroy his crops and to ruin him, and he is eventually murdered for no logical reason by a discontented farm laborer. Again, the mysterious hold of the father over the son, so important in Tozzi's works, explains much of the novel's action. Remigio seems to suffer from a curse brought upon him by his earlier desertion of his father. In addition, while his enemies steal his inheritance from him, Remigio himself feels a strange sense of satisfaction when his property and inheritance are ruined, an obvious sign of the resentment he feels for his father and his subconscious need to rebel.

Two brief novels are also worthy of note: *Gli egoisti* (1923, The Egotists) and the more important *Ricordi di un impiegato* (1920, Diary of a Clerk). The second treats the life of a provincial clerk named Leopoldo Gradi, a figure who has been compared to Svevo's* Alfonso Nitti in *Una vita* and to Kafka's Gregory Samsa in "The Metamorphosis."

It was perhaps impossible for the Italian reading public or its critics to appreciate Tozzi's works when they first appeared, for at that time the impact of Freud's ideas and the vogue of the psychological novel in general had yet to penetrate Italian culture. With the passage of time, however, Tozzi's novels have come to be considered accurate reflections of an alienated existence with its roots in the family structure and of the universal experience of growing up which all his readers share with his protagonists. Tozzi's antiheroes and his nonrhetorical literary language now seem integral elements in the historical development of the Italian novel.

Bibliography: Opere, ed. Glauco Tozzi, 4 vols. (Florence: Vallecchi, 1961–70); *Three Crosses,* trans. R. Capellero (New York: Moffat Yard, 1921); Claudio Carabba, *Tozzi* (Florence: La Nuova Italia, 1971); *From Verismo to Experimentalism: Essays on the Modern Italian Novel,* ed. Sergio Pacifici (Bloomington, Ind.: Indiana University Press, 1969); Sergio Pacifici, *The Modern Italian Novel from Capuana to Tozzi* (Carbondale, Ill.: Southern Illinois University Press, 1973); Giosè Rimanelli, "Federigo Tozzi: Misfit and Master," *Italian Quarterly* 14 (1971), 29–76; Ferruccio Ulivi, *Federigo Tozzi* (Milan: Mursia, 1962).

TRAPASSI, PIETRO: *See* METASTASIO, Pietro.

TRILUSSA, pen-name of Carlo Alberto Salustri (1871–1950), Roman poet and journalist. Trilussa's first collection of verse in Roman dialect appeared in 1895. Soon, his skill in evoking the spoken language of the Eternal City and its local color attracted a wide audience. Among the most successful of his collections of poetry may be numbered *Favole romanesche* (1900, Romanesque Fables), *Omini e bestie* (1908, Men and Beasts), and *Lupi e agnelli* (1919, Wolves and Lambs). True to the tradition of popular dialect poetry best represented in Rome by Belli,* Trilussa's verse aimed its satiric barbs at various targets (bureaucrats, women, socialists, politicians) and often employed the moralistic structure of the animal fable. Although he was widely read, his obviously antifascist views prevented official recognition during the Mussolinian era. His nomination as senator for life from the president of the Italian republic came but a short time before his death.

Bibliography: Tutte le poesie, ed. Pietro Pancrazi (Milan: Mondadori, 1951); *Twentieth-Century Italian Poetry: A Bilingual Anthology,* trans. Margherita Marchione (Rutherford, N.J.: Fairleigh Dickinson University Press, 1974); Gaetano Mariani, *Trilussa: storia di un poeta* (Rome: Bonacci, 1974).

TRISSINO, GIAN GIORGIO (1478–1550), literary theorist, poet, and playwright. Born in Vicenza of a noble family, Trissino came to Milan in 1506 to study Greek. In 1512, he was brought to Ferrara under the protection of Lucrezia Borgia, and during the next year he took part in the gatherings at the Orti Oricellari which included Florentine intellectuals such as Machiavelli* and Alamanni.* In 1514, the attraction of Pope Leo X's court drew him to Rome where, the following year, he wrote his important tragedy *Sofonisba* (Sophonisba). The first four parts of his influential critical work, *La poetica (Poetics)* appeared in 1529. The last two sections of the study were not completed for twenty years and were published only in 1563, although they represented critical opinions Trissino had formed much earlier in his life. Trissino became involved in the polemical arguments over the *questione della lingua,** and in 1529 he translated Dante's* *De vulgari eloquentia* into Italian and composed a treatise on language entitled *Il Castellano* (The Castellan). More significantly, in 1547, he published the first nine books of his epic* poem, *La Italia liberata dai Goti* (Italy Liberated from the Goths), the other eighteen books of which appeared the following year.

Before the sixteenth century, Italian dramatists had little opportunity to read Greek plays and had based their Latin tragedies primarily upon Seneca. The appearance of Aldine editions of Sophocles, Euripides, and Aeschylus at the turn of the century prompted Italians to imitate the Greek works directly. Trissino led this movement with *Sofonisba,* which most critics consider the first "regular" modern tragedy based upon Greek practice. With a story taken from the Roman historian Livy, the play followed Greek models rather than Aristotle's *Poetics*. Its principal stylistic innovation was its blank verse *(versi sciolti)*, which replaced the rhymed verse of earlier Italian drama. Trissino was one of the first to establish blank verse as the norm for European heroic and dramatic poetry. He followed the Greek practice of arranging their dramas in episodes and choral odes, but the framework of his play with its prologue and four episodes closely resembles the Roman model. Moreover, he neglects the unity of place, while observing the unities of action and time. Although *Sofonisba* was not staged in Italy until 1562 and was not the first regular tragedy performed in Italy (that honor belongs to Giraldi's* *Orbecche*), its influence exceeded its intrinsic literary merit. Mellin de Saint-Gelais translated it into French around 1559, and it was performed at the castle of Blois before Catherine de' Medici. Numerous European plays devoted to the theme of Sophonisba included works by Jean Mairet and John Marston, and the theme continued to attract neoclassical playwrights all over Europe through the eighteenth century.

Trissino's epic poem was meant to mirror what he considered true Homeric epic poetry rather than the works of Dante, Ariosto,* or even Virgil. He worked on the poem for twenty years and based his hopes for future fame upon its success, but the poem's reception was scarcely better than that accorded to either Petrarch's* Latin epic or Voltaire's later feeble attempts in the genre. The story was taken from the historians Procopius and Vegetius and involved a celebration of the conquest of Italy by Belisarius for the Emperor Justinian in the sixth century. Every possible Homeric stylistic device (catalogues, heavenly messengers, *ekphrasis*) and character find their parallel in Trissino's work, but the poetry never seems truly inspired. Nonetheless, his use of blank verse rather than the *terza rima** of Dante or the *ottava rima** of Ariosto and Boiardo* set an example for the greatest Renaissance* epic poem, Milton's *Paradise Lost*. It appears that Milton knew of Trissino's use of blank verse indirectly through Tasso's* *Il mondo creato* (The Created World), written in blank verse after Trissino's example but devoted to the theme of the earth's creation, the subject Milton himself adopted.

Trissino also composed lyric poems—many of them in the Petrarchan tradition—as well as several Pindaric odes and the first Horatian ode written in Italian. *I simillimi* (1548, The Look Alikes) is an Italian version of Plautus's *Menaechmi* in which he imitates the Greek form of Aristophanic comedy (episodes are divided by choral passages). *La poetica* sets forth, in six parts, many problems of versification—the choice of language and rhetoric (I); the kinds of rhyme (II); the possible combinations of rhyme schemes (III); and the stanzaic forms of the various lyric genres (IV). This treatise is most remarkable for its use of Italian poetry to

522 _Trissino, Gian Giorgio_

illustrate theoretical ideas. The fifth and sixth parts are often nothing more than a translation of Aristotle's _Poetics,_ but the book is one of the earliest poetics written in the vernacular. Although it lacks the elaborate critical apparatus and commentaries that later Cinquecento scholars provided along with Aristotle's text, Trissino's work was nevertheless more useful to the average reader of the time. It reflects a moment in the development of Renaissance poetic theory when Aristotle slowly supplanted Horace as the dominant authority in critical matters.

See also QUESTIONE DELLA LINGUA.

Bibliography: Tutte le opere di Giovan Giorgio Trissino, ed. S. Maffei, 2 vols. (Verona: Vallarsi, 1729); _Literary Criticism: Plato to Dryden,_ ed. Allan H. Gilbert (Detroit, Mich.: Wayne State University Press, 1962)—contains portions of _La poetica_; Marvin T. Herrick, _Italian Tragedy in the Renaissance_ (Urbana, Ill.: Illinois University Press, 1965); Charles Ricci, _Sophonisbe dans la tragédie classique italienne et française_ (Grenoble: Allier Frères, 1904); Bernard Weinberg, _A History of Literary Criticism in the Italian Renaissance,_ 2 vols. (Chicago: University of Chicago Press, 1961).

U

UNGARETTI, GIUSEPPE (1888–1970), poet, translator, and essayist. Born in Alexandria, Egypt, of Tuscan parents, Ungaretti was schooled in the best French tradition of his native city and wrote his first poems in French. At twenty-four, he moved to Paris to continue his education at the Collège de France and the Sorbonne, where he studied under Henri Bergson. In Paris, Ungaretti also came into contact with the major exponents of the French avant-garde—Apollinaire, Picasso, Braque, Léger, and Modigliani—as well as with the then futurist-oriented Papini,* Soffici,* and Palazzeschi.* In 1915, he volunteered for military service and was sent to the Carso front as an officer in the infantry. After the war, while still living in Paris, he worked as a correspondent for Mussolini's *Popolo d'Italia*. In 1921, he moved to Rome where he was employed as a journalist by the Ministry of Foreign Affairs and, until 1936, by the *Gazzetta del popolo*. In that same year, Ungaretti accepted the chair of Italian at the University of São Paulo in Brazil. Returning to Rome in 1942, he was nominated to the Accademia d'Italia and given the chair of contemporary Italian literature at the University of Rome. In 1962, he was unanimously elected president of the European Community of Authors. Two years later, he came to the United States as visiting professor at Columbia University, and in 1969, he was honored as a poet in a special ceremony at Harvard University. Also in recognition of his poetry, numerous international literary prizes, honorary degrees, and distinguished citations have been conferred upon Ungaretti. He died in Milan at the age of eighty-two from the effects of pneumonia.

The basic conception underlying Ungaretti's poetry is that of the existence of a universal, cosmic life to which man is integrally joined in a nonrational, intuitive way. Estranged by history and circumstance from the cosmic life, the poet aspires to unity and harmony, to becoming "a pliant fiber/ of the universe"; poetry must capture what is essential, mysterious, and sensual in universal life. To do this it must abandon its traditional function as statement or description for pure evocation, expressed in a word or brief phrase, such as "M'illumino d'immenso" ("Immensity/ illumines me") or "Morire come le allodole assetate sul miraggio" ("To die at the mirage/ like thirsty skylarks").

Ungaretti inherited his conception of poetry as complex suggestion and verbal music from the French symbolists, in particular Mallarmé and

Apollinaire. From futurist poetics he took certain technical characteristics of his early verse, such as the rejection of meter in favor of free verse, the abolition of capitals and punctuation, and the lyrical function invested in graphic signs. Also, from symbolists and futurists alike, he learned to emphasize the sonoric quality of words in his quest for verbal sensuality—hence his recognition as the master of Italian hermeticism.*

In the best tradition of European *Lebensphilosophie,* Ungaretti's general poetic vision consists of the sublimation of lived experience (mainly the vicissitudes of rootlessness, of the wars and their aftermaths) into life. The comprehensive title of his complete works is, in fact, *La Vita d'un uomo* (1947, Life of a Man), where the word *vita* is meant to connote a personal experience given the objective status of myth and idea. The main poetic themes corresponding to Ungaretti's conception of life are the fusion of self with nature (the recognition of self in things), and the mythical transformation of time, memory, and human emotion. The total poetic form they evince is the rhythmical embodiment of what Ungaretti himself called "a spontaneous and disquieting immediatization with the cosmic essence of things."

Ungaretti's books document the poetic processes of such a realization with varied complexity and with a diversity of posture and technique. In *Allegria dei naufragi* (1919, The Joy of Shipwrecks), what dominates is the quality of pure presence, of a spontaneous, ecstatic belonging to the cosmos, shown in poetic flashes or illuminations. *Sentimento del tempo* (1933, Sentiment of Time), on the other hand, marks the recovery of the temporal dimension and the return to conventional forms of versification and poetic meter. Here the inquietude animating the early poems is sublimated into a quest for an absolute, mythical past and primordial innocence, lyrically, a quest for the *canto italiano,* the essence of an Italian poetic voice. The most representative and elaborate poems of this collection are "Sirene" (Sirens) and "L'isola" ("The Island"), in which a union with the cosmos is attained through the sensuous mirage of illusion. In the second half of *Sentimento del tempo,* Ungaretti's preoccupation with the absolute brings him to confront the question of an order of reality beyond the poetic mind, the existence of God, and the crises and torments of the dynamics of belief, dramatically expressed in the hymns "La Pietà," ("La Pietà"), "Caino" ("Cain"), and in the seven cantos of "La morte meditata" ("The Meditated Death"). The poems comprising Ungaretti's third book *Il Dolore* (1947, The Grief) are those of the tragedies he suffered between the years 1937 to 1946: the deaths of his brother and his nine-year-old son, the war, and the Allied occupation of Italy. The poems are written in what Ungaretti calls the baroque style of titanic suffering. In their oblique syntax and polysyllabic diction, they display the poet's search for firm foundations and permanence expressed both in his contemplation of the frailty of his dead son and the ruins of baroque Roman artifacts.

The major poems of Ungaretti's later period are incorporated in the collection *La terra promessa* (1950, The Promised Land), fragments of an incomplete long poem on the mythical rediscovery of Italy, and *Un grido e paesaggi* (1952, A Cry and Landscapes). His translations are contained in the volumes *40 sonetti di Shakespeare* (1946, Forty Sonnets by Shakespeare), *Da Góngora a Mallarmé* (1948, From Góngora to Mallarmé), and *Fedra di Jean Racine* (1950, Phaedre by Jean Racine).

See also HERMETICISM.

Bibliography: Vita d'un uomo: Tutte le poesie, ed. Leone Piccione (Milan: Mondadori, 1969); *Vita d'un uomo: Saggi ed interventi,* eds. Mario Diacono and Luciano Rebay (Milan: Mondadori, 1974); *Selected Poems of Giuseppe Ungaretti,* trans. Allen Mandelbaum (Ithaca, N.Y.: Cornell University Press, 1975); Glauco Cambon, *Giuseppe Ungaretti* (New York: Columbia University Press, 1967); Joseph Cary, *Three Modern Italian Poets: Saba, Ungaretti, Montale* (New York: New York University Press, 1969); G. Singh, "The Poetry of Giuseppe Ungaretti," *Italian Studies* 28 (1973), 64-82; *Books Abroad* 44, No. 4 (1970)—special Ungaretti issue.

Robert S. Dombroski

V

VALLA, LORENZO (1407–1457), humanist, philologist, and scholar. Valla was born in Rome, studied at the University of Pavia, and became secretary to King Alfonso of Aragon in 1437. After his return to Rome in 1448, he became papal secretary and taught at the university there until his death. Valla's works reflect the diversity of interests common to Italian Renaissance* humanists. His popular treatise, *Elegantiae linguae latinae* (1444, On the Elegance of the Latin Language), set out to establish the correct usage of ancient Latin and to remedy the linguistic and grammatical corruption which had set in during the succeeding centuries. For several centuries after Valla's death, it was used as a Latin textbook.

Of greater import, however, are Valla's more philosophical writings. The early humanist dialogue *De voluptate* (1431, On Pleasure), later entitled *De vero bono* (1432, On The True Good), presents an inquiry into the nature of the true good for man by three spokesmen representing the Stoic, Epicurean, and Christian positions. Valla himself supported the Christian arguments, although he admired some aspects of the other two views. *De libero arbitrio* (1435–43, *On Free Will*), likewise in dialogue form, makes a contribution to the argument that God's foreknowledge and man's freedom are compatible. Most consequential in terms of both its political and its philological impact was Valla's exposure of the Donation of Constantine as a forgery, thus undermining the traditional, medieval papal claim to sovereignty over temporal rulers. *De falso credita et ementita Constantini donatione declamatio* (1440, *The Treatise of Lorenzo Valla on the Donation of Constantine*) proved that the document could not have been sent by the Emperor Constantine to Pope Sylvester, since an examination of the language of the text revealed a Latin style uncommon until several centuries after the date of the alleged donation. This crucial philological method came to be used against the church during the Reformation.

See also HUMANISM.

Bibliography: The Treatise of Lorenzo Valla on the Donation of Constantine (New Haven, Conn.: Yale University Press, 1922); *The Renaissance Philosophy of Man* (Chicago: University of Chicago Press, 1948); Paul Oskar Kristeller, *Eight Philosophers of the Italian Renaissance* (Stanford, Calif.: Stanford University Press, 1964).

VARCHI, BENEDETTO (1503–1565), critic, historian, and academician. Varchi was born in Florence. His father intended that he become a notary after studying at Pisa, but Varchi was attracted to literature, and after his father's death, he learned Greek and taught himself Provençal. Because of his early support for Florentine republicans, he was forced to flee from Florence after the siege of the city in 1530 resulted in the return of the Medici. After traveling around Italy for some years, he was recalled to Florence by Cosimo I de' Medici. Received into the Accademia Fiorentina in 1543, Varchi became its consul in 1553 and the friend of many distinguished literary and artistic figures of sixteenth-century Italy, including Salviati,* Cellini,* Michelangelo,* Bembo,* and Aretino.* He was the official lecturer on Petrarch* in the Academy for many years. Although he lost the support of his Medici patrons several times during his career, his life was closely bound to them and reflects the increasing importance of princely patronage in Florentine cultural life in the sixteenth century.

Varchi's vast literary production encompasses Italian versions of many important Greek and Latin works, including Boethius' *Consolation of Philosophy* and a treatise by Seneca; many lyric poems in all forms and styles; a comedy in Terence's style entitled *La suocera* (1569, The Mother-in-Law); numerous orations on state funerals and in commemoration of the demise of notable citizens such as Michelangelo and Pietro Bembo; and a number of substantial lectures on the works of Dante* and Petrarch, delivered before the academy. He also served as editor of the second edition of Bembo's *Prose della volgar lingua* (Writings in the Vernacular Language). His principal works, however, are his *Storia fiorentina* (Florentine History), begun in 1547 at Cosimo's request but first published in 1721, and the *Ercolano* (1570, The Dialogue of Ercolano), an unfinished dialogue between Varchi and Count Cesare Ercolano. While defending the theories of Caro* against Castelvetro* and disputing those of Trissino* on the *questione della lingua** in the *Ercolano,* Varchi emphasizes the supremacy of the vernacular over Latin as Gelli* had done, asserts its autonomy, and sets down his own theories on the origins of the vernacular which differ from those of Bembo with his belief in its essentially oral nature. The sixteen books of his history of Florence deal with the period from 1527 until 1538, continuing—at least in its use of the vernacular—the tradition established by Machiavelli* and Guicciardini.* The work naturally praises Cosimo de' Medici, often at the expense of the other, more famous branch of the family which produced Pope Clement VII. Many critics have seen this obvious desire to flatter his patron as proof of Varchi's unreliability as a historian. However, Varchi's careful consideration of his sources deserves praise, and the defects of his history lie, instead, in its weakness of thought and its lack of a philosophical basis rather than in mere historical bias. Many of the opinions expressed in his extensive lectures on various literary and philosophical topics reveal his basically Aristotelian point of view in critical matters.

See also QUESTIONE DELLA LINGUA.

Bibliography: Opere, 2 vols. (Milan: Bettoni, 1834); Umberto Pirotti, *Benedetto Varchi e la cultura del suo tempo* (Florence: Olschki, 1971), and "Aristotelian Philosophy and the Popularization of Learning: Benedetto Varchi and Renaissance Aristotelianism," pp. 168–208, in *The Late Italian Renaissance 1525–1630,* ed. Eric Cochrane (London: Macmillan, 1970); Rudolf von Albertini, *Firenze dalla repubblica al principato* (Turin: Einaudi, 1970).

VASARI, GIORGIO (1511–1574), architect, painter, and biographer. Vasari was born in Arezzo. Having provided training in drawing for him at an early age, Vasari's family obtained the assistance of Pope Clement VII's representative, Cardinal Silvio Passerini, who arranged for Vasari to study with Michelangelo* in Florence. When Michelangelo left for Rome, Vasari worked with Andrea del Sarto. After his patron, Duke Alessandro de' Medici, was assassinated in 1537, Vasari fell ill. Having recovered, he traveled throughout Italy, gathering much of the information on the works and lives of the artists he later published, and returned to Florence only four years later. In 1549–50, the first version of *Le vite de' più eccellenti architettori, pittori, e scultori italiani (The Lives of the Artists)* appeared from the Torrentino Press. Returning to Florence to enjoy the patronage of the ruling Medici, Vasari was named architect of the Palazzo Vecchio, began the paintings in the *palazzo,* started the construction of the building now known as the Uffizi Museum, and founded the Accademia del disegno (1563), one of the first art academies. The second and enlarged version of the *Vite* was published in 1568 by the Giunti Press, confirming his earlier reputation as the foremost biographer of his day. Vasari's own artistic and architectural compositions—including the Uffizi, the Palazzo dei Cavalieri (Pisa), Michelangelo's tomb, and the frescoes in the Vatican's Sala Regia —display the mannerist style of the Florentine court in his day and have never been as highly regarded by art historians as his literary masterpiece.

Vasari's collection of the lives of famous Italian artists is not uncomplicated. Besides the some two hundred biographies of Italy's most prominent artists from the time of Cimabue to his own, there are three treatises on architecture, painting, and sculpture known as the *Tre arti del disegno (Vasari on Technique)*, a general preface to all the biographies, and briefer introductions to each of the work's three sections. Vasari's use of the term *rinascita* several times in the course of his work makes him one of the first to express the concept of an artistic Renaissance* which has now become a scholarly commonplace. Viewing the arts as a living organism evolving by stages of growth and development, Vasari divided Italian art into three periods: the early stage of its infancy (the late thirteenth and fourteenth centuries, represented by Giotto and Cimabue); the period of youthful vigor (the fifteenth century of Donatello, Brunelleschi, and Ghiberti); and the mature period of perfection (the sixteenth century, dominated by Michelangelo, Leonardo,* and Raffaello). Because the first version of the collection was criticized for its Florentine bias and its praise of Michelangelo above all other artists and local styles, the second version gave more space to artists from outside Florence (in particular, Venice) and other masters besides Michelangelo. Nonetheless, the grand design of the work—the progress of the arts leading inexorably from the revolutionary new discoveries of Giotto through the rise of perspective to the perfection of Michelangelo—abides. Although Vasari's biographies often err in factual details, they remain a primary document in the study of Italian Renaissance art today. Vasari is at his best when he describes a work of art which has fired his imagination or when he recounts anecdotes about an artist in a manner worthy of the best Tuscan *novellieri*. One of his essential critical criteria for judging a work of art is its *grazia* (or "grace"), a quality to be distinguished from beauty and connected to an indefinable element dependent upon critical judgment which does not go hand in hand with simple craftsmanship. Often synonymous with sweetness and softness, it is never associated with laborious or painstaking effort. In the final analysis, it is derived from birth and genius, the gift of nature rather than the product of study. The entire concept owes much to Castiglione's* *Il cortegiano (The Book of the Courtier)* and his discussion of *sprezzatura* ("nonchalance") in human relations. Besides providing readers of many centuries with the most appealing portraits of great artists ever assembled, Vasari succeeded in creating a literary myth with his biographies, the dramatic picture of an emerging Italian art, and its heroic culmination in the Titanic genius of Michelangelo.

See also BUONARROTI, Michelangelo; CASTIGLIONE, Baldesar.

Bibliography: Le opere, ed., Gaetano Milanesi, 9 vols. (1906; rpt. Florence: Sansoni, 1973); *La città ideale,* ed. Virginia Stefinelli (Rome: Officina, 1970); *The Lives of the Artists,* trans. George Bull (Baltimore: Penguin, 1971); *Vasari on Technique,* trans. G. B. Brown (London: Dent, 1907); Anthony Blunt, *Artistic Theory in Italy 1450–1600* (New York: Oxford University Press, 1940); T. S. R. Boase, *Giorgio Vasari: The Man and the Book* (Princeton, N. J.: Princeton University Press, 1978).

VERGA, GIOVANNI (1840–1922), novelist, short-story writer, and playwright, leading figure in *verismo*.* Verga was born in Catania, but went to Florence, then the capital of Italy, in 1865 and spent most of his time first there and afterwards at Milan until his final return to Catania in 1894. His earliest novels were historical and patriotic. In Florence, he established contact with other writers and began to produce the novels which extended to 1875: *Una peccatrice* (1866, A Woman Sinner), *Storia di una capinera* (1871, Story of a Blackcap), *Eva* (1873, Eva), *Eros* (1875, Eros), and *Tigre reale* (1874, Royal Tigress). The first two are set in Sicily, the *Storia* enjoying popularity through its theme of a girl being forced into a convent, and the others focus on aristocratic and middle-class society in Florence. The woman in these works is presented in artificial circumstances—the elegance of social occasions or on the stage—and represents an escape into illusion for the hero. In *Eros* and *Tigre reale,* she becomes a literary *femme fatale. Eva* shows touches of realism, with Eva, a dancer, aware of the artificiality of her life. In the preface, Verga states that the story is true or could have happened and that art both reflects and exposes society. *Tigre reale* shows an advance in style and technique and, with the return of La Ferlita to the family and the quiet strength of Erminia, indicates future developments.

In Milan, Verga encountered the *scapigliati,* a vaguely bohemian group which cultivated a certain realism, other prominent writers, and also French novels up to Zola. He was a close friend of his fellow Sicilian, Luigi Capuana,* the main exponent in Italy of French naturalist doctrine.

In 1874, Verga wrote the "Sicilian sketch" *Nedda,* the turning point in his literary career, although less abrupt a shift in style than is often supposed. Nedda, a farm worker, has a child by Janu (who meanwhile has died of malaria), is ostracized, and loses the child through starvation. The story deals with the lowest level of society and is narrated in a language and with an outlook that approximates its milieu, although literary influence is still discernible. Verga was forsaking the artificiality of bourgeois life for the genuine tragedies of the poor.

Primavera e altri racconti (1876, Spring and Other Stories) deals in part with Milan, but Verga was now elaborating a new technique for presenting the life of his native Sicily. The short stories of *Vita dei campi* (Life in the Fields) were published in 1880. If French realism described city life, *verismo* reflected the life of the varied regions. In these works, Verga is no longer the omniscient author using a literary language and interpreting from his own viewpoint; the restricted outlook and language belong to his humble characters. Passions and reactions are not governed by middle-class conventions: vengeance for violation of marriage is death. "Cavalleria rusticana," from which the *libretto* was drawn for Mascagni's opera, is of this type, but includes the conventions and the "rustic chivalry" of a village society. In "Rosso Malpelo" ("Rosso Malpelo"), a miner in a sand quarry accepts his lot as the lowliest of all, bereft of human charity and cooperation. "Fantasticheria" (Reverie) is a foretaste of *I Malavoglia* (1881, *The House by the Medlar Tree*), representing a rejection of bourgeois elegance for the life of humble fishermen.

Verga proposed to write a series of five novels exemplifying the struggle for existence, which underlies progress, as it manifests itself at each level of society. Each book was to have a distinct form, deriving from its content and the means of expression of its social class, conscientiously observed. For Verga, this was sincerity in art and realism. Verga, in the age of Darwinism, regarded the struggle for existence and progress as facts. The final title of the series, *I Vinti* (The Vanquished), shows his concentration on the victims of the struggle. The preface of *I Malavoglia* develops these ideas: first, the struggle for material needs, then greed for wealth, aristocratic vanity, ambition, and finally the man who combines all of these and is consumed by them.

The Malavoglia, fishermen of Aci Trezza, transport a cargo of lupins, their boat is wrecked, and they lose their house through failure to pay back the borrowed purchase price. After being drafted into the navy at Naples, 'Ntoni is unwilling to accept the ancestral way of life, the "religion" of the house and family represented by his grandfather. He wounds a customs guard in a smuggling expedition and goes to prison. On his return, a wiser man, he wishes to rejoin the family and Aci Trezza but must "atone" for his sin by wandering through the world. Meanwhile, his younger brother has married and, by buying back the house, has reestablished the family's previous position. Aci Trezza is a pre-industrial society governed by rigid conventions handed down from its ancestors in the form of incontestable proverbs, mostly economic. As Mena ('Ntoni's sister) realizes, love lacks significance in such circumstances. It is outside history, its past, present, and future identical. In fact, history is now touching it through the new united Italy and through the beginnings of a capitalist outlook in some inhabitants. Verga is the impersonal narrator of a story told from within Aci Trezza in its language and thought patterns, often in direct or indirect discourse, without any formal presentation of characters or places. Comment on events and characters comes from other characters or through a collective comment or "chorus," although Verga intervenes for Mena and her mother. The abrupt shifts of scene and event reflect the haphazard character of life. Verga had earlier spoken of a story that tells itself, with no sign of its origin or the directing hand of its author.

After *Il marito di Elena* (1882, Helen's Husband), the story of a woman yearning for luxury and pleasure, Verga published the short-story collection *Novelle rusticane* (1883, *Little Novels of Sicily*). The moral feeling of the Malavoglia family gives place to the pessimistic presentation of characters dominated by material considerations, by the effort to acquire and keep *la roba* (property) at the expense of all else. Although Verga was writing short stories of lowly life in Milan, *Per le vie* (1883, In the Streets), in part developing the manner of his youth, he was also working on the second novel of the *Vinti, Mastro-don Gesualdo* (1889, *Mastro-don Gesualdo*). A bricklayer accumulates wealth, buys land, and marries the noble but impoverished Bianca Trao. He cannot rise socially, however, and, in fact, he betrays his origins. He can never establish mutual comprehension with his wife and daughter Isabella. His daughter, already pregnant, marries a nobleman from Palermo, in whose palace Gesualdo dies amid the indifference of servants. The novel falls into four parts, thus lacking the compact unity of *I Malavoglia,* and extends over a longer period, with the inclusion of both a plague and the revolts of 1820 and 1848. Life is dominated by *la roba,* and a bitter irony expresses this pessimistic atmosphere. The only exception is the genuine feeling between Gesualdo and the submissive peasant girl, Diodata. Again, Verga does not present characters formally, but the effect is ultimately far more vivid. He enters into the psychology of some characters, however, as with Isabella in the countryside at the time of her love for Ninì, and especially when Gesualdo contemplates his past labors and experiences, and their meaning. Verga had a keen sense of literary mission in the technique of his two major novels, despite the incomprehension of others, although he was always sustained by the judgments of Capuana. He was no mere imitator of Zola, whose work he did not hesitate to criticize.

Verga wrote only a chapter of the third novel of *I Vinti, La Duchessa di Leyra* (The Duchess of Leyra). Other short stories followed, dealing rather nostalgically with love in middle-class society or with provincial life, and he also wrote a novel from the play, *Dal tuo al mio* (1905, From Yours to Mine). Although he had no true bent for the theatre, Verga wrote or adapted several plays from short stories. One of these plays, *Cavalleria rusticana* (1883), achieved notable success on its first performance in Turin with Eleonora Duse.

Although he was a member of the landed gentry and a conservative, Verga portrayed with sympathetic feeling the poverty, struggles, and psychology of Sicilians burdened with centuries-old misery. However, he was no socialist anticipating future changes: he viewed their condition as constant and inevitable. Rather, he looked back to an unspoilt primitive society, which was now being superseded. Verga's reputation is securely established in Italy, and his influence on modern realism is obvious. Although some of his works have been translated by D. H. Lawrence, his undoubted depth and originality have brought him little recognition outside of Italy.

See also VERISMO.

Bibliography: Cavalleria Rusticana, and Other Stories, trans. D. H. Lawrence (1926; rpt. Westport, Conn.: Greenwood Press, 1975); *The House by the Medlar Tree,* trans. Eric Mosbacher (1953; rpt. Westport, Conn.: Greenwood Press, 1975); *Little Novels of Sicily,* trans. D. H. Lawrence (1953; rpt. Westport, Conn.: Greenwood Press, 1975); *Mastro-don Gesualdo,* trans. D. H. Lawrence (1923; rpt. Westport, Conn.: Greenwood Press, 1976); *The She-Wolf and Other Stories,* trans.

Giovanni Cecchetti, 2nd ed. (Berkeley, Calif.: University of California Press, 1973); Alfred Alexander, *Giovanni Verga* (London: Grant & Cutler, 1972); Thomas G. Bergin, *Giovanni Verga* (1931; rpt. Westport, Conn.: Greenwood Press, 1969); Sergio Pacifici, *The Modern Italian Novel* (Carbondale, Ill.: Southern Illinois University Press, 1967); Olga Ragusa, *Verga's Milanese Tales* (New York: Vanni, 1964); Luigi Russo, *Giovanni Verga,* 6th ed. (Bari: Laterza, 1959).

S. B. Chandler

VERISMO, an Italian literary movement in the second half of the nineteenth century, whose aim was to achieve objectivity in artistic representation through a scientific method of observation and stylistic impersonality. On philosophic grounds, *verismo* grew out of the development of romantic idealism into positivistic materialism; historically, it corresponded to the fading of the Risorgimento ideals into the concrete problems of the administration of united Italy; and on literary grounds, it was both the development of romantic realism and the reaction against romantic oversentimentality.

Francesco De Sanctis* was perhaps the most important literary figure who pushed Italian literature in the direction of *verismo.* A scholar of Vico* and Hegel, an admirer of Zola (and through Zola, of Compte, Taine, and Darwin), De Sanctis advocated a literature capable of uniting the ideal with the real, thus obtaining the true. His criticism and theoretical statements provide the most self-conscious voice of the Italian literature of the period. But the two most influential and long-lasting spokesmen of *verismo* were without doubt Luigi Capuana* and Giovanni Verga.* Together (although in different ways reflecting their individual personalities) they advocated the theoretical tenets of the movement in their letters to each other and in various critical statements that were more theoretical and systematic in Capuana, and more pragmatic and scattered in Verga. They wrote literary texts embodying these tenets with valuable artistic results.

Capuana was particularly influenced by French naturalism, the literary movement in which the positivistic belief in the scientific approach to the study of nature and reality found its artistic expression. He accepted the naturalists' experimental method of observation derived from Claude Bernard's medical treatise, and, fusing it with his Hegelianism, applied it very successfully to "pathological cases," such as those portrayed in his *Giacinta* and "Profumo." The results of his "materialistic psychology" were so subtle and far reaching that today he can rightly be called a forerunner of Freud. But the cold detachment with which Capuana observed and rendered the psychopathological cases under his scrutiny had its limitation in his too optimistic belief in the possibility of treatment as return to normalcy, as reestablishment of the bourgeois order.

Unlike Capuana, Verga was more influenced by both Italian and French realism. He inherited and carried forth the Manzonian poetics of the humble people and developed the Flaubertian poetics of authorial impersonality in his own original terms. Particularly significant is his letter to Salvatore Farina, opening the short story "L'amante di Gramigna" ("Gramigna's Mistress"). There he states that when a work of art's "manner and reason for being" are "so necessary that the artist's hand remains absolutely invisible," then this work of art "will have the imprint of a real event, will seem to *have been made by itself,* to have ripened and originated spontaneously, as a natural fact, without keeping any point of contact with its author." He also states that he has written the story "more or less with the same, simple and picturesque words of the popular narrative." Verga's concern for representing all strata of society, but particularly the humble people, and his deliberate search for authorial impersonality had tremendous consequences for his own art as well as for subsequent Italian literature. On the one hand, by taking popular narrative as a model for his best writings and by blending dialectal patterns and syntax with literary Italian, he made it a strong, lively, and broadly accepted language. On the other hand, by disappearing as author, he overcame his youthful romantic tendencies toward excessive sentimentality and achieved the kind of objectivity that opened the way to the modern novel. For example, consider the importance of the *discours indirect libre* (free indirect discourse) used by Verga as an interior monologue *in nuce* and as a lyric-epic prose capable of carrying choral qualities. Traces of it can be found in Pavese* and Vittorini,* not to speak of Joyce, who masterfully exploited all the possibilities of such a technique.

Verismo was particularly strong and influential in two centers of Italian culture between 1860 and 1890, Florence and Milan. In Florence, Telemaco Signorini (1835–1901) formulated the theoretical views of the group of *Macchiaioli* painters, Pasquale Villari (1826–1917) expounded his positivistic philosophy, Luigi Capuana was particularly active as drama critic, and De Sanctis's view of Italian literature was highly influential. In Milan, the *Scapigliati* group (Emilio Praga*; Igino Ugo Tarchetti, 1830–1869; Carlo Dossi, 1849–1910; Felice Cameroni, 1844–1913, among others) embraced the social concerns of *verismo,* while furthering their linguistic expressionism and experimentalism that were to lead to the decadent movement later on. It was not by chance that precisely during those years Verga went from his native Sicily to Florence and Milan.

A secondary aspect of *verismo,* which is too often overestimated by critics, is its insistence on regionalism and on economic factors. This insistence was contingent upon the reality of newly united Italy with its enormous problems of civil and industrial development as a modern nation, rather than imbedded in any theoretical foundations of the literary movement as such. Among the best representatives of this kind of *verismo* were

Salvatore Di Giacomo* and Matilde Serao* from Naples, Federico De Roberto* from Sicily (especially with his historical novel *I Vicerè*[1894, *The Viceroys*]), and the *bozzettisti,* or writers of sketches, from Tuscany.

With its "lay and empiricist character," *verismo* was perhaps the most successful effort of Italian literature in its fight for truth and against its own "reluctance" (as Carlo Dionisotti, 1908–   , called it) to face historical and social reality. As such, it was the Italian contribution to that "representation of reality in Western literature" which Auerbach called *mimesis* and Lukàcs "critical realism." It was also, and perhaps above all, the first Italian form of the "modern" narrative technique. Without *verismo* it would be impossible to understand the development and the achievements of the contemporary novel—from Svevo,* Pirandello,* and Tozzi* to the neorealists and the avant-garde.

See also CAPUANA, Luigi; DECADENTISMO; DE SANCTIS, Francesco; NEOREALISM; ROMANTICISM; VERGA, Giovanni.

Bibliography: Luigi Capuana, *Saggi sulla letteratura contemporanea,* Vol. 2 (Catania: Giannotta, 1882); Francesco De Sanctis, *Saggi critici,* Vol. 3 (Bari: Laterza, 1952); Giovanni Verga, *Lettere a Luigi Capuana* (Florence: Le Monnier, 1975); Roberto Bigazzi, *I colori del vero* (Pisa: Nistri-Lischi, 1969); Giovanni Cecchetti, "Verga and *Verismo*: The Search for Style and Language," in *Petrarch to Pirandello: Studies in Italian Literature in Honour of Beatrice Corrigan,* ed. Julius Molinaro (Toronto: University of Toronto Press, 1973), pp. 169–85; Giacomo Debenedetti, *Verga e il naturalismo* (Milan: Garzanti, 1977); Carlo Madrignani, *Capuana e il naturalismo* (Bari: Laterza, 1970); Vittorio Spinazzola, "Verismo e positivismo artistico," *Belfagor* 25 (1970), 247–76.

Gian-Paolo Biasin

VERRI, COUNT ALESSANDRO (1741–1816), Milanese novelist and poet. Although separated by thirteen years from his older and better known brother Pietro,* a sincere friendship between them enabled Pietro to guide the younger Alessandro along a systematic program of readings which emphasized the French and English Enlightenment* philosophers. Alessandro's first published work (1762) was a defense of a minor treatise by Cesare Beccaria;* in 1765, he rose to defend Beccaria's *Dei delitti e delle pene (On Crimes and Punishments).* Between 1761 and 1765, Verri worked on a monumental history of Italy from Romulus to 1760, interrupting this grandiose plan only to work with Pietro on *Il Caffè,* to which he contributed thirty-two articles.

In 1766, Alessandro accompanied Beccaria on his celebrated journey to Paris, but after Beccaria's return to Milan with the favor of Parisian society and the admiration of most of Enlightenment Europe, Verri continued on to London. His friendship with Beccaria cooled, but that with his brother grew and produced a body of correspondence which constitutes an invaluable source of historical information about the Europe of those times. During his stay abroad, Alessandro met such individuals as Diderot, Charles Fox, Benjamin Franklin, d'Alembert, and d'Holbach. In 1767, he returned to Italy via Paris, Turin, Genoa, and Florence and settled in Rome. There, he devoted himself to a number of scholarly and linguistic activities, studying French, English, and Greek. In 1777, he completed but never published a version of Shakespeare's *Hamlet*, and in 1789, he published a translation of Homer's *Iliad*. After a number of tragedies based upon classical or medieval themes, Verri published a first novel entitled *Le avventure di Saffo* (1780, The Adventures of Sappho) which influenced the more famous poem on Sappho by Leopardi.* The discovery of the Roman tombs of the Scipioni outside the San Sebastiano gate in that same year inspired the novel *Le notti romane al sepolcro degli Scipioni (The Roman Nights at the Tomb of the Scipios),* part of which appeared in 1792 and the remainder in 1804. A "best seller" of monumental proportions in its day, it enjoyed fifty Italian editions between 1792 and 1823 and at least four English versions by 1850, not to mention many translations in other languages. With echoes of writers both classical and contemporary (i.e., Livy, Plutarch, Machiavelli,* Cicero, Alfieri,* Young, and *Ossian*), *Le notti romane* is structured around a number of visions at the tombs in which the shades of various Roman figures appear and raise questions of greater interest to the Enlightenment intellectual than to men from classical times —the state of nature and the noble savage, a comparison of republics and monarchies, the papacy, the quarrel of the ancients and the moderns, and a comparison of ancient and modern Rome. Today, the novel seems less compelling because of its declamatory, pre-romantic style. Among Verri's later works are to be found another novel, several classical translations, and a critical edition of the works of Annibale Caro.*

See also BECCARIA, Cesare; ENLIGHTENMENT; VERRI, Pietro.

Bibliography: Le notti romane, ed. Renzo Negri (Bari: Laterza, 1967); *Illuministi settentrionali,* ed. Sergio Romagnoli (Milan: Rizzoli, 1962); *The Roman Nights at the Tomb of the Scipios* (Philadelphia: J. Ball, 1850); D. Chiomenti Vassalli, *I fratelli Verri* (Milan: Ceschina, 1960); James T. S. Wheelock, "Verri's *Notti romane:* A New Edition and Some Old Translations," *Italica* 46 (1969), 58–68.

VERRI, COUNT PIETRO (1728–1797), Milanese reformer and social thinker. Verri completed his studies in Milan, Rome, and Parma before joining the Austrian army in 1759 in a campaign against the Prussians. Returning from the war after a year, he met an Englishman named Henry Lloyd who introduced him to the science of political economy which was to become his lifelong preoccupation. At the same time, he and his brother Alessandro met Cesare Beccaria* and other like-minded young intellectuals who eventually formed the Accademia dei Pugni (The Academy of the Fists), the nucleus around which Verri later established his important periodical, *Il Caffè*. In 1763, he published a treatise, *Meditazioni sulla felicità* (Meditations on Happiness) which forms a hedonistic basis for his social thought and directly bears upon his constant efforts to propose administrative and legal reforms in the governments of his day in order to increase the standards of living enjoyed by their citizens. He forwarded such a plan to the Austrian government in the same year, its most innovative proposal being the abolishment of certain unfair and anachronistic taxes.

In 1764, Verri founded *Il Caffè* (The Coffee House). During its brief, two-year existence, Verri published contributions by respected reformers, among whom Cesare Beccaria was the most important. Modeled on such famous periodicals of the period as the English *Spectator, Il Caffè* had profound consequences, introducing revolutionary literary, political, and economic ideas into Italian culture. During his life, Verri held a number of government positions, most of which concerned the regulation of public finances. An immediate success in Italy and abroad, his *Meditazioni di economia politica* (1771, Meditations on Political Economy) presented a plan designed to produce the maximum amount of happiness for the citizens of a state and also questioned some of the assumptions underlying the works of his friend Beccaria. Among Verri's later works are a history of Milan, published in its entirety only after his death; a treatise on torture; a discussion of the French Revolution; and a number of interesting letters. When Napoleon entered Milan in 1796, Verri became a spokesman for moderation and refused to retire to his villa, as had so many other noblemen, remaining a part of that government until his death.

See also BECCARIA, Cesare; ENLIGHTENMENT; VERRI, Alessandro.

Bibliography: Storia di Milano, ed. Alberto Crescentini, 3 vols. (Milan: Dall'Oglio, 1962); *Illuministi settentrionali*, ed. Sergio Romagnoli (Milan: Rizzoli, 1962); *Lettere inedite*, ed. Mario Zolezzi (Milan: Editrice Vita e pensiero, 1965); Nino Valeri, *Pietro Verri* (Florence: Le Monnier, 1969); Franco Venturi, *Italy and the Enlightenment* (New York: New York University Press, 1972), and *Settecento riformatore* (Turin: Einaudi, 1969).

VESPASIANO DA BISTICCI (1421–1498), bookdealer and biographer. A Florentine by birth, Vespasiano rose to become the most celebrated bookdealer of his time in Europe. Before the invention and diffusion of printing presses, bookdealers sold only expensive manuscripts copied by hand and illustrated by artists. Vespasiano's manuscripts had an excellent reputation for their fidelity to the original copy and for their artistic merits. He helped to build the three greatest libraries of his time for Cosimo de'

Medici, Federico da Montefeltro, and Pope Nicholas V; he supplied books
to all the Medici, the Este family, the House of Aragon, the king of
Hungary, and many other rich and influential readers. His extensive connections with his prominent customers enabled him to compose one of the
essential collections of biographical portraits of the Renaissance* after he
retired in 1480 to his country villa. *Le vite d'uomini illustri del secolo XV
(Renaissance Princes, Popes & Prelates)* was known to many scholars for
centuries but was published only in 1839 by Cardinal Angelo Mai. Jacob
Burckhardt declared that reading this work inspired his monumental interpretation of the Italian Renaissance. The collection is written in an unpretentious Italian, but its attention to detail and its many portraits of the
major clerics, political figures, and artists of the time make it an intriguing
source of historical information, unequaled in Italy until Vasari's* collection of artists' lives appeared in the next century.

Bibliography: Renaissance Princes, Popes & Prelates, trans. W. George and
Emily Waters (New York: Harper, 1963); Giuseppe M. Cagni, *Vespasiano da
Bisticci e il suo epistolario* (Rome: Edizioni di storia e letteratura, 1969).

VETTORI, FRANCESCO (1474–1539), diplomat and historian. A member
of one of Florence's upper-class families, Vettori was named envoy to
Emperor Maximilian of Germany (1507-09), a post initially denied to
Niccolò Machiavelli,* the protégé of the head of the Florentine Republic,
through patrician opposition. Machiavelli eventually joined Vettori in
Germany, and the two men became close friends. Named ambassador to
the Papal Court in Rome in 1512, Vettori represented Florence before
Pope Julius II and, from 1513 to 1515, also before Pope Leo X. Back in
Florence after the restoration of the Medici, Vettori became one of the
favorites of the city's ruler, Lorenzo de' Medici, duke of Urbino (to whom
Machiavelli dedicated *The Prince*). He also worked to obtain Machiavelli's
release from the prison in which he had been incarcerated briefly upon the
Medici's return to power. The correspondence between the two men
contains some of the most important letters in Italian literature, particularly that describing Machiavelli's composition of *The Prince*. Much
of Vettori's life after 1515 was spent in the service of the Medici family.

As an historian, he is best remembered for a dialogue on the Sack of
Rome in 1527, a life of the duke of Urbino, and, primarily, for his *Sommario della storia d'Italia dal 1511 al 1527* (A Summary of Italian History
from 1511 to 1527), which was probably composed in 1529 but was never
printed until the nineteenth century. One of the first European diplomatic
histories, the work places Italian affairs within a broad, European context
much as Guicciardini's* more influential *History of Italy* did some years
later. It reveals fortune as the omnipotent and unfathomable ruler of human
history and presents two engaging literary portraits of Leo X and Clement

VII, the two Medici popes. Guicciardini continued this comparison in his history. Although Vettori's history resembles those of both Machiavelli and Guicciardini in its emphasis upon politics as a struggle of basically selfish and egotistical men, he knew the classical historians and had even examined Thomas More's *Utopia* before completing his own work.

See also GUICCIARDINI, Francesco; MACHIAVELLI, Niccolò.

Bibliography: Sommario della storia d'Italia dal 1511 al 1527, ed. A. von Reumont, *Archivio storico italiano* (1848), Appendix vi, pp. 287–382; Rudolf von Albertini, *Firenze dalla repubblica al principato: storia e coscienza politica* (Turin: Einaudi, 1970); Rosemary Devonshire-Jones, *Francesco Vettori: Florentine Citizen and Medici Servant* (London: Athlone Press, 1972); Felix Gilbert, *Machiavelli and Guicciardini: Politics and History in Sixteenth-Century Florence* (Princeton, N.J.: Princeton University Press, 1965).

VICO, GIAMBATTISTA (1668–1744), philosopher, historian, and social scientist. Vico was born in Naples, and except for a period of nine years when he served as a tutor in the residence of the Rocca family at Vatolla, some sixty miles south, he never left his native city. His father Antonio was the proprietor of a small bookstore. The family was poor but far from ignorant—indeed, it was avidly devoted to learning. Vico was educated partly in Jesuit schools, partly by private tutor, and to a considerable extent by himself; he was a gifted and precocious scholar. His early interests were jurisprudence and philosophy. At the age of eighteen, he defended his father in a lawsuit, although he did not matriculate in the Faculty of Law until three years later. He received his LL.D. in 1694. In the same year, under the avowed inspiration of Cicero and Petrarch,* he composed a panegyric in honor of the Elector Maximilian of Bavaria. This work was followed by an epithalamium for the marriage of that prince to Princess Theresa of Poland. Both exercises were subsequently published, as he tells us in his autobiography. (Vico was to compose many such "occasional" eulogies during his lifetime.)

In 1699, having won the competition for the post, Vico was appointed to the professorship of rhetoric at the University of Naples; he held the chair until his retirement in 1741. In this role, he delivered seven "Inaugural Orations" (the first in 1699, the last in 1708), traditionally given at the beginning of the academic year. His professorship, however, was not one that carried great prestige or even an adequate stipend; the chief function of rhetoric was to prepare students for the study of law. Vico's ambition was to become the professor of civil law. For reasons still obscure, this appointment was denied him when he tentatively presented his candidacy in 1723. The frustation deeply embittered him (he was, as he confesses, choleric by nature in any case). It also spurred him on to the composition of his great work *La Scienza Nuova (The New Science),* the first edition of which appeared in 1725 and the third and final version shortly after his death in 1744.

Vico's personal life was in the main uneventful. In the *Autobiography,* covering the years from birth to 1731, the only specific events he mentions are a fall from a ladder in his father's bookstore at the age of seven and his visit to Vatolla; the rest of the work describes only his readings and his contacts with various teachers and mentors. His notion of an autobiography was a record of intellectual development, but in any case there seem to have been no especially noteworthy episodes in his life. A youthful poem, "Gli affetti di un disperato" (1692, Accents of despair), seems to suggest a real emotional crisis but, although deeply felt, the nature of the crisis is undefined. In 1699, the first year of his professorship, he married Caterina Destitito, a poor and illiterate woman. The marriage seems to have been a happy one for Vico. Caterina bore him two sons, one of whom, Gennaro, succeeded him in the chair of rhetoric, and two daughters of whom the elder, Luisa, delighted her father with her agile mind and gift for writing verses. (Vico mentions neither his wife nor his children in the *Autobiography.*) Although he felt—and rightly—that he was not properly recognized by the intellectual world, he did not entirely lack appreciation in his city. He was elected to the Arcadia* and various other learned societies, and in 1735, he was appointed royal historiographer by the new king, Charles of Bourbon. Such honors were by no means lucrative, and Vico lived on the edge of utter poverty all his life, being compelled to supplement his salary by hours of private tutoring.

One may say that in their unexciting tranquility Vico's times were not unlike the tenor of his life. Italy was affected by the dynastic wars of the period, but for the most part the decisive battlefields lay beyond her frontiers. During Vico's lifetime, Naples and its ancient realm passed from the hands of Spain to Austrian domination (1707) and subsequently to the victorious Charles of Bourbon, who restored the independence of the kingdom (1734). As far as the city itself was concerned, however, the transitions were peaceful. With all due recognition of the military genius of Marborough or Prince Eugene and the statesmanship of kings and emperors, Vico's years are less notable for political change than for intellectual activity. Indeed, the time of his maturity is known as the Enlightenment,* and Locke, Voltaire, and Diderot were all active at some period in his lifespan. Although Naples, a faithful daughter of the church and immunized against emancipated speculation by the conservatism of the Counter-Reformation (in Vico's youth the Inquisition still flourished, and some of his friends were penalized for "Epicureanism"), did not participate fully in the new movement, Vico's inquiring mind could not be restrained. His study of law and philosophy inevitably channeled his interest towards research into the problems of the origins of society and the nature of human institutions which had engaged the attention of such forerunners of the Enlightenment as Machiavelli* and Bacon. Descartes too attracted him, although Vico professes distaste for Cartesian "inconsistency." He learned much from Hobbes and Grotius (whose work he would have annotated, save that it seemed inappropriate for a Catholic to annotate the work of a heretic).

Such readings, as well as his study of classical authors of which he found Plato and Tacitus most valuable, are chronicled in the *Autobiography*. In effect, the *Autobiography* is a kind of bibliographical introduction to *The New Science,* his magnum opus and the goal, at first dimly sensed, to which his lifetime's labors and studies were directed. The basic theme of the work is the establishment of a consistent and eternal pattern in the origin and development of human institutions. Its essential postulate is that it is possible to find such a pattern since the sources can be sought in the human mind itself. In the case of primitive man, his mentality may be probed by approaches through mythology and philology, as well as through such chronicles as have come down to us somewhat fragmentarily from Greek history and more copiously through Latin historians. For Vico's purposes, epic* poetry and folklore (as it was later to be called) were no less significant than erudite annals. *The New Science* is tangential, discursive, repetitious, and sometimes obscure, but it is also full of original discoveries and charged with a poetic intensity. Two subsidiary themes of special interest may be cited: the cyclical theory of history and the concept of a guiding Divine Providence. Vico argues that the pattern of human things prescribes a cyclical movement from anarchy to oligarchy to democracy to monarchy and, with inevitable decadence, back to anarchy. The history of Rome exemplifies the thesis, with the Dark Ages cast in the role of the anarchy initiating the successive cycle. Vico's survey follows only the Gentile nations, the Jews, having special revelation, are excluded, although the pattern of their progress also indicates the operations of a Divine Providence. Men, acting under immediate and contingent urgencies, invariably bring about results unforeseen by them but in keeping with the Divine plan.

The New Science was rewritten twice. The first edition appeared in 1725, the second in 1730, and the third and definitive version shortly after Vico's death in 1744. Many of its peripheral insights, if not its central argument, are well ahead of Vico's time. No doubt, for that reason it did not attract much attention outside of Italy for some time after the author's death. Not until an abridged translation of the work by the French historian Jules Michelet appeared in 1824 did it receive European recognition. Since then, it has grown in prestige among philosophers and historians. In our century, Benedetto Croce* has been the most eloquent interpreter and champion of Vico's thought.

Although unique for its scope and originality, *The New Science* is not Vico's only notable work. We have already mentioned the *Autobiography* (1728–29, with a posthumous addition in 1818), an unusual account of an intellectual trajectory. Another is his *De nostri temporis studiorum ratione* (1709, *On the Study Methods of Our Time*), which is a defense of humanistic education against the rigidities of pure intellectualism that Vico found in Descartes. *De antiquissima Italorum sapientia* (1710, On Ancient Italian Wisdom) is in some sense a precursor of *The New Science*. In *De rebus gestis Antonii Caraphaei* (1716, *Life of Antonio Carafa*), although the work was commissioned by the family of the subject, Vico displays his objectivity and his talents as a historian.

Bibliography: *The New Science of Giambattista Vico,* trans. T. G. Bergin and M. H. Fisch (Ithaca, N.Y.: Cornell University Press, 1968); *The Autobiography of Giambattista Vico,* trans. M. H. Fisch and T. G. Bergin (Ithaca, N.Y.: Cornell University Press, 1963); *On the Study Methods of Our Time,* trans. E. Gianturco (Indianapolis, Ind.: Bobbs-Merrill, 1965); H. P. Adams, *The Life and Writings of Giambattista Vico* (London: Allen & Unwin, 1935); Isaiah Berlin, *Vico and Herder: Two Studies in the History of Ideas* (New York: Viking, 1976); A. R. Caponigri, *Time and Idea: The Theory of History in Giambattista Vico* (Notre Dame, Ind.: University of Notre Dame Press, 1968); Benedetto Croce, *The Philosophy of Giambattista Vico,* trans. R. G. Collingwood (London: Howard Latimer, 1913); R. Manson, *The Theory of Knowledge of Giambattista Vico* (Hamden, Conn.: Archon Books, 1969); Leon Pompa, *Vico: A Study of the "New Science"* (London: Cambridge University Press, 1975).

Thomas G. Bergin

VIDA, MARCO GIROLAMO (1485–1566), Cremonan poet. After a classical education in Mantua, Vida moved to Rome in 1510 where he encountered the learned scholars and poets at the papal court—Bembo,* Jacopo Sadoleto (1477–1547), Castiglione,* Navagero,* Giovio,* and others. Leo X gave him a benefice, so that he could devote his time to poetry. After the completion of his major epic* poem, he was rewarded with the bishopric of Alba in 1535, a post he held for the remainder of his life. As a churchman, he was also an active participant in the Council of Trent.

Vida is best known for several Latin works. His epic poem, *Christiados libri sex* (1535, *The Christiad*), is Virgilian in style and written in six books which celebrate Christian redemption and the heroism of Christ as Virgil had the founding of Rome and the bravery of Aeneas. Central to the Renaissance* debate over the nature of the Christian heroic poem, Vida's epic influenced those of both Tasso* and Milton. Pope's *Essay on Criticism* cites the work approvingly in a reference to the "Immortal Vida." *De arte poetica* (1527, *The Art of Poetry*) treats the place of heroic poetry in education, the method of composing works based upon the models of

Homer and Virgil, and the problems of epic style and imitation. As a work of art in its own right, this treatise joined the earlier tradition established by Horace and provided inspiration for future poetic works in this genre by Boileau and Pope. Less important but no less popular were his *Scacchia ludus* (1527, *The Game of Chess*), a tale of a game of chess between Apollo and Mercury in a mock-heroic vein later translated by Oliver Goldsmith, and *De bombyce* (1527, *The Silkworm*), a didactic poem celebrating the industry vital to northern Italian commerce. Vida, with Sannazaro,* Pontano,* Mantuan,* and others, played a major role in revitalizing neo-Latin literature in the sixteenth century.

See also SANNAZARO, Jacopo.

Bibliography: The "De Arte Poetica" of Marco Girolamo Vida, ed. and trans. Ralph G. Williams (New York: Columbia University Press, 1976); *An Edition of Vida's Christiad*, trans. G. G. Coyne (Ph.D. Dissertation, Cornell University, 1939); *The Game of Chess: Marco Girolamo Vida's Scacchia Ludus*, ed. Mario Di Cesare (Nieuwkoop: B. De Graaf, 1975); *The Silkworm*, trans. Samuel Pullein (Dublin: S. Powell, 1750); Mario A. Di Cesare, *Bibliotheca Vidiana: A Bibliography of Marco Girolamo Vida* (Florence: Sansoni, 1974), and *Vida's Christiad and Vergilian Epic* (New York: Columbia University Press, 1964).

VILLANI, GIOVANNI (circa 1275–1348), Florentine historian and businessman. Villani was associated with the most powerful of the city's banking firms and was a member of the Black faction in Florence's internecine struggles. Widely traveled both in Italy and abroad, in France and Flanders, Villani occupied a number of municipal offices between 1316 and 1341, and enjoyed the prestige and comfort typical of the rich burgher of his day. However, the last decade of his life was filled with misfortunes. The collapse of the Buonaccorsi Company (1338) cost him a term in prison for debt; the subsequent failures of the Bardi and Peruzzi Companies further increased his financial difficulties. Already embittered in his last years by what he felt was the gradual eclipse of his class's political and economic power, he died in the terrible Black Plague of 1348. In the thirty-sixth chapter of the eighth book of his historical masterpiece, the *Cronica* (first published in 1537–54, *Chronicle*), Villani announces that while in Rome on the occasion of the jubilee of 1300 he was inspired to write his city's history in order to achieve for Florence the fame won for the Eternal City by the classical historians, now that Florence was about to surpass Rome in importance. Internal evidence from the text which has survived indicates, however, that Villani actually began composing his history no earlier than the 1320s. The fact that Villani points to the symbolic year of 1300, a date that is also crucial in the composition of Dante's* *Divine Comedy*, suggests that Villani may have intended his history to represent more than a mere historical record of the past.

The chronicle opens with a presentation of the early legends surrounding Florence's origins that were the common property of all Florentines (including Dante). Divided into twelve books, the work covers Florence's legendary past up to the year 1346: the first six books (256 chapters) open with the description of the destruction of the Tower of Babel and conclude in 1264; the last six books (1125 chapters) carry the narrative to Villani's own times. The first section reflects the combination of numerous sources and legends, many with little or no historical foundation; the second deals with events Villani himself experienced and observed or discussed with eyewitnesses. Although Villani's ideas mark him as a man of Dante's generation, his work is a necessary first step toward the development of an historiography based upon natural rather than supernatural processes. His narrative, organized along traditional annalistic lines, is given continuity by a broad conception of history in which human sin is inevitably punished by retribution. The downfall of many rulers, including the Hohenstaufens and several French monarchs, is cited as proof of this universal process. For today's readers, however, the importance of Villani's *Cronica* lies in its invaluable description of life during the most crucial period of Florence's late medieval history. Furthermore, his work shows an interest in statistics which is a remarkably reliable tool for the study of changes and developments in Florentine population, revenues, expenditures, food supplies, education, professions, economic development, and the like. Although his work is not characterized by the attention to style, form, and structure which marks both his humanist successors in Latin and the vernacular historians of the Cinquecento (all of whom were to use his history as a major source), Villani's faith in the didactic lessons taught by history qualify him as one of the forerunners of the humanist view of the past.

After Giovanni's death, his brother Matteo (circa 1285–1363) continued the chronicle and brought the narrative to the year 1363 when he, too, perished from the plague. His narrative style is considerably inferior to Giovanni's, and his tendency to view history in strictly moralistic terms represents a step backward from his brother's accomplishments. Matteo's picture of Florentine history after the plague of 1348 reflects a deep pessimism and a crisis of moral values which contrast with Giovanni's firm belief that history demonstrated the ultimate validity of traditional ethical principles. After Matteo's death, his son Filippo (circa 1325–circa 1405), at one time chancellor of the Comune of Perugia and public lecturer on Dante, added an additional book to the history in order to bring the narrative through the year 1364. Filippo is also the author of a Latin commentary on the first canto of Dante's epic* poem and a Latin work entitled *Liber de origine civitatis Florentinae et eiusdem famosis civibus* (after 1400, Book on the Origin of the City of Florence and Its Illustrious

Citizens), which contains several interesting biographies of eminent Florentine citizens.

See also COMPAGNI, Dino.

Bibliography: Croniche di Giovanni, Matteo e Filippo Villani, 2 vols. (Trieste: Lloyd Austriaco, 1857–58); *Villani's Chronicle: Being Selections from the First Nine Books of the Croniche Fiorentine of Giovanni Villani,* trans. Rose Selfe and ed. Philip Wicksteed (London: Constable, 1906); Louis Green, *Chronicle into History: An Essay on the Interpretation of History in Florentine Fourteenth-Century Chronicles* (Cambridge: Cambridge University Press, 1972).

VILLANI, MATTEO: *See* VILLANI, GIOVANNI.

VITTORINI, ELIO (1908–1966), novelist, essayist, translator, critic, and editor. Vittorini was born in Sicily, where his father was a railroad employee. His childhood was spent in isolated country stations surrounded by "a desert of malaria." He was to become an accountant but was far more interested in travel and literature. His third attempt to flee from home and school was successful and took him to Gorizia, where he worked on a road and bridge-building gang, an experience that gave him a permanent faith in the working class and in human resourcefulness. In 1929, he moved to Florence, writing for *Solaria* and working as a proofreader and journalist. He moved to Milan in 1936, where he translated from the English and American and did editorial work, rising to become editor for Bompiani, Einaudi, and Mondadori.

Vittorini's importance as a novelist and essayist is equaled by his role as a cultural entrepreneur: he was among the group who introduced American authors, helping to air the stuffy prewar Italian literary scene. He founded and directed two of the most controversial and important postwar Italian periodicals: *Il Politecnico* (1945–47) and *Il Menabò* (1959–67). The first, an "enlightenment" attempt to create a meeting place for both Sino-Soviet and Western culture after twenty years of fascist censorship, was also to serve as a point of encounter for workers and intellectuals. The avant-garde *Il Menabò* focused on the literary problems of effective innovation in style and language. Vittorini also directed Einaudi's *I Gettoni* (Telephone Tokens), a series founded in 1951 that published translations and innovative work by young authors like Calvino.* In 1964 and 1965, he founded Mondadori's *Nuovi scrittori stranieri* (New Foreign Writers) and Einaudi's *Nuovo Politecnico* series. They were to introduce the latest international trends to the Italian public and published everything from Myrdal's *Report from a Chinese Village* to Barthes's *Elements of Semiology.*

Vittorini's development is typical of his generation. In the 1920s, he believed in "pure literature"; later, he moved gradually to a position of commitment. His basic attitude did not change, although he went from left-wing fascism to communism, which was rejected in its turn as too rigid, and finally to liberal socialism. His ideas, courage, and open-mindedness played a large part in the development of Italian literature from the 1930s until his death. His own novels, highly interesting and individual in style, are the result of his passionate and lyrical temperament, combined with the various influences of *prosa d'arte,* hermeticism,* the European novelists such as Proust and Joyce that interested the *Solaria* group, and his beloved modern American writers.

Vittorini's first book, *Piccola borghesia* (1931, Petty Bourgeoisie), is a stylistically elegant series of ironic studies. *Nei Morlacchi–Viaggio in Sardegna* (1936, In the Morlacchi—Voyage to Sardinia) is a highly lyrical prose poem followed by an impressionistic diary of a trip through Sardinia with overtones of social indignation. The theme of nostalgia for "magic" childhood is strong in both. *Il garofano rosso* (1933, *The Red Carnation,* published in 1948) is a psychological novel that studies the themes of adolescence, sex, violence, and revolution in the 1920s. Vittorini later called it a documentary of fascism's attraction for his generation. His growing sympathy for leftist ideals, already clear in *Il garofano,* exploded in *Erica e i suoi fratelli,* a 1936 unfinished work published in 1956 with *La Garibaldina* (English translation of both: *The Dark and the Light*). It is a Marxist affirmation of the basic human right to work, the story of a child abandoned by her parents during a depression who must resort to prostitution to feed herself and her younger brother and sister. Its importance lies in its poetic and fabulistic structure. The injustice of a world in which some must accept charity in order to live is viewed through the vital innocence of childhood and is told as a fable whose conscious use to state a social message adds universality as well as poetry to the work. For years, Vittorini had been seeking a style that would combine commitment and the emotional immediacy of music ("poetry" as he called it). *Conversazione in Sicilia* (1941, *In Sicily*), written under the impact of the Civil War in Spain, was the result. It allegorically states the necessity to reform "the evil in the suffering world" in a new and daring style relying heavily on parataxis and rhythmic repetition, combining Vittorini's own lyricism with lessons learned from Faulkner and Hemingway. The book became a banner for antifascist intellectuals and, together with his generosity to young writers, vociferous political morality, and avant-garde eclecticism, helped make him a leader among postwar intellectuals.

Uomini e no (1945, Men and Non-Men), cited as *the* example of neo-realism, is a bad pastiche of *Conversazione* and Hemingway, written while Vittorini was working for the resistance. *Il Sempione strizza l'occhio al Fréjus* (1947, *The Twilight of the Elephant*), stylistically his most perfect work, is the intense, lyrical, allegorical story of Grandfather Elephant, an old worker representing humanist civilization, whose enormous appetite is ruining his family. He is persuaded to seek death by the magic tune of a dying construction worker. *Le donne di Messina* (1949, *Women of Messina*, revised edition 1964) is an attempt at epic. A small group of people founds a postwar commune and attempts to survive in spite of the pressures of a rebuilt capitalist country and the "fascism" (egoism) in one of its leaders. Vittorini rewrote the book to show that an agricultural commune is an anachronism in an improved technological world. *La Garibaldina* (1950, *The Garibaldina*) is an apparently gay, but very bitter, portrait of a Sicily whose social structure is still feudal. It is the last of Vittorini's fiction. *Diario in pubblico* (1957, Public Diary) contains excerpts from his nonfiction. This intellectual biography is completed by *Le due tensioni* (1967, Two Tensions), an important posthumous collection of thoughts and sketches for essays. Also posthumous are *Le città del mondo* (1969, Cities of the World), a collection of fragments from a planned triple novel, and *Nome e lagrime* (1972, Tears and a Name), a collection of prose fragments published in periodicals during the 1930s and 1940s. Vittorini's fiction has been gathered in a two-volume *Opere* (Works), published in 1974.

Bibliography: Opere, ed. Maria Corti, 2 vols. (Milan: Mondadori, 1974); *The Dark and the Light* (New York: New Directions, 1960); *The Red Carnation*, trans. Anthony Bower (1952; rpt. Westport, Conn.: Greenwood Press, 1972); *The Twilight of the Elephant and Other Novels: A Vittorini Omnibus* (New York: New Directions, 1973); *Women of Messina* (New York: New Directions, 1973); Donald Heiney, *Three Italian Writers* (Ann Arbor, Mich.: University of Michigan Press, 1968); Sergio Pautasso, *Elio Vittorini* (Milan: Rizzoli, 1977).

Joy Hambuechen Potter

VITTORINO DA FELTRE, pen-name of Vittore dei Rambaldoni (circa 1373–1446), humanist and educator. After studying at Padua and Venice and striking up a friendship with the famous teacher Guarino da Verona (1374–1460), Vittorino taught rhetoric at the University of Padua but resigned that post after one year to direct a school in Venice for young noblemen. In 1423, he went to Mantua and became the tutor of Gianfrancesco Gonzaga. Among his students there were Ludovico Gonzaga and Federico da Montefeltro. His school was famous for its progressive curriculum; among its offerings were the Greek and Latin classics as well as music, dance, and physical education. It stressed rigid discipline and a moral as well as a Scholastic education. It lasted twenty years after his death. Vittorino's teaching was of considerable consequence; his pedagogical example contributed to the emerging Renaissance* ideal of the humanist disciplines, continuing the principles of his great predecessor

Petrarch.* Vittorino is also credited with writing a treatise on Latin orthography.

See also HUMANISM.

Bibliography: Eugenio Garin, *L'educazione umanistica in Italia* (Bari: Laterza, 1949), and *Il pensiero pedagogico del umanesimo* (Florence: Sansoni, 1958); William Harrison Woodward, *Studies in Education During the Age of the Renaissance* (1906; rpt. New York: Russell & Russell, 1965), and *Vittorino da Feltre and Other Humanist Educators* (1897; rpt. New York: Teachers College, Columbia University, 1963).

VOLPONI, PAOLO (1924–   ), poet and novelist. Volponi, born in Urbino, received a law degree in 1947 before publishing his first volume of verse, *Il ramarro* (1948, The Green Lizard). His association with the Olivetti firm began in 1950 and lasted until 1971. This early poetry was influenced by the avant-garde poetry journal *Officina,* founded by Pier Paolo Pasolini* and other like-minded intellectuals who had been attracted by post-hermetic ideas and Gramscian concepts concerning the relationship of literature and culture. Volponi continued writing poetry with some success and published two more collections, *L'antica moneta* (1955, The Old Coin) and *Le porte dell'Appennino* (1960, The Gates of the Appennines), the latter of which was awarded the Viareggio Prize in 1960.

Volponi turned from the lyric to the novel as much to solve his own personal intellectual problems as to offer formalistic solutions to the problems of another genre. His first novel, *Memoriale* (1962, *My Troubles Began*), was received as a masterpiece by many of Italy's best writers. One of the so-called industrial novels published since the war, *Memoriale* depicts the struggle of Albino Saluggia, a worker in a modern factory who contracts a lung disease. Told in the first person from Saluggia's point of view, the narrative offers a nightmarish vision of bureaucratic indifference and personal alienation. A second novel, *La macchina mondiale (The Worldwide Machine)* was awarded the Strega Prize in 1965. It is the diary of a madman, Anteo Crocioni, a landowner whose obsession with a mad scientific theory ruins his life. Like his classical namesake Antaeus, the protagonist is destroyed by losing touch with the earth, just as modern man is alienated from his natural existence by a world of machines and technology.

Volponi continues to contribute to Italian periodicals and has recently published *Corporale* (1974, The Body Factor), which has aroused a good deal of critical debate, and *Il sipario ducale* (1975, The Ducal Curtain), which received the Viareggio Prize in 1975. *Corporale* deals with a schoolteacher, Gerolamo Aspri, who builds a refuge from the bomb and who hopes to emerge from the future conflagration as one who is closer to the animal world, closer to "the body factor." Like the central characters of the earlier novels, Aspri is yet another manifestation of contemporary alienated man.

Bibliography: Corporale (Turin: Einaudi, 1974); *My Troubles Began,* trans. Belén Sevareid (New York: Grossman, 1964); *The Worldwide Machine,* trans. Belén Sevareid (New York: Grossman, 1967); Vittoria Bradshaw, *From Pure Silence to Impure Dialogue* (New York: Las Americas, 1971)—contains poems in translation; Gian Carlo Ferretti, *Volponi* (Florence: La Nuova Italia, 1972).

Z

ZANELLA, GIACOMO (1820–1888), poet and scholar. Ordained at the age of twenty-three after a seminary education in Vicenza, Zanella taught in Verona, earning a degree in philosophy from the University of Padua in 1847. Forced to abandon this post between 1853 and 1857 for his political beliefs, he returned to his profession and worked in Venice, Vicenza, and Padua before being called to the professorship of Italian literature at Padua in 1866. After 1878, an illness restricted him to life at a country villa, where he remained until his death.

Zanella's originality as a poet lay in his sensitive reaction in verse to science and his use of scientific themes as a source of literary inspiration. In a narrative poem entitled "Milton e Galileo" (1868, Milton and Galileo), Zanella recreates the meeting of the two men at Arcetri, discusses the problems of scientific truth and religious revelation, and underlines man's need for both religious faith and the knowledge of science. His most famous poem, "Sopra una conchiglia fossile nel mio studio" (1864, "On a Fossil Shell in My Study"), reconciles the discoveries of science with men's religious faith. An able translator of foreign literatures, he rendered Longfellow, Heine, and Shelley, among others, as well as biblical and classical texts, into Italian. The critical essays *Paralleli letterari* (1885, Literary Parallels) are early and excellent examples of Italian comparative literature, which analyze the relationships of Addison and Gozzi,* Shelley and Leopardi,* Gray and Foscolo,* and many other Italians influenced by literatures from abroad. His *Storia della letteratura italiana dalla metà del Settecento ai giorni nostri* (1880, History of Italian Literature from the Mid-Eighteenth Century Until Our Time) is one of the more important critical reinterpretations of the literature of that period written in the last century.

Bibliography: Poesie di Giacomo Zanella (Florence: Le Monnier, 1928); *Paralleli letterari: studi* (Verona: Münster, 1885); *Storia della letteratura italiana dalla metà del Settecento ai giorni nostri* (Milan: Vallardi, 1880); *From Marino to Marinetti,* trans. Joseph Tusiani (New York: Baroque Press, 1974).

ZANZOTTO, ANDREA (1921–), lyric poet. Zanzotto, born in Pieve di Soligo (Treviso), received a degree in literature from the University of Padua in 1942 and has lived in his birthplace for most of his life, working as a teacher. Although his verse is most often set in the surrounding countryside, he is by no means a provincial poet. His collections of verse include *Dietro il paesaggio* (1951, Behind the Landscape), *Elegia e altri versi* (1954, Elegy and Other Verse), *Vocativo* (1957, Vocative), *IX Ecloghe* (1962, Nine Eclogues), *La beltà* (1968, Beauty), and *Pasque* (1973, Easters). Zanzotto inherited a poetic tradition indebted to the hermeticism* of the masters of the early twentieth century (Montale,* Ungaretti*) and to the works of younger poets such as Luzi* and Sereni.* His verse has attracted attention and praise from notable poet-critics such as Montale, Ungaretti, and Pasolini.* While his earliest works seemed to continue the hermetic tradition, reflecting the idyllic, pastoral mood of the bucolic surroundings of his hometown, with *La beltà* Zanzotto initiated an experimental phase that has sharply divided his critics. Among his works are some genuine masterpieces, including his "Ecloga IV" ("Eclogue IV") from *IX Ecloghe*; and "L'elegia in petèl" ("The Elegy in Petèl") from *La beltà,* a remarkable composition which embodies the poet's desire to seek out a new poetic language. Like much of contemporary Italian fiction, Zanzotto's recent poetry has apparently been informed by the insights of linguistics and semiotics.* Many Italian critics consider Zanzotto to be the most important living poet in Italy today.

Bibliography: Selected Poetry of Andrea Zanzotto, trans. Ruth Feldman and Brian Swann (Princeton, N.J.: Princeton University Press, 1975)—contains bilingual selections, plus critical essays by Glauco Cambon and Gino Rizzo.

Appendix A:

TIME LINE

ITALIAN LITERATURE		WORLD LITERATURE	
		1071-1127	Guilhem de Peitieus, the first troubadour
		circa 1098	*The Song of Roland*
		circa 1100-	
		circa 1155	Geoffrey of Monmouth's *History of the Kings of England*
		circa 1135-	
		circa 1190	Chrétien de Troyes
		1148-1195	Bernart de Ventadorn
		circa 1160	Benoît de Sainte-Maure, *The Romance of Troy*
		1167-1184	Marie de France
		circa 1174-1186	Andreas Capellanus, *The Art of Courtly Love*
1194-1250	Frederick II of Hohenstaufen	circa 1200	*The Owl and the Nightingale*
circa 1220-circa 1295	Brunetto Latini	circa 1225-1275	*The Romance of the Rose* (Guillaume de Lorris and Jean de Meun)
circa 1240-1276	Guido Guinizzelli		
circa 1240-1300	Guido Cavalcanti		
1249	Death of Pier della Vigna		
1260-1313	Cecco Angiolieri		
circa 1267	Jacopo Da Varazze, *The Golden Legend*		

POLITICAL THEORY, HISTORY, AND RELIGION		PHILOSOPHY, SCIENCE, AND THE ARTS	
1202-04	Fourth Crusade		
1204	Crusaders take Constantinople		
1208	Albigensian Crusade		
1209	Foundation of Franciscan order		
1215	Foundation of Dominican order; Lateran Council; Magna Carta		
1226	Death of St. Francis		
1228-29	Sixth Crusade led by Frederick II		
1248-54	Seventh Crusade led by Louis IX		
		Introduction of Arabic numerals in Europe	
		1259-60	Nicola Pisano, pulpit in Pisan Baptistery
1260	Florentines defeated at battle of Montaperti		
1261	Greeks retake Constantinople		
1266	Charles of Anjou becomes king of Naples		
1266-73	St. Thomas Aquinas (d. 1275) writes *Summa Theologica*		
1280	Eighth Crusade led by Louis IX	circa 1280	Cimabue, *Madonna Enthroned*

ITALIAN LITERATURE		WORLD LITERATURE	
1287	Guido Delle Colonne, *Historia destructionis Troiae*		
1292-1300	Composition of Dante's *New Life*		
circa 1298	Composition of Marco Polo's travel journal		
1306	Dante begins *The Divine Comedy*		
1310-12	Compagni, *Chronicle*		
		circa 1316-28	*Ovid Moralized*
circa 1320	Villani begins his *Chronicle*	circa 1320	*Sir Orfeo*
		circa 1330-1408	John Gower
		circa 1332- circa 1400	William Langland *(Piers Plowman)*
1335-36?	Boccaccio, *Filostrato*	1337-1405	Jean Froissart
1340-41	Boccaccio, *The Book of Theseus*		
1341	Petrarch crowned poet laureate in Rome		
1342-43	Petrarch begins the *Canzoniere, The Triumphs,* and the *Secretum*		
circa 1347	Fazio degli Uberti, *The Book of the World*		
1349-50	Boccaccio, *The Decameron*		

POLITICAL THEORY, HISTORY, AND RELIGION		PHILOSOPHY, SCIENCE, AND THE ARTS	
1285	Marco Polo returns from Kublai Khan	late 1280s	Giovanni Pisano, facade of Sienese Cathedral
1294-1303 circa 1295	Papacy of Boniface VIII Marco Polo returns from China by sea	circa 1294	Construction of Santa Croce Cathedral in Florence begins
		1298-1301	Giovanni Pisano, pulpit in Pistoia
		1299-1310	Palazzo Vecchio in Florence constructed
		circa 1305	Giovanni Pisano, *Virgin and Child* in Padua
		1305-06	Giotto, Arena Chapel frescoes
1308-77	Papacy in Avignon	1308-11	Duccio, *Maestà*
1312-1447	Visconti rule in Milan		
		1333	Simone Martini, *Annunciation*
1337	Outbreak of the Hundred Years' War	1338-39	Lorenzetti, *Allegory of Good Government*
		1340	Palazzo Ducale in Venice begun
1346	Battle of Crécy		
1347-48	The Black Death		
		circa 1350	Francesco Traini, *Triumph of Death* at Pisan Campo Santo

ITALIAN LITERATURE		WORLD LITERATURE	
circa 1354	Passavanti, *The Mirror of True Penitence*		
1356?	Boccaccio, *The Corbaccio*	circa 1356	*The Travels of Sir John Mandeville*
		circa 1360-1400	The Gawain Poet *(Sir Gawain and the Green Knight; Pearl)*
1361-74	Petrarch, *Letters of Old Age*		
		1369-70	Chaucer, *The Book of the Duchess*
		1372-73	Chaucer's first visit to Italy
1378	Giovanni Fiorentino, *The Pecorone*	1378	Chaucer's second visit to Italy
		circa 1385	First English adaptation of a Petrarchan sonnet in Chaucer's *Troilus and Criseyde*
1392-97?	Sacchetti, *The Three Hundred Novelle*		
		1394-1465	Charles d'Orléans
end of the century	*The Novellino: The Hundred Old Tales*		
		circa 1431-?	Francois Villon

POLITICAL THEORY, HISTORY, AND RELIGION		PHILOSOPHY, SCIENCE, AND THE ARTS	
		1368	Cathedral of Florence begun
1378	Ciompi Revolt in Florence		
1378-1418	Great Schism in the Western church		
		1386	Cathedral of Milan begun
1400	Salutati, *A Treatise on Tyrants*	circa 1400-circa 1474	Guillaume Dufay
1402	Death of Gian Galeazzo Visconti		
1403-04	Bruni, *In Praise of the City of Florence*	circa 1405-08	The Boucicaut Master, *Hours of the Maréchal de Boucicaut*
		1413-16	*Très Riches Heures du Duc de Berry*
1414-18	Council of Constance		
		1420-36	Brunelleschi, dome of the Cathedral of Florence
		1423	Gentile da Fabriano, *Adoration of the Magi*
		circa 1425	Masaccio, *Tribute Money* fresco in Brancacci Chapel
		1425-50	Ghiberti, *Gates of Paradise* (Florentine Baptistery)
		1430-32	Donatello, *David*
1431	Joan of Arc executed		
1431-49	Council of Basel		
1432	Battle of San Romano		

ITALIAN LITERATURE		WORLD LITERATURE	
1433-39	Alberti, *The Books of the Family*		
1438-52	Bracciolini, *The Facetiae*		
1444	Enea Silvio Piccolomini (Pius II), *The Tale of Two Lovers*		
		1447-1511	Philippe de Commynes
1452-53	Biondo, *The Decades;* Manetti, composition of *On the Dignity of Man*		
1470	First printed edition of Petrarch's *Canzoniere* and *The Triumphs*		
1471	Poliziano, *Orpheus*		
circa 1474	Lorenzo de' Medici, *Nencia from Barberino*		
1475	Masuccio Salernitano, *The Novellino*		
1476	Bracciolini, *History of Florence*		
1481	Landino's commentary on Dante		
1483	Pulci, *The Greater Morgante*		
		1485	Malory, *Morte d'Arthur*
1486	Pico della Mirandola, *Oration on the Dignity of Man*		

POLITICAL THEORY, HISTORY, AND RELIGION		PHILOSOPHY, SCIENCE, AND THE ARTS	
1434	Medici ascendancy in Florence begins with Cosimo de' Medici	1434	Van Eyck, *Arnolfini Wedding*
		1436	Alberti, *De pictura*
1438-45	Council of Ferrara— Florence attempts to unite Eastern and Western churches		
1440	Florence and Venice defeat Milan at the battle of Anghiari; Valla, *On the Donation of Constantine*	circa 1445	Bernardo Rossellino, tomb of Leonardo Bruni
1447-55	Papacy of Nicholas V		
		1450	Invention of printing
		circa 1450	Alberti, *De re aedificatoria* and Malatesta Chapel in Rimini
1453	Fall of Constantinople to Turks		
1458-61	Papacy of Pius II		
		1461	Alberti, facade of Palazzo Rucellai
		after 1466	Mantegna, *Dead Christ*
1469-92	Lorenzo de' Medici controls Florence		
1471-84	Papacy of Sixtus IV		
1478	Pazzi Conspiracy against Medici	circa 1478	Botticelli, *Primavera*
		circa 1483	Da Vinci, *Madonna of the Rocks*
1484	Publication of Ficino's translations of Plato		

ITALIAN LITERATURE		WORLD LITERATURE	
1494	Aldine press established by Aldo Manuzio	1494	Brant, *The Ship of Fools*
1495	Boiardo, *Orlando in Love*		
1499	Francesco Colonna, *Hypnerotomachia Poliphili*	circa 1500	*Everyman*
1501	Bembo's Aldine edition of Petrarch's Italian poetry		
1502	Sannazaro, *Arcadia*		
1505	Bembo, *Gli Asolani*		
1509	Ariosto, *The Pretenders*	1509	Erasmus, *In Praise of Folly*
1514	Trissino, *Sophonisba*		
1516	Ariosto, first edition of *Orlando Furioso;* Pomponazzi, *On the Immortality of the Soul*		
1518	Machiavelli, *The Mandrake Root;* Aldine editions of Pontano's bucolic lyrics in Latin		
1521	Bernardo Dovizi ("Il Bibbiena"), *The Follies of Calandro*		
1525	Aretino, *The Courtesan;* Bembo, *Writings in the Vernacular Language*		

POLITICAL THEORY, HISTORY, AND RELIGION		PHILOSOPHY, SCIENCE, AND THE ARTS	
1492	Death of Lorenzo de' Medici; Moors expelled from Granada; Columbus discovers a New World		
1494	French invasion of Italy		
1498	Execution of Savonarola in Florence; voyage of Vasco da Gama	1498	Dürer, *Self-Portrait*
		1501-04	Michelangelo, *David*
		1503-06	Da Vinci, *Mona Lisa*
1505	Treaty of Blois	circa 1505-10	Hieronymus Bosch, *Garden of Delights*
		1508-11	Michelangelo, Sistine Chapel frescoes
1509	Henry VIII ascends English throne	1510-11	Raphael, *School of Athens*
1513	Leo X elected pope		
		circa 1515	Titian, *Sacred and Profane Love*
1516	More, *Utopia*		
1517	Publication of Luther's Theses	circa 1517	Raphael, portrait of Pope Leo X
		1519-34	Michelangelo, tombs of Medici Chapel
1519	Charles V elected emperor of the Holy Roman Empire		
1521	Luther excommunicated		
1522	Luther's *New Testament* in German		
1523	Clement VII elected pope		
1524-25	Peasants' War in Germany		
1525	Battle of Pavia	1525-94	Giovanni Pierluigi da Palestrina

ITALIAN LITERATURE		WORLD LITERATURE	
1526	Beolco (Ruzzante), *Ruzzante Returns from the Wars;* Sannazaro, *The Virgin's Childbirth*	1526	Boscán's experiments with Italian verse forms in Spain begin
1528	Castiglione, *The Book of the Courtier;* Palmieri, *On Civic Life*		
1530	Da Porto, *Romeo and Juliet;* Guicciardini, final version of the *Maxims;* Fracastoro, *Syphilis or The French Disease*		
1531	Alciati, *Emblem Book;* Machiavelli, *Discourses* published		
1532	Machiavelli, publication of *The Prince*	1532	Rabelais, *Pantagruel*
		1533	Boscán's translation of *The Book of the Courtier*
		1534	Rabelais, *Gargantua*
1535	Vida, *The Christiad*		
1540	Giannotti, *On the Venetian Republic*		
1541	Giraldi ("Il Cinzio"), *Orbecche;* Daniello's commentary on Petrarch		
		1544	Scève, *Délie*
		1546	Rabelais, *Tiers Livre*
1547-48	Trissino, *Italy Liberated from the Goths*		
1548	Grazzini's edition of Berni's lyrics; Robortello's commentary on Aristotle's *Poetics*	1548	Loyola, *Spiritual Exercises*

POLITICAL THEORY, HISTORY, AND RELIGION		PHILOSOPHY, SCIENCE, AND THE ARTS	
1527	The Sack of Rome		
1529	The Peace of Cambrai		
1534	Henry VIII founds Anglican church; Ignatius Loyola founds Society of Jesus		
1535	Execution of Sir Thomas More		
1536	Calvin, *Institutes of the Christian Religion*	1536-41	Michelangelo, *Last Judgment* in Sistine Chapel
		1538	Titian, *Venus of Urbino*
		1543	Copernicus, *De revolutionibus orbium coelestium*
1545-63	Council of Trent	1545-54	Cellini, *Perseus and Medusa*
		1548	Tintoretto, *St. Mark Freeing a Christian Slave*

ITALIAN LITERATURE		WORLD LITERATURE	
1549	Gelli, *Circe;* Bernardo Segni, Aristotle's *Poetics* rendered into Italian for the first time	1549	Du Bellay, *L'Olive* and *Deffence et Illustration de la langue francoyse*
		1550	Ronsard, *Odes*
1552	Folengo, *Baldus;* Grazzini's edition of lyrics by Domenico di Giovanni ("Il Burchiello")	1552	Rabelais, *Quart Livre;* Jodelle, *Captive Cleopatra*
1552-53	Doni, *The Marble Steps* and *The Worlds*		
1554	Bandello, first part of *The Novels*	1554	*Lazarillo de Tormes*
		1557	*Totel's Miscellany*
1558	Della Casa, *Lyric Poems* and *Galateo*	1558	Du Bellay, *Les Regrets*
		1558-59	Marguerite de Navarre, *Heptaméron*
		1559	Montemayor, *Diana;* Amyot's *Plutarch's Lives*
1561	Scaligero, *Poetics* ·		
1563	Minturno, *The Art of Poetry*	1563	*The Mirror for Magistrates*
1565	Giraldi ("Il Cinzio"), *The Hundred Stories*		
1568	Vasari, *Lives of the Artists*		
1570-76	Castelvetro's commentary on Aristotle's *Poetics*		
		1572	Ronsard, *The Franciad;* Camoens, *Os Lusiadas*
1573	Tasso, *Aminta*		
1574	Guazzo, *Civil Conversation*		
		1579	North's *Plutarch's Lives;* Spenser, *Shepherd's Calender*
		1580	Sidney, *Apologie for Poetrie*
		1580-88	Montaigne, *Essais*

POLITICAL THEORY, HISTORY, AND RELIGION		PHILOSOPHY, SCIENCE, AND THE ARTS	
1549	First Book of Common Prayer		
		1550	Palladio, Villa Rotunda begun in Vicenza
		circa 1553-99	Luça Marenzio (madrigals)
1555	Peace of Augsburg		
1558-1603	Reign of Elizabeth I in England		
1559	Peace of Cateau-Cambrésis		
		1560-1613	Gesualdo, prince of Venosa (madrigals)
		1560-80	Vasari, Palazzo degli Uffizi
1561-64	Guicciardini, *History of Italy*	circa 1561-62	Bruegel, *Triumph of Death*
		1567-1643	Claudio Monteverdi
		1569	Mercator's map of the world
1571	Battle of Lepanto		
1572	St. Bartholomew's Day Massacre	1573	Veronese, *Feast in the House of Levi*
1576	Bodin, *Six Books of the Republic*		
1580	Sir Francis Drake circumnavigates the world		

ITALIAN LITERATURE		WORLD LITERATURE	
1581	Tasso, *Jerusalem Delivered;* Caro's translation of *The Aeneid*		
1582	Bruno, *The Candle Bearer;* Salviati's expurgated edition of Boccaccio's *Decameron*		
1584-85	Bruno: *The Ash Wednesday Supper, The Expulsion of the Triumphant Beast,* and *The Heroic Frenzies*		
1589	Della Porta, *The Sister*	circa 1589	Marlowe, *Doctor Faustus*
1590	Guarini, *The Faithful Shepherd*	1590	Spenser, *The Faerie Queene;* Alonso de Ercilla y Zuniga, *The Poem of Araucania*
1591	Della Valle, *The Queen of Scotland*	1593-98	Donne, *Songs and Sonets*
1594	Tasso, *Discourses on the Heroic Poem;* Ammirato, *Discourses on Cornelius Tacitus*	circa 1595	Shakespeare, *Romeo and Juliet*
1600	Chiabrera, *The Abduction of Cephalus*		
		1603	Shakespeare, *Hamlet*
1605-15	Boccalini, *Advertisements from Parnassus*	1605-16	Cervantes, *Don Quijote*
		1607	d'Urfé, *Astrée*

POLITICAL THEORY, HISTORY, AND RELIGION		PHILOSOPHY, SCIENCE, AND THE ARTS
	1582	Pope Gregory XIII introduces Gregorian calendar
1588	Defeat of the Spanish Armada	
1589	Botero, *Reason of State*	
	1597	First opera performed: *Dafne* by Peri and Rinuccini
	1597-1600	Carracci, ceiling fresco in Palazzo Farnese (Rome)
1598	Edict of Nantes	
1600	Bruno burned at the stake	circa 1600	Camerata dei Bardi and rise of monodic style
	circa 1600-10	El Greco, *Toledo*
	circa 1601	Caravaggio, *Conversion of St. Paul*
1602	Campanella, *City of the Sun*	
	1608	Invention of the telescope
	1609-19	Kepler's laws of planetary motion
1610-17	Sarpi, *History of the Council of Trent* composed; regency of Maria de' Medici in France (Louis XIII reigns from 1610 until 1643)	

ITALIAN LITERATURE		WORLD LITERATURE	
		1611	Chapman's translation of *The Iliad*
1612	First edition of the Accademia della Crusca's dictionary		
1613	Adreini, *Adam;* Testi, *Rhymes*		
1614	Marino, *The Lyre*	1614	Webster, *The Duchess of Malfi*
		1621	Burton, *The Anatomy of Melancholy*
1622	Tassoni, *The Rape of the Bucket*		
1623	Marino, *Adonis;* first edition of Michelangelo's lyrics		
		1630	Tirso de Molina, *The Trickster of Seville*
1634-36	Basile, *The Pentameron*		
		1635	Calderón, *Life Is a Dream*
		1637	Milton, *Lycidas;* Corneille, *The Cid*

POLITICAL THEORY, HISTORY, AND RELIGION		PHILOSOPHY, SCIENCE, AND THE ARTS	
1611	King James Bible		
		1614-18	Rubens, *Fall of the Damned*
1618	Thirty Years' War begins		
1620	Landing of the May- flower	1621-25	Rubens, *Henry IV Receiving the Portrait of Maria de' Medici*
		1622-24	Bernini, *Apollo and Daphne*
1624-42	Cardinal Richelieu min- ister to King Louis XIII	1628	Velázquez, *Triumph of Bacchus;* Poussin, *Inspiration of the Poet;* Harvey describes the circulation of the blood
		1632	Galileo, *Dialogue Con- cerning the Two Chief World Systems;* Rem- brandt, *Anatomy Lesson of Dr. Tulp*
		1635	Richelieu founds the French Academy
		1637	Poussin, *Rape of the Sabines;* Descartes, *Dis- course on Method*
		1641	Lorrain, *Embarkation of Saint Ursula*
		1642	Rembrandt, *Nightwatch*
1643-61	Cardinal Mazzarin governs France during minority of Louis XIV	1643	Torricelli discovers principle of the barometer
		1645-52	Bernini, *Ecstasy of Saint Theresa*
1648	Treaty of Westphalia ends Thirty Years' War	circa 1648	Lorrain, *Marriage of Isaac and Rebecca*

ITALIAN LITERATURE	WORLD LITERATURE

1655	Tesauro, *The Aristotelian Telescope*		
1656-57	Pallavicino, *The History of the Council of Trent*		
		1667	Milton, *Paradise Lost;* Racine, *Andromaque*
		1669	Molière, *Tartuffe*
1685	Redi, *Bacchus in Tuscany*		
1689	Frugoni, *The Dog of Diogenes*	1689	Perrault, *Parallel Between the Ancients and the Moderns*
1690	Foundation of the Arcadia		
1694	Rosa, *Satires*		
1695	Magalotti, *Letters on Buccheri*		
1698	Maggi, *The Competition of the Meneghinis*		
		1700	Congreve, *The Way of the World*

POLITICAL THEORY, HISTORY, AND RELIGION		PHILOSOPHY, SCIENCE, AND THE ARTS	
1649	Charles I beheaded; Cromwell's Commonwealth begins		
1651	Hobbes, *Leviathan*		
		1653-1713	Arcangelo Corelli
		1656	Velázquez, *Las Meninas*
		1660	Boyle's Law
		1662	Charles II charters Royal Society
		circa 1665	Vermeer, *Allegory of the Art of Painting*
1666	Great Fire of London		
		1667-70	Perrault, east facade of the Louvre
1668	Peace of Aix-la-Chapelle		
		1669	Rembrandt, *Self-Portrait*
1670	Spinoza, *Tractatus Theologico-Politicus*		
		1675-1710	Wren, St. Paul's Cathedral in London
		1676-1741	Antonio Vivaldi
1677	Spinoza, *Ethics*		
1678	Bunyan, *Pilgrim's Progress*	1678	Hardouin-Mansart and Lebrun begin Hall of Mirrors at Versailles
1682-1725	Reign of Peter the Great in Russia		
1685	Louis XIV revokes the Edict of Nantes	1687	Newton, *Principia Mathematica;* completion of Santa Maria della Salute in Venice by Baldassare Longhena
1688	Glorious Revolution in England		
1690	Locke, *Treatises of Government*	1690	Locke, *Essay Concerning Human Understanding*

ITALIAN LITERATURE		WORLD LITERATURE	
1708	Gravina, *On the Nature of Poetry*		
		1711-12	Pope, *An Essay on Criticism* and *The Rape of the Lock*
1713	Maffei, *Merope*		
1723	Giannone, *The Civil History of the Kingdom of Naples*		
1723-50	Muratori, *Historians of Italy*		
1724	Metastasio, *Dido Forsaken*		
		1726	Swift, *Gulliver's Travels*
1728-29	Vico, *Autobiography*	1728	Gay, *The Beggar's Opera*
1729-35	Rolli's translation of *Paradise Lost*	1731	Prévost, *Manon Lescaut*
1732	Metastasio, *Attilius Regulus*		
		1742	Young, *Night Thoughts*
		1749	Fielding, *Tom Jones*
		1751	Gray, *Elegy*
		1759	Voltaire, *Candide*
1760	Goldoni, *The Boors*	1760-67	Sterne, *Tristram Shandy*

POLITICAL THEORY, HISTORY, AND RELIGION		PHILOSOPHY, SCIENCE, AND THE ARTS	
1704	Battle of Blenheim	1704	Newton, *Optics*
		1705-22	Vanbrugh, Blenheim Palace constructed
		1710-36	Giovanni Battista Pergolesi
1713-15	Peace of Utrecht		
1715-74	Reign of Louis XV		
		1717	Fahrenheit system and thermometer; Watteau, *A Pilgrimage to Cythera*
		1721	Bach, *Brandenburg Concertos*
		1725	Vico, *The New Science*
		1737	Linnaeus, *Systema Naturae*
1738	Wesley brothers found Methodism	1738	Excavations at Herculaneum, Paestum, and Pompeii begin
1740-86	Reign of Frederick the Great	1740	Boucher, *Triumph of Venus*
1741-48	War of the Austrian Succession	1741	Handel, *Messiah*
1748	Montesquieu, *The Spirit of the Laws*	1749-1801	Domenico Cimarosa
		1750-53	Tiepolo, frescoes at Würzburg
		1751-72	Publication of the *Encyclopédie*
1755	Lisbon earthquake		
1756-63	Seven Years' War		

ITALIAN LITERATURE		WORLD LITERATURE	
1761-65	Gozzi's fables for the theatre: *Turandot, The King Stag, The Love of Three Oranges*		
1762	Baretti begins publication of *The Literary Whip*		
1764	Pietro Verri begins publication of *Il Caffè*		
		1766	Lessing, *Laokoon;* Goldsmith, *The Vicar of Wakefield*
1767-72	Meli, *The Bucolics*		
1772-82	Tiraboschi, *The History of Italian Literature*		
		1773	Goldsmith, *She Stoops to Conquer*
		1774	Goethe, *The Sorrows of Young Werther*
1775-86	Alfieri, *Saul* and *Mirra*	1775	Beaumarchais, *Barber of Seville*
1777	Baretti, *Discourse on Shakespeare and Mr. Voltaire*		
1781-83	Alfieri, *America the Free: Five Odes*		
1786-90	Da Ponte's *libretti* for Mozart		
		1789	Blake, *Songs of Innocence*

POLITICAL THEORY, HISTORY, AND RELIGION		PHILOSOPHY, SCIENCE, AND THE ARTS	
		1760-1842	Maria Luigi Cherubini
1762	Rousseau, *The Social Contract*		
1762-96	Reign of Catherine II the Great		
1764	Beccaria, *On Crimes and Punishments*		
		1765	Fragonard, *The Bathers*
		1768	Death of Canaletto
1770	Galiani, *Dialogues on the Wheat Trade*	1770	West, *Death of General Wolfe;* Jefferson builds Monticello
		1774	Priestley discovers oxygen
1775-83	American War of Independence		
1776	Gibbon, *Decline and Fall of the Roman Empire;* Smith, *The Wealth of Nations*		
		1778	Houdon, *Voltaire*
1779	Hume, *Dialogues Concerning Natural Religion*		
1780-83	Filangieri, *The Science of Legislation*	1781	Kant, *Critique of Pure Reason*
		1782-1840	Niccolò Paganini
		1784-85	David, *Oath of the Horatii*
		1787	Mozart, *Don Giovanni*
1789	Fall of the Bastille and the outbreak of the French Revolution; Bentham, *Introduction to the Principles of Morals and Legislation*		

ITALIAN LITERATURE			WORLD LITERATURE
		1791	De Sade, *Justine;* Boswell, *The Life of Samuel Johnson*
1797	Cesarotti, *Essay on the Philosophy of Languages*	1797-99	Hölderlin, *Hyperion*
		1798	Wordsworth, *Lyrical Ballads*
1799-1803	Alfieri, *Memoirs*		
1801-04	Parini's complete works appear	1801	Chateaubriand, *Atala*
1804	Alessandro Verri, *The Roman Nights at the Tomb of the Scipios*		
1807	Foscolo, *On Sepulchres*		
		1808	Goethe, *Faust (Part I)*
1810	Monti's translation of *The Iliad*		
		1812	Byron, *Childe Harold's Pilgrimage*
		1813	Austen, *Pride and Prejudice*
		1814	Scott, *Waverley*
1815	Pellico, *Francesca da Rimini*		
1816	Berchet, *On the "Fierce Hunter" and "Leonora" of G. A. Bürger; The Semiserious Letter from Chrysostom to His Son;* Borsieri, *Literary Adventures of a Day;* Di Breme, *Discourse Concerning the Injustice of Some Italian Literary Judgments*	1816	Constant, *Adolph;* Coleridge, *Kubla Khan;* De Staël, "On the Method and Value of Translations"
		1817	Keats, *Poems*
1818-19	Publication of *Il Conciliatore*		
1819	Leopardi, "The Infinite"; Porta, "The Selection of the Chaplain"	1819-24	Byron, *Don Juan*

POLITICAL THEORY, HISTORY, AND RELIGION		PHILOSOPHY, SCIENCE, AND THE ARTS	
1790	Burke, *Reflections on the French Revolution*		
1791-92	Paine, *The Rights of Man*		
		1793	David, *Death of Marat*
1798	Malthus, *An Essay on the Principle of Population*	circa 1798	Jenner discovers small-pox vaccine
		1799	Beethoven, *First Symphony*
		1800	Goya, *Maja desnuda;* Volta invents electric battery
1804	Napoleon crowned emperor		
		1805-07	Canova, *Maria Paulina Borghese, as Venus Victrix*
		1807	Hegel, *Phenomenology of Spirit*
1815	Battle of Waterloo		
		1816	Rossini, *The Barber of Seville*
		1818-19	Géricault, *Raft of the Medusa*
		1819	Schopenhauer, *The World as Will and Idea*

ITALIAN LITERATURE		WORLD LITERATURE	
1821	Casanova, *History of My Life*		
1822	Pindemonte's translation of *The Odyssey*	1823	Stendhal, *Racine and Shakespeare*
		1823-31	Pushkin, *Eugene Onegin*
		1826	Cooper, *The Last of the Mohicans*
1827	Leopardi, *Little Moral Exercises* published (most written in 1824)		
1828	Guerrazzi, *Manfred*		
		1830	Hugo, *Hernani*
1831	Leopardi, *Songs*	1831	Stendhal, *The Red and the Black*
1832	Pellico, *My Prisons*		
1833	D'Azeglio, *Ettore Fieramosca*	1833	Balzac, *Eugénie Grandet;* Tennyson, *Poems*
1834	Grossi, *Marco Visconti*		
1840-42	Manzoni, *The Betrothed*		
		1841-44	Emerson, *Essays*
1843	Gioberti, *The Moral and Civic Pre-eminence of the Italians;* Niccolini, *Arnold of Brescia*		

POLITICAL THEORY, HISTORY, AND RELIGION		PHILOSOPHY, SCIENCE, AND THE ARTS	
1823	Monroe Doctrine		
		1825	Completion of the first steam railroad
		1834	Delacroix, *Women of Algiers*
		1834-38	Berlioz, *Benvenuto Cellini*
1835-40	De Tocqueville, *Democracy in America*	1835	Donizetti, *Lucia di Lammermoor*
1837	Queen Victoria ascends the throne of Great Britain		
		1839	Daguerreotype photographic process introduced
		1840	Turner, *The Slave Ship*
		1844	Morse's telegraph
1848	Marx and Engels, *Communist Manifesto;* Mill, *Principles of Political Economy*		
1848-49	Republican revolts and suppression across Italy and Europe		
		1849	Death of Chopin
		1849-50	Courbet, *A Burial at Ornans*

ITALIAN LITERATURE		WORLD LITERATURE	
		1850	Hawthorne, *The Scarlet Letter*
		1851	Melville, *Moby Dick*
		1855	Whitman, *Leaves of Grass*
		1857	Flaubert, *Madame Bovary;* Baudelaire, *Flowers of Evil*
1858-79	Tommaseo, *Dictionary of the Italian Language*		
1860	Mazzini, *The Duties of Man*	1860-61	Dickens, *Great Expectations*
		1862-69	Tolstoy, *War and Peace*
		1865	Carroll, *Alice's Adventures in Wonderland*
1867	Nievo, *The Castle of Fratta*		
1868	D'Azeglio, *Things I Remember*		
1870-71	De Sanctis, *History of Italian Literature*		
1872	Cossa, *Nero*		
		1873	Pater, *Studies in the Renaissance*
		1876	Mallarmé, "The Afternoon of a Faun"
1877-89	Carducci, *Barbarian Odes*		
1879	Capuana, *Giacinta*		

POLITICAL THEORY, HISTORY, AND RELIGION		PHILOSOPHY, SCIENCE, AND THE ARTS	
		1851	Verdi, *Rigoletto*
1852	Napoleon III proclaimed emperor of France		
1853-56	Crimean War		
1859	Mill, *On Liberty*	1859	Darwin, *Origin of Species*
1860	Burckhardt, *The Civilization of the Renaissance in Italy;* Garibaldi's Expedition of the Thousand		
1861	Cavour proclaims a Kingdom of Italy under Victor Emmanuel II		
1861-65	American Civil War		
		1863	Manet, *Luncheon on the Grass*
		1864	Pasteur's germ theory
		1865	Mendel's experiments in genetics published
1866	Austro-Prussian-Italian War; Venice added to Italy		
1867-94	Marx, *Capital*	1867	Nobel invents dynamite
1870-71	Franco-Prussian War; Rome added to Italy	1871	Darwin, *The Descent of Man*
		1874	Degas, *The Rehearsal*
		1876-79	Invention of the telephone, phonograph, and light bulb

ITALIAN LITERATURE		WORLD LITERATURE	
		1880	Zola, *Nana* and *The Experimental Novel;* Dostoevsky, *The Brothers Karamazov*
1881	Verga, *The House by the Medlar Tree*	1881	James, *Portrait of a Lady*
1883	Lorenzini (Carlo Collodi), *The Adventures of Pinocchio*	1884	Ibsen, *The Wild Duck;* Twain, *Adventures of Huckleberry Finn*
1886	De Amicis, *Heart*		
1886-89	Belli, *Roman Sonnets*		
1890	De Marchi, *Demetrio Pianelli*		
1891	Pascoli, *Myricae;* Marco Praga, *The Ideal Wife*		
1894	D'Annunzio, *The Triumph of Death;* De Roberto, *The Viceroys*		
1895	Zanella, *Literary Parallels*		
1896	Fogazzaro, *The Little World of the Past*	1896	Jarry, *Ubu Roi*
1898	Svevo, *As a Man Grows Older*	1898	Tolstoy, *What Is Art?*
1901	Serao, *The Land of Cockayne*		

POLITICAL THEORY, HISTORY, AND RELIGION		PHILOSOPHY, SCIENCE, AND THE ARTS	
1882	Italy joins Triple Alliance	1882	Wagner, *Parsifal*
		1883-92	Nietzsche writes *Thus Spake Zarathustra*
		1884-86	Seurat, *Sunday Afternoon on the Island of the Grande Jatte*
		1886	Rodin, *The Kiss*
1887-96	Crispi governments		
		1889	Van Gogh, *Self-Portrait* and *The Starry Night*
		1890	Mascagni, *Cavalleria rusticana*
1892	Foundation of the Italian Socialist party	1892	Leoncavallo, *Pagliacci*
		1892-93	Monet, *Rouen Cathedral: The Facade at Sunset*
		1893	Munch, *The Scream*
		1895	Lumière brothers invent cinematograph; Marconi invents wireless telegraphy
1896	Mosca, *The Ruling Class*	1896	Puccini, *La Bohème;* Medardo Rosso, *Madame X*
		1897	Rousseau, *The Sleeping Gypsy*
		1898	Curies discover radium
1900	Umberto I assassinated by Italian-American anarchist	1900	Planck's quantum theory; Pavlov's experiments on reflexes; Bergson, *On Laughter;* Freud, *Interpretation of Dreams*
1902	Pareto, *Les Systèmes Socialistes*	1902	Croce, *Aesthetic*

ITALIAN LITERATURE		WORLD LITERATURE	
1903	Prezzolini and Papini found *Leonardo*	1903	Shaw, *Man and Superman*
1904	Pirandello, *The Late Mattia Pascal*	1904	Chekhov, *The Cherry Orchard*
1906	Carducci receives Nobel Prize		
1908	Pirandello, *On Humor;* Oriani, *The Ideal Revolt*		
1909	Sem Benelli, *The Jest*		
1911	Gozzano, *Conversations*		
1912	Papini, *The Failure*		
		1913	Mann, *Death in Venice;* Apollinaire, *Alcools;* Proust, *Remembrance of Things Past* (completed in 1927)
1914	Campana, *Orphic Songs*		
1916	Chiarelli, *The Mask and the Face*	1916	Joyce, *Portrait of the Artist as a Young Man;* Kafka, *Metamorphosis*
1917	Pirandello, *It Is So! (If You Think so)*		
1918	Antonelli, *The Man Who Met Himself*		
1919	Ungaretti, *The Joy of Shipwrecks*		
1919-23	Publication of *La Ronda*		
1920	Deledda, *The Mother;* Tozzi, *Three Crosses*	1920	Lawrence, *Women in Love;* Lewis, *Main Street*

POLITICAL THEORY, HISTORY, AND RELIGION		PHILOSOPHY, SCIENCE, AND THE ARTS
	1903	Flight of the Wright brothers at Kitty Hawk
1904-05		Weber, *The Protestant Ethic and the Spirit of Capitalism*
1904-14		Giolittian Era
	1905	Einstein formulates special theory of relativity
1906		Dreyfus declared innocent
	1907	Picasso, *Les demoiselles d'Avignon;* Bergson, *Creative Evolution*
	1909	Marinetti, *Futurist Manifesto* published in Paris
	1910-12	Russell and Whitehead, *Principia Mathematica*
	1911	Matisse, *Red Studio*
	1912	Duchamp, *Nude Descending a Staircase*
	1913	Stravinsky, *The Rite of Spring;* Boccioni, *Unique Forms of Continuity in Space;* Mondrian, *Composition in Line and Color;* Kandinsky, *Improvisation 30 (Cannon);* Armory Show in New York
1914	"Red Week" in central Italy; outbreak of World War I	1914 — Kokoschka, *Bride of the Wind*
1915-18	Italy enters war on the side of the Allies	1915 — Griffith, *Birth of a Nation*
1916	Pareto, *The Mind and Society*	
1917	Russian Revolution	1917 — De Chirico, *Italian Square*
	1918	Tzara, Dada manifesto
1919	Treaty of Versailles; Mussolini founds fascist movement; D'Annunzio's march on Fiume	

ITALIAN LITERATURE		WORLD LITERATURE	
1921	Borgese, *Rubè;* Pirandello, *Six Characters*		
1922	Marinetti, *The Untamables;* Pirandello, *Henry IV*	1922	Joyce, *Ulysses;* Eliot, *The Waste Land*
1923	Svevo, *The Confessions of Zeno;* Croce, *European Literature in the Nineteenth Century*	1923	Rilke, *Duino Elegies*
1924	Pirandello, *Each in His Own Way*		
1925	Montale, *Cuttlefish Bones*	1925	Gide, *The Counterfeiters;* Kafka, *The Trial;* Dreiser, *An American Tragedy;* Fitzgerald, *The Great Gatsby*
1927	Deledda receives Nobel Prize	1927	Hesse, *Steppenwolf*
1929	Croce, *History of the Baroque Age in Italy;* Moravia, *The Time of Indifference*	1929	Faulkner, *The Sound and the Fury;* Hemingway, *A Farewell to Arms;* Döblin, *Berlin Alexanderplatz*
1930	Alvaro, *Revolt in Aspromonte;* Pirandello, *Tonight We Improvise*		
		1931	O'Neill, *Mourning Becomes Electra*
1934	Pirandello receives Nobel Prize; Palazzeschi, *The Sisters Materassi*		
1936	Croce, *Poetry;* Flora, *Hermetic Poetry*		
1937	Silone, *Bread and Wine*		
1938-40	Bacchelli, *The Mill on the Po* trilogy	1938	Sartre, *Nausea*
		1938-39	Brecht, *Galileo*

POLITICAL THEORY, HISTORY, AND RELIGION		PHILOSOPHY, SCIENCE, AND THE ARTS	
1921	Foundation of Italian Communist party by Gramsci, Togliatti, and Tasca	1921	Wittgenstein, *Tractatus Logico-philosophicus*
1922	Mussolini's March on Rome		
		1924	Breton, Manifesto of Surrealism
1925-27	Hitler, *Mein Kampf*	1925	Eisenstein, *Potemkin*
		1927	Respighi, *The Birds*
1928	Croce, *A History of Italy 1871-1915*	1928	Buñuel and Dali, *Un chien andalou;* discovery of penicillin
1929	Lateran Pact of Roman church and Mussolini		
		1930	Freud, *Civilization and Its Discontents;* Gentile, *Philosophy of Art;* Ortega y Gasset, *The Rebellion of the Masses*
		1931	Arp, *Torso*
1932	Mussolini and Gentile, *The Doctrine of Fascism;* Croce, *History of Europe in the Nineteenth Century*	1932	Kipchitz, *Song of the Vowels;* Calder displays his mobiles in Paris
		1933	Jung, *Modern Man in Search of a Soul*
		1934	Moore, *Composition*
1936	Mussolini invades Ethiopia	1936	Frank Lloyd Wright, Kaufmann house in Bear Run, Pennsylvania
1936-39	Spanish Civil War	1937	First jet engine constructed
1939-45	World War II	1939	Renoir, *The Rules of the Game*

•

ITALIAN LITERATURE		WORLD LITERATURE	
1940	Buzzati, *The Tartar Steppe*		
1941	Vittorini, *In Sicily;* Pavese, *The Harvesters*	1941	Ransom, *The New Criticism*
		1942	Camus, *The Stranger;* Wellek and Warren, *Theory of Literature*
1944	Malaparte, *Kaputt;* Betti, *Corruption in the Palace of Justice*		
1945	Levi, *Christ Stopped at Eboli*		
1946	De Filippo, *Filumena Marturano*	1946	Auerbach, *Mimesis*
1947	Calvino, *The Path to the Nest of Spiders;* Gramsci, *Letters from Prison;* Quasimodo, *Day After Day;* Ungaretti, *Life of a Man;* Pavese, *Dialogues with Leucò;* Pratolini, *A Tale of Poor Lovers*		
1950	Pavese, *The Moon and the Bonfires*		
		1952	Beckett, *Waiting for Godot*
1954	Cassola, *Timber Cutting;* Soldati, *The Capri Letters*		
1955	Pratolini, *Metello*		
1957	Gadda, *That Awful Mess on Via Merulana;* Pasolini, *The Ashes of Gramsci;* Moravia, *Two Women*	1957	Frye, *The Anatomy of Criticism;* Pasternak, *Doctor Zhivago*

POLITICAL THEORY, HISTORY, AND RELIGION		PHILOSOPHY, SCIENCE, AND THE ARTS	
		1941	Welles, *Citizen Kane*
		1942	Camus, *The Myth of Sisyphus*
		1943	Sartre, *Being and Nothingness*
1945	Mussolini captured and executed; Hitler commits suicide; atomic bomb dropped on Hiroshima; United Nations founded	1945	Rossellini, *Rome Open City*
1946	Gentile, *Genesis and Structure of Society;* Italians vote for a republic		
1947	Marshall Plan begins in Europe		
1947-52	Publication of Gramsci's *Prison Notebooks*		
1948	Assasination of Mahatma Gandhi; Israel established	1948	De Sica, *The Bicycle Thief;* Giacometti, *Three Men Walking*
		1948-49	Nervi, Turin Exhibition Hall constructed
1950-53	Korean War	1950-54	Le Corbusier, Notre Dame du Haut
1953	Death of Stalin	1953	Wittgenstein, *Philosophical Investigations;* Pollock, *Blue Poles;* discovery of the double helical structure of DNA
		1956	De Kooning, *The Time of the Fire*
1957	European Common Market established	1957	Sputnik; Bergman, *The Seventh Seal;* Rothko, *White and Greens in Blue*

ITALIAN LITERATURE		WORLD LITERATURE	
1958	Tomasi di Lampedusa, *The Leopard*	1958	Genet, *The Blacks*
1959	Quasimodo receives Nobel Prize	1959	Spitzer, *Romanische Literaturstudien;* Bellow, *Henderson the Rain King*
1960	Moravia, *The Empty Canvas*	1960	Ionesco, *Rhinoceros*
1961	Saba, definitive edition of *Songbook;* Sciascia, *Mafia Vendetta*	1961	Frisch, *Andorra;* Poulet, *The Metamorphoses of the Circle*
1962	Zanzotto, *Nine Eclogues;* Bassani, *The Garden of the Finzi-Continis*		
1963	Ginzburg, *Family Sayings*		
1964	Berto, *Incubus*		
1966	Quasimodo, *To Give and To Have*		
		1969	Todorov, *Grammaire du Décaméron*
1972	Pasolini, *Heretical Empiricism;* Calvino, *Invisible Cities;* Dessì, *The Forests of Norbio*		
1974	Morante, *History: A Novel;* Sciascia, *One Way or Another*		
1975	Montale receives Nobel Prize; Volponi, *The Ducal Curtain*		

POLITICAL THEORY, HISTORY, AND RELIGION		PHILOSOPHY, SCIENCE, AND THE ARTS	
		1959	Fellini, *La dolce vita*
		1962	Lévi-Strauss, *The Savage Mind;* Fellini, *8½*
1963	John F. Kennedy assassinated	1964	Pasolini, *The Gospel According to St. Matthew*
1965-74	Vietnamese War	1966	Mao launches Cultural Revolution in China; Antonioni, *Blow-Up*
1967	Arab-Israeli Six-Day War	1967	First successful heart transplant
		1969	Fellini, *Satyricon;* Americans land on the moon
1972	Nixon visit to China	1972	Bertolucci, *Last Tango in Paris;* Henry Moore's outdoor exhibition in Florence
1974	Nixon resigns as president of the United States		
		1976	Umberto Eco, *A Theory of Semiotics;* Lina Wertmüller, *Seven Beauties;* Bertolucci, *1900;* Fellini, *Casanova*
1978	Christian Democrats and Communists in Italy conclude a "historic compromise;" Aldo Moro killed by Red Brigade terrorists	1977	Taviani brothers, *Padre, Padrone*

Appendix B:

ENTRIES GROUPED BY SUBJECT MATTER OR CHRONOLOGICAL PERIOD

I. METRICS AND POETIC GENRES OR FORMS

Ballata
Caccia
Canto carnascialesco
 ("Carnival Song")
Canzone
Capitolo
Emblem: *See* Alciati
Epic
Lauda
Madrigal
Melodrama
Novella
Ottava rima
Pastoral
Rispetto: See Strambotto
Sacra rappresentazione
Sestina
Sonnet
Stornello
Strambotto
Terza rima

II. LITERARY OR CRITICAL SCHOOLS, PERIODS, PROBLEMS, OR MOVEMENTS

Arcadia
Baroque
Commedia dell'arte
Decadentismo
Dolce stil nuovo
Enlightenment
Futurism
Grotesque Theatre: *See*
 Teatro grottesco
Hermeticism
Humanism
Neoclassicism
Neo-Platonism: *See*
 Bembo, Pietro;
 Castiglione, Baldesar;
 Della Mirandola,
 Giovanni Pico; Ebreo,
 Leone; Ficino, Marsilio
Neorealism
Petrarchism

Caro, Annibale
Castelvetro, Ludovico
Castiglione, Baldesar
Cellini, Benvenuto
Ciminelli, Serafino De':
　See Serafino Aquilano
Cinzio: *See* Giraldi,
　Giambattista
Colonna, Francesco
Colonna, Vittoria
Daniello, Bernardino
Da Porto, Luigi
Da Vinci, Leonardo
Della Casa, Giovanni
Della Mirandola, Giovanni
　Pico
Della Porta, Giambattista
Domenico Di Giovanni
Doni, Anton Francesco
Dovizi, Bernardo
Ebreo, Leone
Enea Silvio Piccolomini
Ficino, Marsilio
Firenzuola, Angelo
Flaminio, Marcantonio
Folengo, Teofilo
Fracastoro, Girolamo
Gareth, Benedetto: *See*
　Cariteo
Gelli, Giovan Battista
Giannotti, Donato
Giovio, Paolo
Giraldi, Giambattista
Grazzini, Anton Francesco
Guazzo, Stefano
Guicciardini, Francesco
Landino, Cristoforo
Lasca: *See* Grazzini,
　Anton Francesco
Machiavelli, Niccolò
Manetti, Giannozzo
Mantuan: *See* Spagnoli,
　Battista
Manuzio, Aldo ("Aldus
　Manutius")
Masuccio Salernitano

Medici, Lorenzo De'
Minturno, Antonio
Nardi, Jacopo
Navagero, Andrea
Palmieri, Matteo
Pius II: *See* Enea Silvio
　Piccolomini
Polidoro Vergilio
　("Polydore Vergil")
Poliziano, Angelo
　("Politian")
Pomponazzi, Pietro
Pontano, Giovanni
Pulci, Luigi
Robortello, Francesco
Ruzzante
Salutati, Coluccio
Salviati, Lionardo
Sannazaro, Jacopo
Savonarola, Girolamo
Scaligero, Giulio Cesare
Serafino Aquilano
Spagnoli, Battista
Speroni, Sperone
Stampa, Gaspara
Straparola, Gian
　Francesco
Tansillo, Luigi
Tasso, Bernardo
Tebaldeo, Antonio
Trissino, Gian Giorgio
Valla, Lorenzo
Varchi, Benedetto
Vasari, Giorgio
Vespasiano Da Bisticci
Vettori, Francesco
Vida, Marco Girolamo
Vittorino Da Feltre

V. BAROQUE LITERATURE

Ammirato, Scipione
Andreini, Giovan Battista
Basile, Giambattista

Boccalini, Traiano
Botero, Giovanni
Bruno, Giordano
Buonarroti, Michelangelo
Buonarroti, Michelangelo
  ("The Younger")
Campanella, Tommaso
Chiabrera, Gabriello
Croce, Giulio Cesare
Della Valle, Federico
Frugoni, Francesco Fulvio
Galilei, Galileo
Gravina, Gian Vincenzo
Guarini, Battista
Maffei, Scipione
Maggi, Carlo Maria
Marino, Giambattista
Pallavicino, Sforza
Paruta, Paolo
Redi, Francesco
Rosa, Salvatore
Sarpi, Paolo
Tasso, Torquato
Tassoni, Alessandro
Tesauro, Emanuele
Testi, Fulvio

VI. ENLIGHTENMENT LITERATURE

Alfieri, Vittorio
Baretti, Giuseppe
Beccaria, Cesare
Casanova, Giacomo
  Girolamo
Da Ponte, Lorenzo
Fantoni, Giovanni
Filangieri, Gaetano
Galiani, Ferdinando
Giannone, Pietro
Goldoni, Carlo
Gozzi, Carlo
Gozzi, Gasparo
Magalotti, Lorenzo
Mascheroni, Lorenzo
Meli, Giovanni

Metastasio, Pietro
Monti, Vincenzo
Muratori, Lodovico
  Antonio
Parini, Giuseppe
Pindemonte, Ippolito
Rolli, Paolo Antonio
Tiraboschi, Girolamo
Trapassi, Pietro: *See*
  Metastasio, Pietro
Verri, Count Alessandro
Verri, Count Pietro
Vico, Giambattista

VII. NINETEENTH-CENTURY LITERATURE

Aleardi, Aleardo
Belli, Giuseppe
  Gioacchino
Berchet, Giovanni
Boito, Arrigo
Boito, Camillo
Borsieri, Pietro
Capuana, Luigi
Carducci, Giosuè
Carrer, Luigi
Cesarotti, Melchiorre
Collodi, Carlo: *See*
  Lorenzini, Carlo
Cossa, Pietro
D'Azeglio, Massimo
  Tapparelli, Marchese
De Amicis, Edmondo
De Marchi, Emilio
De Roberto, Federico
De Sanctis, Francesco
Di Breme, Ludovico
Ferrari, Paolo
Fogazzaro, Antonio
Foscolo, Ugo
Fucini, Renato
Gallina, Giacinto
Garibaldi, Giuseppe
Gioberti, Vincenzo

Giusti, Giuseppe
Grossi, Tommaso
Guerrazzi, Francesco
  Domenico
Leopardi, Giacomo
Lorenzini, Carlo
Manzoni, Alessandro
Mazzini, Giuseppe
Niccolini, Giovanni
  Battista
Nievo, Ippolito
Oriani, Alfredo
Pascoli, Giovanni
Pellico, Silvio
Porta, Carlo
Praga, Emilio
Praga, Marco
Prati, Giovanni
Rossetti, Gabriele
Rovetta, Gerolamo
Ruffini, Giovanni
Serao, Matilde
Tommaseo, Niccolò
Verga, Giovanni
Zanella, Giacomo

VIII. TWENTIETH-CENTURY LITERATURE

Aleramo, Sibilla
Alvaro, Corrado
Antonelli, Luigi
Bacchelli, Riccardo
Banti, Anna
Bassani, Giorgio
Benelli, Sem
Bernari, Carlo
Berto, Giuseppe
Betocchi, Carlo
Betti, Ugo
Bilenchi, Romano
Bontempelli, Massimo
Borgese, Giuseppe
  Antonio
Bracco, Roberto

Brancati, Vitaliano
Buzzati, Dino
Calvino, Italo
Campana, Dino
Cardarelli, Vincenzo
Cassola, Carlo
Cecchi, Emilio
Chiarelli, Luigi
Corazzini, Sergio
Croce, Benedetto
D'Annunzio, Gabriele
De Céspedes, Alba
De Filippo, Eduardo
Deledda, Grazia
Dessì, Giuseppe
Di Giacomo, Salvatore
Eco, Umberto
Fabbri, Diego
Fenoglio, Beppe
Fo, Dario
Fortini, Franco
Gadda, Carlo Emilio
Gatto, Alfonso
Gentile, Giovanni
Giacosa, Giuseppe
Ginzburg, Natalia
Govoni, Corrado
Gozzano, Guido
Gramsci, Antonio
Jahier, Piero
Jovine, Francesco
Landolfi, Tommaso
Levi, Carlo
Lucini, Gian Pietro
Luzi, Mario
Malaparte, Curzio
Manzini, Giana
Marinetti, Filippo
  Tommaso
Michelstaedter, Carlo
Montale, Eugenio
Morante, Elsa
Moravia, Alberto
Moretti, Marino
Neera
Negri, Ada
Ortese, Anna Maria

REFERENCE AIDS: A SELECTED LIST

I. General Guides to the Study of Italian Literature and Culture

Mollica, Anthony, ed. *A Handbook for Teachers of Italian*. American Association of Teachers of Italian, 1976. Extensive discussion and bibliographical information on pedagogy, ethnic studies, and the teaching of Italian film, literature, and culture. Contributions by a number of American and Canadian scholars.

Momigliano, Attilio, ed. *Problemi ed orientamenti critici di lingua e di letteratura italiana*. 5 vols. Milan: Marzorati, 1948. Individual volumes devoted to bibliography, literary theory and technique, problems and currents in literary history, Italy's literary relations with other major literatures, and aesthetics. Numerous contributors.

Orientamenti culturali: Letteratura italiana. 19 vols. Milan: Marzorati, 1956–74. An indispensable bibliographical tool containing the following: two volumes on literary periods and critical problems; two volumes devoted to "major" authors and four to "minor" authors; six volumes dedicated to "contemporary" writers and five which treat critics from De Sanctis to the present. Numerous contributors.

Puppo, Mario. *Manuale critico bibliografico per lo studio della letteratura italiana*. 12th rev. ed. Turin: Società editrice internazionale, 1974. Invaluable but abbreviated reference work on methodology, stylistics and linguistics, bibliography on major literary periods and writers.

Stych, F. S. *How To Find Out About Italy*. Oxford: Pergamon Press, 1970. A wealth of bibliographical information and a guide to bibliographies related to every aspect of Italian life and culture, including libraries, archives, manuscripts, rare books, encyclopedias, newspapers, societies, literature, fine arts, social sciences, language, applied science and technology, natural sciences, geography, and the like.

II. Italian Metrics and Versification

Elwert, W. Th. *Versificazione italiana dalle origini ai giorni nostri*. Florence: Felice Le Monnier, 1973.

Manna, Francesco. *Dolce stile: nozioni di stilistica, di retorica e di metrica italiana*. Milan: Signorelli, 1967.

Reference Aids

Spongano, Raffaele. *Nozioni ed esempi di metrica italiana.* Bologna: Pàtron, 1966.

III. History of the Italian Language and Italian Grammar

De Mauro, Tullio. *Storia linguistica dell'Italia unita.* Bari: Laterza, 1963; rev. ed., 1970.

Devoto, Giacomo. *Profilo di storia linguistica italiana.* Florence: La Nuova Italia, 1953.

D'Ovidio, Francesco, and Wilhelm Meyer-Lübke. *Grammatica storica della lingua e dei dialetti italiani.* Trans. E. Polcari. Milan: Hoepli, 1932 (first Italian ed. 1906).

Meyer-Lübke, Wilhelm. *Grammatica storica della lingua italiana e dei dialetti toscani,* Ed. Matteo Bartoli, et al. Turin: Loescher, 1967 (first Italian ed. 1901).

Migliorini, Bruno. *Storia della lingua italiana.* Florence: Sansoni, 1960. *The Italian Language.* Rev. ed. and trans. T. Gwynfor Griffith. London: Faber & Faber, 1966.

Rohlfs, Gerhard. *Grammatica storica della lingua italiana e dei suoi dialetti.* 3 vols. Turin: Einaudi, 1966–69.

IV. Italian Literary History

Cecchi, Emilio, and Natalino Sapegno, eds. *Storia della letteratura italiana.* 9 vols. Milan: Garzanti, 1965–69 (includes contributions by a number of authors).

De Sanctis, Francesco. *A History of Italian Literature.* Trans. Joan Redfern. 2 vols. New York: Basic Books, 1959.

Donadoni, Eugenio. *A History of Italian Literature.* 2 vols. Rev. ed. by Ettore Mazzali and Robert J. Clements. Trans. Richard Monges. New York: New York University Press, 1969.

Flora, Francesco. *Storia della letteratura italiana.* 5 vols. Milan: Mondadori, 1972 (original ed. 1940; rev. ed. 1947).

Getto, Giovanni. *Storia delle storie letterarie.* Milan: Bompiani,1942.

Muscetta, Carlo, ed. *La letteratura italiana: storia e testi.* 9 vols. Bari: Laterza, 1970–76 (reprinted by sections in a paperback edition; includes not only literary history but also textual commentary and close readings of key passages by a number of contributors).

Rosa, Alberto Asor, ed. *Storia e antologia della letteratura italiana.* 25 vols. Florence: La Nuova Italia, 1974 (similar in format to the Muscetta collection above with paperback edition and a combination of literary history and textual commentary by a number of authors).

Whitfield, John H. *A Short History of Italian Literature.* Westport, Conn.: Greenwood Press, 1976 (original ed. 1960).

Wilkins, Ernest Hatch. *A History of Italian Literature*. Rev. ed. by Thomas G. Bergin. Cambridge, Mass.: Harvard University Press, 1974.

V. Dictionaries and Reference Encyclopedias

Avery, Catherine, ed. *The New Century Italian Renaissance Encyclopedia*. New York: Appleton-Century-Crofts, 1972.

Bosco, Umberto, ed. *Enciclopedia dantesca*. 5 vols. Rome: Istituto dell'enciclopedia italiana, 1970–76.

Branca, Vittore, ed. *Dizionario critico della letteratura italiana*. 3 vols. Turin: UTET, 1973.

Cordati, Bruna, and Mario Farina, eds. *Dai: Dizionario degli autori italiani*. Florence: D'Anna, 1974.

Enciclopedia dello spettacolo. 12 vols. Rome: Le Maschere, 1954–68.

Enciclopedia filosofica. 2nd rev. ed. 6 vols. Florence: Sansoni, 1968–69.

Enciclopedia italiana di scienze lettere ed arti. 36 vols. Rome: Istituto dell'enciclopedia italiana, 1929–37.

This celebrated work, known as the "Trecani" encyclopedia because of the generosity of its industrialist-patron, was published under the general direction of Giovanni Gentile. Appendices were published in 1938 (one volume), in 1948–49 (two volumes), and in 1961 (two volumes). A revised edition of 1952 includes appendices published prior to that date.

Fusco, Enrico M., ed. *Scrittori e idee: dizionario critico della letteratura italiana*. Turin: Società editrice internazionale, 1956.

Petronio, Giuseppe, ed. *Dizionario enciclopedico della letteratura italiana*. 6 vols. Bari: Laterza, 1966–70.

Preminger, Alex, ed. *Princeton Encyclopedia of Poetry and Poetics*. Princeton, N.J.: Princeton University Press, 1965.

Renda, Umberto, and Piero Operti, eds. *Dizionario storico della letteratura italiana*. 4th rev. ed. Turin: Paravia, 1959.

Ronconi, Enzo, ed. *Dizionario generale degli autori italiani contemporanei*. 2 vols. Florence: Vallecchi, 1974. Abridged paperbound edition available.

Sestan, Ernesto, ed. *Dizionario storico politico italiano*. Florence: Sansoni, 1971.

Toynbee, Paget. *A Dictionary of Proper Names and Notable Matters in the Works of Dante*. Rev. ed. by C. S. Singleton. Oxford: Clarendon Press, 1968.

VI. Scholarly Periodicals Containing Regularly Published Bibliographies on Italian Literature

Italianistica

Italica

Publications of the Modern Language Association

Rassegna della letteratura italiana

Year's Work in Modern Languages

INDEX

The index includes references to names or pseudonyms of writers, artists, musicians, and film directors; literary academies; literary prizes; and journals, newspapers, and periodicals. Historical figures have, for the most part, been omitted, as have general literary periods, movements, or genres.